LIST OF PREDEFINED IDENTIFIERS

Abs	Pack
Arctan	Page
Boolean	Pred
Char	Put
Chr	Read
Cos	Readln
Dispose	Real
Eof	ReSet
Eoln	ReWrite
Exp	Round
False	Sin
Get	Sqr
Input	Sqrt
Integer	Succ
Ln	Text
MaxInt	True
New	Trunc
Odd	Unpack
Ord	Write
Output	Writeln

INTRODUCTION TO COMPUTING AND COMPUTER SCIENCE WITH PASCAL

Little, Brown Computer Systems Series

INTRODUCTION TO COMPUTING AND COMPUTER SCIENCE WITH PASCAL

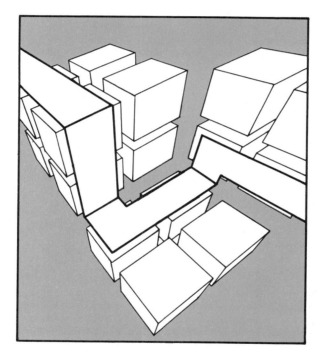

Henry M. Walker

Grinnell College, Grinnell, Iowa

LITTLE, BROWN AND COMPANY
Boston   Toronto

Library of Congress Cataloging-in-Publication Data

Walker, Henry M., 1947-
  Introduction to computing and computer science with
Pascal.

  Includes index.
  1. Electronic digital computers--Programming.
  2. PASCAL (Computer program language) I. Title.
  QA76.6.W3275 1985   005.13'3   85-19856
  ISBN 0-316-91841-5

Library of Congress Catalog Card No. 85-19856

ISBN 0-316-91841-5

9 8 7 6 5 4 3 2 1

HAL

Published simultaneously in Canada
by Little, Brown & Company (Canada) Limited

Printed in the United States of America

Disclaimer of Liabilities: Due care has been exercised in the preparation of this book to ensure its effectiveness. The author and publisher make no warranty, expressed or implied, with respect to the programs or other contents of this book. In no event will the author or publisher be liable for direct, indirect, incidental, or consequential damages in connection with or arising from the furnishing, performance, or use of this book.

Acknowledgments

Syntax diagrams in Appendix A reproduced from OH! PASCAL by Doug Cooper and Michael Clancy, by permission of Doug Cooper and W.W. Norton & Company, Inc. Copyright © 1982 by W.W. Norton & Company, Inc.

To my wonderful wife Terry, and
to my dear daughters, Donna and Barbara,
for their support, encouragement, understanding, and tolerance
during the writing of this book

PREFACE

In the past two decades, computers have streamlined or enhanced a variety of applications, thereby changing many disciplines in fundamental ways. The field of computing and computer science examines all phases of these applications and includes a wide range of topics such as the following:

- Problem solving methodology
- Algorithm design and analysis
- Programming
- Data structures
- Applications
- Computer organizations and systems
- Social implications

Each of these topics can involve considerable complexity and sophistication. Problem solving brings together these topics in a variety of ways.

Introduction to Computing and Computer Science With Pascal provides a solid, integrated introduction to these fundamental topics. Designed to go beyond most existing computing textbooks, this text considers each topic in detail and brings together important relationships between topics.

Main Features

The presentation of this broad range of material includes many features designed to aid the learning process.

- *Problem solving orientation and methodology*

  Structured problem solving and top-down, modular design are emphasized. Most examples begin with a statement of a problem, followed by a problem analysis and an appropriate solution outline. Thus, structured software is presented as a natural consequence of good analysis rather than as a pedagogical nicety.

- *Motivation of topics through applications*

  The role of the computer in solving problems is stressed, and various techniques and language constructs are introduced as a means of finding solutions to given problems.

- *Early treatment of procedures and functions*

  Simple procedures and functions are introduced in Chapters 3 and 4 to emphasize top-down design and modular program structure. Thus, from an early stage, students can incorporate modularization using procedures and functions as an integrated part of their approach to problem solving.

- *Spiral approach*

  Many topics in computing and computer science can be studied at varying levels of complexity and sophistication. For example, procedures and functions can be considered without parameters, with both value and reference parameters on a relatively simple level, or with complex interactions involving multiple declarations and aliases. This text often breaks such topics into logical pieces and then discusses the pieces in separate chapters.

- *Students can start quickly*

  Beginning students can quickly learn to write simple algorithms and programs by following good development principles and by approaching a subject using simple techniques. As these students gain experience, they become prepared for more advanced techniques.

- *Wide variety of applications illustrated*

  The text includes a variety of applications, including a large number of both numeric and non-numeric problems. Many of these applications are introduced through examples, and problems illustrate several possible extensions and additional uses.

- *Pascal based*

  Pascal is a programming language that encourages good problem solving techniques and is sufficiently rich to provide exposure to appropriate control structures and data types seen in modern languages. Pascal is thus ideally suited to the problem solving orientation of this text.

- *Integration of programming with other topics in computer science*

  The various topics mentioned above are integrated as much as possible. For example, the mechanism of calling functions and procedures is discussed using stacks; some social implications of data bases are reviewed as part of the discussion of files; and the implementation of character strings, integers, and real numbers complements the discussion of bits, bytes, and words from computer architecture.

- *Presentation via examples and complete programs*

  The text often introduces algorithms and language constructs via annotated examples and complete programs. Readers see applications of Pascal features, as well as syntax and semantics rules. The many Pascal programs can serve as models for beginners writing their own programs. In addition, since most coding examples are complete programs, readers do not have to guess how individual procedures and functions can be combined to form working programs.

- *Introduction of data structures at several levels, from simple data types to abstract data structures*

  Data types and structures are introduced at various levels. The beginning of the text considers only a few simple data types, so that the variety of data types available does not diffuse the focus on other programming constructs (procedures, functions, loops, conditional statements). Then more simple data types are introduced. Next, data are grouped together in records and sets. Finally, stacks, queues, linked lists, and trees are presented as abstract data structures, with objects and operations.

- *Consistent with recommended introductory sequences*

  The text introduces many of the concepts central to the fields of computing and computer science. This coverage is consistent with recommendations for introductory sequences in computer science made by the Association for Computing Machinery (ACM), the IEEE Computer Society, and the College Board Advanced Placement Development Committee in Computer Science.

- *Adherence to ANSI standard Pascal*

  Except where noted, all sample Pascal programs in the text conform to the ANSI Standard Pascal Programming Language. All programs have been compiled and run, generating the output shown in the text.

- *Concise chapter reviews*

  Each chapter ends with a list of key words, phrases, and concepts; a list of Pascal statements covered in the chapter; and a chapter summary.

- *Many diverse problems*

  Each chapter contains a substantial number of exercises, at varying levels of difficulty.

- *Workbook*

  A workbook containing chapter reviews, additional examples, and short answer questions is available to help guide students through this text.

- *Extensive instructors' materials*

  Instructors may order an *Instructors' Manual, Transparency Masters,* and *Programs in Machine-Readable Form.* The *Instructors' Manual* contains teaching notes, possible course schedules, suggestions for projects, and answers to most even-numbered problems in the text. The *Transparency Master Package* includes listings of all programs in the text for easy reference in class, as well as some additional aids for the presentation of several topics. Finally, all programs in the text and all programming solutions to even-numbered exercises are available in machine-readable form (diskette or tape) for a wide variety of machines.

Prerequisites

The text is largely self-contained, and minimal background is required. Specifically, no prior computing experience is assumed. While some of the beginning stages of programming may proceed more quickly if the reader has worked previously with computers in some way, such background is not necessary.

This text assumes that the reader is comfortable only with mathematics through algebra, although some analysis of algorithms does require a minimal acquaintance with logarithms. However, the appropriate material is covered in Appendix C.1, so prior exposure to logarithms is not necessary.

Acknowledgments

The development of this book has been greatly aided by the contributions of many people, and I would like to express my deep thanks to all those who helped in this process. First, I wish to acknowledge the support received from Little, Brown and Company, particularly from Tom Casson, who followed this project from preliminary discussions to the final production, and Lee Ripley, who was invaluable in the development of the manuscript itself. This text has benefited greatly from the helpful comments and reviews of many people. In particular, I want to thank Derald Boline, Shawnee Mission East High School; Steven Bruell, University of Minnesota; Robert Fischer, De Paul University; Wayne Gibson, Santa Ana College; Peter Henderson, SUNY, Stony Brook; Joseph Kent, University of Richmond; David Rine, W. Illinois and George Mason Universities; Robert Streett, Boston University; Stephen Weiss, University of North Carolina, Chapel Hill;

Patrick Wheatley, California Polytechnic State University; Lawrence Wright, Williams College; and Marvin Zelkowitz, University of Maryland. I also want to thank David Rine for his contributions to the workbook that has been developed in conjunction with this book.

In addition, I want to thank the following people who contributed various exercises: Arnold Adelberg, Charles Duke, Eugene Herman, Thomas Moberg, and John Stone from Grinnell College; and John Vogel.

I also received great encouragement and support from Grinnell College, and special thanks are due Dean Catherine Frazer for her active interest in this project and for her allocation of part of a special grant to Grinnell College from the Exxon Educational Foundation to the preparation of this manuscript. In addition, I want to express my thanks to Ms. Betty Deminoff for her expert typing and editing of various drafts of the manuscript.

Finally, I am deeply grateful to my family, my wife Terry and my daughters Donna and Barbara, for encouraging me throughout the development of this book and for tolerating my moods during the writing and revision process. Their understanding and support were essential to the entire project, and it is to them that this book is dedicated.

BRIEF CONTENTS

CONTENTS

CHAPTER 6   CONDITIONAL STATEMENTS AND
             BOOLEAN DATA TYPE   158

CHAPTER 9   MULTIPLE SUBSCRIPTS: ARRAYS WITH SEVERAL SUBSCRIPTS   268

CHAPTER 10   PROCEDURES AND FUNCTIONS (REVISITED)   299

CHAPTER 11   PROGRAM CORRECTNESS AND ACCURACY   336

CHAPTER 12 SOME SIMPLE PROBLEMS INVOLVING CHARACTERS: ADDITIONAL SIMPLE DATA TYPES 365

CHAPTER 13 COLLECTIONS OF OBJECTS: SETS AND RECORDS 402

CHAPTER 16 THE SOFTWARE LIFE CYCLE AND ITS
IMPLICATIONS   501

CHAPTER 17 STACKS AND QUEUES: SOME ADDITIONAL
DATA STRUCTURES   525

CHAPTER 18   LINKED LIST DATA STRUCTURES: AN INTRODUCTION TO POINTERS   557

CHAPTER 21   UNCONDITIONAL BRANCHING   679

CHAPTER 22   HARDWARE AND OPERATING SYSTEMS   697

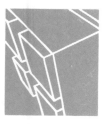

CHAPTER 1

PROBLEM
SOLVING AND
COMPUTING

Over the past several years, we have seen a dramatic rise in the already widespread popularity of computers, and we might think of many possible reasons for this tremendous interest in computing. Computers can be used to play exciting, challenging games; computers give an air of prestige and authority to an office; computers provide convenient targets when something must be blamed for a mistake. All these aspects of computers are interesting topics for study and discussion. We can identify another, more basic reason, however; computers are valuable tools that can help people address questions that could not be answered as quickly or as completely without these sophisticated machines.

When computers are used as tools to help solve problems, people must still take active roles in analyzing the problem, formulating a plan of attack for the problem, and instructing the computer on what steps to follow. Computers can be extremely valuable aids in many ways, but computers depend upon people to specify how a solution to a problem can be obtained. Therefore, we begin our study of computing and computer science by reviewing the process of solving problems and the role that computers play in this process.

| SECTION 1.1 | THE PROCESS OF PROBLEM SOLVING |

When we discuss problem solving, we mean the process of finding answers to questions. The actual process of finding answers frequently depends, however, upon the nature of the questions themselves, and it is very hard to make detailed, meaningful comments about this problem solving process. Many strategies for problem solving depend upon particular characteristics of the subjects involved.

Some Sample Problems
To begin, consider the following questions.

| PROBLEM 1.1 | If a car travels 55 miles per hour along an interstate highway for two hours, how far has the car traveled? |

| PROBLEM 1.2 | If a town discharges its sewer water into a nearby stream, how will the water quality of the stream be affected? |

| PROBLEM 1.3 | To what extent does a woman's nomination as a vice-presidential candidate affect the likelihood that a party's nominees will be elected? |

| PROBLEM 1.4 | What will happen to the Dow Jones Industrial Average next Tuesday? |

We can imagine being asked any of these questions, but we would not proceed in the same way in all cases. For example, Problem 1 gives us sufficient information to solve the problem with little further research. We need only recall the formula

$$\text{distance} = (\text{rate})\,(\text{time}).$$

Problem 2 requires us first to define what constitutes water quality and then to determine how it can be measured. Next, we will probably need to investigate the nature of the town's water and the characteristics of the stream. Finally, we will need to find appropriate relationships among all these items to allow us to finish our computations.

Similarly, Problem 3 requires us to analyze the political process, to determine the significant factors affecting voting patterns, and to study how these factors depend upon the gender of the candidate. Here, however, we should notice that different people might identify distinct political factors, and so conclusions might vary widely.

Problem 4 requires us to predict the future, which is beyond our capacity. We will not be able to answer this type of question definitively until next week (when the question will refer to another Tuesday). The person asking the question might want us to make some informed predictions about the Dow Jones Industrial Average; we might try to analyze market trends and economic indicators to make some predictions. Predictions do not precisely answer the question given, however, and the problem as stated is not solvable.

Undoubtedly, you could suggest many more problems to display still more characteristics, but even these few problems suggest the following features.

- Although some problems may contain adequate information to allow for a solution, other problems may require additional research.
- Some problems may require us to define terms, and our solution may depend upon our definitions.
- The methods for problem analysis may depend greatly upon the nature of the problem. For example, our water quality problem may require the development of formulas relating quality to the characteristics of sewage and stream water, but the problem about a woman as a vice-presidential candidate may require conducting public opinion surveys and analyzing related historical trends.
- Some problems, such as Problem 4, may not be solvable.

General Steps in the Problem Solving Process

Clearly, we must be cautious about oversimplifying the subject of problem solving. Problem solving is not a simple subject, and we must be careful not to trivialize it. We can, however, make some reasonable generalizations that apply to a large number of problems. The main points are illustrated in Figure 1–1.

1. In problem solving, we often begin with an **initial statement of the problem** that is quite general and vague. For example, I may decide to fix my stereo when I notice that something is missing in the sound of records being played.
2. Once we have this general topic, we must sharpen our problem so that we know precisely what we are assuming and what we are looking for (our results). In the stereo example, a more precise statement of the problem might be: No sound comes out of the left speaker when I play records. What needs to be fixed? This formulation of a problem in precise terms is often called the **specification of requirements.**
3. For nontrivial problems, we then need to develop a **general design or plan** to attack the problem. In working with the stereo system, I might approach the problem by trying to identify the component (turntable, amplifier, speaker, connecting wires) where the sound is lost.
4. Once we have developed our general design, we know what approach to take, but not how each part of the plan is to be carried out efficiently. The next step includes developing one or more techniques or **algorithms** to accomplish the individual steps in the general design. To fix the stereo, I must check an owner's manual to determine specific ways of testing the turntable or amplifier. I must also decide which specific connecting wires need testing. I need to specify tests for checking each

FIGURE 1–1 • **Process of Problem Solving**

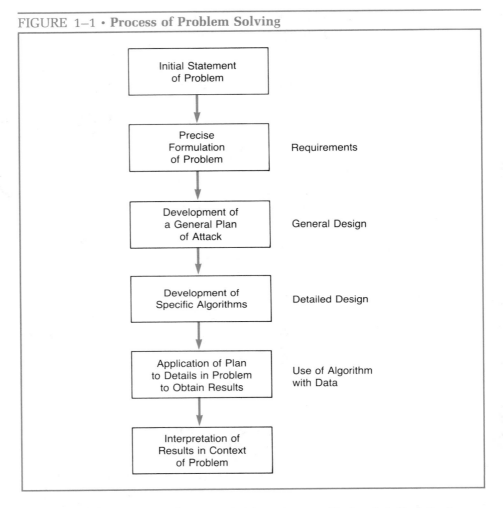

part of the system. This step is sometimes called a **detailed design or plan.** We will discuss algorithm development more in the next section and again in later sections of the book.

5. Once the detailed design is complete, we must apply the algorithms to the data. I might follow through the checklist and tests for the stereo and may find some connections that have become loose.

6. Finally, we need to interpret our results in the context of the problem. Once I have identified a problem with wire connections, I can infer that these connections were the likely cause of the trouble and proceed to fix the stereo.

Of course, the steps in this process may be followed in a systematic manner, or various parts of these steps may be combined. When we analyze many types of problems, however, we see that these steps normally occur.

Some Cautions

These steps may seem obvious enough that the problem solver may try to dismiss some of them as trivial. We need to be cautious about jumping to such conclusions, however. Certainly, some problems are very easy, but we need to develop problem solving skills so that we can tackle hard problems when they arise. By starting with reasonably simple problems, we can learn appropriate techniques that we can then apply to more sophisticated situations.

We can view much of science and engineering as the solving of various problems. A great deal of effort in these disciplines goes into reworking problems until they are understood precisely, and then developing techniques to solve them. Frequently, the hardest work is designing the means to attack a problem; the setup may be extremely difficult. Thus, we should not get discouraged if we cannot find an answer immediately, and we should not ignore any of these stages in the problem solving process.

SECTION 1.2   THE ROLE OF ALGORITHMS

We have noted that the first step in problem solving involves precisely formulating the problem, and the next is developing a plan of attack for solving the problem. In this section we will look more closely at plans of attack.

A plan of attack typically specifies two types of information. First, we must decide how to structure the attack. In other words, we must decide what steps to follow. Second, we must determine how to perform each step. Once we have identified the steps, we must know how to do them. In the process, we have developed an algorithm, which is a logical series of steps we can follow to solve a problem. As we will see throughout this book, effective problem solving depends upon the development of appropriate algorithms to solve the problem.

Writing Algorithms

When writing algorithms, we should be sure to include both the structure and the detail. We need to keep track of the overall ideas as well as the individual pieces. One way of doing this is with flowcharts. Figure 1–1 is one example, where various steps in the algorithm are stated and the progression from one step to another is illustrated by arrows. For complex algorithms, however, flowcharts can be hard to follow. The overall structure can be obscured by a mass of arrows and major steps can become confused with minor details. Flowcharts do not encourage careful structuring of steps, and so flowcharts will not be used much in this text.

Another way to indicate the structure of various steps is to use an outline form, where the major steps are shown at one level and the details are shown to be subsidiary. In contrast to flowcharting, we will see that outlining does work quite well with complex problems. The major headings remain unchanged as more details are added. In this book, therefore, we will concentrate on the use of outlines to develop algorithms to solve problems. Our motivation for learning about computers is our hope that computers can help us in problem solving, and we will see that algorithms written in outline form can be used effectively with computers.

Finally, as we develop algorithms, we must remember several points:

- Some problems may not be solvable. If we cannot find an acceptable plan of attack, we should consider whether we are attempting the impossible.
- Some algorithms may not be feasible. If a solution will require years of work to complete, it may not be of any practical value.
- Some problems may be solvable in several ways. The first solution may not be the best way to proceed. In some cases, one solution may extend to a large number of related problems, but another solution may not generalize at all.
- Sometimes we may be able to develop several algorithms to solve a problem, and we may need to examine each to determine which one is best.

<table>
<tr><td>SECTION 1.3</td><td>THE ROLE OF COMPUTERS AND COMPUTER SCIENCE</td></tr>
</table>

Up to now, our discussion of the general problem solving process has not involved the use of computers at all. The steps of problem formulation and algorithm design are necessary regardless of whether we expect to use computers. To determine when computers can be useful, we need to consider at what tasks computers are particularly good; this will suggest what role computers might play in problem solving. Also, several general questions arise naturally in this use of computers, and these questions will suggest some major topics in the field of computer science.

Computers are extremely effective in performing certain kinds of tasks: following logical steps; repeating steps quickly and accurately; storing and retrieving information; performing arithmetic; and transforming data. With these capabilities, computers are particularly helpful in applying algorithms to the data of a specific problem. Once an algorithm has been designed, the computer can be an effective tool in following the detailed steps of the algorithm.

Translating an algorithm into a form a computer can follow takes considerable effort, however. Thus, normally we will use a computer only if this extra overhead is offset by some gains that the computer can provide. Referring to the list of computer capabilities above, we see that computers can be of particular help in problems that require

- storage and retrieval of large amounts of data,
- transformation of large amounts of data,
- considerable processing of information, and
- repeating many steps with speed and accuracy.

As we continue our study, we will see other areas where the use of computers is particularly helpful. We will even see some cases where the process involved in using the computer can give us new insights for better understanding our own thought processes. Certainly, from the brief list above, it is clear that computers can be an important tool in following algorithms when either the data or the processing of the data is vast. The computer may not help much in developing algorithms, but once an algorithm is determined, the computer may be an effective tool in following some of the steps involved in solving the problem.

In the broadest sense, computer science is the study of how computers can be used effectively to help solve problems. More specifically, computer science contains many subfields that address various aspects of the problem solving process. These include:

Theory of computation: When can we be sure that a problem is solvable? If a solution exists, can we determine whether the solution is feasible?

Artificial intelligence: Can we understand the problem solving process more precisely? Can we analyze the effectiveness of various problem solving strategies?

Hardware design: How can we design machinery to perform the tasks that we need done?

Algorithm analysis and design: How can we develop algorithms effectively? What are some standard algorithms for performing common tasks?

Software design: How can we write an algorithm in a form that our machinery can follow?

Data structures: How can we store data in a machine so that we can retrieve and process the data efficiently?

Even from this incomplete list, we can see that computer science encompasses many facets of the problem solving process. The discipline is certainly more extensive than the typing of instructions or data into a machine.

In the next two sections, we will examine some of the details of actually using a computer. Then we will be able to return to the theme of solving problems.

SECTION 1.4   THE CONCEPT OF A PROGRAM

When we solve problems without computers, we may write out algorithms in a form that we can understand, in normal English sentences with appropriate formulas as needed. Familiarity with English allows us to outline our thoughts informally, and we may be able to infer details without great difficulty. If we expect to carry out our own algorithm, rather than letting others do the work, we may even skip steps in writing it out, because we know what we mean and we will be able to fill in the details later. Algorithm outlines may therefore be sketchy; we may actually write out very little, although occasionally this imprecision may lead to mistakes, such as leaving out steps or not accounting for some special cases.

When you want a computer to perform your algorithms, however, this casual approach to specifying algorithms will not work. In specifying algorithms for a computer, two important differences exist. First, you must write the steps in a form that the computer can interpret; informal English

FIGURE 1–2 • **Process of Problem Solving Using Computers**

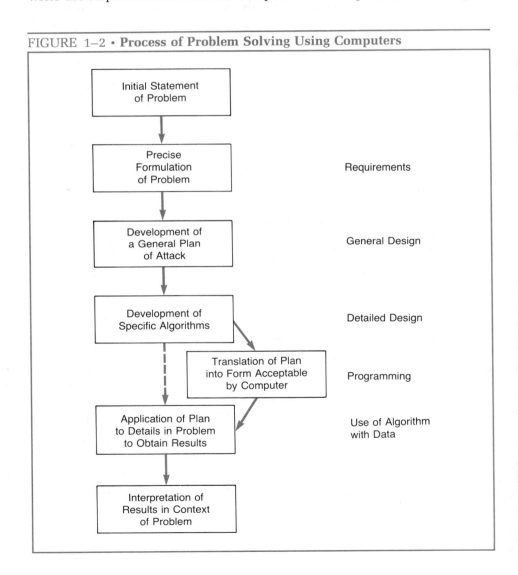

is not a satisfactory medium for communication. Second, you must include all steps in complete detail; the computer cannot guess what you mean where steps are omitted.

Thus, when you expect to use a computer to follow your algorithm, you must describe the algorithm to the computer in an appropriate language and in complete detail. This is the concept of a **computer program.** A computer program is a detailed, step-by-step set of instructions for performing a task, written in a language that a computer can interpret. This writing of a computer program forms an additional step in the problem solving process, **programming** or **coding.** Figure 1–2 shows the expanded problem solving process using a computer.

When writing a program, we must realize that the computer will not make inferences about steps that have been omitted or about the order of steps. We must tell the machine what steps to perform in what order, for a machine will do only what we tell it to do.

Computers can follow instructions very quickly and accurately, but they do not analyze instructions; they perform incorrect operations if we tell them to do so. They make no judgments about what we really mean, if we do not write out our intentions explicitly. They cannot fill in missing steps. They will not correct us if we tell them to perform operations in an incorrect order. They must be given instructions in a carefully defined format. The omission of even a single semicolon may prevent a computer from processing a program.

That machines will only follow our instructions may be quite different from the image of computers in movies or science fiction stories. Computers are often portrayed as having great intellectual powers capable of making incredible inferences at lightning speed. In reality, computers can help us use our algorithms very effectively, but we must tell computers what to do, with great care and precision. This programming effort has the additional benefit that it can help us think through our algorithms more carefully and sharpen our problem solving skills.

SECTION 1.5 ·   USING PROGRAMS TO SOLVE PROBLEMS

We have noted that we must write algorithms in language that computers can interpret if we wish to use computers as a tool in the problem solving process. In this section we will look at this computer language somewhat more carefully and consider some characteristics of the machines we are likely to encounter. In many respects, these details of programming language and hardware are only tangential to the problem solving process, just as setting margins and inserting paper in an electric typewriter are tangential to writing a paper. Thus we will outline only the major points in the process; we will not worry at this point about many subtleties. We do need to have some general overview of the process, however, if we are to understand how we can use computers easily and effectively.

Software Environment

A computer itself is essentially a mass of electrical switching circuits, so our instructions must ultimately take the form of information about circuits. We might write "0" for a circuit where no current flows or where a low voltage is detected and "1" for a circuit where current flows or where a high voltage is found. In this code, instructions must end up in a form such as "01101011," which indicates something about how the computer circuitry is to behave.

Computer Languages. In early machines all instructions were written in the 01 form, and algorithms were translated into appropriate sequences of 0s and 1s, called **machine language.** Even today all instructions must end up in this form before a computer can follow them. Different machines may use different sequences of 0s and 1s to represent an instruction, but each machine does have its own machine language. While this form of language may be essential for machines, we can see that it is not a form that people normally find comfortable or natural.

People like to think more abstractly. Over the years, therefore, a variety of other languages have been developed for computers, and these languages allow us to specify our instructions in a more natural way than is possible with machine language. These people-oriented languages are called **high-level languages,** and programming in them is a two-step operation. First, we write instructions in an appropriate high-level language; then, the program must be translated to machine language for the computer to follow (see Figure 1–3).

Translation to Machine Language. Fortunately, the second step of translation can be done by a computer itself, as long as we have written the program in an appropriate format, following appropriate rules of grammar for that language. This translation can be done in two ways. The whole program may be translated to machine language at one time, before the machine tries to follow the instructions. In this case we say the program is **compiled,** and the translator is called a **compiler.** The second approach is for the instructions to be translated one at a time, with the machine following one instruction before it translates the next. Here we say our language is **interpreted,** and the translator is called an **interpreter.** In either case, instructions in a relatively natural language are translated to machine language, and the computer follows the machine-language versions of the program.

Throughout this text we will have to be aware of both parts of writing programs. We will concentrate on writing instructions in high-level languages, but we will have to be aware of translation. If mistakes are made in writing a program, translation may be impossible; we will identify some errors that are frequently made. Other errors may translate into valid machine-language programs, but produce errors or omissions in logic. We will see some helpful ways to find and correct these errors as well.

Language compilers and interpreters are often part of a general collection of tools that can help us write, modify, test, and run programs. This

FIGURE 1–3 • **Steps for Programming in High-Level Languages**

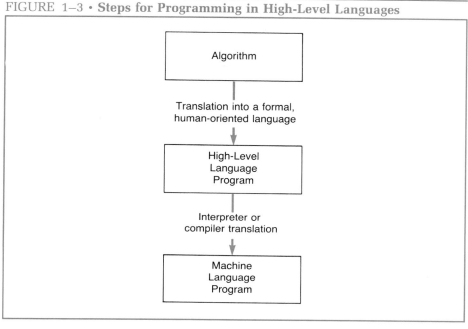

general set of tools comprises a **software environment,** and frequently this environment includes capabilities for editing and monitoring programs, as well as translating and running them.

Pascal.   In this text we will concentrate on one high-level language, called **Pascal,** because this language contains features common to many languages and because this language is particularly well suited to problem solving. Pascal is new enough (it was first introduced about 1970) that it reflects much of what was learned from earlier languages, but Pascal is old enough to be commonly available. In 1982 a National Standard Pascal was adopted by the American National Standards Institute,[1] and so the Pascal found on one machine will usually run on other machines as well. Some versions of Pascal have some extra features, but most versions contain the same fundamental features.

Hardware Environment

The software environment must be built for particular machinery. Each machine has its own machine language and its own special capabilities, although some features are common to most computers. In programming, we

---

[1]*IEEE Standard Pascal Computer Programming Language,* approved September 17, 1981, IEEE Standards Board; approved December 16, 1982, American National Standards Institute. Sponsored jointly by the IEEE Pascal Standards Committee of the IEEE Computer Society and ANSI/X359 of the American National Standards Committee X3. Published by the Institute of Electrical and Electronic Engineers, New York, 1983.

must consider the **hardware environment** as well as the software environment (see Figure 1–4).

Organization of Hardware.   Most computers are organized in much the same way, although details may differ dramatically. The heart of the computer is the **central processing unit (CPU),** which controls all the functioning of the machine. The CPU determines what instructions are performed, how they are performed, what data are to be used, and where the results are to be put. The CPU acts as the manager of the computer, and all other work in the computer is done on command from the CPU.

Connected closely with the CPU itself is the **main memory** of the computer. In most cases, main memory is located physically close to the CPU, often in the same cabinet, and data can move between main memory and

FIGURE 1–4 • **A Typical Hardware Configuration**

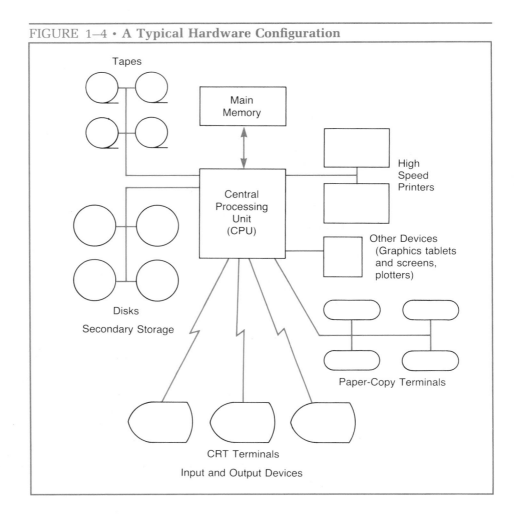

the CPU very rapidly. During processing information is normally stored in main memory, where it can be used quickly and easily.

Most of the other machinery in a computer is designed either to store information or to move information in and out of the CPU and main memory. This equipment, such as keyboards, printers, terminals, and storage devices, is sometimes called the **peripheral equipment** or the **peripherals,** and is often physically distinct from the CPU and main memory, with wires or cables running from one cabinet to the next.

Long-term or **secondary storage** comes in several forms, with the most common being **disks** and **tapes.** Disks have two basic forms: hard disks and floppy disks. Both types of disks look much like phonograph records, and an "arm" moves to the correct band or cylinder to store or retrieve information. Tapes follow the same principle for computers as for audio; information is stored as magnetic impulses and these impulses are read as the tape moves over sensors or heads. Both disks and tapes have the capacity to store large amounts of data, but in each case some mechanical activity is needed to retrieve the data. Thus, disks and tapes require more time to process information than the electronic main memory, but they can store much more information.

Input and output devices also come in several forms. Some devices, such as **high-speed printers,** are designed to print data rapidly, but they are unable to move data into the CPU. Other devices, called **terminals,** allow data to flow both to and from the CPU. Most terminals have keyboards on which users type information to the CPU, while information coming back is either printed on paper or displayed on a **cathode-ray tube (CRT),** which looks like a television screen. On occasions, other approaches are used for moving information in and out of the CPU. Paper cards and paper tape can be punched, with the position of the holes indicating the data. In recent years, however, cards and paper tape have become completely out of date, and magnetic tape is used instead.

In many cases, programming may not require extensive knowledge of these vairous units, but some applications will require planning what information will be stored where, at what time. Thus a basic understanding of the various pieces of hardware is needed for effective use of a computer.

Running a Program. As an example of how these processes work, this outline shows what happens when you run a simple program:

1. From a terminal, type your program into the CPU.
2. The CPU may store the program in main memory or on a disk.
3. To compile the program to get machine language instructions, tell the CPU to use a compiler (which is usually stored on a disk). The CPU follows the directions from the compiler to get the machine instructions needed.
4. The machine instructions are stored in main memory or on a disk.
5. The CPU runs the program, following the machine language instructions.

6. If needed, data for analysis are typed into the CPU from a terminal.

7. The CPU prints the results at a terminal.

Throughout this process, the CPU controls all activities, going to the terminal (for the program or data), main memory (for storing the program and the corresponding machine language instructions), and secondary storage (for the compiler) as needed.

Types of Systems and Modes of Processing. Although this organization is common to most computers, there are also some major differences in the way computers operate. Some computers (particularly microcomputers) are designed to be used for one task at a time. These are **dedicated systems,** doing only one thing at a time. Such systems might be connected to an experiment to collect data. A user of a dedicated system need never worry about interfering with other users.

At the other extreme are **time-sharing systems,** in which computers are designed to work for several users at once. The computer's time may be split among several tasks, with the machine working a fraction of a second on one task, moving on to other tasks, and then returning to the first task. In many cases the programs will be the same regardless of the type of machine we are using. In some cases, however, we can utilize particular features of a dedicated computer or a time-sharing system if we design algorithms in particular ways.

Beyond these distinctions, we can identify two other ways to work with computers. Many computers allow users to interact directly with the machine. We can type information directly into the machine, and we get information from the machine directly on a screen or a printer. This **interactive processing** allows users to monitor what the machine is doing. This type of processing is becoming more and more common.

Other computers perform tasks without much interaction. Such a machine is not slowed down by human activity; it first gathers a set of computer jobs together into what is called a **batch,** and then processes instructions in the batch without user intervention. This **batch processing** often allows a high volume of processing, but at a sacrifice of human interaction and monitoring. Here, too, programs will look the same in many ways, regardless of the type of processing done. At times, however, we will want to make special allowances if we know a particular type of processing will be used.

SECTION 1.6   THE ROLE OF CAREFUL METHODOLOGY

A Top-Down Methodology

At this point it is useful to formulate a general strategy for approaching problems. To begin, we make two observations: First, short, easy problems often require less time and effort than hard problems. Second, we are less likely to make mistakes if the answers are short and straightforward. While these observations may not seem profound, they do suggest a general approach to solving difficult problems. The idea, simply, is to reduce complicated problems to a series of simple ones that we can solve without trouble. This approach, called a **top-down methodology** for problem solving, starts with the major pieces and gets down to the details later.

To be more specific, when we have a hard problem, we will divide it into small, (usually) easier subproblems. When necessary, we will subdivide these smaller problems. At the end of the dividing process, we will have a collection of relatively simple tasks to accomplish, and we can hope to have little difficulty solving these easy pieces.

You will note that this is precisely the process followed in writing an outline, so it is an approach with which we are somewhat familiar. Begin with the major steps or tasks and divide them into smaller, more manageable pieces.

This same approach is seen in the organization of books or large papers. The entire book discusses a subject (e.g., Introduction to Computer Science), but that subject is too big to work with all at once. Thus the book is divided into chapters (e.g., Chapter 1, Problem Solving and Computing), so the author can focus on one part of the topic at a time. The one topic may be too large to be manageable, so the chapter is divided into sections (e.g., Section 6, The Role of Careful Methodology). If the sections are still too big, they can be broken down (e.g., an example about book organization). If the outline is carefully structured, the author will find that each paragraph and sentence contributes to the overall book, and the text has a coherent style and content.

Throughout this text, we will emphasize a structured methodology that will allow us to solve complex problems. We will normally outline solutions before writing programs, and we will structure our algorithms carefully. In some cases, this careful approach may seem unnecessarily formal for the problem at hand. If you can become comfortable with the style of structuring problems and working from general steps to details, however, you will be ready to attack complex problems later on.

SUMMARY

1. The problem solving process frequently involves the following major steps:
   a. Initial statement of problem
   b. Precise formulation of problem—**requirements**
   c. Development of a plan of attack—**general design**
   d. Determination of an efficient **algorithm** to perform each task in the general design—**detailed design**
   e. Use of algorithm with data from problem—algorithm **execution**
   f. **Interpretation** of results

2. When we use a computer to help solve problems, we need to add a step to this process, to translate our algorithms into **computer programs.**
3. **Computer science** studies all aspects of this process, from the initial specification of requirements to the final use of algorithms with data. Computer science involves a very broad range of topics and is not limited to specific uses of particular machines.
4. Within the area of algorithm design and analysis, computer science includes the study of when algorithms exist at all and when such algorithms are feasible.
5. When a computer processes data following an algorithm, the computer requires that instructions be coded in a **machine language,** which can be awkward for people. **High-level languages,** such as Pascal, have emerged to help people communicate with computers. People translate algorithms into high-level language programs, and computers themselves translate **(compile** or **interpret)** the programs into machine language.

EXERCISES

1.1 Write a careful definition of each of the key terms for this chapter.
1.2 The organization of this chapter illustrates the top-down methodology. The major problem solving steps are shown in Section 1.1 and expanded in later sections. Section 1.4 shows that sometimes an analysis

---

KEY TERMS, PHRASES, AND CONCEPTS

Algorithm	Interactive Processing
Algorithm Execution	Machine Language
Batch Processing	Main Memory
Cathode-Ray Tube (CRT)	Pascal
Central Processing Unit (CPU)	Peripherals
Coding	Printer
Compiler	Programming
Computer Program	Requirements
Dedicated Systems	Secondary Storage
Design	Software Environment
Detailed Design	Specifications
Disk	Tape
Hardware Environment	Time-Sharing Systems
High-Level Language	Terminals
General Design	Top-Down Methodology
Interpreter	

of a problem indicates places where the initial structure must be modified.

Outline this chapter, with the major problem solving steps as the main headings. Identify major themes in the sections as secondary headings. Subdivide headings as needed, and organize details under the appropriate headings.

1.3 Small computers are now being used in a large number of home appliances. In each of the following situations, identify what tasks are being repeated frequently, making computers helpful.
    a. microwave ovens
    b. washing machines
    c. clock radios
    d. videotape recorders

1.4 Review the flow of information for running a small program (Section 1.5). At each step, identify what the CPU is doing, where it is getting information, and where it is sending the results of that step.

1.5 Read an article on the use of computers in a field of your choice; identify what tasks are being performed by computers. Are there some tasks for which computers are not being used in that application? Why or why not?

1.6 For each of the following situations, develop a detailed algorithm for performing the desired task.
    a. Filling your car's gas tank and checking the oil.
    b. Obtaining money from an automatic teller banking machine.
    c. Making a cup of coffee. (*Caution:* In this problem you must decide what type of coffee and what type of coffeemaker you will use!)
    d. Paying a baby sitter for hours worked. The sitter receives $1.25 an hour from 6:00 AM to 9:00 PM, $1.00 an hour between 9:00 PM and midnight, and $1.50 an hour for time in the early morning, before 6:00 AM. (This pay scale reflects the family's schedule; the kids go to bed at 9:00 PM. The pay scale also acknowledges that the sitter has early-morning classes, which make late nights difficult.)

1.7 Consider the following three approaches for finding a word in a dictionary.
    Approach A
    • *Step 1.* Look at the first word in the dictionary. Compare this first word with your word. If they match, you have found your word and you may stop.
    • *Step 2.* Look at the second word in the dictionary. Compare this word with your word. If they match, you have found your word and you may stop.
    • *Subsequent steps.* Continue looking at successive words and comparing until you have found your word or until you run out of words in the dictionary.
    Approach B
    • *Step 1.* Look at the first letter of your word. Use the tabs in the dic-

tionary to turn to the page where words beginning with that letter start (i.e., turn to the beginning of the As, or Bs, . . .).
- *Step 2.* Proceed word by word as in Approach A.

Approach C
- *Step 1.* Turn to the middle page of the dictionary. Using the key words at the top of the page, see if your word is before that page, on that page, or after that page. If your word is on that page, proceed with the last step below. Otherwise, you have found which half of the book your word is on; continue with the next step.
- *Step 2.* Divide your half of the dictionary in half again. (You are now determining which quarter of the book your word is in.) See if your word is in the first part, on that page, or in the last part
- *Next Steps.* Continue dividing parts of the dictionary in half until you find the page your word is on.
- *Final Step.* When you find the correct page, go through the words one at a time (as in Approach A) until you find your word.

Each of these approaches will allow you to find your word in the dictionary. Informally analyze each approach. Describe which approach you like best. Is there a fourth approach that you like better than any of these? If so, describe it.

CHAPTER 2

THE FIRST
STEPS WITH
SIMPLE EXAMPLES

In Chapter 1 we observed that a major reason for the widespread use of computers was their capacity to help people solve problems. In this chapter we consider some simple problems, and we will see how to use the computer to help us find the answers.

Throughout the chapter, our applications will be quite elementary; we will use the computer as little more than a simple electronic calculator. This will allow us to become comfortable with much of the form, or syntax, of computer programs written in Pascal. At first the details of format may appear a bit overwhelming, as many pieces must fit together to get a complete program. One analogy would be learning to drive a car. If you know how to drive, you may remember that learning to drive involved many details, including steering, signaling, shifting, braking, and accelerating. Certain specialized maneuvers, such as parking or starting on a hill, had to be mastered. When you were learning to drive you had to think carefully about each detail, and it took time before you could perform the common maneuvers smoothly. After some practice, however, these details became automatic, and you can now concentrate more on general traffic patterns, nearby drivers, etc.

Your experience in programming will be similar. After the first few programs, you can expect many of the beginning details to become familiar and automatic. Eventually, in later chapters, you will be able to look at more complicated problems without being sidetracked by details of form.

EXAMPLE: COMPUTING UNIT PRICING

We begin by considering a simple problem.

PROBLEM 2.1

In a store, we want to compute the unit cost for a package. Write a program that will compute the cost per ounce for a particular package.

Solution to Problem 2.1

To compute unit cost, we will need to know the size of each package and its cost. For convenience, we decide to measure size in ounces (rather than in pounds, grams, or some other weight). Cost can be in dollars.

Our solution can have the following steps.

Outline for Problem 2.1

I. Determine size and cost of the package
    A. Determine size (in ounces)
    B. Determine cost (in dollars)
II. Compute cost per ounce
    The appropriate formula will be

$$\text{cost per ounce} = \text{cost/size}.$$

III. Write down cost per ounce as the final answer

From this outline we can now write a Pascal program that will perform these steps.

```
Program UnitPricing (Output);
```

This Pascal 'Program' is called by the name 'UnitPricing' and this program will print some 'Output'.

```
{This program computes cost per ounce,
given cost and number of ounces.}
```

We describe in words what the program does, as an integral part of the program.

```
Var Ounces, Cost, CostPerOunce: Real;
```

In this program, we will use variables called 'Ounces', 'Cost', and 'CostPerOunce'.

```
Begin                                            Our computations start here.

    {I.  Determine size and cost of the package}   We include our outline in our
         {Determine size (in ounces)}              program as well.

         Ounces := 16.0;                           This size was picked arbitrarily.

         {Determine cost (in dollars)}

         Cost := 1.25;                             This cost was also picked at
                                                   random.

    {II. Compute Cost Per Ounce}

         CostPerOunce := Cost / Ounces;            This is the formula we noted in
                                                   our outline.

    {III.Write down the cost per ounce as the final answer}

         Writeln(CostPerOunce)

End.                                              Our program "End's" here with a
                                                 period.
```

This Pascal program, as written, is complete and ready to be typed into a computer. When our typing is complete, we can tell the machine to compile the program (translate it to machine language) and run it (follow the instructions).

After running the program, the computer prints

7.812500E−02

This output is the same as 7.812500×10^{-2} or 0.078125.

In this particular program, we compute the cost per ounce for a 16 ounce package costing $1.25. We could compute the unit price for a package of a different size or cost by changing the appropriate lines in our program. Once these changes were made, the revised program would be recompiled and run to yield the new unit price.

From this example, we see that Pascal programs can be written in a form that is easy to read and allows us to follow our outline solution very closely. The program includes all the steps we want performed, and these steps are placed in the correct order for solving our problem.

SECTION 2.2   ELEMENTS OF A SIMPLE PROGRAM

The program in Section 2.1 illustrates many of the pieces that make up a Pascal program. In this section we will consider these pieces in some detail.

We will identify three general types of statements:

- Statements that tell the computer about the structure of the program.
- Statements that tell the computer about the work that must be performed at each step.
- Statements that act as notes for ourselves in reading the program and are ignored by the computer.

For each type of statement we will need to distinguish among three topics:

- **Syntax**—the format required for a Pascal program (the "grammar" of the language)
- **Semantics**—the meaning of the statements
- Relationship to solving problems

For convenience, we will refer to the following stripped-down version of the unit-pricing program. We have added line numbers at the left margin for ease of reference. They are *not* part of the program.

```
Reference
  Line
 Number              Actual Pascal Program
 -------     ------------------------------------------

    1        Program UnitPricing (Output);
    2        {This program computes cost per ounce,
    3        given cost and number of ounces.}
    4        Var Ounces, Cost, CostPerOunce: Real;
    5        Begin
    6            Ounces := 16.0;
    7            Cost := 1.25;
    8            CostPerOunce := Cost / Ounces;
    9            Writeln(CostPerOunce)
   10        End.
```

This illustration contains the following pieces, which are found in typical Pascal programs:

program heading (line 1)

comments (lines 2–3)

declarations (line 4)

statements (lines 5–10)

In considering each of these pieces, we will see that the program heading and the declarations indicate structure, the statements indicate specific tasks to be done, and comments act as notes for ourselves. We also will see how various pieces and statements can be formatted so we can read a program easily, making a clear division between one part of a program and the next.

We will now look at the syntax and semantics of each of these pieces in some detail.

Program Heading

Every Pascal program begins with a formal heading, just as every book begins with its title and author on a title page. In the unit-pricing program, the heading was

Program UnitPricing (Output);

This heading has three parts:

- *Program* announces the start of a program.
- The name, *UnitPricing*, we wish to give our program. The program name can help keep track of what the program is about, so we have chosen a one-word name that suggests the purpose of the program.
- A list in parentheses that tells the computer something about how data will move into the CPU and how data will move out of the CPU. We want to print results at a terminal, so we have used the word *Output* on this list. We will consider other possibilities later.

The semicolon at the end of the line separates the program heading from the rest of the program.

To summarize, a Pascal program begins with a program heading, which has the syntax (or form):

Program ProgramName (Output);

where ProgramName is a descriptive name of our choosing and *(Output)* indicates that we will print data at a terminal.

Comments

We may want to remind ourselves, throughout a program, what we are doing or what algorithm we plan to follow. We can make notes to ourselves within a program to aid our memory as we read the code. Such notes are called **comments,** and we can insert comments anywhere in a program by enclosing them in braces { }. In the example, lines 2 and 3 form a comment, since line 2 begins with { and line 3 ends with }.

NOTE: The symbols (* and *) are allowed as alternates for { and }, respectively, in the Pascal Standard. These alternatives are useful if the braces are not available on your terminal.

When we type comments into a program, they appear in the program listings, so we will have the benefit of our notes as we read the code. Comments are ignored by the computer, however, when the program is compiled.

The program in Section 2.1 has comments inserted throughout the program. Comments can start or stop anywhere in a line, regardless of what other material is to appear. Whenever we write comments, the computer will type the text with the program, but the computer will not try to interpret the comment. The comment is for our use, not the computer's. It is good practice to place a comment at the start of each program to describe what task the program performs.

Declarations

After the program heading (and usually some comments), we list the variables that are used in the program. Here we need to consider both what variable names can be used and how to tell the computer about these names.

Identifiers.   In computer science, these names are called **identifiers,** and the example includes several different identifiers. We have already mentioned the identifiers *Program* and *Output*. Other identifiers or names in the program include *Ounces, Cost, CostPerOunce, Writeln, Begin, End,* and *Var.*

More generally, in Pascal identifiers can be any meaningful sequence of letters and digits, provided the first character is a letter. (Most compilers do have a practical limit on the length of identifiers, but that limit may be fairly large.) Spaces are not allowed, but we can use capitalization to "separate" words. The following identifiers are allowed:

    Me2
    ThisIsAVariable
    FourScoreAnd7YearsAgo

These identifiers are *not* allowed:

    2BeOrNot2Be   (starts with a number)
    WOW!!!   (! is not a letter or number)
    Gee Wiz   (contains a space)

Specifying Identifiers.   Now that we know what identifiers are, we need to see how we can tell a computer about them in Pascal. In some cases this is easy, because the names have special meanings in Pascal. For example, the identifier *Program* is used for a special purpose at the beginning of our program, and this identifier may not be used in any other way. Such an identifier is called a **reserved word.** The Pascal language dictates how the identifier will be used, and that use is incorporated into the compiler. (All Pascal reserved words are listed in the front cover of this text for easy reference.)

A few other identifiers have been **predefined** in Pascal, and a compiler will recognize these terms automatically. For example, a compiler interprets the identifier *Output* in a program header to mean that the program will transmit data to a terminal. (The inside front cover also contains a list of predefined identifiers.) Later we will see that we can change the meanings of predefined identifiers, but in practice we can think of reserved words and predefined identifiers in much the same way.

Beyond these few identifiers that are already known to a compiler before we start, we need to tell the computer what identifiers we plan to use as variables, and we need to say what types of values they will have. In our illustration we mention the variables *Ounces, Cost,* and *CostPerOunce,* and we indicate that they will contain **real** numbers. (We will see a variable type **integer** later in this chapter, and we will encounter other types in later chapters.) In specifying these identifiers to the computer, we say that we are **declaring** our variables.

The syntax for this declaration of variables is shown in our sample program, where we have

Var Ounces, Cost, CostPerOunce: Real;

Here we used the reserved word *Var* to begin our declarations. Then we listed the identifiers we will use. Finally, after a colon, we indicate these variables will have *Real* values.

A more extended syntax is possible if we want to declare a larger number of variables. After the keyword *Var* we can list the identifiers and their type *(Real)* on several lines. In the illustration we could replace line 4 with

Var Ounces: Real;
    Cost: Real;
    CostPerOunce: Real;

or

Var Ounces, Cost: Real;
    CostPerOunce: Real;

In each case, we have mentioned the names of all of our variables, and we have indicated that all of these will represent *Real* numbers.

NOTE: Most of the program so far has been quite formal in specifying structure. We have had to worry about syntax (form), but this form has not really helped us solve our problem very much. In time, you will find this initial work does help clarify your thinking, and you will not mind the formalism.

Statements

Once the Program Heading and the Declarations have set up the program, we are ready to tell the computer the steps involved in the algorithm.

The steps themselves (lines 5–10) start with the word *Begin* (line 5) and finish with the word *End* (line 10); the statements between *Begin* and *End* tell the machine what to do and in what order. These statements are sometimes called a **Begin–End Block.**

Assignments and Arithmetic.   In the lines

Ounces : = 16.0;
Cost : = 1.25;
CostPerOunce : = Cost/Ounces;

we are computing values for the variables. First we assign the value 16.0 to the variable *ounces*, and then we assign the value 12.5 to the variable *cost*. These values are then used to compute a value for the variable *CostPerOunce*. In these lines the symbols := are used to denote the **assignment** of values to variables; the computer finds the value on the right side of the := and gives that value to the variable on the left.

Just as the division operator (/) is shown in the illustration, other arithmetic operations may be performed, using +, −, and * for addition, subtraction, and multiplication, respectively. Several operations may be put together on one line, and parentheses may be used to group terms as in arithmetic.

Pascal performs arithmetic operations in the same order as is done in algebra. That is, expressions within parentheses are done first. Multiplication and division are performed before addition or subtraction. We say that multiplication and division have **higher precedence** than addition or subtraction. If multiplications and divisions or additions and subtractions are mixed, then operations are performed from left to right. We say multiplication and division have the **same precedence.** Similarly, addition and subtraction have the same precedence. These rules are summarized in Figure 2–1, and examples follow in Table 2–1.

Note, however, that the computer will not perform algebraic steps with equations, so line 8 is not the same as

    Cost := CostPerOunce * Ounces;

We must be sure that all quantities on the right of an assignment statement have been given values by previous Pascal statements and that the correct variable is on the left.

Printing.   After values have been computed and assigned, we can ask the computer to print the results. In line 9 we have asked the computer to write the value of *CostPerOunce*. If we wanted *Ounces* and *Cost* printed as well, we could replace line 9 with

    Writeln (Ounces, Cost, CostPerOunce);

and the output of the program would be:

    1.6000000E+01   1.2500000E+00   7.812500E-02

FIGURE 2–1 • **Summary of Rules for Evaluating Arithmetic Expressions**

1. Compute within parentheses first.
2. Perform operations of higher precedence before operations on lower precedence.
3. When several operations of the same precedence appear, work left to right.

TABLE 2–1 · Examples

Expression	Result	Comment
7.0*(5.0 − 2.0)	21.0	Subtraction, in parentheses, done first.
7.0*5.0 − 2.0	33.0	With no parentheses, multiplication has higher precedence and so is done before subtraction.
30.0/3.0 * 5.0	50.0	Since division and multiplication have equal precedence, evaluation proceeds from left to right. 30.0/3.0 is computed first; the result, 10.0, is then multiplied by 5.0.

The values of the three variables are printed in the order specified.

The word *Writeln* instructs the computer to print something, and the variables in parentheses indicate what is to be printed. When several variables are listed, these variables are separated by commas.

In the next section we will see how to modify this statement to make the output easier to read. For now, the main point is that we can determine the results of computation by the statement *Writeln*.

Formatting and Punctuation.   As a final element of Pascal syntax, we need to consider how Pascal programs can be formatted, and we need to consider two types of punctuation; the semicolon and the period.

Pascal allows programs to be typed in a rather free format. We may not leave spaces within words (within *CostPerOunce* for example), but we may leave as many spaces between words as we wish. We may even start new words or symbols on new lines, and we may indent as much as we wish. For example, the statement

    CostPerOunce : = Cost/Ounces

could be written on several lines

    CostPerOunce
                : =
                    Cost
                        /
                    Ounces

Several statements could also be written on one line, such as

    Ounces : = 16.0; Cost : = 1.25;

This example also illustrates the need in Pascal for separating one statement from another. The **semicolon** is used to separate any two Pascal statements. Using this convention, we can type programs so they are easy to read. We do not have to cram formulas onto a single line. The semicolon tells the computer when one statement is done and the next is about to start. (If we omit the semicolon, the compiler will not be able to tell where one statement ends and the next begins, and the program will not run.)

Note, however, that since *Begin* and *End* are markers for the ends of the program statements, we do not need a semicolon after *Begin* or before *End*. We do not need to separate the Pascal statements from these markers.

One last element of syntax on this illustration concerns the **period.** Every Pascal program must end with a period. In writing English, we customarily conclude a simple sentence with a period, and Pascal works the same way. (Unlike English, we are not allowed to use marks such as ? or ! in place of the period in Pascal!)

We have now covered many of the basic details of Pascal syntax and semantics, and you can now write many simple Pascal programs. In the next sections we will look at several more examples where Pascal programs can help solve simple problems.

SECTION 2.3	ANOTHER EXAMPLE: COMPUTING SALES TAX AND TOTAL COST

In Section 2.1 we saw an example of a Pascal program that helped us with a problem of Unit Pricing, and in Section 2.2 we used this example to identify the basic parts of a Pascal program. Now we are ready for another example, and we will see how some modifications can make the final results easier to read.

PROBLEM 2.3	Sales tax is to be computed for a particular item. Write a program that will compute the amount of tax and the total purchase price, given the cost of the item and the tax rate.

Our solution to this problem follows a form similar to the solution of Problem 2.1.

Outline for Problem 2.3
  I. Determine item cost and tax rate
   A. Determine cost (in dollars)
   B. Determine tax rate
  II. Compute tax and total purchase price
   A. The appropriate formula for tax will be

$$tax = cost * tax\ rate$$

B. The appropriate formula for total price will be

$$\text{total price} = \text{cost} + \text{tax}$$

III. Write tax and total purchase price as the final answers.

From this outline we can write a Pascal program, following the format we have discussed in Section 2.2. In the problem we have arbitrarily picked the cost of the item to be $25.99 and the tax rate to be 0.07 (7%).

```
Program TaxComputation {Version 1} (Output);

{This program computes the tax and total cost of an item,
 given the original cost of the item and the tax rate}

Var Cost, TaxRate: Real;        {The Givens in our problem}
    Tax, TotalCost: Real;       {Our Desired Results}

Begin

    {Determine Item Cost and Tax Rate}
    Cost := 25.99;
    TaxRate := 0.07;

    {Compute Tax and Total Purchase Price}
    Tax := Cost * TaxRate;
    TotalCost := Cost + Tax;

    {Write out the desired results}
    Writeln (Tax, TotalCost)

End .
```

When this program is run, the computer prints

1.819300E+00   2.780930E+01

We can interpret these numbers by shifting the decimal point appropriately. (Recall that the E+01 indicates we should multiply 2.780930 by 10^1 to get 27.80930; the E stands for the exponent or power of 10.)

Strictly speaking, the program solves the problem, but the output of the program is not ideal for several reasons: We have to interpret the numbers by shifting a decimal point. We have to remember that 1.819300E+00 is the tax and 2.780930E+01 is the total cost. We have to remember what the initial values were for item cost and the tax rate.

We modify the output so we will be able to interpret the results more easily. Consider the following revised program. For convenience, we have added a variable *PerCentTax*, which is the tax rate in percent. The last parts of several *Writeln* statements specify output formatting, which we will describe shortly.

```
Program TaxComputation {Version 2} (Output);

{This program computes the tax and total cost of an item,
 given the original cost of the item and the tax rate}

Var Cost, TaxRate: Real;        {The Givens in our problem}
    PerCentTax: Real;           {The Tax in Percent}
    Tax, TotalCost: Real;       {Our Desired Results}

Begin

    {Determine Item Cost and Tax Rate}
    Cost := 25.99;
    TaxRate := 0.07;
    PerCentTax := TaxRate * 100.0;

    {Compute Tax and Total Purchase Price}
    Tax := Cost * TaxRate;
    TotalCost := Cost + Tax;

    {Write out the desired results}
    Writeln ('This program computes the tax and total cost of an item.');
    Writeln ('Cost of item = $', Cost:6:2);
    Writeln ('Tax Rate =', PerCentTax:4:1, ' %');
    Writeln ('For this purchase, the tax is $', Tax:5:2);
    Writeln ('and the total cost is $', TotalCost:6:2, ' .')

End .
```

When this revised program is run, the output is

```
This program computes the tax and total cost of an item.
Cost of item = $ 25.99
Tax Rate = 7.0 %
For this purchase, the tax is $ 1.82
and the total cost is $ 27.81 .
```

This output is much easier to interpret than the output of the first program. All of the objections raised earlier in this section are resolved.

If we look at how we achieved this better output, we see that our improvements fall into two categories, printing text labels and formatting numbers.

Labeled Output

The example illustrates that we can print text in output by placing the text in single quotes within a *Writeln* statement. Any text placed in single quotes is printed exactly as it is written. All spaces and punctuation marks are printed in the format that we specify, with one exception. If you want a single quote mark printed, you must use two symbols '', for otherwise the single quote would be interpreted as the end of the text. Thus the contraction "Don't" must be typed "Don''t". In all other respects, however, the computer will print text exactly as you type it.

Formatted Output

The example also illustrates how to format real numbers, but we first must consider the form that real numbers have. Real numbers are positive and negative numbers with decimal points, such as 3.1415927 or −12345.67, and these numbers have two characteristics. First, they require a certain number of spaces to print (e.g., both 3.1415927 and −12345.67 require nine symbols). In addition, they contain a certain number of digits to the right of the decimal place. Thus, to format real numbers, you need to specify the total width for the number and a number of digits to the right of the decimal point. In the example, this format is specified by placing both formatting items after the variable. Thus,

Tax: 5: 2

specifies that we want to allow five spaces (including the decimal point) for printing the value for *Tax*, and we want the number rounded to two decimal places.

In the example, Tax: 5: 2 left five spaces for the number, even though the number required less space than five characters. Since 1.82 only required four spaces, the first of the five characters was left blank. In general, if the number does not require all of the space allocated, the first spaces will be left blank; the number is right-justified in the space specified.

On the other hand, if a number requires more space to the left of the decimal point than allocated, then Pascal adds space to the width. Thus, if *Tax* were 135.79 and the format remained Tax:5:2, an extra character would be added to the overall width of the number; 135 requires three characters; the decimal point . requires one character; and we specified two decimal places in our format. The number printed, 135.79, requires six characters total. Further examples are found in Table 2–2, where ____ indicates that space is left in the output.

Formatting Hints

We have seen several ways to add text to output and to format numbers. Now we can discuss some general guidelines for putting these pieces together.

Perhaps the most basic principle is that output should be readable. A user of the program should be able to understand easily what is printed. This implies that enough space should be left on the page so various results can be distinguished. It may even be worthwhile to leave some blank lines between various parts of the output. To leave a blank line insert a *Writeln* followed by a semicolon. This will print out simply as a blank line. To skip several blank lines, just repeat this *Writeln*; statement for each line.

TABLE 2–2 • **Formatting Real Numbers**

Number to be printed	Format specified	Actual output*	Comments
123.46	7:2	__ 123.46	Number right-justified
123.46	7:1	__ __123.5	Number rounded to one decimal place and right justified
123.42	7:1	__ __123.4	Number rounded to one decimal place and right justified
123.5	6:2	123.50	Two decimal places printed
123.46	3:2	123.46	Extra space allocated, as number requires six characters
123.46	3:1	123.5	Number rounded, extra space allocated

*__ __ indicates space left in the actual output.

Numbers should be identified so anyone reading the output will know what each number represents. For example, our previous output included

Cost of item = $25.99

We can follow many approaches to identify results, and any approach that yields readable output can be acceptable. Here we will mention two common approaches, which are summarized in Table 2–3.

Approach 1: Placing results within text. In the revised program to compute tax and total cost we included the results of computations within

TABLE 2–3 • **Formatting Guidelines**

1. Output should be readable.
   a. Leave enough space.
   b. Do not cram.
   c. Label numbers.
2. When numbers appear within text:
   a. specify the appropriate number of decimal places;
   b. underestimate total width;
   c. leave spaces in text both before and after numbers.
3. When numbers appear in a table:
   a. specify titles for the table;
   b. be sure enough room is left for each number.

some text. The output included several sentences. In this particular program we knew how large our various numbers would be, so we could allocate exactly the right amount of space for each number. In this situation, we could determine the appropriate formatting information while we were writing the program. (A tax of $10 seemed unlikely, so we only needed to allow 1 digit to the left of the decimal point when printing this computed tax.) We did have to print a space before the final period, so the number $27.81 would not be crammed next to the period at the end of the sentence. However, all of the information was known ahead of time, and we could specify our formats without great difficulty.

Even if we do not know what output to expect, we still must specify formats. In this situation it is best to decide upon the approximate number of decimal places and then to underestimate the total number of spaces required. For example, we might specify *Tax:1:2*. Here, we know that 1 space is not enough (we need a leading digit, a decimal point, and two decimal places, for a minimum of four spaces). But we also know that Pascal will add spaces as they are needed. The *Tax:1:2* format will allow the computer to print the tax correctly, but we will not have any extra spaces printed at the start of the number. If we specified *Tax:10:2*, we would have plenty of room for our tax of 1.82, but there would be six blank spaces between the $ we printed and the number. *Tax:1:2* gives us adequate space without leaving unnecessary gaps.

To conclude Approach 1, when you print results within some text, you must decide upon the number of decimal places you want printed. To avoid large gaps in the text, guesses about the total width of numbers should be too small rather than too large.

Approach 2: Placing results in tables.   A second way to print output in a readable form is to place results in tables. For example, consider the following version of the tax program:

```
Program TaxComputation {Version 3} (Output);

{This program computes the tax and total cost of an item,
 given the original cost of the item and the tax rate.
 The results are printed in a table.}

Var Cost, TaxRate: Real;        {The Givens in our problem}
    Tax, TotalCost: Real;       {Our Desired Results}

Begin

    {Determine Item Cost and Tax Rate}
    Cost := 25.99;
    TaxRate := 0.07;

    {Compute Tax and Total Purchase Price}
    Tax := Cost * TaxRate;
    TotalCost := Cost + Tax;
```

```
{Write out the desired results}
Writeln ('This program computes the tax and total cost of an item');
Writeln ('when the tax rate is ', TaxRate*100.0:4:2, '% .');
Writeln ;    {skip line}
Writeln ('               Amount');
Writeln ('               (Dollars)');
Writeln ;    {skip line}
Writeln ('Cost of Item:', Cost:10:2);
Writeln (' Tax on Item:', Tax:10:2);
Writeln ('  Total Cost:', TotalCost:10:2)

End .
```

When this program is run, the output is

```
This program computes the tax and total cost of an item
when the tax rate is 7.00%

               Amount
               (Dollars)

Cost of Item:      25.99
 Tax on Item:       1.82
  Total Cost:      27.81
```

All dollar amounts are shown in a column that is clearly labeled and easy to read.

In printing such a table, we must allocate enough room for each number so that the columns of the table are properly aligned. Any guessing about the size of numbers should be on the large size. Allow enough room so that the machine will not add more spaces and ruin the alignment of the columns.

Next, note that the table is easier to read if you insert blank lines to set the table off from other parts of the output. (In some instances, you may want to leave spaces within a table as well, to aid readability.)

Some Programming Aids

There are some further techniques that can help when we place numbers within text or when we format tables. We may need to print long lines of text or numbers, and we may find it difficult to fit this text in a *Writeln* statement comfortably. Here we may proceed in either of two ways.

1. We may divide the text into a few lines within the *Writeln*. For example, the line

Writeln ('This program computes the tax and total cost of an item,')

may be written on two or more lines of a Pascal program:

Writeln ('This program computes the tax and ',
    'total cost of an item,')

Here we broke the long text into two smaller pieces and told the computer to print the first piece and then the second. Each piece was placed in quotes, and the pieces were separated by a comma. Notice that we still included the space after "and," so the pieces would fit together correctly.

2. We may use a varient of *Writeln* for the first parts of the line. For example, the above line may be printed

```
Write ('This program computes the tax and ');
Writeln ('total cost of an item,')
```

Here the *Write* statement works much the same way as *Writeln*, except that the machine does not go on to a new line after the output is printed. (The *ln* of *Writeln* means "line.") Instead, the next output will start where the *Write* finished.

Further, to divide an output line into several pieces, follow the form

```
Write (_ _ _ _);
Write (_ _ _ _);
Write (_ _ _ _);
    .           .
    .           .
    .           .
Write (_ _ _ _);
Writeln (_ _ _ _);
```

All of the material specified will be printed on the same line, with one *Write* starting on the line where the previous one finished. At the end of the line *Writeln* prints its text (if any) and moves on to the start of the next line.

Thus when we have long lines of text or numbers, we can divide the lines into short pieces, as different pieces in the same *Write* or *Writeln*, or in a sequence of *Write* and *Writeln* statements.

Another technique that can simplify programs is also illustrated in the last example. We wanted to print the tax rate in percent, so we needed to compute TaxRate * 100.0 . In Version 2 of the program, we did this as a separate step:

```
PerCentTax : = TaxRate * 100.0
```

Then we printed *PerCentTax*. The computation was not needed for the problem, only for the output.

In Version 3 of the program we included the computation in the *Writeln* statement itself, and we wrote

```
Writeln ('when the tax rate is ', TaxRate * 100.0:4:2, '% .')
```

In this line the first text was printed, and then *TaxRate * 100.0* was computed and formatted. Finally, the last text, '% .', was printed. In the revised program the percentage of tax is relegated to an expression in the output where it logically belongs in the problem.

With these observations and techniques using *Write* and *Writeln* statements, we are now able to print our results in any form that is helpful for our problem. We have sufficient flexibility in designing output to meet the needs of any problem. In the next section we will see how to run programs with different sets of data for input.

| SECTION 2.4 | LABELED INPUT |

We have seen how to write simple programs, and we have learned how to format output so we can interpret the results easily. In this section we will see how to use the same program to help solve several related questions.

Consider the following example.

| PROBLEM 2.4 | Write a program that converts yards, feet, and inches to meters. Once again, the solution follows a familiar form: |

Outline for Problem 2.4

   I. Determine values for yards, feet, and inches.

  II. Compute meters.

     From a handbook we find:

$$1 \text{ inch} = 0.0254001 \text{ meters}$$

$$1 \text{ foot} = 0.304801 \text{ meters}$$

$$1 \text{ yard} = 0.914403 \text{ meters}$$

 III. Print results

     From this outline we develop the following program:

```
Program YardsToMeters {Version 1} (Output);
{This program converts Yards, Feet, and Inches to Meters.}

Var Yards, Feet, Inches:Real;          {The Givens}
    Meters: Real;                      {The Desired Result}

Begin
    {Determine values for Yards, Feet, and Inches}
    Yards := 4.0;
    Feet  := 2.0;
    Inches := 7.0;

    {Compute the corresponding number of meters}
    Meters := 0.914403*Yards + 0.304801*Feet
            + 0.0254001*Inches;
```

```
        {Print the results in a short table}
        Writeln ('Yards    Feet   Inches   =    Meters');        {Write heading}
        Write (Yards:5:2, Feet:8:2, Inches:8:2);                 {Write givens}
        Writeln (Meters:13:2)                                    {Complete output line}
End.
```

When we run the program, we get

```
Yards    Feet   Inches   =   Meters
 4.00    2.00    7.00          4.45
```

(Note how we divided the last output line into pieces. Then we used *Write* to print the first three pieces and *Writeln* for the last piece.)

This program works well for the particular data we used, namely 4.0 yards, 2.0 feet, 7.0 inches. Whenever we want to run other data, we must change the appropriate line(s) in the program and recompile and run the program. Instead we might prefer to write the program so we can type our data at a terminal when the program is run. This suggests the following revised program, where we have added *Input* to our program heading.

```
Program YardsToMeters {Version 2} (Input, Output);
{This program converts Yards, Feet, and Inches to Meters.}

Var Yards, Feet, Inches:Real;          {The Givens}
    Meters: Real;                      {The Desired Result}

Begin
    Writeln ('This program converts yards, feet, and inches to meters.');

    {Determine values for Yards, Feet, and Inches}
    Writeln ('Enter values for yards, feet, and inches');
    Readln (Yards, Feet, Inches);          {Type values at our terminal}

    {Compute the corresponding number of meters}
    Meters := 0.914403*Yards + 0.304801*Feet
              + 0.0254001*Inches;

    {Print the results in a short table}
    Writeln ('Yards    Feet   Inches   =    Meters');        {Write heading}
    Write (Yards:5:2, Feet:8:2, Inches:8:2);                 {Write givens}
    Writeln (Meters:13:2)                                    {Complete output line}
End.
```

When this program is run, the computer begins

```
This program converts yards, feet, and inches to meters.
Enter values for yards, feet, and inches
```

The computer then waits for us to type in our data.

Readln (Yards, Feet, Inches);

specifies that we will enter values for these variables (in the order specified and separated by spaces) when the program is run. If we type

4.0 2.0 7.0

then the computer has the needed values, so it continues and prints

```
Yards  Feet  Inches = Meters
 4.00  2.00    7.00    4.45
```

Thus this revised program performs the same computations as the first version when we enter the same numbers. If we run the program again, we can enter new data without retyping any part of the program. We just need to type our new values in place of 4.0, 2.0, and 7.0. As before, we need to leave one or more spaces between numbers.

Some cautions: Inserting *Readln* statements can greatly increase the flexibility of programs, but they do require the person running the program to enter appropriate values. Whenever you use *Readln*, therefore, you must be sure to tell the user what is expected. In the revised program, this is done in two ways:

- The first *Writeln* in the program tells the user what the program does. The user learns the context of the program.
- The second *Writeln* gives the user specific instructions. The statement
  Writeln ('Enter values for yards, feet, and inches');
  tells the user that three numbers are needed. The user knows what these values represent and in what order to type them.

Without these two *Writeln* statements, a user could still run the program. However, when the computer encountered the *Readln*, the machine would wait for the required values. No messages would be printed, and the user could wait for a long time for something to happen. Even if a user realizes that some information is needed, the user may not know how much data are required or in what order the values should be typed. (Should we type "inches" first or "yards"?). Therefore, it is essential to prompt the user whenever information must be entered from the keyboard.

Programming Aids

We have the same flexibility in reading data that we noted earlier for writing. In particular, a *Read* statement is a variant of *Readln* that allows us to obtain a value from a terminal without moving to a new line. Thus

Readln (Yards, Feet, Inches);

is equivalent to

Read (Yards);
Read (Feet);
Readln (Inches);

In either case we could type

4.0 2.0 7.0

to represent 4.0 yards, 2.0 feet, 7.0 inches.
Alternatively, we could type

4.0 2.0
7.0

on two lines if we wanted more room for our numbers.
On the other hand, the statements

Readln (Yards);
Readln (Feet);
Readln (Inches);

would require us to type our numbers on three separate lines:

4.0
2.0
7.0

If we typed the numbers on the same line,

4.0 2.0 7.0

the *Readln (Yards)* would set *Yards* to 4.0, but the remaining numbers would be skipped. The *ln* indicates we must move to the next line. Thus the machine would still need values for *Feet* and *Inches,* and we would have to enter these values on two succeeding lines. This capacity to skip lines can be convenient, but it can also be a source of errors if we are not careful.

We can gain still more flexibility in labeling data and entering numbers if we combine *Write, Writeln, Read,* and *Readln* in various patterns. For example, we might want to prompt the user for each number on a separate line. In this case we might replace

Writeln ('Center yards, Feet, and Inches');
Readln (Yards, Feet, Inches);

with the lines

Write ('Enter Yards: ');
Readln (Yards);

```
Write ('Enter Feet:   ');
Readln (Feet);
Write ('Enter Inches:   ');
Readln (Inches);
```

When we run this revised program and enter the data 4.0, 2.0, 7.0, we would see the following:

```
Enter Yards:   4.0
Enter Feet:   2.0
Enter Inches:   7.0
```

The computer would pause on each line after printing the text so the user could type the data. The *Write* does not move the machine to the next line, so we are able to type our information on the same line as the prompt. The *Readln* tells the computer we only plan to type one number; other information we might add to the line should be skipped.

By carefully choosing which combination of *Read–Readln* and *Write–Writeln* statements we use, we can tailor our input and output to fit most problems. Users can be prompted at appropriate places, and both input and output can be readable. We should include planning for this user contact as part of our problem solving activities.

SECTION 2.5   INTEGER DATA TYPE

So far, all of our examples have included computations with real numbers. In Pascal, real numbers must have decimal points and at least one digit before and after the decimal point. Thus the real number 3 must be written 3.0 or 3.00, rather than just 3., and the real number ½ must be written 0.5 or 0.50, rather than just .5. Such numbers arise in many settings, and we should recognize their importance.

Many problems require other types of data. In this section we consider numbers that are whole numbers or integers. In Pascal, **integers** are numbers that are written without decimal points—such as 0, 3, and −37—and we must be careful to distinguish these numbers from reals. In fact, Pascal stores real numbers and integers in different ways, so that the numbers 3 and 3.0 are treated differently. (See Appendix B for more details on data storage of reals and integers.)

To begin we consider a simple division problem.

PROBLEM 2.5A   Compute the quotient and remainder when one integer is divided by another.

Outline of Problem 2.5A
I. Determine the dividend and divisor.

II. Compute the quotient and remainder.

III. Print and label all results.

This outline leads to the following program:

```
Program IntegerDivision (Output);
{This Program computes the quotient and remainder when one
 integer is divided by another.}

Var Divisor, Dividend: Integer;
    Quotient, Remainder: Integer;
Begin

    {Determine values for dividend and divisor}
    Dividend := 13;
    Divisor := 5;

    {Compute quotient and remainder}
    Quotient := Dividend Div Divisor;
    Remainder := Dividend Mod Divisor;

    {Print out all numbers in the problem}
    Writeln ('When ', Dividend:1, ' is divided by ', Divisor:1, ' ,');
    Writeln ('the quotient is ', Quotient:1,
             ' and the remainder is ', Remainder:1, ' .')

End.
```

When this program is run, we get the following output.

```
When 13 is divided by 5 ,
the quotient is 2 and the remainder is 3 .
```

This program illustrates several characteristics of integers in Pascal. Integers are numbers without decimal points, and integer data are considered distinct from real data. The variables are declared in the program to be *Integer*, not *Real* as in the past.

When we print integers, we have to specify the number of spaces needed for the number, but we do *not* indicate a number of decimal places. As with real numbers, the total width may be larger than required, in which case the number is right justified. If the width is set too small, extra space is allocated as required. In the program we allowed one space for each number. This was adequate for *Division*, *Quotient*, and *Remainder*, and each number was printed in the space provided. However, *Dividend* required two spaces, so an extra space was added over the specifications.

When we divide one integer by another, we might mean any of three operations. In Pascal, each of these operations has a distinct symbol, as noted in the following chart:

Operation	Symbol	Example
Integer Quotient	Div	22 Div 7 = 3
		20 Div 4 = 5
Remainder	Mod	22 Mod 7 = 1
		20 Mod 4 = 0
Real Quotient	/	13 /6 = 2.1666 . . .
		1 /4 = 0.25

These three forms of division are illustrated further in the next program.

```
Program IntegerDivision (Input, Output);
{This Program illustrates the three types of integer division}

Var Divisor, Dividend: Integer;
    Quotient, Remainder: Integer;
    RealQuotient: Real;

Begin
    {Determine dividend and divisor}
    Write ('Enter Dividend: ');
    Readln (Dividend);
    Write ('Enter Divisor: ');
    Readln (Divisor);

    {Perform various divisions}
    Quotient := Dividend Div Divisor;
    Remainder := Dividend Mod Divisor;
    RealQuotient := Dividend / Divisor;

    {Print results in a table}
    Writeln {Skip Line} ;
    Writeln ('                     Integer            Real');
    Writeln ('Dividend  Divisor   Quotient  Remainder Quotient');
    Writeln ('                     (Div)      (Mod)     ( / )');
    Writeln (Dividend: 5, Divisor: 10, Quotient: 10,
             Remainder: 10, RealQuotient: 12:3)
End.
```

When we use 13 for our dividend and 5 for our divisor, the program produces the following output:

```
Enter Dividend: 13
Enter Divisor: 5
```

Dividend	Divisor	Integer Quotient (Div)	Remainder (Mod)	Real Quotient (/)
13	5	2	3	2.600

We see that Pascal allows us to decide just what type of division we want to perform between two integers. The arithmetic operations of addition, subtraction, and multiplication do not require us to choose the type of operation intended; and these operations are denoted +, −, *, respectively, just as for arithmetic with real numbers.

Conversion Between Integer and Real Types

Although these arithmetic operations may seem the same for integers and real numbers, we need to emphasize that Pascal treats these types of numbers differently, and we cannot interchange the two types directly. As outlined in Appendix B-1, the different types are stored in different ways, and we must consciously change a number from one form to the other.

Conversion from integer to real is straightforward—just add a decimal point and zeros. For example, the integers 17 and − 325 convert to the reals 17.0 and − 325.0, respectively. With this ease of conversion, Pascal allows us to mix integers and reals in the same arithmetic expression, and in each case the integer is converted to a real number before the operation is applied. For example, in computing 17.3 + 14, the 14 is changed to 14.0, then 17.3 and 14.0 are added, to get 31.3. When such conversions are needed, the resulting values are always real.

On the other hand, we have to be careful in converting reals to integers. We would normally want to convert the real 14.3 to the integer 14. However, the conversion of 14.9 is less clear. The number is not as big as 15, so we might want to forget the .9. Still, 14.9 is closer to 15 than to 14, so we might want to convert 14.9 to 15. In Pascal, therefore, conversion from reals to integers is not automatic; you must specify which of two conversions to apply:

Round (14.9) rounds 14.9 to 15

Trunc (14.9) truncates the .9 to 14.

In general, to convert a real number to an integer, apply *Round ( )* to round the number and *Trunc ( )* to discard values to the right of the decimal point. Some examples are listed in Table 2–4.

TABLE 2–4 • Examples

Number	Round(Number)	Trunc(Number)
17.35	17	17
16.89	17	16
0.99999999	1	0

Example: Making Change.   We conclude this section by looking at an example that puts together some of the features of integers and reals in a practical setting.

PROBLEM 2.5B

In a store, a customer is to receive change for a purchase. Write a program that reads the amount of change and determines the number of $10 bills, $5 bills, $1 bills, and the amount in coins that should be paid back to the customer.

   Our outline here is a bit more complex than we have encountered in previous problems.

Outline for Problem 2.5B

I. Determine amount of change.

II. Compute the amount to be given in bills.
Look at the dollar amount, ignoring the cents.

III. Compute the amount to be paid in coins.
Subtract the dollar amount paid from the total amount of the change.

IV. Compute the number of $10 bills.
The number of $10 bills is the integer quotient when the amount in bills is divided by 10.

V. Compute the number of $5 bills.

   A. The amount in bills left to return is the remainder after paying out the $10 bills.

   B. When the amount is divided by $5, the integer quotient gives the number of $5 bills.

VI. Compute the number of $1 bills.
The amount of bills left after paying out $5 bills must be paid in $1 bills.

VIII. Print amount to be paid in coins.

   This outline yields the following program:

```
Program MakingChange (Input, Output);
{This program reads the change due a customer and determines
 number of $10, $5, and $1 bills and the total amount of coins
 that the customer should receive.}

Var TotalChange: Real;
    Bills, Tens, Fives, Ones: Integer;
    BillsAfter10s: Integer;
    Coins: Real;

Begin

    {Determine amount of change}
    Writeln ('This program makes change for a customer.');
    Write ('Please enter the amount of change due:  ');
    Readln (TotalChange);
```

```
{Compute the Number of bills}
Bills := Trunc(TotalChange);

{Compute the Amount to be Paid in Coin}
Coins := TotalChange - Bills;

{Compute the Number of Ten Dollar Bills}
Tens := Bills Div 10;
Writeln ('Ten dollar bills required:   ', Tens:1);

{Compute the Number of Five Dollar Bills}
BillsAfter10s := Bills Mod 10;
Fives := BillsAfter10s Div 5;
Writeln ('Five dollar bills requried:  ', Fives:1);

{Compute the Number of One Dollar Bills}
Ones := BillsAfter10s Mod 5;
Writeln ('One dollar bills required:   ', Ones:1);

{Print Change in Coins}
Writeln ('Change in coins required:  $ ', Coins:1:2)
End.
```

When this program is run using 17.85 as the change due, we get:

```
This program makes change for a customer.
Please enter the amount of change due:  17.85
Ten dollar bills required:   1
Five dollar bills requried:  1
One dollar bills required:   2
Change in coins required:  $ 0.85
```

This program uses the *Trunc* function, as well as the *Div* and *Mod* operations. You should check that each function and operation performs the task required in the outline.

In this program you might also note that several statements can be combined for brevity. For example, the computation of the amount to be paid in five-dollar bills could be written

Fives   : = (Bills Mod 10) Div 5;

The resulting code is shorter, but harder to check with the outline.

SECTION 2.6   CONSTANTS

In our work so far, we have used real numbers and integers, we have seen how to compute and print values from expressions, and we have seen how to assign those values to variables. In using these variables we may expect the values of the variables to change. For example, when we read a value, we do not know what number will be typed until the program is actually run, and different values may be entered if the program is run several times. Some values, however, will remain the same every time the program is run. These objects are **constants,** and we may want to think of these items differently from the variables we have encountered up to now. For example, consider the following problem.

PROBLEM 2.6   Compute the volume and the surface area of a sphere, given its radius.

Outline for Problem 2.6

I. Determine the radius.

II. Compute the volume and surface area from a handbook.

From a handbook, we find

$$volume = 4/3 \ \pi \ r^3$$

and

$$surface \ area = 4 \ \pi \ r^2,$$

where r is the radius and π is the familiar 3.1415926535. . .

III. Print the results.

In these formulas, we may expect the radius under consideration to change from one run to the next, but we know π will always be 3.1415926535. . . . Thus, when we write the program, we declare Pi to be a Constant rather than a Variable:

```
Program Spheres (Output);
{This Program computes the volume and surface area of a sphere,
 given the radius of the sphere}

Const Pi = 3.1415926535;                    {Pi is the constant 3.1415926535}

Var Radius, Volume, Area: Real;

Begin

     {Determine Radius}
     Writeln ('This program computes a sphere''s volume and surface area.');
     Write ('Enter radius:   ');
     Readln(Radius);

     {Compute Volume and Area}
     Volume := 4.0/3.0 * Pi * Radius * Radius * Radius;
     Area := 4.0 * Pi * Radius * Radius;
```

```
{Print Results}
Writeln ('When the radius of a sphere is ', Radius:1:2, ' ,');
Writeln ('then the volume is ', Volume:1:2,
         ' and the surface area is ', Area:1:2)
End.
```

When this program is run, we get

```
This program computes a sphere's volume and surface area.
Enter radius:  2.0
When the radius of a sphere is 2.00 ,
then the volume is 33.51 and the surface area is 50.27
```

In this program, *Pi* is declared at the beginning of the code to be the constant 3.1415926535. Then we use this number in the rest of the program. The resulting program is clear to read, since we can use *Pi* in all the formulas instead of the long, cumbersome decimal that it represents.

MaxInt

There is a special constant that is always defined in Pascal, although its value depends on the particular machine. The constant *MaxInt* is **machine-defined** to be the largest integer allowed on that machine. Pascal requires that all values in the range from $-MaxInt$ to $MaxInt$ (inclusive) are valid for integers. The following program will allow you to determine how large integers can be on your computer:

```
Program FindMaximumInteger (Output);
{This program prints the maximum integer allowed on this machine.}

Begin
    Writeln ('The maximum integer allowed on this machine is ', MaxInt:1)
End.
```

On some machines you may be able to use a few integers that are beyond this range. (On a PDP-11/70, *MaxInt* is 32767, but the smallest allowed integer is -32768.) You can only depend in your programs, however, on integers from $-MaxInt$ to $MaxInt$!

On most machines the limitation on the range of integers is quite severe, and this is one reason why real numbers are used in many applications. The range for real numbers is always considerably larger than for integers, although reals have other limitations. Some of the reasons for these limitations are based on the ways numbers are stored inside a machine; such details are discussed in more depth in Appendix B.

We have now seen how to write sample Pascal programs, and we have seen that constants can help us clarify some of the values in our programs. We will see other uses for constants in later chapters. In the next section we pause to note other ways we can make our programs readable and easy to understand.

SECTION 2.7   STYLE

When we consider the elements of style in the programs we have seen so far, we can distinguish the following categories:

Comments. We have already seen in Section 2.2 that comments can be placed anywhere in a program. Further, all of our sample programs share several characteristics. At the very beginning of each program, we have stated what task the program performs and recorded special features of the algorithms and any limitations that the program might have. Throughout each program we noted in comments the major points of the problem outline, so that any reader will know what each part of the program is supposed to do. Special comments guide us through specific parts of the code. For example, we often identified givens and desired results.

Since comments are so important in describing algorithms, we must be sure to write enough of them. On the other hand, we should not write an essay for each line of a program.

Indenting and spacing. You can also aid the readability of a program by clear formatting of the program. You can use indenting and spacing to show the program's structure. You can skip a space after each logical unit of the program, to separate one piece of code from the next. You can indent consistently following the structure of the code. For example:

- In our declarations we did not indent the word *Var*, but we did indent all declarations in subsequent lines.
- In the statement block, we did not indent the initial *Begin* or the final *End*, but we did indent all statements within the block.
- Whenever a statement continued on more than one line, we indented the second and subsequent lines to show that these lines were logically part of the first one.

If you follow consistent patterns of indenting and spacing, and if you allow enough white space to separate pieces of code, then the visual appearance of a program will indicate its structure, and you will be able to read the code easily and quickly.

Descriptive names.   In our programs, we carefully used descriptive names for all variables and constants. Of course, you could use short abbreviations, such as Y for yards and F for feet. As you need more names, however, these abbreviations become hard to remember. For example, you could use the following variables in the program for making change (Section 2.5):

> *CO* for TotalChange
> *C1* for Coins
> *BO* for Bills
> *B1* for BillsAfter10s

These variable names will work, but as programs get longer, you will find it hard to keep tract of which name represents what quantity. On the other hand, extremely long variable names also invite misspelling and can be cumbersome.

Constants.   Similarly, the use of Constants can help you simplify your code by allowing you to replace a long decimal with a descriptive name.

Input and output.   Sections 2.3 and 2.4 showed how to read and write information in whatever format we desired. In writing programs this means that we should choose a format that will be easy to use and understand. In those sections we noted this formatting could be guided by several principles.

- All results should be identified, so we know what each item is supposed to represent. Placing items within text or in tables often helps identify results.
- Users should be prompted when input is expected. Users must know what information is desired and how that information should be ordered.
- Sufficient space should be allowed between parts of the output, so the results are not jumbled together and hard to read. Inserting blank lines can help separate one set of results from the next.

Each of these elements of style can help you read and understand your programs. In many cases, just reading your code will help you detect and correct errors you might have made. Other times, you will have to rely upon testing to detect errors, and then you will need to read the program to find where and how the error occurred.

Now that you can write programs clearly, you are ready to begin running them.

SECTION 2.8   ## PROGRAM CORRECTNESS AND TESTING

We have seen how to create simple programs that are well structured and easy to read. We cannot be sure, though, that these programs help solve our problems until we know that what we have written works correctly. In this section, we will identify a few ways to check programs.

When you try to compile a program, the compiler may report some errors in syntax or semantics. For example, you may have misspelled an identifier, left out a semicolon between statements, or omitted a right brace at the end of a comment. In these cases, you are told you have made a mistake, but you have to reread the program carefully to find the error. For example, a misspelled identifier in a declaration may only be caught later by the compiler, when you try to use the identifier.

Once errors in syntax and semantics are corrected, the program will compile, and you will have a machine language program to run. Then you are ready to test the program to be sure it works the way you intend. You might begin by running the program with several pieces of data where you know the correct results. If the program works correctly on data that you know or where the answers are obvious, then you may have some confidence that the program will also work correctly on other data.

On the other hand, if the program does not produce correct results with test data, then you need to go through the code line by line to find the mistake. You might find that you mistyped a number or copied a formula incorrectly. In other cases, you might find that the logic in the solution outline was incorrect, and you need to revise your approach to the problem.

As you gain experience in programming, you will find you can recognize and correct errors reported by the compiler more easily and quickly than when you began. In subsequent chapters, you will also see many techniques that can help in writing programs that perform as intended. You will also find, however, that you can never assume a program is working correctly unless you check it carefully. Running code with a variety of test cases is one excellent way to do this checking.

SUMMARY

1. Pascal programs have the following form:
   - **Program Header**
   - **Comments**
   - **Program Block**
     - **Declarations**
     - **Statements**

2. All programs begin with the **header**

   Program ProgramName (Input, Output)

   Input may be omitted if the program will only write results and not read data.

3. You can write **comments** to help you understand your programs. Such notes are placed in braces { }.

4. In Pascal, the compiler must be able to recognize all names, or **identifiers,** that you use in a program. Some identifiers are already known to the compiler, including **reserved words** and **predefined identifiers.** You must **declare** all other identifiers, and you must specify whether each variable represents **Integer** or **Real** data.

5. After the declarations, indicate the steps the machine is to follow, in a **statement block.** Start with *Begin* and conclude with *End.* The steps may include
   - *Input of data.* Use *Read* or *Readln* when you want to type data into the computer from a keyboard.
   - *Arithmetic operations.* Use the arithmetic operations +, −, *, / for real or integer data. Use *Mod* and *Div* for integers.
   - *Conversion of types.* Conversion from integer to real is done automatically. Conversion from real to integer can be done in either of two ways, and you must specify the appropriate function, *Round* or *Trunc.*
   - *Assignments.* Once values have been computed, these values can be assigned to identifiers, using :=.

KEY TERMS, PHRASES, AND CONCEPTS		ELEMENTS OF PASCAL SYNTAX	
Arithmetic Operators and Operator Procedure	Printing Numbers and Text	Arithmetic operations:	Quotes ' ' for text
Assignments	Program Heading	+, −, *,	*Read*
Begin–End Block	Program Readability and Style	/ , *Div, Mod*	*Readln*
Comments	Real Number	*Begin*	*Real*
Constants	Reserved Words	Comments { }	*Round*
Declarations	Semantics	*Const*	Semicolon ;
Formatting Programs and Output	Statements	*End*	*Trunc*
Identifiers	Syntax	Identifier	*Var*
Input of Data	Testing	*Input*	*Write*
Integers	Type	*Integer*	*Writeln*
Output	Type Conversion	*MaxInt*	
Precedence	Variables	*Output*	
Predefined Identifier		*Program*	

- *Output.* Use *Write* or *Writeln* to print numbers or text. With some care, you can identify all results clearly and prompt the user when input is required.
6. Write programs in a style and format that allow you and others to understand them easily and clearly. When writing programs you should make effective use of comments, indenting and spacing, descriptive names, constants, and input and output.
7. After a program is written, **test** it to be sure that it works as intended.

EXERCISES

2.1 Rewrite the Unit Pricing program in Section 2.1 so the output is nicely labeled and formatted.

2.2 Rewrite the Unit Pricing program further so that the cost and the size of the item are entered from the keyboard.

2.3 Section 2.7 lists several features of good programming style. Find a sample program in this chapter to illustrate each feature.

2.4 Section 2.8 suggests selecting test data where the answers are already known or obvious. Determine a good set of test data for checking each of the following programs:
a. The Sales Tax program (Section 2.3)
b. The Change-Making program (Section 2.5)
c. The Sphere program (Section 2.6)

2.5 When shopping for pizza, we can find the best buy by determining the relative cost of each size. Assuming pizzas all have the same thickness, write a program that reads the cost of a pizza and its diameter (in inches) and computes the cost per square inch of pizza.

2.6 In the previous problem, suppose that pizzas can have different thicknesses (e.g., deep-dish and thin crust). Modify your program to include the thickness of the pizza as well as the cost and diameter in determining the cost per unit volume of the pizza.

2.7 As a pizza restaurant owner, you have determined that you can sell your 6-inch pizza for $3.50 to make a reasonable profit and still stay competitive. If your 10-inch, 12-inch, and 14-inch pizzas all have the same thickness, how much should you charge for these sizes?
HINT: Compare the areas of the pizzas.

2.8 In the previous problem, you computed the costs of pizzas based on a thin-crust, 6-inch pizza. Suppose that your price for a deep-dish 6-inch pizza should be $4.50. Write a program that computes the appropriate prices for 6-inch, 10-inch, 12-inch, and 14-inch pizzas for both deep-dish and thin crust styles. Use the relative areas of the pizzas to determine price, and print your results in a table.

2.9 Write a program that computes the molecular weight of a hydrocarbon molecule, given the number of atoms of carbon, oxygen, and hydrogen. From a handbook, we find

Atom	Atomic Weight
Carbon	12.011
Hydrogen	1.0079
Oxygen	15.9994

2.10 *Making Change, Expanded.* Modify the change-making problem of Section 2.5 so that it reads the amount of change a customer is to receive and then determines the number of bills, quarters, dimes, nickels, and pennies to be paid back to the customer.

2.11 A family wants to determine the cost and the efficiency of its car during a trip. Write a program that computes miles per gallon and cents per mile, given total cost, distance, and fuel consumption on the trip.

2.12 Write a program to compute a person's weight in grams, given weight in pounds (1 pound avoirdupois = approximately 473.59 grams).

2.13 A common algorithm for finding the distance between you and a flash of lightning goes like this: When you see the lightning flash, count the seconds before you hear the thunder. If you divide this time by 5, you will have the approximate number of miles between you and the lightning.

This algorithm is based on the fact that sound normally travels about 1100 feet per second. In comparison, light's velocity is almost instantaneous; it takes virtually no time for the light to go from the lightning flash to where you are standing. Thus, the time you count before hearing the thunder gives a good measurement of the time it takes for sound to travel from the lightning to you.

Write a program that will compute the distance in feet and in miles from you to the lightning, given the time delay in seconds before you hear the thunder.

2.14 Write a program that reads a volume in quarts and computes the corresponding volume in liters (1 liter = 1.056710 quarts).

2.15 Write a program that converts temperature in Fahrenheit to Centigrade and Kelvin.

NOTE: Centigrade = 5/9 (Fahrenheit − 32);
        Kelvin = Centigrade + 273.

CHAPTER 3

STRUCTURE IN
PROBLEM SOLVING:
INTRODUCTION
TO PROCEDURES

In Chapter 2 we saw how to write simple programs to help solve fairly straightforward problems. In this chapter we return to our problem solving theme, describing a more complete methodology for finding solutions. We will consider a general approach to problem solving as well as an application of this approach in a practical setting.

SECTION 3.1   PROBLEM SOLVING METHODOLOGY

In Chapter 1 we identified the following basic steps in the problem solving process:

- initial statement of the problem
- precise formulation of the problem—requirements
- development of a general plan of attack—general design
- development of efficient algorithms—detailed design

- application of the plan to the details of the problem—algorithm execution
- interpretation of results

We also discussed one approach for designing algorithms, a **top-down methodology.** In this section we will look at this approach and a second approach in some detail, and we will identify a general-purpose problem solving strategy.

In the precise formulation of a problem, we identify what we are given and determine what results we want. Algorithms then specify the means for getting from our givens to our desired results.

Sometimes you can see immediately how to proceed to get results, but in complex problems the path may not be so obvious. It is worthwhile to analyze why this path may be difficult to find. Although each problem has its own characteristics, the difficulties often fit into one or more categories:

solutions that involve many steps

problems that involve many details

problems that involve some complicated steps

If we analyze these difficulties further, we see that much of the trouble reduces to a fundamental human limitation: Our minds can only keep track of a certain amount of information at a time. We try to focus our attention on the problem at hand, but when the problem gets too big, we cannot keep all parts of the problem in mind at the same time.

For example, if a solution requires many steps, we may be able to keep the basic steps in mind, but we may not be able to look at the overall outline of steps while we figure out the details of each step. Similarly, if a problem contains many details, we may find it hard to remember all of these details at once.

Motivation for a Top-Down Strategy

Once we have made these observations about our own limitations, we can also see how to resolve some of the difficulties. First, we need to organize our work so we do not have to remember everything at once. Second, we need to be able to distinguish between the basic steps and the details of those steps. Sometimes we must worry about details, but we must also be able to step back from the details to see the general task that motivates the details. If we can apply these two principles, then we can avoid being overwhelmed by the complexity or the size of a problem.

When faced with a complex problem, we can begin a solution by identifying the major steps needed to perform the task. Once we know that the major steps fit together logically to give a solution to a problem, we can decide how to do each step in turn.

For example, consider the solution to the Making Change problem in

Section 2.5. The original problem was to determine the number of $10 bills, $5 bills, $1 bills, and coins that are needed to make change for a customer. When considering this problem, we analyzed how we actually make change. Once we knew the amount to be paid, we first counted out tens, then fives, then ones, and finally the amount in coins as needed. This analysis suggested the following initial outline:

Initial Outline for Making Change

    I. Determine the amount of change.
   II. Compute the amount to be paid in bills.
  III. Compute the amount to be paid in coins.
  IV. Compute the number of $10 bills.
   V. Compute the number of $5 bills.
 VI. Compute the number of $1 bills.
VII. Print the amount paid in coins.

This initial outline does not contain any details concerning how the various computations might be made. Rather, this outline covers the main steps needed in a solution. Further, when you read this outline you can see that the problem will be solved if you can do each of these steps. The outline is short enough to keep track of what you are doing, and you can see that these basic steps will fit together correctly. Once you have this initial outline, you can focus your attention on each step individually. For example, in Step IV you only have to determine how to compute the number of $10 bills required, and you can assume that Steps I, II, and III have been performed. Thus your work in Step IV is reduced to finding the number of tens required, given the amount to be paid in bills.

The point is that once an initial outline is developed at a general level, you can look at each step in the outline as a simpler, smaller problem. Then you can focus your attention on each smaller problem in turn, without being distracted by the magnitude of the entire problem. In the example, Step IV presents a relatively simple task to handle, to compute the number of $10 bills required given the total amount to be paid in bills.

While this task may not be trivial, it is certainly much easier than the initial problem. In Section 2.5 we came up with the idea of dividing the amount to be paid in bills by 10 and taking the integer quotient. There might be other approaches that work as well. If you do find several solutions, pick the method that seems best.

This approach of dividing a major problem into steps has a second advantage as well, which is also illustrated in the Making Change problem. The solution of one of the smaller pieces (e.g., Step IV) may suggest similar approaches for solving some of the other pieces (e.g., Steps V, VI, VII). Thus, when we look at the detailed outline in Section 2.5, we find that several of our steps follow the same idea of integer division. (We will expand on this observation shortly.)

This approach to problem solving has the further advantage that once the initial outline is established, you can apply the entire approach to any or all of the steps in turn. If one of the steps still seems quite complicated, you can treat that step as a new problem and find a general outline to finish that task. As a result, one step may contain several headings under it. This process can then continue until the pieces are sufficiently small to work out in detail.

Top-Down Methodology

This general approach is called a top-down methodology, and it will be our major problem solving approach throughout this text. To summarize the strategy we can identify the following features:

1. Start by outlining a solution at a general or abstract level.
2. Consider each step of the outline separately.
3. If necessary, outline specific steps, so some headings are subdivided into subheadings.
4. At each stage in the process, start at a general level and work toward more detailed levels.

Bottom-Up Methodology

Instead of the top-down approach, you might analyze various details and then identify several places where you need to perform the same tasks. For example, in the Making Change problem, we followed the same general approach in computing the number of $10 bills, $5 bills, and $1 bills.

This task identification is called a **bottom-up methodology,** for it generalizes from details and moves toward an overall structure. Note that this bottom-up approach is philosophically opposed to a top-down methodology, where you work from a general outline down to the details.

A Revised Top-Down Strategy

After considering these two strategies, it is apparent that the top-down methodology more effectively allows us to focus attention on a few pieces at a time, so we will always begin working top-down with an initial outline, refining the outline and adding subheadings as appropriate. In analyzing one part of the outline, however, we may also look at other parts to see if there are several places where we want to do the same work. If so, we will determine the details of that task just once, note the details outside the outline, and refer to that common task from the several places.

For example, in designing a wagon, we would start from the general concept of "wagon." Then, once we decide that the wagon must be supported in four places, we will not try to invent the wheel four times!

SECTION 3.2   EXAMPLES OF SIMPLE PROCEDURES

The previous section developed a revised top-down strategy for solving complex problems. In this section we will see how to incorporate this structure in our programs.

PROBLEM 3.2A   Write a program that prints a Tic-Tac-Toe board. More precisely, write a program that generates the following output:

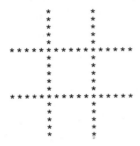

Our first approach to the problem might be to draw the two vertical lines and then the two horizontal lines, for that is how we might proceed if we drew such a board on paper. Few computer terminals and printers, however, can move paper backward or back up on a line. Our approach must therefore proceed from one line to the next down the paper.

With this in mind, we might divide the problem into five basic steps:

  I. Print the upper part of the vertical lines (the top five lines).
  II. Print a horizontal line.
  III. Print the middle part of the vertical lines.
  IV. Print a horizontal line.
  V. Print the bottom part of the vertical lines.

This outline includes all parts of the desired output, so we can be confident that this general outline will solve the problem.

We can now consider the details of each step in turn. First, we consider Step I, print the upper part of the vertical lines:

```
Writeln ('          *     *');
Writeln ('          *     *');
Writeln ('          *     *');
Writeln ('          *     *');
Writeln ('          *     *')
```

Next, we look at Step II, print a horizontal line. Again, the desired output is clearly specified in the problem, and can be accomplished by the following Pascal statement:

```
Writeln ('     * * * * * * * * * * * * * *')
```

Considering Step III, the desired output is exactly the same as for Step I. Skipping ahead, Steps I, III, and V all call for the same output. We have found a common task, which we might call *PrintVertical*. This task consists of the five *Write* statements for Step I and solves three parts of the outline.

Similarly, considering Step IV we need the same work as for Step II. Thus we have identified another common task, which we might call *PrintHorizontal*.

Our outline now reduces to the following abbreviated steps:

I. *PrintVertical*
II. *PrintHorizontal*
III. *PrintVertical*
IV. *PrintHorizontal*
V. *PrintVertical*

We need to write out the details for the tasks PrintVertical and Print-Horizontal, but once those details are given, we have solved the problem, as in the following program. Note that in Pascal tasks are called **procedures.**

```
Program TicTacToe {Version 1} (Output);
{This program prints a Tic Tac Toe board.}

Procedure PrintVertical;
{This procedure prints part of the vertical lines on the board.}

    Begin
        Writeln('         *        *');
        Writeln('         *        *');
        Writeln('         *        *');
        Writeln('         *        *');
        Writeln('         *        *')
    End {PrintVertical} ;

Procedure PrintHorizontal;
{This procedure prints a horizontal line for the board.}

    Begin
        Writeln('    ****************')
    End {PrintHorizontal} ;

Begin {Main Program}

    PrintVertical;
    PrintHorizontal;
    PrintVertical;
    PrintHorizontal;
    PrintVertical;

End {Main Program} .
```

In this program two tasks, Procedure *PrintVertical* and Procedure *PrintHorizontal*, are defined first, as variables were declared in earlier programs. In the last few lines the program uses those procedures (or tasks), following the outline. Pascal allows us to define separate procedures or tasks; once those procedures are specified we can use them anywhere in a program.

When the program runs, the machine starts with the *Begin* of the Main Program. The first instruction is *PrintVertical*, so the machine jumps to this procedure to *Write* the lines specified. Here we say that the Main Program **calls** procedure *PrintVertical*. When those lines are printed, *PrintVertical* is done, so the machine returns to the Main Program.

Since the first *PrintVertical* is done, the machine moves to the next task, *PrintHorizontal*. With this procedure call, the machine again must jump to procedure *PrintHorizontal* to perform this step. In *PrintHorizontal* the machine *Writes* the appropriate line. When this is completed, *PrintHorizontal* is done, and the machine returns to the Main Program. *PrintVertical* comes next, so the machine jumps again to perform this procedure, and the machine returns when that procedure concludes.

The Main Program guides the computer through the main steps of the program, and the machine jumps to the procedures whenever it needs to see the details of a step.

To continue this example, we might break *PrintVertical* into five smaller steps, where each step is to print the single line

*   *

In the next program, this common work is contained in a procedure *PrintDots*, placed inside *PrintVertical* as a subprocedure. We say that *PrintDots* is **nested** inside *PrintVertical*.

```
Program TicTacToe {Version 2} (Output);
{This program prints a Tic Tac Toe board.}

Procedure PrintVertical;
{This procedure prints part of the vertical lines on the board.}

    Procedure PrintDots;
    {This procedure prints the dots for the vertical line.}

        Begin {PrintDots}
            Writeln('            *      *')
        End {PrintDots} ;

    Begin {PrintVertical}

        PrintDots;
        PrintDots;
        PrintDots;
        PrintDots;
        PrintDots

    End {PrintVertical} ;
```

```
Procedure PrintHorizontal;
{This procedure prints a horizontal line for the board.}

    Begin
        Writeln('      ****************')
    End {PrintHorizontal} ;

Begin {Main}

    PrintVertical;
    PrintHorizontal;
    PrintVertical;
    PrintHorizontal;
    PrintVertical;

End {Main} .
```

Again, the procedures *PrintVertical* and *PrintHorizontal* are defined be-fore they are used in the main program. Within *PrintVertical*, however, we have defined a subtask in the procedure *PrintDots*. That task is defined at the start of *PrintVertical*, and after it is defined, it can be used as required in *PrintVertical*.

To conclude this example, note that in this revised form we have iso-lated the details of printing in two lines (one in *PrintDots* and one in *PrintHorizontal*). This isolation has the added advantage that we can mod-ify the program very easily to accommodate changes in the problem. For example, consider the following revision.

PROBLEM 3.2B

Write a program that generates the following output:

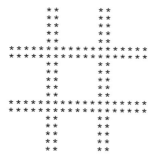

The problem is closely related to the original problem, and we can use the same basic outline for a solution; we only have to change the lines of the Tic-Tac-Toe board to double thickness. The new program is:

```
Program TicTacToe {Version 3} (Output);
{This program prints a Tic Tac Toe board.}
{The lines of this Board are all double thickness.}
```

```
Procedure PrintVertical;
{This procedure prints part of the vertical lines on the board.}

    Procedure PrintDots;
    {This procedure prints the dots for the vertical line.}

        Begin {PrintDots}
            Writeln('          **       **')
        End {PrintDots} ;

    Begin {PrintVertical}

        PrintDots;
        PrintDots;
        PrintDots;
        PrintDots;
        PrintDots

    End {PrintVertical} ;

Procedure PrintHorizontal;
{This procedure prints a horizontal line for the board.}

    Begin
        Writeln('     ******************');
        Writeln('     ******************')
    End {PrintHorizontal} ;

Begin {Main}

    PrintVertical;
    PrintHorizontal;
    PrintVertical;
    PrintHorizontal;
    PrintVertical;

End {Main} .
```

This program has the same structure as the previous ones. We only had to make minor revisions to the procedures *PrintDots* and *PrintHorizontal*.

We now turn to a second example where the structure of the outline gives rise to procedures in a Pascal program. We return to Problem 2.3A, where we were asked to compute the sales tax and total cost of an item, given its cost and the sales tax rate. We used the following initial outline:

I. Determine item cost and tax rate.
II. Compute tax and total purchase price.
III. Write out the desired results.

(See Section 2.3 for the more detailed outline.)

In this problem, the three steps do not have common tasks. Each step is quite independent of the others, and we might use procedures to emphasize that each step is a separate, self-contained entity, as in the following program:

```
Program TaxComputation {Version 2} (Input, Output);

{This program computes the tax and total cost of an item,
 given the original cost of the item and the tax rate}

Var Cost, TaxRate: Real;        {The Givens in our problem}
    Tax, TotalCost: Real;       {Our Desired Results}

Procedure ReadData;
{This procedure determines the Item Cost and Tax Rate.}

    Begin
        Writeln ('This program computes an item''s tax and total cost.');
        Write ('Enter Cost of Item:  ');
        Readln (Cost);
        Write ('Enter Sales Tax Rate:  ');
        Readln (TaxRate)
    End {ReadData} ;

Procedure ComputePrices;
{This procedure computes Tax and Total Purchase Price.}

    Begin
        Tax := Cost * TaxRate;
        TotalCost := Cost + Tax
    End {ComputePrices} ;

Procedure PrintResults;
{This procedure prints the desired results.}

    Begin
        Writeln ('Cost of item = $ ', Cost:1:2);
        Writeln ('Tax Rate = ', TaxRate*100.0:1:1, ' %');
        Writeln ('For this purchase, the tax is $ ', Tax:1:2);
        Writeln ('and the total cost is $ ', TotalCost:1:2, ' .')
    End {PrintResults} ;

Begin {Main}

    ReadData;
    ComputePrices;
    PrintResults

End {Main} .
```

As in the program to draw a Tic-Tac-Toe board, we have defined the separate tasks at the beginning of the program, right after the variable declarations. Once the procedures are specified, we can use them. Finally, the

Main Program is reduced to the three lines corresponding to the outline:

```
ReadData;
ComputePrices;
PrintResults
```

When this program is run, the computer starts with the Main Program, at the *Begin* located five lines from the bottom. The first statement says *ReadData,* so the computer has to go to the *ReadData* procedure to determine what to do. As part of this procedure, some text is printed and some data are read from the terminal. Then *ReadData Ends,* and the computer goes back to the Main Program.

The next statement specifies *ComputePrices,* so the computer must look at this second procedure to determine the next steps. As part of this procedure, *Tax* and *TotalCost* are computed before *ComputePrices* is done, and the computer returns to the Main Program.

Next, the program states *PrintResults,* and the steps in that procedure are executed. When that procedure is finished, the computer goes back to the Main Program and the program *Ends.*

The use of procedures allows the program structure to parallel the solution outline. We have incorporated the revised top-down approach to problem solving in a Pascal program. The overall problem can be divided into major steps, each handled by a procedure. These procedures allow us to separate the details of a step from the overall outline of the solution. When the same task must be done in several places, the program can use the same procedure each time. When tasks are independent, we can define distinct procedures. Thus Pascal programming can be an extension of the problem solving methodology; we do not need to change our perspective when we move from algorithm design to programming.

SECTION 3.3   ELEMENTS OF DEFINING SIMPLE PROCEDURES

The examples in the previous section illustrate the general form for defining and using procedures. This form is outlined in Figure 3–1. First, declare the procedures. In Pascal the program begins with a heading and then a listing of the pieces to be used (variables and procedures).

Second, in the statement block, use any of the variables or procedures that have been defined. In these statements, you use a variable name when you want to store a value you have computed or when you want to use the value later on. Specify a procedure name when you want to perform the task done by that procedure.

This same structure is repeated when you look at the form for defining procedures, as illustrated in Figure 3–2. A procedure starts out with a formal declaration (or heading)

Procedure Name;

FIGURE 3–1 • **Format of a Pascal Program Using Procedures**

Description	Syntax Outline
Heading	*Program* Name *(Input, Output)*
Declarations { Variables	*Var* names: type
	.
	.
	.
Procedures	*Procedure* name
	.
	.
	.
Statement Block	*Begin*
	statements, including references to procedures
	End.

where the name indicates how you will refer to this procedure later. After this heading, the procedure itself may contain some declarations. For example, the second and third Tic-Tac-Toe programs in Section 3.2 contained a procedure *PrintVertical,* and another procedure *PrintDots* was declared within *PrintVertical.* Thus, as with overall programs, a procedure begins with a formal heading and a declaration of the variables and procedures needed in this step of the outline.

After all of these declarations are presented, the procedure concludes with a statement block, where the procedures and variables can be used. As in the Tic-Tac-Toe programs, once *PrintDots* is defined in a procedure *PrintVertical,* you can use *PrintDots* as you wish within *PrintVertical.*

FIGURE 3–2 • **Format of a Pascal Procedure**

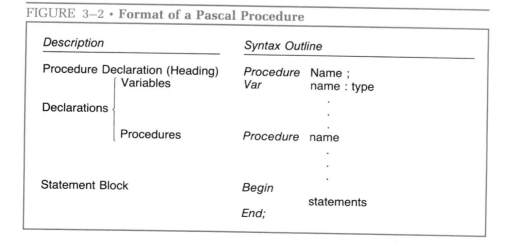

Description	*Syntax Outline*
Procedure Declaration (Heading)	*Procedure* Name ;
Declarations { Variables	*Var* name : type
	.
	.
Procedures	*Procedure* name
	.
	.
Statement Block	*Begin*
	statements
	End;

We will have more to say about some details involving the declaration and use of procedures, but first we need another example.

<table>
<tr><td>

SECTION 3.4

PROBLEM 3.4

</td><td>

EXAMPLE USING SEVERAL PROCEDURES

A florist wants to price flowers to reflect two distinct costs:

</td></tr>
</table>

- Each flower costs a certain amount to grow.
- A clerk must serve each customer.

The florist notes that the time spent by the clerk does not depend upon the number of flowers purchased. For example, the clerk spends the same amount of time showing flowers, offering suggestions, wrapping flowers, and handling money whether one flower or one dozen flowers are purchased.

The florist decides upon a pricing structure in which a price is fixed as the Base Price of a flower. This Base Price reflects the cost to grow the flower, with appropriate profit. (The Base Price may vary with the type of flower.) A service charge is fixed to cover the clerk's time. Once the Base Price and the Service Charge are known, the customer is charged the Base Price for each flower, and the Service Charge is added at the end. Stated as a formula, if n flowers are purchased, then

$$\text{Customer Charge} = n*(\text{Base Price}) + \text{Service Charge}$$

Recently the florist determined the following price schedule:

Base Price of Roses: $2.00

Base Price of Carnations: $.75

Base Price of Mums: $1.00

Service Charge: $.50

Write a program to complete the following chart showing flower charges:

Flower	Single	Half Dozen	Dozen
Roses			
Carnations			
Mums			

In analyzing this program, we will concentrate on the table we need to complete.

Outline for Problem 3.4

I. Print titles at top of table.
II. Compute and print charges for Roses.
III. Compute and print charges for Carnations.
IV. Compute and print charges for Mums.

Each of Steps II, III, and IV involves the same work:

A. Print name of flower.
B. Determine Base Price.
C. Compute and print cost for single flower:

$$\text{Cost} = \text{Base} + \text{Service Charge}$$

D. Compute and print cost for a half-dozen flowers:

$$\text{Cost} = 6*\text{Base} + \text{Service Charge}$$

E. Compute and print cost for a dozen flowers:

$$\text{Cost} = 12*\text{Base} + \text{Service Charge}$$

As part of this work, we must decide how we want the table to look. The following program results.

```
Program Florist (Output);
{This program prints the cost of various types of flowers,
 using a base cost per flower and a service charge.}

Const Service = 0.50;

Var Base: Real;

Procedure PrintHeadings;
{This procedure prints the headings for the price table.}
    Begin
        Writeln ('Table of charges for various quantities of flowers.');
        Writeln;
        Writeln ('                      Flower Charges');
        Writeln ('   Flower      Single   Half Dozen     Dozen')
    End {PrintHeadings} ;

Procedure ComputeCharges;
{This program computes the flower charges and prints those charges
 in the table.}
    Var Single, Half, Dozen: Real;
    Begin
        Single := Base + Service;
        Half  := 6.0*Base + Service;
        Dozen := 12.0*Base + Service;
        Write (Single:7:2);
        Write (Half:12:2);
        Writeln(Dozen:11:2)
    End {ComputeCharges} ;

Procedure Roses;
{This procedure computes and prints the charges for roses.}
    Begin
        Write ('    Roses    ');
        Base := 2.00;
        ComputeCharges
    End {Roses} ;
```

```
Procedure Carnations;
{This procedure computes and prints the charges for carnations.}
    Begin
        Write (' Carnations ');
        Base := 0.75;
        ComputeCharges
    End {Carnations} ;

Procedure Mums;
{This procedure computes and prints the charges for mums.}
    Begin
        Write ('    Mums    ');
        Base := 1.00;
        ComputeCharges
    End {Mums} ;

Begin {Main}

    PrintHeadings;
    Roses;
    Carnations;
    Mums

End {Main} .
```

Once again the Main Program is structured according to the outline, with separate procedures, *PrintHeadings, Roses, Carnations,* and *Mums,* for the outline steps. There is a separate procedure for the common task of computing and printing prices from the Base Price and Service Charge.

This program illustrates many important features of procedures and variables, and we will discuss these points at some length in the next section. Now we will review how the program works (see Figure 3–3). Execution *Begins* in the Main Program.

The first statement refers to procedure *PrintHeadings.*

The computer jumps to that procedure and prints the
appropriate text.

When *PrintHeadings* is over, the computer returns to the
Main Program.

The second statement in the Main Program refers to procedure *Roses.*

The computer jumps to that procedure, writes a title, and computes
Base.

The next statement refers to procedure *ComputeCharges.*

The computer jumps to this new procedure and
computes and prints several values.

When *ComputeCharges* finishes, the computer goes
back to *Roses.*

Procedure *Roses* is now complete, so the computer refers back to the
Main Program.

The next statement in the Main Program refers to procedure *Carnations.*

FIGURE 3-3 · Schematic Diagram for Execution of the Florist Program

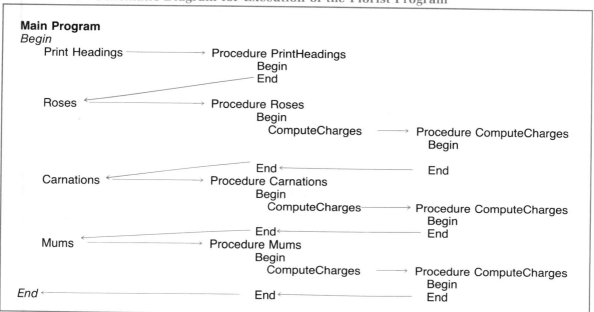

The machine proceeds as it did in procedure *Roses*. Similarly, the machine goes on to procedure *Mums*, from the Main Program.

Note that the *ComputeCharges* procedure has its own variables, *Single, Half,* and *Dozen*. Once these variables are declared, *ComputeCharges* can use them as needed.

This program illustrates the general form of Pascal programs with procedures and variables; we can follow what happens when the program is run. With this understanding, we will consider some details of this program with more care.

SECTION 3.5   SCOPE: LOCAL AND GLOBAL VARIABLES

The example in the previous section illustrates many features of variables and procedures. We will look at these points in more detail in this section.

Variables

At the start of the Florist program we declared

    Const Service = 0.50;
    Var Base: Real;

Then we used these variables in several procedures, including *Compute-Charges, Roses, Carnations,* and *Mums.* In fact, different values were assigned to *Base* in the last three procedures, and these values were used in *ComputeCharges.*

We declared *Service* and *Base* in the Main Program. We say that *Service* is a **global constant** and *Base* is a **global variable.** Global identifiers are declared at the start of a program and can be used anywhere within the program. For example, when we write

Base : = 2.00

in the *Roses* procedure, that value is used throughout the program. We can use that value of *Base* in *ComputeCharges.*

In contrast, in *ComputeCharges,* we have declared some new variables—*Single, Half,* and *Dozen;* these are **local variables.** Local identifiers are declared at the start of a procedure, and they can be used only within that procedure. We can compute and print values for *Single, Half,* or *Dozen* in procedure *ComputeCharges,* but we do not use the variables elsewhere. In fact, if we tried to write the value of *Single, Half,* or *Dozen* within the *Roses* procedure, the program would not compile. Procedure *Roses* knows nothing of the variable *Single!*

This distinction between local and global variables is very important, and you must be sure you understand where various constants and variables can be used. We say that the **scope** of a global variable is the entire program, and the scope of a local variable is the procedure where it is declared. Scope refers to the part of a program where an identifier is defined and can be used. As you gain experience with procedures, you will want to use local constants and variables whenever possible and avoid globals whenever possible. (In Chapter 10 we will discuss ways to eliminate virtually all global variables.) For now, we will use global variables as necessary, but we will be careful to use local variables whenever we can restrict our work with a variable to within a single procedure.

Visually, we can picture scope through the use of a set of nested boxes (see Figure 3–4). The Florist program is a large box containing the constant *Service,* the variable *Base,* and five procedures. Each procedure is represented by its own smaller box, in which all details of that procedure are hidden.

From any point in the box we can look out of our box, and we can look within our box. For example, when working within any procedure, we can look out and use the global variable *Base.* We cannot, however, look inside other boxes to use variables that might be there. It might be useful to think of the box walls as one-way mirrors; we can look out but not in.

Global variables appear outside of all procedures, and we can see them from anywhere in the program. Local variables appear inside smaller boxes—*Single, Half,* and *Dozen* appear in the *ComputeCharges* box. We can see (or use) these variables within the *ComputeCharges* procedure, but

FIGURE 3–4 • **Levels of Declarations for Florist Program**

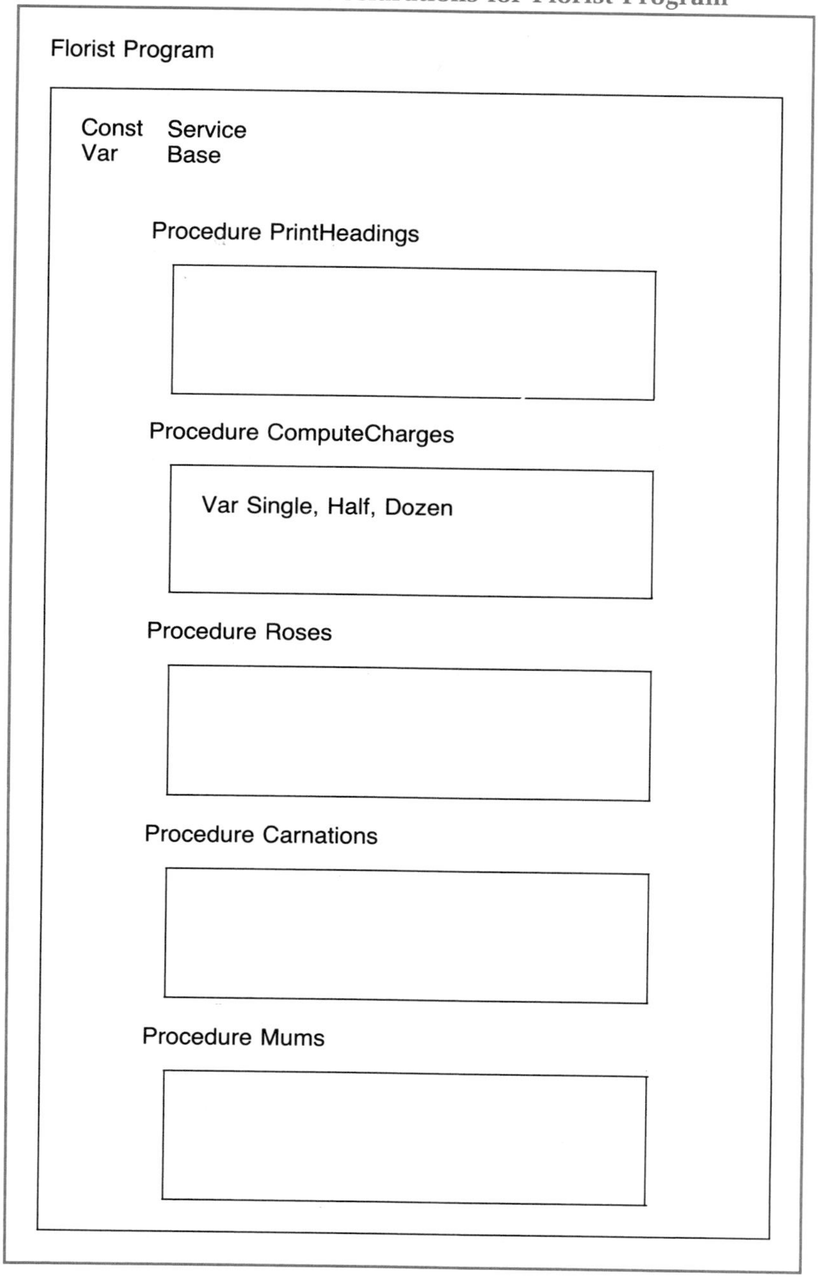

Florist Program

Const   Service
Var   Base

Procedure PrintHeadings

Procedure ComputeCharges

Var Single, Half, Dozen

Procedure Roses

Procedure Carnations

Procedure Mums

these variables are unknown outside that procedure. We cannot see them from the Main Program or from the other procedures.

Similarly, we can discuss where various procedures are known. We can only use a procedure at a given point in the program if we can see the procedure from that point. In the example, we were able to call *Print-Headings, Roses, Carnations,* and *Mums* from the Main Program, because we could see those names from the Main Program. (Here we think of the procedure name as being outside the procedure's box.)

Next, consider another approach for placement of the *ComputeCharges* procedure. We have already seen that we can consider this procedure as performing a common task, and we have defined this procedure globally so it could be used by procedures *Roses, Carnations,* and *Mums.* Alternately, we could consider *ComputeCharges* as a separate task for each of the flower computations. With this orientation, we might want to repeat the *ComputeCharges* procedure in each of the procedures *Roses, Carnations,* and *Mums,* as in this revised program:

```
Program Florist {With Three ComputeCharges Procedures} (Output);
{This program prints the cost of various types of flowers,
 using a base cost per flower and a service charge.}

Const Service = 0.50;

Var Base: Real;

Procedure PrintHeadings;
{This procedure prints the headings for the price table.}
    Begin
        Writeln ('Table of charges for various quantities of flowers.');
        Writeln;
        Writeln ('                          Flower Charges');
        Writeln ('    Flower      Single    Half Dozen     Dozen')
    End {PrintHeadings} ;

Procedure Roses;
{This procedure computes and prints the charges for roses.}

    Procedure ComputeCharges;
    {This program computes the flower charges and prints those charges
     in the table.}
        Var Single, Half, Dozen: Real;
        Begin
            Single := Base + Service;
            Half  := 6.0*Base + Service;
            Dozen := 12.0*Base + Service;
            Write (Single:7:2);
            Write (Half:12:2);
            Writeln(Dozen:11:2)
        End {ComputeCharges} ;
```

```
    Begin {Roses}
        Write ('     Roses    ');
        Base := 2.00;
        ComputeCharges
    End {Roses} ;

Procedure Carnations;
{This procedure computes and prints the charges for carnations.}

    Procedure ComputeCharges;
    {This program computes the flower charges and prints those charges
     in the table.}
        Var Single, Half, Dozen: Real;
        Begin
            Single := Base + Service;
            Half := 6.0*Base + Service;
            Dozen := 12.0*Base + Service;
            Write (Single:7:2);
            Write (Half:12:2);
            Writeln(Dozen:11:2)
        End {ComputeCharges} ;

    Begin {Carnations}
        Write (' Carnations ');
        Base := 0.75;
        ComputeCharges
    End {Carnations} ;

Procedure Mums;
{This procedure computes and prints the charges for mums.}

    Procedure ComputeCharges;
    {This program computes the flower charges and prints those charges
     in the table.}
        Var Single, Half, Dozen: Real;
        Begin
            Single := Base + Service;
            Half := 6.0*Base + Service;
            Dozen := 12.0*Base + Service;
            Write (Single:7:2);
            Write (Half:12:2);
            Writeln(Dozen:11:2)
        End {ComputeCharges} ;

    Begin {Mums}
        Write ('     Mums    ');
        Base := 1.00;
        ComputeCharges {This strange name occurs again!!!}
    End {Mums} ;

Begin {Main}

    PrintHeadings;
    Roses;
    Carnations;
    Mums

End {Main} .
```

This program produces the same output as the first Florist program, but its structure is quite different (see Figure 3–5).

In fact, in this program each of the three *ComputeCharges* procedures is considered as a separate, unrelated item. If we wished, we could write three different procedures with different variable names, and these proce-

FIGURE 3–5 • **Levels of Declarations for Florist Program Using Three Separate ComputeCharges Procedures**

Florist Program {with separate computer charges procedures}

Const   Service
Var   Base

Procedure PrintHeadings

Procedure Roses

Procedure ComputeCharges

Var Single, Half, Dozen

Procedure Carnations

Procedure ComputeCharges

Var Single, Half, Dozen

Procedure Mums

Procedure ComputeCharges

Var Single, Half, Dozen

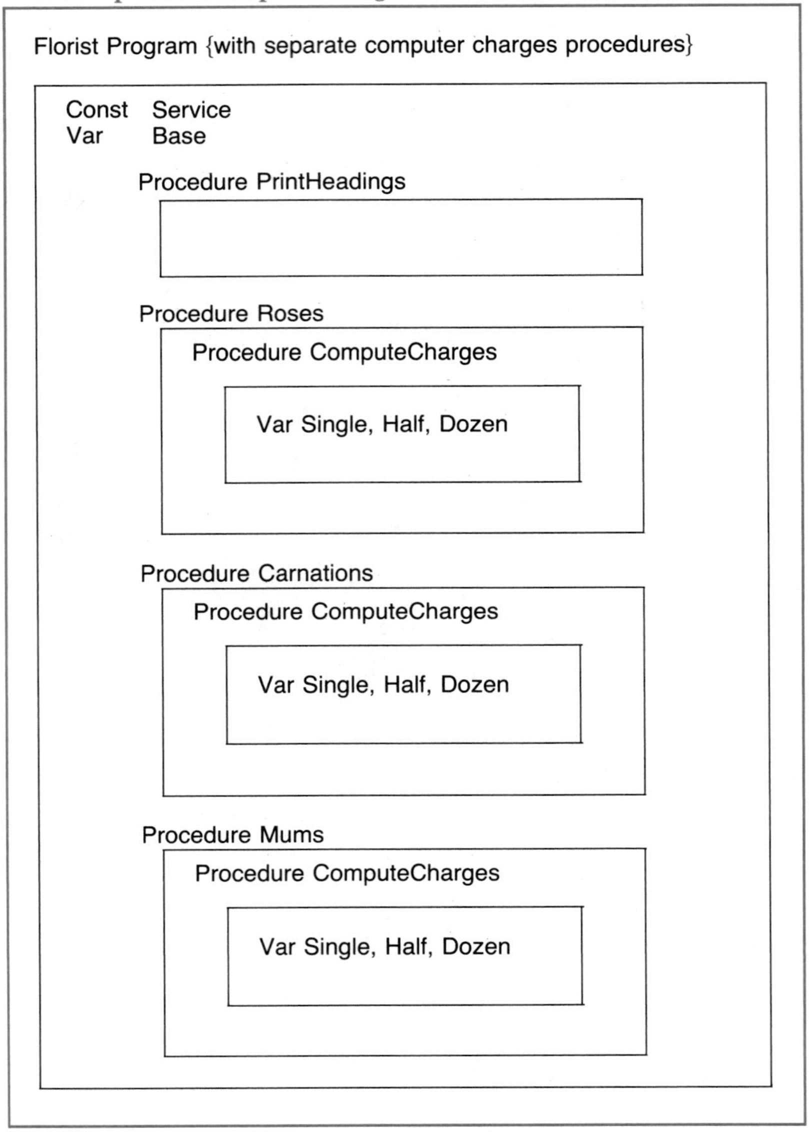

dures could perform separate tasks. What we write inside one procedure has no effect on what we write inside other procedures.

The Forward Statement

We conclude this section by mentioning one more aspect of procedure declaration, which is also illustrated by the Florist example. In the first Florist program, the procedure declarations were, in order, *PrintHeadings*, *ComputeCharges*, *Roses*, *Carnations*, *Mums*.

This order of procedures fits well with the outline for the solution, but the order also had a useful side effect. *ComputeCharges* was declared before it was used in *Roses*, *Carnations*, and *Mums*. Thus, when the compiler got to these last three procedures, it already knew what procedure *ComputeCharges* was. Early declaration of *ComputeCharges* allowed the compiler to use the procedure in the later procedures, and many times this ordering is convenient.

Sometimes, however, you may want to define a procedure after it is referenced. (In Chapter 19, we will see some instances where this is actually necessary.) For example, you might want to declare procedures in alphabetical order, so you can find them easily in the program (output remaining the same). This can be done in two steps. First, early in the program tell the computer that the procedure is coming. Then, later on, you can furnish the details of the procedure.

More precisely, early in the program, before the procedure is used, place the first part of the declaration, followed by the word *Forward*. For example, you might write

Procedure ComputeCharges; Forward;

No other part of the procedure appears at this point; you are only telling the compiler that this procedure is listed eventually. Then, later in the program, repeat

Procedure ComputeCharges;

followed by the complete declaration, including declarations and statement block. The complete program might look like this:

```
Program Florist (Output);
{This program prints the cost of various types of flowers,
 using a base cost per flower and a service charge.}

Const Service = 0.50;

Var Base: Real;
```

```
Procedure ComputeCharges; Forward; {This procedure is defined later}

Procedure Carnations;
{This procedure computes and prints the charges for carnations.}
    Begin
        Write (' Carnations ');
        Base := 0.75;
        ComputeCharges
    End {Carnations} ;

Procedure ComputeCharges; {The full definition is given here}
{This program computes the flower charges and prints those charges
 in the table.}
    Var Single, Half, Dozen: Real;
    Begin
        Single := Base + Service;
        Half := 6.0*Base + Service;
        Dozen := 12.0*Base + Service;
        Write (Single:7:2);
        Write (Half:12:2);
        Writeln(Dozen:11:2)
    End {ComputeCharges} ;

Procedure Mums;
{This procedure computes and prints the charges for mums.}
    Begin
        Write ('    Mums    ');
        Base := 1.00;
        ComputeCharges
    End {Mums} ;

Procedure PrintHeadings;
{This procedure prints the headings for the price table.}
    Begin
        Writeln ('Table of charges for various quantities of flowers.');
        Writeln;
        Writeln ('                    Flower Charges');
        Writeln ('  Flower      Single   Half Dozen    Dozen')
    End {PrintHeadings} ;

Procedure Roses;
{This procedure computes and prints the charges for roses.}
    Begin
        Write ('    Roses   ');
        Base := 2.00;
        ComputeCharges
    End {Roses} ;

Begin {Main}

    PrintHeadings;
    Roses;
    Carnations;
    Mums

End {Main}
```

We have now seen many of the important aspects of procedures and variables. We have distinguished between local and global variables. We have examined the scope of variables. We have defined procedures, and we can determine their scope. We have seen that we can declare procedures in various orders, although we may need the *Forward* statement if we wish to reference a procedure before it is defined. In the next section we will discuss some elements of style that can help in using procedures effectively and easily.

SECTION 3.6	**STYLE**

In this chapter we have refined our approach to problem solving. We start by dividing the solution into steps, and subdivide each step as needed. When a task is required in several places, we consider that step separately. This common task is defined outside the outline, but referred to at each appropriate point.

When we move from an outline to a Pascal program, we can retain the same features of structure (see Figure 3–6). Each solution step, subdivision, or task can be written separately as a procedure. Further, if one step logically contains several subdivisions, we can define several small procedures inside a larger procedure. In fact, virtually all of the principles of organization and formatting discussed for outlines apply to programs. To be more concrete, our remarks on problem solving suggest the following principles of program style:

Procedures
- Divide programs into procedures, where each procedure performs one step, subdivision, or task in the solution outline.
- Keep procedures independent of each other as much as possible, so details of one procedure have little or no impact on others.
- Make procedure statements stand out as major steps in the program or solution and indent details, including local declarations, subprocedures, and *Begin–End* blocks.
- Pick descriptive names for procedures that suggest the work that the procedures perform.

Local and Global Variables
- At each step of the outline, distinguish between data needed within a step and data needed in other steps. Declare variables on the basis of what data are needed where.
- Use global variables and constants only when data are needed in several steps. Use local variables and constants when data are needed within one step only.
- Try to use local variables and constants whenever possible.

FIGURE 3–6 • **Program Form Parallels Outline Form**

```
                              Program
                              Var {global variables}
Common Task A                 Procedure TaskA
                                  Var {local variables}
                                  Begin
                                      .
                                      .
                                      .
                              End;
Common Task B                 Procedure TaskB
                                  Var {local variables}
                                  Begin
                                      .
                                      .
                                      .
                              End

    .                             .
    .                             .
    .                             .
I. Step I                     Procedure StepI
   A. Subdivision 1               Var {local variables}
                                  Procedure SubI
                                      Var {local variables}
                                      Begin
                                          .
                                          .
                                          .
                                  End
   B. Subdivision 2               Procedure Sub2
                                      Var {local variables}
                                      Begin
                                          .
                                          .
                                          .
                                  End
                                  Begin {StepI}
                                  End   {StepI}
II. Step II                   Procedure StepII
    A. Subdivision 1              Var {local variables}
                                  Procedure SubI
                                      Var {local variables}
                                      Begin
                                          .
                                          .
                                          .
                                  End
    B. Subdivision 2              Procedure Sub2
                                      Var {local variables}
                                      Begin
                                          .
                                          .
                                          .
                                  End
                                  Begin {StepII}
                                  End   {StepII}
```

Changes in local variables have no effect on the working of other procedures, so local variables help keep procedures independent. Changes in global variables in one procedure will yield changes for all other procedures as well. Thus, while global variables are needed to transfer data from one step to another, they should be used carefully so that the steps can remain as independent as possible. (We will discuss ways to eliminate even these global variables in Chapter 10.)

Comments

- Use comments within procedures just as you use them for clarifying the structure of a program.
- State the purpose of each procedure in a comment at the start of the procedure.
- Align this initial comment with the *Procedure* statement; the comment should not be indented. (See programs throughout this chapter as examples.)
- Clarify where each procedure ends by placing its name in a comment after the procedure's *End* statement. If the procedure contains several smaller procedures, attach the main procedure's name to the *Begin* statement as well.

When you follow these general guidelines in writing and formatting programs, the style of your programs will follow your solution outlines very closely; the program appears as a carefully written, well-organized outline. The general structure of the program stands out clearly, and the details are contained within appropriate steps.

SUMMARY

1. In an expanded problem solving strategy, we begin with a **top-down** analysis of the problem, dividing the solution into several major steps and subdividing these steps as necessary. When we identify the same required task in several places, we consider that common task separately. A common task is defined outside the outline and referred to within the outline as needed. Identification of common tasks is the basis of a **bottom-up** analysis; we must be careful not to allow the common tasks to obscure our overall approach to solving the problem.

2. **Procedures** allow us to organize programs following the steps of the outline. Define a procedure to perform each step and task in the outline. When steps are split into pieces, define several small procedures inside the large ones.

3. Each procedure can reference **global variables** and **constants** that are needed throughout the program. Within each procedure, however, declare **local variables** and **constants** for the specific details of the step itself. Local variables help to separate the details of one procedure from

those in other procedures. Whenever possible, use local identifiers, so procedures can remain as independent as possible.

4. With some care in writing and formatting programs, they can become extensions of the solution outlines. A program has the same structure as the outline and programming can help organize and clarify our thoughts in the problem solving process.

EXERCISES

3.1   Consider the following Pascal program:

```
Program Problem1 (Input, Output);

Var First, Second: Integer;
    Dividend, Divisor: Integer;

Procedure EnterData;
    Begin
        Write ('Enter First Integer: ');
        Readln (First);
        Write ('Enter Second Integer: ');
        Readln (Second)
    End {EnterData} ;

Procedure PrintHeadings;
    Begin
        Writeln;
        Writeln ('                      Integer             Real');
        Writeln ('Dividend   Divisor   Quotient   Remainder Quotient');
        Writeln ('                      (Div)      (Mod)     ( / )')
    End {PrintHeadings} ;

Procedure IntegerDivision;
    Var Quotient, Remainder: Integer;
        RealQuotient: Real;
    Begin {IntegerDivision}
        Quotient := Dividend Div Divisor;
        Remainder := Dividend Mod Divisor;
        RealQuotient := Dividend / Divisor;
        Writeln (Dividend: 5, Divisor: 10, Quotient: 10,
                 Remainder: 10, RealQuotient: 12:3)
    End {IntegerDivision} ;

Procedure FirstComputations;
    Begin
        Dividend := First;
        Divisor := Second;
        IntegerDivision
    End {FirstComputations} ;
```

```
Procedure SecondComputations;
    Begin
        Dividend := Second;
        Divisor := First;
        IntegerDivision
    End {SecondComputations} ;

Begin {Main}
    EnterData;
    PrintHeadings;
    FirstComputations;
    SecondComputations
End {Main}  .
```

Suppose the user enters the numbers 15 and 4 (in that order) in response to the prompt. Write, in the appropriate format, what is printed by this program.

3.2 The preceding Pascal program has five independent procedures. We can picture the declaration block as follows:

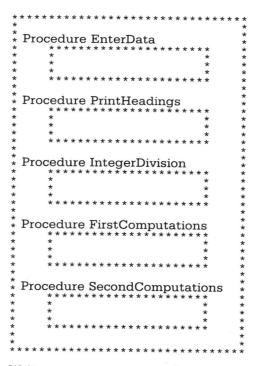

Write a program to print this geometric figure. In your solution, identify the different parts of the pattern, and organize the parts into appropriate procedures.

3.3   Rewrite the program in Problem 3.1 so that the procedures are declared in alphabetical order. (The procedure names and the Main Program should remain unchanged.)

NOTE: A *Forward* statement will be needed.

3.4   In the program in Problem 3.1, we note that a semicolon was not needed before the *Ends* of any of the procedures. A semicolon is required after these *End* statements, however. Please explain why the semicolons are required one place but not another.

NOTE: In Pascal, it is possible to define a "null" or "blank" statement, where no action of any sort is performed. With this information, explain why two semicolons (;;) may appear next to each other in a Pascal program. Also, explain why we could place a semicolon before the *End* statements in the program in Problem 3.1, and the resulting program would still be valid.

3.5   Write a program to print the following geometric pattern:

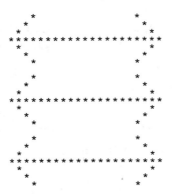

In your solution to the problem, identify different parts of the pattern, and write a procedure for each part.

KEY TERMS, PHRASES, AND CONCEPTS		ELEMENTS OF PASCAL SYNTAX
Bottom-Up	Calls	*Forward*
Methodology	Declarations	*Procedure*
Global Variables	Scope of Constants,	
Local Variables	Procedures, Variables	
Main Program	Top-Down	
Procedures	Methodology	

3.6 Modify your program from Problem 3.5 to make the arrows double thickness. The arrows in the revision should appear as follows:

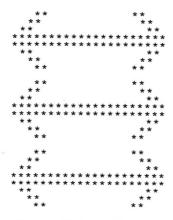

3.7 Rewrite the Making Change problem from Section 2.5, writing a separate procedure for each step of the outline.

3.8 In the revised program for computing florist charges in Section 3.5, the procedure *ComputeCharges* was repeated three times, once inside procedure *Roses*, once in *Carnations*, and once in *Mums*. Explain why this same procedure had to be repeated each time, rather than just being declared the first time, inside *Roses*.

3.9 The Bird Call Travel Agency has negotiated special rates for vacations in Phlatt Cliffs, Po-Dunque, and East Overshoot. In cooperation with Buzzard Airlines and Exotic Hotels, Inc., the full adult costs for a seven-day vacation are:

	Air Travel (Round Trip)	Hotel Room (Full Week)
East Overshoot	$450	$300
Phlatt Cliffs	$550	$400
Po-Dunque	$600	$200

When a family travels together, the following discounts are available:

Hotel Room
    A second adult pays 60% of the room cost.
    Children stay in the room free.
Air Travel
    Each adult pays full fare.
    Each child pays 50% of the adult rate.

Write a program that computes the cost of travel plus lodging for a single adult and for a family of two, three, and four people (two adults plus zero, one, and two children).

Print the results in this table:

	Number of people			
	1	2	3	4
East Overshoot				
Phlatt Cliffs				
Po-Dunque				

3.10 What is printed by the following Pascal program?

HINT: Keep track of the global identifiers and the local identifiers.

```
Program Problem10 (Output);
Var A: Integer;

Procedure FirstOne;
    Var B: Integer;
    Procedure Another;
        Begin
            Writeln ('Another 1:', A:5, B:5);
            A := 2;
            B := -3;
            Writeln ('Another 2:', A:5, B:5)
        End {Another} ;
    Begin {FirstOne}
        A := -1;
        B := 3;
        Writeln ('  First 1:', A:5, B:5);
        Another;
        Writeln ('  First 2:', A:5, B:5)
    End {FirstOne} ;

Procedure SecondOne;
    Var B: Integer;
    Procedure Another;
        Begin
            Writeln ('Another 3:', A:5, B:5);
            A := 5;
            Writeln ('Another 4:', A:5, B:5)
        End {Another} ;
    Begin {SecondOne}
        B := 4;
        Writeln (' Second 1:', A:5, B:5);
        Another;
        Writeln (' Second 2:', A:5, B:5)
    End {SecondOne} ;

Begin {Main}
    A := 1;
    Writeln ('   Main 1:', A:5);
    FirstOne;
    Writeln ('   Main 2:', A:5);
    SecondOne;
    Writeln ('   Main 3:', A:5)
End {Main} .
```

3.11 Draw a diagram showing the declaration block of the procedures in the program from exercise 3.10.

3.12 An avid gardener regularly prepares stewed tomatoes for freezing, using tomatoes, peppers, and various herbs and spices from the garden. Over the past several years, the gardener has found that a pint of stewed tomatoes requires between five and seven tomatoes, depending upon their size.

Write a program that computes the number of pints that the gardener can expect from 50, 100, and 150 tomatoes, assuming that five, six, or seven tomatoes are needed for each pint. The output of the program should be in the form of the following table:

Number of Tomatoes	Pints Produced		
	Minimum	Middle	Maximum
50			
100			
150			

Use a procedure to print the headings and another procedure to perform the actual computations.

3.13 An engineer uses a micrometer to measure the diameter of ball bearings that are used in a particular machine. The micrometer can measure accurately to three decimal places, so all readings are correct within 0.0005 cm. When four bearings of one size are measured, the diameters are found to be 0.491 cm, 0.498 cm, 0.506 cm, and 0.512 cm. Compute the volume of each of these bearings, using the actual measurements. Also compute the volume taking into account the possible errors in each reading. Express your results in a table of the form

Measured Radius	Minimum Volume	Measured Volume	Maximum Volume

Use procedures to structure your program clearly.

3.14 A person wishes to drive to a conference 500 miles away, and the individual wants to determine how the car's miles-per-gallon performance will affect the trip. The car's gas tank holds 18 gallons, and the individual fills the tank just before leaving town. Assuming gas costs $1.40 per gallon, write a program to fill in the following table for the round trip to the conference and back.

Miles per Gallon	Cost of Gas on Trip	Number of Refueling Stops	Gas Left at Destination
18			
21			
24			
27			
32			
36			

Use procedures to help structure your program.

3.15 The lyrics of many familiar songs have the following organization:
- Verse 1
- Chorus
- Verse 2
- Chorus
- Verse 3
- Chorus
- etc.

Several verses are sung, with a chorus or refrain repeated after each verse. (Sometimes this chorus is sung before the first verse as well.)

Pick a song that has this form, and write a program to print the lyrics. In your program, use a procedure to write each separate verse, and use another procedure to print the chorus.

CHAPTER 4

SIMPLE

FUNCTIONS

AND PARAMETERS

In Chapter 3 we refined our approach to problem solving and divided the overall solution into small pieces. Procedures allow us to use this problem solving strategy easily in programs.

In this chapter we look at the special case when one step requires computing exactly one result. In particular, we will study a variant of procedures, called **Functions,** which compute and represent single values. We will use functions in mathematical expressions when the general solution outline requires determining one specific value. As with procedures, functions allow us to separate the final result of a step from the details of computation. In using functions we do not care how our final results are obtained, as long as we can get them. Thus the philosophy behind functions and procedures is quite similar.

Then as an extension of our discussion of functions, we will see how we can pass values into functions and procedures and how we can get values returned. This introduces the important idea of **parameters.**

SECTION 4.1 **STANDARD FUNCTIONS**

In Pascal, functions allow us to perform some operations beyond the simple arithmetic computations of addition, subtraction, multiplication, and division. In particular, we can use functions in mathematical expressions

87

to perform specific computations. For example, in Chapter 2 we already used the functions *Trunc* and *Round* in various expressions to convert real numbers to integers. A complete list of the standard functions available in

---

TABLE 4–1 · Standard Arithmetic Functions

Function Code	Meaning	Examples

Abs(x)	Compute the absolute value of x.
	  If x is real, then Abs(x) is real.
	  If x is an integer, then Abs(x)
	  is also an integer.
		3.2 = Abs(3.2)
		5.1 = Abs($-$5.1)
		0.0 = Abs(0.0)
		3 = Abs(3)
		2 = Abs($-$2)

Sqr(x)	Compute the square of x.
	  As with Abs(x), Sqr(x) will be
	  the same type (real or
	  integer) as x.
		1.44 = Sqr(1.2)
		9.61 = Sqr($-$3.1)
		0 = Sqr(0)
		64 = Sqr(8)

Sqrt(x)	Compute the nonnegative square root of x.
	  x must be a nonnegative
	  number, although x may be
	  either real or integer.
	  Sqrt(x) is always real.
	  (If x < 0, then Sqrt(x)
	  produces an error.)
		2.0 = Sqrt(4.0)
		1.414. . .
		  = Sqrt(2.0)
		0 = Sqrt(0.0)
		ERROR
		  = Sqrt($-$103)

Logarithms and Exponentials[1]

Function Code	Meaning	Examples

Exp(x)	Compute e^x, i.e., raise the
	  number e to the exponent x.
	  x may be real or integer, but
	  Exp(x) is always of real
	  type.
		1.0 = Exp(0)
		2.718. . . = Exp(1)

Ln(x)	Compute the natural logarithm
	  of x; $\log_e x$
	  x must be a positive number,
	  although x may be either
	  real or integer.
	  Ln(x) is always real
	  (If x ≤ 0, then Ln(x) produces
	  an error.)
		0.0 = Ln(1.0)
		1.0 = Ln(2.718)

---

[1]e is the base of the natural logarithms, e ≈ 2.718281828459. . . . See Appendix C-1 for a brief introduction to logarithms.

Function Code	Meaning	Examples
	Trigonometry[2, 3]	
Sin(x)	Compute the sine of x. x may be real or integer. Sin(x) is always real.	0.0 = Sin(0.0) 1.0 = Sin(Pi/2.0)
Cos(x)	Compute the cosine of x. x may be real or integer. Cos(x) is always real.	1.0 = Cos(1.0) 0.0 = Cos(Pi/2.0)
Arctan(x)	Compute the principal value of the arctangent of x. x may be real or integer. Arctan(x) is always real.	0.78 ≈ Arctan(1) (Recall 0.78 ≈ Pi/4.0)

[2]A knowledge of trigonometry is not required for this text, although some exercises do use this background. These problems will be marked specifically, and they may be skipped without loss of continuity.

[3]All angles are measured in radians. In the examples in this section, assume Pi is the constant 3.14159265. To convert from degrees to radians, use the formula

$$radians = \frac{\pi}{180} \ degrees$$

Pascal is given in Table 4–1. When any of these functions are used, a value is computed for the function, and this value is substituted for the function in the arithmetic expression.

The following problem shows how these functions might be used. The problem also illustrates that these functions often can be quite important for solving problems.

PROBLEM 4.1

Each fall, you need to clean the gutters on your house, and you need a ladder to get to the roof. We can measure the length of the ladder, and we can estimate the height of the house.

Compute the distance that the base of the ladder should be from the house so that the top of the ladder will reach the roof (see Figure 4–1).

Solution for Problem 4.1

We know the length and the height in our Figure, and we want to find the base distance for the ladder. We assume here that this information was measured correctly and that it will be entered into the computer correctly. In a later chapter, we will see how this entry might be controlled. Using the Pythagorean theorem, which relates these quantities, we find

$$(Length)^2 = (Base)^2 + (Height)^2.$$

With this equation, we can outline the solution.

FIGURE 4–1 · **A Ladder from the Ground to the Top of a House**

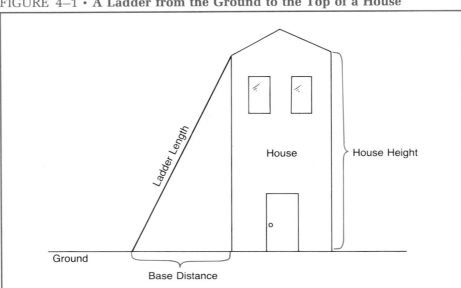

Outline for Problem 4.1

   I. Determine house height and ladder length.

  II. Compute the base distance for the ladder.

      The correct formula is

$$\text{Base} = \sqrt{(\text{Length})^2 - (\text{Height})^2}$$

 III. Print results.

Discussion of Problem 4.1

While this outline follows the same general form as many earlier outlines, we cannot compute the required square root with the simple arithmetic operations from Chapter 2. From Table 4–1, however, we see that Pascal can compute square roots using a function called *Sqrt*. We can compute a square root of a number x by writing *Sqrt(x)*.

    With the *Sqrt* function, we are ready to write a program for Problem 4.1.

```
Program Ladder (Input, Output);
{This program computes the distance required between the base of a ladder
 and a house, if the top of the ladder is to reach the roof of a house.}

Var Height, Base, Length: Real;
    BaseSquared: Real;
```

```
Begin {Main}

    {Determine Length and Height}
    Writeln ('This program determines the distance between the base of a');
    Writeln ('ladder and a house, so the ladder reaches a house''s roof.');
    Write ('Please enter the length of the ladder: ');
    Readln (Length);
    Write ('Please enter the height (in feet) of the house: ');
    Readln (Height);

    {Compute the length of the ladder}
    BaseSquared := Length*Length - Height*Height;
    Base := Sqrt(BaseSquared);

    {Print Results}
    Writeln;
    Writeln ('Position the base of the ladder ', Base:1:1,
             ' feet from the house.')

End {Main} .
```

When this program is run with a house height of 18 feet and a ladder length of 20 feet, we will have the following interaction with the computer.

```
This program determines the distance between the base of a
ladder and a house, so the ladder reaches a house's roof.
Please enter the length of the ladder: 20
Please enter the height (in feet) of the house: 18

Position the base of the ladder 8.7 feet from the house.
```

This program first computes the square of the desired base distance, then it applies the *Sqrt* function to obtain the desired base distance. The computations proceed as in earlier problems, except that we have used *Sqrt* to compute the needed square root, with this statement:

Base := Sqrt (BaseSquared)

BaseSquared is the appropriate distance squared, and we apply the square root function *Sqrt* to the value.

In fact, we could do all of the computation in one line, without reference to the intermediate value *BaseSquared*. In this version, we would replace the two lines in the computation section with

Base := Sqrt (Length*Length − Base*Base)

The value

Length*Length − Base*Base

is computed first, then the square root of the quantity is determined. The computer works first with the expression inside parentheses and then applies *Sqrt*.

Pascal also has a squaring function, *Sqr* (see Table 4–1). The solution could therefore take the following form:

```
Program Ladder {Revised} (Input, Output);
{This program computes the distance required between the base of a ladder
 and a house, if the top of the ladder is to reach the roof of a house.}

Var Height, Base, Length: Real;

Begin {Main}

    {Determine Length and Height}
    Writeln ('This program determines the distance between the base of a');
    Writeln ('ladder and a house, so the ladder reaches a house''s roof.');
    Write ('Please enter the length of the ladder: ');
    Readln (Length);
    Write ('Please enter the height (in feet) of the house: ');
    Readln (Height);

    {Compute the length of the ladder}
    Base := Sqrt( Sqr(Length) - Sqr(Height) );

    {Print Results}
    Writeln;
    Writeln ('Position the base of the ladder ', Base:1:1,
            ' feet from the house.')

End {Main} .
```

In this program the computation of *Base* is reduced to one line, as before, and the *Sqr* function is used twice—*Sqr(Length)* computes *Length*Length*; *Sqr(Height)* computes *Height*Height*. In computing the value of this expression, the computer again starts inside the parentheses. First, *Sqr(Length)* and *Sqr(Height)* are computed. Then, these values are added. Finally, the *Sqrt* function is applied to the sum.

You can use any of the standard arithmetic functions in Pascal programs, in the same way that you use the other operations of arithmetic, such as addition and subtraction. These functions are easy to use, and they expand the range of computations you can do.

Finally, note that these functions do not require understanding any details about performing the computations. For example, you need not know how square roots are computed. The details of computation are hidden within the functions themselves, and you can ignore the details when you use the functions. This use of functions is completely consistent with the problem solving methodology discussed earlier. You can think of these functions as performing common tasks; you can distinguish between the steps of the outline and the technical details of various tasks.

SECTION 4.2   **EXAMPLE OF A USER-DEFINED FUNCTION**

Section 4.1 presented several functions that could be useful in solving some problems. Many problems, however, require functions that are not included in the list of Standard Pascal functions (Table 4–1). Therefore you will find it helpful to be able to write your own functions. In this section we look at a specific example that illustrates how to define your own functions. The next section considers the subject in more detail.

PROBLEM 4.2 ___   Suppose you deposit a specific amount of money in a bank account at a given rate of interest. Determine how the money in the account would grow over a year if the interest is compounded annually, semiannually, quarterly, monthly, and daily. With these computations, you will be able to conclude which compounding gives the best return on your money.

Discussion of Problem 4.2.
From handbooks or texts you can find the following formula:

$$\text{Balance} = \text{Principal} \ (1 + \text{rate/frequency})^{\text{frequency}}$$

where

   Balance is the amount in the account at the end of the year,

   Principal is the amount deposited at the start of the year,

   rate is the annual interest rate,

   frequency is the number of times interest is compounded during the year.

Restatement of Problem 4.2
Given the *Principal* and *rate* for a bank account, compute the *Balance* in the account for *frequency* = 1, 2, 4, 12, 365.

   Results will be easy to read if output is in the form of a table.

Outline for Problem 4.2
   I. Determine Principal and interest rate.
   II. Print headings for table.
   III. Compute the Balance using the formula

$$\text{Balance} = \text{Principal}(1 + \text{rate/frequency})^{\text{frequency}}$$

for

   A. frequency = 1
   B. frequency = 2
   C. frequency = 4
   D. frequency = 12
   E. frequency = 365

   Translating this outline into a Pascal program, two observations come to mind in part III. First, we can apply the same formula to each computation. Further, we are not particularly interested in the formula for computation; we want to focus on the *Balance* itself. Therefore, we would like to write a program in a way that focuses on the *Balance* for the given *Principal*, *rate*, and *frequency*.

Second, the formula requires taking the quantity (1 + *rate/frequency*) to the power *frequency*. We do not care about the details of the computation, but we do need to compute with this exponent. Unfortunately, Pascal does not allow us to perform this exponentiation directly. Instead, to compute r^s in Pascal, we need to write the expression *exp(s*ln(r))*, which uses the two Pascal functions *exp* and *ln*. (See Appendix C on logarithms for a derivation of this formula.)

In the problem at hand, the formula is tangential to our focus on bank interest, so we can write a program where the formulas for computing balances and powers are removed from the main steps of the outline, as in the following program.

```
Program BankInterest {Version 1} (Input, Output);
{This program computes one's bank balance after one year.}

Var Principal: Real;
    Interest: Real;

Function Powers (Base, Exponent: Real): Real;
{This function raises Base to the power Exponent.}
    Begin
        Powers := Exp(Exponent * Ln(Base))
    End {Powers} ;

Function Balance (Prin, Rate, Freq: Real): Real;
{This function computes the Balance in a bank account,
 given the Principal, annual interest Rate,
 and the Frequency of compounding.}
    Begin
        Balance := Prin * Powers (1 + Rate/Freq, Freq)
    End {Balance} ;

Begin {Main Program}

    {Determine Principal and Interest}
    Writeln ('Computation of Bank Balances');
    Writeln;
    Write ('Enter Principal and Interest Rate:   ');
    Readln (Principal, Interest);

    {Print Headings for the Output}
    Writeln;
    Writeln (' Number of');
    Writeln ('Compounding');
    Writeln ('  Periods      Balance');
```

```
{Compute and Print the Balances}
Writeln (   1:6, Balance(Principal, Interest,   1.0):15:2);
Writeln (   2:6, Balance(Principal, Interest,   2.0):15:2);
Writeln (   4:6, Balance(Principal, Interest,   4.0):15:2);
Writeln ( 12:6, Balance(Principal, Interest, 12.0):15:2);
Writeln (365:6, Balance(Principal, Interest,365.0):15:2);

End {Main Program}.
```

Before we look at how this program works, note the output when we specify a *Principal* of $1500 at an annual interest *rate* of 8 percent:

```
Computation of Bank Balances

Enter Principal and Interest Rate:   1500.0   0.08

 Number of
Compounding
    Periods       Balance
        1         1620.00
        2         1622.40
        4         1623.65
       12         1624.50
      365         1624.98
```

Now we are ready to trace the execution of this program. In many respects, this program works much the same way as the programs in the last chapter, which used procedures.

The program starts with the *Begin* of the Main Program. After printing some text the computer reads values for *Principal* and for *Interest*. This completes Step I of the outline.

The next three lines print the headings for the table, completing Step II. So far, we are proceeding straight through the program.

In Step III the execution becomes more involved. The first line reads

Writeln (1:6, Balance(Principal, Interest, 1.0):15:2);

This tells the computer to print two numbers in specified formats. The computer will write the numbers one at a time. First the computer prints the number 1, allowing six spaces. Then the computer must print *Balance*. It proceeds in several steps. For this example we will use *Principal* = 1500 and *Interest* = 0.08.

Step 1: Function *Balance* is called.

Program{

Function Balance (Prin, Rate, Freq: Real): Real;

Writeln (1:6, Balance; Principal, Interest, 1.0):15:2);
                       1500.   .08

The values for *Prin, Rate,* and *Freq* in the function are supplied in the *Writeln* statement:

The value (1500.0) for *Principal* will be used for *Prin* on the function; the value (0.08) for *Interest* will be used for *Rate* in the function; The number 1.0 will be used for *Freq* in the function.

Step 2: Computation within function *Balance* begins.

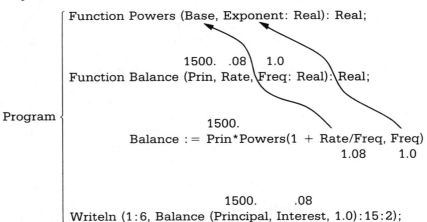

Since we have values for *Prin, Rate,* and *Freq,* computation begins with 1 + *Rate/Freq.* From earlier data, we have

$$1 + \text{Rate/Freq} = 1 + 0.08/1.0 = 1.08$$

Before the program can go on, however, it must evaluate *Powers.*

Step 3: Function *Powers* is called.

As at the start of the *Balance* function, function *Powers* requires two starting values, *Base* and *Exponent.* These two values are determined by the call in the *Balance* function.

The value 1 + *Rate/Freq* (1.08) will be used for *Base;* the value *Freq* (1.0) will be used for *Exponent.*

Step 4: Computation within function *Powers* begins.

$$
\begin{aligned}
&\qquad\qquad\qquad 1.08 \qquad 1.0 \\
&\text{Function Powers (Base, Exponent: Real): Real;} \\
&\qquad\qquad\qquad\qquad\quad 1.0 \qquad 1.08 \\
&\qquad \underline{\text{Powers} := \text{Exp (Exponent*Ln(Base))}} \\
&\qquad\qquad\qquad\qquad 1.08 \\
&\qquad\qquad\quad 1500. \ .08 \quad 1.0 \\
&\text{Function Balance (Prin, Rate, Freq: Real): Real;} \\
&\qquad\qquad\qquad\qquad 1500. \qquad\qquad\quad 1.08 \quad 1.0 \\
&\qquad \text{Balance} := \text{Prin*Powers (1 + Rate/Freq, Freq)} \\
\\
&\qquad\qquad\qquad 1500. \qquad `.08 \\
&\text{Writeln (1:6, Balance (Principal, Interest, 1.0):15:2);}
\end{aligned}
$$

Program { (bracketing the above block)

The values for *Base* and *Exponent* are used in the Standard Pascal Functions *Ln* and *Exp* to give a value (1.08) for *Powers*. Note that the value is a real number, which agrees with the declaration

Function Powers (. . .): Real;

Step 5: Function *Powers* concludes.

When we reach the *End* of the *Powers* function, the computed value for *Powers* is returned to *Balance*, where it was requested.

$$
\begin{aligned}
&\qquad\qquad 1.08 \quad 1.08 \qquad 1.0 \\
&\text{Function Powers (Base, Exponent: Real): Real;} \\
\\
&\qquad\qquad\qquad 1500. \quad .08 \quad 1.0 \\
&\text{Function Balance (Prin, Rate, Freq: Real): Real;} \\
\\
&\qquad\qquad\qquad\qquad 1500. \qquad\qquad\qquad 1.08 \qquad 1.0 \\
&\qquad \text{Balance} := \text{Prin*Powers (1 + Rate/Freq, Freq)} \\
\\
&\qquad\qquad\qquad 1500. \qquad .08 \\
&\text{Writeln (1:6, Balance (Principal, Interest, 1.0):15:2);}
\end{aligned}
$$

Program { (bracketing the above block)

Then function *Powers* disappears, as it is no longer needed, and the computer goes back to function *Balance* to continue the computations.

$$
\text{Program}
\begin{cases}
\quad\quad\quad\quad \text{1500.} \quad .08 \quad 1.0 \\
\text{Function Balance (Prin, Rate, Freq: Real): Real;} \\
\\
\quad\quad\quad\quad\quad\quad \text{1500.} \quad 1.08 \quad\quad 1.08 \quad\quad 1.0 \\
\quad\quad \text{Balance} := \text{Prin*Powers (1 + Rate/Freq, Freq)} \\
\\
\quad\quad\quad\quad\quad\quad \text{1500.} \quad\quad .08 \\
\text{Writeln(1:6, Balance (Principal, Interest, 1.0):15:2);}
\end{cases}
$$

Step 6: Computation within function *Balance* resumes.

$$
\text{Program}
\begin{cases}
\quad\quad\quad\quad \text{1500.} \quad .08 \quad 1.0 \\
\text{Function Balance (Prin, Rate, Freq: Real): Real;} \\
\\
\quad\quad\quad\quad\quad\quad \text{1500.} \quad 1.08 \quad\quad 1.08 \quad\quad 1.0 \\
\quad\quad \underline{\text{Balance} := \text{Prin*Powers (1 + Rate/Freq, Freq)}} \\
\quad\quad\quad\quad\quad\quad\quad\quad\quad \text{1620.00} \\
\\
\quad\quad\quad\quad\quad\quad \text{1500.} \quad\quad .08 \\
\text{Writeln (1:6, Balance (Principal, Interest, 1.0):15:2);}
\end{cases}
$$

From function *Powers* the program has a value (1.08) which we can substitute for Powers (1 + Rate/Freq) in the line

Balance := Prin * Powers(1 + Rate/Freq, Freq)

Now the program can complete the computation to obtain a value (1620.00) for *Balance*. Again, note that *Balance* is a real number, which agrees with the function declaration:

Function Balance (. . .): Real;

Step 7: Function *Balance* concludes.

After computing *Balance,* the function *Ends.* As with *Powers,* two actions occur at this point. The computed *Balance* is returned to the Main Program from the function *Balance.*

$$
\text{Program}
\begin{cases}
\quad\quad\quad\quad \text{1620.00 1500.} \quad .08 \quad 1.0 \\
\text{Function Balance (Prin, Rate, Freq: Real): Real;} \\
\\
\quad\quad\quad\quad\quad\quad\quad\quad \text{1500.} \quad\quad .08 \\
\text{Writeln (1:6, Balance (Principal, Interest. 1.0):15:2);}
\end{cases}
$$

Function *Balance* then disappears and the computer goes back to the Main Program.

$$
\text{Program}
\begin{cases}
\quad\quad\quad \text{1620.00} \quad\quad \text{1500.} \quad\quad .08 \\
\text{Writeln (1:6, Balance (Principal, Interest, 1.0):15:2);}
\end{cases}
$$

Conclusion of the Writeln Statement

The Main Program has a value for *Balance,* so the computer can print that value in the format designated (:15:2). The computer prints 1620.00 to complete this line of the Main Program.

Execution of Subsequent Lines

Once the first *Writeln* statement is finished, the computer moves on to subsequent *Writeln* statements. For each *Writeln* statement, the computer repeats the steps just described, using new values for *Freq* as specified. In each case the computer prints the resulting balance and goes on to the next statement.

The output shows that daily compounding gives a little more money in the account at the end of the year, but that amount is not much more than the other compounding possibilities.

Overview and Summary of the Example

The outline uses the same formula to determine various bank balances, and the focus is on the balances. The Main Program emphasizes each *Balance* and the values *(Principal, Interest, Frequency)* that it depends upon. The details of the formula are isolated in a function separate from the main steps in the outline.

Looking at the *Balance* formula itself, we need to compute various powers. Again, the details of computing the powers are tangential to our interest in the *Balance* formula, so we have moved those details to a function *Powers.*

For *Balance* and for *Powers,* we need to compute a value, and we want to separate the computational details from the main point of our work. We can use functions for these details, and the separation can be reflected in the Pascal code.

SECTION 4.3   ELEMENTS OF DEFINING SIMPLE FUNCTIONS

Section 4.2 presented some illustrations of functions defined by the programmer. We gave a function some values at the start, then let the function perform a computation, and finally concluded with a specific value. In this section we look at these functions more formally.

The general form of Pascal functions is illustrated by an example from the previous section:

```
Function Balance (Prin, Rate, Freq: Real): Real;
    Begin
            Balance : =  Prin*Powers(1 + Rate/Freq, Freq)
    End
```

We will examine each part of this function in some detail.

Function Name

Functions always start with the reserved word *Function*, followed by an indentifier we wish to use to refer to our function.

Parameter List

Next, in parentheses, list the values you will need for computation, and give those values names. In the example, we needed three real numbers to begin the computation—*Prin*, *Rate*, and *Freq*. This list of variables, or **formal parameters**, declares some of the identifiers to be used within the function. The example also shows that when the function is called in a program initial values are assigned to the formal parameters.

In the declaration and initialization you must be consistent in the order of parameters, because the computer matches up formal parameters with values, or **actual parameters**, each time the function is used. From the example, the function declaration begins

Function Balance (Prin, Rate, Freq: Real)

and the function is used with the statement

Balance (Principal, Interest, 1.0)

Here *Prin*, *Rate*, and *Freq* are the formal parameters, referred to within the function itself. *Principal*, *Interest*, and 1.0 are the actual parameters, used to initialize the formal parameters. It is important to note the order used to specify the parameters. The first formal parameter, *Prin*, is given the value of the first actual parameter, *Principal*, in the function call. Similarly, the second formal parameter, *Rate*, is given the value from the second actual parameter, *Interest*. Finally, the third elements on each list, *Freq* and 1.0, are matched. Be sure to list the formal parameters in the same order that you write the actual parameters. If you change the order of elements in a formal parameter list, you must be sure to change the order of the actual parameters as well. If you list formal parameters in a different order from the actual parameters, computations will be based on inappropriate data and will give erroneous results.

The formal parameter list at the start of the function specifies the type of each of the formal parameters. *Prin*, *Rate*, and *Freq* were declared to be real. As with other variables discussed in earlier chapters, parameters may be declared individually or in groups. All of the following parameter lists are equivalent:

(Prin, Rate, Freq: Real)
(Prin: Real; Rate: Real; Freq: Real)
(Prin, Rate: Real; Freq: Real)
(Prin: Real; Rate, Freq: Real)

In each case, the formal parameters have the same type (real) and are listed in the same order. In contrast, the parameter list

(Prin, Freq: Real; Rate: Real)

is not equivalent to those above, since the parameters appear in a different order.

In summary, the parameter list in a function declaration serves three purposes: It specifies the names of the formal parameters to be used in a function; it specifies the order of the parameters; and it specifies the type—real or integer—of the parameters. Each time that the function is used, be sure that the actual parameters have the same order and type specified in the function's parameter list.

Function Type

After the parameter list, specify the type of value—real or integer—that the function computes. In the example, we specify that the final *Balance* would be a real number.

Variable Declarations

As with procedures, you may declare additional variables for use within a function. For example, you might want to perform computations in several steps, and you might need to store the results of each step for later use in the function. As a specific illustration, we could rewrite the function *Balance* so the computation proceeded in several steps:

```
Function Balance (Prin, Rate, Freq: Real): Real;
    Var Quotient, Factor: Real;
    Begin
        Quotient : = 1 + Rate/Freq;
        Factor : = Powers(Quotient, Freq);
        Balance : = Prin*Factor
    End;
```

Here we declared two new variables, *Quotient* and *Factor*, for use within the function. As with procedures, these are local variables, and we may not refer to these variables outside the function.

Function Block

Once all variables have been defined, you can proceed with actual computations. Function syntax has the same form as for procedures. The work starts with *Begin* and concludes with *End;* . Between these keywords statements are specified, separated by semicolons.

Unlike procedures, however, you must be aware of one constraint on statements in functions. Our motivation for using functions is to compute a specific result that can be used later. Therefore, at some point in each function, you must assign the function a value. For example, in our illustrations in this section we have written

```
Balance : = Prin*Powers(1 + Rate/Freq, Freq)
```

or

```
Balance : = Prin*Factor
```

In each case, we performed some computations and stored a result under the function name *Balance* for use when the function finishes.

In a function block you can use local and global variables and formal parameters in computations, and you must assign a value to the function name before the function is done. Until you have more background, however, you should not use the function name within the function itself as part of the computations on the right side of the assignment statements.

This completes our description of the pieces that make up a function. In the next section we will see more examples using this form.

| SECTION 4.4 | EXAMPLES |

In Section 4.2 we used one function to compute bank interest and another function to compute an expression involving exponents. We separated the details of computation from the main flow of the program, and we used a function to perform the specific steps of each task. Now we consider additional examples to clarify the use of local variables, global variables, and parameters.

Compounding Bank Interest (Revisited)

You can use parameters to highlight certain aspects of a computation. In the bank balance program we wrote:

> Function Balance (Prin, Rate, Freq: Real)

When we used the function, we wrote

> Balance (Principal, Interest, 1.0);
> Balance (Principal, Interest, 2.0);

Here we specified *Principal* and *Interest* in each function call, even though those variables never changed.

As an alternate approach, you might want to highlight the changing frequencies while deemphasizing *Principal* and *Interest*, which are constant. We can define the function with just one parameter, *Freq*, and write

> Function Balance (Freq: Real)

With this change, the function calls emphasize the changing compounding frequencies:

> Balance (1.0);
> Balance (2.0);

Principal and *Interest* will still be needed for computation, so they are declared in the function as global variables. Finally, we compute *Balance* in two steps, using an intermediate value called *Factor*. The following program produces the same output as the one in Section 4.2.

```
Program BankInterest {Version 2} (Input, Output);
{This program computes one's bank balance after one year.}
{Here, Balance is a function of one variable only.}

Var Principal: Real;
    Interest: Real;

Function Powers (Base, Exponent: Real): Real;
{This function raises Base to the power Exponent.}
    Begin
        Powers := Exp(Exponent * Ln(Base))
    End;

Function Balance (Freq: Real): Real;
{This function computes the bank balance after one year,
 if interest is compounded Freq times in the year.}
    Var Factor: Real;
    Begin
        Factor := Powers (1 + Interest/Freq, Freq);
        Balance := Principal * Factor
    End;

Begin {Main Program}

    {Determine Principal and Interest}
    Writeln ('Computation of Bank Balances');
    Writeln;
    Write ('Enter Principal and Interest Rate:  ');
    Readln (Principal, Interest);

    {Print Headings for the Output}
    Writeln;
    Writeln ('Number of');
    Writeln ('Compounding   Balance');

    {Compute and Print Balances}
    Writeln (1:6,   Balance(  1.0):15:2);
    Writeln (2:6,   Balance(  2.0):15:2);
    Writeln (4:6,   Balance(  4.0):15:2);
    Writeln (12:6, Balance( 12.0):15:2);
    Writeln (365:6,Balance(365.0):15:2);

End {Main Program} .
```

To clarify how the various variables work in the program, consider Figure 4–2. The main program contains two global variables, *Principal* and *Interest*. These variables may be used directly by all procedures.

Function *Powers* uses no outside variables at all, and no local variables are declared either. When *Powers* is called we must specify all values as parameters, and these values are used exclusively in the computation.

Function *Balance* is more complex. Within *Balance* is the local variable *Factor*, which may be used only within *Balance*. Neither *Powers* nor

FIGURE 4–2 • A Schematic Diagram for Variables and Parameters in the Revised Bank Balance Program

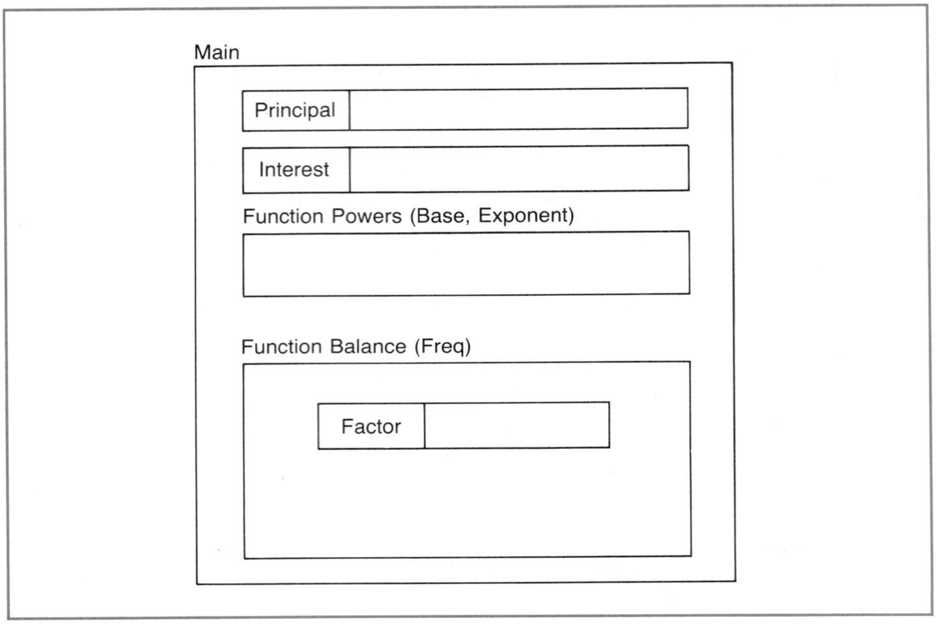

the Main Program is allowed to use *Factor*. (As with procedures, we cannot see into a function from the outside.) On the other hand, *Balance* can use the global variables *Principal* and *Interest*. Note that in this revision of the program we cannot use the names *Prin* and *Rate* in the function, as those names are different from our desired global variables. Finally, we use the parameter *Freq*, which is given a value each time the function is called.

With this mixture of local and global variables and parameters we have enhanced the clarity of the program by focusing on the one variable that changes in the computation. The function of one variable highlights the main element of each computation. A selective use of parameters has helped our work.

The Forward Statement

The Bank Interest program can also illustrate what to do to declare functions in various orders. In each example so far, we defined function *Powers* first, and then we used *Powers* in function *Balance*. In the last chapter we noted that to declare procedures in different orders you sometimes need the *Forward* statement (see Section 3.5). This same comment applies to functions.

To present the functions in Bank Interest in alphabetical order, *Balance* would come before *Powers*. Here we must tell the compiler that function

Powers will be coming, so the compiler will know how to handle the reference to *Powers* in function *Balance*. As with procedures, we declare *Powers* in two parts. First, early in the program we specify the function and its formal parameters in a *Forward* statement:

Function Powers (Base, Exponent: Real): Real; Forward;

Later in the program we give the rest of the information about the function (note that we do not repeat the parameters in the second part):

Function Powers;
    Begin
        Powers : = Exp(Exponent * Ln(Base))
    End;

The first statement tells the computer what *Powers* will look like, with its parameters and resulting type; the second part fills in the details. Here is the revised program:

```
Program BankInterest {Version 3} (Input, Output);
{This program computes one's bank balance after one year.}
{Here we put the functions in alphabetical order}
{As in Version 2, Balance is a function of one variable only}

Var Principal: Real;
    Interest: Real;

Function Powers (Base, Exponent: Real): Real; Forward;
{The details of this function are given below;
 the parameters and the function-type are declared here.}

Function Balance (Freq: Real): Real;
{This function computes the bank balance after one year,
 if interest is compounded Freq times in the year.}
    Var Factor: Real;
    Begin
        Factor := Powers (1 + Interest/Freq, Freq);
        Balance := Principal * Factor
    End;

Function Powers;
{This function raises Base to the power Exponent.}
{The details of this function are specified here.}
    Begin
        Powers := Exp(Exponent * Ln(Base))
    End;

Begin {Main Program}

    {Determine Principal and Interest}
    Writeln ('Computation of Bank Balances');
    Writeln;
    Write ('Enter Principal and Interest Rate:   ');
    Readln (Principal, Interest);
```

```
{Print Headings for the Output}
Writeln;
Writeln ('Number of');
Writeln ('Compounding   Balance');

{Compute and Print Balances}
Writeln (1:6,   Balance(  1.0):15:2);
Writeln (2:6,   Balance(  2.0):15:2);
Writeln (4:6,   Balance(  4.0):15:2);
Writeln (12:6,  Balance( 12.0):15:2);
Writeln (365:6,Balance(365.0):15:2);

End {Main Program} .
```

Functions, like procedures, allow us to organize our work following our original outline. We can declare functions and procedures in whatever order we find easiest to remember. We may sometimes need a *Forward* statement to tell the compiler of steps that are detailed later in a program.

A Random Number Generator

We now turn to another use of functions, as our next example. We will describe a special type of function called a **random number generator,** which will be of considerable use in subsequent chapters. You need more experience and background before you can use this function effectively, so we will postpone actual applications until Section 6.4. For now we will focus on what a random number generator is and how to define it.

A random number generator on a typical computer is a function which produces a value between 0 and 1. Such functions simulate a random selection process. For example, the program segment

```
Writeln(Random);
Writeln(Random);
Writeln(Random);
Writeln(Random);
Writeln(Random)
```

would print five random numbers at the terminal.

Numbers Between 0 and 1.   The function *Random* itself may be defined in any of several ways. We will discuss one of the most common of these approaches, which generates numbers between 0 and 1. In this approach, the numbers will not be strictly random, as the function follows an algorithm to compute one from the previous. The numbers obtained, however, will be distributed fairly well in the interval between 0 and 1, and there will not be any apparent pattern in the numbers. (Statistical tests also indicate that these numbers look quite random.)

This approach depends upon a global variable *Seed*, which yields the random number. The idea is to use the function *Random* to change *Seed* each time in a way that appears fairly random. In a typical form for these functions, A, C, and M are all global integer constants and $Seed$ is a global integer variable:

```
Function Random: Real;
    Begin
            Seed : = (A*Seed + C) Mod M;
            Random : = Seed/M
    End;
```

The function takes the old value of Seed, computes a new value

$$(A*Seed + C) \text{ Mod } M$$

and the new value becomes the new *Seed* value. Each *Seed* value then generates a new *Random* value.

With appropriate choices for A, C, and M, this function will work well for many applications. Unfortunately, the specific choices depend upon the particular computer available, and the technical details are well beyond the scope of this book![1] We can give some guidelines, however:

a. Choose M to be (MaxInt + 1).
This is usually a power of 2.
b. A should meet three conditions:
   i. Sqrt(MaxInt) $< A <$ MaxInt $-$ Sqrt(MaxInt)
   ii. MaxInt/100 $< A <$ MaxInt/2
   iii. A Mod 8 = 5
c. C should be the odd number closest to
$$M*0.2113248654$$

On many machines (called 16-bit machines), $M = 32768$, $A = 3373$, $C = 6925$ satisfies these conditions.

Once the constants are determined, the only other thing you need to do is to pick an initial value for *Seed*. This may be done in several ways. You could ask the user to type in a number when the program is run. You could use a time of day function, if such a function is available on your computer. You could pick an initial value in the program. Using the last option, the program always starts at the same place, so you will get the same sequence of "random numbers" each time the program is run.

Numbers Between R and S. The *Random* function just examined produces values between 0 and 1. For numbers in another range, you can scale the results from *Random*. To get numbers between 0 and the value S you can use S*Random. Thus 2.0*Random will produce numbers between 0 and 2. To get numbers between R and S, you can use $(S-R)*Random + R$.

---

[1] For an extensive discussion of random number generators, see Donald F. Knuth, *The Art of Computer Programming, Volume 2, Seminumerical Algorithms*; Chapter 3—Random Numbers. Addison Wesley Publishing Company, Reading, MA, 1969. A summary of the discussion is found in Knuth's Section 3.6.

NOTE: When *Random* is 0 this expression is R. When *Random* is 1, this expression is S. As *Random* increases from 0 to 1, this expression gives values from R to S.

Integers from 1 to N. You can also use *Random* to obtain integers in a specified range, with appropriate scaling and conversion to integers. Since *Random* gives values between 0 and 1, N*Random gives values between 0 and N. (The *Random* function defined earlier never actually equals 1, so N*Random never actually equals N.) N*Random + 1 gives values between 1 and N + 1. Finally, the expression *Trunc*(N*Random + 1) gives integer values between 1 and N.

Example: Rolling a Die. We can use *Random* to write a program to simulate the rolling of a die six times. We will generate integers from 1 to 6, to correspond to the faces on the die cube.

The following program will run on many machines just as it appears, although the *Random* function as written fails to conform to the Pascal Standard, for a technical reason. Appendix C-2 describes the complex function that does conform to the Standard. Note that the following program calls procedure *InitializeRandomFunction* early in the program to give an initial value to the *Seed* variable.

```
Program RollDie (Output);
{This program uses a random number generator to simulate the
 rolling of a die.}

Var
    {The following variable is needed for the Random Number Function}
    Seed: 0..65535; {Seed is an integer between 0 and 65535}

Procedure InitializeRandomFunction;
    {Procedure initializes variable Seed for the Random Number Function}
    {A value for Seed was picked at random; if a time or date function
     were available, then the following statement might be appropriate
                    Seed := trunc (Time * 1000.0)
    }
    Begin
        Seed := 345
    End {InitializeRandomFunction} ;

Function Random: Real;
    {Function returns a random number between 0 and 1}
    Begin
        Random := Seed / 32768.0;
        Seed := (Seed * 13077 + 6925) mod 32768;
    End { Random };
```

```
Function Random1To6: Integer;
    {Function uses the Random function to get an integer
     between 1 and 6.}
    Begin
        Random1To6 := Trunc(6.0*Random + 1.0)
    End {Random1To6} ;

Begin {Main}
    {Get ready for using the random number generator}
    InitializeRandomFunction;

    {Simulate rolling the die}
    Writeln ('The following shows the results of rolling a die 6 times');
    Writeln (Random1To6);
    Writeln (Random1To6);
    Writeln (Random1To6);
    Writeln (Random1To6);
    Writeln (Random1To6);
    Writeln (Random1To6)
End {Main} .
```

In each of the examples in this section you have seen various ways to use functions to help in writing programs, and you have seen how to use parameters with functions to apply functions to appropriate values. In fact, Pascal allows you to use parameters with procedures as well; you can specify appropriate values to procedures just as we have to functions. Functions and procedures thus share many advantages. You will use both extensively to organize your work, following your outlines to solutions of problems.

SECTION 4.5   PROCEDURES AND PARAMETERS

In the last three sections, we could pass information into functions using parameters and we could base our computations in the functions on these initial values. When we work with procedures, we can use parameters in a similar way so that we can begin computations with some initial values. However, in some cases, we want procedures to return values as well, and in these situations, we need to use a different type of parameter. Such a situation is illustrated in the following problem.

PROBLEM 4.5   Applying Paint

Many latex wall paints specify that one gallon of paint will cover about 400 square feet. Varnishes and stains specify one gallon for 500 square feet.

Write a program that reads the dimensions (length and height) of a wall and computes the number of gallons of paint and of varnish needed for the wall.

Solution for Problem 4.5

In this problem, we can proceed using steps which are similar to several of our earlier problems.

Outline for Problem 4.5

    I. Determine Length and Height of Wall
    II. Compute Gallons Needed
        A. Determine Area of Wall
        B. Compute Gallons of Paint

$$\text{Paint Gallons} = \text{Area} / 400$$

        C. Compute Gallons of Varnish

$$\text{Varnish Gallons} = \text{Area} / 500$$

    III. Print Results

Discussion of Problem 4.5

When we program using this outline, we may try to structure our code by using a separate procedure or function for each of the three major steps. However, in both Steps I and II, our computations require us to obtain more than one value; Step I needs two values, and Step II computes three values. Thus, in this program, functions are not adequate for performing each major step. Instead, we use procedures with parameters for the appropriate values. This gives rise to the following program.

```
Program Paint (Input, Output);
{This program computes the amount of paint needed to cover a wall.}

Var Length, Height: Real;
    GalPaint, GalVarnish: Real;

Procedure FindDimensions (Var Length, Height: Real);
{This procedures computes the dimensions of the wall}
    Begin
        Write ('Please enter the length of the wall: ');
        Readln (Length);
        Write ('Please enter the height of the wall: ');
        Readln (Height)
    End {FindDimensions} ;

Procedure Compute (Length, Height: Real; Var Paint, Varnish: Real);
{This procedures computes the area of the wall and the amount of
 paint and varnish needed to cover this area}
    Const PaintSqFeet = 400.0;    {Number of square feet covered by}
          VarnishSqFeet = 500.0;  {a gallon of paint or varnish}
    Var Area: Real;
    Begin
        Area := Length * Height;
        Paint := Area / PaintSqFeet;
        Varnish := Area / VarnishSqFeet
    End {Compute} ;
```

```
Procedure Print (Length, Height, Paint, Varnish: Real);
{This procedure prints the results of tne computation}
    Begin
        Writeln;
        Writeln ('For a wall measuring ', Length:1:1, ' by ',
                Height:1:1, ',');
        Writeln ('we need ', Paint:1:2, ' gallons of paint, or ',
                Varnish:1:2, ' gallons of varnish.')
    End {Print} ;

Begin {Main}
    Writeln ('This program computes the amount of paint and varnish');
    Writeln ('needed to paint a wall.');
    FindDimensions (Length, Height);
    Compute (Length, Height, GalPaint, GalVarnish);
    Print (Length, Height, GalPaint, GalVarnish)
End {Main} .
```

When this program is run using the dimensions for a rather large living room, we get the following.

```
This program computes the amount of paint and varnish
needed to paint a wall.
Please enter the length of the wall: 25
Please enter the height of the wall: 9

For a wall measuring 25.0 by 9.0,
we need 0.56 gallons of paint, or 0.45 gallons of varnish.
```

Value and Reference Parameters

This program provides another example of the type of parameters used in the previous sections, and the program also illustrates a second type of parameter. In particular, in the Print procedure, we use values that have been computed earlier in our program, and we use parameters as before. The declaration:

Procedure Print (Length, Height, Paint, Varnish: Real);

indicates that we must supply four values to the Print procedure. Here, we specify four parameters, called **Value Parameters,** and Procedure Print uses the values specified in its work.

In contrast, in the FindDimensions procedure, we need to return values from the procedure to the main program. In order to return these values, we add the keyword *Var* to our declaration:

Procedure FindDimensions (Var Length, Height: Real);

The addition of this *Var* keyword allows this procedure to return values to the calling program, and these parameters are called **Reference Parameters.**

Finally, in the Compute procedure, we need to use both types of parameters. We begin with values for length and height, and we use value parameters (without the *Var*) for these parameters. Then, we want to compute values for the amount of paint and varnish, and we want these values returned so we can use them later. Thus, we use reference parameters (with the *Var*) for these values.

To summarize: When we want to start computations within a procedure or a function but we do not want revised values when the procedure or function is done, we use value parameters, and we omit *Var* in our procedure declarations. However, when we want parameters to have new or revised values after a procedure or function is completed, we use reference parameters, and we preceed them with the keyword *Var* in our procedure declarations.

SECTION 4.6 STYLE

Throughout the discussion of functions and procedures we have focused upon using Pascal features to program a step in the solution to a problem. Functions and procedures allow us to separate major steps from details, and these constructs allow us to handle common tasks efficiently. Further, we can pass parameters to both functions and procedures, to specify values that might be appropriate within a step. In Chapter 3 we mentioned some consequences of using procedures, and these remarks apply to functions as well. For example, indenting and formatting of functions and procedures can reflect the structure of the solution outline. Each program in this chapter illustrates how to indicate program structure by program format. For example, indenting indicates where various variables are defined. Local variables are known only within functions, and indenting the declaration of these variables within a function illustrates this. On the other hand, the function name and the parameter list are links between the function and the Main Program, so these aspects of the function are not indented.

Choosing Local and Global Variables and Parameters

The solution outline can help you decide when to use local variables, global variables, and parameters in functions: you can see how each value fits into the general solution. When a computation and result are needed only within one step of the outline, then the corresponding function or procedure should use local variables. The variables are logically meaningful only within the function or procedure, and the program should reflect this.

When you need initial values to start a step, then parameters are appropriate. Parameters form a convenient link between the Main Program and a function. When the computations require continuity through several steps, we maintain that continuity through the use of parameters. We can use either value or reference parameters to bring values into functions or procedures. In contrast, we must use reference parameters when procedures or functions will return new or revised values to those parameters.

Here are some general guidelines:

- Use local variables, rather than global ones, whenever possible in functions and procedures.
- Use parameters to link the Main Program with a function and to highlight the key initial values for a function.
- Try to minimize the use of global variables, so that functions and procedures can remain independent of each other as much as possible.

SECTION 4.7   TESTING

Dividing a program into separate procedures and functions not only allows you to read and understand your programs better, it also helps you check that your programs and solutions are correct.

Since each function or procedure should be largely self-contained, you can test each piece separately before you put the pieces together. For example, the Bank Interest program in Sections 4.2 and 4.4 used

Function Powers (Base, Exponent)

to compute $Base^{Exponent}$. Once we have written this function, we can check that it does the appropriate computation, using a simple program:

```
Program TestPowers (Output);
{This program tests the function Powers.}

Function Powers (Base, Exponent: Real): Real;
{This function raises Base to the power Exponent.}
    Begin
        Powers := Exp(Exponent * Ln(Base))
    End;

Begin {Main}

    Writeln (Powers(2.0, 0.0));
    Writeln (Powers(1.0, 9.0));
    Writeln (Powers(3.0, 2.0));
    Writeln (Powers(2.0, 3.0))

End {Main} .
```

This program does not solve the Bank Interest problem, but it does test *Powers* in several easy cases. In particular, the program computes 2^0, 1^9, 3^2, and 2^3. When running this test program yields the desired results, you can be fairly confident that function *Powers* works correctly.

You can follow this same approach whenever you have functions or procedures in a program. You can test each piece of the program and can correct errors until you are reasonably sure that each piece works as you expect. Then, when you put the pieces together in the final solution to a problem, you should expect that most bugs have been found. There may be some troubles with the functions and procedures interacting in unexpected ways, so you still need to test the final program. If you keep the steps independent, however, potential interaction problems will be minimized.

In later chapters we will see that **modular testing,** where each procedure and function is tested separately, is particularly helpful when programs are fairly long. A long program contains many steps, and it is easy to make a simple mistake in one of the steps. If an error can be isolated in a small procedure, it often can be found and corrected without much difficulty. Testing each procedure and function allows you to perform this error isolation before you must contend with the whole program.

SECTION 4.8 — COMPILING AND LINKING

In this chapter you have seen how to use functions as well as procedures to perform specific tasks. With this background, we will look a little more closely at the process that builds complete machine-language programs from Pascal programs. This process actually proceeds in two steps (see Figure 4–3).

As noted in Chapter 1, whenever you write a Pascal program, you must use a compiler to translate the program to machine language. Programs normally use some standard Pascal functions and procedures, however. Some of the programs in this chapter have used *Sqr*, *Ln*, and *Exp*, and almost all programs use the procedures *Write*, *Writeln*, *Read*, and *Readln*. Before a program can run, the various parts of these functions and procedures must be added to the code.

This addition of standard functions and procedures is done in a second step by a **linker.** The machine instructions for standard tasks are normally stored in a Pascal library on a disk that is accessible to programmers. After the compiler has generated machine code for a Pascal program, the linker adds the appropriate machine instructions from a Pascal library and links the two parts together into a complete machine language program.

Later, in Chapter 10, we will see that some compilers and linkers even allow you to write your own procedures in separate pieces. With this capability you can compile various parts of a program at different times and then link the pieces together.

On some computers, the linker is called automatically after the compiler is used, and you may never be aware that linking and compiling in-

FIGURE 4–3 • **The Compiling and Linking Process**

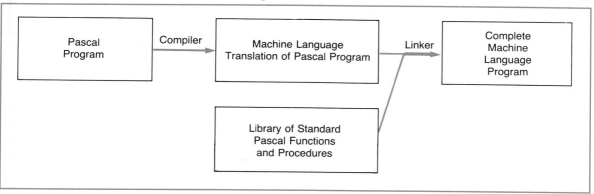

volve two separate steps. On other machines you must run the compiler and the linker with two distinct commands.

Whichever way you produce complete machine language programs, you will use functions and procedures throughout your work. You can write your own functions and procedures to accomplish special tasks that arise in particular problems, and you can rely upon a Pascal library for tasks, such as *Read* and *Write*, that arise in many problems.

SUMMARY

1. Pascal **functions** can be helpful in problem solving when one step of a solution to a problem involves computing exactly one value.
2. The **Pascal library** already contains the functions you need for some computations. You can use these basic functions when your work requires some simple algebra or computation with logarithms, exponents, or trigonometry.
3. When you need to **define your own functions,** proceed in much the same way as with procedures. Declare the function, stating the computations it will perform and specifying a final value for the function to return. The form for function declarations is quite similar to the form for programs and procedures.
4. Once a function is defined you can use it whenever appropriate. In this way, the details of computation are separated from the main idea of the task.
5. Both functions and procedures can start with certain values; you can specify **parameters** that you need to get going. Define functions and procedures with **formal parameters,** and state the **actual parameters** each

time the function or procedure is used. Parameters form a link between the Main Program and a function or procedure, and this link can take on two forms. **Value parameters** allow us to pass values into a function or procedure, while **reference parameters** allow new or revised values to be returned. Finally, global variables extend throughout the entire program and local variables are restricted to one specific function or procedure.

6. This chapter presented several examples of functions, including a special **random number generator.** To use the *Random* function, first call procedure *InitializeRandomFunction* to set up your work. Then, whenever you want another random number between 0 and 1, use the special function.

7. In previous chapters we had already used some standard Pascal procedures, such as *Readln* and *Writeln*. These procedures and other standard functions are normally stored in a special Pascal library, and they must be added to a compiled program. Thus, after you **compile** a Pascal program, **link** your code with the required instructions in the Pascal library to obtain a complete machine language program.

EXERCISES

4.1 Write a program to input a number and print that number with its square root and cube root.

4.2 *Purchasing a Ladder.* A ladder will be used to reach the roof of a

KEY TERMS, PHRASES, AND CONCEPTS		ELEMENTS OF PASCAL SYNTAX
Compiler	Parameters	*Function*
Functions	Actual Parameters	Functions:
Function	Formal Parameters	Abs
Declaration	Parameter List	Arctan
Function	Reference Parameters	Cos
Block	Value Parameters	Exp
Function	Procedures with Parameters	Ln
Parameters	Random Number Generator	Round
Standard	Seed	Sin
Pascal		Sqr
Library		Sqrt
Linker		Trunc
Modular		
Testing		

garage, and the ladder must extend over some bushes next to the garage. For safety, the ladder must extend beyond the roof by more than one foot. Also, in practice, ladders are available only in certain sizes. Find the length of the ladder you should purchase if

a. ladders are available in any whole-foot length;

b. (more challenging) ladders only come in lengths divisible by 2 (e.g., 10 feet, 12 feet, 14 feet)

4.3 *Mortgage Payments.* You can compute monthly mortgage payments as follows. Suppose you borrow an amount A, at a rate of I per cent per year, and suppose you want your mortgage to be paid off in N years. Your monthly payment P is determined by the formulas

$$R = I/1200$$
$$P = AR/(1 - (1 + R)^{-12N}).$$

a. Write a program that reads the amount, interest rate, and length of the mortgage and computes the monthly payment. This payment should be computed in a function, with parameters for amount, rate, and length.

b. [Optional] Compute and print the total amount paid over the life of the loan.

4.4 *Slope of a Line.* Write a function that computes the slope of a line between two points, where the x and y coordinates of the points are specified as function parameters. Use the function in a program that has the coordinates of two points as parameters and that returns the slope of the line containing those points.

As part of your testing, see what your program does when the line is vertical, but do not try to correct your program to handle this special case.

4.5 *Equation of a Line.* Expand the previous problem to compute the equation of the line passing through two points.

4.6 *Composition of a Function.* Write a program that contains two functions $f(x)$ and $g(x)$. For various values of x, compute $f(x)$, $g(x)$, $f(g(x))$, and $g(f(x))$. Run the program several times using different functions of your own choosing for $f(x)$ and $g(x)$. Compare (by hand) the values of $f(g(x))$ and $g(f(x))$.

4.7 Use a random number generator to print five random real numbers between 6 and 14.

4.8 Use a random number generator to print five random integers between 6 and 13.

4.9 *Coin-Toss Simulation.* You can use a random number generator to simulate the tossing of a coin by associating heads with the number 0 and tails with the number 1.

Use a random number generator to print out the results when a coin is tossed five times.

Once the program is run, write (by hand) an interpretation of the output.

4.10 *Dice-Rolling Simulation.* Write a program that simulates the rolling of a pair of dice and generates a table in the following form:

Die 1	Die 2	Total
____	____	____
____	____	____
____	____	____
____	____	____
____	____	____
____	____	____

Your program should define a procedure *Roll* that uses a random number generator to roll each die and prints one line of the table. The Main Program should initialize the random number generator, print headings, and call *Roll* six times.

4.11 *Read and Write Parameters.*
  a. Suppose you were asked to code the familiar "Read" procedure in Pascal. In your procedure, would you use value or reference parameters? Explain your answer.
  b. Answer the same question if you were coding the "Write" procedure.

4.12 Rewrite the Florist program from Section 3.4 so that procedure *ComputeCharges* has *Base* as a formal parameter.

4.13 (This problem revises the Pizza program from Problem 8 of Chapter 2.) As a pizza restaurant owner you have determined that you can sell your 6-inch thin-crust pizza for $3.50 to make a reasonable profit and still stay competitive. You have also decided that the appropriate price for a 6-inch deep-dish pizza is $4.50.

Write a program that computes the appropriate prices for 6-inch, 10-inch, 12-inch, and 14-inch pizzas for both deep-dish and thin-crust styles. Use relative areas of the pizza to determine price, and print your results in a table.

In your program, define a procedure *SetPrice* that has the 6-inch price as a formal parameter and computes and prints a line of the table based on that price.

4.14 *Logarithms.*
  a. Write a program that reads positive numbers a and b and prints $\log_b a$.
  b. Write a program that reads a positive number a and computes the common logarithm of a.
  (Logarithms are discussed in some detail in Appendix C-1.)

4.15 *Other Trigonometric Functions.* Write a program that reads the measure of an angle in radians and computes the sine, cosine, tangent, cotangent, secant, and cosecant of that angle. (Hint: Since all trigonometric functions can be defined in terms of sine and cosine, the exercise can be done using the two standard Pascal functions *Sin* and *Cos.*)

4.16 *Radian Measure*

a. Write a program that reads the measure of an angle in degrees and uses a function *Rad* to find the size of the angle in radians.

b. Define functions *DegSin* and *DegCos* with an angle in degrees as formal parameter and that use the *Rad* function from part (a) and the standard *Sin* and *Cos* functions to compute the sine and the cosine of the angle, respectively.

c. Use your functions in a program that reads the measure of an angle in degrees and prints the sine and cosine of that angle.

(The conversion between degrees and radians is given in a note to Table 4–1.)

4.17 *Reference Parameters and Functions.* A common programming guideline states that reference parameters normally should not be used with functions. Discuss why reference parameters might be philosophically opposed to the concept of a function which returns a single value.

CHAPTER 5

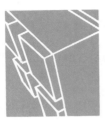

SIMPLE LOOPS:
THE FOR–DO
STATEMENT

In our work up to now, we used the computer to calculate various values. When we considered a problem, we divided the problem into steps, identified appropriate formulae to help with these steps, and translated the formulae into Pascal. In this process we typed various declarations, and we wrote a line of Pascal code for each value we needed. With all of this effort in developing a Pascal program, you may have felt that the computer was little if any help in problem solving. We used the computer as a simple calculator, but instead of pushing buttons on a calculator we had to write, compile, and link a Pascal program, and we still had to enter the data. In these applications a calculator would have been quicker and equally useful.

In this chapter we describe some ways that computers can go beyond a calculator to reduce the work of solving problems. In particular, once we set up a process, we can ask the computer to repeat that process many times. This repetition of work is the notion of a **loop,** and we will see that a loop can be a great aid in solving problems. In this chapter we will consider one basic approach to loops. In Chapter 7 we will look at two other approaches.

| SECTION 5.1 | EXAMPLE: CHART OF SECONDS PER MILE VERSUS MPH |

We introduce our discussion of loops with an example.

PROBLEM 5.1　　When driving along an Interstate Highway, we know that if we travel 60 miles per hour (MPH), then we will travel one mile in one minute. To see how long it will take to travel a mile at different speeds we can construct a chart:

Seconds Per Mile	Miles Per Hour
55	.
.	.
.	.
.	.
60	60
.	.
.	.
75	.

With such a chart we can check that our car speedometer is working properly by timing our travel between two mile markers.

Print a chart relating seconds per mile (SPM) with miles per hour (MPH), where SPM ranges between 55 and 75.

Discussion of Problem 5.1

In attacking this problem, it is clear that we need to perform the same conversion from SPM to MPH many times. Thus computations can proceed in two major steps: Determine how to convert SPM to MPH; tell the computer to repeat these computations for SPM between 55 and 75.

To convert SPM to MPH we will need the formulae

$$time(hours) = time(seconds)/(60*60)$$
$$rate(MPH) = 1(mile) / time(hours)$$

Outline for Problem 5.1

I. Print headings for the chart.

II. Repeat the following steps for time(seconds) = 55, 56, . . . , 75.

    A. Compute time(hours)

$$time(hours) = time(seconds)/3600.0$$

    B. Compute MPH

$$MPH = 1/time(hours)$$

    C. Print time(seconds) and MPH

The following program demonstrates that this outline can be translated into Pascal quite easily. In this program, note that steps A, B, and C of Part II are put together by placing these Pascal statements between the keywords *Begin* and *End*.

```
Program MPHChart (Output);
{This program prints a chart of Seconds Per Mile
 versus Miles Per Hour.}

Var Seconds: Integer;
    Hours, MPH: Real;

Begin
    Writeln('A Chart of Seconds Per Mile Versus Miles Per Hour');
    Writeln;    {Skip Line}

    {Print Headings}
    Writeln('  Seconds        Miles');
    Writeln(' Per Mile      Per Hour');

    {Repeat Computations}
    For Seconds := 55 To 75
        Do Begin
            Hours := Seconds / 3600.0;
            MPH := 1.0 / Hours;
            Writeln (Seconds:6, MPH:14:1)
        End {For}

End {Main} .
```

When this program is run, we get the following output:

```
A Chart of Seconds Per Mile Versus Miles Per Hour

  Seconds        Miles
 Per Mile      Per Hour
    55          65.5
    56          64.3
    57          63.2
    58          62.1
    59          61.0
    60          60.0
    61          59.0
    62          58.1
    63          57.1
    64          56.3
    65          55.4
    66          54.5
    67          53.7
    68          52.9
    69          52.2
```

70	51.4
71	50.7
72	50.0
73	49.3
74	48.6
75	48.0

This example shows that Pascal allows us to repeat computations quite easily. Once we decide what we want done, we can ask the computer to repeat the steps many times. In this program we used a *For–Do* statement to ask the computer to repeat the steps. More generally, when we want the computer to repeat some statements several times, we need a **loop structure** or a **loop** in the program to instruct the computer what to repeat and how often these steps are to be repeated.

Syntax and Semantics of the For–Do Loop

The only new element in this program is the For–Do statement itself. A common syntax for this For–Do loop was illustrated in the MPH Chart program:

For ControlVariable *:=* InitialValue *To* FinalValue *Do* Statement

In the example, we have the following correspondences.

ControlVariable	Seconds
InitialValue	55
FinalValue	75
Statement	Begin
	Hours := Seconds/3600.0;
	MPH := 1.0/Hours;
	Writeln (Seconds:6, MPH:14:1)
	End;

The **Control Variable** must be an integer variable, and the **Initial Value** and the **Final Value** must be integers. Real numbers are not allowed. (We will see other possible data types in Chapter 12.) The statement is repeated for ControlVariable = InitialValue, InitialValue + 1, InitialValue + 2,. . ., FinalValue.

In this syntax, we note that only one statement will be repeated. For example, if you write

```
For Number := 1 to 3
        Do Writeln('Going');
        Writeln('Gone');
```

the output will be

```
Going
Going
Going
Gone
```

Only the first *Writeln* (*'Going'*) is repeated.

ELEMENTS OF A LOOP

In this section we will look at the process of **iteration** or **repetition** more carefully. We will begin by identifying the elements typically found in a loop, then we look at the Pascal syntax for the *For–Do* loop from Section 5.1. With this background we can trace the computer's execution of the program in Section 5.1.

Anatomy of a Loop

Programs that contain loops, such as the example in Section 5.1, have four major elements:

Initialization (optional): Before a loop begins, we may need some statements to get started. In the example, we printed a title for the table before the loop began. Titles should be printed only once, at the top of the table, so we need a *Writeln* statement before any other work is done. The printing of the titles cannot be part of the loop itself, for we do not want to repeat the titles many times.

Repetitive statement: We need a statement that instructs the computer to repeat some work. In the example the *For–Do* statement specified that something should be done several times.

Loop block: We must specify what statements are to be repeated. In the example we repeated the computation of hours, the computation of MPH, and some printing.

Conclusion (optional): Just as we may need to perform some work before a loop begins, once a loop is over other tasks may be needed. In the example the program stopped after the loop, so this step was omitted. We might have repeated the printing of titles, however, or we might have written some concluding notes. If any output was needed after the table, we would need some concluding statements after the loop.

In applying this general loop structure to a *For–Do* loop structure, we see that the *For–Do* statement itself includes an initialization, since the control variable is given an initial value. The *For–Do* statement is the repetitive statement that tells the computer to repeat something, and the statement following the *Do* is the loop block that is repeated.

A loop block may contain any single statement, such as a *Read* or *Write*, a procedure call, or a function. Just one statement can be repeated, however. There are several ways to have more than one operation performed several times. In the example in Section 5.1 we placed multiple statements inside a *Begin–End* block. In this situation, the several statements are considered part of one compound statement, and the entire compound statement is repeated. We could also place several operations in a separate procedure and call that procedure in the *For–Do* statement, as in the following program:

```
Program MPHChart {With a Procedure} (Output);
{This program prints a chart of Seconds Per Mile
 versus Miles Per Hour.}

Var Seconds: Integer;

Procedure ComputeAndPrintMPH (TimeInSeconds:Integer);
    {This procedure computes and prints MPH.}
    Var Hours, MPH: Real;
    Begin
        Hours := TimeInSeconds / 3600.0;
        MPH := 1.0 / Hours;
        Writeln (TimeInSeconds:6, MPH:14:1)
    End {ComputeAndPrintMPH} ;

Begin
    Writeln('A Chart of Seconds Per Mile Versus Miles Per Hour');
    Writeln;      {Skip Line}

    {Print Headings}
    Writeln(' Seconds        Miles');
    Writeln(' Per Mile      Per Hour');

    {Repeat Computations}
    For Seconds := 55 To 75
        Do ComputeAndPrintMPH(Seconds)

End {Main} .
```

Here all computations and printing are done in procedure *ComputeAndPrintMPH*, and the *For–Do* only specifies that this procedure should be repeated. We do not need a *Begin–End* statement after the *For–Do* in this case, as only one statement is needed to call a procedure.

In each of these examples, one statement (a compound *Begin–End* or a procedure) is repeated several times. We now trace the execution of a loop, so we are sure we know how the computer performs its work.

Tracing a Loop

We consider the loop from the example in Section 5.1:

```
For Seconds := 55 to 75
        Do Begin
                Hours := Seconds/3600.0;
                MPH := 1.0/Hours;
                Writeln(Seconds, MPH)
        End;
```

When the computer begins this section of code, several events occur.

Step 1:

- The computer sets

  Seconds : = **55**

- This value is immediately checked against the final value (75).
- Since *Seconds* is no bigger than 75 (the final value), the computer performs the steps in the *Begin–End* block:

  Hours becomes 55/3600.0, or 0.01528;

  MPH becomes 1.0/0.01528, or 65.5;

  Seconds and *MPH* (55 and 65.5) are printed.

- Since it has reached the *End* statement for 55 seconds, the machine goes back to the beginning of the segment of code (back to the *For*).

Step 2:

- The computer goes on to the next value for *Seconds*, 56.
- Since *Seconds* is no bigger than 75, the computer performs the steps in the *Begin–End* block:

  Hours becomes 56/3600.0, or 0.01556;

  MPH becomes 1.0/0.01556, or 64.3;

  the values for *Seconds* and *MPH* (56 and 64.3) are printed.

- The work is done for 56 seconds, so the machine goes back to the beginning of the segment of code.

Successive Steps. The same process continues for 57 seconds, 58 seconds, etc., up to 75 seconds:

Step 21:

- The computer goes on to the next value for *Seconds*, 75.
- Since *Seconds* is no bigger than 75, the computer performs the steps in the *Begin–End* block:

  Hours becomes 0.02083;

  MPH becomes 1.0/0.02083, or 48.0;

  the values for *Seconds* and *MPH* (75 and 48.0) are printed.

- The work is done for 75 seconds, so the machine goes back to the beginning of the segment of code

Step 22:

- The computer recognizes that the last value for seconds, 75, is the final value designated in the *For* statement. All computations specified in the loop have been done, and the loop is completed. The computer moves to any concluding statements that may follow the *For–Do* and its *Begin–End* block.

This tracing illustrates how the computer methodically repeats the statements specified in the loop block. The control variable, *Seconds*, takes on succeeding values from the initial value (55) to the final value (75). Once the computer finishes with the final value, the loop is over and the computer moves on to any subsequent code in the program.

Variables and Assignments

Tracing the program also illustrates that variables may change value during the course of a program. To understand this process more clearly, we will now consider how variables are given values in a computer.

We can envision the main memory of a computer as a collection of storage locations, in much the same way as a post office contains a number of post-office boxes. When you declare a variable in a program, one of these locations is reserved for that variable. Thus when we declared, in the original *MPH Chart* program,

    Var Seconds: Integer;
        Hours, MPH: Real;

we reserved three "mail boxes" for the three variables *Seconds*, *Hours*, and *MPH* (see Figure 5–1). In the language of computer science, we even talk of the **address** corresponding to a variable. Whenever you assign a value to a variable, the computer stores the value at that variable's address. Whenever you use a value in a computation, the computer looks up the value in the corresponding location.

For example, consider the loop

    For Seconds : = 55 to 75
            Do Begin
                    Hours : = Seconds/3600.0;
                    MPH : = 1.0/Hours;
                    Write (Seconds, MPH)
            End

At the start there are no values stored in *Seconds*, *Hours*, or *MPH*, so main memory looks much like Figure 5–1. When the *For–Do* statement

FIGURE 5–1 • **Variables Seconds, Hours, and MPH in Main Memory**

Seconds	
Hours	
MPH	

FIGURE 5–2 • **Assigning Values to Locations in Main Memory**

a. Seconds := 55

Seconds	55
Hours	
MPH	

b. Hours := Seconds/3600.0
   MPH := 1.0/Hours

Seconds	55
Hours	0.01528
MPH	65.5

c. Seconds := 56

Seconds	56
Hours	0.01528
MPH	65.5

starts, the initial value 55 is placed in the *Seconds* mailbox (see Figure 5–2a). Next, values are computed for *Hours* (0.01528) and then for *MPH* (65.5). These values are stored in main memory and are found when the computer must print out numbers for *Seconds* and *MPH* (Figure 5–2b).

When the loop starts over again, *Seconds* is changed to 56 (Figure 5–2c). Note that while Seconds has a revised value, the computer has not yet changed *Hours* or *MPH*. Only when the loop block is done the second time do the values for *Hours* and *MPH* get updated.

From this discussion, you may note that the assignment statement has a different interpretation from that of an equal sign (=) in algebra. In particular, if we write

Hours := Seconds/3600.0;

the machine goes to its memory and finds the value in the location for *Seconds*. This value is divided by 3600.0 and the result is stored in the location for *Hours*. The computer does nothing with the location *Hours* until after the computation is completed (see Figure 5–3).

This same sequence can be used to explain the statement

Sum := Sum + 3.0

FIGURE 5–3 • **Performing Hours := Seconds/3600.0**

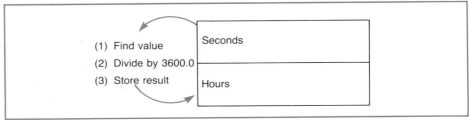

(1) Find value
(2) Divide by 3600.0
(3) Store result

Seconds
Hours

FIGURE 5–4 • **Performing Sum := Sum + 3.0**

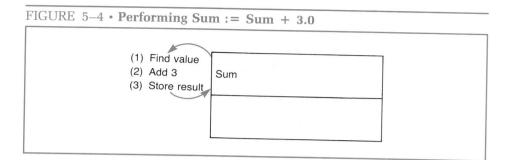

Certainly, this is not valid mathematically, but it makes sense to the computer (see Figure 5–4). The machine finds the old value of *Sum*, adds 3.0, and stores the new value in location *Sum* (destroying the previous value).

In the next section we will use this type of statement effectively in several applications. First, we need a few more observations to complete our formal discussion of Syntax and Semantics.

Alternate Syntax: DownTo

Consider how you might proceed with the following revision of Problem 5.1:

PROBLEM 5.2

Print a chart relating seconds per mile to miles per hour, where seconds per mile = 75, 74, 73, . . . , 55.

This problem is very similar to the earlier one, except that you want the chart to start at 75 rather than 55. The solution outline can have the same form as the outline for Problem 5.1, but you must be a little careful in using the *For–Do* construction. If you write

      For Seconds := 75 To 55
           Do . . .

nothing will be printed in the loop! The difficulty is that when you start with 75 seconds you are already bigger than the final value of 55. The machine skips the loop block completely.

To solve this difficulty, replace the word *To* with *DownTo*:

```
Program MPHChart {Using 'DownTo'} (Output);
{This program prints a chart of Seconds Per Mile
 versus Miles Per Hour.}

Var Seconds: Integer;
    Hours, MPH: Real;

Begin
    Writeln('A Chart of Seconds Per Mile Versus Miles Per Hour');
    Writeln;     {Skip Line}
```

```
{Print Headings}
Writeln(' Seconds         Miles');
Writeln(' Per Mile      Per Hour');

{Repeat Computations}
For Seconds := 75 DownTo 55
    Do Begin
        Hours := Seconds / 3600.0;
        MPH := 1.0 / Hours;
        Writeln (Seconds:6, MPH:14:1)
    End {For}

End {Main} .
```

The program works the same as the earlier ones, but the chart starts wih 75 seconds rather than 55. When you want a control variable to take on ascending values, use *To* in the *For* statement. If you want the control variable to descend, use *DownTo*. With either form you instruct the computer to repeat a task as the control variable progresses through a range of values.

SECTION 5.3   EXAMPLE: AVERAGING NUMBERS

We now consider one more example, which will illustrate several additional techniques that can be very helpful in using loops.

PROBLEM 5.3

Find the average of the numbers $(0.5)^2$, 1^2, $(1.5)^2$, 2^2,. . ., $(9.5)^2$, $(10)^2$.

Discussion of Problem 5.3

To solve this problem you must address two more basic problems, how to compute an average and how to compute the squares of 0.5, 1.0,. . ., 10.0.

Averages.   Recall that the average of the n numbers a_1, a_2,. . ., a_n is

$$average = (a_1 + a_2 +. . .+ a_n)/n.$$

To decide how to do this computation, consider how you might proceed without the help of a computer.

You would start with a *Sum = 0.0*, then add succeeding numbers one at a time until all of the numbers were included. To write it more formally,

A. Start with the initial

$$Sum := 0.0$$

B. Repeat the following for $j = 1, 2, 3, 4,. . ., n$

$$Add\ the\ number\ a_j.$$
$$Sum := Sum + a_j.$$

(In the last step, recall that you are taking the "old" sum and adding a_j; the result is the "new" sum.)

Computing Squares.   Next you need to determine how to get the computer to compute the squares you need. You can proceed in two steps. First identify a pattern for going from one number to the next; the numbers start with 0.5 and move up 0.5 at a time. Next apply the *Sqr* function to each number in turn.

Outline for Problem 5.3

I. Set up starting values:
>> Number := 0.0
>> Sum := 0.0

II. Repeat for 20 terms:
>> Number := Number + 0.5;
>> Square := Sqr(Number);
>> Sum := Sum + Square;

III. Compute *Average*.

IV. Print results.

Use two variables to keep track of the terms to be averaged. *Number* starts at 0.0 and grows by 0.5 each time through the loop, so it takes on the values 0.5, 1.0,. . ., 10.0. *Square* is $Number^2$, so *Square* takes on the values $(0.5)^2$, $(1.0)^2$,. . ., $(10.0)^2$ which we want to sum and average. The outline has been followed in this program. In this program, steps I and II require more than a single line of code, so we perform these steps in separate procedures.

```
Program Average20Squares (Output);
{This program averages the squares of 0.5, 1, 1.5, ... , 9.5, 10}

Var Number. Real; {next number in the series}
    Sum, Average: Real;

Procedure Initialize (Var Number, Sum: Real);
{This procedure sets values to 0.0}
    Begin
        Number := 0.0;
        Sum := 0.0
    End {Initialize} ;

Procedure ComputeSum (Var Number, Sum. Real);
{This procedure computes desired sum for 20 terms}
    Var j. Integer;    {Control variable to count terms processed}
        Square: Real; {Square term to be added}
    Begin
        For j := 1 to 20
            Do Begin
                Number .= Number + 0.5;
                Square .= Sqr(Number);
                Sum := Sum + Square
            End
    End {Compute} ;
```

```
Begin {Main}
    Writeln ('This program averages the squares of');
    Writeln ('   0.5, 1, 1.5, 2, ...  , 9.5, 10 .');

    Initialize (Number, Sum);

    ComputeSum (Number, Sum);

    {Compute the average}
    Average := Sum / 20.0;

    {Print results}
    Writeln ('The average of these numbers is ', Average:1:2, ' .')
End {Main} .
```

The program does not ask for any user input; it just prints:

```
This program averages the squares of
    0.5, 1, 1.5, 2, ...  , 9.5, 10 .
The average of these numbers is 35.87 .
```

This program illustrates the parts of a loop:

1. Initialization

    Number : = 0.0;
    Sum : = 0.0;

2. Repetitive statement

    For J : = 1 to 20 Do

3. Loop block

    Number : = Number + 0.5;
    Square : = Sqr(Number);
    Sum : = Sum + Square;

4. Conclusion

    Average : = Sum/20.0

SECTION 5.4   STYLE

There are several important stylistic principles for programs that use loops. Of course, the principles of structure and form discussed in earlier chapters still apply, so you might want to review the earlier sections on style. Here we will focus on some additional points that deal specifically with loops.

As with other programming constructions, the format of a loop should reflect the structure of the outline. An outline would use the form

1. Repeat the following steps for a range of values
    a.
    b.
    c.

To write loops in programs, use a similar form:

```
For                          For
     Do     ;                     Do Begin
                                  End
```

In each case the *For* statement is aligned with other major headings, and the *Do* phrase is indented. When several statements are included between *Do Begin* and *End*, each is indented further. The statements are enclosed by the *Do Begin* and *End* and the starting and stopping points have the same level of indentation.

The steps performed within the loop should be clearly designated; the loop should be clean and easy to read, so the overall structure of the loop is clear. If the steps within a loop involve many details, code the steps as separate procedures.

In a *For–Do* loop, use the control variable to methodically step through a designated range of variables. For example, write

```
For Index : = 3 to 9
    Do
```

to repeat a task for Index = 3, 4, 5, 6, 7, 8, 9. Be careful not to change the control variable within the loop, as in

```
For Index : = 3 to 9
    Do Begin
        Write (Index);
        Index : = Index + 1            {NO!!!}
    End;
```

Here changing Index interferes with the meaning of the *For–Do* loop. Changing control variables within a loop is illegal in Pascal. The compiler may generate an error message if you attempt such a change.

The control variable should be considered local to the loop. One step in the outline tells you to repeat a task, and the repetition is restricted to that one basic step. You should not declare control variables globally, unless the loop is in the Main Program itself, and you may not use the control variable in computations after the loop until it is assigned a new value. In fact, in Pascal, a Control Variable must be declared as local to the procedure or function where the loop is defined (see Figure 5–5).

In general, these principles all follow from the philosophy of structuring solutions to the problems. Loops may arise as major steps, and they

FIGURE 5–5 • **Declaration of a Control Variable**

```
Procedure A;                              Procedure A;
    Procedure B                               Var Index:   Integer;
        Var Index:   Integer;                 Procedure B
        Begin                                     Begin
        For  Index :=   3 to 9                        .
            Do ————                                   .
        End {B}                                       .
    Begin   {A}                                   For Index  :=   3 to 9
    End   {A}                                          Do  ————
                                              End {B}
                                          Begin   {A}
                                          End  {A}


Correct                                   Wrong
Index declared in                         Index is declared
the procedure where                       outside the procedure that
the loop is.                              defines the loop.
```

may contain several smaller tasks. When you outline solutions, you naturally incorporate these structures in your writing. Your programs need to follow a similar form.

SECTION 5.5

EXAMPLE: APPROXIMATING AREA

In many subjects—such as probability, economics, physics, and engineering—you may need to compute the area under a curve. For example, the area under the graph of velocity versus time corresponds to distance travelled. This motivates the following problem:

PROBLEM 5.5

Area Under a Curve

Suppose we are given function $y = f(x)$. Find the area under the graph between $x = a$ and $x = b$. (Figure 5–6 illustrates the area under the curve between $x = 1$ and $x = 3$ when $f(x) = x^2$.)

Discussion of Problem 5.5

In our solution, we will not try to compute the desired area exactly. Rather, we will consider a fairly simple approach, called the **trapezoidal rule,** which can give us good approximations to the area. In this approach, we break down a large area into small pieces and approximate each of the small pieces by a trapezoid (see Figure 5–7). From geometry, we can easily compute the area of each trapezoid (see Figure 5–8). Then we can approximate the entire area under the curve by adding up the areas of the trapezoids.

FIGURE 5–6 • Area under f(x) = x² between x = 1 and x = 3

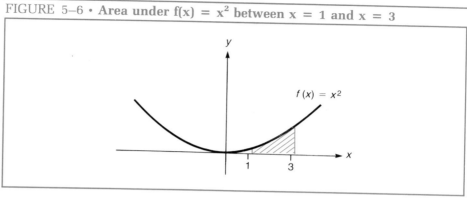

More precisely, we first divide the interval $[a,b]$ into n equal pieces $a = x_0, x_1, x_2, \ldots, x_{n-1}; x_n = b$. Then we use the pieces to divide the overall area into trapezoids. After we compute the area of each trapezoid, we add up these small areas. The final formula is

Approximate
area $= h[f(x_0)/2 + f(x_1) + f(x_2) + \ldots + f(x_{n-1}) + f(x_n)/2]$,
under curve

where $h = (b - a)/n$ and $x_j = a + jh$ for $j = 0, 1, 2, \ldots n$. This is the formula for the trapezoidal rule. (The interested reader should consult books in calculus or numerical methods for the details of this and other methods.)

To make this formula more concrete, we apply it to $f(x) = x^2$ between $x = 1$ and $x = 3$ (Figure 5–6) and divide the interval $[1, 3]$ into five pieces. This gives: $n = 5; a = 1; b = 3$. The overall interval $[1, 3]$ has length 2; we divide it into five subintervals of length $h = 2/5 = 0.4$ The x values are

FIGURE 5–7 • Approximating Area by Trapezoids

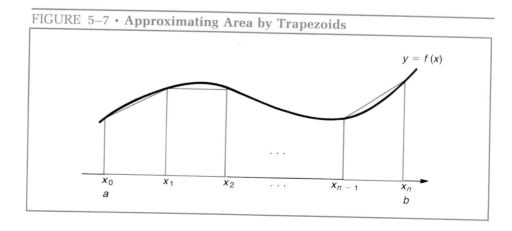

FIGURE 5–8 • Area of a Trapezoid is $(b^1 + b^2)\, h/2$

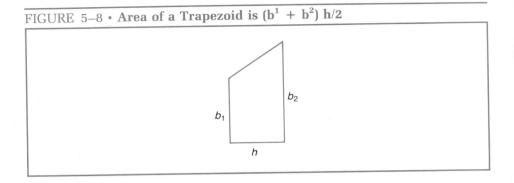

$x_0 = 1$, $x_1 = 1.4$, $x_2 = 1.8$, $x_3 = 2.2$, $x_4 = 2.6$, $x_5 = 3$. The trapezoidal rule gives

$$\text{Approximate Area} = h[f(x_0)/2 + f(x_1) + f(x_2) + f(x_3) + (x_4) + f(x_5)/2]$$
$$= 0.4[f(1)/2 + f(1.4) + f(1.8) + f(2.2) + f(2.6) + f(3)/2]$$
$$= 0.4[1^2/2 + (1.4)^2 + (1.8)^2 + (2.2)^2(2.6)^2 + 3^2/2]$$
$$= 8.72.$$

Accuracy of the Trapezoidal Rule

While it is hard to predict the accuracy of approximations with the trapezoidal rule, we can make several useful observations.

- The trapezoidal rule relies upon the actual area under the graph being close to the area under the trapezoid.
- If the graph of the function is a straight line, then the trapezoids should give exact results. Otherwise the trapezoidal rule cannot be expected to be exactly correct.
- If we divide the interval [a, b] into a large number of pieces, we can expect each trapezoid to be close to the actual area under the graph.
- As n gets bigger, the approximation of area using the trapezoidal rule should get better. (Note, however, that computational errors can appear if n is too large. We will discuss such errors in Chapter 11.)

Programming the Trapezoidal Rule

In the problem we were given a function $y = f(x)$ and an interval [a, b]. We can decide ahead of time how many pieces to work with; i.e., we can choose n. Thus the key to approximating the area is the computation of

$$h\,[\, f(x_0)/2 + f(x_1) + f(x_2) + \ldots + f(x_{n-1}) + f(x_n)/2].$$

To compute this sum, we proceed in much the same way that we did to compute averages in Section 5.3.

Since $x_0 = a$ and $x_n = b$, we start by computing the first and last terms of the sum,

$$Sum = f(x_0)/2 + f(x_n)/2$$

or

$$Sum = [f(a) + f(b)]/2.$$

Then we add the middle terms to this sum one at a time until all terms in the formula are included. This suggests the following approach.

A. Compute the first two terms.

$$Sum := [f(a) + f(b)]/2$$

B. Repeat for $j = 1, 2, 3, \ldots, n - 1$
    1. Compute x_j

$$x_j = a + jh$$

    2. Add $f(x_j)$ to the sum.

$$Sum := Sum + f(x_j)$$

This approach for adding successive terms is the heart of the following outline.

Outline for Problem 5.5

  I. Determine $f(x)$, a, b, n, h.
    A. $f(x)$ will be a function declared in the program.
    B. a and b will be constants.
    C. Read n
    D. Compute h:

$$h = (b - a)/n.$$

 II. Compute approximation.
    A. Compute the first and last terms:

$$Sum := [f(a) + f(b)]/2.0$$

    B. Repeat for $j := 1, 2, 3, \ldots, n - 1$:
      1. Compute x_j:

$$x_j = a + jh.$$

      2. Add $f(x_j)$ to Sum:

$$Sum := Sum + f(x_j).$$

    C. Finish the formula:

$$\text{Approximate Area} := h*Sum$$

III. Print results.

This outline suggests the following program, using $f(x) = x^2$, $a = 1$, $b = 3$.

```
Program TrapezoidalRule (Input,Output);
{This program approximates the area under a graph y = f(x)
 between x = a and x = b using the Trapezoidal Rule.}

Const a = 1;
      b = 3;
Var n: Integer;                {number of subdivisions}
    h: Real;                   {width of each subdivision}
    ApproximateArea: Real;     {result of approximation}

Function f(x:Real): Real;
{y = f(x) is the graph under consideration}
    Begin
        f := x*x
    End {f};

Procedure SetUp;
{Procedure determines the initial values needed in the Trapzoidal Rule.}
    Begin
        {f(x), a, and b are already specified above}

        {determine the number of pieces}
        Write ('Enter the number of subdivisions: ');
        Readln(n);

        {Compute h, the width of each piece}
        h := (b - a) / n;
    End {SetUp} ;

Procedure ComputeArea;
{Procedure to apply the Trapzoidal Rule with n subdivisions}
    Var j: Integer; {control variable for sum}
        Sum, x: Real;
    Begin
        {Compute the first two terms}
        Sum := (f(a) + f(b)) / 2.0;

        {Repeat for j := 1, 2, 3, ..., n-1}
        For j := 1 to n-1
          Do Begin
             x := a + j*h;
             Sum := Sum + f(x)
          End;

        {Finish Formula}
        ApproximateArea := h * Sum

    End {ComputeArea} ;

Begin {Main}
    Writeln ('The area under a graph is approximated, ',
             'using the Trapezoidal Rule.');
```

```
{Determine f(x), a, b, n, h for the Trapezoidal Rule}
SetUp;

{Compute Approximation}
ComputeArea;

{Print Results}
Writeln ('When ', n:1, ' subdivisions are used, ',
         'the approximate area is ', ApproximateArea:1:2)
End {Main} .
```

When we run this program with n = 5 we get

```
The area under a graph is approximated, using the Trapezoidal Rule.
Enter the number of subdivisions: 5
When 5 subdivisions are used, the approximate area is 8.72
```

NOTE: The correct answer to two decimal places is 8.67, according to calculus. This answer could be achieved with this program by using at least 13 subdivisions.

This program shows the various features of loops that we encountered before, but here the steps require a bit more care. The computation of the formula

$$h [f(x_0)/2 + f(x_1) + . . .+ f(x_{n-1}) + f(x_n)/2]$$

proceeded in three steps. It started with *initialization,*

> Sum := (f(a) + f(b))/2

A *loop* added successive terms:

> x := a + j*h
> Sum := Sum + f(x)

The *conclusion* finished the formula:

> Area := h*Sum

We needed to repeat a computation for $x = a + h$, $x = a + 2h$, $x = a + 3h,$. . . . To accomplish this repetition we set up a control variable j and repeated the computation for a range of j values, namely $j = 1, 2, 3,$. . ., $n - 1$. Then, within the loop, we used j to compute the x values. The control variable j allowed us to repeat the computations the correct number of times. The x values increased in parallel with the control variable j as the loop was executed. In Pascal, control variables cannot be real numbers, so fractional x values cannot be used for the control variable. Using a counter like j and then computing x solves this problem.

Using a function for f and constants for a and b made this program easy to modify for other areas as well. You can easily insert different functions for f, and you can change a and b without having to search through the entire program. This ease of program modification illustrates another important reason why functions, procedures, and constants can be particularly helpful in writing programs.

SECTION 5.6   NESTED LOOPS

Once you understand the idea of repeating some work several times, it is natural to consider situations where repeated work itself includes a loop. This situation, where one loop is inside another one, is called a **nested loop.** In this section we will look at a problem that involves nested loops.

PROBLEM 5.6   Car Loan Payment Tables

If you are planning to buy a car, you want to know what your monthly payments would be on a loan, which you expect to pay off over five years. Determine the monthly payments for loans of $5000, $6000, $7000,. . ., $15,000 at annual interest rates of 9%, 10%, 11%,. . ., 15%.

Discussion of Problem 5.6

The results will be most helpful if you plan to produce a table of the following type:

Loan Amount	Annual Interest Rates						
	9%	10%	11%	12%	13%	14%	15%
$5000							
$6000							
$7000							
.							
.							
.							

The key task will be to print one line of the table. On each line print the loan amount, then repeat the same calculation for each interest rate. Thus, for one line, we have the following outline:

A. Print loan amount.
B. Repeat for rates 9%, 10%,. . ., 15%.
    1. Compute monthly payment.
    2. Print payment.
C. Move to next line.

From a handbook, here is the formula for computing the monthly payment:

$$\text{Payment} = \text{Loan} * i/[1 - (1 + i)^{-n}],$$

where n = number of months of loan (60 months, or 5 years), and i = monthly interest rate (annual rate/12). Once you know how to compute one line, you can repeat the process for each loan amount. This suggests the following outline:

Outline for Problem 5.6

I. Print table headings.

II. Print payments for loans of $5000, $6000,. . ., $15000.

    A. Print loan amount.

    B. Repeat for rates 9%, 10%,. . ., 15%.

        1. Compute monthly payment.

        2. Print payment.

    C. Move to next line.

To translate this outline into a Pascal program, use functions to compute the messy payment formula. In addition, as each major step of the outline requires several lines of code, we write procedures for each of these major steps. Otherwise, the program follows the outline very closely:

```
Program LoanPayments (Output);
{This program computes the monthly payments needed to pay off
 various loans at various interest rates over 5 years.}

Function Powers (Base, Exponent: Real). Real;
{Function raises the base to the given exponent.}
    Begin
        Powers := exp(Exponent * Ln(Base))
    End {Powers} ;

Function MonthlyPayment (Loan, Rate. Real): Real;
{Function computes the monthly payment for a loan at the given
 monthly rate to be paid in 5 years (60 months).}
    Var Top, Bottom. Real;
    Begin
        Top .= Loan * Rate;
        Bottom .= 1 - Powers(1+Rate, -60.0);
        MonthlyPayment := Top / Bottom
    End {MonthlyPayment} ;

Procedure PrintHeadings;
{This procedure prints the headings for the table of payments.}
    Begin
        Writeln ('Computation of monthly payments for various 5-year loans');
        Writeln;
        Writeln (' Loan                      Annual Interest Rates');
        Writeln ('Amount      9%        10%       11%',
                '        12%       13%       14%       15%');
    End {PrintHeadings} ;
```

```
Procedure PrintPayments;
{This procedure prints payments for loans of 5000, 6000, 7000, ..., 15000}
    Var Loan: Real;
        Thousand. Integer; {Loan amounts in thousands}
        AnnRate: Integer;  {annual interest rate}
        MonRate: Real;     {monthly interest rate}
        Payment: Real;
    Begin
        For Thousand := 5 To 15
          Do Begin
            {Print loan amount}
            Loan := 1000.0 * Thousand;
            Write (Loan.5:0);

            {Repeat for each rate}
            For AnnRate .= 9 to 15
              Do Begin
                MonRate := AnnRate / 1200.0;
                Payment := MonthlyPayment(Loan, MonRate);
                Write (Payment.8:2)
              End {AnnRate};

            {Move to next line}
            Writeln
          End {Thousand}

    End {PrintPayments} ;

Begin {Main}
    PrintHeadings;
    PrintPayments;
End {Main} .
```

Notice how the indenting in this program clarifies the nested loops. When the program is run, we get

```
Computation of monthly payments for various 5-year loans
```

Loan Amount	Annual Interest Rates						
	9%	10%	11%	12%	13%	14%	15%
5000	103.79	106.23	108.71	111.22	113.76	116.34	118.95
6000	124.55	127.48	130.45	133.47	136.52	139.61	142.74
7000	145.31	148.73	152.20	155.71	159.27	162.88	166.53
8000	166.07	169.98	173.94	177.96	182.02	186.15	190.32
9000	186.82	191.22	195.68	200.20	204.78	209.41	214.11
10000	207.58	212.47	217.42	222.44	227.53	232.68	237.90
11000	228.34	233.72	239.16	244.69	250.28	255.95	261.69
12000	249.10	254.96	260.91	266.93	273.04	279.22	285.48
13000	269.86	276.21	282.65	289.18	295.79	302.49	309.27
14000	290.62	297.46	304.39	311.42	318.54	325.76	333.06
15000	311.37	318.70	326.13	333.67	341.29	349.02	356.85

This example illustrates one general situation that arises when a problem contains several distinct variables, each varying over a range of values. The result is a table. To create this table, we first considered what we needed to do for a single row or a particular loan amount. For a particular loan, we needed to compute payments at various interest rates, and we used a loop to make these various payment computations. For this loop, we had an initialization *Write(Loan)*, a repetitive statement *For AnnRate*, a loop block, and a conclusion *Writeln*.

When we had identified what we needed to do for a given loan amount, we repeated that computation for the various loan amounts. As a result, we had one large loop (for loan amounts) which contained a smaller loop (for various interest rates); the loop for interest rates was nested inside the loop for loan amounts.

| SECTION 5.7 | SIMULATION OF CONTINUOUS PHYSICAL PROCESSES |

Many subjects in engineering and in the physical sciences involve quantities that are constantly changing. For example, the rate of a chemical reaction changes as the reaction proceeds; the velocity and the position of a rocket change during flight. In such situations various mathematical models can help predict what will happen. In practice, however, the equations in many such models can be too hard to solve. Thus, the computer is often used to help get good approximate answers to these questions.

This use of the computer to simulate physical processes can involve very sophisticated methods, and a full study of the subject is certainly beyond the scope of what we can cover here. In this section we will consider a simple application that gives some indication of the more complex problems that could be considered.

| PROBLEM 5.7 | The Jump of a Pole Vaulter |

An olympic pole vaulter jumps up into the air at the rate of 33 ft/sec. Approximate the heights achieved over a period of two seconds.

Discussion of Problem 5.7

As the pole vaulter moves upward, gravity pulls on him continually. Physics tells us that velocity decreases 32 ft/sec each second the vaulter is in the air. Also, we know that if velocity is constant, then

$$\text{distance} = (\text{rate})(\text{time})$$

In the present problem, rate or velocity changes a considerable amount in one second, so the distance formula does not apply very well.

Over short periods of time (fractions of a second), however, velocity would not change very much. Thus, over short time intervals we could use the distance formula to approximate the distance traveled.

Outline for Problem 5.7

I. Print table headings.

II. Determine initial velocity and distance.

    A. velocity = 33 ft/sec

    B. distance = 0 ft (The vaulter has not yet left the ground.)

III. Repeat every 0.1 seconds:

    A. Update distance:

$$\text{new distance} = \text{old distance} + (\text{velocity})(0.1 \text{ sec}).$$

    B. Update velocity:
    (velocity decreases by 3.2 every 0.1 sec):

$$\text{new velocity} = \text{old velocity} - 3.2.$$

    C. Print updated information

In the following program, note how constants are used to clarify many of the numbers in the outline.

```
Program PoleVaulter (Output);
{This program follows a pole vaulter jumping into the air}

Const TotalTime = 2.0;
      IntervalLength = 0.1;
      InitialVelocity = 33.0;
      Acceleration = -32.0;           {acceleration due to gravity in a second}

Var NumberOfIntervals: Integer;
    Velocity, Height: Real;

Procedure Headings;
{This procedure prints table headings}
    Begin
        Writeln ('Simulation of a pole vaulter in the air,',
             ' starting at ', InitialVelocity:1:1, ' ft/sec');
        Writeln;
        Writeln ('  Time');
        Writeln ('Interval  Velocity  Height');
    End {Headings} ;

Procedure Initialize (Var Velocity, Height: Real;
                      Var NumberOfIntervals: Integer);
{This procedure determines initial velocity and height}
    Begin
        Velocity := InitialVelocity;
        Height := 0.0;
        NumberOfIntervals := Round (TotalTime / IntervalLength) ;
        Writeln (0.0:6:1, Velocity:12:3, Height:10:3);
    End {Initialize} ;
```

```
Procedure FollowVaulter (Velocity, Height: Real; NumberOfIntervals: Integer);
{This procedure follows the path of the vaulter during the jump}
    Var TimeInterval: Integer;
        Time: Real;
    Begin
        For TimeInterval := 1 to NumberOfIntervals
            Do Begin
                {Compute Time}
                Time := TimeInterval * IntervalLength;

                {Update Height}
                Height := Height + Velocity * IntervalLength;

                {Update Veloctiy}
                Velocity := Velocity + Acceleration * IntervalLength;

                {Print results}
                Writeln (Time:6:1, Velocity:12:3, Height:10:3)
            End {TimeInterval}
    End {FollowVaulter} ;

Begin
    Headings;
    Initialize (Velocity, Height, NumberOfIntervals);
    FollowVaulter (Velocity, Height, NumberOfIntervals)
End {Main} .
```

The program produces the following output:

```
Simulation of a pole vaulter in the air, starting at 33.0 ft/sec

  Time
Interval   Velocity    Height
   0.0      33.000      0.000
   0.1      29.800      3.300
   0.2      26.600      6.280
   0.3      23.400      8.940
   0.4      20.200     11.280
   0.5      17.000     13.300
   0.6      13.800     15.000
   0.7      10.600     16.380
   0.8       7.400     17.440
   0.9       4.200     18.180
   1.0       1.000     18.600
   1.1      -2.200     18.700
   1.2      -5.400     18.480
   1.3      -8.600     17.940
   1.4     -11.800     17.080
   1.5     -15.000     15.900
   1.6     -18.200     14.400
   1.7     -21.400     12.580
   1.8     -24.600     10.440
   1.9     -27.800      7.980
   2.0     -31.000      5.200
```

This problem illustrates one fundamental approach for simulating physical phenomena. We started the work at a known point (velocity = 33, distance = 0), then we used this information to determine the changes in velocity and distance over short time intervals, where we could use algebra to approximate the changes.

Here, however, the velocity changes considerably in 1 second. Therefore, we approximate distance by working with short time intervals of 0.1 seconds. Each distance computation assumes constant velocity, and we approximate this assumption more accurately when time intervals are shorter. This solution can be expanded to a very general approach called **Euler's method.** The interested reader should consult books on differential equations or numerical methods for more details.

| SECTION 5.8 | TESTING AND DEBUGGING |

In earlier chapters, our programs followed simple formulas and the amount of computation performed was rather small. Such programs were fairly easy to check. We had little difficulty following the formulae, and we could easily test that the programs produced correct results. The task of checking programs that contain loops can be harder. The computer may be performing many more computations, and it may be impractical for us to do the same work. Similarly, once we discover that a program produces incorrect results, we may have a hard time locating the bugs.

In this section we will begin a discussion of ways to test programs and find bugs when we use loops. We will review some ways of selecting good test data for checking programs; then we will identify places in loops where errors are frequently made. Finally, we will mention some techniques for locating specific errors. This discussion will allow us to get started testing and correcting many programs that contain loops. After we have some experience (by Section 7.5), we will consider a few additional ideas for testing and debugging.

Choosing Test Cases

Back in Chapter 2 we tested programs by running them with data where we knew the answer ahead of time. When the programs worked correctly on the test cases, we felt fairly confident that the programs would work on other cases as well.

This idea still applies, but we need to select test cases carefully. It would be best to avoid long, involved computations, even if the computer will perform the work. We may be able to identify special cases where we know an answer without doing all the steps. Here are two illustrations:

Use of Special Data: We know the average of several numbers is a "middle" value. Thus, we could pick data where the "middle" can be determined at a glance. The average of 2, 2, 2, 2, 2 is clearly 2. The average of 1 and 2 is clearly 1.5. The average of 9, 10, 12, 13 is 11.

FIGURE 5–9 • Area under f(x) = 3 between x = 1 and x = 5

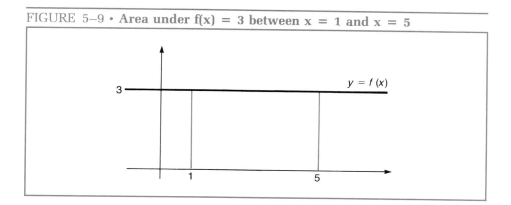

Use of Special Functions: The program for computing areas in Section 5.5 requires many approximations, and checking the accuracy of each would be tedious. By choosing certain functions, however, we may be able to find an area by simple geometry. For example,

a. Suppose $f(x) = 3$ and we want the area between $x = 1$ and $x = 5$ (see Figure 5–9). The region is a rectangle with length 4 and height 3, and geometry tells us that the area should be 12.

b. Suppose $f(x) = 3x$ and we want the area between $x = 1$ and $x = 5$ (Figure 5–10). The region is a trapezoid, and geometry tells us that the area should be $1/2(3 + 15) \times 4 = 36$.

c. Suppose $f(x) = \sqrt{9 - x^2}$ and we want the area between $x = -3$ and $x = 3$ (Figure 5–11). Here the region is a semicircle of radius 3. The area of the whole circle is $\pi 3^2 = 9\pi$. Thus the area of the region is $9\pi/2$, or about 14.137.

FIGURE 5–10 • Area under f(x) = 3x between x = 1 and x = 5

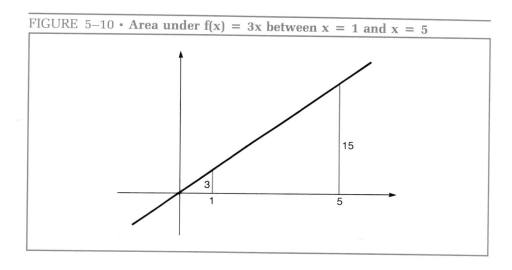

FIGURE 5–11 • **Area under f(x) $= \sqrt{9 - x^2}$ between x $= -3$ and x $= 3$**

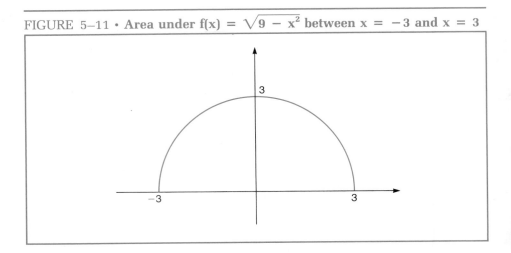

Since the Trapezoidal Rule uses trapezoids to approximate area, we would expect the program to give exact results for cases a and b. For case c we would not expect exact results. As the number of trapezoids increases, however, we would expect the results of the program to get fairly close.

NOTE: This use of special functions reinforces earlier comments on the use of independent procedures and functions. Here, we are testing procedures *SetUp* and *ComputeArea* (from program Trapezoidal Rule) by making appropriate choices for the function *f*. The tests involve changes in two constants and in a function, but these modifications do not require changes in the code that actually computes area, so the special cases should help test the area computations. You can test functions and procedures separately when you divide your programs into independent modules.

In all of the special cases discussed here, we used general knowledge (of averages and geometry) to select test cases with known answers. We did not need to repeat the work of the program to test it.

Finding Errors

After a program is run with test data, you may know that the program contains an error, or **bug.** The next task is to find and correct the error, often called **debugging.** We will now consider a few ways to find errors.

Common Errors. While errors can occur in many places, you often can find an error quickly if you check the places where troubles most frequently arise. These common errors in writing loops are summarized in Table 5–1; you might start your debugging work by reading the code to try to correct these potential errors.

TABLE 5–1 · Common Errors in Writing Loops

Error	Description
Initialization	First datum often either omitted completely or counted twice.
Moving from case to case	One variable often not updated or changed incorrectly.
Ending at the right time	Steps in a loop may be done one time too many or one time too few.
Putting too much or too little in the loop	Part of the initialization or conclusion of a loop may be inside the loop itself. For example, a sum may be reset to 0.0 each time in a loop.
Changing the control variable	If you change the control variable in a loop, you lose track of how many repetitions have occurred.

Tracing Execution.   A second important technique is to trace through the program with your data, printing out what the computer is doing at each step. Two tracing techniques are helpful. You can go through the program step by step, using notepaper to keep track of each variable and computation; you "play computer," following each instruction in the program.

You could also insert *Write* statements at various places in the program, to see what the computer has done. For example, you could write out the values of variables at the beginning or end of each procedure and before and after loops. In this technique you let the computer perform the computations, but you monitor the program as the work proceeds. Placing *Write* statements in a loop often helps identify errors in initialization, conclusion, and moving from case to case in a loop.

Frequently you can combine these two techniques effectively. First you might insert a few *Write* statements to determine what section of code the bug is in. If the program has correct values before a piece of code and incorrect values after, then there must be an error in that piece. Once you have narrowed down the location of the bug, you can trace the program yourself, on paper, to find the error.

When the bugs are found and corrected, remove the extra *Write* statements after rechecking the program with the test cases. While you are becoming proficient in the tracing process, you may find some suggestions helpful:

- When you insert *Write* statements, it is helpful to print where the statements are. Then, when the program is run, you know what statement produced what output.
- Extra *Write* statements should be identified in some way in the pro-

gram listing, so they can be found quickly and removed easily after the program is corrected.

- When tracing through a program, be sure you keep track of enough information. When inserting *Write* statements, print enough data to trace through the next part of the program if necessary.

A sample of a *Write* statement inserted for debugging is shown in Figure 5–12.

Loop Invariants. When developing loops, you may find it helpful to write out explicitly what you need to be true each time you start the loop. For example, our program to average the numbers $(0.5)^2,. . ., (10.0)^2$ contained the statements

```
Number : = 0.0;
Sum : = 0.0;
For J : = 1 to 20
     Do Begin
          Number : = Number +0.5;
          Square : = Sqr(Number);
          Sum : = Sum + Square
     End;
```

Here, each time the loop repeats, we can check that *Number* is the last value processed and *Sum* equals the sum of the squares from 0.5 up to *Number*. These two conditions are called **loop invariants** in this program; we need them to be true each time we start or finish our loop.

Once you have identified loop invariants, you can check that initialization and updating of variables keeps the statements true. If they are not true, you can check the list of common errors to see if you have forgotten to update a variable appropriately, or if initialization allows the loop to start correctly the first time. To trace a program's execution, you can insert *Write* statements at the beginning of a loop to see if the loop invariants really do hold each time the loop begins. In many cases, once you write out explicitly what the loop invariants should be, you can locate and correct errors quite effectively.

FIGURE 5–12 • **Inserting a Write Statement for Debugging**

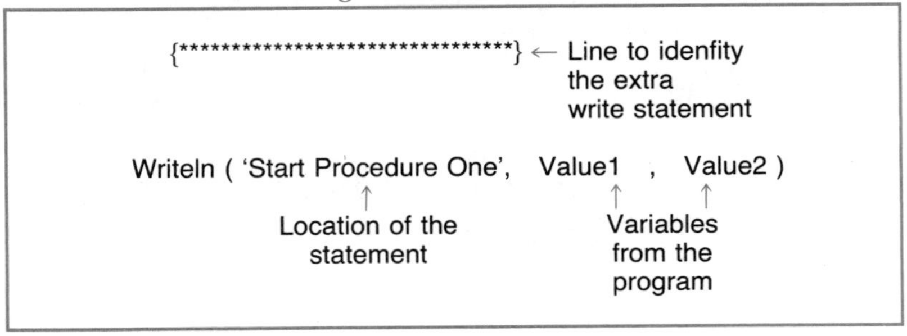

SUMMARY

1. A **loop** is a repetitive structure that allows you to repeat steps several times. This process of **repetition,** or **iteration,** has the following basic steps:

   I. **Initialization:** Before the loop begins, you may need to get ready for the loop.
   II. Loop itself
      A. Repetitive statement: A statement that tells the computer to repeat something.
      B. Loop block: Specifies what statements must be repeated.
   III. **Conclusion:** After the loop is over, you may have some final work to do.

2. This chapter presents two forms for repetitive statements:

   For ControlVariable : = InitialValue *To* FinalValue *Do* LoopBlock

   and

   For ControlVariable : = InitialValue *DownTo* FinalValue *Do* LoopBlock

   The loop block can be either a single Pascal statement or a **Begin–End block.**

3. Within the loop itself, you may need to start the loop each time with certain conditions being true. You need to update variables at the end of the loop for the **loop invariants** to be true when you start the next iteration of the loop. The loop block often contains two parts: Perform work for this iteration; get ready for next iteration.

4. When you test a program, you may need to **trace** through the code to determine what the computer is doing. You can review what the computer has done by inserting extra *Write* statements, and you can follow the instructions yourself using pencil and paper to keep track of your work.

5. Finally, this chapter includes many applications. Some applications involve simple loops. In other cases, you need **nested loops,** with one loop inside another.

EXERCISES

5.1 *Converting Quarts to Liters.* Write a program that shows the conversion of quarts to liters, for quarts in the range 1, 2, 3,. . ., 20. Label the columns of the table "Quarts" and "Liters."
   NOTE: 1 liter = 1.056710 quarts.

5.2 *Temperature Conversion.* Write a program to produce a table of Fahrenheit temperatures with corresponding centigrade and absolute (Kelvin) temperatures. The Fahrenheit temperatures in the table should include 0, 1, 2,. . ., 212. Label the columns of the table "Fahrenheit," "Centigrade," and "Kelvin." The appropriate conversion formulas are:

$$\text{Centigrade} = 5/9(\text{Fahrenheit} - 32)$$
$$\text{Kelvin} = \text{Centigrade} + 212$$

5.3 *Sum of Cubes.* For $n = 1, 2, 3,$. . ., 50, compute both n^3 and the sum

$$1^3 + 2^3 + 3^3 + \cdots + (n - 1)^3 + n^3.$$

Print the results in a table with headings "N," "N Cubed," and "Sum."

5.4 *Table of Roots and Powers.* Write a program to print a table where each row contains a number N with its square, square root, cube, and cube root. The table should cover numbers $N = 1, 2, 3,$. . ., 50. Label each of the columns in the table appropriately.

5.5 *Approximating π.* It can be shown that π can be approximated by any of the following series:

a. $\pi/4 = 1 - \frac{1}{3} + \frac{1}{5} - \frac{1}{7} + \cdots$

b. $\pi^2/6 = 1 + \frac{1}{2^2} + \frac{1}{3^2} + \frac{1}{4^2} + \cdots$

c. $\pi^2/12 = 1 - \frac{1}{2^2} + \frac{1}{3^2} - \frac{1}{4^2} + \cdots$

d. $\pi^2/8 = 1 + \frac{1}{3^2} + \frac{1}{5^2} + \frac{1}{7^2} + \cdots$

e. $\pi^2/24 = \frac{1}{2^2} + \frac{1}{4^2} + \frac{1}{6^2} + \frac{1}{8^2} + \cdots$

To use any of these series to approximate π, first compute the first n terms of the right side to get an approximate value for the series, then solve for π using the approximate value for the series.

For example, using the first 20 terms from formula d, $\pi^2/8$ is approximately 1.2212. Thus π^2 is about 8 * 1.2212, and π is about Sqrt(8 * 1.2212) = (3.125).

Problems a through e. Use the above series to approximate π; try 10, 20, 30, and 40 terms.

5.6 *Generating Random Numbers.* Write a program to generate 100 random numbers and print them out in five side-by-side columns. (Section 4.4 discusses a random number generator.)

KEY TERMS, PHRASES, AND CONCEPTS		ELEMENTS OF PASCAL SYNTAX
Address	Iteration	*Begin–End Block*
Bug	Loop	*For–To–Do*
Conclusion of a Loop	Loop Block	*For–DownTo–Do*
Control Variable	Loop Invariants	
Debugging	Nested Loops	
Euler's Method	Repetition	
Initial Value	Repetitive Statement	
Final Value	Tracing Program	
Initialization of a	Execution	
Loop	Trapezoidal Rule	

5.7 *Converting Quarts and Gallons to Liters.* Print a table that shows the conversion of quarts and gallons to liters. In the table, use the format

	Quarts			
Gallons	0	1	2	3
0				
1				
2				
3				
.				
.				
.				
10				

NOTE: one liter = 1.056710 quarts.

5.8 *Converting Feet and Inches to Centimeters.* Print a table that shows the conversion of feet and inches to centimeters. In the table, use the headings

	Inches					
Feet	0	1	2	3	. . .	12
0						
1						
2						
3						
4						
5						

NOTE: one inch = 2.54 centimeters.

5.9 *Extended Chart for Seconds Per Mile Versus Miles Per Hour.* Write an extended table relating seconds per mile to miles per hour, where seconds per mile covers the range 30, 31, 32,. . ., 129. The output should be in the form of a compact chart:

Seconds Per Mile	Units									
Tens	0	1	2	3	4	5	6	7	8	9
3 --						.				
4 --						.				
5 --						.				
6 --	- - - - - - - - - - - - .									
7 --										
8 --										
9 --										
10 --										
11 --										
12 --										

The chart illustrates how to look up 65 seconds per mile. Move down the left column to find the 6 in 65, then move across the row to find the column labeled 5.

5.10   *Mortgage Payments (1)*. Given the length of a mortgage (read from the terminal), determine the monthly payments on mortgages of 15,000, 20,000,. . ., 80,000 at annual interest rates of 7%, 8%, 9%,. . ., 15%. Display the results in a chart:

| Mortgage | Annual Interest Rate | | | | | | | | |
Amount	7	8	9	10	11	12	13	14	15
15000									
20000									
25000									
.									
.									
.									
80000									

5.11   *Mortgage Payments (2)*. Given an annual interest rate (read from the terminal), determine the monthly payments on mortgages of 15,000, 20,000, 25,000, 30,000,. . ., 80,000 for periods of 15 years, 20 years, 25 years, 30 years, and 35 years. Display the results in a chart:

Annual Interest Rate: _____

| Mortgage | Length of Mortgage in Years | | | | |
Amount	15	20	25	30	35
15000					
20000					
25000					
30000					
35000					
.					
.					
.					
80000					

5.12   *Mortgage Payments (3)*. Investigate the monthly payments on mortgages of 15,000, 20,000, 25,000, . . . , 80,000 at annual interest rates of 7%, 8%, 9%, . . . , 15% over periods of 15 years, 20 years, 25 years, 30 years, and 35 years. Display your results in a series of charts, where each chart has the form shown in the previous problem.

5.13   *Windchill Temperature*. In cold weather the windchill temperature is used to indicate the effect of the wind and temperature on cooling the body. Suppose the wind is measured at W miles per hour, and suppose the thermometer shows a temperature of F degrees Fahrenheit. The approximate windchill temperature is given by the formula

$$T = 1.05 + 0.93T - 3.65W + 3.62 \sqrt{W} + 0.103T\sqrt{W} + 0.0439W^2.$$

Compute the windchill temperature for temperatures of 10°, 9°, 8°, . . . , −30° Fahrenheit and for winds 0, 5, 10, . . . , 40 MPH. Display the results in a table labeled as follows:

Temperature	0	5	10	15	20	25	30	35	40
				Wind Speed					
10									
9									
8									
.									
.									
.									

NOTE: In practice, the windchill temperatures reported by the weather bureau are modified from a formula such as the one above. We therefore cannot expect a formula to give exact windchill temperatures.

5.14 *Table of Natural Logarithms.* Ln(x) can be shown to be closely approximated by the formula

$$2[y + y^3/3 + y^5/5 + \cdots + y^{2n-1}/(2n - 1)],$$

where $y = (x - 1)/(x + 1)$, and where n is sufficiently large. Use this formula to compute ln(x) for x = 1, 1.1, 1.2,. . ., 4 with $n = 8$, and compare the results with the Pascal Ln function. Display the output in the form

X	Computed Ln(x)	Pascal Ln(x)
1.0	0.000	0.000
1.1		
1.2		
.		
.		
.		

Programming Notes:

Use a function *MyLn(x)* to compute the value from the above formula. (In the function, declare n to be the constant 8.)

In this problem you must use multiplication to compute powers of y. You may not use the *Powers* function discussed in Section 4.2.

In practice, the Pascal *Ln(x)* function uses formulas similar to this to compute natural logarithms. Other such formulas are used for *Exp(x)*, *Sin(x)*, *Cos(x)*, etc.

5.15 Write a table that contains the values of n, n^2, $\log_2(n)$, $n*\log_2(n)$, and $10n*\log_2(n)$ for $n = 2, 4, 8, 16, 32, \ldots, 16384$. Display your computations in a table with the appropriate headings.

   NOTE: When we analyze various algorithms in later chapters, you will find numbers such as these will tell you the amount of work required for n pieces of data. Thus comparisons of this type can help you pick the best algorithms to solve certain problems.

5.16 What are the loop invariants in the programs in Sections 5.1, 5.3, and 5.5?

5.17 *The Jump of a Pole Vaulter.* In Problem 5.7 we divided time into intervals of 0.1 seconds, and we assumed the velocity of the pole vaulter remained constant during that time interval. If we used shorter time intervals, the change in velocity over each interval would be less, and we could expect our results to be more accurate.

   Modify the program for Problem 5.7 so the time intervals have length 0.02 seconds. Your program should still follow the vaulter over a total time of two seconds.

5.18 *Height of a Rocket.* Suppose a rocket engine expels gas at the constant rate of a gm/sec with constant velocity b m/sec ($a > 0$, $b > 0$). Ignoring gravity, the change in velocity in a short time interval (one second) is approximated by the equation

$$\text{change in velocity} = ab/(M_0 - at),$$
   in 1 second

where t is the number of seconds elapsed and M_0 is the mass of the rocket at time 0.

   a. Find the velocity of the rocket and the distance traveled by the rocket over a period of 15 seconds, assuming

$$a = 500 \text{ gm/sec}$$
$$b = 1000 \text{ m/sec}$$
$$M_0 = 10{,}000 \text{ gm,}$$
   initial distance $= 0$ meters
   initial velocity $= 0$ meters/second

   b. Modify your program from part a to account for the force of gravity. In particular, if the rocket starts on the ground and moves straight up, the gravity decreases velocity by 9.8 meters/second each second. (We ignore variations in gravity as the distance changes.) The change in the velocity in one second would be approximated by

$$\text{change in velocity} = ab/(M_0 - at) - 9.8.$$

   c. Modify your program from part b so that the velocity and distance of the rocket are computed every ½ second. (The change in velocity in 0.5 seconds should be half the change that would occur in 1 second.)

FIGURE 5–13 • **Discharging Sewage into a Tank**

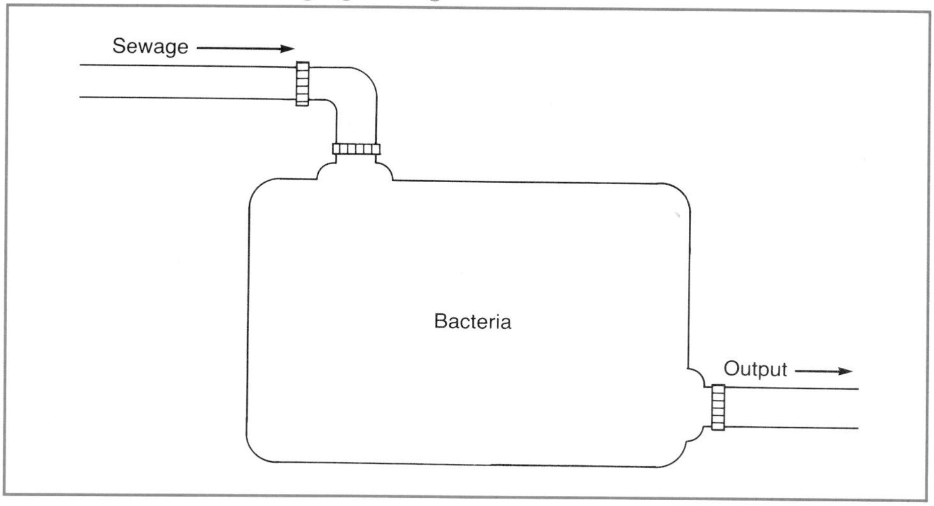

5.19 *Discharge of Pollutants.* When sewage is discharged into a holding tank, bacteria feed on the sewage and neutralize it. The more sewage that is present, the more the bacteria grow, and the more sewage is neutralized. Suppose sewage at the concentration 1000 grams of pollutants per gallon is pumped into a 2000-gallon tank at the rate of 60 gallons of sewage per hour (see Figure 5–13). The contents of the tank are well mixed, so the new sewage is combined uniformly with the solution already in the tank. This combined solution then leaves the tank at the same rate, of 60 gallons/hour. Bacteria reduce the level of sewage by a factor of $\frac{1}{10}$ each hour. Investigate the concentration of pollutants in the output pipe, assuming the tank contains fresh water at the beginning.

The equation for the change in pollutants over five minutes is approximated by the equation

$$\text{change in pollutants} = 5000 - P/120 - P/400,$$
$$\text{in 5 minutes}$$

where P is the amount of pollutants in the tank.

What can you say about the level of pollutants discharged from the tank after several hours?

CHAPTER 6

CONDITIONAL

STATEMENTS

AND

BOOLEAN DATA TYPE

In our work up to this point, we have always followed the same steps every time we ran a program. *For–Do* statements allow us to repeat some steps, but even then we always repeat exactly the same statements.

In this chapter we address problems where some steps apply in certain circumstances and other steps apply in other cases. Much of this work depends upon expressions that are true or false. Such expressions are called **conditional** or **Boolean expressions,** and we will introduce a new **Boolean data type** for these values. With this new material you will be able to write programs where the solutions involve dividing problems up into different cases, with different work required for each case.

SECTION 6.1	EXAMPLE: COMPUTING THE COST OF A TELEPHONE CALL

We begin with a rather simple problem, where one step of the solution must be performed only in some circumstances. Later we will add some details to make the problem somewhat more complex. Then we will want to divide the solution into separate cases and handle each case separately.

PROBLEM 6.1A   Compute the cost of a daytime telephone call from Grinnell, Iowa, to Chicago, Illinois.

Discussion of Problem 6.1A

The telephone company has supplied the following daytime rate schedule for station-to-station calls: (Basic Rate) first minute $0.58; each additional minute $0.39. Thus, the cost of a five-minute call would be computed as follows:

First minute	$0.58
4 minutes at $0.39	$1.56
Total cost	$2.14

Further, in computing costs, times are always rounded up, so that a call lasting 4 minutes, 10 seconds is rounded up to count as a five-minute call. This computation suggests the following steps:

1. The first minute (or less) of the call is $0.58.
2. If the call lasts over one minute, then $0.39 is added for each minute beyond the first.

We now can outline the solution.

  I. Determine the length (in minutes) of the call.
 II. Charge for the first minute: *Cost := $0.58.*
III. Charge for any time beyond the first minute
     If the call lasts over one minute, then $0.39 is added for each minute beyond the first.
 IV. Print results

In Pascal we can code this outline as follows:

```
Program TelephoneCall {Version 1} (Input, Output);
{This program computes the cost of a daytime telephone call
 from Grinnell, Iowa (Where?) to Chicago, Illinois}

Const FirstMinute = 0.58;
      AdditMinute = 0.39;

Var Length: Integer;    {The length of the call in minutes}
    Cost: Real;         {the cost of the call in dollars}

Begin
    Writeln ('This program computes the cost of a daytime telephone call');

    {Determine data about the call}
    Write ('Please enter the length of the call in minutes: ');
    Readln (Length);

    {Charge for the first minute}
    Cost := FirstMinute;
```

```
{Charge for any time beyond the first minute}
If Length > 1
    Then Cost := Cost + AdditMinute * (Length-1);

{Print results}
Writeln ('The cost of the call was $', Cost:1:2)

End {Main} .
```

When this program is run for a three-minute call, the following appears:

```
This program computes the cost of a daytime telephone call
Please enter the length of the call in minutes: 3
The cost of the call was $1.36
```

Describing and Handling Two Distinct Possibilities

One new feature appears for step III of the outline, to charge for time beyond the first minute. In this step there are two distinct possibilities; the call may last more than one minute, or the call may last one minute or less. In the first case we have extra work to do, but the second case does not require further computations.

This situation prompts the use of an *If–Then* statement:

> If Length > 1
>   Then Cost : = Cost + AdditMinute*(Length − 1)

When the computer executes this command, the machine first looks at the condition *Length* > 1. In the test run, where *Length* is 3, this condition is true, so the computer performs the *Then* part of the statement. If *Length* is 1, however, the condition *Length* > 1 is false and the *Then* statement is skipped by the computer.

This program illustrates two important points. When solving problems, you may want to divide a solution into cases. An *If–Then* statement allows you to perform work for a specified case. This work is omitted if the condition specified is not met.

This capability of performing operations for particular cases also allows us to look at a more general problem:

PROBLEM 6.1B

Compute the cost of a telephone call from Grinnell, Iowa to Chicago, Illinois.

Discussion of Problem 6.1B

Complete telephone rate information for this call is given in the chart below.

Basic rate:	$0.58 for the first minute
	$0.39 for each additional minute
Evening rate:	discount of 40% from the basic rate
(5 PM to 11 PM)	(charge is 60% of the basic rate)
Night rate	discount of 60% from the basic rate
(11 PM to 8 AM)	(charge is 40% of the basic rate)

If a five-minute call is made at 9:30 in the morning, the cost of the call would be $2.14, as we computed earlier. If a five-minute call begins at 4:00 AM, however, the cost of the call is 40% of $2.14, or $0.86.

Note that the rate charged for the call depends only on the time the call begins. A five-minute call starting at 7:58 AM would all be charged at the night rate ($0.86), and a five-minute call starting at 4:58 PM would all be charged at the basic rate ($2.14).

With this rate schedule, you need two more pieces of data to compute the cost of a call from Grinnell to Chicago, the length of the call (in minutes) and the hour when the call started. To avoid ambiguity in distinguishing between AM and PM, you might use a 24-hour clock; 2 PM would be written 14:00.

Outline for Problem 6.1B
I. Determine data about the call:
A. *Length* (in minutes) of the call
B. *Hour* when call started.
II. Use *Length* to compute the basic *Cost*.
III. Use *Hour* to determine the appropriate discount (if any).
A. If *Hour* is between 5 PM (17:00) and 11 PM (23:00), *Cost* is 60% of the basic *Cost*.
B. If *Hour* is before 8 AM or after 11 PM (23:00), *Cost* is 40% of the basic *Cost*.
IV. Print results.

This outline yields the following program:

```
Program TelephoneCall {Version 2} (Input, Output);
{This program computes the cost of a telephone call
 from Grinnell, Iowa (Where?) to Chicago, Illinois}

Const FirstMinute = 0.58;
      AdditMinute = 0.39;

Var Length: Integer;    {the length of the call in minutes}
    Hour: Integer;      {the hour when the call began}
    Cost: Real;         {the cost of the call in dollars}
```

```
Begin
    Writeln ('This program computes the cost of a daytime telephone call');

    {Determine data about the call}
    Write ('Please enter the length of the call in minutes: ');
    Readln (Length);
    Write ('Enter the hour when the call started: ');
    Readln (Hour);

    {Compute the cost of the call}
    If Length = 1
        Then Cost := FirstMinute        {Call lasts one minute}
        Else Cost := FirstMinute + AdditMinute * (Length-1);

    {Compute discount, if any}
    If (Hour >= 17) And (Hour < 23)     {Evening Rate Applies}
        Then Cost := 0.60 * Cost;
    If (Hour < 8) or (Hour >= 23)       {Night Rate Applies}
        Then Cost := 0.40 * Cost;


    {Print results}
    Writeln ('The cost of the call was $', Cost:1:2)

End {Main}
```

This program illustrates two additional points about programming for distinct cases. First, to compute the basic cost, observe that the problem has only two distinct cases (Case A, one minute; Case B, longer). In the program we wrote

> If Length = 1
>   Then Cost : = FirstMinute
>   Else Cost : = FirstMinute + AdditMinute*(Length − 1)

When the computer executes this statement, it first determines whether the call lasted one minute. If this condition is true (Case A), the *Then* clause is executed. If the condition is false (Case B), the *Else* clause is performed. Again, the work of the computer depends upon the initial condition.

Second, this program illustrates that the condition for a discount can be split into pieces, and these pieces can be put together with *And* and *Or*. The computer cannot make two comparisons at once, so $17 <= Hour < 23$ is beyond the capabilities of the machine. Such expressions can be split up into pieces, however, so that only two items are being compared in each piece. (Hour is compared to 17 in one piece and to 23 in another.) In Pascal, a variety of comparisons are possible. The complete list of comparison operators is listed in Table 6–1.

Let us look at *If* statements more carefully.

TABLE 6–1 · Logical
Operators Between Numbers

<	less than
<=	less than or equal to
=	equal to
>	greater than
>=	greater than or equal to
<>	not equal

SECTION 6.2   ELEMENTS OF CONDITIONAL EXECUTION

Section 6.1 illustrated the two basic forms of the conditional *If* statement:

> *Form 1*
> If   Condition
>   *Then* Statement
> *Form 2*
> If   Condition
>   *Then* Statement 1
>   *Else* Statement 2

NOTE: In the second form, the *If–Then–Else* is all considered one statement, so no semicolon is used after Statement 1.

In either form, *Condition* is an expression that has a true-or-false value. *Statement, Statement 1,* and *Statement 2* are any single Pascal statements or compound *Begin–End* blocks.

When the computer encounters an *If* statement, it first evaluates the condition to see if that condition is true or false. In either form, if the condition is true the computer executes the *Then* clause, performing the work specified in the statement or statements. When this work is finished, the computer moves to the next command after the *If* statement. (If there is an *Else* clause, it is skipped.)

If the condition is false, the *Then* clause is skipped. The computer goes on to the next statement following the *If,* or executes the *Else* clause if it is there. These patterns of execution are illustrated in the following examples:

```
If Rain > 0                          If Rain > 0
   Then Writeln('It is Raining');       Then Writeln('It is Raining')
   Writeln ('Tomorrow may be nice')     Else Writeln ('No Rain Today');
                                        Writeln ('Tomorrow may be nice')
```

In either example, if the code is run with *Rain* having the value 1, the result would be

```
It is Raining
Tomorrow may be nice
```

In each case, the condition *Rain* > *0* is true (1 is greater than 0), and the *Then* clause applies. After the *Then* clause is executed, the computer goes to the *Writeln* statement after the *If*. The *Else* clause in the second example is not executed for this value of *Rain*. The examples give different output, however, if the code is run with *Rain* set to 0. The first example prints only one line,

Tomorrow may be nice

The second example prints two lines:

No Rain Today
Tomorrow may be nice

The condition *Rain* > *0* is false, so the *Then* clause is skipped. In the first example the computer goes on to the next statement, which is a *Writeln*. In the second example the false condition causes the *Else* clause to be executed. When the *Else* clause is finished, the computer continues with the next statement, the last *Writeln*.

To summarize, in a conditional statement, the condition is first evaluated. If the condition is true, the *Then* clause is executed. If the condition is false, an *Else* clause is executed, if such a clause exists. These three steps complete the execution of the *If* statement. When the *If* statement is done, the computer goes on to whatever statement comes next.

Compound Statements Within an *If* Statement

In either form of conditional statement, you can ask the computer to perform multiple steps as part of a *Then* or *Else* clause by using a *Begin–End* block for the statement. For example, in the first program to compute telephone charges, we might print out a message if the length of the call exceeded one minute. The revised statement might be

```
If Length > 1
    Then Begin
        Writeln ('Call took over one minute');
        Cost := Cost + AdditMinute*(Length − 1)
        End;
```

Two tasks would be done if we talked for more than one minute. First a message would be written. Second, the cost for the additional time would be computed. You can also have multiple statements in the *If–Then–Else* form of conditional statement, using a *Begin–End* block in either or both of the *Then* and *Else* clauses. For example, you could write

```
If Length = 1
    Then Cost := FirstMinute
    Else Begin
        Writeln ('You talk too much');
        Cost := FirstMinute + AdditMinute*(Length − 1)
        End;
```

This points out a general concept: A *Begin–End* block can be used anywhere in a Pascal program where a single statement is used. Whenever a *Begin–End* block is used, think of the block as being a single entity. The statements within the block can be considered pieces of one big step.

Use *Begin–End* blocks with *For–Do* statements and with *If* statements when you want several pieces of work done as part of a single step. You can also use a *Begin–End* block to clarify how various pieces fit together, such as when you put *If* statements together.

Nested *If* Statements

Many times, you will want to consider several distinct cases. For example, in the Telephone Call Problem 6.1B, we can distinguish three cases:

Basic rate	Calls originating between 8 and 17 o'clock
Evening rate	Calls starting after 17 o'clock, but before 23 o'clock
Night rate	Calls starting after 23 o'clock or before 8 o'clock

These cases are mutually exclusive; if one rate applies, then the other rates do not apply. If the *Hour* of the call implies the basic rate, there is no reason to check further to see if we should use an evening or night rate. We include these observations in the following revised outline, which also tells how to print the rate used in the computation.

Revised Outline for Problem 6.1B

I. Determine data about the call:
   A. *Length* (in minutes) of the call.
   B. *Hour* when call started.
II. Compute the *Cost* of the call.
   A. Determine whether basic rate applies ($8 \leqslant Hour \leqslant 17$).
   B. If so,
      1. Make appropriate computations using basic rate.
      2. Print that basic rate is used.
   C. If not, determine whether the evening rate applies
      ($17 < Hour \leqslant 23$).
      1. If the evening rate applies,
         a. Make appropriate computations using the evening rate.
         b. Print that evening rate is used.
      2. If the evening rate does not apply, then we must use the night rate. (We have already checked for basic and evening rates, and these rates do not apply. The only other possibility is the night rate.)
         a. Make appropriate computations using the night rate.
         b. Print that night rate is used.
III. Print Results

From this outline we write the following program. As in our previous programs, we use procedures here for steps I and II which involve several lines of code.

```pascal
Program TelephoneCall {Version 3} (Input, Output);
{This program computes the cost of a telephone call
 from Grinnell, Iowa (Where?) to Chicago, Illinois}

Const FirstMinute = 0.58;
      AdditMinute = 0.39;

Var Length: Integer;     {the length of the call in minutes}
    Hour: Integer;       {the hour when the call began}
    Cost: Real;          {the cost of the call in dollars}

Procedure DetermineCallData (Var Length, Hour: Integer);
{This procedure reads the necessary data about the call}
    Begin
        Write ('Please enter the length of the call in minutes: ');
        Readln (Length);
        Write ('Enter the hour when the call started: ');
        Readln (Hour)
    End {DetermineCallData} ;

Function BasicRate (Length: Integer; First, Additional: Real): Real;
{This function computes the basic rate for the call}
    Begin
    If Length = 1
        Then BasicRate := First      {Call lasts one minute}
        Else BasicRate := First + Additional * (Length-1)
    End {BasicRate} ;

Procedure ComputeCost (Length, Hour: Integer; Var Cost: Real);
{This procedure computes the cost of the call, using the appropriate rate}
    Begin
        If (8 <= Hour) And (Hour < 17)
          Then Begin
              Writeln ('Basic Rate Applies');
              Cost := BasicRate (Length, FirstMinute, AdditMinute);
          End
          Else Begin
            If (Hour >= 17) And (Hour < 23)
                Then Begin
                    Writeln ('Evening Rate Applies');
                    Cost := 0.60 * BasicRate (Length, FirstMinute, AdditMinute)
                End
                Else Begin
                    Writeln ('Night Rate applies');
                    Cost := 0.40 * BasicRate (Length, FirstMinute, AdditMinute)
                End
          End {Else}
    End {ComputeCost} ;

Begin
    Writeln ('This program computes the cost of a daytime telephone call');

    DetermineCallData (Length, Hour);

    ComputeCost (Length, Hour, Cost);

    {Print results}
    Writeln ('The cost of the call was $', Cost:1:2)

End {Main}
```

This program uses a second *If* statement within the *Else* clause of the first *If*. The program does not explicitly test that the night rate applies, because that rate can be inferred if the other rates do not apply. Read this code carefully to be sure you understand the program logic.

The first *Begin–End* block is not actually needed in the *Else* clause. An *If* statement is a single Pascal statement, so an *If* could be used directly in a *Then* or *Else* clause. The computation for this program could also be written as follows:

```
{Compute the cost, using the appropriate rate}
If (8 <= Hour) And (Hour < 17)
    Then Cost * = BasicRate             {Basic Rate Applies}
    Else If (Hour >= 17) And (Hour < 23)
        Then Cost := 0.6*BasicRate      {Evening Rate Applies}
        Else Cost := 0.4*BasicRate      {Night Rate Applies}
```

Here the *Begin–End* is not needed, but can make the program clearer.

Common Errors

We conclude this section on the elements of the *If* statement by noting four common errors.

1. Ambiguity can arise when you combine *If–Then* statements with *If–Then–Else* statements. In particular, the code *If–Then–If–Then–Else* has two reasonable interpretations, as suggested by indenting:

```
If A > 0
    Then If B > 0
        Then Writeln('One')
        Else Writeln('Two')

If A > 0
    Then If B > 0
        Then Writeln('One')
    Else Writeln('Two')
```

The issue here is whether *Else Writeln* ('Two') goes with the first *If (A > 0)* or with the second *If (B > 0)*. In computer science, different languages address this difficulty in various ways. In Pascal the *Else* always goes with the most recent *If–Then* (the first interpretation). If you want to use the second interpretation, put the *If B > 0* statement inside a *Begin–End* block. It is good practice to use *Begin–End* blocks for clarity even when they are not needed technically.

2. There is a tendency to forget the *Begin–End* in a *Then* or *Else* clause when you want several steps done. For example, we may write

```
If Length = 1
    Then
            Writeln ('One Minute Call');
            Cost := FirstMinute
    Else  Cost := FirstMinute + AdditMinute*(Length − 1);
```

Here we omitted the *Begin–End*, and *Else* is separated from the *If–Then*. The compiler would not be able to tell where the *Else* belongs, and the program would not compile.

A similar, but more subtle error occurs when you forget the *Begin–End* in an *Else* clause or in a *Then* with no following *Else*. For example, we may write

```
If Length = 1
    Then Cost : = FirstMinute
    Else Cost : = FirstMinute + AdditMinute*(Length – 1);
        Writeln ('You talk too much');
```

Here we indented the *Writeln* to be part of the *If–Then–Else*. As written, however, the *Writeln* is a separate statement, and the message is always printed. The program contains a logical error, but the syntax is correct; the program will compile, but will not give the expected results.

3. The third common error is the addition of a semicolon immediately after the word *Then*. For example, consider the statement

```
If Length > 1 Then ;
    Cost : = Cost + AdditMinute * (Length – 1)
```

Here the semicolon separates the *If–Then* statement from the computation of *Cost*. Thus this cost computation is always performed; the computation is not part of the *Then* clause of the *If* statement, and it will always be performed.

4. A similar error is the insertion of a semicolon before an *Else* clause. Philosophically, the *If–Then–Else* is all part of one statement. There is a strong tendency, however, to type a semicolon after the *Then* clause. When a semicolon is included there the *Else* is separated from the *If–Then* and the program normally will not compile.

SECTION 6.3   EVALUATING A LOGICAL STATEMENT

In Sections 6.1 and 6.2 we saw how to use conditional statements to solve problems. Before looking at further examples, you must be sure you know how to write conditions effectively.

Logical Operators

Every conditional expression ends with a value of True or False, and it often begins with some numbers to compare. When comparing two numbers, use any of the operators $<$, $<=$, $=$, $>$, $>=$, $<>$ (see Table 6–1). You could write

$x < y$	(x is less than y)
$6 <> x$	(6 is not equal to x)
$5.0 >= y$	(5.0 is greater than or equal to y)

In each case the expression is true or false, depending upon the values of x and y. For example, if x = 2 and y = 5, then all three expressions would be true, but if x = 6 and y = 5.5, then each statement is false. In these comparisons the numbers can be real or integer, and you can mix these two types in your expressions.

You can put comparisons together with the operators *Not, And,* and *Or,* which have the following meanings: Suppose E, E_1, and E_2 are expressions that have values of True or False:

Not E	true if E is false
	false if E is true
E_1 *And* E_2	true if both E_1 and E_2 are true
	false if either E_1 or E_2 is false (or if both are false)
E_1 *Or* E_2	true if either E_1 or E_2 is true (or if both are true)
	false if both E_1 and E_2 are false

Examples

Expression	Value	Comment
Not (3 < 4)	False	(3 < 4) is true, so *Not* (3 < 4) is false
(3 < 4) *Or* (4 < 3)	True	(3 < 4) is true, so the result is true. The value of (4 < 3) does not matter.
(3 < 4) *Or* (4 < 5)	True	(3 < 4) is true, so the result is true. The value of (4 < 5) does not matter.
(3 > 4) *Or* (4 > 5)	False	Both (3 > 4) and (4 > 5) are false, so the result is false.
(3 < 4) *And* (4 < 3)	False	(4 < 3) is false, so the result is false. The value of (3 < 4) does not matter.
(3 < 4) *And* (4 < 5)	True	Both parts of the expression are true.
(3 > 4) *And* (4 > 5)	False	(3 > 4) is false, so the result is false. The value of (4 > 5) does not matter.

Putting Operators Together: Parentheses and Operator Precedence

You can put the logical operators together in many ways, and you can even mix logical and arithmetic operators. As with arithmetic expressions, however, you must be careful that your expressions will be evaluated as you intend. Table 6–2 shows the precedence of the various operators. When an expression uses several operators of the same precedence, execution proceeds from left to right.

The expression *3*5 < 20* is a valid expression with value True. From

TABLE 6–2 • Precedence of Operators

First Precedence	Not
Second Precedence	* / Div Mod And
Third Precedence	+ − Or
Fourth Precedence	= <> < > <= >=

the table, * has higher precedence than <, so the multiplication 3*5 is done first, and we have 15 < 20; the < operator is applied, and the result is True.

The expression 3 < 4 And 4 < 5 is not valid. And has higher precedence than <, so the computer will first try to evaluate 4 And 4. And can only be applied to true and false values, not to numbers, so 4 And 4 cannot be evaluated and the expression 3 < 4 And 4 < 5 is invalid. If our intention was to apply the And to (3 < 4) and (4 < 5), then we must add parentheses to our expression, to get (3 < 4) And (4 < 5).

This example illustrates a general situation in Pascal. Whenever logical expressions involving <, <=, >, >=, =, <> are put together with Not, And, or Or, use parentheses to form expressions. You may elect to add parentheses to other expressions, for clarity, but you have no choice when using Not, And, or Or with operators of lower precedence.

As a final example, consider

$$(3 > 4) \text{ And } (5 = 5) \text{ Or } (6 = 6)$$

The parentheses make this a valid expression. From Table 6–2, And has higher precedence than Or, so the computer will apply And first. The expression is evaluated as if parentheses were added as follows:

$$((3 > 4) \text{ And } (5 = 5)) \text{ Or } (6 = 6)$$

If we wanted Or to be applied before And, we would need to place parentheses differently:

$$(3 > 4) \text{ And } ((5 = 5) \text{ Or } (6 = 6))$$

The original expression is true, but this revised statement is false.

These examples suggest several general principles. While we can put logical and arithmetic operators and terms together in a wide variety of ways, we must be careful to apply arithmetic operations to numbers and logical operations to Boolean (true–false) values.

Precedence rules govern what operations will be performed in which order; we can add parentheses to alter this order. You may add parentheses to help you understand what you have written, even if parentheses are not strictly needed. The addition of parentheses can help avoid mistakes in writing long or complex expressions.

SECTION 6.4	EXAMPLE: MONTE CARLO METHOD

Conditional statements can be helpful in solving a wide variety of problems. Section 6.1 illustrated an application where a problem could be divided naturally into cases. In this section we will obtain results by simulating events. For example, we can "roll dice" or "pick points at random" using the random number generator from Section 4.4. After we have simulated a large number of games with the computer, we can draw some conclusions. These examples are typical of a general approach to problem solving called the **Monte Carlo Method.** In this method we simulate a game or event a large number of times, using a random number generator, and base our conclusions on these simulations.

PROBLEM 6.4A	**Rolling Dice**

In a game of dice, two dice are thrown. Team A wins if the sum of the faces of the dice is 7, 8, 9, 10, or 12. Otherwise, Team B wins. Which team is the safer bet?

Discussion of Problem 6.4A

To solve this problem we might simulate the rolling of dice and tabulate the results. We might use the random number generator to toss the dice 10,000 times. For each roll, look at the sum of the faces to see if the winner is Team A or Team B.

If the numbers of wins for Team A and Team B are recorded in the variables *AWins* and *BWins*, then a single roll of the dice would involve the following steps:

A. Roll Die 1
B. Roll Die 2
C. Compute the sum of Die 1 and Die 2
D. If the sum is 7, 8, 9, 10, 12, then increase *AWins* by 1. Otherwise increase *BWins* by 1.

These steps are included in an overall program outline.

Outline for Problem 6.4A

I. Initialize
  A. Initialize random number generator.
  B. Number of wins for each team is 0. (*AWins* := 0; *BWins* := 0).
  C. Print headings
II. Repeat the roll of the dice 10,000 times.
  A. Roll Die 1
  B. Roll Die 2
  C. Compute the sum of Die 1 and Die 2.
  D. If the sum is 7, 8, 9, 10, 12, then *AWins* := *AWins* + 1. Otherwise *BWins* := *BWins* + 1.
III. Print results of the simulation.

In the program from this outline, we will use a function *DieRoll* to roll one die. *DieRoll* yields a random integer between 1 and 6, following the approach described in Section 4.4.

NOTE: In the program listing, the random number generator is not shown, since each random number generator must be tailored to the machine where it is run. Refer to Section 4.4 and Appendix C–2 for details.

```
Program RollingDice (Output);
{This program simulates the tossing of two dice}
{Side A wins if the sum of the dice is 7, 8, 9, 10, or 12}
{Side B wins otherwise}

Const NumberOfRolls = 10000;

      {Constants for the random number generator must be included here}

Var AWins, BWins: Integer;      {Number of wins for Side A and B}

    {Variables for the random number genertor must be included here}

Procedure InitializeRandomFunction;
    {Body of this procedure must be included here}

Function Random: Real;
    {Body of this function must be included here}

Function DieRoll: Integer;
{This function gives the result when a die is rolled}
    Begin
        DieRoll := Trunc(6.0*Random) + 1
    End {Roll} ;

Procedure Initialization (Var AWins, BWins: Integer);
{This procedure initializes the random number generator and the
 number of wins for each player}
    Begin
        InitializeRandomFunction;
        {Neither side has any wins yet}
        AWins := 0;
        BWins := 0;
    End {Initialization} ;

Procedure SimulateRolls (Var AWins, BWins: Integer) ;
{This procedure simulates the rolling of dice many times}
    Var Die1, Die2: Integer;   {Roll on each of the two dice}
        Roll: Integer;         {Control variable to keep track of the rolls}
        Sum: Integer;          {the sum of the rolls}
```

```
    Begin
        For Roll := 1 to NumberOfRolls
          Do Begin
             {Roll Die 1 and Die 2}
             Die1 := DieRoll;
             Die2 := DieRoll;

             {Compute the sum}
             Sum := Die1 + Die2;

             {Determine who wins the roll}
             If ((Sum >= 7) And (Sum <= 10)) Or (Sum = 12)
                 Then AWins := AWins + 1
                 Else BWins := BWins + 1

        End {Roll} ;
    End {SimulateRolls} ;
Procedure PrintResults (AWins, BWins: Integer) ;
{This procedure prints the results of the simulation}
    Begin
        Writeln ('When the dice were rolled ', NumberOfRolls:1, ' times,');
        Writeln ('Side A won ', AWins:1, ' times or ',
                AWins/NumberOfRolls*100.0:1:1, ' percent');
        Writeln ('Side B won ', BWins:1, ' times or ',
                BWins/NumberOfRolls*100.0:1:1, ' percent')
    End {PrintResults} ;

Begin {Main}
    {Print Headings}
    Writeln ('This program simulates a game of dice');
    Writeln ('Side A wins on a roll of 7, 8, 9, 10, 12');
    Writeln ('Side B wins otherwise');

    Initialization (AWins, BWins) ;
    SimulateRolls (AWins, BWins) ;
    PrintResults (AWins, BWins)
End {Main} .
```

When the program is run, we get

```
This program simulates a game of dice
Side A wins on a roll of 7, 8, 9, 10, 12
Side B wins otherwise
When the dice were rolled 10000 times,
Side A won 5308 times or 53.1 percent
Side B won 4692 times or 46.9 percent
```

This program illustrates that the number returned by one call of the *Random* function is independent of the result from its previous call. Thus,

```
Die1 := DieRoll;
Die2 := DieRoll;
```

give two different results. The function *DieRoll* returns a different random number each time. In fact, we could simplify our program a bit by omitting the variables *Die1* and *Die2* completely and writing

Sum := DieRoll + DieRoll;

The two mentions of the *DieRoll* function generate two separate rolls of the dice.

From this simulation we can go back to the problem and conclude that Side A is a better bet, but the two values are fairly close. (Side A is better, but not by too much.)

PROBLEM 6.4B   ## Throwing Darts and Computing π

Given a 2 × 2 foot dart board, draw a circle of radius one foot inside the board so that the circle just touches each edge (see Figure 6–1).

Now suppose you throw a dart (at random) that hits the board. Determine how likely the dart is to land inside the circle. That is, if you throw many darts at the board, determine the fraction of the times you can expect the dart to land inside the circle.

Discussion of Problem 6.4B

If we introduce coordinates for the dart board as shown in Figure 6–1, a dart on the board has coordinates (x,y) where $-1 < x < 1$ and $-1 < y < 1$. The dart is in the circle if $x^2 + y^2 < 1$.

FIGURE 6–1 • **A Circle of Radius 1 Foot Inside a 2 × 2 Foot Dart Board**

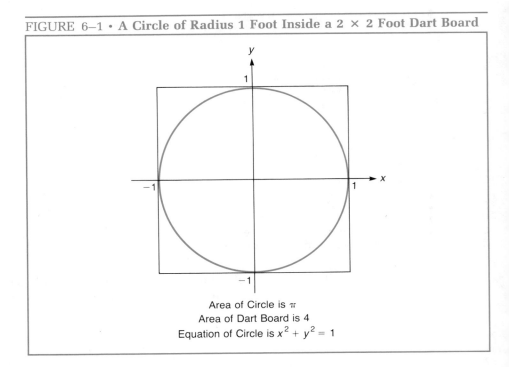

Area of Circle is π
Area of Dart Board is 4
Equation of Circle is $x^2 + y^2 = 1$

To simulate throwing darts, we can now pick many points (x,y) with $-1 < x < 1$, $-1 < y < 1$ and check these points against the equation of the circle to see how many lie inside. We can perform this simulation many times, to see what range of values is computed.

Outline for Problem 6.4B

I. Initialize
  A. Initialize *Random* function
  B. Print headings
II. Repeat the following simulation 20 times.
  A. At the start of a simulation, no points are in the circle.
  B. Simulate the picking of points 10,000 times
    1. Choose x and y in the unit square.
    2. Check whether the point is in the circle. If so, record 1 point in the circle.

Further Discussion of Problem 6.4B

The number of points lying inside the circle should depend upon what part of the area of the square lies inside the circle. The bigger the area of the circle, the more points should be in the circle. Thus we should have

$$\frac{\text{Points in circle}}{\text{Total points}} = \frac{\text{Area of circle}}{\text{Area of square}}$$

From geometry we know that the area of a circle of radius 1 is π and the area of a square of side 2 is 4. Thus the equation can be written

$$\frac{\text{Points in circle}}{\text{Total points}} = \frac{\pi}{4}$$

If we multiply by 4, this problem also will allow us to approximate the value of π! Include this additional computation in the outline as

II. C. Print Approximate Value of π

$$\text{Approximation} = \frac{4 * (\text{Points In Circle})}{\text{Total Points.}}$$

The revised outline produces the following program. As before, we omit the code for the random number generator.

```
Program MonteCarloDartsAndPi (Output);

{Simulation of the tossing of darts at a dart board to determine
 the fraction that land in a circle.  Since this fraction should
 be Pi/4, this simulation should also give an approximate value
 for Pi.}

Const NumberOfTrials = 20;
   NumberOfPoints = 10000;
   {Constants for the random number generator must be included here}
```

```
Var Trial: Integer;
    {Variables for the random number generator must be included here}

Procedure InitializeRandomFunction;
    {Procedure must be included here}

Function Random: Real;
    {Function must be included here}

Procedure ThrowDarts (Trial: Integer) ;
{This procedure throws darts at the board a prescribed number of times
 and computes and prints the results}
    Var x, y: Real;
        NumPts, PointsIn: Integer;

    Begin
        {Initially, no points are in the circle}
        PointsIn := 0;

        {Simulate picking points}
        For NumPts := 1 to NumberOfPoints
          Do Begin
            {Pick x and y in the square}
            x := -1.0 + 2.0*Random;
            y := -1.0 + 2.0*Random;

            {Check if point is in circle}
            If (x*x + y*y) <= 1
                Then PointsIn := PointsIn + 1;
          End;

        {Print value of Pi}
        Writeln (Trial: 5, PointsIn / NumberOfPoints:12:6,
                 4*PointsIn / NumberOfPoints:12:6)

    End {ThrowDarts} ;

Begin {Main Program}
    InitializeRandomFunction;

    {Write Output Headings}
        Writeln(' Trial    Fraction   Approximate');
        Writeln('Number  in Circle    Pi Value');
        Writeln;

    {Repeat the simulation several times}
    For Trial := 1 to NumberOfTrials
        Do ThrowDarts (Trial)

End {Main Program}.
```

This program produces the following output.

Trial Number	Fraction in Circle	Approximate Pi Value
1	0.783400	3.133600
2	0.784700	3.138800
3	0.780500	3.122000
4	0.787000	3.148000
5	0.783100	3.132400
6	0.781700	3.126800
7	0.787400	3.149600
8	0.781100	3.124400
9	0.784400	3.137600
10	0.785300	3.141200
11	0.781700	3.126800
12	0.789200	3.156800
13	0.781000	3.124000
14	0.784000	3.136000
15	0.784600	3.138400
16	0.783600	3.134400
17	0.785000	3.140000
18	0.783900	3.135600
19	0.784100	3.136400
20	0.783200	3.132800

Each simulation with 10,000 points was able to approximate π correctly to about two digits, but there is some variability in the third digit.

Some Limitations of this Approach

The solution to Problem 6.4B illustrates that the Monte Carlo Method, which uses random numbers to simulate events, can give fairly good approximations to the desired results. You should be aware of several limitations, however. First, this method relies upon the picking of points at random, so you cannot even attempt to use it unless you have a good random number generator. The generator must produce numbers that are well distributed and have no obvious pattern.

Second, random number generators normally depend on a positive integer, which we called *Seed* in Section 4.4. Once the value of *Seed* is specified, a random number is explicitly calculated. To perform several simulations you must start *Seed* at a different value each time, so the simulation will be based on a different random value each time.

Finally, since *Seed* is a positive integer, its values are severely limited to a range between 1 and *MaxInt*. After a certain point, *Seed* must start to repeat itself. Once *Seed* and the random number generator start to repeat, the simulation will just be using the same points over again; you will not be getting new information in your simulation. Thus, in using the Monte Carlo method you must be aware that any computer's random number generator will repeat eventually, and this repetition will limit the accuracy of your results.

Even with these limitations the Monte Carlo Method can be a very useful approach to problem solving. You can simulate events many times to determine what outcomes are likely to occur. Note that this method is usually feasible only with the capabilities of computers. The computer can perform the appropriate computations fast enough to try a large number of experiments with a problem. Thus the Monte Carlo Method shows that the computer can be helpful not only in solving problems in traditional ways; the computer also can allow you to try new types of solutions.

SECTION 6.5   BOOLEAN DATA TYPE

In each of the previous examples in this chapter we used a conditional statement (*If* statement) to determine which case we should execute at a particular point. In these examples we evaluated a true-or-false expression and acted accordingly. Sometimes, however, you may want to evaluate a conditional expression at one time and then act upon the result later. In this case you must store a True or False value for later reference.

In other cases the details of a Boolean expression may be complicated while the idea is simple. You may want to separate the complex details from use of the idea, so you may want to use a function as we did in Chapter 4. These considerations require another type of data, **Boolean Data Type.** Boolean data type allows you to work with True and False values, just as real and integer data types allow you to consider numbers.

In this section we will discuss this new data type and consider some examples. We begin with a particularly simple problem.

PROBLEM 6.5

Read two numbers, divide the smaller into the bigger to find the quotient and remainder, and print which number is bigger.

The following outline may be inelegant, but the solution is correct and elementary.

Outline for Problem 6.5
   I. Determine Two Numbers, A and B.
  II. Decide whether A is bigger.
 III. Compute quotient.
     A. If A is bigger, compute A *Div* B.
     B. If B is bigger, compute B *Div* A.
 IV. Compute remainder.
     A. If A is bigger, compute A *Mod* B.
     B. If B is bigger, compute B *Mod* A.
  V. Print which is larger.
     A. If A is bigger, print A.
     B. If B is bigger, print B.

To program from this outline you must decide, in Step II, whether A is bigger than B, and use the conclusion in Steps III, IV, and V. In this process, you must record the result of Step II for future use. Since the result of Step II is a true or false value, use a Boolean variable *AIsBigger*, which will have values *True* or *False*.

```
Program Bigger (Input, Output);
{This program prints a quotient and remainder when the smaller
 of two numbers is divided into the larger.}

Var A, B: Integer;     {Our two  given numbers}
    Quotient, Remainder: Integer; {results of division}
    AIsBigger: Boolean;   {True if A > B}

Begin
    Writeln('This program divides a smaller number into a larger one');
    Writeln('to get a quotient and a remainder');

    {Determine two numbers, A and B}
    Write('Enter two numbers: ');
    Readln (A, B);

    {Decide if A is bigger}
    AIsBigger := (A > B);

    {Compute quotient}
    If AIsBigger
        Then Quotient := A Div B
        Else Quotient := B Div A;
    Writeln (Quotient:1, ' is the quotient');

    {Compute remainder}
    If AIsBigger
        Then Remainder := A Mod B
        Else Remainder := B Mod A;
    Writeln (Remainder:1, ' is the remainder');

    {Print which is bigger}
    If AIsBigger
        Then Writeln(A:1, ' is the larger number')
        Else Writeln(B:1, ' is the larger number')

End {Main} .
```

If you run this program with the numbers 4, 13, you get the following:

```
This program divides a smaller number into a larger one
to get a quotient and a remainder
Enter two numbers: 4 13
3 is the quotient
1 is the remainder
13 is the larger number
```

The same output results if you reverse the numbers, typing 13 4.

This example illustrates the following points about Boolean data type: To assign *True* or *False* values to a variable you first must declare the variable to be of type *Boolean*. In the declarations we wrote

AIsBigger: Boolean;

The form of declaration is the same as for numbers; just replace "Real" or "Integer" with the word "Boolean."

Once a variable is declared to be Boolean, you can use it to record the results of Boolean expressions. We wrote

AIsBigger : = (A > B);

Here the expression $(A > B)$ has a true-or-false value, depending upon the values of A and B. This value is stored in the Boolean variable specified.

You can use Boolean variables in conditional statements. Recall that the *If* statement has the form

If Condition
    Then Statement 1
    Else Statement 2

Here *Condition* is an expression that is true or false. Since the value is recorded in a Boolean variable, it makes sense to use the variable as the *Condition* in the *If* statement. In the example,

If AIsBigger
    Then Quotient : = A Div B
    Else Quotient : = B Div A;

we compute *A Div B* if *AIsBigger* is *True*, and we compute *B Div A* if *AIsBigger* is *False*.

You can use Boolean data in much the same way that you use numbers. The values of the data are *True* or *False*, and you can work with this data in any context where true or false makes sense.

You can use Boolean variables within other Boolean expressions. For example, you could write

Var A, B: Integer;
    AIsBigger, BIsBigger, Not Equal: Boolean;

AIsBigger : = (A > B);
BIsBigger : = (B > A);
Not Equal : = AIsBigger Or BIsBigger

This bit of code also illustrates a second way that Boolean variables can be useful. If you need to evaluate a complex Boolean expression, Boolean variables allow you to break the expression into pieces. You do not have to write out the whole expression at once.

Pascal contains Boolean constants *True* and *False*, so you can initialize Boolean variables. For example, you could write

Fun : = True;

.
.
.

If (Rain > 0) Or (Homework > 0)
    Then Fun : = False;

You can write out the value of a Boolean variable. You could say

Write (AIsBigger);

The result would be the word *True* or the word *False*. To format the *True* or *False* value, specify the number of spaces that should be used in the printing. If you write

AIsBigger : = True;
Write (AIsBigger :10);

you would see ten spaces allocated for the word *True*. As this word only requires four spaces, the first six spaces would be left blank. On the other hand, if you write

AIsBigger : = True;
Write (AIsBigger :1);

then only the initial "T" will be printed. The word is truncated after the number of characters specified. You should note that this formatting is different from writing numbers, where spaces are added automatically if more room is needed.

While you can write Boolean values, Pascal does not allow you to read them. You cannot write

Read(YesOrNo)

where *YesOrNo* is a Boolean variable.

You can compare Boolean values with the logical operators $<$, $<=$, $>$, $>=$, $=$, $<>$. If you write $E = F$, you mean both E and F are true or both are false, as you might expect. Pascal also uses the convention that *False* is less than *True*. Thus $E < F$ is true only if E is *False* and F is *True*.

Pascal contains standard Boolean functions, just as it contains various numerical functions such as *Sqrt* and *Round*. One of the Boolean functions is *Odd*. For the integer x, $Odd(x)$ is true if x is odd and false if x is even. Thus $Odd(x)$ gives the same value as the Boolean expression

$$((x \; Mod \; 2) \; = \; 1)$$

Finally, as with variables, we can define Boolean functions and Boolean parameters by using the word "Boolean" instead of "Integer" or "Real."

SECTION 6.6	EXAMPLE: SCORING A BOWLING GAME

In this section we consider a somewhat complex problem that will tie the topics of conditional statements and Boolean data type from this chapter with the topics of procedures and loops from previous chapters.

PROBLEM 6.6

Write a program to score a bowling game.

Review of Scoring in Bowling: A game of bowling is divided into ten frames. In each frame each bowler is allowed to throw two balls at ten pins in an attempt to knock them down. Roughly speaking, the score is the total number of pins knocked down over the course of ten frames. If a player knocks down five pins on the first ball and three pins on the second, the score for the frame is eight pins. If this pattern of knocking down eight pins is repeated in each of the ten frames, the score for the game would be 80.

This simple idea is complicated, however, by two basic "bonus" opportunities. If you knock down all ten pins on the first ball, you have rolled a "strike." In this case, you count those ten pins for that frame, plus what you roll on the next two balls. The pins knocked down in those next two balls are counted both in the frame when a strike was rolled and in their own frame(s).

If you take two balls to knock down all ten pins in a frame, you have rolled a "spare" (i.e., you do not get all ten on the first ball, but the second ball gets all the pins missed on the first ball). In this case, the score is ten plus the pins you roll on the next ball.

To clarify these scoring rules look at four short examples, illustrated in Figure 6–2. In Example A the bowler knocked down 8 pins (7 on the first ball, 1 on the second). Since all 10 pins were not knocked down, this is called an "open frame," and there are no bonus points. The score for the frame is 8.

In Example B the bowler got a strike (shown by the "X" in the small box) in Frame 1 and then 8 (7 on the first ball, 1 on the second) in Frame 2. In Frame 1 the bowler scores 10 plus the score on the next two balls (7 + 1), for a total of 18. The balls from Frame 2 are added without bonus for Frame 2, so the score after two frames is 26.

Example C is similar to Example B, except the bowler got a spare in Frame 1 instead of a strike. Only the first ball (7 pins) in Frame 2 is added as a bonus.

Example D shows the special case of strikes in successive frames. Here, as a bonus for the first strike, you count the next two balls (10 from Frame 2, 7 on first ball of Frame 3 for a total of 27). You get 18 more in Frame 2, as in Example B, for a total of 45 through two frames. Frame 3 gives 8 additional pins, as in Example A.

Finally, if you get a spare or a strike on the tenth frame, entitling you

FIGURE 6–2 • **Sample Bowling Games**

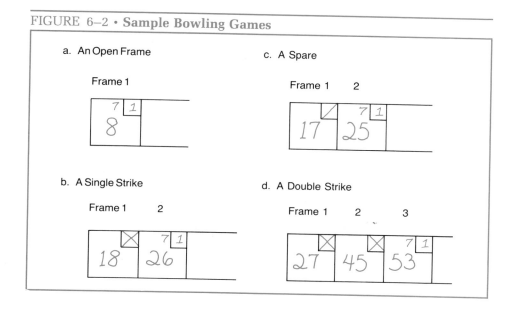

to count your pins on the next one or two rolls, you are allowed the appropriate extra rolls to knock down bonus pins.

Discussion of Problem 6.6

To attack this problem, we try to find a pattern that we you can apply frame by frame.

General Design for Problem 6.6

I. Initialize conditions before the game.
    A. Score starts at 0.
II. Repeat scoring for ten frames.
    A. Roll first ball.
    B. Score first ball.
    C. If first ball not a strike,
        1. Roll second ball.
        2. Score second ball.
III. Roll extra balls for tenth frame if necessary.
IV. Print final score.

This general outline gives the main steps to follow, but we still need to determine the details of the scoring. There are three special conditions: *Double strike*–strikes in the previous two frames; *Strike*–a strike in the previous frame (this includes the possibility of a double strike); *Spare*–a spare in the previous frame. These conditions call for the following outline for scoring a particular frame:

A. First ball in a frame:
1. Count the pins knocked down.
2. If on a strike or spare, count the pins from the previous frame.
3. If on a double strike count the pins from the last two frames.

B. Second ball in a frame (if needed):
1. Count the pins.
2. If on a strike, count the pins from the previous frame.

To include these details of scoring in the general outline, two additions are necessary. First, note that at the start of the game there are no spares, strikes, or double strikes. Next we consider how to go from one frame to the next, under the following rules:

A. Ten pins on first ball:
1. If previous frame is a strike, then we have a double strike. Otherwise, we do not have a double strike.
2. We now have a strike and not a spare.

B. Less than ten pins on the first ball:
1. We cannot have a strike or double strike.
2. We must roll the second ball.
3. If sum of pins on two balls is ten, then we have a spare. Otherwise, we do not have a spare.

With this discussion, we can fill in the outline for scoring a bowling game.

Detailed Algorithm for Problem 6.6

I. Initialize conditions before the game.
- **A.** Score starts at 0.
- **B.** We have not rolled spares, strikes, or double strikes.

II. Repeat scoring for ten frames:
- **A.** Roll first ball.
- **B.** Score first ball:
  1. Count the pins.
  2. If on a strike or spare, count the pins for the previous frame.
  3. If on a double strike, count the pins for the last two frames.
- **C.** If the first ball is not a strike:
  1. Roll second ball.
  2. Score second ball:
     - **a.** Count the pins.
     - **b.** If on a strike, count the pins for the previous frame.
- **D.** Prepare for next frame.
  1. Ten pins on first ball:
     - **a.** If previous frame is a strike, then we have a double strike. Otherwise, we do not have a double strike.
     - **b.** Regardless of past history, we now have a strike, not a spare.
  2. Less than ten pins on the first ball:
     - **a.** We consider our score on both balls.

If sum of pins on two balls is 10, then we have a spare.
Otherwise, we do not have a spare.
  b. We cannot have a strike or double strike.
III. Roll extra balls for tenth frame if necessary.
   A. If on a strike, roll ball.
      1. Count pins.
      2. If on double strike, count pins for ninth frame.
   B. If on a strike or spare, roll ball.
      1. Count pins.
IV. Print final score.

Writing a program from this extended outline, we find that the algorithm is quite detailed at several places, so we will use procedures for many of the more involved steps. Also, to keep track of the conditions *DoubleStrike, Strike,* and *Spare,* we use Boolean variables. When we need these values for scoring, we can use the variables as parameters in procedures.

```
Program BowlingScore (Input, Output);
{This program scores a bowling game}

Var First, Second: Integer; {pins knocked down on first
                             or second ball in a frame}
    Score: Integer;   {Our current score in the game}
    Frame: Integer;   {Control variable to determine current frame}
    Double, Strike, Spare: Boolean;   {Results of previous frames}

Procedure Initialize;
{Procedure to initial conditions before game}
    Begin
        Score := 0;
        Double := False;
        Strike := False;
        Spare := False
    End {Initialize} ;

Procedure ScoreFirstBall (Mark, Double: Boolean);
{Procedure tallies score after first ball.}
{Procedure checks if there is a double strike and
 if there was a mark (spare or strike) in the previous frame}
    Begin
        Score := Score + First;
        If Mark
            Then Score := Score + First;
        If Double
            Then Score := Score + First
    End {ScoreFirstBall} ;
```

```
Procedure ScoreSecondBall (Strike: Boolean);
{Procedure tallies score after second ball.}
{Procedure checks if ;there is a strike in the previous frame}
    Begin
        Score := Score + Second;
        If Strike
            Then Score := Score + Second
    End {ScoreSecondBall} ;

Procedure PrepareNextFrame;
{Procedure updates Double, Strike, and Spare for the next frame}
    Begin
        If (First = 10)

        Then Begin
            {We now have a double if we had a strike before}
            Double := Strike;
            {We have a strike, not a spare}
            Strike := True;
            Spare := False
            End {Strike}

        Else Begin {Consider second ball}
            {We cannot have a strike or a double}
            Strike := False;
            Double := False;
            {If sum of balls is 10 then we have a spare}
            Spare := (First+Second = 10)
            End {Second ball}

    End {PrepareNextFrame} ;

Procedure ExtraRoll (Strike, Double: Boolean);
{Procedure rolls the extra balls needed to finish 10th frame}
    Begin
        If Strike

        Then Begin
            {Roll Ball}
            Write ('Enter first extra ball: ');
            Readln (First);

            {Count Pins}
            Score := Score + First;

            If Double
                Then Score := Score + First
            End {First strike ball} ;

        {Roll last ball}
        Write ('Enter last extra ball: ');
        Read (Second);

        {Count pins}
        Score := Score + Second
    End {ExtraRoll} ;
```

```
Begin {Main}
    Initialize; {conditions before game}

    {repeat scoring for 10 frames}
    For Frame := 1 to 10
      Do Begin

        {Roll First Ball}
        Write ('Frame ', Frame:1,':  Enter first ball count: ');
        Readln (First);

        ScoreFirstBall (Strike Or Spare, Double);

        If (First <> 10)
          Then Begin
            {Roll Second Ball}
            Write ('Enter second ball: ');
            Readln (Second);

            ScoreSecondBall (Strike)
          End;

        PrepareNextFrame

      End; {Frame}

    {Roll extra balls for 10th frame if necessary}
    If Strike Or Spare
        Then ExtraRoll (Strike, Double);

    {Print final score}
    Writeln ('The Final score of the game is ', Score:1)
End {Main} .
```

Running this program with the scores from a good game, we get the following output:

```
Frame 1:  Enter first ball count: 10
Frame 2:  Enter first ball count: 7
Enter second ball: 3
Frame 3:  Enter first ball count: 8
Enter second ball: 1
Frame 4:  Enter first ball count: 10
Frame 5:  Enter first ball count: 10
Frame 6:  Enter first ball count: 10
Frame 7:  Enter first ball count: 6
Enter second ball: 4
Frame 8:  Enter first ball count: 7
Enter second ball: 2
Frame 9:  Enter first ball count: 9
Enter second ball: 1
Frame 10:  Enter first ball count: 10
Enter first extra ball: 6
Enter last extra ball: 3
The Final score of the game is 188
```

This program illustrates several points.

Problem Solving: In solving this problem, we started with an initial, general outline, which described the main steps required for a solution, then we added detail to some steps to concentrate on specific parts of the problem. We did not have to consider the problem as a whole. Thus we followed the top-down methodology discussed early in this book (Chapters 1 and 3).

Procedures: While the outline contained various steps involving considerable detail, the program retained the same concise form of the initial, general outline. Procedures allowed us to separate the details of these steps from the main tasks of the program.

Boolean Data Type: We used Boolean variables to record the results (strike, double strike, spare) of one frame for scoring in subsequent frames. The Boolean variables were used as parameters in the procedures for scoring and in conditions for *If* statements. When assigning values to Boolean variables, we used the constants *True* and *False*, and we also evaluated appropriate logical expressions.

SECTION 6.7 | STYLE

The last section illustrated several ways to use Boolean variables and conditional statements with procedures and loops to solve problems. We will now consider several elements of style that can help in writing clear, easy-to-read, correct programs.

Formatting and Structure

In previous sections we have seen that it is easier to understand how various parts of a program fit together if the form of the program reflects the structure of the outline. To apply this idea to *If* statements, indent *Then* and *Else* clauses further than the *If*, since the execution of the *Then* or *Else* depends upon the *If* condition. When you use a *Begin–End* to include several statements within a *Then* or *Else* clause, these statements are all dependent upon the *Then* or *Else* and should be indented further. For example, you might write

```
If Rain
    Then Begin
            Writeln ('Sky is cloudy');
            Writeln ('Tennis match is canceled')
         End
```

The *Then* is indented beyond the *If*, and the *Writeln* statements within the *Begin–End* are indented beyond the *Then*. (You must be careful however not to indent so far that you reach the right margin!)

Within a *Begin–End* block, use procedures or functions if necessary, so that details of a *Then* or *Else* clause do not overwhelm the basic structure for the conditional statement. Always use procedures or functions when details are complex.

Elegance and Simplicity in Programs

Whenever you try to solve problems, look for ways to simplify your work. Of course, simple, elegant answers do not always exist, but it is astonishing how often a complex solution indicates that you have overlooked something in your analysis. *When you find yourself bogged down in a mass of details you should spend some time trying to find an easier way.* Search for an elegant solution, particularly when your first effort is messy. Moreover, you should actively seek opportunities to simplify and clarify your work.

Simplification Opportunities

The above comments on simplicity and elegance apply to all phases of the problem solving process. Here, we identify four ways to simplify Boolean expressions and conditional statements, namely negation and double negation, DeMorgan's laws, turning conditions around, and omitting redundant or impossible conditions. In the following discussion, we will consider simplifications that are possible in each of these areas, and we will examine some elementary examples. The main points of this discussion are outlined in Tables 6–3 and 6–4.

Negation and Double Negation.   The *Not* operator has many useful applications, but you should always ask whether a *Not* expression can be rewritten in a more elementary way. For example, when you apply *Not* to a simple comparison, you often can rewrite the condition without the *Not* by changing the comparison. For example *Not (A > B)* means "*A* should not be greater than *B*." Another way to express this relationship is "*A* is less than or equal to *B*," i.e., *(A <= B)*. Similarly, *Not (A = B)* is equivalent to *(A <> B)*.

TABLE 6–3 · Simplification Opportunities for Boolean Expressions

1. *Not* applied to a simple comparison
   Simplification: Turn comparison around
2. Double Negation *Not(Not(E))*
   Simplification: Omit both *Not* operators to get just *E*
3. DeMorgan's laws:
   (Not E) Or (Not F) = Not (E And F)
   (Not E) And (Not F) = Not (E Or F)

TABLE 6–4 · Simplification Opportunities for Conditional Statements

1. Turn conditional statements around:

> If Condition
>> Then Statement 1
>> Else Statement 2

is equivalent to

> If Not Condition
>> Then Statement 2
>> Else Statement 1

2. Omitting redundant or impossible conditions:

> If E_1
>> Then Begin
>>> If E_2
>>>> Then —
>> End

Check whether the result of test E_2 can be inferred from test E_1.

Similarly, the double negation $Not(Not(E))$ is equivalent to E itself. (If E is true, $Not(E)$ is false, so $Not(Not(E))$ is true again.) Whenever you find a double negative, remove both Not operators.

DeMorgan's Laws. Two relationships can help when an expression involves Not in conjunction with And or Or. If E and F are two Boolean expressions, the following formulas are called **DeMorgan's Laws:**

> (Not E) Or (Not F) = Not(E And F)
> (Not E) And (Not F) = Not(E Or F)

Both of these formulas can be proven rigorously, but we omit the proofs here. (The interested reader should consult a book on logic.) Instead, consider two examples that illustrate how these laws can help simplify expressions, particularly when used in conjunction with the simplifications of negation and double negation.

Not((A > 1) And (B <= 3))
     = (Not(A > 1)) Or (Not(B <= 3))   DeMorgan's laws
     = (A <= 1) Or (B > 3))   Simplification of negatives
Not((A > 1) Or Not(B <= 3))
     = (Not(A > 1)) And (Not(Not(B <=3)))   DeMorgan's laws
     = (A <= 1) And (B <= 3)   Simplification of negative and double negative

In each case, we can replace the initial expression by an equivalent one which is shorter and clearer.

Turning Conditions Around. When you use Boolean expressions in *If* statements, you often can simplify your code significantly by turning the condition around. For example, consider

```
If ((x < -1) Or (x > -1)) And ((x < 2) Or (x > 2))
    Then Write ('Neither -1 or 2')
    Else Write ('-1 or 2')
```

If you analyze this condition, you will find that the statement is true for any value of x except -1 and 2. If you turn the statement around, you can replace a complex condition with

```
If (x = -1) Or (x = 2)
    Then Write ('-1 or 2')
    Else Write ('Neither -1 or 2')
```

Omitting Redundant or Impossible Conditions. When you put various conditions together, some conditions become redundant or impossible, and these can be omitted. For example, consider the code

```
If A > 1
    Then Begin
        If   A > 0
            Then Write ('A is big enough')
        End
```

Here, the test $A > 0$ is redundant. We can only execute the statement *If A > 0* when the test *A >1* is true. If *A* is greater than 1, however, *A* must be greater than 0. This compound statement is logically equivalent to the simpler

```
If A > 1
        Then Write ('A is big enough')
```

All of these simplifications are possible fairly frequently in practice, and each can help you write much cleaner, easier-to-read code. If you combine these simplifications with the guidelines for good formatting and structure, your programs will be relatively easy to test, correct, and modify.

SECTION 6.8   TESTING

Typically, you will use conditional statements when you have divided a solution into various cases. In testing programs that handle these cases, you can be guided by two basic ideas. First, check that the results for each case are correct. Then be sure the program shifts from one case to the next at the appropriate time. These goals are met by two guidelines for choosing test data, **every-path testing** and **boundary value testing**.

Every-Path Testing

Test all possible ways that a program might be executed. For example, to test

> If A > 0
> > Then Statement 1
> > Else Statement 2

pick data where $A > 0$ and where $A <= 0$. With these two test cases, you can check that both Statement 1 and Statement 2 are correct.

The same idea applies when you put several conditions together. To test

> If A > 0
> > Then If B > 0
> > > Then Statement 1
> > > Else Statement 2
> > Else Statement 3

choose data where (1) $A > 0$ and $B > 0$, (2) $A > 0$ and $B <= 0$, and (3) $A < 0$. Only with these three sets of test data can you check all three statements in the program.

Similarily, you need to check the various possibilities when one *If* statement follows another. For example, consider

> If A > 0
> > Then Statement 1
> > Else Statement 2 ;
> If B > 0
> > Then Statement 3
> > Else Statement 4

Here you must check four cases: (1) $A > 0$, $B > 0$; (2) $A > 0$, $B <= 0$; (3) $A <= 0$, $B > 0$; (4) $A <= 0$, $B <= 0$. All these data sets are needed to test that both Statement 3 and Statement 4 work correctly after either Statement 1 or Statement 2.

Putting these ideas together for the Bowling Score program from Section 6.6, we must check games that contain open frames, as well as spares, strikes, double strikes, and sequences of these possibilities. For example, we might check what happens when a spare or open frame follows a strike or a double strike.

Boundary Value Testing

While every-path testing demonstrates that your work is correct for each case, you must also check that each case is performed at the correct time. To test this, select data at the boundary of each case. For example, in the telephone call program in Section 6.1, rates change at 8 AM, 5 PM, and 11 PM. To test this program, check the times 7:59 and 8:00, 17:00 and 17:01, 23:00 and 23:01 to see that the correct rates are used when the time periods change.

Similarly, to test the Bowling Score program, check the results when you knock down nine pins instead of ten. You must be sure that a frame that is "close" to a spare or a strike is not scored as a spare or strike.

Testing and Modularity

When programs are long and complex, there may be very large numbers of possible paths and boundary values. It may not be practical to test all these cases. In such situations, testing will probably be incomplete, but you can still find most bugs if you divide large programs into several procedures and then test the individual procedures.

Procedures can be short enough to test the appropriate paths and boundary values for these pieces. Then, when you know the pieces are correct, select some representative sets of data to see if the pieces fit together in an appropriate way. This selective testing may fail to find some subtle interactions among procedures, but you should find many of the bugs that might exist.

In practice, you are likely to find occasional errors in large programs, even if these programs have been used for many years. You may try a new path in the program, or the data may land on a new boundary between cases. These cases always allow the chance for a new error to be discovered. After a point, such bugs are relatively rare when you use a program normally, but such errors can arise when complete testing is impractical. Testing of individual pieces can help reduce the number of remaining bugs, but more persistent bugs may remain.

SUMMARY

1. **Conditional Statements** allow you to break your work into pieces to handle separately. These statements come in two forms:

    If Condition   *If* Condition
        Then Statement   *Then* Statement 1
                        Else Statement 2

    Here the Condition is a **Boolean expression** that has a *True* or *False* value, and each Statement is a single Pascal statement or a *Begin–End* block.

2. You can form Boolean expressions by comparing various items with the Boolean operators $<$, $<=$, $>$, $>=$, $=$, and $<>$, and you can put these comparisons together using the operators *And, Not,* and *Or.*

When you form such expressions, **precedence rules** determine the order in which the operators will be applied. Use parentheses if you wish to use operators in another order.

3. **Boolean variables and functions** may be declared and used when you need to consider the values *True* and *False*. These variables and functions may be used in logical expressions and in the conditions of *If* statements. You may Write (but not Read) the values of such variables.

4. Boolean variables can be helpful when you compute a *True* or *False* value at one place in a program and use it later on, and to divide a complex Boolean expression into simple pieces.

5. Boolean functions help separate the technical details of a condition from the idea of the test.

6. An important application of conditional statements is the **Monte Carlo Method**, which allows you to simulate activities to determine likely results.

7. In writing Boolean expressions, you may be able to simplify your work by eliminating **negation** and **double negation**, by applying **DeMorgan's laws**, by **turning conditions around**, and by **omitting redundant or impossible conditions.**

8. Apply the principles of **every-path testing** and **boundary value testing** to help determine if a program works correctly.

EXERCISES

6.1   *A, B, C,* and *D* are integer variables; *E, F,* and *G* are Boolean variables. The variables have been given the following values:

$$
\begin{array}{ll}
A := 1 & E := True \\
B := 2 & F := False \\
C := 3 & G := True \\
D := 6 &
\end{array}
$$

Determine which of the following expressions make sense, and evaluate those that have logical values.

a. Not $A >= B$
b. $A*B < C - D$
c. $A = B$ Or E
d. $F = (Not\ E\ And\ G)$
e. $(A < B)$ And $(C > D)$
f. Not $(E >= F)$
g. $(A >= B)$ Or $(C <= D)$
h. Not $(F <> E)$ And $(B*C = D)$
i. E And $(A = B)$ Or F
j. Not E And Not F Or Not F

6.2 Simplify the following Boolean expressions. *(A, B, C, D are integer variables; E, F, G are Boolean variables.)*
  a. *Not (A >= C)*
  b. *Not (Not E And Not F)*
  c. *(A <= C) And (A >= C)*
  d. *Not ((A < B) Or (C < B))*
  e. *Not ((A < B) And Not (C < B))*
  f. *Not E and Not G Or E*

6.3 Simplify the following pieces of code. *A, B, C* are integer variables, and *S, T, U* are procedures.
  a. If A >= 3
       Then If A >= 4
               Then S

  b. If A < C
       Then If (A = B) And (B > C)
               Then S
               Else T

  c. If A < 2 And C > 1
       Then If B < 2 and A > 1
               Then S
               Else T

  d. If A < 2
       Then Begin
             If B < 3
                   Then S
                   Else T
           End
       Else Begin
             If B >= 3
                   Then T
                   Else S
           End

KEY TERMS, PHRASES, AND CONCEPTS		ELEMENTS OF PASCAL SYNTAX	
Boolean Data Type	*If–Then–Else*	*Boolean*	Logical Operators:
Expressions	DeMorgan's Laws	*Else*	<, <=, >, >=, =, <>
Functions	Double Negation	*False*	*And, Not, Or*
Parameters	Elegance and Simplicity	*If*	*Then*
Variables	Every-Path Testing		*True*
Boundary Value	Logical Operators and		
Testing	Precedence		
Conditional	Monte Carlo Method		
Statements	Negation		
If–Then			

6.4 *Quadratic Formula.* Find all real solutions of the quadratic equation

$$ax^2 + bx + c = 0.$$

Use the discriminant, $b^2 - 4ac$, to compute and print the number of real solutions as well as the values for the existing real solutions. Your work should allow for the case where $a = 0$.

6.5 *Windchill Danger.* In the problems for Chapter 5, we stated that the windchill Temperature T may be approximated from the Fahrenheit temperature F and the wind speed W by the formula

$$T = 1.05 + 0.93F - 3.65W + 3.62\sqrt{W} + 0.103F\sqrt{W} + 0.0439W^2$$

Windchill temperatures are rated in the following categories (for covered skin):

Little danger of freezing	above 0°F
Moderate danger of freezing	0°F to −30°F
Extreme danger of freezing	Below −30°F

Write a program that reads the current Fahrenheit temperature and wind speed (in MPH) and prints the appropriate windchill danger category.

6.6 Write a program that reads three numbers and prints out the smallest of the numbers.

6.7 Write a program that reads an integer N followed by N numbers, and then computes and prints the largest of these numbers. (You should not assume that the numbers will be entered in order.)

6.8 *Wind Strength.* Table 6–5 gives the terms used by the U.S. Weather Service to describe winds of various strengths. Write a program that reads the speed of the wind (in MPH) and then prints the corresponding descriptive term.

TABLE 6–5 · Wind Speed Terms Used by the U.S. Weather Service

Velocity (MPH)	Term
Less than 1	Calm
1–7	Light
8–12	Gentle
13–18	Moderate
19–24	Fresh
25–38	Strong
39–54	Gale
55–75	Whole gale
Above 75	Hurricane

6.9   *Integer Factoring*

a. Write a program that will compute all factors of a given positive integer.

NOTE: *N* is divisible by *I* if the remainder after dividing *N* by *I* is 0.

b. An integer is *prime* if its only factors are 1 and itself. Modify the program in part (a) so that after the factors are printed the program states whether or not the given integer is prime.

6.10 *Paying a Baby Sitter.* A baby sitter charges $1.50 per hour until 9:00 PM (while the kids are still up) and $1.00 per hour thereafter (when the kids are in bed.)

Write a program that reads the sitter's starting time in hours and minutes and the ending time in hours and minutes and then computes the sitter's fee. Assume all times are between 6:00 PM and 6:00 AM. *(Optimal Simplification:* Assume all times are between 6:00 PM and 12:00 midnight.)

[This problem was initially suggested by John Vogel.]

6.11 *Dice Simulation.* Write a program that simulates the rolling of two dice 1000 times and determines the number of times that a 7 or an 11 is rolled.

6.12 *Coin-Tossing Simulation.*

a. We wish to toss a fair coin 1000 times and count the number of heads. Write a procedure that simulates these tosses and prints out the number of heads.

b. Investigate the range we might expect in the number of heads. Include the procedure for part (a) in a program that repeats part (a) 20 times, printing out the number of heads each time.

NOTE: In your simulation, just print out the number of heads obtained on the 1000 tosses; do not print the result of each toss!

6.13 *Limitations of Coin-Tossing Simulations.* If *MaxInt* is the maximum integer allowed on your computer, write a procedure *TOSS* that simulates the tossing of a coin that number of times and prints the number of heads obtained.

a. Write a main program that initializes the random number generator and then applies procedure *TOSS* 20 times.

b. Rerun your program, modifying procedure *TOSS* so the number of times is *MaxInt* + 1.

c. What do you observe about your simulations? Why?

6.14 *Coin-Toss Simulation—String of Heads.* Simulate the tossing of a coin 1000 times and determine the length of the longest sequence of consecutive heads.

6.15 *Tax Computation.* Table 6–6 presents the 1984 Tax Rate Schedule for single taxpayers of the federal income tax. The following example shows how this table is read:

If my taxable income is $12,000, I find the line where $12,000 falls in the table, over $10,800 but not over $12,900. From the next

---

TABLE 6–6 · 1984 Tax Rate Schedule for Single Taxpayers

Taxable Income is

Over	But not over	Tax is	Of the Amount Over
$0	$2,300	—$0—	
2,300	3,400	11%	$ 2,300
3,400	4,400	121 + 12%	3,400
4,400	6,500	241 + 14%	4,400
6,500	8,500	535 + 15%	6,500
8,500	10,800	835 + 16%	8,500
10,800	12,900	1,203 + 18%	10,800
12,900	15,000	1,581 + 20%	12,900
15,000	18,200	2,001 + 23%	15,000
18,200	23,500	2,737 + 26%	18,200
23,500	28,800	4,115 + 30%	23,500
28,800	34,100	5,705 + 34%	28,800
34,100	41,500	7,507 + 38%	34,100
41,500	55,300	10,319 + 42%	41,500
55,300	81,800	16,115 + 48%	55,300
81,800	———	28,835 + 50%	81,800

Source: 1984 Form 1040 Federal Income Tax Forms and Instructions, page 33. (U.S. Government Printing Office 1984 – 423–003 23–188–5979)

---

two columns, my tax is $1203 plus 18% of the amount over $10,800,

$$\$1203 + 0.18(\$12000 - \$10800), \text{ or } \$1419.$$

Write a program that reads taxable income and computes the taxpayer's tax.

6.16 *Unusual Canceling.* The fraction $^{64}/_{16}$ has the unusual property that its reduced value of 4 may be obtained by "canceling" the 6 in the numerator with that in the denominator. Write a program to find the other fractions whose numerators and denominators are two-digit numbers and whose values remain unchanged after "canceling."

NOTE: Suppose ab is the two-digit number n (e.g., if $n = 64$, then $a = 6$, $b = 4$.) Then we have

$$n = 10\,a + b$$
$$a = n \text{ Div } 10$$
$$b = n \text{ Mod } 10.$$

6.17 *Details in Then or Else Clauses.* Section 6.7 suggests using procedures and functions when details of *Then* and *Else* clauses are complex.

This principle becomes particularly clear when we see a program with all details included in *Then* and *Else* clauses.

Rewrite the Bowling Score program from Section 6.6 without using any procedures or functions. Compare your program with the program in Section 6.6 for readability.

CHAPTER 7

CONDITIONAL
LOOPS

In Chapter 5 we saw one way to tell the computer to repeat some operations a specific number of times. Since then, we have used these loops in several applications to tackle problems that would otherwise be quite tedious. In each application we specified the number of iterations for the loop when we started.

In many applications, however, we do not know the appropriate number of repetitions until we solve the problem. In this chapter we will consider two new types of loops, where the number of iterations is not fixed from the start, and we will apply these new loop structures to several applications. In addition, we will look more carefully at program correctness, expanding the concept of loop invariants, mentioned briefly in Section 5.8.

SECTION 7.1:   **EXAMPLE: FAMILY SIZE**

We will begin with a brief review of the basic parts of any loop and consider an example that illustrates a *Repeat–Until* loop, which is one of the new repetitive statements.

Basic Loop Components

The loops used in previous chapters have the following fundamental components:

1. *Initialization* to set up the work before the loop begins.
2. *Repetition* of a certain number of steps within the loop.
3. *Exit condition* to indicate when the loop is to stop.

For example, in the *For–Do* loop

```
For I := 1 to 10
    Do Writeln (I);
```

the initialization sets I equal to 1, the *Writeln* is in the repetition component, and the limit of 10 implies an exit condition.

In the following problem you will need a somewhat different type of exit condition.

PROBLEM 7.1

A couple decides that they want to raise at least one boy and one girl. They decide to keep having children until they have one child of each gender, and then stop having children. Assume that having a boy or a girl is equally likely, and assume that the gender of one child has no influence on the gender of the next. Investigate how many children such a couple could expect to have.

Discussion of Problem 7.1

To solve this problem, you might use a simulation where a random number generator determines the gender of a child. You can keep track of the number of girls and boys the couple has, and continue the simulation until there is at least one child of each gender.

We can identify many of the same parts of a loop that we have just reviewed. Before the loop starts, initialization must set the number of boys and the number of girls to 0. Within the loop we need a statement that will add one boy or one girl, according to the random value. (You might decide upon a boy if the random number is less than 0.5 and a girl otherwise.) We do not know, however, how many times to repeat the loop. The exit condition here must involve an expression such as $((Boy > 0) \text{ And } (Girl > 0))$.

Outline for Problem 7.1

I. Initialization: Set number of boys and number of girls to 0.
II. Continue until there is at least one boy and one girl.
   A. Determine gender of next child.
   B. If child is a boy, increase number of boys by 1.
   C. If child is a girl, increase number of girls by 1.
III. Print number of boys, number of girls, and total number of children.

In the program we have used a repetitive statement that allows writing out this more involved exit condition. We have also implemented the outline as a procedure *FamilySize* and repeated this procedure 20 times to help answer the initial problem. As in the earlier programs involving random numbers, we omit the details of the random number generator in the program listing.

```
Program FamilySimulation (Output);
{This program prints a table of family sizes for couples who
 wish to continue having children until they have at least one
 boy and at least one girl.}

Const NumberOfCouples = 20;
        {Constants for the random number generator must be included here}

Var Couple: Integer;
    {Variables for the random number generator must be included here}

Procedure InitializeRandomFunction;
    {Procedure must be included here}

Function Random: Real;
    {Function must be included here}

Procedure FamilySize (Couple: Integer);
{This procedure performs the simulation for one Couple}
    Var Boy, Girl: Integer;
    Begin
        {Initialization}
        Boy := 0;
        Girl := 0;

        {Repetitive Statement}
        Repeat
            If Random < 0.5
                Then Boy := Boy + 1
                Else Girl := Girl + 1
        Until ((Boy > 0) And (Girl > 0));

        {Conclusion:  Print results}
        Writeln (Couple:4, Boy:7, Girl:7, Boy+Girl : 7)

    End {Family Size} ;

Begin {Main}
    {Initialize Random Function}
    InitializeRandomFunction;

    {Print Headings}
    Writeln ('Couple  Boys   Girls   Total');

    {Repeat simulation for several couples}
    For Couple := 1 To NumberOfCouples
        Do FamilySize (Couple)
End {Main} .
```

In this program we placed the steps to be repeated for a couple within a *Repeat–Until* loop. These steps are then repeated until the specified exit condition is met. When we run this program with a particular random number generator, we get the following output:

Couple	Boys	Girls	Total
1	2	1	3
2	1	2	3
3	2	1	3
4	4	1	5
5	1	1	2
6	2	1	3
7	1	1	2
8	1	1	2
9	3	1	4
10	1	2	3
11	2	1	3
12	2	1	3
13	1	3	4
14	1	1	2
15	1	1	2
16	1	6	7
17	2	1	3
18	1	3	4
19	1	4	5
20	4	1	5

This output suggests that a couple wishing to have at least one child of each gender can expect to have a total of two to four children, although there is some possibility that the family could be somewhat larger. (Of course, these conclusions depend upon our initial assumptions about the gender of successive children, and we have not examined those assumptions.)

This program illustrates several important points. In Pascal you can repeat a sequence of steps in several different ways. Here we used *Repeat–Until* instead of the *For–Do* construction we used earlier. When you use the *Repeat–Until* construction, place the statements you want repeated in the loop between the *Repeat* and the *Until*.

Repeat–Until has no control variable, so no variables are updated automatically; you must write out all operations explicitly. You also must specify when you want the loop to stop. Here we said the loop was to stop when $((Boy > 0) \ And \ (Girl > 0))$.

In contrast to the *Repeat–Until* loop for the steps involved for a particular couple, we used a *For–Do* loop to count the number of couples, since we knew exactly how many couples we wanted to consider.

The *Repeat–Until* construction allows considerable flexibility in writing loops; you do not need to know the results when you start.

ELEMENTS OF CONDITIONAL LOOPS

In this section we will discuss the syntax and semantics of two forms of repetitive statements, the *Repeat–Until* construction from the previous section and the *While–Do* construction. Each form allows you to specify exit conditions explicitly, although they work in slightly different ways. The two forms give you considerable flexibility in specifying loops.

Syntax and Semantics of Repeat–Until Statements

As the program in Section 7.1 illustrates, the *Repeat–Until* statement has the following syntax:

> Repeat
> > Statements
> Until   Condition

Here, "Statements" may include any number of Pascal statements (separated by semicolons), and "Condition" is a Boolean condition.

This syntax is interpreted as follows: The statements are executed once, and the condition is then evaluated. If the condition is true, the loop stops. If the condition is false, the computer goes back to Step 1 and repeats the process. With this form, we see

- Initialization normally precedes the *Repeat*.
- The specified statements form the body of the repetition.
- The condition gives the exit condition.

Figure 7–1 shows these elements for the Family–Size Simulation program of Section 7.1. For brevity, we have omitted the parts of the program not strictly related to the loop.

Before looking at the next type of repetitive statement. we need to note

FIGURE 7–1 • Loop Elements for the Family–Size Program of Section 7.1

```
Procedure FamilySize (Couple: Integer);
    Begin
        Boy := 0;  ⎫
        Girl := 0; ⎭              Initialization

        Repeat
            If Random < 0.5   ⎫
                Then Boy := Boy + 1   ⎬  Repetition
                Else Girl := Girl + 1 ⎭
        Until ((Boy > 0) And (Girl > 0)); ⎭  Exit Condition
    End { Family Size} ;
```

two other important points about the *Repeat–Until* construction. First, the statements are executed once before the condition is evaluated. Second, since the exit condition is tested at the very end of the loop, you do not have to initialize all variables needed in the condition before the loop starts. You may do some computations in the loop and use the results of these computations in the exit condition. In the *Repeat–Until* statement you compute new values before you need to test them in the condition. Thus, the statements are always repeated once, and they can initialize some values needed in the condition.

Syntax and Semantics of While–Do Statements

Next we turn to another form of repetitive statement, the *While–Do* construction. This statement has many of the characteristics of the *Repeat–Until* statement, but there are also some important differences. This statement has the following syntax:

> While Condition
> > Do Statement

Here the "Condition" is a Boolean statement and the "Statement" is a single Pascal statement or a *Begin–End* block.

The semantics of this statement are similar to those of *Repeat–Until*, but the order of events is different. In particular, in a *While–Do* statement, the condition is evaluated. If the condition is true, the loop continues; if the condition is false, the loop stops. As long as the loop continues, the statement is executed. Here,

- Initialization must be done before the *While* statement.
- The condition gives the exit condition.
- The statement forms the body for the repetition.

As a specific example, we translate the loop from Section 7.1 into this alternate form (see Figure 7–2).

The main ideas of the loop are the same in both constructions, but there are a few differences. In *While–Do*, the exit condition is evaluated immediately after initialization. (All variables used in the condition must be initialized before the loop.) The condition for the *While* is reversed from that for the *Repeat*. The *While* continues as long as the condition is true; the *Repeat* keeps going as long as the condition is false. If the repetitive part of the statement is more than one line, you must place the steps to be repeated in a *Begin–End* block. In Figure 7–2 the repetitive part contains only one line, so the *Begin* and *End* were not technically necessary. However, we added the reserved words anyway, for clarity.

Because of the position of the condition, all initialization must be done before a *While* loop. You cannot rely on values being computed the first time through the loop. This position of the condition also implies that the body of a *While* loop may not be executed at all. If the condition is false when you start, the body of the loop will be omitted.

FIGURE 7–2 • **Loop Elements for the Family–Size Program of Section 7.1 Using the While–Do Construction**

```
Procedure FamilySize (Couple: Integer);
    Begin
        Boy : = 0;  ⎱            Initialization
        Girl : = 0; ⎰
        While ((Boy = 0) Or (Girl = 0)) ⎱  Exit Condition
            Do Begin
                If Random < 0.5          ⎱
                    Then Boy : = Boy + 1  ⎬  Repetition
                    Else Girl : = Girl + 1 ⎰
            End;
    End {Family Size};
```

SECTION 7.3   EXAMPLE: CREDIT-BALANCE PAYMENTS

In Section 7.1 we saw an example that used the *Repeat–Until* construction. Before we compare the details of the various types of loops, consider a problem that illustrates the use of the *While–Do* construction.

PROBLEM 7.3   Credit-Balance Payments

You have charged the cost of an item on your credit card, planning to make fixed monthly payments to pay for the purchase. Compute the monthly balance of the credit account for the life of the loan. Compute the final payment and the total interest paid.

Discussion of Problem 7.3

Each month of the loan, the account will see activity of two types: Interest will be charged at the start of each month, and a payment will be made sometime during the month.

Monthly payments will continue until the loan is paid off. We will have to pay the full payment until the last month, when we will pay a (perhaps smaller) amount that just covers the final balance plus the appropriate interest.

In the outline, keep track of the following items:

Cost = cost of item purchased

Rate = monthly interest rate

Payment = normal monthly payment

Balance = balance in the account at the start of a month, before interest has been added

Interest = interest for a given month

TInterest = total interest accumulated to the current time

Month = Number of months the loan has run so far

Outline for Problem 7.3

I. Determine *Cost, Rate, Payment.*

II. Print table headings.

III. Set up account for first month:
Month := 1
Balance := *Cost*
Interest := *Balance*Rate*
TInterest := *Interest*

IV. Continue normal monthly payments as long as *Payment* does not exceed *Balance* plus *Interest:*

    A. Add *Interest* and deduct *Payment* activity for the month:
    Balance := *Balance* + *Interest* − *Payment.*

    B. Print results.

    C. Set up for the next month:

        1. Compute *Interest* to start the next month:
        Interest := *Balance*Rate.*

        2. Update total interest for the next month:
        TInterest := *TInterest* + *Interest.*

        3. Update *Month:*
        Month := *Month* + 1.

V. Make final payment:
Payment := *Balance* + *Interest*

The program from this outline uses a *While–Do* loop, for two reasons. First, the loop needs to continue as long as a certain condition is true. Philosophically, this is how the *While* construction works.

Second, note that it is possible for the normal monthly payment to exceed the initial cost. (For example, the item might cost $5.76 and the normal payment might be $10.00.) In this case we would not pay the normal payment at all; we would skip Step IV completely. Skipping the loop is possible with the *While* construction, but not with *Repeat.*

```
Program CreditBalancePayments (Input, Output);
{This program follows the balance of a charge account
 month by month as monthly payments are made.}

Var Cost: Real;          {Cost of item purchased}
    Rate: Real;          {Monthly interest rate}
```

```pascal
    Payment: Real;          {Normal monthly payment}
    Balance: Real;          {Account balance at start of month,
                             before interest has been added}
    Interest: Real;         {Interest for month}
    TInterest: Real;        {Total accumulated interest}
    Month: Integer;         {Month number}

Procedure SetUpCharge (Var Cost, Rate, Payment: Real);
{This procedure determines Cost, Rate, Payment}
    Begin
        Write ('Enter cost of item purchased: ');
        Readln (Cost);
        Write ('Enter monthly interest rate: ');
        Readln (Rate);
        Write ('Enter normal monthly payment: ');
        Readln (Payment);
    End {SetUpCharges} ;

Procedure PrintHeadings;
{This procedure prints the headings for the payment table}
    Begin
        Writeln;
        Writeln ('        Month''s   Total');
        Writeln ('Month Interest  Interest     Balance');
        Writeln (0:3, Cost:32:2);
    End {PrintHeadings} ;

Procedure SetUpFirstMonth (Cost: Real; Var Month: Integer;
                           Var Balance, Interest, TInterest: Real);
{This procedure sets up the account for the first month}
    Begin
        Month := 1;
        Balance := Cost;
        Interest := Balance * Rate;
        TInterest := Interest;
    End {FirstMonth} ;

Procedure ProcessNormalMonth (Cost, Payment: Real; Var Month: Integer;
                              Var Balance, Interest, TInterest: Real);
{This procedure continues normal monthly payments while appropriate}
    Begin
        While (Payment <= Balance + Interest)
          Do Begin
            Balance := Balance + Interest - Payment;
            Writeln (Month:3, Interest:10:2, TInterest:10:2, Balance:12:2);
            Interest := Balance * Rate;
            TInterest := TInterest + Interest;
            Month := Month + 1
          End;
    End {ProcessNormalMonth} ;

Procedure FinalPayment (Balance, Interest, TInterest: Real; Var Payment: Real);
{This procedure makes the final payment}
    Begin
        Payment := Balance + Interest;
        Writeln;
        Writeln ('Interest for final payment is ', Interest:1:2);
        Writeln ('The final payment is ', Payment:1:2);
        Writeln ('The total interest charged was ', TInterest:1:2)
    End {FinalPayment} ;
```

```
Begin {Main}
    Writeln ('This program follows the balance of a charge account.');

    SetUpCharge (Cost, Rate, Payment);
    PrintHeadings;
    SetUpFirstMonth (Cost, Month, Balance, Interest, TInterest);
    ProcessNormalMonth(Cost, Payment, Month, Balance, Interest, TInterest);
    FinalPayment (Balance, Interest, TInterest, Payment)

End {Main} .
```

When we run this program for a charge of $1000 at a monthly interest rate of 1 percent and a normal monthly payment of $100, we get the following output:

```
This program follows the balance of a charge account.
Enter cost of item purchased: 1000.00
Enter monthly interest rate: 0.01
Enter normal monthly payment: 100.00

        Month's   Total
Month  Interest  Interest   Balance
  0                         1000.00
  1     10.00     10.00      910.00
  2      9.10     19.10      819.10
  3      8.19     27.29      727.29
  4      7.27     34.56      634.56
  5      6.35     40.91      540.91
  6      5.41     46.32      446.32
  7      4.46     50.78      350.78
  8      3.51     54.29      254.29
  9      2.54     56.83      156.83
 10      1.57     58.40       58.40

Interest for final payment is 0.58
The final payment is 58.98
The total interest charged was 58.98
```

When the program is run with a charge of $50 at a monthly interest rate of 1 percent and a normal monthly payment of $100, we get this output:

```
This program follows the balance of a charge account.
Enter cost of item purchased: 50.00
Enter monthly interest rate: 0.01
Enter normal monthly payment: 100.00

        Month's   Total
Month  Interest  Interest   Balance
  0                           50.00

Interest for final payment is 0.50
The final payment is 50.50
The total interest charged was 0.50
```

In this case, the loop was never executed, as the normal monthly payment exceeds the amount due, $50.50.

This example illustrates how to use the *While–Do* loop effectively in programming. The example also demonstrates the advantage of testing the condition at the beginning of a loop.

SECTION 7.4 **CHOOSING AMONG *FOR, REPEAT,* AND *WHILE***

We have seen the three major constructions available for looping in Pascal, namely:

For–Do

Repeat–Until

While–Do

In this section we will discuss how to choose the right construction for a particular situation. Figure 7–3 summarizes the discussion.

Definite Repetition

The problems in Chapters 5 and 6 required repetition of work a specified number of times. We knew how many iterations we would need in a loop before we started. In the pole vaulting problem, for example, we knew we wanted to follow the vaulter over 20 time intervals. In such situations the *For–Do* loop applies, since the control variable counts the number of iterations exactly.

FIGURE 7–3 · **Choosing Among *For, Repeat,* and *While***

```
Definite repetition (number of iterations known)
      For–Do
            Control variable counts iterations.

Conditional repetition (number of iterations not known)
      While–Do
            Test at top of loop.
                  Loop may never be performed.
            Continue looping while condition true.
            Stop looping when condition false.
      Repeat–Until
            Test at bottom of loop.
                  Loop is always performed at least once.
            Continue looping while condition false.
            Stop looping when condition true.
```

Conditional Repetition

This chapter has studied problems where the number of iterations is not known ahead of time. Here we must evaluate a condition each time and decide whether to continue on the basis of that condition. For conditional repetition we have two possible constructions, *Repeat–Until* and *While– Do.* These statements have the following major features:

While–Do tests a condition at the beginning of the loop; the loop is executed only if the condition is true. If the condition is false initially, then the loop is never executed at all. Looping continues as long as the condition is true and stops when the condition is false.

Repeat–Until tests a condition at the bottom of the loop; the loop continues only if the condition is false. The loop is executed once before the condition is ever checked. Looping continues as long as the condition is false and stops when the condition is true.

The major difference between these two constructions is in when the condition is evaluated. The *While* loop may never be executed; the *Repeat* loop is always performed at least once. The examples in Sections 7.1 and 7.3 show how to exploit this difference effectively in certain problems.

In the Credit-Balance Payment problem, we needed to allow the possibility that the normal payment would be too much. The *While* loop tested this condition *before* making a normal payment. A *Repeat* loop would have required at least one normal payment, because we would check the balance only *after* making a normal payment.

In contrast, in the Family Size simulation, a couple needed some children before we could stop the simulation. Thus, we used the *Repeat* statement, to be sure the couple had at least one child. Similarly, to compute an average, you must process at least one number before work can stop, and you would use a *Repeat* statement to guarantee this initial processing. From this discussion we derive the following major guideline for choosing between *While* and *Repeat.*

Major Guideline for Conditional Repetition

- Choose *While* when you need a test at the top of the loop.
- Choose *Repeat* when you want to delay the test to the bottom of the loop.

In any problem, first determine whether the steps in the loop must be carried out at least once, or if there are cases when you definitely want to skip those steps. By applying the answers to these questions to the above guideline, you often can choose the correct construction.

In cases where the answers to the questions are less clear, however, the solution may not depend on whether the loop is executed once, and you may have trouble applying this guideline. In these cases, write out the loop using each construction and compare the resulting code.

The following additional guidelines may help you choose:

When problems can be solved using either the *While* or the *Repeat* construction, one solution may be much cleaner and more elegant than the other. For example, in one looping form you find special cases arise that do not occur in the other form. *When you can find solutions using both While and Repeat, choose the cleaner, more elegant program.*

When you write an outline, ask how you are thinking of the loop.

- Do you want to continue until something happens (e.g., until the couple has at least one child of each gender), or
- Do you want to continue while something holds true (e.g., while you need to make your full monthly payment)?

Philosophically, the *Repeat* applies when you answer yes to the first question, and the *While* applies when you answer yes to the second. *Thus your thinking about the nature of the loop can suggest which construction to use.*

In practice, these guidelines almost always suggest how to program a loop. As you write programs, the choice of *For* loops may be relatively clear, but you may have to work harder to choose between *While* and *Repeat*. The above guidelines can help while you get the practice you need to make this choice more comfortably.

SECTION 7.5   PROGRAM STYLE AND CORRECTNESS

We have seen how to write various types of loops, and we have some guidelines for choosing among Pascal's three loop constructions. Now we turn our attention to program correctness.

Chapter 5 discussed several important and relevant topics, including indenting and formatting, local declaration of variables, choosing test cases, tracing program execution, and common errors. These comments apply generally to all types of loops. In this section we will expand briefly on the topic of indenting and formatting for the *Repeat* and *While* constructions. Good program structure remains a vital part of program correctness, but we will not repeat the other topics here.

Then we expand the concept of loop invariants, mentioned briefly in Chapter 5. This latter topic is becoming recognized as a particularly important one in the area of program correctness, so we will consider loop invariants at some length.

Indenting and Formatting

Throughout our discussion of programming, we have stressed that the form of a program should reflect its structure. Our basic principle has been to indent when one piece of code depends upon another. Applying this principle to the new loop constructions of this chapter, we can identify the words *Repeat–Until* and *While–Do* as major headings, and we can consider the details of a loop as being dependent upon these headings. These considerations suggest the following basic forms:

Repeat
    Statement 1;
    Statement 2;
    .
    .
    .
    Statement n
Until Condition ;

While Condition
    Do Statement;

In each case the main repetitive statement stands out, and the details of the loop are shown as being dependent. As in the past, if you replace the statement of the *While* loop with a *Begin–End* block, indent the individual parts of the block further.

Loop Invariants

We now turn to a second topic that can be helpful in developing correct programs—loop invariants. In Chapter 5 we said that a **loop invariant** is a condition that is expected to be true at the beginning or at the end of a loop. Each time the loop is repeated, that same condition must be valid.

More generally, we can speak of an **assertion** in a program. An assertion is a condition that must be true at a given point in a program. Comparing the definitions of assertions and loop invariants, we see that an assertion located at the start or the end of a loop is a loop invariant.

To see how assertions and loop invariants can be of help in writing correct programs, consider an example.

PROBLEM 7.5

Given a list of numbers, find their mean (or arithmetic average), and the maximum and minimum values.

Discussion of Problem 7.5

In attacking this problem we analyze how we might proceed without the help of a computer. Since we discussed computing means in Section 5.3, we will focus here on finding maximum and minimum values.

Computing Maximums. To find a maximum by hand (without a machine), we might scan down the list, looking for bigger and bigger numbers. More formally, we might proceed as follows:

1. Start with the first number. So far, that is the maximum (and the minimum, too).
2. Look at the second number. If the second number is bigger than the first, you have a new maximum.
3. Look at the third number. If the third number is bigger than the previous maximum, you have a new maximum.

The same process continues down the list of numbers. A similar process would work for computing the minimum.

Determining Loop Invariants. We want to process other numbers on the list one by one, following the patterns we have identified for computing means, maximums, and minimums. After we have processed any of the numbers, we will want the following:

Maximum = maximum value read thus far

Minimum = minimum value read thus far

Sum = sum of numbers read thus far

N = number of items read thus far

These invariants will guide us in writing a loop in the outline. Two more topics need discussion before we write out all the steps, namely initialization and the exit condition.

Initialization. Applying the loop invariants after the first item on the list is processed, we have the following:

Maximum = first number

Minimum = first number

Sum = first number

N = 1

One clear way to accomplish this initialization is to read and process the first item on the list separately.

Exit Condition. The problem does not specify how many items appear on the list. It would be good to be able to run the program with a variety of sets of data, and not to have to count the items before you enter data. Thus, you must have some flexible way to decide when to stop processing numbers. One very useful approach is to place some special value at the end of the list of numbers. You would keep reading until you read this special value. (The special value is not processed; it just marks the end of the list.) In programming we call this special value (or values) a **sentinel.**

For example, you might put the number −9999 at the end of the list, or you might decide the list will contain only positive numbers and read until you find the value 0 (or maybe a negative number). In these cases, −9999 and 0 would be sentinels. With a sentinel marking the end of the list, the exit condition from a loop is a test for the sentinel value. Of course, you must be sure the sentinel is not included in the data processing itself (the sentinel should not be included in the computation of an average, a maximum, or a minimum).

With these comments, we can suggest an outline for solving the problem. Since we must check the sentinel before processing, we have restated the loop invariants slightly.

Outline for Problem 7.5

I. Read and process first item on the list:
  A. Read item.
  B. Initialize *Minimum, Maximum, Sum* to the item.
  C. Set $N = 1$.
II. Read next item.
III. Continue processing as long as the last item read is not the sentinel:
  Loop Invariants at Top of Loop:
     Maximum = maximum value read prior to this latest value.
     Minimum = minimum value read prior to this latest value.
     Sum = sum of numbers read prior to this latest value.
     N = number of items read prior to this latest value.
  Steps
     Update *Maximum* and *Minimum*, if needed.
     Update *Sum*.
     Update N.
     Read next item.
IV. Compute *Average*.
V. Print results.

Using the value 31416 as the sentinel, this outline yields the following program. Note that the sentinel is declared as a constant within the program.

```
Program FindMaxAndMin (Input, Output);
{This program computes the mean, maximum, and minimum
 for a list of numbers.}

Const Sentinel = 31416.0;

Var Number: Integer;          {number of items read}
    Sum: Real;                {sum of items read}
    Maximum, Minimum: Real;   {extremes of items read}
    Average: Real;            {average of items}

Procedure FirstRead (Var Sum, Max, Min: Real; Var N: Integer);
{This procedure reads and processes first item on list}
    Var Item: Real;
    Begin
        Writeln ('Enter numbers; finish by typing ', Sentinel:1:1);
        Read (Item);
        Sum := Item;
        Max := Item;
        Min := Item;
        N := 1
    End {FirstRead} ;
```

```
Procedure ProcessRemainder (Var Sum, Max, Min: Real; Var N: Integer);
{This procedure reads and processes the second and subsequent input items.}
    Var Item: Real;
    Begin
        {Read next item}
        Read (Item);

        {Process items until sentinel is read}

        While (Item <> Sentinel)
          Do Begin
            If Item > Max
                Then Max := Item;
            If Item < Min
                Then Min := Item;
            Sum := Sum + Item;
            N := N + 1;
            Read (Item)
          End {Processing of items} ;
    End {ProcessRemainder} ;

Procedure PrintResults (Var Avg, Max, Min: Real);
{This procedure prints the average, maximum, and minimum data values}
    Begin
        Writeln ('The average of the items on the list is ', Avg:1:2);
        Writeln ('The largest number is ', Max:1:2);
        Writeln ('The smallest number is ', Min:1:2);
    End {PrintResults} ;

Begin {Main}
    Writeln ('Computation of mean, maximum, and minimum ',
            'for a list of numbers');

    FirstRead (Sum, Maximum, Minimum, Number);
    ProcessRemainder (Sum, Maximum, Minimum, Number);
    Average := Sum / Number;
    PrintResults (Average, Maximum, Minimum)
End {Main} .
```

Study Step III to be sure you know why we used a *While* loop. You should also check that the loop invariants are valid. When we run this program for the list 7.0, 5.0, 1.0, 11.0, 9.0, 3.0, we have the following interaction. Note that the sentinel value, 31416, is entered after the last item.

```
Computation of mean, maximum, and minimum for a list of numbers
Enter numbers; finish by typing 31416.0
7.0
5.0
1.0
11.0
9.0
3.0
31416.0
The average of the items on the list is 6.00
The largest number is 11.00
The smallest number is 1.00
```

Practical Uses of Assertions and Loop Invariants

This discussion demonstrates that loop invariants can help in writing correct programs, in several ways. They encourage precision in stating assumptions. By writing down what you expect, you can see ambiguities and contradictions. For example, you can check that the meanings of variables have not changed from one part of a program to another.

Loop invariants can also help you examine various parts of a program carefully. Loop invariants located at the beginning of a loop can help you check initialization and repetitive statements. With care you can also check exit conditions and any concluding statements.

When loop invariants or assertions include Boolean expressions, you can evaluate these expressions within a program. Thus, a program can monitor itself for errors. For example, after computing new maximums and minimums in a loop, you could check that the maximum was never smaller than the minimum with the statement

> If (Minimum > Maximum)
>   Then Writeln('Invalid Minimum or Maximum');

As software quality becomes more and more important to computer users, loop invariants and assertions are being incorporated into programming languages.

Loop invariants and assertions may be used to prove that a program is correct, just as axioms are used to prove theorems in geometry.

Assertions can help you check various parts of a program carefully, and spot places where your thinking may be fuzzy or contradictory. Specifying and checking loop invariants and assertions can also complement your use of test data in finding bugs and reducing errors.

| SECTION 7.6 | **EXAMPLE: FINDING WHERE GRAPHS CROSS AN AXIS** |

To conclude this chapter, we consider one more problem that draws on the notion of loop invariants to develop a solution. This problem will also show another application for conditional loops.

| PROBLEM 7.6 | **Approximating Roots** |

Given a function $y = f(x)$, find a root of f. In other words, find a number x_0, where $f(x_0) = 0$. (This is the place where the graph of the function crosses the x axis. See Figure 7–4.)

This is such a common problem in all sciences, engineering, and mathematics that many approaches have been developed. Here we will consider a simple method that works in a very wide range of cases.

Bisection Method for Approximating Roots. We will assume that we know (or can find) values a and b $(a < b)$ so that $f(a)$ and $f(b)$ have opposite

FIGURE 7–4 · **The Root of a Function**

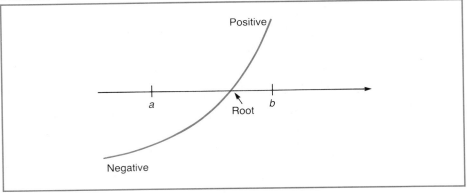

signs. As long as f is continuous (i.e., has no jumps), then f must have a root in the interval $[a,b]$. (In Figure 7–4, $f(a)$ is negative and $f(b)$ is positive.) In this situation, we can get better and better approximations to the root.

We begin with two observations: Since the root lies between a and b, one approximation for the root is the midpoint c of the interval $[a,b]$, where $c = (a + b)/2$. Second, if $[a,b]$ is a small interval, then c would be a good approximation. In particular, if $[a,b]$ has length L, then c must be within $L/2$ of the actual root.

From the cases in Figure 7–5 we can see how to use the midpoint c to narrow down the interval where the root lies. There are three possibilities. If $f(c) = 0$, we have found a root. If $f(a)$ and $f(c)$ have opposite signs, a root must be in $[a,c]$. If $f(a)$ and $f(c)$ have the same sign, then $f(c)$ and $f(b)$ must have opposite signs, and a root must be in $[c,b]$.

In the first case, we can stop. Otherwise we cut the interval containing a root in half, from $[a,b]$ to either $[a,c]$ or $[c,b]$. We can then repeat this process until either we have found the root or the interval is small enough to ensure we have a good approximation.

Example: $\sqrt{2}$ is a root of $f(x) = x^2 - 2$. Here we find $\sqrt{2}$ to two decimal places (error < 0.005), so the final interval must have a length < 0.01.

We know $1 < \sqrt{2} < 2$, so we begin with $[a,b] = [1,2]$. Figure 7–6 shows the first two steps, and Table 7–1 gives all of the calculations.

The last subinterval has length 0.0078125, which is less than the 0.01 required. Thus the midpoint 1.4180 of this last subinterval

$$[1.40625, 1.421875]$$

is within 0.005 of the desired root. We use 1.4180 as our approximation of $\sqrt{2}$. (Note: This agrees with the true value of $\sqrt{2}$, 1.41431, to two decimal places.)

In the following outline we have included appropriate loop invariants.

FIGURE 7–5 • **Cases for the Bisection Method**

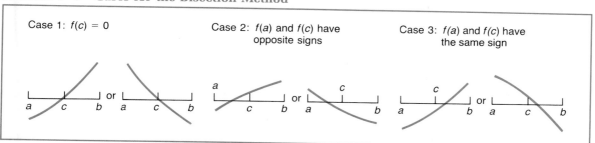

Outline for Problem 7.6

I. Initialization:

    A. Determine a, b, and maximum error allowed.

    B. Note root not yet found.

II. Continue as long as root not found and length of interval $[a,b]$ exceeds twice the allowed error:

    Loop Invariants

        $f(a)$ and $f(b)$ have opposite signs

        Desired root lies in interval $[a,b]$

    Steps

        Compute midpoint:

            $c = (a + b)/2$.

        If $f(c) = 0$, then root has been found.

        Otherwise,

            if $f(a)$ and $f(c)$ have opposite signs,

                then root is in $[a,c]$;

                else root is in $[c,b]$.

FIGURE 7–6 • **Approximating $\sqrt{2}$**

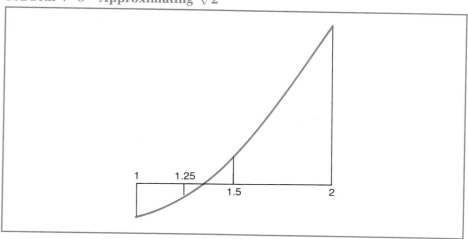

TABLE 7–1 • The Bisection Method Used to Find the Root of *Sqr(x)* − 2

Step	Interval	Midpoint	Function Values	Roots Lie in This Subinterval
1	[1.0000, 2.0000]	1.5000	f(1.0000) = −1.0000 f(1.5000) = 0.2500 f(2.0000) = 2.0000	[1.0000, 1.5000]
2	[1.0000, 1.5000]	1.2500	f(1.0000) = −1.0000 f(1.2500) = −0.4375 f(1.5000) = 0.2500	[1.2500, 1.5000]
3	[1.2500, 1.5000]	1.3750	f(1.2500) = −0.4375 f(1.3750) = −0.1094 f(1.5000) = 0.2500	[1.3750, 1.5000]
4	[1.3750, 1.5000]	1.4375	f(1.3750) = −0.1094 f(1.4375) = 0.0664 f(1.5000) = 0.2500	[1.3750, 1.4375]
5	[1.3750, 1.4375]	1.4063	f(1.3750) = −0.1094 f(1.4063) = −0.0225 f(1.4375) = 0.0664	[1.4063, 1.4375]
6	[1.4063, 1.4375]	1.4219	f(1.4063) = −0.0225 f(1.4219) = 0.0217 f(1.4375) = 0.0664	[1.4063, 1.4219]
7	[1.4063, 1.4219]	1.4141	f(1.4063) = −0.0225 f(1.4141) = −0.0004 f(1.4219) = 0.0217	[1.4141, 1.4219]

An approximate root is 1.4180

III. Print approximation to root:
If root found, then *c* is root.
Otherwise midpoint of [*a,b*] is an approximate root.

In programming from this outline, note that *f(a)* and *f(c)* have opposite signs if their product is negative. In the following program we have chosen $f(x) = x^2 - 2$ as the function.

```
Program BisectionMethod (Input, Output);
{This program uses the Bisection Method to compute the
 root of the function f(x) in the interval [a,b], with
 an error not exceeding a given tolerance.}

Var a, b: Real;        {interval for the root}
    c: Real;           {midpoint of the interval}
    TwiceError: Real;  {Twice the prescribed tolerance}
    Found: Boolean;    {specifies if actual root found}
```

```
Function f(x: Real): Real;
{This is the function under consideration}
    Begin
        f := Sqr(x) - 2.0
    End {f} ;

Procedure Initialize (Var a, b, TwiceError: Real; Var Found: Boolean);
{This procedure initializes variables for the Bisection Method.}
    Var Error: Real;           {prescribed tolerance}
    Begin
        Write ('Enter the endpoints of the interval containing the root: ');
        Readln (a, b);
        Write ('Enter maximum error allowed: ');
        Readln (error);
        TwiceError := 2.0 * Error;
        {Note that root has not yet been found}
        Found := False;
    End {Initialize} ;

Procedure FindRoot (Var a, b, c, TwiceError: Real; Var Found: Boolean);
{This procedure continues while root not found and length of
 interval [a,b] too big}
    Begin
        While (Not Found) and (Abs(b-a) >= TwiceError)
            Do Begin

                {Compute midpoint}
                c := (a + b)/2.0;

                {Check function}
                If f(c) = 0.0
                    Then Found := True
                    Else Begin
                        {check signs of f(a) and f(c)}
                        If (f(a)*f(c) < 0.0)
                            Then b := c                {root in [a,c]}
                            Else a := c                {root in [c,b]}
                    End

            End {While} ;
    End {FindRoot} ;

Procedure PrintResults (a, b, c: Real; Found: Boolean);
{This procedure prints the root or its approximation.}
    Begin
        If Found
            Then Writeln ('The exact root is ', c:1:4)
            Else Writeln ('An approximate root is ', (a+b)/2.0 :1:4)
    End {PrintResults} ;

Begin {Main}
    Writeln ('The Bisection Method is used to find the root of a function');

    Initialize (a, b, TwiceError, Found);
    FindRoot (a, b, c, TwiceError, Found);
    PrintResults (a, b, c, Found)
End {Main} .
```

When we run this program with $a = 1$, $b = 2$, and error $= 0.005$, as in the example, we get the following output:

```
The Bisection Method is used to find the root of a function
Enter the endpoints of the interval containing the root: 1 2
Enter maximum error allowed: 0.005
An approximate root is 1.4180
```

Table 7–1 shows each step in this loop.

This program combines conditional loops and loop invariants, as suggested in this chapter, with Boolean variables and conditional statements, from Chapter 6. The loop invariants make the program easy to check. The conditional loop depends on a two-part Boolean expression.

This practical problem arises in many applications and uses many of the concepts and constructions developed thus far. The final result is a relatively short, but somewhat sophisticated solution to the problem.

SUMMARY

1. This chapter introduced the *Repeat–Until* construction and the *While–Do* construction for writing loops and compared them with the *For–Do* loop introduced in Chapter 5.
2. Initialization, repetition, and exit conditions are specified in any loop.
3. *For–Do* gives **definite repetition;** you must know the number of iterations before you start a loop.
4. *Repeat* and *While* specify **conditional repetitions;** you do not know the number of iterations when you start. *Repeat* or *While* specifies an **exit condition** that determines when the loop continues and when it terminates. *While* tests the exit condition at the top of the loop; *Repeat* tests the exit condition at the bottom of the loop.
5. **Assertions** and **loop invariants** can help in developing a solution to a problem and in specifying what conditions should be true at various places in a program.

EXERCISES

7.1 Rewrite the Credit-Balance Payment program from Section 7.3, using a *Repeat–Until* construction instead of *While–Do*.
   a. First ignore the possibility that the normal monthly payment might exceed the cost of the item.
   b. Modify your program from part (a). to include the possibility that

the normal monthly payment might exceed the cost of the item. (You will need to put your loop in an *If* statement.)

   c. Compare your program with the *Repeat–Until* loop with the program in the text, which uses a *While–Do* loop.

7.2   *Rewriting the* For *in Pascal.* Rewrite the Pascal construction

      For I: = A to B
         Do Statement

   a. into a loop using the *While* construction.

   b. into a loop using the *Repeat* construction.
      Caution: What happens in Pascal if $A > B$?
      NOTE: In either (a) or (b), feel free to use an *If* statement when you need to.

7.3   *Proving Program Correctness.* Consider the Credit-Balance Payment program from Section 7.3.

   a. Develop loop invariants for *Month, Balance, Interest,* and *TInterest* at the beginning of each month.

   b. Use your assertions in part (a). to argue the validity of the program in Section 7.3.

7.4   *Family-Size Simulation, Expanded.* Expand the Family-Size simulation from Section 7.1 to simulate the number of children expected from 1000 such couples. Compute and print the average for number of children, but do not print the number of children for each individual couple.

7.5   *Assertions—Finding Errors.* Consider the following program that claims to solve the Credit-Balance Payment problem from Section 7.3. (The program is simplified from several attempts made by students in various programming classes.)

```
Program CreditBalancePayments (Input, Output);
{This program follows the balance of a charge account
 month by month as monthly payments are made.}

Var Cost: Real;            {Cost of item purchased}
    Rate: Real;            {Monthly interest rate}
    Payment: Real;         {Normal monthly payment}
    Balance: Real;         {Account balance at start of month,
                            before interest has been added}

    Interest: Real;        {Interest for month}
    TInterest: Real;       {Total accumulated interest}
    Month: Integer;        {Month number}

Begin {Main}
    Writeln ('This program follows the balance of a charge account.');
```

```
{Determine Cost, Rate, Payment}
Write ('Enter cost of item purchased: ');
Readln (Cost);
Write ('Enter monthly interest rate: ');
Readln (Rate);
Write ('Enter normal monthly payment: ');
Readln (Payment);

{Print table headings}
Writeln;
Writeln ('        Month''s   Total');
Writeln ('Month Interest  Interest    Balance');
Writeln (0:3, Cost:32:2);

{Set up account for first month}
Month := 0;
Balance := Cost;
Interest := 0.0;
TInterest := 0.0;

{Continue normal monthly payments while appropriate}
While (Payment < Balance)
  Do Begin
    Month := Month + 1;
    Interest := Balance * Rate;
    TInterest := TInterest + Interest;
    Balance := Balance + Interest - Payment;
    Writeln (Month:3, Interest:10:2, TInterest:10:2, Balance:12:2);
  End;

{Make Final Payment}
Interest := Balance * Rate;
TInterest := Interest + TInterest;
Payment := Balance + Interest;
Writeln;
Writeln ('Interest for final payment is ', Interest:1:2);
Writeln ('The final payment is ', Payment:1:2);
Writeln ('The total interest charged was ', TInterest:1:2)

End {Main} .
```

KEY TERMS, PHRASES, AND CONCEPTS		ELEMENTS OF PASCAL SYNTAX	
Assertions	Loop Invariants	Do	Until
Conditional	Placing of Exit Condition	Repeat	While
Repitition	Test at Bottom of Loop		
Definite Repetition	Test at Top of Loop		
Exit Condition	Sentinel		
Initialization			

a. Following the example in Section 7.5 as a model, write out some possible assertions and loop invariants for this program.

b. Use your assertions from part (a) to find an error in this program. If you run this program with the test cases from Section 7.3, the program output is exactly the same as the output shown for the correct program. Thus, the error is subtle. The precision of your loop invariants should be helpful in finding the bug.

(HINT: You might try the test case *Cost* = 1037.50, *Rate* = 0.01, *Payment* = 100.00.)

7.6 *Doubling Your Bank Balance.* Suppose you deposit a certain amount of money in a savings account at a specified annual interest rate, compounded monthly. Follow the balance in the account month by month until the balance doubles. Compute the balance, monthly interest, and total interest each month until the new balance is at least twice the initial balance.

7.7 *Rolling Doubles.* Simulate rolling a pair of dice, and count the number of times the dice must be thrown until doubles appear. Repeat this simulation 1000 times and compute the average and standard deviation of the number of rolls required.

7.8 N^{th} *Roots.* Write a program that computes the Nth root of the positive number R to three decimal places, using the bisection method from Section 7.6.

Read the values of N and R and check your program using the *Powers* function of Section 4.2. $\sqrt[N]{R}$ is a root of $f(x) = x^N - R$.

7.9 *Syracuse Numbers.* Consider the following iteration procedure, applied to a positive integer n_0 to generate a sequence $n_0, n_1, n_2, n_3, \ldots$ Once the integer n_j is known, the next integer n_{j+1} is computed by the rules

$$(1)\ n_{j+1} = n_j/2 \qquad \text{if } n_j \text{ is even;}$$
$$(2)\ n_{j+1} = 3n_j + 1 \quad \text{if } n_j \text{ is odd.}$$

We call the original number n_0 *Syracuse* if the number 1 appears in the sequence $n_0, n_1, n_2, n_3, \ldots$

Example: The number 5 is Syracuse, because if the iteration begins with $n_0 = 5$, the sequence is 5, 16, 8, 2, 1, ...

Write a program to show that all integers between 1 and 2000 inclusive are Syracuse.

[This problem was suggested by Professor Arnold Adelberg.]

7.10 *Insipid Integers.* Consider an iteration procedure that begins with a positive integer n_0 and generates a sequence by the rule

$$n_{j+1} = \text{sum of the squares of the digits of } n_j.$$

Remarks

1. If any term in the sequence equals 1, then all successive terms are 1.

2. If any term in the sequence equals 58, then the sequence cycles:

$$. . ., 58, 89, 145, 42, 20, 4, 16, 37, 58, 89,. . .$$

3. It is known that either Condition 1 or 2 must occur.
Definition
An integer n_0 is called *insipid* if condition 1 occurs.

Find all integers between 1 and 99 that are insipid.

NOTE: It is interesting to investigate what patterns occur if the integers are represented in a number base other than base 10.

[This problem was suggested by Professor Arnold Adelberg.]

7.11 *Gambling Simulation.* In a private game, a gambler sets the following personal limits. The gambler starts the evening with $20; he bets $2 on each game and stops when he either runs out of money or has a total of $50.

Investigate the likelihood of the gambler winning by simulating games each evening over a period of 1000 evenings. Count the number of nights the gambler wins the $50 and the number of nights the gambler is cleaned out. In your simulation, enter the payoff from winning a game and enter the probability of winning a game. (In a fair game, these might be a $2 payoff with chances of winning ½, or 0.5.)

7.12 *Winning at Racquetball.* Racquetball is a game played by two players on an indoor, enclosed court. Scoring proceeds as follows:

The score starts at 0–0.
Player *A* starts serving.
When Player *A* wins a volley, she scores a point and is allowed to serve again.
When Player *A* loses a volley, she loses the serve but no points are scored.
Player *B* then begins serving.
Player *B* scores a point for each volley she wins while serving.
When Player *B* loses a volley, she loses the serve but no points are scored.

A player can only score points while she has the serve. A player loses the serve when she loses a volley, but no points are scored on the change of serve.

Play continues until either the score is 11–0, which is a shut-out, or one player scores 21 points. (The rules do *not* require a player to win by two points.)

Investigate the relationship between winning a volley and winning the game. Enter the probability of winning a volley, then use this probability to simulate 500 games. Record the number of wins for each player and the percentage of wins. Also record the number of shut-outs for each player.

7.13 *Winning at Volleyball.* Volleyball is a game played on a court by two teams, separated by a net. Scoring proceeds much the same way as in racquetball (see Exercise 7.12).

Scoring starts at 0–0. A team can only score points while it serves. A team loses the serve when it loses a volley, but no points are scored on the change of serve. Play continues until one team scores 15 points, and a team must win by at least two points (if the score is 15–14, play must continue until one team leads by 2 points).

Investigate the relationship between winning a volley and winning the game. Enter the probability of winning a volley, then use this probability to simulate 500 games. Record the number of wins for each team and the percentage of wins.

7.14 *Finding Prime Numbers.* A prime number is a positive integer (greater than 1) that is divisible only by itself and 1—2, 3, and 5 are prime integers, while 6 is not (6 is also divisible by 2 and 3).

Write a Boolean function *Prime(N)* that returns *True* if N is a prime number and *False* otherwise. Use the function *Prime* to write out the first 100 primes.

CHAPTER 8

SIMPLE
SUBSCRIPTING:
ONE-DIMENSIONAL
ARRAYS

All of our applications up to this point have had the common feature that little information was needed at any particular time. We have specified separate variable names for each item, and we have needed only a fairly small number of such variables.

In this chapter we will consider problems that require keeping track of more pieces of information, which would make it cumbersome to write out separate variables for each piece of data. Instead, we can use one name to refer to several items, and this collection of data items is called an **array**. We can distinguish among various items in an array by giving each piece of data a separate label, called a **subscript.**

SECTION 8.1   **EXAMPLE: PRINTING DATA IN VARIOUS ORDERS**

To motivate our work in this chapter, we begin with two closely related problems.

PROBLEM 8.1 Read 25 integers and then print them out as follows:
  a. Print the numbers in reverse order.
  b. Print all of the odd integers and then print all of the even integers.

Discussion of Problem 8.1

Each part of this problem requires storing some of the numbers as they are read. For part (a), you cannot start printing anything until all 25 numbers are read, because the last number read will be the first number printed. For part (b), you cannot print any even integers until all of the numbers are read, since you will not know when the odd integers are finished printing until all of the numbers have been read. To solve these problems, therefore, you will need to store all 25 numbers.

Outline for Problem 8.1

  I. Read all 25 numbers.
  II. Print the 25 numbers in reverse order:
    A. Print the last number.
    B. Print the next-to-last number.
    Etc.
  III. Print the odd integers and then the even ones:
    A. Print the odd integers:
      1. Check each number to see if it is odd.
      2. Print each odd number.
    B. Print the even integers:
      1. Check each number to see if it is even.
      2. Print each even number.

Further Discussion of Problem 8.1

As you program from this outline, you might choose a separate name for each number; for example, you might pick names A, B, C,. . ., Y. However, if you use this approach, your reading would be

    Read (A);
    Read (B);
    Read (C);
    etc.

Even if you try to condense these *Read* statements, reading 25 numbers will be quite tedious. Writing the numbers in reverse order would be equally tedious. For Step III A you would have to test each number separately, using Pascal's *Odd* function. This part of our program might begin

    If Odd (A)
        Then Write (A:5);

Similar coding would be repeated for each of the other variables. When the odd numbers were printed, you would have to repeat a similar process to print the even numbers. The resulting code would be long, tedious, and error prone.

The problem becomes much simpler if you call the numbers $Item_1$, $Item_2$, $Item_3$,. . ., $Item_{25}$. Each number is an "Item", and you can distinguish among the items with subscripts, as you may have seen in algebra.

Look at the reading step again with this notation:

Read ($Item_1$);
Read ($Item_2$);
Read ($Item_3$);

.

.

.

Read ($Item_{25}$);

While this coding looks just as tedious as $Read(A)$; $Read(B)$; . . ., there is a pattern here, reading successive $Items$. In fact, this code can be abbreviated:

Read ($Item_i$);

for i = 1, 2,. . ., 25. Since subscripts are difficult to type on a computer terminal, place them in square brackets [ ]. In Pascal, a subscripted variable such as $Item$ is called an **array.**

Repetition over a sequence of values for i suggests a For loop, where we replace the long sequence of $Read$ statements with

For I : = 1 to 25
    Do Read (Item [I]);

This simple statement reads all 25 values.

A similar approach works for printing out the values. To print

Write ($Item_{25}$)
Write ($Item_{24}$)

.

.

.

the pattern is

Write ($Item_i$:5)

where i = 25, 24,. . .1. We can program this with the statement

For I : = 25 DownTo 1
    Do Write (Item[I]:5);

We can also use loops and subscripts to solve the odd–even part of the problem, as in the following program:

```
Program ChangeOrder (Input, Output);
{This program reads a sequence of 25 integers and prints
 the sequence in two ways:
    1.   the sequence is printed in reverse order
    2.   the odd integers are printed first followed
         by the even integers in the sequence}

Const NumberOfItems = 25;       {the problem specifies 25 items}

Var I: Integer;                 {we use I as a subscript}
    Item: Array[1..NumberOfItems] of Integer; {integers in sequence}

Begin
    Writeln ('A sequence of integers is printed in various ways.');

    {Read all items in the sequence}
    Writeln('Enter sequence of ', NumberOfItems:1, ' integers:');
    For I := 1 to NumberOfItems
        Do Read(Item[I]);

    {Print integers in reverse order}
    Writeln;
    Writeln('Sequence in reverse order');
    For I := NumberOfItems Downto 1
        Do Write(Item[I]:5);

    {Print the odd integers in the sequence}
    Writeln;
    Writeln;
    Writeln('Sequence with odd integers followed by even ones');
    For I := 1 To NumberOfItems
        Do If Odd(Item[I])
            Then Write(Item[I]:5);

    {Print the even integers in the sequence}
    For I := 1 to NumberOfItems
        Do If (Not Odd(Item[I]))
            Then Write(Item[I]:5)

End {Main} .
```

Running this program with a sequence of integers picked at random, we would get

```
A sequence of integers is printed in various ways.
Enter sequence of 25 integers:
3 8 11 15 19 21 23 1 18 17 16 12 7 4 2
25 22 20 10 9 6 5 13 24 14

Sequence in reverse order
    14    24    13     5     6     9    10    20    22    25     2     4     7    12    16
    17    18     1    23    21    19    15    11     8     3
```

```
Sequence with odd integers followed by even ones
    3    11    15    19    21    23     1    17     7    25      9     5    13     8    18
   16    12     4     2    22    20    10     6    24    14
```

This program illustrates several important features about the use of subscripts in Pascal programs. Declarations with subscripts are somewhat modified. First, state explicitly that the variable *Item* will be subscripted, and then state what range of subscripts might be possible; here the subscripts are in the range from 1 to the constant *NumberOfItems* (25). Next, state what type of information is being stored in the array; here the subscripted variables are integers. Finally, after the array is declared, place the subscripts in square brackets.

Let us look at the use of subscripted variables more closely.

SECTION 8.2   ELEMENTS OF ARRAYS

In this section we will discuss with some care the syntax and semantics of arrays. The discussion divides naturally into three pieces: array declarations, storage of arrays in main memory, and use of arrays in programs.

Array Declarations

To use a subscripted variable, the declarations must include four features: the name of the subscripted variable; the specification that the variable will be an array; the range for the subscripts; the type of data to be stored in the subscripted variable. The formal syntax for this array declaration is illustrated by the example in Section 8.1:

> Item: Array [1 . . 25] of Integer

Start an array declaration with an identifier (e.g., *Item*), which will be the name of the array. After a colon and the reserved word *Array*, write the range for the subscripts in *square* brackets []. Specify the lowest possible subscript and the highest possible subscript, and place 2 periods between them. In the example above, the subscripts ranged from 1 to 25, so we wrote [1 . . 25]. Finally, after the reserved word *of*, indicate what type of data will be stored within the array; in the example, the array data was of type *Integer*.

We can store any type of information, integer, real, or Boolean, in an array. For example, we might record whether the integers in the array *Item* were positive, by declaring

> Positive: Array [1 . . 25] of Boolean;

Positive[1] might be true if $Item_1$ is positive and false otherwise. This array would store Boolean values (*True* or *False*) rather than integers. In other cases we might want an array of real numbers.

However, each array can store only one type of data. If $Item_1$ is to be an *Integer*, then $Item_2$ through $Item_n$ must be integers, not reals or Booleans.

Turning to our subscripts, we have noted that the array declaration must specify the range for the subscripts: the range [1 . . 25] indicates that all the subscripts will be between 1 and 25, inclusive. In Pascal we have considerable flexibility in giving this range, as seen in Table 8–1.

From this discussion of syntax and semantics, we can see what types of arrays are possible and what subscript restrictions we have. Next, we will see that we can understand these declarations better if we consider how our declared arrays are stored in main memory.

Storage of Arrays in Main Memory

One of the major purposes of array declarations is to allow the computer to allocate appropriate space for the data when you run a program. For example, if you have declared

Var Item: Array [1. .10] of Integer;

the computer must allocate enough space for the variable *Item* to store 10 integers. In main memory, an integer takes up a certain amount of space, and this declaration reserves the space for 10 integers (see Figure 8–1).

TABLE 8–1 · Specifying Ranges in Array Declarations

Rule or Principle	Example	Comment
Not all subscripts specified must be used	For range [−10. .50] you may use only 1,2,3,. . .,25	You may declare ranges larger than needed
Subscripts used must be in range specified	For range [−10. .50] you may not use 57 as a subscript	You may not declare ranges smaller than needed
Constants can be used in range declarations	We used [1. .NumberOfItems] in the declaration of *Item* earlier in this section	Constants allow easy modification of code for other sizes of data
Range declarations may not include variables or expressions	The following are invalid: [7/7. .30−5] [1. .N]	The second example assumes *N* is a variable
Ranges may include Booleans or integers, but not real numbers	[Boolean] is valid [1.0. .2.0] is invalid	

FIGURE 8–1 • **Storage Allocation for Array Declarations**

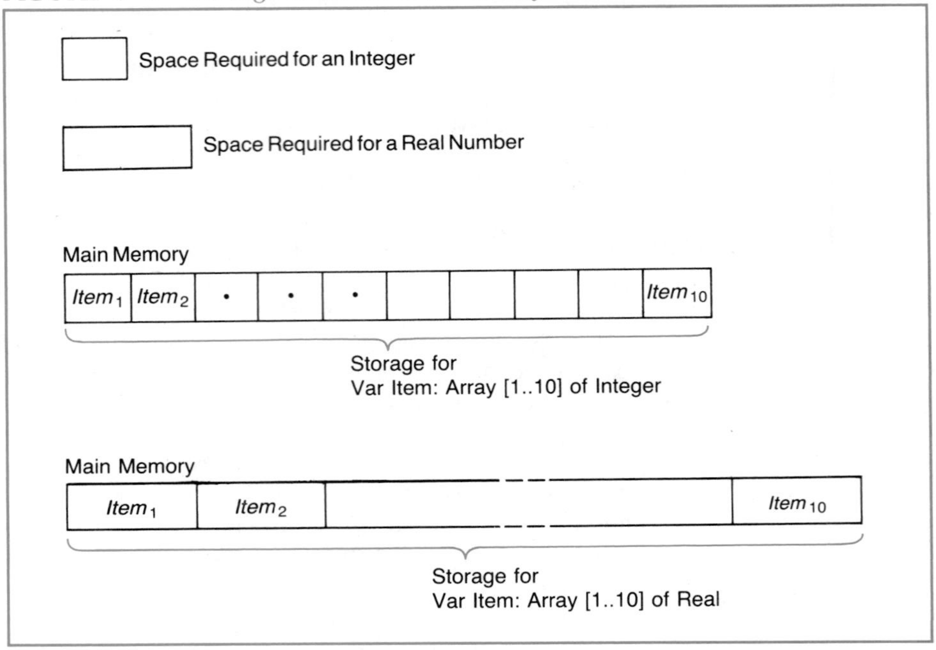

Within this block of space, the first integer will hold the value of $Item_1$, the second integer is for $Item_2$, etc.

On the other hand, if you write

Var Item: Array [1. .10] of Real;

you would again reserve enough space for 10 distinct numbers, but you must store real numbers rather than integers. Real numbers require a different amount of space from that for integer values, so an array of integers is physically different from an array of reals (see Figure 8–1). Boolean variables have still different space requirements.

An array declaration tells the computer two major pieces of information about an array. First, the range of subscripts allows the computer to determine how many spaces must be allocated (it specifies the number of boxes in the array). Second, the array type tells the computer how much space is required for each value (the size of each box).

This notion of storage allocation may clarify the variety of options noted in Table 8–1. You can use Boolean or integer subscripts, because the computer can determine how many subscripts are possible. Two Boolean subscripts, *True* and *False,* can be used. Also, you can use integer ranges

[−27. .−3] or [−12. .12] or [0. .24].

Thus, you are free to choose any range of Boolean or integer subscripts that makes sense in a problem. (However, you cannot use real subscripts, since a range of real numbers would require too much space.)

Use of Arrays in Programs

Once storage space in main memory is allocated on the basis of the information in the array declaration, you can use the array in a program in either of two ways. You may work with the elements of an array one at a time, or you may consider the entire array as a whole.

Individual Array Elements. In Section 8.1 we referred to a specific item in an array by putting a subscript in brackets. In working with array elements, however, we must be careful to distinguish between the value of a subscript and an item stored within the array. For example, 1 might be a subscript, while *Item* [1] refers to the value stored in the first location of the array *Item*.

Arrays as a Whole. In some situations, Pascal also allows us to consider an entire array as a complete unit. For example, in Section 8.4 we will see that Pascal allows us to copy whole arrays. We will also use entire arrays as parameters in functions and procedures. In these cases, we will think of an array as a single entity (containing several parts), and we will work with that entire collection of data.

In many cases, however, we cannot use an entire array, for various philosophical or technical reasons. For example, consider the arrays in Figure 8–2, where it is not clear whether the expression *Item* < *Stuff* is true or false. Similarly, we cannot perform arithmetic operations, such as addition or multiplication, on arrays, and we cannot read or write an entire array in Pascal.

FIGURE 8–2 · **Comparison of Arrays Is Not Allowed**

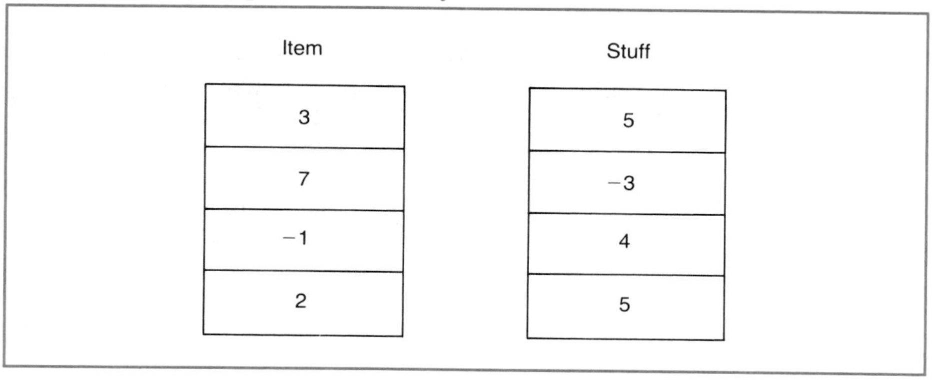

Item	Stuff
3	5
7	−3
−1	4
2	5

Thus, while Pascal does allow use of entire arrays for assignments and parameters, we cannot directly use an entire array in other contexts. These restrictions do not apply to the elements of arrays, since those elements are just numbers or Boolean values.

SECTION 8.3   **EXAMPLE: SEQUENTIAL (LINEAR) SEARCH**

A very common task in many computer applications involves searching a set of data to find a particular item. In this section we will consider two simple variations of this problem and an elementary algorithm to solve it. A second algorithm, which can be much more efficient in certain cases, is presented in Section 8.6.

PROBLEM 8.3   Given an array filled with data, suppose we are given a particular item of information.

   a. Determine whether the particular item is in the array.
   b. Determine how many times the particular item is in the array.

Discussion of Problem 8.3 part (a)

To determine whether a particular item is in an array, you could simply look at each element in the array until either you find the desired element or you run out of items in the array. This elementary approach suggests the following outline:

Outline for Problem 8.3 part (a)

   I. Read the data:
      A. Determine item of interest
      B. Determine array of data
   II. Search through successive array elements until the desired item is found or until you run out of elements.
   III. Print results of the search.

NOTES: (1) You can search through successive elements by changing the subscripts. For example, to consider $Element_1$, $Element_2$, $Element_3$,. . ., check $Element_J$, starting J at 1 and increasing J by 1.

(2) After you finish the search, you must see why you stopped: You might have found the desired item, or you might have run out of array elements. You must distinguish between these two cases.

This outline suggests the following program, which is designed for arrays of 10 elements. The details of reading data are in procedure *ReadData*. The search algorithm is in a separate Boolean function, which returns *True* if the element is found and *False* otherwise.

```
Program LinearSearch (Input, Output);
{This program determines if a particular Item is included
 in a specified array of data.}

Const Max = 10;          {Our array contains this many numbers}

Var Item: Integer;       {The desired element}
    Element: Array [1..Max] of Integer;    {Our array of numbers}

Procedure ReadData (Var Number: Integer);
    {This procedure reads the appropriate data from the terminal}
    Var I: Integer;      {Array subscript for reading}

    Begin
        {Determine Particular Item of Interest}
        Write ('Enter Desired Number: ');
        Readln (Number);

        {Determine Element of Data}
        Writeln ('Enter the ', Max:1, ' array elements.');
        For I := 1 to Max
            Do Read(Element[I]);

    End {ReadData} ;

Function ItemFound (Number: Integer): Boolean;
{This function searches for the Item in the Array}
    Var J: Integer;      {Array subscript for search}

    Begin
        {Set up for search}
        J := 0;

        {Search through Array}
        Repeat
            J := J + 1
        Until ((Number = Element[J]) Or (J = Max));

        {Determine if Number found at end of search}
        ItemFound := (Number = Element[J])

    End {ItemFound} ;

Begin {Main}
    Writeln ('An array of data is searched for a particular item.');

    ReadData (Item);

    {Search for Item and Print Results}
    If ItemFound (Item)
        Then Writeln (Item:1, ' was found in the array.')
        Else Writeln (Item:1, ' was not found in the array.')

End {Main} .
```

Two sample runs of this program are shown below:

```
First Trial Run

An array of data is searched for a particular item.
Enter particular item: 7
Enter the 10 array elements.
3 1 4 7 5 9 2 6 3 8
7 was found in the array.



Second Trial Run

An array of data is searched for a particular item.
Enter particular item: 13
Enter the 10 array elements.
3 1 4 7 5 9 2 6 3 8
13 was not found in the array.
```

A similar approach applies to part (b) of the problem, although there is one significant difference. You still need to determine the particular item to consider, and you need to read the elements of the array. In this case, however, you cannot stop after the desired element is found; you must continue through the rest of the array to see if that element appears again. This suggests the following outline:

Outline for Problem 8.3 part (b)

I. Read the data
   A. Determine item of interest
   B. Determine array of data
II. Check each array element
   A. Start with a count of 0
   B. For each array element that matches the desired element, increment the count by 1
III. Print results

The second program is again for arrays of 10 elements, with the details of reading data in the same *ReadData* procedure. Here, however, the counting details are in a separate procedure rather than in a function.

```
Program LinearSearchWithCount (Input, Output);
{This program determines how often a particular Item is present
 in a specified collection of data.}

Const Max = 10;          {Our array contains this many numbers}

Var Item: Integer;                      {The desired element}
    Element: Array [1..Max] of Integer;    {Our array of numbers}
    TimesFound: Integer;                {Frequency count}
```

```
Procedure ReadData (Var Number: Integer);
    {This procedure reads the appropriate data from the terminal}
    Var I: Integer;     {Array subscript for reading}

    Begin
        {Determine Particular Item of Interest}
        Write ('Enter particular item: ');
        Readln (Number);

        {Determine Array of Data}
        Writeln ('Enter the ', Max:1, ' array elements.');
        For I := 1 to Max
            Do Read(Element[I]);

    End {ReadData} ;

Procedure SearchForNumber (Number: Integer; Var Times: Integer);
{This procedure searches for the Item in the array}
    Var J: Integer;     {Array subscript for search}

    Begin
        Times:= 0;

        For J := 1 To Max
            Do If (Number = Element[J])
                Then Times := Times + 1

    End {SearchForNumber} ;

Begin {Main}
    Writeln ('A collection of data is searched for a particular item.');

    ReadData (Item);

    SearchForNumber (Item, TimesFound);

    {Print Results}
    If (TimesFound = 0)
        Then Writeln (Item:1, ' was not found in the array.')
        Else Writeln (Item:1, ' was found in the array ',
                        TimesFound:1, ' time(s).')

End {Main} .
```

Three sample runs of this revised program are shown below.

```
First Trial Run

A collection of data is searched for a particular item.
Enter particular item: 7
Enter the 10 array elements.
3 1 4 1 5 9 2 6 5 3
7 was not found in the array.
```

```
A collection of data is searched for a particular item.
Enter particular item: 9
Enter the 10 array elements.
3 1 4 1 5 9 2 6 5 3
9 was found in the array 1 time(s).


Third Trial Run

A collection of data is searched for a particular item.
Enter particular item: 5
Enter the 10 array elements.
3 1 4 1 5 9 2 6 5 3
5 was found in the array 2 time(s).
```

These programs illustrate three additional points. First, we can perform the same process with several values in an array by changing a subscript in a loop. Second, we can use a constant to specify the size of an array and then write all other work in terms of that constant. (We used the constant *Max* in this program.) Thus, we can adapt the programs to different amounts of data with only minor changes in the code.

Finally, in both of these problems we followed the same basic algorithm, which is called a **sequential** or **linear search.** It starts with the first element in an array and continues element by element through the array.

Evaluation of Efficiency of a Linear Search

Now that we have seen one method for finding a particular item in an array, let us analyze how much work the algorithm requires. In general, take an array of n elements (in the example, $n = 10$).

In part (a), the search stopped once we found the desired item. Sometimes, the item is near the beginning of the array; other times it is near the end. On the average, we might expect to examine about half of the array elements to find the desired item. The times when we found the item early will be balanced by other times when the item occurs late in the array.

On the average, then, if we find the desired item, we will need about $n/2$ checks or comparisons. On the other hand, if the desired item is not in the array, we must check all of the array elements. We will not know the item is missing until the entire array has been examined; we will need n checks or comparisons to conclude the desired item is not present.

In part (b), we always have to search the entire array. If the item is found, we need to search the rest of the array to find possible repetitions. Again, we do not know the desired item is missing until all array elements are checked. Thus, in the solution to part (b), we always perform n comparisons or checks to obtain the answer. The same work is required whether the item is present or not.

This is our first illustration of an analysis of the work required to perform a specified task. The analysis tells us, for example, that if we have an array of 1000 elements ($n = 1000$), then we would have to perform an average of 500 comparisons ($n/2 = 500$) to find a particular item in the array. If we want to look up items frequently, then this same amount of work would be required each time.

In this text, we will see other algorithms, and we will be able to analyze them as well. Our results will suggest how to choose among various algorithms to use the best algorithm for a particular application.

SECTION 8.4	TYPE STATEMENTS

In previous chapters, we have seen how to define our own constants, variables, procedures, and functions. We have discussed real, integer, and Boolean data, and we have seen how to put this data together in an array. In this section we will introduce defining our own types, and we will see some applications of type declarations when using arrays. We will expand considerably upon this discussion in Chapter 12.

We begin with an example. We have rewritten the first linear search program from the previous section, declaring a new type of data, *Array-OfData*, and using our array *Element* as a parameter in the *ItemFound* function. The revised program produces the same output as the original version.

```
Program LinearSearch {With new array type} (Input, Output);
{This program determines if a particular Item is present
 in a specified array of data.}

Const Max = 10;          {Our array contains this many elements}

Type ArrayOfData = Array [1..Max] of Integer;   {The type of array}

Var Item: Integer;       {The desired element}
    Element: ArrayOfData;   {Our Array of elements}

Procedure ReadData (Var Number: Integer; Var Info: ArrayOfData);
    {This procedure reads the appropriate data from the terminal}
    Var I: Integer;      {Array subscript for reading}

    Begin
        {Determine Particular Item of Interest}
        Write ('Enter Desired Number: ');
        Readln (Number);

        {Determine Array of Data}
        Writeln ('Enter the ', Max:1, ' array elements.');
        For I := 1 to Max
            Do Read(Info[I]);

    End {ReadData} ;
```

```
Function ItemFound(Number: Integer; Info: ArrayOfData): Boolean;
{This function searches for the Item in the array}
    Var J: Integer;    {Array subscript for search}

    Begin
        {Set up for search}
        J := 0;

        {Search through array}
        Repeat
            J := J + 1
        Until ((Number = Info[J]) Or (J = Max));

        {Determine if Item found at end of search}
        ItemFound := (Number = Info[J])

    End {ItemFound} ;

Begin {Main}
    Writeln ('A collection of data is searched for a particular item.');

    ReadData (Number, Element);

    {Search for Item and Print Results}
    If ItemFound (Number, Element)
        Then Writeln (Item:1, ' was found in the array.')
        Else Writeln (Item:1, ' was not found in the array.')

End {Main} .
```

In this program, we declared

Type ArrayOfData = Array [1. .Max] of Integer;

You can use a type *ArrayOfData* as well as the types *Real, Integer, Boolean*. *ArrayOfData* designates an array with a particular range of subscripts.

Once we defined the type, we declared

Var Element: ArrayOfData;

The variable *Element* has the new type *ArrayOfData*, which we have just described.

So far, the declaration of *Element* seems equivalent to the more familiar declaration

Var Element: Array [1. .Max] of Integer;

The new type, however, offers an important additional capacity. You can use this new type to declare the formal parameter in procedure *ReadData* and in the *ItemFound* function:

Procedure ReadData (Var Number: Integer; Var Info: ArrayOfData);

and

Function ItemFound (Number: Integer; Info: ArrayOfData): Boolean;

The formal parameter *Info* has the same type as the global variable *Element*, so you can use *Element* as an actual parameter in the main program. Declaring the new type *ArrayOfData* enables you to use the array *Element* as a parameter both in procedure *ReadData* and in the function *ItemFound*.

Agreement of Formal and Actual Parameter Types

When we discussed parameters for functions and procedures, we distinguished between formal parameters and actual parameters, and we said that the declaration of a function specifies the type of parameter for the function. Actual parameters must have the same type as the formal parameters. In Pascal, this notion of the same type is interpreted very strictly. In particular, you must have names for all formal parameters, and the type names for formal and actual parameters must agree.

In the revised Linear Search program we declared a new type, *ArrayOfData*, and both the formal paramenter *Info* and the actual parameter *Element* for function *ItemFound* had this type. Pascal would not allow declaring *Info* and *Element* separately as

Array [1. .Max] of Integer

Thus when you want to use arrays as parameters in Pascal, you must declare an appropriate type first in a *Type* statement. Then, you can use that type to declare formal parameters and appropriate variables. This use of a *Type* statement guarantees that formal parameters and actual parameters actually have the same type, since the type names are identical.

Type Statements for Assignments

The philosophy of the same type also applies to the transfer of data from one array to another. If you declare

Var Stuff, Item: Array [1. .4] of Integer

Then you may write

Stuff : = Item

Here *Stuff* and *Item* are arrays of the same type, and you can transfer data from one array to the other. The line

Stuff : = Item

is equivalent to

Stuff[1] : = Item[1];
Stuff[2] : = Item[2];
Stuff[3] : = Item[3];
Stuff[4] : = Item[4];

More generally, Pascal allows the transfer of data from one variable to another whenever the variables have the same type. Here Pascal again interprets the word "same" very strictly. The assignment

A := B

is only valid when A and B are declared in the same declaration statement or when their type has the same identifier as a name. To declare A and B in different lines or in different procedures, you must use the Type statement to give the variables the same type. Thus, you could write

Type   Data = Array [−2. .6] of Integer
Var   A: Data;
        B: Data;
   .
   .
   .
      A: = B

since A and B are explicitly the same type.

Summary

This discussion of Pascal types and Type statements raises four major points.

1. Pascal allows us to define data types, using Type statements.
2. Pascal has a very strict interpretation of types. It does not analyze different declarations to determine whether two variables have the same type. We must be explicit if we want two variables to have the same type.
3. Type statements allow us to specify arrays as parameters in functions and procedures; formal parameters and actual parameters can be declared to be the same type, through Type statements.
4. When variables have the same type, we can transfer data from one to the other with the simple assignment statement A := B.

We will now look at some more examples that use arrays to solve common problems.

SECTION 8.5   **EXAMPLE: SORTING**

In Section 8.3 we looked at one approach for solving the common problem of locating a particular item in an array of data. In this section we consider a different, but related problem.

PROBLEM 8.5   Write a program to put a collection of data in ascending order.

The process of putting data in order is called **sorting.** As with the searching problem, sorting problems arise in many applications, and many sorting algorithms have been developed. In this section we will look at two elementary solutions to this problem.

Discussion of Problem 8.5

To begin, consider n pieces of data, $a_1, a_2, \ldots, a_n$.

General Design. The key step will be to consider the elements $a_1, \ldots, a_i$ and find the biggest. We will then move this biggest value to the ith position in the array, at element a_i. First, we do this step for $i = n$; this will move the biggest element to the end of the array. Then, we do this for $i = n-1$, to place the next largest element next to the end of the array, and continue for all the elements. This gives the following general outline:

I. Repeat for $i = n, n-1, n-2, \ldots, 2$:
  A. Consider the elements $a_1, \ldots, a_i$, comparing a_1 with a_2 and then looking at $a_3, a_4, \ldots, a_i$.
  B. Move the largest element found to a_i.

Adding Detail. From the general design we need to go into more detail about how to do the searching and how to end with the largest element in its proper place. There are two ways to accomplish these tasks. You could move items as you go through the array, so the largest item moves into place as you search, or you could locate the largest item during the search process and move that element into place when the search is done.

These two ways of proceeding yield two distinct sorting algorithms—two distinct detailed designs based on one general design. We will consider each, after we make an important technical observation.

Swapping Data. In either approach you will need to interchange two pieces of data, $a[I]$ and $a[J]$. For example, if $a[1] = 8$ and $a[2] = 5$, you may want to swap which value is stored where to end with $a[1] = 5$ and $a[2] = 8$. A first attempt at this task might be

```
a[I] := a[J];
a[J] := a[I];        {Incorrect}
```

Unfortunately, this code does not work as desired. In the example,

```
a[1] := a[2]
```

sets both $a[1]$ and $a[2]$ to 5; you have lost data item 8.

When you swap data, you need to keep track of one item before you move the other. This is done by introducing a new storage location, which we will call *Temp*. The correct code, then, is

```
Temp := a[I];
a[I] := a[J];
a[J] := Temp;        {Correct}
```

The value 8 is stored in $Temp$ before you assign $a[1] := a[2]$. Then the value 8 can be retrieved from $Temp$ and placed in $a[2]$ as desired.

We can now complete the first approach to sorting.

Exchange or Bubble Sort

In this approach, the key step is to swap elements as you search through the array elements $a_1, \ldots, a_i$, so the largest element ends as item a_i. We proceed as follows:

Step 1 Compare a_1 and a_2.
  Swap a_1 and a_2, if necessary, so a_2 is bigger than a_1.
Step 2 Compare a_2 and a_3.
  Swap a_2 and a_3, if necessary, so a_3 is bigger than a_2 (a_3 will also be bigger than a_1, by Step 1).

The process continues until all i elements $a_1, \ldots, a_i$ have been compared. We exchange adjacent elements through the array, so this is sometimes called an **exchange sort.** You might think of an analogy between this process and drops of oil in water. The heavy bubbles of oil sink to the bottom, just as the bigger numbers in the array move downward. This algorithm is therefore also called a **Bubble Sort.**

Detailed Design for the Exchange or Bubble Sort. Outlining this approach, you need to be careful to compare just the right number of items each time. This suggests the following:

  I. Determine an array of N numbers $a_1, \ldots, a_N$.
  II. Exchange or bubble sort:
    Repeat for $I := N, N-1, \ldots, 2$:
      Repeat for $J := 2, 3, \ldots, I$:
        If $a_{J-1} > a_J$, then swap a_{J-1} and a_J.
  III. Print sorted array.

This outline yields the following program, written for arrays of ten elements.

```
Program BubbleSort (Input, Output);
{program uses a Bubble Sort to order data.}
Const Max = 10;    {Number of elements to be sorted}

Type Data = Integer;    {Our array elements will be integers}
     ArrayOfData = Array [1..Max] of Data;

Var A: ArrayOfData;      {Elements to be sorted}

Procedure EnterData (Var Info: ArrayOfData);
```

```
{Determine elements to be sorted}
    Var I: Integer;    {Array subscript}
    Begin
        Writeln ('Enter the elements to be sorted');
        For I := 1 To Max
            Do Read(Info[I])
    End {EnterData} ;

Procedure BubbleSort (Var Item: ArrayOfData);
    Var I, J: Integer;    {Array subscripts}
        Temp: Data;
    Begin
        For I := Max DownTo 2
            Do For J := 2 To I
                Do If Item[J-1] > Item[J]
                    Then Begin
                        Temp := Item[J-1];
                        Item[J-1] := Item[J];
                        Item[J] := Temp
                    End {comparison}
    End {BubbleSort} ;

Procedure PrintData (Info: ArrayOfData);
    Var I: Integer;    {Array subscript}
    Begin
        Writeln;
        Writeln ('The sorted data are shown below:');
        For I := 1 To Max
            Do Write (Info[I]:5)
    End {PrintData} ;

Begin {Main}

    Writeln ('This program sorts ', Max:1, ' elements');
    Enterdata (A);
    BubbleSort (A);
    PrintData (A)

End {Main} .
```

Running this program on some test data, we get

```
This program sorts 10 elements
Enter the elements to be sorted
3 7 4 1 8 9 2 6 5 3

The sorted data are shown below:
    1    2    3    3    4    5    6    7    8    9
```

Trace through the Bubble Sort procedure to see how the solution outline is reflected in the program.

Straight Selection Sort

The second approach also focuses on the elements $a_1, \ldots, a_i$, but first finds the biggest element, and only swaps at the end.

To find the biggest element, start with the first element and let $Max := 1$. $A[Max]$ is the largest (and only) element encountered so far. Next look at the second, third, etc. elements to see if any of them are bigger.

Detailed Design for the Straight Selection Sort.

I. Determine an array of N elements, $a_1, \ldots, a_N$.
II. Straight selection sort:
   Repeat for $I := N, N-1, \ldots, 2$:
   A. Start with $Max := 1$.
   B. Repeat for $J := 2, \ldots, I$:
      If $A_J > A_{MAX}$
         Then the biggest must be updated
            (i.e., $Max := J$).
   C. Swap A_J and A_{MAX}.
III. Print sorted array.

Comparing this outline with the bubble sort outline, we see only Step II is different, so only the second procedure is revised in the following program:

```
Program StraightSelectionSort (Input, Output);
{Program uses a Straight Selection Sort to order data.}
Const Max = 10;     {Number of elements to be sorted}

Type Data = Integer;        {Our array elements will be integers}
     ArrayOfData = Array [1..Max] of Data;

Var A: ArrayOfData;         {Elements to be sorted}

Procedure EnterData (Var Info: ArrayOfData);
{Determine elements to be sorted}
     Var I: Integer;    {Array subscript}
     Begin
         Writeln ('Enter the elements to be sorted');
         For I := 1 To Max
             Do Read(Info[I])
     End {EnterData} ;

Procedure StraightSelectionSort (Var Item: ArrayOfData);
     Var I, J: Integer;     {Array subscripts}
         MaxElt: Integer;   {Subscript of the largest element}
         Temp: Data;
```

```
Begin
    For I := Max DownTo 2
        Do Begin
            {Find location of biggest remaining element}
            MaxElt := 1;
            For J := 2 To I
                Do If Item[J] > Item[MaxElt]
                    Then MaxElt := J;

            {Swap}
            Temp := Item[MaxElt];
            Item[MaxElt] := Item[I];
            Item[I] := Temp
        End
End {StraightSelectionSort} ;
Procedure PrintData (Info: ArrayOfData);
    Var I: Integer;      {Array subscript}
    Begin
        Writeln;
        Writeln ('The sorted data are shown below:');
        For I := 1 To Max
            Do Write (Info[I]:5)
    End {PrintData} ;
Begin {Main}

    Writeln ('This program sorts ', Max:1, ' elements');
    Enterdata (A);
    StraightSelectionSort (A);
    PrintData (A)

End {Main} .
```

The selection sort program gives the same output as the Bubble Sort program.

Evaluation of Efficiency

Each approach follows the same general design—the key step looks at the elements $a_1, \ldots, a_i$ and finds the biggest. Either method compares a_1 with a_2, then looks at $a_3, a_4, \ldots, a_i$. We need $i-1$ comparisons for either method.

This key step is then repeated for $i = n, n-1, n-2, \ldots, 2$. Tabulating this work, we get

Step	Value of I	Number of Comparisons
1	n	$n-1$
2	$n-1$	$n-2$

(continued)

Step	Value of I	Number of Comparisons
3	$n-2$	$n-3$
.	.	.
.	.	.
.	.	.
$n-2$	3	2
$n-1$	2	1

Totaling the work over all steps, we find

Total Number
of Comparisons $= (n-1) + (n-2) + (n-3) + . . .+ 2 + 1$

Using algebra, one can show this sum equals

$$(n^2 - n)/2$$

To appreciate this analysis, consider Table 8–2. The number of steps required to perform a Straight Selection Sort increases very rapidly as the number of data items increases. Even though a computer can perform individual steps quickly, you may still have to wait a long time for either of these sorting methods to work. A Bubble Sort has to exchange items frequently, so the overall work required actually is substantially more than the above analysis indicates.

Thus, while the Bubble Sort and the Straight Selection Sort are easy to understand and program, they are not practical if you must consider data

TABLE 8–2 · Values of $\dfrac{(n^2-n)}{2}$ for

Various Values of *n*

n	$\dfrac{n^2-n}{2}$	Time* for $\dfrac{n^2-n}{2}$
100	4950	0.5 seconds
200	18,800	1.9 seconds
.		
.		
.		
1000	499,500	50 seconds
5000	12,247,500	20 minutes
10000	49,995,000	83 minutes
20,000	199,980,000	5 hours

*Assuming 10,000 comparisons per second.

sets of any size. Bubble Sorts and Straight Selection Sorts are fine when you need to handle only a few items. For many applications, however, you will need to find better ways to sort.

Improved Bubble Sort

Two small improvements will streamline the Bubble Sort to eliminate some extraneous steps. First, in iterations that go through the array without exchanging any elements, subsequent steps are unnecessary—the array is already in order. Second, you may search the elements a_1, a_2, . . ., a_i, and find no exchanges after element a_j. Then, in the array a_1, a_2, . . ., a_j, . . ., a_i, you know a_j, . . ., a_i are already in order.

To make these changes in the Bubble Sort, use a Boolean variable *Done* to check whether changes were made. Start the inner loop with *Done* set to *True*, change it to *False* if a swap is made, and then continue the outer loop until *Done*. (The outer *For* is replaced by *Repeat–Until*.) In addition, use an integer variable *Last* to keep track of when the last swap was made. The inner loop then becomes

      For J : = 1 To Last

rather than

      For J : = 1 To I

In later sections we will use other sorting algorithms that yield more efficient programs by attacking the problem in different ways.

SECTION 8.6   EXAMPLE: BINARY SEARCH

Section 8.3 presented one approach to searching an array for a particular item. This section presents a much more efficient approach for an array that has already been sorted.

We begin with an array of data a_1, . . ., a_n, and we want to find a particular item P. Whereas, in the Linear Search, you potentially had to look at the entire array a_1, . . ., a_n, in a Binary Search you can eliminate much of the data without having to look at them directly. In particular, the Binary Search allows you to divide the amount of data under consideration in half each time.

To understand how this is done, consider how you might look up a name in a telephone book. To begin, open the telephone book to the middle. If you are lucky, you will see the name on the page in front of you. Even if you are unlucky, however, you can tell which half of the book contains the name you want.

Once you know which half the name is in, turn to the middle of that half. Again, you might be lucky and find the name immediately. Otherwise, you can restrict your attention to just the part where the name must be (now just one-quarter of the original book).

Continue looking at the middle page of the section remaining and dividing that section in halves until you find the name or until you run out of pages to look at.

Algorithm Design. Writing this approach as a formal algorithm, you must keep track of four things in the general step: You need to know the first element, a_F, in a short array; the last element, a_L; the middle element, a_M; and the desired element, P.

Outline for Binary Search. With this notation we have the following outline.

I. Read the data:
   A. P.
   B. The array of data $a_1, \ldots, a_N$.
II. Binary search:
   A. Initialize search:
$$F := 1$$
$$L := N$$
   B. Repeat until P is found or there are no elements left to consider:
     1. Find the middle element: $M := (F + L)/2$.
     2. Check P and a_M:
        If $P = a_M$, then element found.
        If $P < a_M$, then $L := P - 1$.
        If $P > a_M$, then $F := P + 1$.
   C. Determine whether the element is found.
III. Print results.

This outline yields the following program, which produces the same output as the Linear Search program from Section 8.3.

```
Program BinarySearch (Input, Output);
{This program determines if a particular Item is present
 in a specified array of data.}

Const Max = 10;          {Our array contains this many elements}

Type ArrayOfData = Array [1..Max] Of Integer;

Var Item: Integer;        {The desired element}
    Element: ArrayOfData ;   {Our array of elements}

Procedure ReadData (Var Number: Integer; Var Info: ArrayOfData);
{This procedure reads the appropriate data from the terminal}
    Var I: Integer;     {Array subscript for reading}

    Begin
        {Determine Particular Item of Interest}
        Write ('Enter Desired Number: ');
        Readln (Number);
```

```
    {Determine Array of Data}
    Writeln ('Enter the ', Max:1, ' array elements.');
    For I := 1 To Max
        Do Read(Info[I])

End {Read Data} ;

Function ItemFound (Number: Integer; Info: ArrayOfData): Boolean;
{This function searches for the Item in the array}
    Var First, Last: Integer;   {Binary Search of
                                   Info[First] to Info[Last]}

        Middle: Integer;  {the middle of our array}

    Begin
        {Initialize Search}
        First := 1;
        Last := Max;

        {Perform search}
        Repeat
            Middle := (First + Last) Div 2;
            If Number < Info[Middle]
                Then Last := Middle - 1
                Else First := Middle + 1;
        Until (Number = Info[Middle]) Or (Last < First) ;

        {Determine if item found}
        ItemFound := (Number = Info[Middle])

    End {ItemFound} ;

Begin {Main}
    Writeln ('A collection of data is searched for a particular item.');

    ReadData (Item, Element);

    {Search for Item and Print Results}
    If ItemFound (Item, Element)
        Then Writeln (Item:1, ' was found in the array')
        Else Writeln (Item:1, ' was not found in the array')

End {Main} .
```

Evaluation of Efficiency.   This algorithm works very efficiently, because inferences can be made about the array after each comparison. In particular, it halves the number of array elements considered in each iteration. For example, if you start with N elements, then after one step, the number of remaining elements is $N/2$. After two steps, the number of remaining elements is $N/4$.

In general, after m steps, the number of elements left to check is $N/2^m$. You can continue this process until you either find the element or run out of elements. If you are lucky, you might find the element very quickly, so you might stop very soon. Even if you are unlucky, however, you will run out of elements quite fast.

In particular, you can stop when the number of elements left to check is less than 1. You can stop by m steps

if

$$N/2^m < 1,$$

or

$$N < 2^m,$$

or

$$\log_2 N < m,$$

or

$$1 + \log_2 N \leq m$$

(see Appendix C-1 for a review of logarithms).

Thus, for an array of N elements, the Binary Search will finish in no more than $1 + \log_2 N$ steps. By the nature of logarithms, this analysis shows that if you double the size of the array, you only add one iteration to the loop. Other comparisons are shown in Table 8–3.

Choosing Between Linear and Binary Search Algorithms

Our analysis and Table 8–3 show that if you have sorted data, then the Binary Search is vastly superior to the Linear Search. Thus, you should choose the Binary Search whenever a problem involves sorted data.

In addition, the Binary Search should be used whenever you will need to search the same data many times. In this situation, the time spent ordering the data is offset by the gain in each Binary Search. This general "divide and conquer" approach applies to many other applications as well. For example, this same idea formed the basis of the Bisection Method in Section 7.6.

On the other hand, if the data are not sorted, and if you do not need to search the data very often, then a Linear Search is the preferred algorithm.

TABLE 8–3 · Steps Required for Two Searching Methods, Based on _n_ Elements of Data

	Linear Search		Binary Search
n	Average number of Steps (n/2)	Maximum Number of Steps n	$1 + \log_2 n$
100	50	100	8
1000	500	1000	11
10000	5000	10000	14

In this situation, the time required to sort data is not balanced by the faster Binary Search.

This Binary Search example also shows that an effective way to improve a program may well be to change the algorithm. Sometimes, you can polish the code to make it run more efficiently. When you need dramatic improvements, however, you may need a different approach to the problem altogether.

SECTION 8.7   EXAMPLE: MAINTAINING LINEAR STRUCTURES

In previous examples, we first entered data and then worked with them. In this section we will see how to edit data. Then we will apply these ideas to get another, somewhat improved sorting algorithm.

PROBLEM 8.7   Simple Editing

Write a procedure that starts with some elements in an array and then allows you to edit the data. You must be able to insert new items and delete existing ones.

Discussion of Problem 8.7

In the past, we have always used a constant *Max* to specify the maximum number of elements to be stored in an array, and we always used this full number. Here, we want to allow additions and deletions to the elements, so we need two changes. We must allow more space than we might need initially, so we have room for additions, and we must keep track of the exact number of elements present at any time. In the program, therefore, we need to set *Max* larger than in the past, and we need a distinct variable *Number* to record the current number of data items.

Suppose an array is declared

Var A: Array[1. .Max] of Integer

and suppose we have already entered some data, so *Number* > 0. When we add a piece of data *P*, we must increment *Number* by 1. (Of course, if this new *Number* is bigger than *Max*, then we cannot store any more data and must stop.)

With *Number* increased, we next need to decide where to place the new piece of data *P*. If the array is not sorted, then we can place *P* at the end of the array,

A[Number] : = P

However, if the array is sorted and we want to keep it sorted, then we must proceed in two steps (see Figure 8–3): slide values bigger than *P* down in the array to make room for *P*, then insert *P* in the vacant space.

FIGURE 8–3 • **Insertion in a Sorted Array**

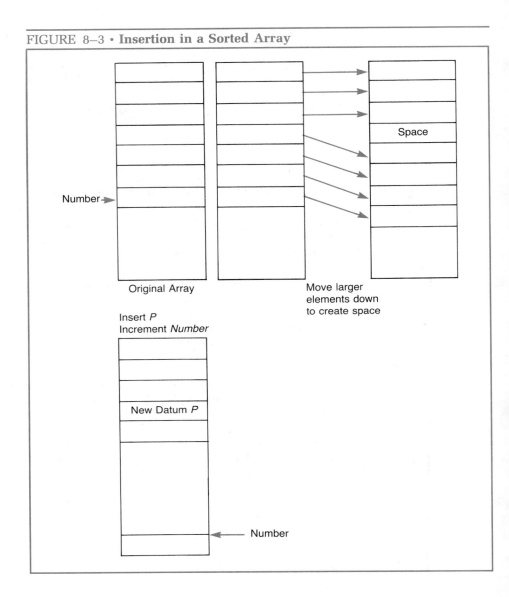

Outline for Insertion. One way to perform this insertion task is outlined below.

   I. Check that there is room for another item in the array.

   II. Use binary search to find where the new item should go.

  III. Slide elements beyond this point down.

  IV. Insert the item and increment *Number*.

This suggests the following code:

```
{Procedure Insert and Function ItemLocation assume that
    Max    is declared as a constant,
    Data   is declared as a type of data, such as integer or real,
    ArrayOfData is declared as "Array [1..Max] of Data"}

Function ItemLocation (Item: Data; Number: Integer;
                       Info: ArrayOfData): Integer;
{This function searches for the Item in the Array}
    Var First, Last: Integer;   {Binary Search of Info[First] to Info[Last]}
        Middle: Integer;   {the middle of our array}

    Begin
        If Item > Info[Number]
            Then ItemLocation := Number + 1
            Else Begin {Binary Search}
                {Initialize Search}
                First := 1;
                Last := Number;

                {Perform search}
                Repeat
                    Middle := (First + Last) Div 2;
                    If Item < Info[Middle]
                        Then Last := Middle - 1
                        Else First := Middle + 1;
                Until (Item = Info[Middle]) Or (Last < First) ;

                {Record where Item should be}
                If Item <= Info[Middle]
                    Then ItemLocation := Middle
                    Else ItemLocation := Middle + 1
            End {Binary Search}

    End {ItemLocation} ;

Procedure Insert (Item: Data; Var Number: Integer; Var Element: ArrayOfData);
{This procedure inserts the specified Item from the Array}
    Var ItemIndex: Integer;    {Location of Item on Array}
        Index: Integer;        {Array subscript}

    Begin
      {Check if there is room in the array}
      If Number = Max
        Then Writeln ('Array is Full - Insertion is impossible')
        Else Begin
            {Find Where New Item Should Go}
            ItemIndex := ItemLocation (Item, Number, Element);

        {Slide Subsequent Elements Down}
        For Index := Number DownTo ItemIndex
            Do Element[Index+1] := Element[Index];
```

```
    {Insert Item}
    Element[ItemIndex] := Item;
    Number := Number + 1
    End {Insertion of Item}

End {Insert} ;
```

This coding uses the efficient binary search to locate where the new element should go, so it allows us to insert new data efficiently.

Deletion of Items.   To delete elements, the process is reversed:

   I. Locate the element in the array to be deleted.
      (If the item is not found, print an error message.)
   II. Move subsequent elements down to close up "space" left by deleted element.
   III. Decrement *Number* by 1.

When we write the corresponding procedure for deletion, we use the same *ItemLocation* function we used for insertion. We omit the listing of this *ItemLocation* function in the following deletion procedure.

```
{Procedure Delete assumes the following declarations:
    Max     is declared as a constant,
    Data    is declared as a type of data, such as real or integer,
    ArrayOfData is declared as "Array [1..Max] of Data" }

Procedure Delete (Item: Data; Var Number: Integer; Var Element: ArrayOfData);
{This procedure deletes the specified Item from the Array}
    Var ItemIndex: Integer;     {Location of Item in Array}
        Index: Integer;         {Array subscript}

    Begin
        {Locate Item in Array - Using Binary Search}
        ItemIndex := ItemLocation (Item, Number, Element);

        {Check if element found}
        If (Element[ItemIndex] <> Item)
            Then Writeln ('Item not in array - deletion impossible')
            Else Begin
                {Shift subsequent elements down}
                For Index := ItemIndex To Number-1
                    Do Element[Index] := Element[Index+1];

                {Decrement Number by 1}
                Number := Number - 1

            End {Deletion of Item Completed}
    End {Delete} ;
```

With these pieces, we can present an outline for the entire editing process:

Outline for Problem 8.7

I. Enter initial data:
   A. *Number* of items in array initially.
   B. Initial *Items*:
      1. Read each *Item*.
      2. Place *Items* in array so result is ordered.
II. Edit data:
   Repeat as long as insertions or deletions are required:
   A. If insertion is desired, follow insertion outline.
   B. If deletion is desired, follow deletion outline.
III. Print final array.

We leave the complete editing program based on this outline as an exercise and turn to another use of the insertion process.

Insertion Sort

We can incorporate the insertion process into a sorting algorithm very easily for two arrays. Start with array A and end with array B, which contains the values from A, in order.

Outline for Two-Array Insertion Sort. The approach is very simple; start with elements $A[1], \ldots, A[N]$.

I. Put first element into array B, using the insertion algorithm.
   Number = 1 in array B, and $B[1] := A[1]$.
II. Repeat for element $A[2], A[3], \ldots, A[N]$
   (i.e., repeat for $I := 2, 3, \ldots, N$):
   A. Insert item $A[I]$ into array B and increment *Number*.

This outline yields the following procedure:

```
Procedure InsertionSort (A: ArrayOfData; Var B: ArrayOfData);
{This procedure moves the elements of data from Array A
 to a sorted array B using an Insertion Sort}
    Var NumberInserted: Integer;   {Number of items inserted}
        I: Integer;          {Array subscript for insertion}

    Procedure Insert (Item: Data; Var Number: Integer; Var B: ArrayOfData);
    {This procedure inserts the specified Item into B}
        Var ItemIndex: Integer;    {Location of item on B}
            Index: Integer;        {Array subscript}

        Function ItemLocation (Item: Data; Number: Integer;
                            B: ArrayOfData): Integer;
        {This function searches for the Item on the B}
            Var First, Last: Integer;  {Binary Search of B[First] to B[Last]}
                Middle: Integer;   {the middle of our array}
```

```
        Begin
            If Item > B[Number]
                Then ItemLocation := Number + 1
                Else Begin {Binary Search}
                    {Initialize Search}
                    First := 1;
                    Last := Number;

                    {Perform search}
                    Repeat
                        Middle := (First + Last) Div 2;
                        If Item < B[Middle]
                            Then Last := Middle - 1
                            Else First := Middle + 1;
                    Until (Item = B[Middle]) Or (Last < First) ;

                    {Record where Item should be}
                    If (Item <= B[Middle])
                        Then ItemLocation := Middle
                        Else ItemLocation := Middle + 1
                End {Binary Search}

        End {ItemLocation} ;

    Begin
        {Find Where New Item Should Go}
        ItemIndex := ItemLocation (Item, Number, B);

        {Slide Subsequent Elements Down}
        For Index := Number DownTo ItemIndex
            Do B[Index+1] := B[Index];

        {Insert Item}
        B[ItemIndex] := Item;
        Number := Number + 1

    End {Insert} ;

Begin {InsertionSort}
    {Insert First Element Into B}
    NumberInserted := 1;
    B[1] := A[1];

    {Insert subsequent elements}
    For I := 2 To Max
        Do Insert(A[I], NumberInserted, B)

End {InsertionSort} ;
```

Outline for One-Array Insertion Sort. In each insertion step you add the element $A[I]$ into the array $B[1], \ldots, B[I-1]$ to get a new array $B[1], \ldots, B[I]$. If you store the value of $A[I]$ first, however, you do not actually need the array B at all. The revised outline is as follows.

    I. First element begins in place.
    II. Repeat for $I := 2, \ldots, N$:
       A. Store value of $A[I]$:
          $Value := A[I]$
       B. Insert $Value$ into array $A[1], \ldots, A[I-1]$.

The revision of the two-array procedure to use just one array is left as an exercise.

Observation for Problem Solving

In these examples, you can see illustrations of another general problem solving principle: Once you solve one problem (e.g., Binary Search or editing an array), you may find a similar idea applies elsewhere (e.g., inserting an element or sorting). If you have written a program with distinct procedures for solving one problem, you may be able to use the same procedures to solve other problems as well.

SECTION 8.8 ## EXAMPLE: STATISTICS

Now that you have seen how to enter, edit, and sort data, let us look at two elementary ways to analyze data, measures of the middle and measures of central tendency and dispersion.

Measures of the Middle

Two values are commonly used to refer to the middle of a sample of data $a_1, \ldots, a_n$. The **mean,** or arithmetic average, is computed by the familiar formula

$$mean = (a_1 + \ldots + a_i + \ldots + a_n)/n.$$

We have discussed earlier how to compute such expressions (Section 5.3). One possible difficulty with this mean is that it can be influenced considerably if one value is much bigger or smaller than the others. One very large number can greatly increase the mean.

    The second value, the **median,** is not affected as much by occasional outliers. Conceptually, the median is the middle data element; that is, a_i is the median if the same number of data items lie above a_i as lie below. For example, given the data 1, 2, 3, 7, 8, the median value is 3; two values (1, 2) lie below 3 and two (7, 8) lie above.

    One natural way to compute the median proceeds in two steps:

I. Sort the array.
II. Determine the middle element.

We have already seen several ways to sort arrays, and we will not comment further on Step I. Step II does require a little discussion.

    In the example, 1, 2, 3, 7, 8, we had no trouble picking the "middle" element. The middle is less clear, however, for the numbers 1, 2, 3, 7, 8, 9. In this example there are two middle elements, 3 and 7. You can average these to get $(3 + 7)/2 = 5$ as the one middle value. More generally, the middle value is chosen as follows:

I. Sort the array $a_1, \ldots, a_n$.
II. Determine the middle value:
Let $m := (n + 1)$ *Div* 2.
Then there are two cases:
  A. If n is odd, then median $= a_m$.
  B. If n is even, then median $= (a_m + a_{m+1})/2$

Measures of Central Tendency and Dispersion

While median and mean can give some idea of the middle of the data, you may want some information about the "spread" of the data. For example, the sample 5, 5, 5, 5, 5, 5, and the sample 1, 1, 1, 9, 9, 9 both have medians and means of 5, but the samples have rather different characters. (If these were the test scores for a ten-point test in a class of six students, you would hardly say the class performances were the same.) You need a measure that reflects the distance from each datum to the median.

A natural first approach is to consider the distance between the mean m and a point a_i. This distance is $|a_i - m|$ or $abs(a_i - m)$. To put these distances together, you might find an average:

$$\text{average distance} = \frac{|a_1 - m| + |a_2 - m| + \cdots + |a_n - m|}{n}.$$

Unfortunately, it turns out that the absolute values in this formula cause some technical problems when they are used in various ways. Thus, while this average is conceptually easy, it is technically hard to work with and thus it is rarely used.

You can arrive at a similar result if you replace the absolute value by a square, $(a_i - m)^2$. These values are all nonnegative and you can put them together by averaging as before. This gives

$$\text{variance} = \frac{(a_1 - m)^2 + (a_2 - m)^2 + \cdots + (a_n - m)^2}{n}.$$

and

$$\text{standard deviation} = \sqrt{\text{variance}}$$

Returning to the example, the standard deviation of the numbers 5, 5, 5, 5, 5, 5 is 0 (no values are different from the mean). The standard deviation of the numbers 1, 1, 1, 9, 9, 9 is 4 (all values are 4 away from the mean). The standard deviation provides a reasonable way to distinguish between these different types of data.

Those interested in using computers for more complex statistical computations should note that various statistical programs or packages are available on many machines. These packages often have extensive capabilities for entering and editing data, and they perform a wide range of statistical tests. You might want to investigate such common packages as SPSS, BMDP, Minitab, or RS/1.

SUMMARY

1. **Arrays** allow you to use subscripts to help solve problems that require you to keep track of many pieces of data at once.
2. To use subscripted variables, declare the name of the array, the type of subscript and the range of values allowed, and the type of data stored in the array. With this declaration the computer can allocate the appropriate storage space in main memory to store the data.
3. Arrays may be used in two ways: Individual elements in the array may be referenced by placing the appropriate subscript in square brackets [   ]. The entire array may be considered as a single entity for assignments and for parameter passage.
4. You can define your own type of data with a *Type* statement. Use a *Type* statement to declare several variables or parameters to have the same type.
5. Several common applications of arrays include **searching** through an array of data to find a particular item, **sorting** a set of data to put the data in order, and computing statistics.
6. Particular algorithms introduced include **linear** or **sequential search, binary search, bubble** or **exchange sort, straight selection sort,** and **insertion sort.**
7. Statistical analysis includes computation of the **mean,** the **median,** the **variance,** and the **standard deviation.**
8. Once you have developed an algorithm to perform a task, you can analyze the algorithm to evaluate its **efficiency.**

EXERCISES

8.1 *Modified Linear Search.* Modify the Linear Search program from Problem 8.2 so that the computer prints where the item is in the array in the case that the element is found.
(Hint: Determine the array subscript where the item is located.)

8.2 *Improved Bubble Sort.* Modify the Bubble Sort to include the improvements suggested in Section 8.5.

8.3 In the first approach to inserting items into an array (Section 8.7), we used a Boolean function to determine when a shift was needed. Look at the condition for shifting and discuss why the function was used.

8.4   Write a complete editing program, following the outline from Section 8.7.

8.5   The Binary-Search Insert procedure in Section 8.7 fails if the array contains no elements (i.e., if *Number* = 0), since in the initial test, *Item* > *Element*[*Number*], the subscript of *Element* is not between 1 and *Max*. Correct the procedure to allow for this special case.

8.6   Throughout Section 8.7, a *Type* statement is used to specify the form of data under consideration in the array. Discuss why you think this approach was used.

8.7   *One-Array Insertion Sort*. Modify the Insertion Sort procedure in Section 8.7 so that only one array is used.

8.8   *Comparison of Bubble and Insertion Sorts*. Write a program that uses the Bubble, Improved Bubble, and Insertion Sorts to order data. Have your program count the number of loop iterations and the number of comparisons between array elements in each algorithm.

Use an initialization procedure to establish the original array. Run your program with the following arrays:

a. data in ascending order

(e.g., *For I* := 1 *To N Do A*[*I*] := *I*)

b. data in descending order

c. random data

(e.g., *For I* := 1 *To N Do A*[*I*] := *Random*

KEY TERMS, PHRASES, AND CONCEPTS		ELEMENTS OF PASCAL SYNTAX

Analysis of
Algorithms
Array
  Declarations
  As Parameter
  Use for Data
    Storage And
    Retrieval
Array Manipulation
  Data Deletion
  Data Insertion
Efficiency
Searching Algorithms
  Binary
  Sequential (or
    Linear)
	Sorting Algorithms
	  Bubble or Exchange
	  Improved Bubble
	  Insertion
	  Straight Selection
	Statistics
	  Mean
	  Median
	  Standard Deviation
	  Variance
	Subscript
	Type Specification
		Array [. .] *of* Type
		Subscript [--]
		Type

where *Random* is the random number generator from Section 4.4 or Appendix C-2)

Compare your results (by hand).

8.9 *Comparing Linear and Binary Searches.* Write a program that uses both Linear and Binary Searches to find elements in an array of data. Have your program count the number of iterations required to find the desired item or to conclude the element is missing.

Use an initialization procedure to establish the original array. Run your program on sorted data containing at least 100 items (e.g., *For I :=* 1 *To N Do A[I] :=* 2*I). Choose a variety of items to search for.

Compare your results (by hand).

8.10 *Counting Repetitions.* Write a program that reads 20 integers into an array and then prints the distinct integers together with the number of times each integer appears. For example, if the initial data were

3, 1, 4, 1, 5, 9, 2, 6, 5, 3, 5, 8, 9, 7, 9, 3, 2, 3, 8, 4

then the output might be

Element	Number of Occurrences
0	0
1	2
2	2
3	4
4	2
5	3
6	1
7	1
8	2
9	3

8.11 *Elementary Statistical Package.* Combine various procedures in this chapter to produce a program with the following steps:

A. Enter data.

B. Edit data (insert, delete, change one value to another).

C. Sort data.

D. Compute statistics:
  mean
  median
  variance
  standard deviation

8.12 *Sieve of Eratosthenes.* In ancient Greece, Eratosthenes gave the following algorithm for determining all prime numbers up to a specfied number *M*:

I. Write down the numbers 2, 3, . . ., *M*.

II. Cross out numbers as follows:

A. Keep 2, but cross out all multiples of 2 (i.e., cross out 4, 6, 8 . . .).
B. Keep 3, but cross out all multiples of 3 (i.e., 6, 9, . . .) (Note: While 6 is crossed out twice, it only matters that it has been crossed out. We will attach no significance to the number of times the 6 is crossed out.)
C. Since 4 is already crossed out, go on to the next number that is not crossed out (i.e., 5). Keep 5, but cross out all multiples of 5 (i.e., 10, 15, . . .).

General Step. In general, suppose you have just processed the number P. Go on to the next number that is not crossed out—Q.

Keep Q, but cross out all multiples of Q.

After you have finished all the crossing out, the numbers remaining are primes.

This method is called the **Sieve Method of Eratosthenes.** Write a program to implement this method, where M is a constant defined in the program. Run your program for $M = 100$ and $M = 500$.

Programming Hints. Use an array

Var Keep: Array [2. .M] of Boolean

to record which elements are still kept and which are crossed out.

Begin with each *Keep[I] set equal to True.* When you cross out the number *I*, set *Keep[I]* to *False.*

8.13 *Tabulating Polynomial Functions.* Polynomial functions are often written in the form

$$p(x) = a_n x^n + a_{n-1} x^{n-1} + \cdots + a_2 x^2 + a_1 x + a_0.$$

Write a program that reads the coefficients $a_n, a_{n-1}, \ldots, a_2, a_1, a_0$ and then uses these coefficients to compute $p(x)$ for $x = 0, 0.5, 1, 1.5, 2.0, \ldots, 10$.

NOTE: One efficient way to compute $p(x)$ without using powers is to use algebra to rewrite the polynomial. Here are two examples of the general technique:

$$2x^3 - 3x^2 + 5x - 6 = x(2x^2 - 3x + 5) - 6$$
$$= x[x(2x - 3) + 5] - 6.$$

$$a_4 x^4 + a_3 x^3 + a_2 x^2 + a_1 x + a_0 = x(a_4 x^3 + a_3 x^2 + a_2 x + a_1) + a_0$$
$$= x[x(a_4 x^2 + a_3 x + a_2) + a_1] + a_0$$
$$= x\{x[x (a_4 x + a_3) + a_2] + a_1\}$$
$$+ a_0.$$

Optional Problems. This general factoring approach is called **Horner's method.** This approach is quite efficient for evaluating general polynomials.

a. Find the general formula to compute p(x) using this factoring process, and incorporate this approach in your program.

b. Determine the number of additions and multiplications required to compute p(x) using Horner's method.

8.14 *Racquetball Simulation.* Simulate a game of racquetball, given the probability of one player winning a given point. (Racquetball rules are outlined in Chapter 7, Exercise 12.) Run your simulation 20,000 times and record who wins and the score of the loser.

a. Present your results in tabular form, such as

Player A has probability _____ of winning a volley.

Wins for Player A			Wins for Player B		
B's Score			A's Score		
0:	0.5%		0:	1.3%	
1:	1.0%		1:	2.5%	
2:			2:		
3:			3:		
·			·		
·			·		
·			·		
20:			20:		

b. Compute the mean, median, and standard deviation of A's score.

8.15 *Coin Tossing Until Heads Appears.* A coin is to be tossed until a head appears. Simulate this activity and record the number of tosses required. Determine the average and median number of tosses and the standard deviation.

Programming Hints. You might store the number of tosses in an array

Var Tosses:[1. .Max] of Integer

where *Tosses[I]* records the number of times you stop in exactly *I* tosses.

Since it is possible that the number of tosses required in one trial is larger than *Max*, you might want to have a separate variable *ExcessiveTosses* to lump together the records of all trials that require more than *Max* tosses. For example, you might write

If Throws < = Max
    Then Tosses[Throws] : = Tosses[Throws] + 1
    Else ExcessiveTosses : = ExcessiveTosses + 1

CHAPTER 9

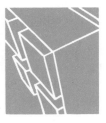

MULTIPLE SUBSCRIPTS:
ARRAYS WITH
SEVERAL SUBSCRIPTS

$\mathbf{W}$e began the previous chapter by considering problems that required keeping track of all of our data at once; we could not process one item and discard it when we moved on to the next item. For example, to sort we needed to have all the data inside the machine at once. To tackle these problems we used one name (e.g., *Element*) to represent the information as a whole, and we used single subscripts (e.g., *Element*[1], *Element*[2]) to distinguish among the particular pieces of data.

In this chapter we will consider problems where a single subscript is not adequate to outline a solution easily. For example, to consider data in tabular form, we want to indicate a row and column within the table. This chapter will expand our work with arrays to allow multiple subscripts.

SECTION 9.1   **EXAMPLE: WAREHOUSE INVENTORY**

We begin our work with an example.

PROBLEM 9.1   A manufacturer requires eight types of parts, which are stored in five warehouses. Table 9–1 shows the cost of each part and the inventory level of the various parts in the different warehouses.

TABLE 9–1 · Warehouse Inventory

Part number	Part cost	Warehouse 1	2	3	4	5
1	$1.25	3	1	4	1	5
2	$3.37	9	2	6	5	3
3	$0.79	5	8	9	7	9
4	$4.73	3	2	3	8	4
5	$1.97	6	2	6	4	3
6	$0.67	3	8	3	2	7
7	$2.29	9	5	0	2	8
8	$3.85	8	4	1	9	7

a. Compute the total number of parts and the total cost of these parts in each warehouse.

b. Compute the total number of each type of part.

Discussion of Problem 9.1

Table 9–1 contains two types of information, cost data and inventory levels. The table associates cost information with each type of part and organizes the inventory data in tabular form. Thus, to solve the problem, we want to think of cost data as depending upon part number, and we want to maintain the tabular form for inventory data.

To notate this data, we can use a single subscript for cost. $Cost_1$, $Cost_2$, . . ., $Cost_8$ can represent the costs of various parts, and we might use an array *Cost* to store the information. Considering the inventory table, however, we need to know both the part number and the warehouse. We might notate this data with two subscripts, in the general form *Inventory* $_{Part, Warehouse}$ for the inventory of the particular part in the specified warehouse.

This representation of data allows us to work with our table directly. We can use this tabular form to guide our solution to the problem. In particular, we can find the total number of parts in a warehouse [part (a) of the problem] by adding down each column in the table. We can find the total number of each type of part [part (b)] by adding across each row. Here is the outline for this problem:

Outline for Problem 9.1

 I. Enter table information:
   A. Part costs.
   B. Inventory levels:
     1. Read a row of inventories at a time, for the warehouse levels of a given part.
 II. Compute totals for each warehouse:
   A. Print headings for warehouse totals.

B. Repeat the following for each warehouse:
1. Totals start at 0:
   Number of parts := 0
   Cost of parts := 0.
2. Add down the column for the warehouse for each type of part:
   a. Add part inventory.
   b. Add cost of part.
3. Print totals for each warehouse.

III. Compute totals for each part:
Repeat the following for each part:
A. Totals start at 0:
   Part inventory := 0
B. Add across the row for the part.
   For each warehouse:
   1. Add part inventory.
C. Print total part inventory.

The addition process is similar to work we have done previously. It starts with Sum := 0, then we add successive numbers (down a column or across a row). A new feature is the use of two subscripts for referencing the inventory. The following program illustrates how to include double subscripts in Pascal code. Again, we use type statements so that we can specify that the procedure parameters are tables.

```
Program Inventory {Version 1} (Input, Output);
{This program reads part-warehouse information and
 computes and prints various totals.}

Const MaxPart = 8;      {Number of types of parts}
      MaxWare = 5;      {Number of warehouses}

Type CostArray = Array[1..MaxPart] of Real;
     Table = Array[1..MaxPart, 1..MaxWare] Of Integer;

Var Price: CostArray;
    InventoryLevel: Table;

Procedure EnterData (Var Cost: CostArray; Var Inventory: Table);
{Procedure to enter Part Costs and Inventory Levels}

    Var Part, Warehouse: Integer;   {Control Variables}

    Begin
        {Read Cost Information}
        Writeln ('Enter the cost of each type of part');
        For Part := 1 To MaxPart
          Do Begin
            Write ('Cost of Part Type ', Part:1, ': ');
            Readln (Cost[Part])
          End;
```

```
                {Read Inventory Levels one row at a time}
                For Part := 1 To MaxPart
                    Do Begin
                        Writeln ('Enter inventory levels for part type ',
                                Part:1, ' for the ', MaxWare:1, ' warehouses');
                        For Warehouse := 1 To MaxWare
                                Do Read(Inventory[Part, Warehouse])
                    End
        End {EnterData} ;

Procedure ComputeWarehouseTotals (Cost: CostArray; Inventory: Table);
{Procedure to compute number of parts in each warehouse and the
  total cost of those parts}

        Var Part, Warehouse: Integer;   {Control Variables}
            Number: Integer;     {Total number of parts for given warehouse}
            PCost: Real;         {Total cost of parts for warehouse}

        Begin
            {Print Warehouse Headings}
            Writeln;
            Writeln ('Warehouse Totals');
            Writeln;
            Writeln ('                Number      Cost');
            Writeln ('                  of         of');
            Writeln ('Warehouse        Parts      Parts');
            Writeln;

            For Warehouse := 1 To MaxWare
                Do Begin

                    {Totals start at 0}
                    Number := 0;
                    PCost := 0.0;

                    {Add down columns of the table}
                    For Part := 1 To MaxPart
                        Do Begin
                            Number := Number + Inventory[Part, Warehouse];
                            PCost := PCost + Inventory[Part,Warehouse] * Cost[Part]
                        End;

                    {Print warehouse totals}
                    Writeln (Warehouse:5, Number:11, PCost:11:2)

                End {Warehouse computation}

        End {ComputeWarehouseTotals} ;

Procedure ComputePartTotals (Inventory: Table);
{Procedure to compute to total number of each type of part}

        Var Part, Warehouse: Integer;   {Control Variables}
            Total: Integer;      {Total number of parts of given type}

        Begin
            Writeln;
            Writeln ('Part Totals');
            Writeln;
```

```
      For Part := 1 To MaxPart
         Do Begin
            Total := 0;

            {Add part inventories accross a row}
            For Warehouse := 1 To MaxWare
                Do Total := Total + Inventory[Part, Warehouse];

            {Print total}
            Writeln ('There are ', Total:1, ' parts of type ',
                Part:1, '.')

         End {Part computation}

   End {ComputePartTotals} ;

Begin {Main}
     Writeln ('This program computes various part-warehouse totals.');

     EnterData (Price, InventoryLevel);

     ComputeWarehouseTotals (Price, InventoryLevel);

     ComputePartTotals (InventoryLevel)

End {Main} .
```

When this program is run using the data from Table 9–1, we get the following results:

```
This program computes various part-warehouse totals.
Enter the cost of each type of part
Cost of Part Type 1: 1.25
Cost of Part Type 2: 3.37
Cost of Part Type 3: 0.79
Cost of Part Type 4: 4.73
Cost of Part Type 5: 1.97
Cost of Part Type 6: 0.67
Cost of Part Type 7: 2.29
Cost of Part Type 8: 3.85
Enter inventory levels for part type 1 for the 5 warehouses
3 1 4 1 5
Enter inventory levels for part type 2 for the 5 warehouses
9 2 6 5 3
Enter inventory levels for part type 3 for the 5 warehouses
5 8 9 7 9
Enter inventory levels for part type 4 for the 5 warehouses
3 2 3 8 4
Enter inventory levels for part type 5 for the 5 warehouses
6 2 6 4 3
Enter inventory levels for part type 6 for the 5 warehouses
3 8 3 2 7
Enter inventory levels for part type 7 for the 5 warehouses
9 5 0 2 8
```

```
Enter inventory levels for part type 8 for the 5 warehouses
8 4 1 9 7
```

```
Warehouse Totals

                Number       Cost
                  of          of
Warehouse       Parts       Parts

    1             46        117.46
    2             32         59.92
    3             32         64.20
    4             38        109.92
    5             46         98.26
```

```
Part Totals

There are 14 parts of type 1.
There are 25 parts of type 2.
There are 38 parts of type 3.
There are 20 parts of type 4.
There are 21 parts of type 5.
There are 23 parts of type 6.
There are 24 parts of type 7.
There are 29 parts of type 8.
```

SECTION 9.2   ELEMENTS OF ARRAYS (MULTIPLE SUBSCRIPTS)

With the inventory example in the previous section, we are ready to consider the use of two or more subscripts in Pascal more closely.

Two Subscripts

The previous section illustrates one way that Pascal allows us to use multiple subscripts in programs. In the program, we declared

> Var Inventory: Array[1. .MaxPart, 1. .MaxWare] of Integer

Then we could refer to a particular entry in the table by writing *Inventory [7, 3]* or *Inventory [Part, Warehouse]*.

More generally, we can declare an array

> *Var* Name: *Array* [Range$_1$,Range$_2$] *of* DataType

where *Name* is the variable name (or identifier) for the array; *Range$_1$* specifies the possible values for the first subscript; *Range$_2$* specifies the possible values for the second subscript; and *DataType* specifies the type of data stored in the array. In the example, we had the correspondences:

> *Inventory—Name*
> 1. .*MaxPart—Range$_1$*
> 1. .*MaxWare—Range$_2$*
> *Integer—DataType*

To refer to an item in the array, then, specify the identifier *Name*, and give the specific values for the subscripts in square brackets [ ]. Once you declare an array, you can solve problems by working with this table. Use of a table motivated the program in the previous section.

Many Subscripts

In other problems, we may want more than two subscripts. For example, for weather forecasting we may want to record the temperature at various places on the earth and at various heights above the earth. Thus, we may want a temperature with subscripts for latitude, longitude, and height. If we measure latitude and longitude in tens of degrees and height in thousands of feet above the earth, then we might declare

> Var Temp: Array[0. .18, 0. .36, 0. .10] of Real;

We can refer to the temperature at latitude 20°, longitude 50°, height 10,000 feet by *Temp*[2, 5, 10].

In fact, Pascal allows you to use as many subscripts as you wish in arrays. In this general setting, declarations have the form

> *Var* Name: *Array* [Range$_1$,. . ., Range$_n$] *of* DataType

In this declaration, we specify the name of the array and the subscripts allowed. For each subscript we state the type of subscript (e.g., integer, Boolean) and the range of values (e.g., 0. .10, *False. .True*). We also specify the DataType being stored in the array (e.g., real temperature values). When we want to use the data, we can refer to particular items by specifying the array name and the appropriate subscript values.

While Pascal does not limit the number of subscripts available, in practice, particular compilers may have some limitations. Most compilers will allow several subscripts (up to 6 or 7), but they may not be able to work with more levels of subscripts. (We may have trouble with that many subscripts as well!)

Two Views

At this point in our discussion of subscripting, we have implicitly assumed one of two views of data. We can think of data as a whole (e.g., the entire table of inventories or an entire set of temperature readings), or we can focus on one particular piece of data (e.g., *Inventory*[7,3] or *Temp*[2,5,3]). Chapter 8 illustrated how a *Type* statement can support a view of data as a whole, defining a new type that is an entire array. We can then work with that array as a single entity when making assignments and when passing parameters.

Similar comments apply to using tables; we can use a *Type* statement to define a table as a separate entity. Thus, in the inventory program in Section 9.1, we might write

> Type Table = Array[1. .MaxPart, 1. .MaxWare] of Integer;
> Var Inventory: Table;

Here, we view our table of inventories as a single object, and we can work with the entire table. If we also declared

Var NewItems: Table;

we could set one table equal to the other by writing

NewItems : = Inventory

Similarly, we could use a table as a parameter for procedures and functions.

More Views of Data

This two-level view of arrays (entire array and specific array elements) often is quite adequate for many applications, particularly when you only want one subscript. You may find, however, that some intermediate views can also be helpful when considering tables (or several subscripts.) For example, in the inventory problem you may want to focus on the rows of the table, or on the columns.

In Pascal, the *Type* statement allows us to work with some of these intermediate views. For example, when we viewed the table of inventories as a whole, we wrote

Type Table = Array[1. .MaxPart, 1. .MaxWare] of Integer;
Var Inventory: Table;

Alternately, we could think of the table as being made up of rows, with one row for each type of part. In this case, we could write

Type PartTotals = Array[1. .MaxWare] of Integer;
        Table = Array[1. .MaxPart] of PartTotals;
Var   Inventory: Table;

Here, we have the same choices for arrays with several subscripts that we had in the previous chapter, for arrays with one subscript. We can work with any array as a complete collection of data, and we can reference individual items. For example, after writing

NewItems : = Inventory

we can print a specific item in the table, such as

Writeln (NewItems[7, 3]);

With these declarations we could also consider the inventory levels for Part 1 or Part 2. When we focus on the inventory for a specific part, we use one row of the table. With this view of our data, we could write *Inventory* [1] to stand for the entire row for PartType 1. *Inventory* [1] represents the row:

3 1 4 1 5

Thus, *Inventory* [1] is an array with five elements. More precisely, *Inven-*

tory [1] has the data type *PartTotals,* which we declared as

PartTotals = Array[1. .MaxWare] of Integer;

Within this row, we can ask about the third piece of data (the inventory for Warehouse 3). To be more precise, we ask about element [3] in *Inventory* [1], and we write *Inventory* [1] [3]. Alternatively, Pascal allows us to simplify the notation, omitting the middle brackets, so we can write this as *Inventory* [1, 3].

With these declarations, then, we can view our data in three ways:

Inventory represents the entire table.

Inventory[7] represents the seventh row of the table.

Inventory[7, 3] or *Inventory*[7][3] represents the element in the third column of row seven.

As an illustration of these views of our data, we have rewritten the inventory program with these alternate declarations of Type *Table* and Array *Inventory.* In the first part of the program, we still enter the data with two subscripts, just as we did earlier. In Step II, to work with columns, we can still proceed by referring to each item in a given column. In Step III, however, we use a row as a separate entity, and we pass each row of the table to a procedure to compute and print the totals.

```
Program Inventory {Version 2} (Input, Output);
{This program reads part-warehouse information and
 computes and prints various totals.}

Const MaxPart = 8;       {Number of types of parts}
      MaxWare = 5;       {Number of warehouses}

Type CostArray = Array [1..MaxPart] of Real;
     PartTotals = Array[1..MaxWare] Of Integer;
     Table = Array [1..MaxPart] Of PartTotals;

Var Price: CostArray;
    InventoryLevel: Table;

Procedure EnterData (Var Cost: CostArray; Var Inventory: Table);
{Procedure to enter Part Costs and Inventory Levels}

    Var Part, Warehouse: Integer;   {Control Variables}

    Begin
        {Read Cost Information}
        Writeln ('Enter the cost of each type of part');
        For Part := 1 To MaxPart
          Do Begin
             Write ('Cost of Part Type ', Part:1, ': ');
             Readln (Cost[Part])
          End;
```

```
      {Read Inventory Levels one row at a time}
      For Part := 1 To MaxPart
        Do Begin
          Writeln ('Enter inventory levels for part type ',
              Part:1, ' for the ', MaxWare:1, ' warehouses');
          For Warehouse := 1 To MaxWare
              Do Read(Inventory[Part, Warehouse])
        End
  End {EnterData} ;

Procedure ComputeWarehouseTotals (Cost: CostArray; Inventory: Table);
{Procedure to compute number of parts in each warehouse and the
  total cost of those parts}

    Var Part, Warehouse: Integer;  {Control Variables}
        Number: Integer;      {Total number of parts for given warehouse}
        PCost: Real;          {Total cost of parts for warehouse}

    Begin
        {Print Warehouse Headings}
        Writeln;
        Writeln ('Warehouse Totals');
        Writeln;
        Writeln ('              Number      Cost');
        Writeln ('              of          of');
        Writeln ('Warehouse     Parts       Parts');
        Writeln;

        For Warehouse := 1 To MaxWare
          Do Begin

            {Totals start at 0}
            Number := 0;
            PCost := 0.0;

            {Add down columns of the table}
            For Part := 1 To MaxPart
              Do Begin
                Number := Number + Inventory[Part, Warehouse];
                PCost := PCost + Inventory[Part,Warehouse] * Cost[Part]
              End;

            {Print warehouse totals}
            Writeln (Warehouse:5, Number:11, PCost:11:2)

          End {Warehouse computation}

    End {ComputeWarehouseTotals} ;

Procedure TypeTotal (Row: PartTotals; PartNumber: Integer);
{This procedure computes the total number of parts,
  given the inventory levels in each warehouse.}

    Var Warehouse: Integer;   {Control Variable for Warehouse}
        Total: Integer;       {Part total for the given type}
```

```
Begin
    Total := 0;

    {Add part inventories accross a row}
    For Warehouse := 1 To MaxWare
        Do Total := Total + Row[Warehouse];

    {Print total}
    Writeln ('There are ', Total:1, ' parts of type ',
        PartNumber:1, '.')

End {TypeTotal} ;
Procedure ComputePartTotals (Inventory: Table);
{Procedure to compute to total number of each type of part}

    Var Part: Integer;     {Control Variable for Part Type}

    Begin
        Writeln;
        Writeln ('Part Totals');
        Writeln;

        For Part := 1 To MaxPart
            Do TypeTotal(Inventory[Part], Part)

    End {ComputePartTotals} ;

Begin {Main}
    Writeln ('This program computes various part-warehouse totals.');

    EnterData (Price, InventoryLevel);

    ComputeWarehouseTotals (Price, InventoryLevel);

    ComputePartTotals (InventoryLevel)

End {Main} .
```

This program follows the same outline as the example in Section 9.1 and produces identical output, but it illustrates how to work with rows of a table, as well as with individual elements.

We can make one additional observation. Pascal allowed us to define a row *PartTotals* and then put these rows together to get an entire table. Once we work with rows, however, we have no mechanism to work with columns at the same time. Pascal does not allow us to consider both rows and columns of the same table in a program. If we decide *Inventory*[2] will represent a row of the table, we cannot decide that this symbol will also represent a column later on.

In the next section we will look at another example involving several subscripts.

SECTION 9.3 — EXAMPLE: STORING GAME BOARDS AND MAPS

Multiple subscripting can be useful in a great many applications. In this section, we consider an example of storing data on game boards or maps. To be concrete, we focus on the game of Tic-Tac-Toe.

PROBLEM 9.3 — Tic-Tac-Toe

Two people play Tic-Tac-Toe, alternately writing Xs and Os on a game board. Write a program that reads successive moves, prints out the board after each move, and stops either when one player wins or when all squares are filled.

Discussion of Problem 9.3

When we picture a Tic-Tac-Toe board (Figure 9–1), we can identify three rows and three columns. Thus, we can consider the board as a 3-by-3 table or array. The upper right square would be in Row 1, Column 3, and we might refer to the element $Board[1, 3]$.

For each square we can identify three possible situations: The square could be blank; the square could contain an X; or the square could contain an O. For convenience, we will code these choices as integer constants as follows:

Square	Code
X	-1
blank	0
O	1

A game is won when there are all Xs or all Os in a row, in a column,

FIGURE 9–1 • A Tic-Tac-Toe Board with Labeled Rows and Columns

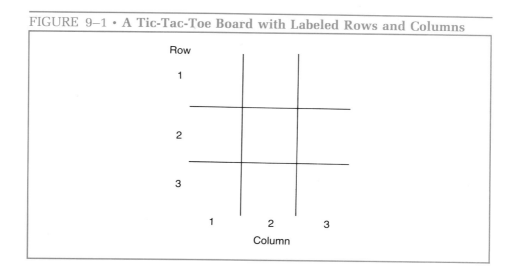

or on a diagonal. With our coding, this says that a game is won when the sum of the entries in a row, a column, or a diagonal is $+3$ or -3. Thus, after each play, we could find the sum of each row, each column and each diagonal. If any of these sums is $+3$ or -3, then the game is over.

To check for a win after each move, we can reduce our work considerably by some additional analysis. When we write an X or an O, we will change only the row and the column that contain this move. Other rows and columns are not affected.

We can check if the move is on a diagonal by carefully analyzing the square (see Figure 9–2). Row = Column means the square is on the diagonal moving down to the right. Row + Column = 4 means the square is on the diagonal moving up to the right.

Finally, note that after nine moves the game must be done, since the board contains only nine squares.

Outline for Problem 9.3

I. Initialize board:
   A. All squares are blank.
   B. Number of moves is 0.
   C. Neither side has won.
   D. X will play first.
II. Repeat the following for each move until one side wins or until all nine squares are filled:
   A. Read move (row and column).
      1. Increase number of moves by one.
      2. Check move is legal (check that row and column are on board; check the square was blank).
      3. Record move.

FIGURE 9–2 • **A Tic-Tac-Toe Board with Diagonals Analyzed**

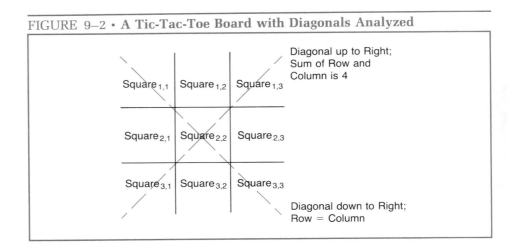

  B. Print revised board:
   1. Print board, one row at a time.
   2. Print dashes between rows.
  C. Check if game is won.
  D. Other player will move next.
 III. Record outcome of game:
  Either X wins, O wins, or there is a draw.

Checking User Input

Before we write the program based on this outline, we note a special feature in reading data, which we have not seen before. In reading a move, we can check the input to see if the move is legal. In particular, we can check that the row is 1, 2, or 3; the column is 1, 2, or 3; and the square chosen is blank. If any of these conditions is violated, then the information entered cannot be correct, and we can ask the user to correct the data.

 This is a specific example of a general principle, which we can incorporate into many programs. When we ask a user to enter data, we should try to determine if the data are reasonable. Unreasonable data may indicate a typographical error. When requesting data, we should allow for the possibility of error, and we should plan how the program will respond to incorrect information.

 In the present program, we ask the user to retype data that is obviously wrong. In other programs, we might allow the user to modify all or part of the data before continuing, or we might require the user to run the program all over again.

 We now write the program based on the outline. Note how it tests data for a legal move. Note also that it uses a Boolean variable *PlayerXMoves* to indicate if X moves next or not.

```
Program PlayTicTacToe (Input, Output);
{This program reads moves in Tic-Tac-Toe,
 prints out the board after each move, and
 stops when either one player wins or
      when all squares are filled.}

Const X = -1;          {our code for the play "X"}
      O = 1;           {our code for the play "O"}
      Blank = 0;       {our code for a blank square}

Type RowOfBoard = Array [1..3] Of Integer;
     GameBoard = Array[1..3] Of RowOfBoard;

Var Board: GameBoard;              {the game board}
    XWins, OWins: Boolean;         {Record of the winner}
    PlayerXMoves: Boolean;         {True if "X" moves next}
    Moves: Integer;                {Number of moves in the game}
```

```
Procedure InitializeBoard (Var Board: GameBoard; Var Moves: Integer;
                           Var XWins, OWins, XMoves: Boolean);
{This procedure sets up the board and initializes variables}
    Var Row, Col: Integer;
    Begin
        {Each square is blank}
        For Row := 1 to 3
            Do For Col := 1 to 3
                Do Board[Row. Col] := Blank;

        {No moves so far}
        Moves := 0;

        {Neither side has won}
        XWins := False;
        OWins := False;

        {"X" will play first}
        XMoves := True;
    End {InitializeBoard} ;

Procedure ReadMove (Var Moves, Row, Col: Integer; XMoves: Boolean;
                    Var Board: GameBoard);
{This procedure reads a legal move from the terminal}
    Var Legal: Boolean;
    Begin
        Moves := Moves + 1;
        If XMoves
            Then Writeln ('X moves next')
            Else Writeln ('O moves next');
        Writeln ('Enter row and column for move ', Moves:1);

        {Read until a legal move is entered}
        Repeat
            Read (Row, Col);

            {Determine if move is legal}
            Legal := (1 <= Row) And (Row <= 3) And
                     (1 <= Col) And (Col <= 3);
            If Legal
                Then Legal := (Board[Row, Col] = Blank);
            If Not Legal
                Then Writeln ('Move is not valid,',
                               ' please re-enter row and column')
        Until Legal;

        {Record move}
        If XMoves
            Then Board[Row, Col] := X
            Else Board[Row, Col] := O

    End {ReadMove} ;

Procedure PrintSquare (Square:Integer);
{Procedure prints the given square of the board}
    Begin
        If Square = X
            Then Write ('  X  ');
```

```pascal
        If Square = 0
            Then Write ('  O  ');
        If Square = Blank
            Then Write ('     ')
    End {PrintSquare} ;

Procedure PrintRow (Row: RowOfBoard);
{Procedure prints the specified row of the board}

    Begin {PrintRow}
        Writeln ('     |     |');

        {Print each square in the row}
        PrintSquare (Row[1]);
        Write ('|');
        PrintSquare(Row[2]);
        Write ('|');
        PrintSquare(Row[3]);
        Writeln;

        Writeln ('     |     |');
    End {PrintRow} ;

Procedure PrintBoard (Moves: Integer; Board: GameBoard);
{Procedure prints the Tic-Tac-Toe Board}

    Begin {PrintBoard}
        Writeln;
        Writeln ('Board position after move', Moves:2);
        Writeln;

        PrintRow(Board[1]);
        Writeln ('-----+-----+-----');
        PrintRow(Board[2]);
        Writeln ('-----+-----+-----');
        PrintRow(Board[3]);

        Writeln
    End {PrintBoard} ;

Procedure Check (Code: Integer; Var XWins, OWins: Boolean);
{Procedure checks if Code gives a win for X or for O}
    Begin
        If Code = -3
            Then XWins := True;
        If Code = 3
            Then OWins := True
    End {CheckForWin} ;

Procedure CheckForWin (Var XWins, YWins: Boolean; Board: GameBoard;
                       NRow, NCol: Integer);
{This procedure checks to see if the latest move has causes
 either player X or player O to win}
    Begin {CheckForWin}
        {Check row for possible win}
        Check(Board[NRow,1] + Board[NRow,2] + Board[NRow,3], XWins, OWins);
```

```
            {Check column for possible win}
            Check(Board[1,NCol] + Board[2,NCol] + Board[3,NCol], XWins, OWins);

            {Check diagonals, if appropriate}
            If NRow = NCol
                Then Check(Board[1,1] + Board[2,2] + Board[3,3], XWins, OWins);
            If (NRow + NCol = 4)
                Then Check(Board[1,3] + Board[2,2] + Board[3,1], XWins, OWins)
    End {CheckForWin} ;

Procedure PlayGame (Var Board: GameBoard; Var Moves: Integer;
                    Var XWins, OWins, PlayerXMoves: Boolean);

{This procedure plays Tic-Tac-Toe, reading successive moves
 from the terminal}
    Var NewRow, NewCol: Integer;   {The square for the new move}


    Begin {Playgame}
        Repeat
            ReadMove (Moves, NewRow, NewCol, PlayerXMoves, Board);
            PrintBoard (Moves, Board);
            CheckForWin (Xwins, OWins, Board, NewRow, NewCol);
            {Note other player moves next}
            PlayerXMoves := Not PlayerXMoves
        Until XWins Or OWins Or (Moves = 9)
    End {PlayGame} ;

Procedure CheckGameOutcome (XWins, OWins: Boolean);
{This procedure prints the final outcome of the game}
    Begin
        If XWins
            Then Writeln('"X" has won the game');
        If OWins
            Then Writeln('"O" has won the game');
        If Not(XWins or OWins)
            Then Writeln('The game ends in a draw')
    End {CheckGameOutcome} ;

Begin {Main}
    Writeln ('This program records the moves in a game of Tic-Tac-Toe');
    InitializeBoard (Board, Moves, XWins, OWins, PlayerXMoves);
    PlayGame (Board, Moves, XWins, OWins, PlayerXMoves);
    CheckGameOutcome (XWins, OWins)
End {Main} .
```

Note how the various parts of the outline are coded concisely as procedures, and how the program is divided into simple, modular procedures. While this program is somewhat long, each module is very easy to check; this program ran correctly the first time it was compiled!

A sample game is shown below:

```
This program records the moves in a game of Tic-Tac-Toe
X moves next
Enter row and column for move 1
1 1

Board position after move 1
```

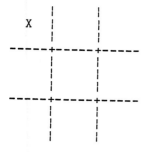

```
O moves next
Enter row and column for move 2
2 1

Board position after move 2
```

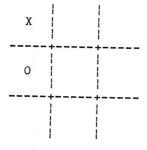

```
X moves next
Enter row and column for move 3
2 2

Board position after move 3
```

```
O moves next
Enter row and column for move 4
3 3

Board position after move 4

       |     |
   X   |     |
       |     |
-----+-----+-----
       |     |
   O   |  X  |
       |     |
-----+-----+-----
       |     |
       |     |  O
       |     |

X moves next
Enter row and column for move 5
1 3

Board position after move 5

       |     |
   X   |     |  X
       |     |
-----+-----+-----
       |     |
   O   |  X  |
       |     |
-----+-----+-----
       |     |
       |     |  O
       |     |

O moves next
Enter row and column for move 6
3 1

Board position after move 6

       |     |
   X   |     |  X
       |     |
-----+-----+-----
       |     |
   O   |  X  |
       |     |
-----+-----+-----
       |     |
   O   |     |  O
       |     |
```

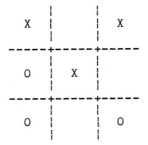

```
X moves next
Enter row and column for move 7
1 1
Move is not valid, please re-enter row and column
1 2

Board position after move 7
```

```
  X  |  X  |  X
     |     |
-----+-----+-----
     |     |
  0  |  X  |
     |     |
-----+-----+-----
     |     |
  0  |     |  0
     |     |
```

```
"X" has won the game
```

This Tic-Tac-Toe problem shows how to use an array with two subscripts to record information about a game board. A similar approach could be used to record information on a map, where *Map[Lat, Long]* represents the elevation (or temperature, or rainfall, etc.) at the given latitude and longitude.

<hr>

SECTION 9.4   ## STORAGE AND INDEXING OF ARRAYS

In using arrays to solve problems in this chapter and the previous one, we outlined only briefly how the information was actually stored; we did not have to worry about the details involved in using this data. This same situation is found in many other applications as well. We can use arrays without any knowledge of the internal structure of the data. In some circumstances, however, we may find a knowledge of this internal structure is useful. In this section, we will discuss some principles of this structure.

Storage of Singly Subscripted (One-Dimensional) Arrays

As we mentioned in Section 5.2, a computer's main memory is organized into distinct pieces, and each piece has its own **address** (see Figure 9–3). Each piece of memory has the same size, and the addresses are numbered consecutively.

When we work with an array, a block of main memory is used to store the array values. Thus, if we declare

Var List: Array[0. .10] of Integer

FIGURE 9–3 • **Main Memory in a Computer**

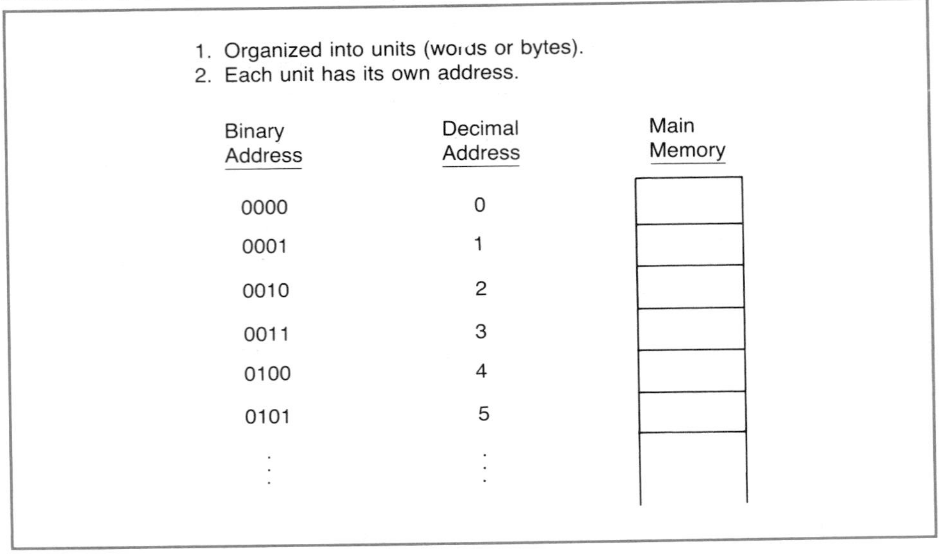

1. Organized into units (words or bytes).
2. Each unit has its own address.

Binary Address	Decimal Address	Main Memory
0000	0	
0001	1	
0010	2	
0011	3	
0100	4	
0101	5	
⋮	⋮	

and if we assume an integer requires one unit of space (as is often the case), then the computer will need to reserve a block of 11 units to work with this array. If this block of space started at decimal address 120, then the array would occupy locations 120–130, as shown in Figure 9–4.

When we look at this block of space, we see a pattern between the address in main memory and the elements of our array.

List[0] is stored in address 120.

List[1] is stored in address 121.

List[2] is stored in address 122.

.

.

.

List[10] is stored in address 130.

In particular, the first array element, List[0], is stored in address 120. To find the location of List[I], then, we can count I units from the starting address. More formally, List[I] is stored in address 120 + I. In fact, all arrays can be stored using this same idea. First, we need to know where the first element of the array is stored. This is the **base address** for the array. To determine where subsequent array elements are located, count from this first element. This counting gives us an **offset** from the base ad-

FIGURE 9–4 · Space Reserved for Var List: Array [0. .10] of Integer;

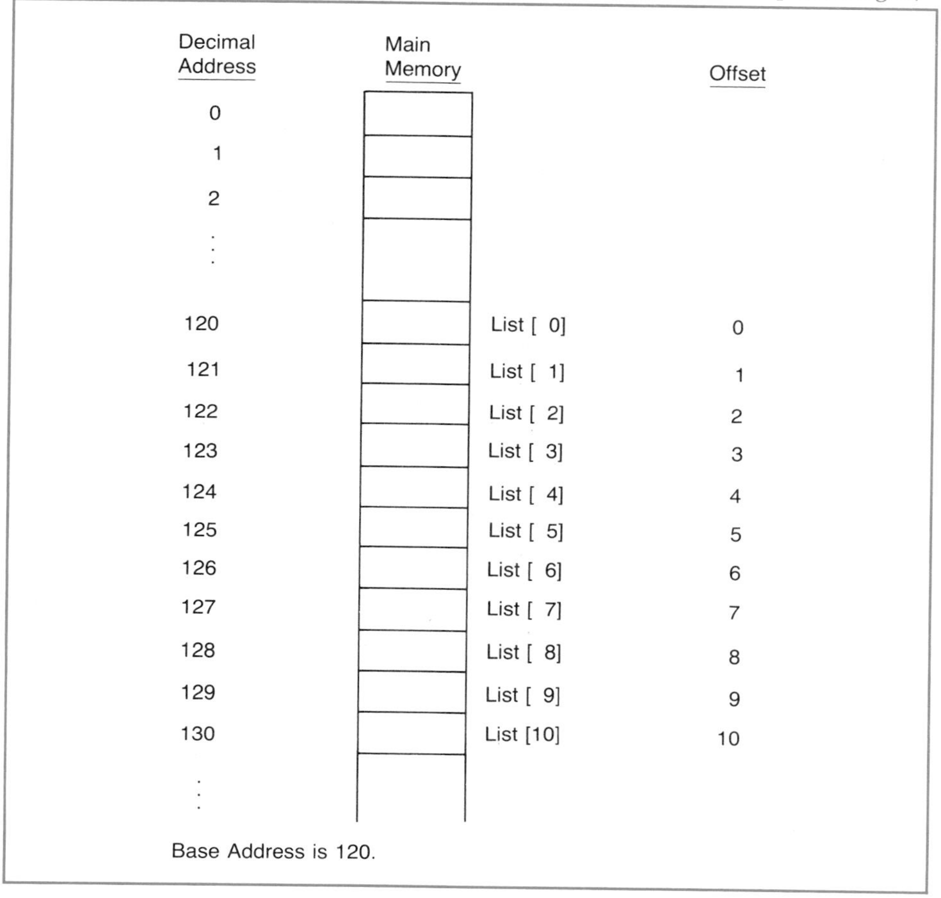

Decimal Address	Main Memory		Offset
0			
1			
2			
:			
120		List [0]	0
121		List [1]	1
122		List [2]	2
123		List [3]	3
124		List [4]	4
125		List [5]	5
126		List [6]	6
127		List [7]	7
128		List [8]	8
129		List [9]	9
130		List [10]	10
:			

Base Address is 120.

dress. Thus, to determine where a particular array element is stored, compute the base address (where the array starts) and the offset (distance from the base). Then desired address := base address + offset.

Storage of Doubly Subscripted Arrays

The approach is similar to store a doubly subscripted array, but we have to be more careful with some details. In particular, while we consider a table as existing with rows and columns, this data must be organized in one long sequence of values in main memory. To see how this can be done, consider the declaration:

Var Table: Array[0. .10, 1. .5] of Integer;

Alternately, we could declare

> **Type Row = Array[1. .5] of Integer;**
> **Var Table: Array[0. .10] of Row;**

In either form, we can use item *Table*[7, 4], but the second set of declarations gives more guidance in how to proceed.

We think of a table as a collection of rows (see Figure 9–5). In this situation, each row stores five integers, so each row requires five storage locations. Thus, we can store the table one row at a time as shown in Figure 9–6, where we use location 1000 as the base address.

With this storage allocation scheme, we compute where the array element *Table*[I, J] is stored using three steps. First, determine the base address for the entire table. Next, determine where Row I starts by counting the number of rows that preceed Row I and allowing space for these full rows. In the example

$$\text{RowOffset} := \underset{\substack{\text{number of array} \\ \text{rows from start}}}{(I - 0)} \quad * \quad \underset{\substack{\text{number of elements} \\ \text{in each row}}}{5}$$

Finally, determine where element J appears in the row. In the example,

$$\text{Offset Inside Row} := (J - 1).$$

FIGURE 9–5 • **Organization of a Table by Rows**

Type Row = Array [1 .. 5] of Integer
Var Table: Array [0 .. 10] of Row
or
Var Table: Array [0 .. 10, 1 .. 5] of Integer

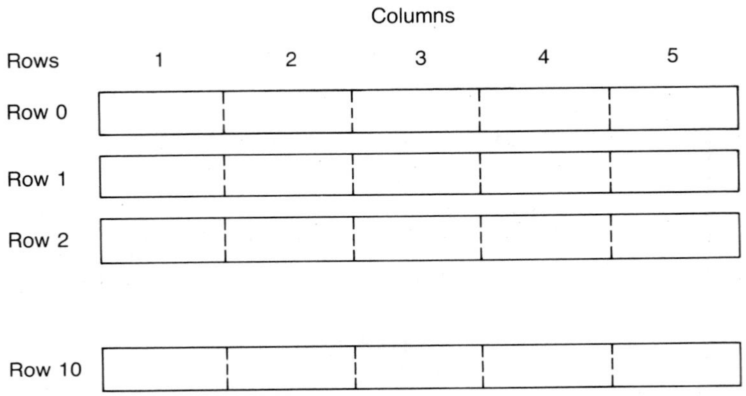

Columns

Rows	1	2	3	4	5
Row 0					
Row 1					
Row 2					
Row 10					

FIGURE 9–6 • **Space Reserved for a Table**

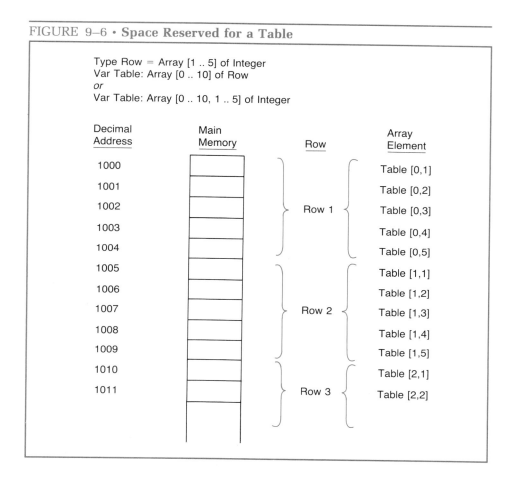

Type Row = Array [1 .. 5] of Integer
Var Table: Array [0 .. 10] of Row
or
Var Table: Array [0 .. 10, 1 .. 5] of Integer

Putting these pieces together, we get

$$\text{desired address} := \text{base address} + \text{row offset} + \text{offset within row}$$
$$:= \quad 1000 \quad + (I - 0) * 5 + \quad (J - 1)$$

As with one-dimensional arrays, we can compute the desired location from a base address, but the work must proceed in a few steps. For *Table*[I, J], we must find how many rows the desired item is from the start of the array (row offset); and find the number of items the desired item is from the start of the row (offset within row). This computation gives the formula desired:

$$\text{address} := \text{base address} + \text{offset}$$

where offset := row offset + offset within row.

An Application of Storage in Pascal

All of our analysis of addresses and storage location was based on the idea that we could store a table one row at a time. This storage format is called **row major form,** and we have already touched upon one consequence of this storage format at the end of Section 9.3. In the revised inventory program, we noted that we could declare

Type PartTotals = Array[1. .MaxWare] of Integer;
       Table = Array[1. .MaxPart] of PartTotals;
Var   Inventory: Table

Then we had a declaration

Procedure TypeTotal (Row: PartTotals);

which we called with the statement

TypeTotal (Inventory[Part])

Here, *Inventory[Part]* represents a row in a table, and that table is stored in a certain block of main memory. This block of main memory forms the basis for initializing the block called *Row* in procedure *Type-Table.* The point here is that *Inventory[Part]* and *Row* are both stored as blocks of main memory, so the data in one can be used in the other. This storage of tables by row allows individual rows of tables to be used as parameters.

This storage allocation does not, however, allow us to work with tables by column. We cannot pass a column of a table to a procedure, because the elements of the column are not stored as a single block. As Figure 9–6 illustrates, the elements of a column are spread out over a large area in main memory.

Thus, while Pascal allows us to think of rows of a table as distinct entities, the storage allocation for Pascal prevents our using columns in the same way. In some other languages data are stored column by column; this format is called **column major form.** In column major form, we might be able to work with columns as distinct entities, but we could not work with rows as easily.

SUMMARY

1. This chapter considers problems where we want to use more than one subscript, such as inventory by warehouse, recording positions on a game board, or recording features on a map. In each case, we first consider the type of data we want to analyze, and we decide that several subscripts would be helpful in discussing the data (e.g., we want to record data in a table).

2. Pascal allows us to use subscripts in several ways. To begin, declare an array:

Var Name: *Array*[Range$_1$,. . ., Range$_n$] *of* DataType

where *Name* specifies the name of the array; *Range$_1$,. . ., Range$_n$* specifies the type of each subscript (e.g., integer or Boolean) and the range of values (e.g., 0. .10, False. .True); and *DataType* describes the type of data being stored. This *DataType* can be one already defined in Pascal (e.g., Integer, Real, Boolean), or we can use a *Type* statement to define our own types.

3. Once arrays are declared, we can work with them on several levels, including as individual array elements—Table [7, 3]; as entire arrays—*BoxScores* := *Table*; as parts of arrays—row 7 of *Table*, by writing *Table*[7].

4. The **address** for a particular array element is computed in two parts, a **base address** for the start of the array and an **offset** to the particular element. In Pascal, tables are stored row by row, in **row major form.** This storage of arrays explains some constraints in parameter usage in Pascal.

EXERCISES

9.1 *Baseball League Standings.* In a baseball league, we want to record team standings in a table such as that shown below:

<u>Team</u>   <u>Wins</u>   <u>Losses</u>   <u>Total</u>   <u>Games</u>   <u>Percentage Wins</u>

For simplicity, we will assume teams are numbered 1, 2,. . . .

a. Write a program that will read the team number and the number of wins and losses, and then will fill out the table.

KEY TERMS, PHRASES, AND CONCEPTS		ELEMENTS OF PASCAL SYNTAX
Address in Main Memory	Column Major Form	User-Defined *Type*
Array	Offset	
Elements of User-Defined Types	Row Major Form	
Multiple Subscripts	Checking User Input	
Storage	Conceptualization of Data in Tabular Form	
Base Address	User-Defined Types	

b. (Optional) Expand the program in part (a) so the ranking of the teams is also computed and printed. Add a column to the table for this ranking.

c. (Optional) Modify your program in part (a) so the teams are printed out in the order of their league ranking, with the best team in the league printed first.

Hint: For parts (b) and (c) you might want to use a sorting algorithm on the rows of the table, with order determined by percentage wins.

9.2 *Interpreting a Program.* Consider the following program:

```
Program Interpretation (Output);
Const N = 21;
Var I: Integer;
    Some, One, First: Boolean;
    Result: Array[1..4] of Boolean;
    Test: Array[1..4] of Integer;

Begin {Main}
    Test[1] := 2;
    Test[2] := 3;
    Test[3] := 5;
    Test[4] := 7;

    For I := 1 To 4
        Do Result[I] := ((N Mod Test[I]) = 0);

    Some := False;
    For I := 1 To 4
        Do Some := Some Or Result[I];
    Writeln ('Some =', Some:6);

    First := False;
    I := 1;
    While (I <= 4) And Not First
      Do Begin
        First := Result[I];
        I := I + 1
      End;
    Writeln ('I =', I:2, '    First =', First:6);

    If Not Some
        Then One := False
        Else Begin
            One := True;
            While (I <= 4) and One
              Do Begin
                One := Not Result[I];
                I := I + 1
              End;
            End;
    Writeln ('One =', One:6)
End {Main} .
```

Assume that both integer variables and Boolean variables require one unit of storage. Also assume that storage for variables is allocated in the order that variables are declared, and that the first address assigned is address 0.

a. Draw a diagram showing where each of the variables in this program is stored.

b. What item is stored in address 3? In address 10?

c. What is printed by this program?

9.3 *Three-Dimensional Tic-Tac-Toe*. Three-dimensional Tic-Tac-Toe is a generalization of Tic-Tac-Toe to three dimensions. The board consists of four layers, each of which is 4-by-4, and we think of the layers being stacked on top of each other to form a cube (see Figure 9–7).

As in conventional Tic-Tac-Toe, two players alternately play Xs and Os until one player gets four in a row (horizontally on one layer,

FIGURE 9–7 · **A Board for Three-Dimensional Tic-Tac-Toe**

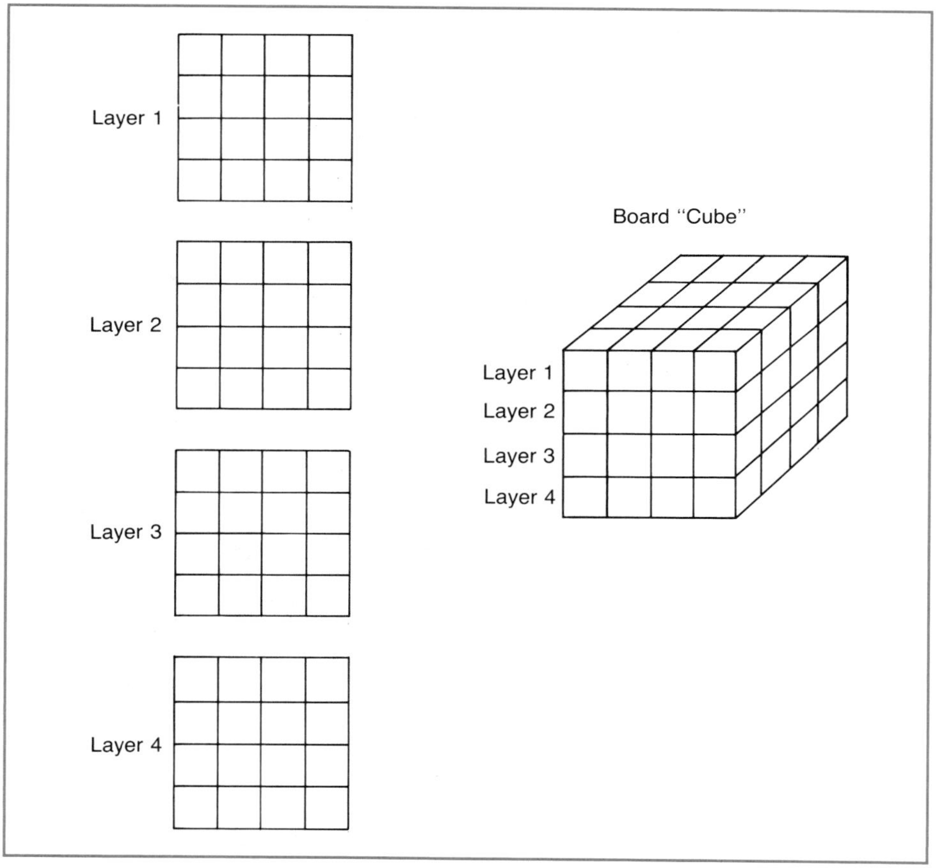

vertically through all four layers, diagonally on one layer, or diagonally through all four layers). If all squares become filled with no winner, the game ends in a draw.

Write a program generalizing Problem 9.3 to read successive moves from this three-dimensional game and to stop when one player wins or when all "squares" are filled.

9.4 *Storing Maps.* Information from a map can be stored in a table by introducing a grid system (e.g., latitude and longitude). For example, Figure 9–8 shows various elevations on an island at each point on a 5-by-5 grid. (Places off the island are in the water and so have an elevation of 0 feet above sea level.)

    a. Write a program that reads this elevation information into an appropriate table.

    b. Compute the grid coordinates for the highest point on the island.

    c. Find the average height on the island. (Do not count height 0 in the average, as that height is in the water.)

    d. Given a point on the island, find the nearest adjacent location on the island of minimum height. [For example, in the figure the lowest spot adjacent location (3,4) is a height of 2.0 feet at location (2,5).]

9.5 *Play Selection.* In football, a defense often will try to anticipate what play the opposing offense will run next. While this guessing of the next play can involve a very sophisticated analysis of many details, we can suggest some basic ideas here. First, we number each of the

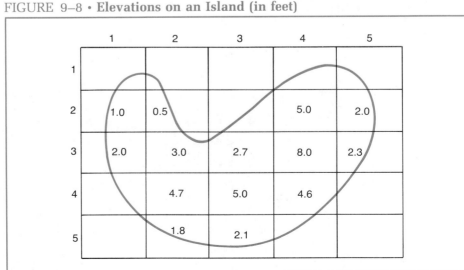

FIGURE 9–8 • **Elevations on an Island (in feet)**

plays that the opponent might try. (For example, play 43 might be a run up the middle by the fullback.) Then we review previous games by recording the down, yards to go, and play number for each play. Next we tabulate how many times each play was run in each situation. (For example, we may find that play 43 was tried in 18 of 22 times when it was third down and less than 3 yards to go.) Write a program that

a. reads the play selection information for all previous games.

b. prints all plays run for each down according to these yards categories:
   - less than 3 yards to go
   - 3 to 6 yards to go
   - 7 to 10 yards to go
   - over 10 yards to go

   (After each play, write the number of times it was run.)

c. prints the five most common plays for each down and yardage category.

NOTES:

1. Your program should check the data input when possible.

2. Your program should not assume that all categories will be represented in the data. (For example, we may never see a first down with less than 3 yards to go.)

9.6 *Computing Addresses—Singly Subscripted Arrays.* Consider the declaration

> Var List: Array[−3. .17] of Integer

Assume an integer requires one unit of storage space.

a. How much storage is required for this array?

b. If the first element of this array is stored in location 537, where is *List*[14] stored?

c. Answer questions (a) and (b) assuming integers require two units of storage space.

9.7 *Computing Addresses—Doubly Subscripted Arrays.* Consider the declaration

> Var Table: Array[−2. .50, 13. .38] of Real;

Assume a real number requires two units of storage.

a. How much storage is required for this array?

b. If the first element of this array is stored in location 200,
   i. Where is the last element stored?
   ii. Where is *Table* [−2, 23] stored?
   iii. Where is *Table* [20, 20] stored?

9.8 *Addresses with Many Subscripts.* The same approach used for computing storage locations with one or two subscripts can be generalized to three or more subscripts as well.

a. Compute the general location for *Piece* [I, J, K], where *Piece* is declared

Var Piece: Array[Low1. .High1, Low2. .High2, Low3. .High3] of Integer

In your computation, assume an integer requires one unit of storage.

b. Modify the previous formula for an array of type *Data* = . . . instead of type *Integer*.

c. As a special case of (b), suppose we declared

Var Piece: Array[− 1. .5, 2. .8, − 3. . − 1] of Real

Suppose *Piece* starts at location 1000, and suppose a real number takes up two units of storage. Find the addresses used to store the real number *Piece*[1, 6, − 2].

9.9 *Recording Moves in Checkers*

a. Write a program that records successive moves in a checker game and prints the position of the board after each move.

b. Expand the program in part (a) to check user input.
In particular,

   i. Check that all moves are legal (to blank squares or jumps).

   ii. Check that a player jumps whenever possible.

   iii. Check that only "Kings" move backward.

c. Expand the program in part (b) to stop when one player wins. (Do not try to check for draws!)

CHAPTER 10

PROCEDURES
AND FUNCTIONS
(REVISITED)

Throughout this book, we solve problems by breaking them down into pieces, and we structure our programs according to these logical pieces using procedures and functions. Further, in declaring procedures, we use reference and value parameters to move information both in and out of those procedures.

In this chapter we re-examine our use of parameters and local and global variables, and we identify a wide variety of situations that can occur. With this discussion we will be able to develop guidelines for structuring programs so we can use these capabilities while minimizing the likelihood of introducing errors into our programs.

SECTION 10.1   **VALUE AND REFERENCE PARAMETERS**

To begin, we need to look at procedures and function parameters more closely, so we can understand the difference between value parameters and reference parameters more clearly.

Parameter Passage by Value
When we pass information into procedures or functions using parameters, we normally have declared parameters by specifying indentifiers and their types (omitting an initial keyword *Var*.) More formally, this connection be-

tween an actual parameter and a formal parameter is called **parameter passage by value** and has the following characteristics.

1. When a procedure or function is called, a new storage location is created for the formal parameter.
2. The value of the actual parameter is copied into this new address.
3. After this copying, the actual parameter and the formal parameter are considered separate, unrelated entities. Either of these can be changed without changing the other.
4. When the procedure or function ends, the storage location for the formal parameter is ignored in future work. Only the actual parameter remains.

With this form of parameter passage, we cannot use these parameters to return new values. In a procedure, formal parameters have their own storage locations, which are unrelated to any global variables. Thus, while we can store values in locations allocated to our formal parameters, all of these values are lost when the procedure finishes.

Parameter Passage by Reference

In contrast, when we add the keywork Var to our parameter declaration, we maintain a tie between the actual and formal parameters, and we can use this **Parameter Passage by Reference** to get data out of a procedure. This parameter passage has the following characteristics.

1. When a procedure or function is called, a new storage location is created for the formal parameter.
2. This new location is used to store the address of the actual parameter.
3. All subsequent uses of the formal parameter then refer back to the address of the actual parameter. Thus, a reference to either the formal or the actual parameter involves the data stored for the actual parameter.
4. When the procedure or function ends, the storage location for the formal parameter is ignored in the future, but any changes in the actual parameter remain.

To clarify the distinction between these two types of parameters further, we consider the following example. (Here, we have added line numbers along the left-hand side for future reference.)

Line Number	Program Listing

```
1      Program Parameter (Output);
2      {A value is passed into a procedure, but nothing is returned.}
3
4      Var A :Integer;
5
```

```
 6        Procedure InAndOut (Var X: Integer);
 7            Begin
 8                Writeln ('Procedure 1:', A:5, X:5);
 9                X := 18;
10                Writeln ('Procedure 2:', A:5, X:5)
11            End {InOnly} ;
12
13        Begin {Main}
14            Writeln ('   Location      A     X');
15            A := 15;
16            Writeln ('       Main 1:', A:5);
17            InAndOut (A);
18            Writeln ('       Main 2:', A:5)
19        End {Main} .
20
```

When this program is run, we get the following output:

```
   Location      A     X
       Main 1:   15
Procedure 1:     15    15
Procedure 2:     18    18
       Main 2:   18
```

From the output of this program, we see that the addition of the reserved word *Var* before the formal parameter *X* has allowed procedure *InAndOut* to change the value of the actual parameter *A*. Figures 10–1 to 10–4 describe in more detail how this change occurs. The key point here is that in parameter passage by reference, the formal parameter always refers back to the actual parameter, so a change in the formal parameter is reflected by a change in the actual parameter.

In contrast, when we pass parameters by value (leaving out the *Var* reserved word) we get the following output:

```
   Location      A     X
       Main 1:   15
Procedure 1:     15    15
Procedure 2:     15    18
       Main 2:   15
```

Here, the actual parameter is not changed because the values of the actual parameter and formal parameter are kept separate, as shown in Figure 10–5. Then, when the procedure is finished and the storage for *InAndOut* is freed for other use, only the storage for the main program remains. (See Figure 10–1.) *A* retains the value 15.

FIGURE 10–1 • **Schematic of Program Parameter after Executing Line 15**

Main

A	15

As the Main Program starts, A is assigned the value 15 and this value is written.

FIGURE 10–2 • **Schematic of Program Parameter after Procedure InAndOut Is Called**

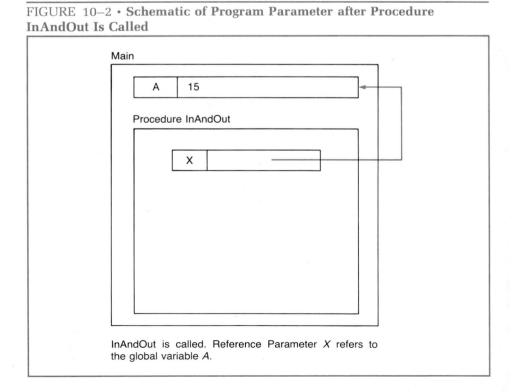

Main

A	15

Procedure InAndOut

X	

InAndOut is called. Reference Parameter X refers to the global variable A.

FIGURE 10–3 • **Schematic for Program Parameter after Executing Line 9 (in Procedure InAndOut)**

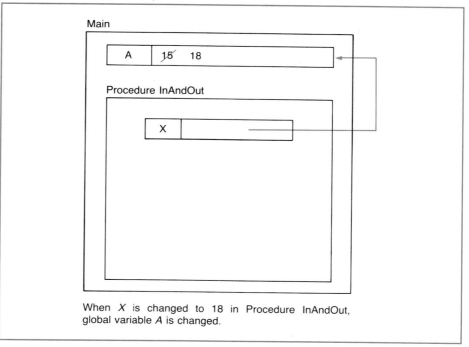

When *X* is changed to 18 in Procedure InAndOut, global variable *A* is changed.

FIGURE 10–4 • **Schematic of Program Parameter after Executing Line 18 in the Main Program**

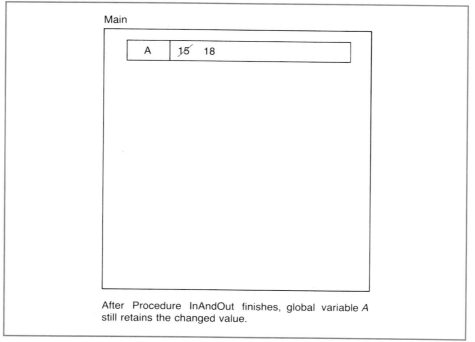

After Procedure InAndOut finishes, global variable *A* still retains the changed value.

FIGURE 10–5 • Schematic of Program Parameter after Executing Line 9 (in Procedure InAndOut)

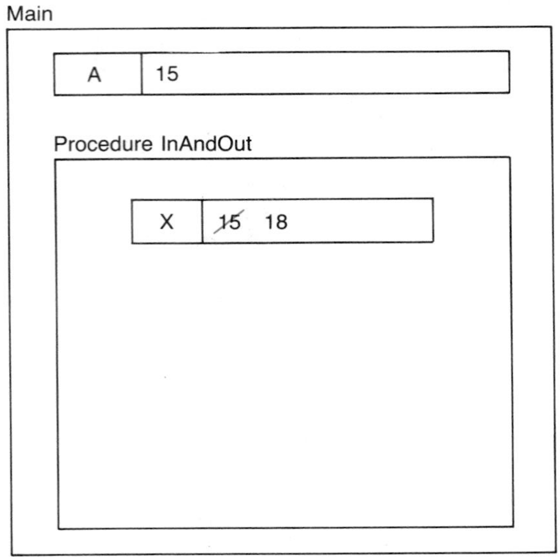

When InAndOut is called, the value of *A* is copied into a new location for Parameter *X*. A revision in *X* then does not affect *A*.

This example illustrates Pascal's two types of parameter passage very clearly, and we summarize our conclusions in Table 10–1. From this table and our examples in this section, we see that we can use either reference or value parameters when we want to supply procedures with initial values. However, only reference parameters allow procedures to return values.

SECTION 10.2   SCOPE OF IDENTIFIERS

While parameters are vital to the effective use of procedures and functions, we find that the use of parameters, especially reference parameters, can also involve some subtleties that we may not anticipate. If we are not careful, the interplay between various parameters and local and global variables can cause errors in our programs that can be difficult to locate and correct.

Thus, in this section and the next, we examine some of the interrelationships that can exist among the various types of parameters and vari-

TABLE 10–1 · Reference and Value Parameters

Passage by Reference	Passage by Value
1. A new storage location is reserved for the formal parameter when a function or procedure is called. This location is used to refer to other locations.	1. A new storage location is reserved for the formal parameter when a function or procedure is called. This location is used to store values of the formal parameters.
2. The address of the actual parameter is stored in this new location.	2. The value of the actual parameter is copied into this new location.
3. Thereafter, the formal parameter refers to the actual parameter.	3. Thereafter, the formal parameter and actual parameters are considered separately.
4. Any change in either formal or actual parameter changes the other.	4. A change in either the formal or actual parameter does not change the other.
5. The actual parameter remains changed after a procedure finishes.	5. The actual parameter cannot be changed by the formal parameter.

ables. Then, in Section 4, we state some guidelines for using parameters and variables effectively while minimizing the potential for errors. We begin by clarifying which identifier refers to which storage location.

Multiple Declarations

In the following program, we use the identifier A for both a local and a global variable.

Line Number	Program Listing
1	Program TwoAs (Output);
2	{This program uses the identifier A for both a global
3	and a local variable.}
4	
5	Var A: Integer;
6	
7	Procedure P;
8	Var A: Integer;
9	Begin
10	A :=18;
11	Writeln ('Procedure:', A:5)
12	End {P} ;
13	

```
14        Begin {Main}
15            Writeln (' Location      A');
16            A := 15;
17            Writeln ('    Main 1:', A:5);
18            P;
19            Writeln ('    Main 2:', A:5)
20        End {Main} .
```

When this program is run, we get the following output:

```
 Location      A
    Main 1:    15
Procedure:    18
    Main 2:    15
```

When we analyze this program, we find that the declaration of *A* in our procedure specifies a new variable with a new address. Then, within the procedure all references to the identifier *A* refer to this new storage location. When the procedure finishes, this local variable is no longer defined, and *A* refers to the global variable. The details of this program are shown in Figures 10–6 to 10–8.

FIGURE 10–6 • **Schematic of Program TwoAs after Executing Line 16 in the Main Program**

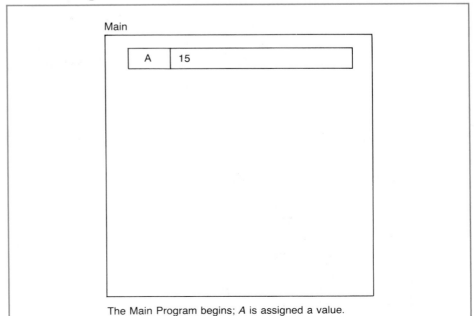

The Main Program begins; *A* is assigned a value.

FIGURE 10–7 • **Schematic of Program TwoAs after Executing Line 10 in Procedure P**

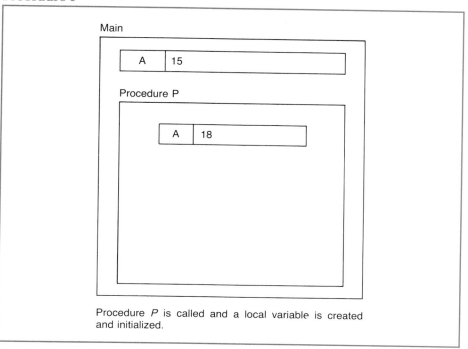

Procedure *P* is called and a local variable is created and initialized.

FIGURE 10–8 • **Schematic of Program TwoAs after Procedure P Returns**

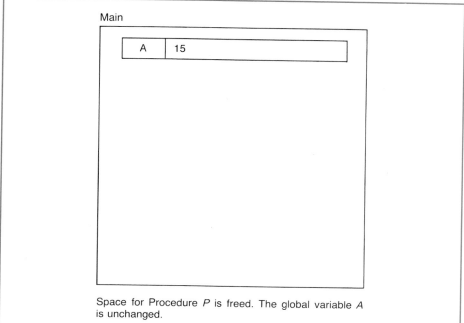

Space for Procedure *P* is freed. The global variable *A* is unchanged.

In general, we find that the declaration of an identifier within a procedure takes precedence over declarations outside the procedure. Inside a procedure or function, local variables or formal parameter names are used first. Global names apply only if these identifiers have not been redefined.

Aliasing

Although we cannot access these global variables directly, the computer still retains storage space for them. We can access this space using reference parameters, as shown in the following example.

```
Line
Number        Program Listing

  1           Program AliasA (Output);
  2           {This program uses the identifier A for both a global
  3            and a local variable and a formal parameter X.}
  4
  5           Var A: Integer;
  6
  7           Procedure P(Var X: Integer);
  8               Var A: Integer;
  9               Begin
 10                   Writeln ('Procedure 1:', X:10);
 11                   A := 13;
 12                   X := 25;
 13                   Writeln ('Procedure 2:', A:5, X:5)
 14               End {P} ;
 15
 16           Begin {Main}
 17               Writeln ('    Location      A     X');
 18               A := 7;
 19               Writeln ('     Main 1:', A:5);
 20               P(A);
 21               Writeln ('     Main 2:', A:5)
 22           End {Main} .
```

When this program is run, we get the following output:

```
    Location      A     X
        Main 1:    7
Procedure 1:             7
Procedure 2:   13    25
        Main 2:   25
```

Figures 10–9 to 10–12 trace this program in some detail. In this program, the identifier A was used as a local and a global variable. In the Procedure P, the identifier A refers to the local variable, not the global one; however, notice that X is used as an alternate name for accessing the global

FIGURE 10–9 · Schematic for Program AliasA after Executing Line 18 in the Main Program

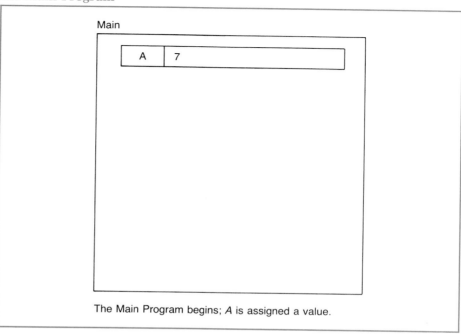

The Main Program begins; *A* is assigned a value.

FIGURE 10–10 · Schematic of Program AliasA after Calling Procedure P (at Line 9)

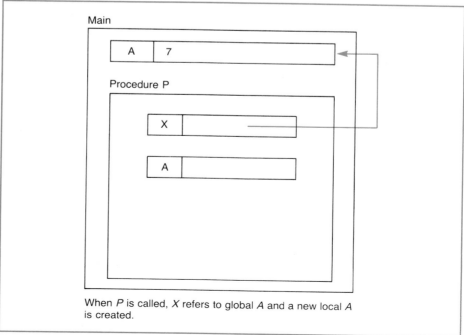

When *P* is called, *X* refers to global *A* and a new local *A* is created.

FIGURE 10–11 • Schematic of Program AliasA after Executing Line 12 in Procedure P

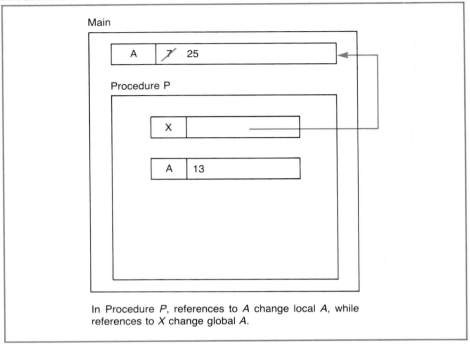

In Procedure *P*, references to *A* change local *A*, while references to *X* change global *A*.

FIGURE 10–12 • Schematic for Program AliasA after Completing Procedure P (Line 21)

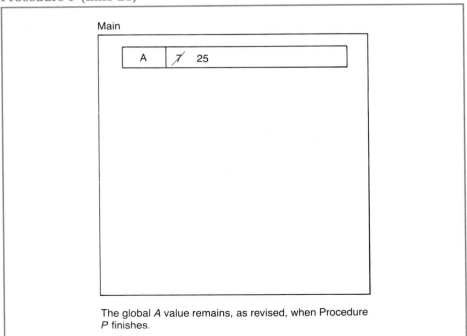

The global *A* value remains, as revised, when Procedure *P* finishes.

data. Here we say that X is an **alias** for the global variable A. Both global A and formal parameter X refer to the same storage location.

Scope of Identifiers

The **scope of an identifier** is that part of the program where an identifier is defined. In Chapter 3, we noted that global identifiers exist throughout the running of a program, whereas local identifiers (and formal parameters) exist only within the procedures where they are defined. Thus, the scope of global identifiers is the entire program; the scope of local identifiers is limited to specific procedures.

These basic scope rules can be complicated in several ways. For example, the *TwoAs* program shows that identifiers can be **redefined** with procedures. Also, the *AliasA* program shows that a reference parameter allows the same storage location to be specified under a different name, or alias.

Line Number	Program Listing

```
 1   Program Environment (Output);
 2   {This program illustrates one way that the compiler environment
 3    determines the scope of identifiers.}
 4   Var A: Integer;
 5
 6   Procedure One;
 7       Begin
 8           Writeln (' One 1:   A = ', A:1);
 9           A := 32;
10           Writeln (' One 2:   A = ', A:1)
11       End {One} ;
12
13   Procedure Two;
14       Var A: Integer;
15       Begin
16           A := 13;
17           Writeln (' Two 1:   A = ', A:1);
18           One;
19           Writeln (' Two 2:   A = ', A:1)
20       End {Two} ;
21
22   Begin {Main}
23       A := 7;
24       Writeln ('Main 1:   A = ', A:1);
25       Two;
26       Writeln ('Main 2:   A = ', A:1)
27   End {Main} .
```

Our example illustrates another subtlety concerning the scope of identifiers. We will see that identifiers in functions and procedures refer to storage locations as they are declared at the time of compilation.

When this program is run, we get the following output:

```
Main 1:   A = 7
 Two 1:   A = 13
 One 1:   A = 7
 One 2:   A = 32
 Two 2:   A = 13
Main 2:   A = 32
```

When we trace through this program to understand the output, the first part of the program execution in which the Main Program calls Procedure Two is similar to our previous examples. (See Figure 10–13.)

Procedure Two calls Procedure One, and we must determine which variable we mean when we use identifier A. Here, we could argue that Procedure One is declared outside of Procedure Two, and with this declaration, One cannot use the local variable A declared inside Procedure Two. (See Figure 10–14.)

Alternatively, we could claim that Procedure One is called by Procedure Two, and within Two, local variable A has superceded global A. (See Figure 10–15.)

In Pascal and several other languages, the first argument is followed, and the global variable A is used inside Procedure One. Here, it does not matter that One was called by Two; the local variables of Procedure Two have no effect on Procedure One. Because it is declared separately from Procedure Two, Procedure One will always refer to global variable A regardless of where it is called from. (We say the scope of A is determined at **compile time** not at **execution time.**)

The rest of the execution of this program is detailed in Figures 10–16 and 10–17.

In this program, identifier A was used both as a global and a local variable. The scope of local variable A was confined to statements inside Procedure Two, and this local variable became inactive when we called Procedure One which was declared outside Two. The scope of global variable A extended to all statements outside of Procedure Two, including the Main Program and Procedure One.

FIGURE 10–13 • **Schematic for Program Environment after Executing Line 17 in Procedure Two**

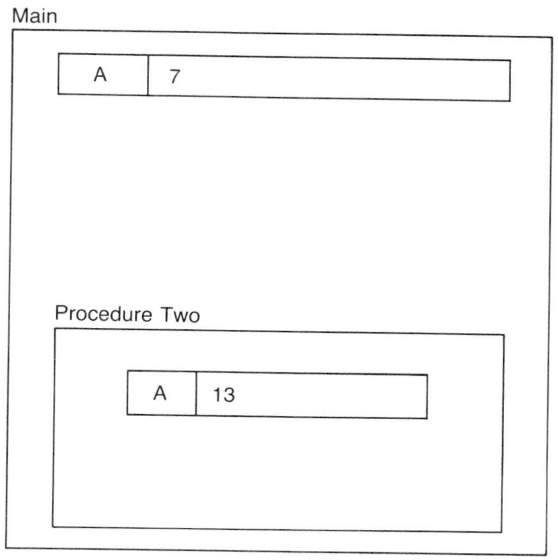

Main

A | 7

Procedure Two

A | 13

When Procedure Two is called, storage is allocated for two identifiers *A*.

FIGURE 10–14 • **Schematic for Program Environment after Calling Procedure One (Line 8) Based on Procedure Environment at Time of Compilation**

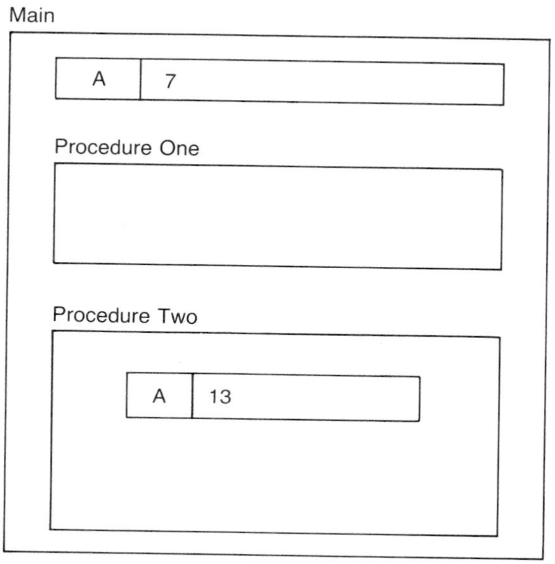

Main

A | 7

Procedure One

Procedure Two

A | 13

In Pascal, Procedure One is declared outside Procedure Two, and One does not have access to local *A* in Two. Rather, *A* in One refers to global *A*.

Main

A | 7

Procedure Two

A | 13

Procedure One

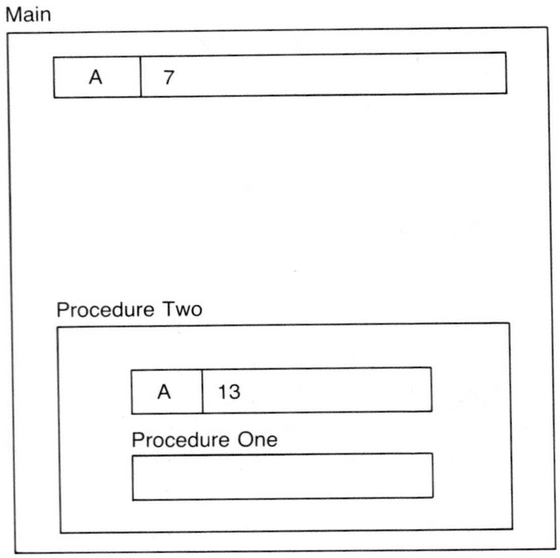

At run-time, One is called from inside Procedure Two.
(This view is not followed in Pascal.)

FIGURE 10–16 · Schematic for Program Environment after Executing
Line 9 in Procedure One

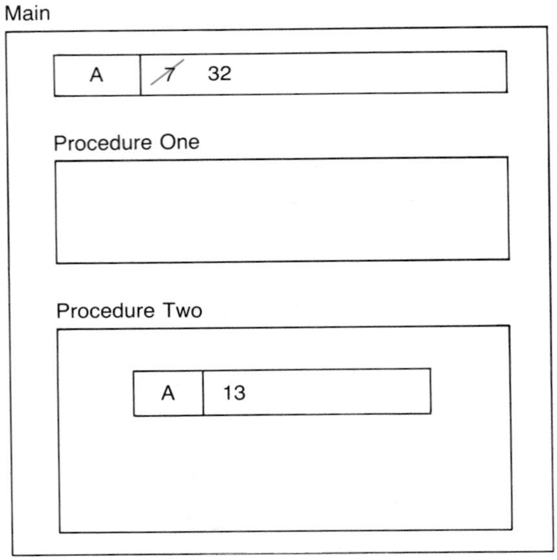

Main

A | ⁄ 32

Procedure One

Procedure Two

A | 13

Procedure One changes global A.

FIGURE 10–17 • **Schematic for Program Environment after Executing Line 19 in Procedure Two**

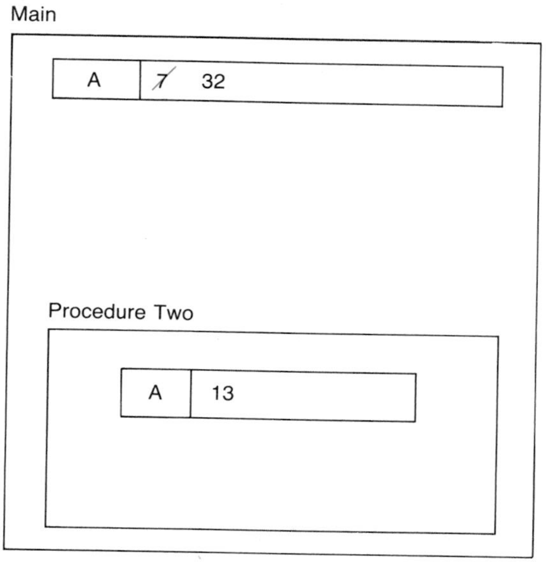

When One finishes, we return to Two, where local *A* is still active.

SIDE EFFECTS

In the previous section, we saw how scope, identifier redefinition, aliases, and program environment can all fit together in a program. In this section, we look at some consequences of these features. We will see that Pascal allows us great flexibility in solving problems, but we will also see that this freedom can get us into trouble.

One type of difficulty is illustrated in the following.

PROBLEM 10.3

Suppose we measure the time (in seconds) that it takes us to travel one mile. Compute our speed in miles per hour, and compute the number of minutes it takes us to travel 30 miles.

This problem is related to Problem 5.1, and we use some of the ideas from Section 5.1 to develop the following outline.

Outline for Problem 10.3

I. Determine time (seconds).
II. Compute MPH.

    A. time(hours) := time(seconds)/3600.0
    B. MPH := 1.0/time(hours)
III. Compute minutes to travel 30 miles.
    A. time(seconds) for 30 miles := 30.0 * time(seconds) for 1 mile
    B. time(minutes) := time(seconds) / 60.0 for 30 miles
IV. Print results.

Our outline is correct and straightforward. In our programming, we decide to compute Steps II and III by using functions. This yields the following program, which contains a common error.

```
Program MPHAndTime {Wrong, but good idea} (Input, Output);
{This program computes speed in miles per hour and time in minutes
 for 30 miles, given time in seconds for one mile.}

Var Time: Real;        {Our time in seconds}
    MPH: Real;         {Our speed in miles per hour}
    TimeFor30: Real;   {Our time in minutes for 30 miles}

Function ComputeMPH (Seconds: Real): Real;
{Compute MPH, given time in "Seconds" for 1 mile}
    Begin
        {Convert time to seconds}
        Time := Seconds / 3600.0;

        {Compute MPH}
        ComputeMPH := 1.0 / Time
    End {ComputeMPH} ;

Function FindMinutes (Seconds: Real): Real;
{Compute time in minutes for 30 miles, given "Seconds" for 1 mile}
    Begin
        {Find time in seconds for 30 miles}
        Time := Seconds * 30.0;

        {Change to minutes}
        FindMinutes := Time / 60.0
    End {FindMinutes} ;

Begin {Main}
    Writeln ('This program computes information about speed and time.');

    {Determine time(seconds)}
    Write ('Enter your time in seconds for 1 mile: ');
    Read (Time);

    {Compute MPH}
    MPH := ComputeMPH (Time);

    {Compute minutes to travel 30 miles}
    TimeFor30 := FindMinutes (Time);

    {Print results}
```

```
    Writeln ('When you travel 1 mile in ', Time:1:2, ' Seconds,');
    Writeln ('your speed is ', MPH:1:2, ' miles per hour,');
    Writeln ('and you will travel 30 miles in ', TimeFor30:1:3, ' minutes.')
End {Main} .
```

When we analyze this program, we note that our Main Program follows our outline exactly. We enter *Time* in seconds. Then we use that to compute miles per hour and time in minutes for 30 miles. Finally, we print the results. These steps correspond exactly to our outline.

However, when we look at our functions, we see that we are using this same global *Time* variable for other things. In *Function ComputeMPH* we use *Time* to mean "time in hours," and in *Function FindMinutes* we use *Time* to mean "time in seconds for 30 miles." Thus, in this program, we are using one global variable for three different things.

In each function, we change the value of *Time* for that particular interpretation. Here we say that the global variable *Time* is changed as a **side effect** of the function. *Time* is not a parameter of the function. In fact, in reading the Main Program, we cannot tell that our function has any effect on *Time* whatsoever. We mean to compute *MPH* or *TimeFor30* from a *Time*, and we do not expect other changes to be made.

This is an example where a side effect causes errors in our program. In each function, we want to use *Time* for a particular purpose, but that purpose is restricted to the function. There is no reason to depend on a global variable for this detail within the function. Thus, we need to introduce a local *Time* variable in each function to correct this problem due to side effects.

Side Effects Can Cause Ambiguity

In previous examples, we have seen instances in which side effects cause errors and others in which side effects can clarify our code. In each instance, we could predict what our code would produce, although sometimes the results were incorrect.

The following example illustrates a situation where side effects can produce ambiguous results; we cannot predict what will be printed.

```
Program Ambiguous (Output);
{A program where side effects produce ambigious results.}

Var A, B, X: Integer;

Function F(U: Integer): Integer;
    Begin
        B := 2 * U;
        F := B - 4
    End;
```

```
Begin
     Writeln ('  A     B      X');

     A := 3;
     B := 4;
     X := B + F(A);
     Writeln (A:3, B:5, X:5, '   B + F(A)');

     A := 3;
     B := 4;
     X := F(A) + B;
     Writeln (A:3, B:5, X:5, '   F(A) + B')
End.
```

This code could produce any of the following four results, depending on the compiler.

Compiler 1

A	B	X	
3	6	8	B + F(A)
3	6	8	F(A) + B

Compiler 2

A	B	X	
3	6	6	B + F(A)
3	6	6	F(A) + B

Compiler 3

A	B	X	
3	6	6	B + F(A)
3	6	8	F(A) + B

Compiler 4

A	B	X	
3	6	8	B + F(A)
3	6	6	F(A) + B

Let us look at the program with some care. We find that Function F does two things: B is given the value 6 as a side effect, and F is given the value 2.

Now let us consider the two computations of X in the main program:

$$X := B + F(A)$$
$$X := F(A) + B$$

In these lines, we know F will have the value 2, but we cannot be sure of the value of B. If the initial value of B is used, then X becomes $2 + 4 = 6$. If the later value of B is used, then X becomes $2 + 6 = 8$. Thus, the value of X depends upon whether B is considered before or after the function F(A) is computed. Since the Pascal Standard says that the terms B and $F(A)$ can be evaluated in either order, any of the four results are possible.

From these examples, we see that we must be careful in our procedures and functions to control side effects. Side effects can change global variables unintentionally. We should use parameters to transmit data both to and from procedures and functions. This transmission with parameters is much cleaner and less error-prone than with global variables.

SECTION 10.4   GUIDELINES ON DECLARING AND USING VARIABLES AND PARAMETERS

The previous sections suggest that unanticipated or inadvertant side effects can cause a wide variety of subtle changes and errors, and we need to control such side effects if we are to write correct programs. In this section, we develop some guidelines which will allow us to use various parameters and variables effectively while we control side effects and minimize the chances for errors.

Global Variables

In the previous sections, a large number of the subtleties we encountered were due to side effects. Procedures and functions used global variables directly rather than referring to them in a more controlled way through appropriate parameters. Further, we might change global variables accidentally if we forget to redeclare identifiers locally within a function or procedure. For example, our miles per hour program in Section 10.3 contained several errors because we omitted the declaration of some local variables.

Unfortunately, whenever we use global variables we always face the possibility that these values will be changed inadvertently by side effects because we omitted a needed declaration in a function or a procedure. Our programs may be syntactically correct, but we risk having procedures interfere with each other because they change global variables.

These observations about side effects and this potential for introducing subtle errors motivates the following major guidelines.

Guideline 1. All programs should be written in a way that eliminates all global variables, unless we can identify truly extraordinary arguments otherwise. Most programs we write should have *no* global variables.

The second guideline emphasizes this principle and suggests a way to accomplish this goal in many cases.

Guideline 2. To avoid global variables, move global declarations together with the steps of the main program to a separate, independent procedure. Then, allow the main program to call this separate driver procedure, and use parameters to transfer all values between the driver and other functions and procedures in the program.

To clarify this approach further, we rewrite the Miles Per Hour Program of Section 10.3 in this style.

```
Program MPHAndTime (Input, Output);
{This program computes speed in miles per hour and time in minutes
 for 30 miles, given time in seconds for one mile.}

{This version uses procedure ControlProcessing to eliminate all
 global variables}
```

```
Function ComputeMPH (Seconds: Real): Real;
{Compute MPH, given time in "Seconds" for 1 mile}
    Var Time: Real;
    Begin
        {Convert time to seconds}
        Time := Seconds / 3600.0;

        {Compute MPH}
        ComputeMPH := 1.0 / Time
    End {ComputeMPH} ;

Function FindMinutes (Seconds: Real): Real;
{Compute time in minutes for 30 miles, given "Seconds" for 1 mile}
    Var Time: Real;
    Begin
        {Find time in seconds for 30 miles}
        Time := Seconds * 30.0;

        {Change to minutes}
        FindMinutes := Time / 60.0
    End {FindMinutes} ;

Procedure ControlProcessing;
{This procedure controls the processing required for the overall problem.}
    Var Time: Real;          {Our time in seconds}
        MPH: Real;           {Our speed in miles per hour}
        TimeFor30: Real;     {Our time in minutes for 30 miles}
    Begin
        {Determine time(seconds)}
        Write ('Enter your time in seconds for 1 mile: ');
        Read (Time);

        {Compute MPH}
        MPH := ComputeMPH (Time);

        {Compute minutes to travel 30 miles}
        TimeFor30 := FindMinutes (Time);

        {Print results}
        Writeln ('When you travel 1 mile in ', Time:1:2, ' Seconds,');
        Writeln ('your speed is ', MPH:1:2, ' miles per hour,');
        Writeln ('and you will travel 30 miles in ',
                 TimeFor30:1:3,' minutes.')
    End {ControlProcessing} ;

Begin {Main}

    Writeln ('This program computes information about speed and time.');
    ControlProcessing

End {Main} .
```

Following Guidelines 1 and 2, we see that this program has no global variables at all. Instead, we define our globals in a new *ControlProcessing* procedure, which controls all computations. Our main program is now reduced to printing an initial title and calling Procedure *ControlProcessing*. Then, *ControlProcessing* uses the same functions we used before.

However, here, we are unlikely to change values inadvertantly by side effects. With no global variables, we must use parameters to transfer data, so we see explicitly how all information is entering and leaving each function and procedure.

Value Versus Reference Parameters

Eliminating global variables forces us to use parameters to move data to and from procedures and functions. Thus, our next task is to develop guidelines for choosing the appropriate type of parameters and these guidelines will depend upon the main distinctions between value and reference parameters from Section 10.1. When we use *value* parameters, the value of the actual parameter is copied into a new location for a formal parameter, and a change in the formal parameter does not change the actual parameter. In contrast, with *reference* parameters, the formal parameter refers to an actual parameter; the copying of values is not needed; and for arrays, only the base address must be transmitted from actual to formal parameters. In addition, a change in formal parameters does change actual parameters.

In reviewing these differences, one consideration needs to be stressed: *Reference parameters can change actual parameters.* This fact has two major implications. First, many of the problems associated with side effects apply to reference parameters. Actual parameters can be changed accidently by procedures and functions when reference parameters are used. Such changes cannot occur with value parameters, so value parameters are safer. Second, when data must be returned by a procedure, value parameters cannot be used. Reference parameters are mandatory when we want to get data from a procedure. These two observations will motivate our guidelines for choosing between value and reference parameters.

However, there is one other important consideration: *Value parameters require values to be copied.* Again, this has two implications. First, for simple data types (Boolean, integer, real), the work required to copy a value is about the same as the work required to set up the reference from the formal parameter to the actual one. Storage requirements are similar as well. Second, for arrays, value passage requires considerably more work and storage. In value passage, a completely new array must be created and all values in the array copied. On the other hand, in reference passage, only the base address must be transferred to the formal parameter and stored. With large arrays, this difference can be considerable; value passage requires much more work. Also, depending on the computer, it is possible that the machine will run out of space when it tries to set up another large array.

These comments suggest the following guidelines for choosing between value and reference parameters.

Guideline 3. Use reference parameters to return data from procedures.

Guideline 4. Use value parameters whenever data need not be returned.

Exception. When dealing with a large array, use reference parameters to reduce storage and copying overhead. Be careful not to make inadvertant changes in actual parameters.

Mistakes involving procedures often are caused by the wrong choice of parameter passage. If a procedure or function seems to be working by itself but does not seem to work when it is put in the program, we always should check the choice of parameter passage.

Data Encapsulation

With the guidelines we have now established, we are ready to tackle a wide variety of problems with little further discussion. However, in some cases, we also should be aware of one additional idea.

To explain this principle, we return to our simulations that used a random number generator, and we consider the structure of those simulation programs carefully. In particular, each simulation used a function *Random* to obtain random numbers, and we ignored the details of that function in our application. However, these details did have two important consequences. First, the *Random* function depended on a *Seed* value that was changed from one function call to the next. For each computation, we needed one *Seed* value to compute the next. Second, to start our simulation, we needed to initialize this *Seed* value using an *InitializeRandomFunction* procedure.

Conceptually, this situation is illustrated in Figure 10–18. We think of the *InitializeRandomFunction* procedure and the *Random* function as being accessible to our simulation program, but we think of their details as being outside our simulation. Further, we think of the variable *Seed* as being shared by these two procedures. More generally, a **shared variable** is one that is needed by a few specific procedures or functions, but which is logically separate from the rest of the program. When this situation arises, we often want to separate these shared variables from the rest of our work so that they are not changed inadvertently by other procedures or functions. With this view, we want to declare shared variables as belonging to only a few designated procedures and functions, as in Figure 10–18. In computer science, this form of declaration is called **data encapsulation,** in which specific variables can be accessed only by certain tasks.

On a practical level, we can think in terms of shared variables as we develop our programs. However, data encapsulation is only available in some recent languages, such as Modula-2 and Ada. Pascal does not have any provision to declare separate shared variables. Thus, in implementing the concept of data encapsulation, we may need to use other constructions. We observe that a shared value cannot be stored in a local variable, because

FIGURE 10–18 • **Seed as a Shared Variable**

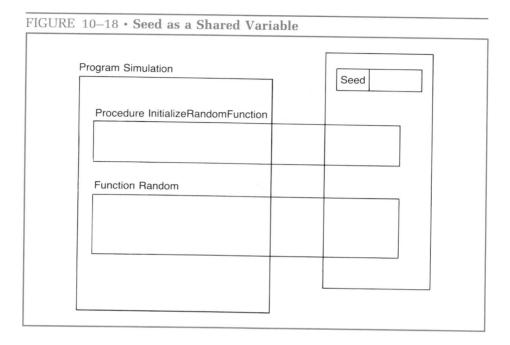

local variables are not carried from one procedure or function call to the next. This leaves us with the possibility of using either parameters or global variables. With this choice, we will always pick a parameter as long as that use of the parameter does not distract from the rest of the application. However, as with our random number example, we will sometimes declare global variables for shared values when we want to deemphasize the technical details of a task.

This discussion motivates the following guideline.

Guideline 5. In implementing the concept of shared variables in Pascal, it is permissible to use global variables as the least objectionable of several weak options.

This guideline is the primary exception to our earlier comments to eliminate all global variables, and it is important that this guideline be applied only after using the concept of shared variables throughout the design process. (In Chapter 20, we will encounter one other exception, which is based on some other specific limitations in Pascal.)

With these five guidelines, our primary goal is to control the flow of data between procedures and functions as much as possible so that we do not make inadvertant changes in our values, yielding unexpected results. As we proceed through the rest of the text, we will be motivated by these guidelines, and we will frequently write programs that have no global variables at all.

SECTION 10.5   MODULARITY: INDEPENDENCE OF PROGRAM UNITS

We have now seen all of the fundamental pieces of procedures and functions, and we have stressed ways that we can make these procedures and functions independent. We now look at this work more formally. We also consider some additional techniques that can be helpful in developing algorithms and in writing and testing programs.

Coupling and Cohesion

Throughout our work, we have followed a basic top-down approach to problem solving—we divide complex problems into small, manageable pieces, and we may identify some tasks that are common to several steps. This approach leads us to an algorithm written in outline form, in which major steps are differentiated from small details. Function and procedures then allow us to structure our code to parallel this outline form.

In our problem analysis, we have tried to keep our steps independent, so these steps do not interfere with each other, and the guidelines from the previous section will help us write procedures and functions so they will be independent. More formally, we can consider the **coupling** of functions and procedures in our programs. Here coupling describes the amount that various procedures and functions depend upon each other, and our principles of independence suggest that we want to minimize coupling in our programming.

In addition, in writing procedures and functions, we write a separate function or procedure for each part of our outline. We should not combine outline steps into a single piece of our program, since our program should retain the same structure and clarity found in our outline. We want the statements within a procedure or function to relate to a single task, and we do not want other tasks disrupting our central focus. In computer science, this relating of the various statements in a procedure or function to a central theme is called **cohesion,** and we should strive to write short, cohesive procedures and functions for each part of our solution outline.

Specifications with Pre- and Post-Assertions

Once we write our outline for a complex problem, we may find it useful to describe the work of each step formally. In large development projects, different people may be assigned to work on different steps, and the overall job will run correctly only if those steps fit together. In such a situation, the work of each step must be specified very carefully, so there can be no confusion about what each step does.

One way to formalize the work required for a step is through the specification of **pre-assertions** and **post-assertions.** Pre-assertions specify what can be assumed when the step begins; post-assertions specify what must be true when the step ends. For example, consider a step that computes the mean, median, and standard deviation of a set of numbers

$$a_1, \ldots, a_n.$$

Pre-assertions for the step might be

1. n is an integer.
2. $n > 1$.
3. $a_1, \ldots, a_n$ are declared as real numbers.
4. $a_1, \ldots, a_n$ have all been given values.

Post-assertions for the step might be

1. *Mean* is the arithmetic average of $a_1, \ldots, a_n$.
2. *Med* is the median of $a_1, \ldots, a_n$.
3. *StdDev* is the standard deviation of $a_1, \ldots, a_n$.
4. n and $a_1, \ldots, a_n$ remain unchanged by the step.
5. No global data are accessed within the step.
6. Nothing is read or printed by the step.

When we want to translate this step into a procedure, we also need one additional piece of information, the **calling format,** which is a precise statement of the procedure name, and the number, type, and meaning of parameters. For example, we might specify a calling format

    Stat(A, N, Mean, Med, StdDev)

where

Stat is the procedure name,

A is a real array of type *ArrayType,*

N is the number of elements in the array, and

Mean, Med, StdDev are real parameters that return the values specified in the post-assertions.

Once we know the calling format and the pre- and post-assertions, we can program the procedure without knowing anything more about how the step will be used. For example, we could begin

    Procedure Stat (A:ArrayType; N:Integer;
                    Var Mean, Med, StdDev:Real);

Next, we could declare any local variables we might need. From the post-assertions, we know what we must compute; that we will not use any *Read* or *Write* statements; and which values we must return when the procedure finishes.

When we use pre- and post-assertions, we should keep in mind two things. First, the pre- and post-assertions do not say how we will do our work in the step; the algorithm is not specified. In fact, we could try several algorithms to see which was most efficient. Second, when we write code on the basis of pre- and post-assertions, we should include these assertions as comments at the beginning of each procedure and function. These comments specify what each piece of code is supposed to do and thus help us understand our program. Also, these comments can help us in testing.

Testing Procedures with Small Driver Programs

The division of programs into independent pieces with clearly specified pre- and post-assertions has several important consequences for program testing.

When procedures and functions are independent, we can test them individually before we try to put them together. One way to proceed uses a small **driver program** that includes the function or procedure in a context that has just enough variables so we can run our procedure or function with test data. More precisely, a driver program to test a given procedure or function contains global declarations, initialization of required variables to meet all pre-assertions, a procedure or function call, and printing or evaluation of all post-assertions.

For example, if we are writing a complete statistics package that includes data entry, data editing, computation of many statistics, and printing of graphs, we could look at these parts separately. In particular, if we use a Procedure *Stat* to compute means, medians, and standard deviations as described earlier in this section, we could write a driver program as follows:

```
Program TestStat(Input, Output);
{Driver to test Stat procedure}

Const N = 6;

Type ArrayType = Array [1..10] of Real;

Var B: ArrayType;
    Mean, Med, StdDev: Real;
    I: Integer;

Procedure Stat
    {Details of this procedure are given here}

Begin
    {Initialize Variables}
    Writeln ('Enter values');
    For I := 1 To N
        Do Read (B[I]);

    {Test Routine}
    Stat (B, N, Mean, Med, StdDev);

    {Print Results}
    Writeln ('Array elements:');
    For I := 1 To N
        Do Write (B[I]);
    Writeln ('Mean =', Mean:5:2);
    Writeln ('Median =', Med:5:2);
    Writeln ('Standard Deviation =', StdDev:5:2);
End {Test} .
```

This program allows us to test Procedure *Stat* easily for a variety of test cases. However, it does not require us to write extensive data entry procedures. We do not have to worry about editing our data nor about drawing graphs. This simple driver program allows us to focus on a single procedure (or group of procedures) rather than the entire complex solution.

Stubbing

A second aid to testing and debugging independent procedures is the use of **stubbing.** In this approach, we write our main program with all of the outlined steps as procedures or functions. However, the body of these procedures is either greatly abbreviated or omitted.

For example, if we want to test our statistics package, the controlling procedure might contain the following procedure calls:

```
Begin {Control Processing}
      EnterData(A, N);
      EditData(A, N);
      Stat (A, N, Mean, Med, StdDev);
      PrintStatistics(A, N, Mean, Med, StdDev);
      PrintHistogram(A, N, Mean, Med, StdDev)
End {ControlProcessing};
```

This program involves many steps, but we can begin by simplifying several of them. For example, our editing procedure could be the following stub:

```
Procedure EditData(Var A: ArrayType; N: Integer);
      Begin
            Writeln('Data Editing Not Available at this Time!')
      End;
```

When we run our program, we can call *EditData,* and the procedure will tell us that it is being used. We still could test other procedures.

This same approach could apply to our *Stat* procedure, but here our post-assertions require that *Mean, Median,* and *StdDev* be given values by our procedure. Thus, our procedure stub might be the following:

```
Procedure Stat(A:ArrayType;N:Integer;Var Mean, Med, StdDev:Real);
      Begin
            Mean  : = 3.0;
            Median : =  3.3;
            StdDev : =  1.0
      End;
```

Obviously this stub does not perform the required computations. However, if our short-term goal is to test our data entry and printing routines, then this stub is adequate. Later, when the input and output procedures are completed, we can come back to this computational procedure.

Debugging Print Procedures

Another aid to testing includes writing special procedures to help in the debugging process. For example, in debugging we often need to print out various values to help us trace the execution of the program. This debugging task is so common that we may decide to write a debugging print procedure that we can call whenever we need to monitor the progress of our program.

A simple way to do this is to declare the folowing:

```
Procedure PrintValues(B: ArrayType; N: Integer;
                        VarMean, Med, StdDev:Real);
        Var I: Integer;
        Begin
            Writeln;
            For I : = 1 TO N
                Do Write(B[I]);
            Writeln ('Mean =', Mean:5:2);
            Writeln ('Median =', Med:5:2);
            Writeln ('Standard Deviation =', StdDev:5:2)
        End;
```

With this procedure, we simply insert a call to *PrintValues* in our code whenever we want to trace what our program is doing. If we already have a print procedure as part of our problem solution, we can use it without modification. We do not need special formatting for our debugging, so we could use any form we want elsewhere.

In more complex problems, we may want to keep our tracing statements in the code even after we believe we have tested our program fairly well. Long programs often contain subtle bugs that we find only after considerable use. When such bugs arise, we want to follow our program through the special cases without having to add our *Write* statements all over again.

One approach for these long programs involves the addition of a global Boolean constant *Debug*. Our program begins

```
Const Debug = True;
```

and our debugging procedure is

```
Procedure DebuggingPrint ( . . . );
        Begin
            If Debug
                Then Begin
                    Writeln . . .
                        .
                        .
                        .
                    Writeln . . .
                    End
        End
```

With this code, we call *DebuggingPrint* whenever we wish to trace our program. When we test our program, we set global constant *Debug* to *True*, and all the data we need to follow our program is printed. When our testing is done, we edit the program and set *Debug* to *False*, and then recompile. This simple change eliminates all of our extra printing. Then, if we need to trace our code at a later time, we just set *Debug* to *True*. Thus, a simple constant can allow us to include extra printing statements in our code for use in special circumstances.

Separate Compilation Sometimes Allowed

One final technique that can save considerable time in writing and debugging programs involves the separate compilation of procedures and functions. In Chapter 4, we noted that after we write our Pascal program, two steps are required before we can run it. First, our program must be compiled; Pascal must be translated to machine language. Second, references to functions and procedures must be added at appropriate places in a linking stage.

In some, but not all, Pascal compilers, independent procedures and functions can be compiled separately. Then, when all pieces are compiled, they can be linked together.

When this feature is available, we can save a great deal of time in several ways. To begin, we write and compile procedures and functions separately, and then, we write and compile small drivers for various procedures and functions as separate entities. Next, by linking a driver to its specific procedures and functions, we can test individual parts of our code. Here, as changes are needed, only a single function or procedure must be revised and recompiled. We do not need to recompile other pieces of code. The revised function or procedure is then linked again to the driver. Further, as we add features, individual stubs can be expanded to full working procedures and functions. Again, only the new pieces must be recompiled before linking. In the end, our final program can utilize the separate working pieces without further editing or copying. We just link the various pieces together in the complete main program.

Thus, with the capability of separate compilation, we can take full advantage of the independence of program parts in the ways we have mentioned in this section. Writing, testing, and changing code can be done one piece at a time; we do not have to recompile the entire program just to change one piece. Thus, independence of program units not only helps us in the early stages of problem solving, but also can help us minimize our work in writing, correcting, and compiling our code.

SUMMARY

1. **Parameter passage** can occur in two ways.
   a. With *value* passage, a new storage location is created for the formal parameter, and the value of the actual parameter is copied to the new location.

b. With *reference* passage, the formal parameter refers to the value of the actual parameter.

2. Various identifiers can be active at different times.

   a. The *scope* of an identifier is the time it is active.

   b. Identifiers can be *redefined*.

   c. A parameter may refer to another variable *(aliasing)*.

   d. Scope is based on the program environment at compile time, not at execution time.

3. A variable may be changed as a **side effect** of a function or procedure.

4. When writing programs, we should *eliminate* global *variables*, except perhaps when a few values must be *shared* by a certain limited number of procedures.

5. In developing and testing independent procedures, we may use the following techniques.

   a. procedure specifications with **calling format, pre-assertions,** and **post-assertions**

   b. testing procedures with small **driver programs**

   c. **stubbing**

   d. **debugging print procedures**

   e. **separate compilation** of functions and procedures.

EXERCISES

10.1 *Redefinition of Identifiers.* Write a program in which identifier *A* is used in different places as a formal parameter in a function, an actual parameter, a global variable, a local variable, and a procedure name.

KEY TERMS, PHRASES, AND CONCEPTS

Alias	Program Environment
Ambiguous Evaluation	Defined at Compile
of code	Time
Cohesion	Defined at
Coupling	Execution Time
Data Encapsulation	Redefinition of
Debugging Print	Identifiers
Procedures	Scope of Identifiers
Driver Program	Separate Compilation
Parameter Passage	Shared Variables
by Reference	Side Effect
by Value	Stubbing
Procedure Specification	
Calling Format	
Post-Assertion	
Pre-Assertion	

10.2 Describe several ways that the value of a global variable can be changed during a procedure call.

10.3 *Effect of Parameter Passage.* Write a procedure that returns different results depending upon whether the parameters are passed by value or by reference.

10.4 *Parameter Passage-1.* What is printed by the following program?

```
Program Passage (Output);
Var w, x, y, z: Integer;

Function F(x: Integer; Var y: Integer): Integer;
    Begin
        x := x - 3;
        y := y + 3;
        w := w Div 2;
        f := w + x + y + z;
        Writeln('F    ', w, x, y, z)
    End {F} ;

Function G(Var w: Integer): Integer;
    Var x, z: Integer;
    Begin
        x := 2;
        w := 3;
        z := 4;
        z := F(x, w);
        G := w + x + y + z;
        Writeln('G     ', w, x, y, z)
    End {G} ;

Begin {Main}
    x := 1;
    y := 2;
    w := 5;
    z := 3;
    z := F(x, y);
    Writeln('Main1', w, x, y, z);
    z := G(x);
    Writeln('Main2', w, x, y, z)
End {Passage}.
```

10.5 *Parameter Passage-2.* What is printed by the following program?

```
Program MorePassage (Output);
Var A, B, C, D: Integer;

Function F(A: Integer; Var B: Integer): Integer;
    Var C: Integer;
```

```
      Begin
          Writeln ('Function 1', A:5, B:5,  D:10);
          C := A + B;
          D := B + C;
          A := C + D;
          B := D + A;
          F := 3*A - 2*B;
          Writeln ('Function 2', A:5, B:5, C:5, D:5);
      End {F} ;

Begin {Main}
      Writeln (' Location     A    B    C    D');
      A := -1;
      B := 2;
      C := -3;
      D := 4;
      Writeln ('    Main 1', A:5, B:5, C:5, D:5);
      D := F(A, B);
      Writeln ('    Main 2', A:5, B:5, C:5, D:5);
      B := F(C, D);
      Writeln ('    Main 2', A:5, B:5, C:5, D:5)
End {Main} .
```

10.6 *Ambiguity with Parameters.* The following program could print several sets of output. What are they?

```
Program Ambiguous (Output);
Var A, X: Integer;
Function F(Var U: Integer): Integer;
      Begin
          U := 2 * U;
          F := U - 4
      End;
Begin
      Writeln (' A    X');
      A := 3;
      X := A + F(A);
      Writeln (A:3, X:5);
      A := 3;
      X := F(A) + A;
      Writeln (A:3, X:5)
End.
```

10.7 *Finding Errors.* The following program was written to find the average of 10 or fewer numbers. Numbers are read until a sentinel value is encountered. Find four of the six errors in the program.

NOTE: The semicolons are correct. The errors are fundamental errors; that is, the program will not compile in its present form and correcting the syntax errors still leaves a program that produces incorrect results. Do not count issues of style; that is, ignore the lack of user prompting and the form of the output.

```
Program Errors (Input, Output);

Const Max = 10;

Type ArrayType = Array[1..Max] of Integer;

Var I, J, Item: Integer;
    B: ArrayType;
    Avg: Integer;

Procedure FindMean (A: ArrayType; N: Integer; Mean: Real);
    Var Sum: Integer;
    Begin
        Sum := 0;
        For I := 1 To Max
            Do Sum := Sum + A(I);
        Mean := Sum / N
    End {FindMean} ;

Begin {Main}
    {Initialize}
    For I := 1 To Max
        Do B[I] := 0;
    J := 0;

    {Read data}
    Read (Item);
    While (Item <> -3.1416)
      Do Begin
        J := J + 1;
        B[J] := Item;
        Read (Item)
      End;

    {Compute and Print Average}
    FindMean (B, J, Avg) ;
    Writeln (Avg)

End {Main} .
```

10.8 *Potpourri.* What is printed by the following program?

```
Program Potpourri (Output);
{This program illustrates many ways that identifiers can
 be redefinited and changed.}

Var A, B, C: Integer;

Function TwiceSum (Var X, Y: Integer; B: Integer): Integer;
    Var A: Real;
    Procedure Double(Var A: Integer; B: Real);
        Begin
            Writeln ('     Double 1:', A:5, B:6:1, C:4, X:5, Y:5);
            A := 2 * A;
            B := A;
            Writeln ('     Double 2:', A:5, B:6:1, C:4, X:5, Y:5);
        End {Minus} ;
    Begin {TwiceSum}
        A := 2.7;
        Writeln ('  TwiceSum 1:', A:6:1, B:4, C:5, X:5, Y:5);
        C := X + Y;
        X := B + C;
        Double (X, A);
        TwiceSum := X;
        Writeln ('  TwiceSum 2:', A:6:1, B:4, C:5, X:5, Y:5)
    End {TwiceSum} ;

Procedure PartTwo(X: Integer; Var Y: Integer);
    Var C: Integer;
    Function A: Integer;
        Begin
            Writeln ('Function A 1:', B:10, C:5, X:5, Y:5);
            C := X + Y;
            A := 2 * C;
            Writeln ('Function A 2:', B:10, C:5, X:5, Y:5);
        End {FunctionA} ;
    Begin {PartTwo}
        C := -3;
        Writeln ('   PartTwo 1:', B:10, C:5, X:5, Y:5);
        B := A + TwiceSum(X, Y, B);
        Writeln ('   PartTwo 2:', B:10, C:5, X:5, Y:5)
    End {PartTwo} ;

Begin {Main}
    {Print Headings}
    Writeln ('      Location     A     B     C     X     Y');

    {Initialization}
    A := 1;
    B := 2;
    C := 3;
    Writeln ('      Main 1:', A:5, B:5, C:5);

    {Apply Function TwiceSum}
    C := TwiceSum (A, A, B);
    Writeln ('      Main 2:', A:5, B:5, C:5);

    {Apply Procedure PartTwo}
    PartTwo (A, B);
    Writeln ('      Main 3:', A:5, B:5, C:5)
End {Main} .
```

10.9 *Test Driver Programs.* Section 8.7 includes an insertion procedure, a deletion procedure, and an insertion sort procedure. Write driver programs to test these procedures.

CHAPTER 11

PROGRAM

CORRECTNESS

AND ACCURACY

Our work to this point has included a top-down methodology for attacking problems and various programming techniques that allow us to translate our solution outlines into Pascal programs. In this chapter, we consider how we can be sure that our final programs produce correct answers.

To begin, we identify various potential sources of error. Then, we examine what we mean by the correctness of a program, and we discover that we can view correctness at two different levels. Finally, this background allows us to identify strategies to improve the quality of our programs at several stages in the development process.

SECTION 11.1   POTENTIAL SOURCES OF ERROR

From our programming up to now, we are probably quite familiar with typographical errors, because they are often caught by the compiler when we try to compile our program. However, these errors represent only one of the many places that difficulties can arise. Mistakes can occur in our work before we even start coding. Also, in some situations, "correct" programs may produce unsatisfactory output.

When we think of problem solving as a process that starts with problem design and analysis and ends with the running of a program, we find we might make errors at each stage in this process. When we analyze these errors, we might divide them into the following categories.

Logical Errors. These arise from mistakes, inconsistencies, or omissions in our approach to a problem.

Numerical Errors. Many real numbers cannot be stored exactly in computers. The resulting numerical errors may significantly affect our answers in some cases.

Algorithm Selection Errors. The algorithm we select may not produce answers in a reasonable amount of time, or the answers may not be sufficiently accurate.

Coding Errors. We may make mistakes in translating our detailed algorithm into program code.

Data Entry Errors. Even when a program is correct, we may obtain incorrect results if we have not entered our data correctly.

In the next five sections, we look at each of these types of error in more detail. Then, in the later part of this chapter we will develop strategies to find or avoid these problems early in the problem solving process.

SECTION 11.2	LOGICAL ERRORS

Logical errors arise from mistakes in our approach to a problem. Of course, people demonstrate considerable creativity in making mistakes, and we cannot possibly describe all ways that people can go wrong. However, we can identify some of the most common errors, including

- incorrect or unstated assumptions;
- faulty algorithm choice or specification;
- omissions; and
- inconsistencies.

Assumptions

As we work on a problem, we should be aware of the assumptions we are making. For example, we may assume that a user usually will enter all of the required data on one line, or that the data will be in ascending order. Similarly, when we choose an algorithm to perform a particular task, we may assume that certain conditions are true. For example, to use the extremely efficient Binary Search Algorithm, our data must be ordered. Further, when we develop a formula to compute a desired quantity, our work may rest on certain conditions. For example, if we use the following variation of the standard deviation formula

$$\text{Standard Deviation} = [(x_1 - \overline{x})^2 + \ldots + (x_n - \overline{x})^2]/[n - 1]$$

the formula assumes $n > 1$.

In any of these cases, we need to identify what our assumptions are, so we can be sure they are met. For example, we must notify the user if we assume something about the way data will be entered. Similarly, we must decide how to proceed if our data violate the conditions that we need. (How will we deal with standard deviation if n = 1?)

In general, we must be sure we know what our assumptions are, so we can take them into account in the problem solving process and so our resulting programs will be correct and accurate.

Algorithms

When we choose or develop an algorithm to accomplish a task, we obviously want our final algorithm to do the work required. Clearly, our choice of algorithm is correct if the algorithm does the right job, and our choice is wrong otherwise. For example, we would hardly pick an algorithm that does a population growth simulation if we want to sort data. Blatant problems in algorithms may be easy to find, but more subtle errors frequently occur that are much harder to locate.

Two examples illustrate ways that trouble can arise if we are not absolutely clear what the algorithm is to do. In the first one, suppose we are to search a list of data for a particular item. Here, we need to know what result we want when the search is complete. Do we want a result "True" or "False" indicating whether the item is found? Or, do we want to know the location on the list where the specified item is located? Similar searching algorithms could address either question, but the details of these two algorithms would be different.

As a second example, suppose we are to insert a new item into our ordered list of data, and we specify a function to locate the place for our insertion. Here, the function might return either the location of the next smaller datum in the list or the location of the next larger datum. If our algorithm returns one of these when we expected the other, our problem solution will be wrong. If our algorithm sometimes returns one of these and sometimes the other, the error in our solution may be quite hard to find.

In a related matter, we must be sure that any loops start and stop correctly. For example, if we want to read data entered from a terminal until we encounter a sentinel value, we must be sure the sentinel is not included in our processing. Similarly, if we want to add

$$(1.0)^2 + (1.5)^2 + \ldots + (9.5)^2 + (10.0)^2$$

we must account for 19 terms. If we miscount these terms, so we have 18 or 20 items instead, our result will be related to the correct answer, but the algorithm will be wrong.

Once we describe carefully what an algorithm is to do, we may be able to check that a particular algorithm works correctly. Errors frequently arise when our algorithm specification is not sufficiently precise. When we are a bit sloppy, our algorithm may look fine, but it may answer a slightly different question than we are asking.

Omissions

Another common source of trouble is the omission of important considerations. For example, we can ask the following.

Do all loops stop? We must check each loop to be sure that the exit condition will eventually be met. For example, in a search, our loop must stop even if an item is not found.

Are all cases covered? For example, in tabulating a survey, we must consider the case where no one answers a particular question.

Do we need a special case for the first or last step in a loop? We must check whether the processing for the first or last iteration in a loop follows the general pattern. For example, in an Insertion Sort, we do not check the first item against previous ones before inserting it in a list, but we do check subsequent items.

Will our subscripts always be within proper bounds? We may need to check subscripts to ensure they will not be too big or too small. For example, we should be sure that there is space to add an item to a list of data stored in an array.

Each of these questions has many implications for problem solving. When we neglect special cases, we may find that our resulting programs work sporadically. Sometimes the programs seem to work fine, but other times they stop abruptly. Such bugs can be hard to locate.

Inconsistencies

Inconsistencies arise most often in large programs, when we change our perspective from one step to another. Thus, when we look at successive steps in our solution outline, we should ask the following.

Are we using consistent variable names? Variable names may be confused in different parts of the program. The use of two names may be interchanged from one procedure to another.

Are our data types the same? Data may be considered in tabular form one place in a program but in list form later on. Double subscripting in one procedure will not agree with single subscripting elsewhere.

Are reference parameters accidentally changed by side effects? We may use reference parameters by mistake instead of value parameters, or we may inadvertently change reference parameters in a function or procedure.

Problems in these areas may be found in almost every beginning programming class, when reasonably long programs (more than 200 lines) are required. Problems arising from the use of global variables in inconsistent ways are particularly common. Many of these problems are reduced if we write out what each step in our outline is to do, where it is to get its data from, and how it is to return its results. In short, a careful top-down approach to problem solving normally prevents most inconsistencies from occurring. However, shortcuts in this approach regularly yield programs that are hopelessly confused because of the inconsistent use of data types and variables.

SECTION 11.3   NUMERICAL ERRORS

Computers may not store real numbers exactly, because of various practical limitations on storage. In particular, a computer can store only a certain number of significant digits of a real number, and when real numbers require more than that degree of accuracy, **round-off error** results. The amount of round-off error may vary from one machine to another, but such an error is always potentially present. In contrast, integers are stored exactly, so they need not involve round-off error. (More details of this storage are given in Appendix B.)

Decimal-Binary Conversion

Storage of real numbers is further compounded by the way computers are built. In particular, electrical devices depend upon closed and open circuits (current flowing or not), and this circuitry is then used to represent numbers. For example, when writing numbers, a computer might interpret 1 as current flowing or high voltage and 0 as no current flowing or low voltage. Thus, numbers are usually represented using two digits 0 or 1 rather than in decimal form. The resulting numbers are called **binary numbers,** and we defer the details of these numbers to Appendix C. For now, our main concern is that not all decimals translate exactly into a few binary digits.

Example: ⅓ does not translate into an exact decimal that can be stored by a computer. If we store 8 significant digits, then ⅓ = 0.33333333. All of the places beyond the eighth are lost.

The same situation arises when various decimal numbers are stored in binary form. For example, 0.1 cannot be stored exactly in a computer in binary form.

This leads to the following basic principle which we must recognize.

Whenever we work with real numbers in a computer, we cannot assume the numbers are exact; there is always the potential for a numerical error.

Consequences of Numerical Errors

This potential for numerical error has several practical consequences in programming. Here, we consider

- writing Boolean expressions;
- writing exit conditions;
- non-associativity;
- promulgation of errors; and
- use of index or control variables.

A few illustrations dramatize these consequences particularly well.

Boolean Expressions.   Consider the following program:

```
Program LongLoop (Output);

Const Inc = 0.1;          {Increment added each time through loop}
Var Sum: Real;            {The result of our additions}
    Difference: Real;     {Difference between Sum and 1.0}

Begin
    Writeln ('We add 0.1 successively, starting at 0.0 until we reach 1.0');
    Writeln;
    Writeln ('    Sum        Difference from 1.0');

    Sum := 0.0;
    Repeat

        Difference := 1.0 - Sum;
        Writeln (Sum:10:8, Difference:18:10);
        Sum := Sum + Inc

    Until (Sum = 1.0);

    Writeln('Program Done')
End.
```

When we ran this program on one particular machine the output began as follows.

```
We add 0.1 successively, starting at 0.0 until we reach 1.0

    Sum        Difference from 1.0
0.00000000      1.0000000000
0.10000000      0.9000000000
0.20000000      0.8000000000
0.30000000      0.7000000000
0.40000000      0.6000000000
0.50000000      0.5000000000
0.60000000      0.4000000000
0.70000000      0.3000000000
0.80000010      0.1999999000
0.90000010      0.0999999000
1.00000000     -0.0000001192
1.10000000     -0.1000001000
1.20000000     -0.2000002000
1.30000000     -0.3000002000
1.40000000     -0.4000002000
1.50000000     -0.5000002000
1.60000000     -0.6000003000

    .
    .
    .
```

Here, the computer continues to produce output beyond the point we expect. The program starts at 0 and adds 0.1 until we get to 1.0, so we expect our program will stop after 10 iterations.

However, here the 0.1 is not stored exactly. When we add 0.1 several times, this inaccuracy grows and our sum never actually equals 1.0. Our sum does equal 1.0 to six decimal places, but our result contains a small numerical error. *Program Done* is never printed.

This example shows that when we compare real numbers, we may want to allow for possible error. Thus, in this program, instead of continuing until *Sum* = 1.0, we might substitute a test for proximity:

$$\text{Abs}(Sum - 1.0) < 0.001$$

Exit Conditions. A modification of the above program illustrates a related problem with Boolean expressions as exit conditions.

```
Program ShortLoop (Output);

Const Inc = 0.1;        {Increment added each time through loop}
Var Sum: Real;          {The result of our additions}

Begin
    Writeln ('We add 0.1 successively, starting at 0.0 ',
            'while we do not exceed 1.0');
    Writeln;

    Sum := 0.0;
    While (Sum <= 1.0)
      Do Begin
         Write (Sum:5:1);
         Sum := Sum + Inc
      End;

    Writeln('    Program Done')
End.
```

Here, we want to continue our loop but not exceed 1.0. However, our output appears to skip the final case where *Sum* = 1.0. The actual output is

```
We add 0.1 successively, starting at 0.0 while we do not exceed 1.0

 0.0  0.1  0.2  0.3  0.4  0.5  0.6  0.7  0.8  0.9    Program Done
```

When we look at the output from the previous program, we see the difficulty is that the numerical error gives us results that are slightly too large. In particular, the machine computes 1.000001192 instead of 1.0 during the 10th time through the loop. Thus, while we expected a *Sum* of 1.0 to be printed at the end of our loop, this case was skipped. The loop stopped one iteration before we expected. Here, numerical errors have shortened our loop by one iteration.

This example illustrates the following:

> *We cannot depend upon real variables to count loop iterations; numerical errors may cause steps to be skipped when real variables are incremented and tested in exit conditions.*

This potential for numerical error is precisely the reason why Pascal does not allow real variables as control variables. Some other languages do not have this restriction, but they always have the potential for unexpected results when a particular iteration is skipped. Pascal eliminates this possibility of error in control variables.

Non-Associativity. Another consequence of real number storage is that arithmetic no longer follows the familiar rules that we depend upon in much of our traditional thinking about numbers. In particular, *addition is not associative*. In other words, we cannot assume that

$$(a + b) + c = a + (b + c)$$

for all real numbers a, b, c. Instead it may matter if we perform $(a + b)$ or $(b + c)$ first.

As an example, suppose that our computer stores exactly 8 digits of accuracy and suppose that it rounds to those 8 digits after each operation. Now, suppose we add

$$1.0000000 + 0.00000004 + 0.00000004$$

in two ways.

a. If we add the first two numbers, we get

> $1.0000000 + 0.00000004$
> $= (1.00000004)$
> $= 1.0000000$ rounding to 8 significant digits
>   (including the 1).

Thus

> $(1.0000000 + 0.00000004) + 0.00000004$
> $= (1.0000000) + 0.00000004$ first addition with rounding;
> $= 1.0000000$ second addition with rounding.

b. If we add the second two numbers first, we get

$$0.00000004 + 0.00000004 = 0.00000008$$

and

$$1.0000000 + (0.00000004 + 0.00000004)$$
$$= 1.0000000 + (0.00000008) \quad \text{first addition;}$$
$$= (1.00000008) \quad \text{second addition before rounding;}$$
$$= 1.0000001 \quad \text{second addition after rounding.}$$

These three numbers demonstrate that the order of addition matters. When we add small numbers to large numbers, the small numbers can be lost completely (as in a. above). On the other hand, if we add small numbers first, the small pieces can accumulate enough to affect the large number (as in b. above).

When we are adding many such numbers, the cumulative effect of these errors can be quite noticeable. For example, consider the following:

PROBLEM 11.3   It can be shown that

$$\pi^2 = 6 + 6/2^2 + 6/3^2 + 6/4^2 + \ldots$$

Use this series to approximate the value of π.

Discussion of Problem 11.3

The above formula indicates that we can approximate π^2 by adding more and more terms of this series. In other words,

$$\pi^2 \approx 6 + 6/2^2 + 6/3^2 + 6/4^2 + \ldots + 6/n^2$$

where n is a large integer.

When we compute the right hand side of this equation, we will get an approximate value of π^2. Then by taking the square root, we can approximate π.

When we look at this series carefully, we see that the terms get smaller continually as the denominators get bigger. Thus, we must be careful when we add up our terms. If we start with the first term 6, we will have our large numbers first, and the small terms will not affect these large results. If we start with the small terms, the small values can accumulate. This difference is illustrated in the following program.

```
Program Series (Output);
{Approximation of Pi}
{Using the series Sqr(Pi) = 6 + 6/Sqr(2) + 6/Sqr(3) + ...}
Var SumUp, SumDown, IReal: Real;
    Index, N: Integer;

Begin {Main}
    {Determine number of terms to be used in the approximation}
    Writeln ('The value of Pi is approximated by using N terms of a series.');
    Write('Enter N: ');
    Readln(N);
```

```
    {Compute terms in ascending order}
    SumUp := 0.0;
    For Index := 1 to N
      Do Begin
        IReal := Index;
        SumUp := SumUp + 6.0/Sqr(IReal);
      End;

    {Compute terms in descending order}
    SumDown := 0.0;
    For Index := N DownTo 1
      Do Begin
        IReal := Index;
        SumDown := SumDown + 6.0/Sqr(Ireal)
      End;

    {Print Results}
    Writeln;
    Writeln(' Number Of        Approximations to Pi');
    Writeln('  Terms      Biggest First     Smallest First');
    Writeln(N:7, Sqrt(SumUp):17:10, Sqrt(SumDown):17:10)
End {Main} .
```

When this program is run for various values of n, we get the following output:

```
First Trial Run

The value of Pi is approximated by using N terms of a series.
Enter N: 1000

 Number Of        Approximations to Pi
  Terms      Biggest First     Smallest First
   1000      3.1406390000       3.1406380000


Second Trial Run

The value of Pi is approximated by using N terms of a series.
Enter N: 3000

 Number Of        Approximations to Pi
  Terms      Biggest First     Smallest First
   3000      3.1412800000       3.1412740000


Third Trial Run

The value of Pi is approximated by using N terms of a series.
Enter N: 3543

 Number Of        Approximations to Pi
  Terms      Biggest First     Smallest First
   3543      3.1413630000       3.1413230000
```

```
Fourth Trial Run

The value of Pi is approximated by using N terms of a series.
Enter N: 5000

    Number Of          Approximations to Pi
      Terms      Biggest First    Smallest First
      5000       3.1413630000     3.1414020000


Fifth Trial Run

The value of Pi is approximated by using N terms of a series.
Enter N: 30000

    Number Of          Approximations to Pi
      Terms      Biggest First    Smallest First
     30000       3.1413630000     3.1415610000
```

This output illustrates several important points:

- When we add a series in one order, we can get different results than if we add it in another order.
- When we add terms in descending order, the large terms dominate and small terms can be lost. In this program, when we add the large terms first, our approximation for π does not change after $n = 3542$. After this, the additional terms are too small to affect the already large sum.
- When we add terms in ascending order, the small terms can contribute. When we add the small terms first, our approximation for π continually improves as we add more terms.

Propagation of Errors. The previous example also illustrates that when we put real numbers together, the size of the numerical errors can increase. Each real number may be off by a small amount; when we combine these numbers, we may combine these errors. This error can be particularly significant when we subtract two numbers of about the same size, for then our result depends largely on the least accurate parts of the original numbers.

SECTION 11.4   CHOICE OF ALGORITHM

Any algorithm that we might select for a program must meet at least two fundamental criteria, namely efficiency and accuracy. The algorithm must be efficient enough to produce results in a reasonable length of time, and the results must be sufficiently accurate to solve the problem. In this section, we look at some practical consequences of each of these criteria.

Efficiency

Algorithm efficiency can be divided into two fairly obvious parts. First, we must be confident that an algorithm eventually will stop. A program containing an infinite loop cannot be helpful. Second, once we know the algorithm will stop, we can analyze how much time will normally be required for the output.

While these points may seem obvious in considering program efficiency, they do have important practical implications in our design of algorithms. Consider the following:

- A simulation may require a process to continue until a certain condition is met. (We may need to flip a coin until three consecutive heads appear.) However, if that condition happens only rarely, we may need to make a special provision so that our loop stops. (In tossing coins, we may limit the total number of tosses allowed. If the number of tosses exceeds this maximum, we may report the results as a special case.)
- Given the possibility of numerical errors discussed in the previous section, Boolean expressions and exit conditions must allow for small differences between real numbers that theoretically should be the same.
- If an algorithm requires a great deal of computer time to produce an answer, we may want to find a better way to proceed. In some cases, we may be able to streamline a given algorithm to make it work more effectively. In other cases, we may have to discard one algorithm completely, and we may need to discover a new approach to the problem. For example, when data are ordered, we changed our approach from the simple linear search to develop the substantially better binary search.

Accuracy

In the last section, we saw that arithmetic cannot be assumed to be associative. Thus, when adding many numbers, we should add the smallest ones first. Similarly, we saw round-off error can accumulate; when adding many numbers, our results may include some error even when the results theoretically should be getting very close to the "correct" answers.

Thus, in choosing an algorithm, we must have confidence that our final results will be sufficiently accurate to be helpful. Here, we can distinguish three types of algorithms.

- Some algorithms (e.g., the Trapezoidal Rule) tend to accumulate round-off error. Any inaccuracy in one step is compounded in the next step. For these algorithms, we must be aware that numerical errors can accumulate, and we must be careful not to expect too much accuracy in our results.
- Other algorithms (e.g., the Bisection Method of Section 7.6) do not tend to accumulate errors. In these algorithms, each step starts fresh, and

previous computations are not used again. Thus, in these algorithms, numerical error does not tend to accumulate.

- Some algorithms may even be self-correcting. In these algorithms, any errors in previous steps tend to be corrected in subsequent steps. (For example, in finding the solutions of an equation, two common algorithms, called Newton's Method and the Method of False Position, are self-correcting. More details on these algorithms may be found in texts on calculus or numerical methods.)

Coding Implications

These comments on efficiency and accuracy have several coding implications.

In some programs, such as simulations, we may want to count the number of times that a loop is executed. If the number exceeds a specified limit, we might want to stop the loop as a special case, thereby avoiding the possibility of an infinite loop.

When we are unsure about the efficiency of an algorithm, we may want to write the algorithm as a separate procedure. Then, if the algorithm does not run as efficiently as required, a new algorithm can be substituted in the program by changing only this procedure.

We can code our algorithms to minimize possible numerical errors. For example, we can identify two ways to compute

$$(0.1)^2 + (0.2)^2 + \ldots + (100.0)^2.$$

Approach 1:

```
Sum := 0.0;
XValue := 0.1;
While   (XValue <= 100.0)
        Do  Begin
                Sum := Sum + Sqr(XValue);
                XValue := XValue + 0.1
        End;
```

Approach 2:

```
Sum := 0.0;
For   I := 1 to 1000
        Do Begin
                XValue := I/10.0;
                Sum := Sum + Sqr(XValue)
        End;
```

In looking at the first approach, we see two problems. First, our exit condition does not allow for possible error in *XValue*, and we may stop one iteration too soon in our loop. In addition, any inaccuracy in the storage of 0.1 will be compounded as the loop proceeds, since the values of *XValue* depend upon previous values.

In contrast, the second approach does not allow these errors to accumulate. Since our loop depends on an integer control variable, we will continue our loop the correct number of times. Further, *XValue* is recomputed from the exact integer *I* each time in the loop. Previous inaccuracies in *XValue* are not included.

SECTION 11.5	CODING ERRORS

Once we have chosen our algorithm and outlined our solution, we are ready for coding. Here, we can distinguish two principal types of errors.

- Typographical errors
- Errors in translating from our algorithm or outline to our Pascal program.

Typographical Errors

As early as Section 2.8, we saw that a compiler will find many typographical errors, since each variable, function, and procedure we use must agree with an identifier we have declared. However, Section 2.8 also noted that some typographical errors cannot be caught by a compiler. For example, a compiler cannot find errors in literal numbers, characters, or Booleans (3.1416 might be written 3.1614). Similarly, the comiler will not detect substitutions of one identifier for another. For example, if both I and J are declared, I might be used for J on a particular line.

The first of these errors can be minimized by the wise use of constants. For example, if we declare

$$\text{Const Pi} = 3.1416$$

then we only need to check the digits of the constant once. Thereafter, we can refer to it symbolically as *Pi*.

The elimination of the second class of these errors depends upon careful proofreading. We must examine our code in detail to be sure we have typed what we meant. This is a major point where program formatting and style become important. If our code reads naturally, we often can find typographical errors fairly easily. Descriptive identifiers are particularly useful here, for the names tell us what we are doing. For example, we will find it harder to confuse identifiers *Quarts* and *Liters* than the abbreviations *Q* and *L*.

Translation Errors

Errors also can arise in translating from our algorithms and solution outline into Pascal. One way this might happen is if we implement particular steps incorrectly. Translation errors also may result if our outline is not sufficiently complete so that logical errors may occur as we add the required details to our code.

In each of these areas, careful formatting and the division of our program into procedures and functions can help us check our work. Normally, details are easy to check if they are isolated in short pieces of code. Also, the major flow of our program is clear if details are separated from major steps. In short, programs that are well structured generally are easy to proofread and correct.

Caution

This discussion of program structure assumes considerable preliminary work in structuring solutions. When this preliminary work is not done, the task of developing algorithms and writing details falls into the coding process. In any approach to problem solving, we must complete all details before we are done. Thus, if we avoid the details at one stage, we must face them later on.

When we consider the programming process, it is easier to correct programs before they are written. Adding details at coding time is a highly error-prone venture. Experience suggests that we take the time to write out our design carefully, before we are committed to particular pieces of code.

| SECTION 11.6 | DATA ENTRY ERRORS |

In Section 9.3, we noted that even a correct program can produce inappropriate results if the program is given incorrect data. Thus, in planning a program, we should consider the possibility that errors will be found in the program input. These input errors fall into three classes:

> input that is impossible;
>
> input that is unlikely, but possible; and
>
> plausible input that is incorrect.

For each of these types of errors, we may need to proceed differently.

Impossible Input

In some situations, we may be able to determine that a particular input value could not possibly be correct. The following examples illustrate such situations.

In the Tic-Tac-Toe game of Section 9.3, our move must be in row 1, 2, or 3 and in column 1, 2, or 3. Further, we cannot mark a square that has been taken previously. If we try to move into row 5 or if we try to move on an occupied square, our move is invalid.

If we are recording telephone numbers, we know the form of our input should be

(area code)-(exchange)-(number).

Further, we know

the area code contains 3 digits, and the second digit is 0 or 1;

the exchange contains 3 digits and the second digit cannot be a 0 or 1; and

the number contains 4 digits.

Thus, we can conclude that each of the following telephone numbers is invalid.

123-456-7890 second digit of area code incorrect
312-5555-8901 wrong number of digits for exchange
312-515-5432 incorrect second digit of exchange

Many credit card numbers include digits for checking typing. For example, in a 10-digit number, the 10th digit might be chosen so the sum of the digits is 0 mod 10. Thus,

1234567895 is possible
0123456789 is impossible

In any of these cases, we can state rules that can be used to check if an input value is possible. Then, in programming we can check this, and we can request users to reenter data that is definitely wrong.

This checking is particularly important if we write our programs based on certain assumptions in the data. For example, in the Tic-Tac-Toe program of Section 9.3, we want to write

Read (Row, Column)

.
.
.

Board [Row, Column] := X

Here, we must know our *Row* and *Column* will have values 1, 2, or 3. Any other values will cause our array subscript to be out of bounds, and our program will terminate prematurely. Thus, in this program, invalid data could halt processing if we do not check each input value first.

Possible but Unlikely Input

In other applications, we may want a user to double check an input value before we continue. Here, we might expect values of a certain type or range, but we cannot rule out the possibility of other values.

- In a grocery store, we expect most individual items to be between $0.00 and $100.00 (exclusive). Items over $100.00 are very unlikely, although they are possible. (For example, one side of beef from the meat department could exceed this amount.)

- Test scores rarely exceed 100% although extra credit sometimes brings scores over this point.
- Few customers have a birth date before the year 1900, but a few might.

In these cases, we need to scan an input value to see if it is unlikely to be correct, and we may ask the user to verify the correctness of the datum. For example, if a grocery item costs $150.00, we may wonder if the cashier has entered an extra "0," and we may give the cashier an opportunity to correct this value. However, since this value is possible, our program must allow this value to be processed.

Possible but Incorrect Input

In the previous two cases, we have been able to identify input data that were suspect. Our job of verifying input is much harder if the values seem plausible. For example, if a grocery item costing $3.29 is incorrectly marked as $2.39, we will have difficulty spotting an error. The $2.39 value seems to be a reasonable cost for an item, and we would have no reason to suspect a mistake unless we checked an inventory list or invoice.

In such situations, we may elect several approaches to data entry.

1. We may decide that such errors are too costly or time consuming to find, and we may elect to ignore them.
2. We may supply the user with a print out of all data entered, so the user can check the values manually. (The paper receipt at the grocery store allows this type of checking.)
3. We may add digits to our data, so the data can be checked automatically. For example, after a cost, we may write the sum of the digits (mod 10) and the product of the odd digits (mod 10). Thus, for $3.29

$$\text{sum of digits} = 3 + 2 + 9 = 14$$
$$\text{product of odd digits} = 3 * 9 = 27$$

and 3.29 would be coded

$$3.29 - 4 - 7$$

Such checks do not completely eliminate the possibility of error, but these checks could spot many typographical errors. In general, the field of Coding Theory includes the study of how these check-digits can be added to numbers so that many types of data errors can be identified.

Implications in Programming

In practice, we may find that we want to combine several types of checks for input data. Some values may be impossible. Other values may be possible, but unlikely. When checking input data, we often write the details of data entry in a separate procedure:

Procedure Enter (Var Value: Data)

This procedure reads the value, checks it for being impossible or unlikely, asks the user for corrections, if necessary, and returns a "correct" value. All details of data entry are buried inside this procedure, so the rest of the program can rely upon this procedure for obtaining correct values. Checking is not required outside the procedure.

SECTION 11.7 — DEGREES OF PROGRAM CORRECTNESS

Now that we have seen how various types of errors can arise, we can put several of these ideas together in our development of correct programs.

Of course, any program is correct and useful only if it answers the questions that we are asking. Thus, in evaluating a program, we first must specify explicitly what the program is to do. Then the correctness of the program depends upon whether it meets this specification. We cannot discuss the correctness of a program in isolation; we must know what problem we are solving before we can evaluate a program.

Testing and Correctness

Once we know what a program is supposed to do, we can try to determine if the program performs correctly. Here, we should be careful to distinguish between two categories of statements:

"This program produces correct answers for all possible values of data."

"This program *seems* to produce correct answers." (At least, we have not found any instances where incorrect results are obtained.)

The first of these statements asserts that the program is correct, while the second asserts that the program is *likely* to be correct. In the first case, we can rely upon our results, for we know that no bugs are present in our program. In the second case, we know we have not found any bugs, but we cannot rule out the possibility that a subtle error might exist somewhere. Thus, the first statement is much stronger than the second.

To clarify this distinction, we consider the following.

PROBLEM 11.7 — Prime Numbers

A positive integer is *prime* if it is divisible only by 1 and itself. Thus, 2, 3, and 5 are prime, but 6 is not. (6 is divisible by 2 and 3 as well as by 1.)

Write a program that reads a positive integer and determines if the number is prime.

Let us consider the following attempt to solve this program.

```
Program PrimeMaybe (Input, Output);
{This program attempts to determine if a given Number is prime.}
Var Number: Integer;
Begin
    Writeln ('Prime tester');
    Write ('Enter integer to be tested: ');
    Readln (Number);
    If (Number = 2) Or
        ((Number > 1) And ((Number Mod 2) = 1))
          Then Writeln ('The number is prime.')
          Else Writeln ('The number is not prime.')
End .
```

When we run this program for the test cases 1, 2, 3, 4, 5, 6, 7, and 8, we find the program gives correct results. Further, if we try larger numbers such as 28, 29, 30, 31, 101, 102, 103, and 104, the program works correctly. From these tests, we may conclude that our program *seems* to be correct, and we might expect that these sixteen test cases are more than adequate to check our code. However, we cannot conclude that the program works correctly for all possible values, and in fact, the program incorrectly identifies the integer 9 as a prime number. (More generally, the program fails for odd, non-primes larger than 1.)

This example illustrates two important points.

1. When we say a program is correct, we mean that the program will produce correct results for all possible input values.
2. Testing specific values of input cannot prove a program is correct, unless we actually test all possible input values.

When we test a program by using selected data, we may be able to conclude that our program is not correct. Certainly, we know that a bug is present if our answers are wrong. However, correct test runs cannot prove our programs work for all input values unless we have tested all such values. We must be careful not to infer too much from a few test cases. Test cases may give us some confidence about our work, but they do not prove the work.

Determining Program Correctness

Next, we need to ask how we could conclude that a program is correct. This can be done in two basic ways: exhaustive testing and verification.

Exhaustive Testing. In some problems, we can actually test all possible cases. For example, if we want the computer to print the number of days in each month for the year 1986, we can check the output in complete detail. Similarly, if our problem only makes sense for integer values between −5 and 10 (inclusive), then we could enter each value and check the results. This approach to proving program correctness is called **exhaus-**

tive testing, and it is feasible only when the number of possible cases in our problem is fairly small.

Verification.   If the number of data items in our problem is large, exhaustive testing is not feasible, and we must proceed differently. One approach that has sparked a great deal of research in computer science is called **program verification.** Here, the task of the program is specified in precise, formal terms, and a formal proof is constructed to show that the program does the desired task.

For example, when proving results about a procedure or function, we can begin with some pre-assertions which we assume to be true. From these givens, we might prove in a formal way that our post-assertions hold. The approach is similar to the approach used in geometry where axioms (pre-assertions) are assumed to be true and theorems (post-assertions) are then proven. In this process, we may find it convenient to make statements about what happens in the middle of a procedure or function. These intermediate statements are the assertions and loop invariants that we discussed in Sections 5.8 and 7.5.

Throughout this approach, we do not rely on testing to check that a program seems to run correctly. Rather, formal logic is used to make conclusions about a program. Then, whenever we run our program, we know our results will be correct (according to our post-assertions) for any input data meeting our pre-assertions.

SECTION 11.8	METHODS OF PROGRAM TESTING

In the previous section, we said that exhaustive testing can guarantee that a program is correct, but we noted that such testing is rarely feasible. In this section, we look at how we might select test data when our tests cannot cover all cases. Here, we hope that some carefully selected test runs can help us eliminate many bugs that might be in our code initially. In particular, we can identify two basic approaches for testing.

Top-Down Testing.   When we have organized our program into modules, we can first test each module separately. Then, when our testing has helped us correct any errors within each module, we can put these pieces together and test that the pieces interact properly.

In this approach, we can use stubbing and small driver programs, which we discussed in Section 10.5. Also, where a compiler allows procedures and functions to be compiled and linked separately, we can save time in correcting individual pieces and in putting them together.

Bottom-Up Testing.   We can assemble our entire program first and then run tests for the entire code. Here, when a program produces an error for a test, we trace our code line-by-line and module-by-module until we find a bug.

With either of these approaches, we want to select tests to uncover as many bugs as possible. Occasionally, our problem may allow the exhaustive testing that we discussed in the previous section. With such problems, our test data can include all possible cases, and our selection of test cases is straightforward.

When exhaustive testing is not feasible, we must select some sample test data. Here, we can apply the ideas of **every-path testing** and **boundary value testing** from Section 6.8 in two ways; we can focus on our statement of our problem or we can concentrate on our code. This suggests the following possibilities.

Problem Analysis, Every-Path Testing. We can identify the various cases that can arise in our problem, and we can test our program with representative data for each case.

Problem Analysis, Boundary Value Testing. We can identify the conditions that separate one case from another, and we can check that our program moves from one case to another at the appropriate time.

Code Analysis, Every-Path Testing. Within our code, we can try to identify all possible ways that a computer can execute our program, and we can test each of these execution paths.

Code Analysis, Boundary Value Testing. We can identify and test that the computer shifts from one execution path to another at the appropriate time.

Comparison of Top-Down and Bottom-Up Testing

When we apply these guidelines with a Top-Down or Bottom-Up approach to testing, we can make several useful observations. First, when the total number of possible cases in our problem or program is small, then either testing approach can work well. We can manage the various cases without being overwhelmed. On the other hand, when the total number of possible cases is large, we may find that the complete set of cases may not be feasible to check. In this situation, we may need to structure our testing to reduce the number of possibilities. With our top-down testing strategy, such structuring is possible because our modules can be relatively simple. We can try each procedure or function under a variety of situations. Then, in putting the modules together, we can limit our attention to the possible interaction of the modules. We may not have to test how every possibility for one module works with every possibility for another module. Unfortunately, this structuring of our testing is not compatible with the bottom-up testing strategy, and we may not be able to manage a large number of cases with this alternate approach.

Testing Simulations

To conclude this discussion of testing and to illustrate many of our points, we apply our comments to simulation programs. In all of our comments so far, we have assumed that we could check a program by running a program with test data and then determining if the program produced correct results. However, when we perform simulations, we may not know what results to expect. Thus, we need to examine how we can use our principles of testing when we do not know the outcome.

In testing simulations, we can begin by following many of the ideas in our top-down strategy. In particular, while the final results of our program may be unclear, often we can test individual modules. For example, we could print out values returned by a random number generator to see if they appear random; or we could run some modules with driver programs to see if they process various values correctly.

Then, when we put the modules together, we may be able to check various parts of our output in two ways, even if we do not know all of the details. For example, we can check that our results seem **reasonable.** (If we simulate economic growth, we should see how our results compare with our intuition about how the economy should behave.) Also, we can check that our results are **consistent.** (If we toss a coin 1000 times, then the number of heads plus the number of tails should be 1000.)

While the testing of modules and the review of final results does not eliminate the possibility of error, we can expect that many (if not all) of our bugs have been discovered and corrected.

SECTION 11.9   WRITING CORRECT SOLUTIONS

The previous section has outlined several techniques that we can use to test whether our programs work correctly. In this section, we observe that these same ideas can be applied fruitfully to the earlier phases of the problem solving process.

We have seen that programming is only one step in a process that begins with specifications, design, and choice of algorithms. Each of these steps builds on our earlier work, so we can expect errors (e.g., omissions, inconsistencies) from one step to be reflected in our subsequent work. If we can correct difficulties before we start to code, we will not have to change our programs to correct such trouble after the programs are written. Programs are easiest to correct before they are written, so we can find it worthwhile to analyze and check each problem solving step before we move to the next one. More specifically, we can analyze each of these steps to see if we can spot errors or potential problems. Table 11–1 lists some questions we should address throughout the problem solving process.

Walk Throughs

When our problems are relatively simple, we may tend to be somewhat casual about such questions. For example, we may decide just to proofread our specifications or design. On the other hand, complex problems require

---

TABLE 11–1 · **Checklist for the Problem Solving Process**

Specifications	Are the specifications complete?
	Have we omitted any cases?
	Have we indicated what is required in each case?
	Do the specifications state what is actually meant?
	Are the specifications contradictory?
	Do some cases overlap?
Design	Have we broken our problem into logically independent pieces?
	Will the pieces fit together to meet the specifications?
	Have we left cases out?
	Are the cases contradictory?
	Have we defined each piece clearly and unambiguously?
Algorithm Selection	Does each algorithm do the task required?
	Have we considered all cases?
	Is the algorithm accurate, or could numerical errors reduce the usefulness of our results?
	Is the algorithm efficient?
	Will the algorithm always finish?

---

more care. In such cases, we can formally review our work for various sample data sets to see if our outlines are adequate. Here, our review is called a **walk through,** and we begin with particular data from the problem, checking that our work leads us methodically to a correct result. For example, we may trace our design step-by-step for a given set of data, just as we may trace the execution of our programs when we are testing with test data.

In major software development projects, where problems are complex and several people are involved in the work, special meetings are often scheduled for this testing. **Design reviews** allow many people to check through the details of the algorithms and design. Before that, software developers meet formally with clients to check that specifications address the desired job.

Throughout this chapter, we have identified various ways that errors can arise and we have seen techniques to help reduce or eliminate errors. When we consider the questions mentioned in this section and the possibilities for testing, we see that our techniques for coding apply equally well to the earlier stages of problem solving. When we apply these techniques, we often can eliminate errors before they require a major revision of much of our work.

SUMMARY

1. Programs are correct when they produce the results required by a problem.
2. Errors in our final programs may be introduced at any of the stages of the problem solving process, including specifications, design and algorithm selection, and programming.
3. Potential sources for errors include **logical errors,** such as mistaken assumptions, omissions, or inconsistencies; **numerical errors,** which may arise from **round-off error,** real arithmetic, or decimal-binary conversions; **poor selection of algorithms,** since some algorithms may compound error, affecting the **accuracy** of the results, while others may not be **efficient; coding errors,** which arise when we translate our algorithms into programs; **data entry errors,** which may produce undesired results.
4. We may establish program correctness either by **testing** or **verification.**
   a. **Testing** involves the use of test data and may proceed in either a **top-down** or **bottom-up** manner. Testing can occur at each phase of the problem solving process. Thus, testing can include **walk throughs** for specifications, design, and algorithms as well as the identification of test data for checking programs.
   b. **Verification** uses assertions and loop invariants to produce logical proofs that a program performs correctly in all cases.

EXERCISES

11.1   *Computing Infinity.* Consider the following program.

```
Program Infinity (Output);
Var Index: Integer;
    OldSum, Sum: Real;

Begin
    Writeln('This program adds 1.0 to a sum until the sum stops changing.');
    Sum := 0.0;
    Repeat
        OldSum := Sum;
        Sum := Sum + 1.0
    Until (Sum = OldSum);
    Writeln ('The sum stopped changing when it reached the value ',
            Sum:1:1, ' .')
End.
```

When this program is run on one particular machine, the output is

```
This program adds 1.0 to a sum until the sum stops changing.
The sum stopped changing when it reached the value 33554430.0 .
```

- Explain this result.
- (Optional) What happens when this program is run on your local system?

11.2 *Harmonic Series: A Small Infinity.* In mathematics, one can show that the sum

$$1 + \tfrac{1}{2} + \tfrac{1}{3} + \tfrac{1}{4} + \ldots$$

approaches infinity. (This sum is called the *Harmonic Series* and is sometimes said to *diverge.*) From this viewpoint, the following program should never stop.

```
Program HarmonicSeries(Output);
Var Index: Real;
    Sum: Real;
Begin
    Writeln('This program computes the limit ',
            'of the harmonic series.');
    Sum := 0.0;
    Index := 1.0;
    Repeat
        Sum := Sum + 1.0/Index;
        Index := Index + 1
    Until (Sum = Sum + 1.0/Index);
    Writeln ('After ', Index:1:1, ' terms,');
    Writeln ('the harmonic series converges to ', Sum:1:5, ' !')
End.
```

KEY TERMS, PHRASES, AND CONCEPTS

Algorithm	Non-Associativity
Accuracy	Round-Off
Efficiency	Program Verification
Binary Numbers	Testing
Design Reviews	Bottom-Up
Errors	Boundary Value
Coding	Consistency
Data Entry	Every-Path
Logical	Exhaustive
Numerical	Reasonableness
Decimal-Binary	Top-Down
Conversion	Walk Throughs
Finite Storage	
of Reals	

Run this program on a computer and explain what happens.

11.3   *Convergent Series.*[1] In mathematics, the convergence of series is defined as a limit of partial sums. In particular, we let

$$S_n = \sum_{i=1}^{n} a_i,$$

and then we define

$$\sum_{i=1}^{\infty} a_i = \lim_{n \to \infty} S_n.$$

With this definition, many tests for convergence and divergence are well established. One theorem states,

Theorem: If $\sum_{i=1}^{\infty} a_i$ converges, then $\lim_{n \to \infty} a_n = 0.$

However, the Harmonic Series shows that the converse of this theorem is not true.

a. Use what you know about numerical errors to prove that the converse is true if the partial sums are evaluated by computer.

b. Find a series in which partial sums do converge on your computer but where $\lim_{n \to \infty} a_n \neq 0.$

11.4   *Comparison of Algorithms.* Consider the following problem.

After a fly settles on a table, a person tries to hit the fly with a flyswatter. In particular, the person starts with the flyswatter 1 yard from the table and the person moves the flyswatter at the rate of 1 yard/second. Does the person hit the fly? If so, when? (You may assume the fly remains still and the person has good aim.)

Now consider two solutions.

Plato's Paradox. We divide time into various intervals. In the first time interval, the flyswatter moves from 1 yard to ½ yard from the table. In the second interval, the flyswatter moves half the remaining distance, from ½ yard to ¼ yard from the table. In the third interval, the distance is again halved. In subsequent time intervals, this halving of distance continues. With all of these time intervals, the flyswatter never reaches the table.

Another Approach. The flyswatter travels 1 yard per second. Thus, in 1 second the flyswatter travels 1 yard. Since this is the distance from the initial position of the flyswatter to the table, the flyswatter must hit the table (and thus the fly) in 1 second.

a. Explain the apparent contradictory conclusions of these algorithms.

---

[1]This problem requires a knowledge of convergent series. Students without this background should skip this problem.

    b. Write programs that implement each of these algorithms and compare the output of these programs.

11.5 *Checking Input Data.* In each of the following, develop appropriate tests to determine if input data are impossible, implausible, or plausible.

    a. Scholastic Aptitude Scores (SATs) are always between 200 and 800, inclusive.

    b. Test grades normally range between 0 and 100. However, sometimes up to 20 points of extra credit are possible.

11.6 *Checking Telephone Numbers.* Write a procedure that will read a telephone number and check that it has the appropriate form:

$$\text{(area code)-(exchange)-(number).}$$

If a number of the wrong form is entered, the procedure should ask the user to reenter the number.

11.7 *Checking Input Data—Check Digits.* A particular product code has the form

$$\text{(number)-(check)}$$

where "number" is a four digit number, and "check" is a check digit, derived from the number by adding the digits (mod 10). Thus,

    1234-0 is a valid number (check = 1 + 2 + 3 + 4, mod 10)
    5827-1 is invalid (check should be 2 if number is valid).

Write a procedure that reads a product code and checks that the code is legal. If the code is not legal, the procedure should ask the user to reenter the code.

11.8 *Checking for Unlikely Input.* In a grocery store, we expect most individual items to be between \$0.00 and \$100.00 exclusive. Costs below \$0.00 or above \$300.00 are considered impossible, and costs between \$100.00 and \$300.00 (inclusive) are considered possible, but unlikely.

    a. Write a program that
- reads the costs of successive items until the sentinel value of \$0.00 is read;
- asks the user to verify possible, but unlikely, values;
- finds impossible input values and asks the user to reenter these values; and
- computes the total bill for the grocery items.

    b. Modify your program so that all valid grocery costs are recorded and then printed after the bill total. (You may assume no more that 100 items will be purchased at one time.)

11.9 *Selection of Test Data.* Choose test data for the following:

    a. The Baby Sitter Problem (Exercise 6.11.)

    b. The Bowling Score Program of Section 6.6.

    c. The Credit Balance Program of Section 7.3.

    d. The Improved Bubble Sort Program (Exercise 8.2.)

11.10 *Testing Simulations.* Section 11.8 noted that the difficulty of testing simulations was compounded when the correct results were not known. Develop specific strategies to test solutions to each of the following.

    a. The Dice Rolling Simulation of Section 6.4.

    b. The Family Size Simulation of Section 7.1.

    c. The Racquetball or Volley Ball Simulations of Exercises 7.12 and 7.13.

In each case, specify how you could test each module, how you could test various combinations of modules, and how you could test the final results for reasonableness and consistency.

11.11 *Social Implications of Program Correctness in Administering Medicines.* In this chapter, we have seen several ways that can help us write correct programs, but we have also noted that these methods can be very hard to apply when dealing with large, complex programs. Certainly, we cannot use exhaustive testing for such programs. Similarly, we may find that it is not feasible even to list all possible cases for processing, so that every-path testing and boundary value testing are not possible or practical. Similar practical difficulties arise in applying the details of program verification to prove program correctness. Thus, we can identify circumstances where we cannot know if programs are correct. This uncertainty about a program's correctness presents many interesting philosophical problems when we try to use computers in various applications.

Consider the use of computers to monitor the condition of patients in hospitals. In some cases, certain changes in a patient's condition may require a very fast response for the life to be saved.

At least two approaches can be developed to meet these conditions.

1. While monitoring a patient, a computer could call hospital personnel whenever a significant change in the patient's condition occurs. The personnel then are responsible for responding in time.

2. To save time and labor, the computer could be allowed to administer needed medicines in response to a change in condition.

This second approach eliminates the possibility that hospital personnel will be delayed, but it relies upon the computer responding correctly in all cases.

    a. Discuss some implications of the uncertainty of program correctness in this situation.

    b. (Optional) If either approach is followed, suppose a bug results in the death of a patient. Who do you think should be legally liable, the programmer(s)? the hospital personnel? both? Explain your answer.

11.12 *Accumulation of Round-Off Error.* Use the Trapezoidal Rule from Section 5.5 to compute the area under the function

$$y = f(x) = \sqrt{1 - x^2}.$$

Since this is the equation for the top half of a circle of radius 1, the area should be $\pi/2$ and twice this area should equal

$$3.1415926535 \ldots .$$

Run your program where the number of subdivisions ranges from 1000 up to values close to *MaxInt*. In theory, the accuracy of your results should improve as the number of subdivisions increases. Does your output agree with this theoretical result? Explain your answer.

CHAPTER 12

SOME
SIMPLE PROBLEMS
INVOLVING CHARACTERS:
ADDITIONAL SIMPLE DATA TYPES

U p to this point, we have limited the complexity of our problems by restricting our attention to applications that involve numbers. In this chapter, we shift our focus to applications that involve nonnumeric information, such as alphabetical data. For example, we will see how we can process data typed at a terminal by dealing with one character at a time. We also will see how we can introduce our own simple data types, so our work can closely reflect the problems we are solving.

SECTION 12.1   **CHARACTERS**

We introduce the general subject of **character data** with a simple extension of our first Unit Pricing Problem from Section 2.1.

PROBLEM 12.1   **Unit Pricing Revisited**

Write a program that computes the unit price of several items. More precisely, write a program that computes the cost per ounce of an item, given its cost in cents and its weight in ounces. After each computation, ask if the user wishes to continue this series of computations. The program should then respond to a "Yes" or "No" typed by the user.

Discussion of Problem 12.1

In this problem, the unit pricing computation can follow the same outline we used in Chapter 2, so here we focus on the exchange between the user and the computer about whether to continue.

This exchange may follow these steps:

I. The computer prints:
  "Do you want to continue?"
II. The user responds appropriately.
  (e.g., "Yes," "Yeah," "Yup," "No," "Nope.")
III. The computer repeats the unit pricing computation, until the user responds in the negative.

While the first of these steps can be implemented with a simple *Write* statement, we must consider Steps II and III with some care. Our sample responses above suggest that we should allow many possible answers from the user. In handling this variety, we might prepare a list of all reasonable user responses and then write our program to handle each anticipated answer, or we may identify a pattern in the various possible responses and then proceed on the basis of this pattern.

Here, we use the second approach. When we consider the possible responses, we see that negative responses normally start with the letter *N*. Similarly, the affirmative answers normally begin with *Y*. Thus, we write our program so that it responds to an initial *N* or *Y*. We will ignore all subsequent characters that the user may type on the response line.

From this discussion, we develop the following outline.

Outline for Problem 12.1

I. Repeat until the user types the letter *N*.
  A. Compute unit price.
  B. Determine if user wants to continue.
    1. Print the question: "Do You Want To Continue?"
    2. Read the user's response, keeping the first character and discarding the rest.

This outline yields the following program.

```
Program UnitPricing {Revised} (Input, Output);

{This program computes the cost per ounce of an item,
 given cost and number of ounces.  The program continues processing
 data until the user tells the program to stop.}

Var Ounces, Cost, CostPerOunce: Real;
    Answer: Char;
```

```
Begin

    Repeat

        {Compute Unit Price}
        Write  ('Enter size of item in ounces and cost in dollars:');
        Readln (Ounces, Cost);
        CostPerOunce := Cost / Ounces;
        Writeln ('Cost per ounce = $ ', CostPerOunce:1:2);

        {Determine if user wants to continue}
        Write ('Do you want to continue?');
        Readln (Answer);

    Until (Answer = 'N') or (Answer = 'n')

End .
```

A sample run of this program might be:

```
Enter size of item in ounces and cost in dollars:12 3.60
Cost per ounce = $ 0.30
Do you want to continue?yes
Enter size of item in ounces and cost in dollars:5  1.10
Cost per ounce = $ 0.22
Do you want to continue?YUP
Enter size of item in ounces and cost in dollars:3 .99
Cost per ounce = $ 0.33
Do you want to continue?no
```

This program illustrates several important features of character data. When we want to process character information (rather than numbers), we can declare our variables to be type *Char*. For example,

Var Answer: Char

specifies that the identifier *Answer* will be used to store *one character* of information, such as a letter, a digit, or a punctuation mark.

We can declare characters in just the same way that we declare reals, integers, and Booleans. Then, we can use character variables in much the same way as other variables.

1. We can input a character from the terminal using either *Read* or *Readln*.
2. We can specify one piece of character data by putting the character in quotes. For example, we can write 'N' and 'n'.

3. We can compare one character value against another. For example, we can test

    (Answer = 'N') Or (Answer = 'n')

4. Similarly, we can use assignment statements, procedures, and functions with character data.

5. We can print character data using *Write* and *Writeln*, and we can specify formatting information. For example,

    Writeln(Answer:5);

specifies that we should allow 5 spaces to print the character stored in *Answer*. (The character will be right-justified in the wide field.)

The last test in this unit pricing program also illustrates that the computer distinguishes between uppercase and lowercase letters. In fact, each individual character that we can type on our terminal is represented in a coded form inside the machine, and a different code is used for lowercase letters than for uppercase. Similarly, each punctuation mark and each digit has its own code. We will discuss some features of this coding in more detail in the next section.

Since character data are different from numeric data, some numeric operations do not apply to characters.

- The arithmetic operations $+$, $-$, $*$, $/$, *div*, *mod* cannot be used with character data.
- Numeric functions such as *abs*, *ln*, *exp*, and *sin* cannot be used with character data.
- Character data are stored differently from integer or real data, and the machine will not automatically convert from one to another (just as Pascal does not allow us to convert from reals to integers automatically).

To illustrate these distinctions, consider the statements:

Var Ch1, Ch2 : Char;
    I: Integer;
    R: Real;
Begin
    Ch1 := 'Q';
    Ch2 := 'Z';
    I := 7;

With this initialization, the following statements do not make sense and are illegal in Pascal.

Statement	Comment
Ch1 := Ch1 + Ch2	No single character could represent two letters.

R   := Ch1   No real number corresponds to a 'Q'.
Ch2 := I   The number 7 is distinct from character '7'.

This same distinction between character and numeric data make the following more subtle expressions invalid.

I := '7'   Again, the number 7 and the
'7' = 7   character '7' are distinct!

In all cases, we can work with numeric data or with character data, but we cannot mix the two types. Pascal expects us to be precise in specifying what form of data we have and how we expect to use it.

To conclude this section, we apply these comments on character data to give a better, more complete solution to Problem 12.1.

Further Discussion of Problem 12.1

Our first solution to Problem 12.1 continues as long as the user does not type the letter 'N' or 'n'. Any other response is considered to be an affirmative answer to the question.

In a more complete solution, we should check that the user types the 'Y' or 'N' expected, and we should ask the user to retype the answer if neither of these responses is given.

These details complicate our work considerably, and we can identify two special tasks that need to be done:

Task 1. We need to be able to determine if a character that we enter is 'Y', 'y', 'N', or 'n'.

Task 2. We need to continue asking for user input until an acceptable response is given.

In the following revised program, we separate these details by using functions and procedures, and we control our overall processing in another procedure.

```
Program UnitPricing {Revised Again} (Input, Output);

{This program computes the cost per ounce of an item,
 given cost and number of ounces.  The program continues processing
 data until the user tells the program to stop.}

Function YOrN (Ch: Char): Boolean;
{This function is True if the character Ch is a 'Y' or 'N'
 (upper or lower case) and False otherwise.}
    Begin
       YOrN := (Ch = 'Y') or (Ch = 'y') or (Ch = 'N') or (Ch = 'n')
    End {YOrN} ;
```

```
Procedure GetResponse (Var Ch: Char);
{This procedure askes if the user wants to continue,
and the procedure continues to process responses
until the user responds with a "Yes" or "No".}
    Begin

        Write ('Do you want to continue?');
        Repeat
            Readln (Ch);
            If Not YOrN(Ch)
                Then Write ('Please answer "Yes" or "No":')
        Until YOrN(Ch)

    End {GetResponse} ;

Procedure ControlProcessing;
{This procedure organizes our solution to the unit pricing problem.}
    Var Ounces, Cost, CostPerOunce: Real;
        Answer: Char;

    Begin
        Repeat

            {Compute Unit Price}
            Write ('Enter size of item in ounces and cost in dollars:');
            Readln (Ounces, Cost);
            CostPerOunce := Cost / Ounces;
            Writeln ('Cost per ounce = $ ', CostPerOunce:1:2);

            {Determine if user wants to continue}
            GetResponse(Answer)

        Until (Answer = 'N') or (Answer = 'n')
    End {ControlProcessing} ;

Begin {Main}
    ControlProcessing
End {Main} .
```

This program produces the same output as before, but it also allows for other user responses, as shown below.

```
Enter size of item in ounces and cost in dollars:7 14.49
Cost per ounce = $ 2.07
Do you want to continue?maybe
Please answer "Yes" or "No":who me?
Please answer "Yes" or "No":Yes
Enter size of item in ounces and cost in dollars:13 1.69
Cost per ounce = $ 0.13
Do you want to continue?No, Thank you!!
```

This program illustrates many aspects of character data that we have seen in this section. Character data can be used in functions and procedures, assignments and comparisons. Further, we can *Write* or *Read* character data to and from our terminal. This program shows how we can take advantage of functions and procedures when processing characters so that the details of our work can be separated from the program's main steps.

We expand our capabilities for processing characters in the next section, where we consider some special character functions.

SECTION 12.2   SPECIAL FUNCTIONS

In the previous section, we saw some simple ways to process character data. Pascal allows us to declare character variables and to do the familiar operations of reading, writing, assigning, and comparing character data. We also noted that each character is stored in some coded form, and this code distinguishes between uppercase and lowercase letters. Thus, in our programs of the previous section, we read characters, and then we compared them with the letters 'Y', 'y', 'N', and 'n' to see if the user wanted to continue.

While our resulting program worked correctly, we did have to check our input against both uppercase and lowercase letters. When we give the user more choices in other applications, this distinction between uppercase and lowercase can become quite tedious. Thus, we may need to solve the following.

PROBLEM 12.2   Capitalizing Letters.

Write a function CAPITALIZE that capitalizes lowercase letters, while leaving punctuation and digit characters unchanged.

To solve this problem, we will take advantage of some special Pascal functions. These functions connect characters with their computer codes, and we will see how we can utilize these codes to solve our problem. We begin with a discussion of the codes themselves.

Character Codes

When working with character data, the computer uses a specific coded value for each possible character. Thus, when we press a key at our terminal, the terminal translates our keystroke into the appropriate code, and this code is transmitted to the computer. Similarly, when the CPU wants some data printed at a terminal, the CPU translates this data into a sequence of **character codes.** These codes are sent to our terminal, and our terminal responds to these codes by displaying the characters that we recognize.

As a specific example, one commonly used code is the American Standard Code for Information Interchange, called the ASCII code. Part of this code is shown in Table 12–1. Here, we see that the number '2' is represented by the binary code 00110010 (code number 50), the letter 'A' is

TABLE 12–1 · A Portion of the ASCII 8-Bit Code

Binary Code	Decimal Code Number	Character or Comment
00110000	48	0
00110001	49	1
00110010	50	2
00110011	51	3
00110100	52	4
00110101	53	5
00110110	54	6
00110111	55	7
00111000	56	8
00111001	57	9
00111010	58	:
00111011	59	;
00111100	60	<
00111101	61	=
00111110	62	>
00111111	63	?
01000000	64	@
01000001	65	A
01000010	66	B
01000011	67	C
01000100	68	D
01000101	69	E
01000110	70	F
01000111	71	G
01001000	72	H
01001001	73	I

Source: United States of America Standards Institute, Standard X3.4-1968.

represented by the binary code 01000001 (code number 65), and the semi-colon ';' is represented by 00111011 (code number 59). Other ASCII codes not included in Table 12–1 are the carriage return (code number 13), the tab (code number 9), and the letter 'a' (code number 97). In fact, each key or combination of keys on our terminal corresponds to a distinct code number in ASCII.

Table 12–1 also suggests another key consequence of machine codes, for the table provides an ordering for the various characters. For example, in the ASCII code, 'B' comes after 'A', ';' (code 59) comes before '<' (code 60), and '?' (code 63) comes before 'a' (code 97). Of course these relationships depend upon the particular code used on a specific machine, but the underlying ideas of coding and ordering apply to all computers.

Once we understand this idea of character coding and ordering, we find that Pascal allows us to utilize these ideas in several ways.

Functions Ord and Chr

Two functions, *Ord* and *Chr*, allow us to translate easily between characters and the underlying code. In particular,

Ord(Ch)	gives us the code number for the character *Ch* specified. For example, if we are using the ASCII code, then $\qquad$ Ord('A') = 65 and $\qquad$ Ord(';') = 59.
Chr(N)	gives us the character with code N. For example, in the ASCII code, $\qquad$ Chr(65) = 'A' and $\qquad$ Chr(59) = ';'.

Functions Pred and Succ

Two functions, *Pred* and *Succ*, utilize the ordering of characters. In particular,

Succ(Ch)	gives us the character that is the successor to *Ch* in our coding table.
Pred(Ch)	gives us the character that is the predecessor to *Ch* in our coding table.

For example, if we use the ASCII code, we have

$$\text{Pred('B')} = \text{'A'}$$
$$\text{Succ('A')} = \text{'B'}$$

and

$$\text{Succ(';')} = \text{'<'}$$

Inequalities

The ordering of characters also allows us to make **comparisons of characters** within Boolean expressions. For example, in the ASCII code, we find that all capital letters are between 'A' and 'Z.' Thus, the following function can be used to test if a given character is a capital letter (for the ASCII code).

```
Function CAP(Ch: Char): Boolean;
    Begin
        CAP := (Ch >= 'A') And (Ch <= 'Z')
    End
```

In the ASCII code, any capital letter has a code between 65 (code for 'A') and 90 (code for 'Z'), so any capital letter satisfies the test in the above function. Similarly, any other character is not in this range on the ASCII code, so other characters will not meet the above test.

Notes on Various Codes and Some Cautions

Unfortunately, the exact ordering of characters depends upon the specific code used by a particular machine, so that we must be careful when comparing different characters in our programs. For example, in some codes, such as the ASCII, the capital letters come before the small letters so 'A' comes before 'a'. In other codes, such as the Extended Binary Coded Decimal Interchange Code or the EBCDIC code, the small letters come first.

On the other hand, in virtually all codes, the capital letters are in order, so

$$\text{'A'} < \text{'B'} < \text{'C'} \ldots < \text{'Z'}$$

Similarly, the small letters are in order, and the digits '0', '1', . . . , '9' are in order. Thus, regardless of the specific code used in a particular machine, we can use inequalities, such as '<' and '>', for alphabetizing letters and for ordering strings of digits. Beyond these general statements, however, we need to consult a manual for our specific machine to learn any details of the coding in a particular situation.

Capitalization: An Application

With these capabilities for working with characters and their codes, we now can return to our Capitalization Problem which began the section. Our problem requires a two-part solution:

I. Identify if a given character is a lowercase letter.
II. If the character is lowercase:
   A. Then capitalize it.
   B. Otherwise, leave it alone.

We consider each part separately:

I. We already have seen how to identify a capital letter in the ASCII code. A similar approach applies to lowercase letters.
II. Most codes (including both ASCII and EBCDIC) arrange their lowercase and uppercase letters in the same pattern. Thus, we can use the following approach to perform the actual capitalization.
   A. Given the letter Ch, determine how far it is from the start of the lowercase alphabet. This is done by

$$\text{Distance} := \text{Ord(Ch)} - \text{Ord('a')}$$

   B. Find the letter that is this prescribed distance from 'A'. This is given by

$$\text{Chr (Ord('A') + Distance)}$$

For example, if we wish to capitalize 'c', we note:

A. 'c' is two letters beyond 'a' (Distance := 2)

B. Our desired letter is coded 2 letters beyond 'A'. Thus, we want the letter whose code is

Ord('A') + 2

that is, we want

Chr (Ord ('A') + 2)

These steps are coded in the following function, which produces correct results for virtually any coding system (including ASCII and EBCDIC).

```
Function CAPITALIZE(Ch: Char): Char;
{This function capitalizes a lower case character Ch,
 but the function leaves other characters unchanged}

    Begin
       If (Ch >= 'a') And (Ch <= 'z')
          Then CAPITALIZE := Chr( Ord(Ch) - Ord('a') + Ord('A') )
          Else CAPITALIZE := Ch
    End {CAPITALIZE} ;
```

In this function, we compare various characters, and we use character codes and Pascal functions to transform character data from one form to another. In the next section, we see how to apply these same ideas in the processing of several characters.

SECTION 12.3 — SEQUENCES OF CHARACTERS

The previous two sections have illustrated how we can process individual characters. In this section, we begin an investigation of techniques for processing several characters by considering two ways we can use arrays with character data. We will continue this study in the next two chapters.

Our first approach uses arrays of characters with integer subscripts.

PROBLEM 12.3A — Message Decoding

Decode a message by replacing each letter in the message by an appropriate alternate letter. More precisely, begin with a 'real' alphabet and a 'cipher' alphabet. Then decode a message by looking up each letter of the message in the cipher alphabet and replacing it by the corresponding letter in the real alphabet.

For example, suppose we are given

RealAlphabet   = ABCDEFGHIJKLMNOPQRSTUVWXYZ 0123456789
CipherAlphabet = 3456217089ACB QRSTUVWXYZDEFGHIJKLMNOP

Then the coded message

8 FHKPIF5QCWB4WUFU38C26FV02FQ523 F4CW2

becomes

IN 1492 COLUMBUS SAILED THE OCEAN BLUE

(To encipher a message, we just interchange the real and cipher alphabets.)

Discussion of Problem 12.3A

In this problem, we need to work with several pieces of character information. In particular, we need a real alphabet, a cipher alphabet, and a coded message, and we must produce a decoded message. One natural way to store each of these is to use arrays, and we can declare

```
Const AlphabetLength = 37;
      MaxLen = 80; {Number of characters on a line of a terminal}
Type  Alphabet = Array [1..AlphabetLength] of Char;
      CharLine = Array [1..MaxLen] of Char;
Var   RealAlphabet: Alphabet;
      CipherAlphabet: Alphabet;
      Message: CharLine;
      CodedMess:CharLine;
```

Here, we store the first letter of our cipher alphabet as

CipherAlphabet[1]

and the corresponding letter in the real alphabet as

RealAlphabet[1].

Then, with this storage of our alphabets, we can decode each character of our message easily.

For each character in our coded message, we search through the cipher alphabet to find the position of the character in this cipher alphabet. Then we take the corresponding character from that position in the real alphabet to obtain the decoded letter.

With this deciphering process specified, we next examine how we can determine the two alphabets and the coded message. One simple approach for the alphabets is to ask the user to enter them. Since we know these alphabets will each contain exactly 37 characters, we can perform this task simply. For example,

```
For Index := 1 to 37
    Do Read (RealAlphabet [Index])
```

However, in reading this character data, we must be a little careful when we come to the end of a line. After we read each alphabet, we want to start our next input on a new line. Thus, we need to be sure we move to the next line each time we finish a line. (When we read numbers, the computer automatically moves ahead to new lines when necessary, but this is not true in reading characters.) Therefore, after we read each alphabet, we need to insert a *Readln* in our program so we will be ready for the next line of data. The *Readln* clears the present line and moves to the next one.

Next, when we try to read our message, we note that we may not know the length of our input before we start. Thus, we will have to allocate some maximum amount of space in our program declaration and then count the actual number of characters as our coded message is entered.

These comments suggest the following solution to our problem.

Outline for Problem 12.3A

I. Enter alphabets.
   A. Enter *RealAlphabet* one character at a time.
   B. Enter *CipherAlphabet* one character at a time.
II. Enter the coded message.
   A. Start count of message length at 0.
   B. Continue reading until we reach the end of line and as long as we still have room to store the coded message.
      1. Increase the letter count by one.
      2. Read the character.
III. Decipher the coded message. For each letter in the coded message:
   A. Find the position of the letter in the *CipherAlphabet*.
   B. Take the corresponding character in the *RealAlphabet* for our message.
IV. Print
   A. The original message.
   B. The decoded message.

This outline yields the following program. Here, for clarity, each step is written as a separate procedure.

Also, in this program, we must be able to test when we have read the last character on a line. To make this test, we use the function *EOLN* (End Of Line) from the Pascal library. This Boolean function is true when we have read the last character on a line, and false if more characters remain.

```
Program DecipherMessage (Input, Output);
{This program deciphers a message which has been coded
  according to a monoalphabetic substitution code.}

Const AlphabetLength = 37;
      MaxLen = 80;

Type Alphabet = Array [1..AlphabetLength] of Char;
     CharLine = Array [1..MaxLen] of Char;
```

```
Procedure EnterAlphabets (Var RealAl, CipherAl: Alphabet);
{Procedure asks user to enter the real and cipher alphabets
 for the deciphering.}
    Var Index: Integer;
    Begin
        Writeln ('Please enter the real alphabet');
        For Index := 1 To AlphabetLength
            Do Read (RealAl[Index]);
        Readln;   {Clear input line of any extra characters}
        Writeln ('Below each letter in the real alphabet, please enter');
        Writeln ('the corresponding letter of the cipher alphabet');
        For Index := 1 To AlphabetLength
            Do Write (RealAl[Index]);
        Writeln;
        For Index := 1 To AlphabetLength
            Do Read (CipherAl[Index]);
        Readln    {clear input line of any extra characters}
    End {EnterAlphabets} ;

Procedure EnterLine (Var CodedMess: CharLine; Var CodeLen: Integer);
{Procedure enters the coded message to be deciphered.}
    Var Index: Integer;

    Begin
        Writeln ('Please enter your coded message:');
        CodeLen := 0;
        While (Not Eoln) And (CodeLen < MaxLen)
            Do Begin
               CodeLen := CodeLen + 1;
               Read (CodedMess[CodeLen])
            End;
        If Not Eoln
            Then Writeln ('Your coded message was too long; ',
                          'message truncated to ', MaxLen:1, ' characters');
        Readln;     {Clear input line}
    End {EnterLine} ;

Procedure Decipher (Code: CharLine; Var Plain: CharLine; Length: Integer;
                    RealAl, CipherAl: Alphabet);
{Procedure deciphers Coded message by looking up letters in the CipherAl,
 and using the corresponding letters in RealAl to get the Plain message}
    Var Index: Integer;
        Position: Integer;

    Procedure Find (Var Position: Integer; Letter: Char; Alpha: Alphabet);
    {Procedure finds the Position of the given Letter in the given Alpha.}
        Begin
            Position := 1;
            While (Letter <> Alpha[Position])
                Do Position := Position + 1
        End {Find} ;

    Begin {Decipher}
        For Index := 1 To Length
            Do Begin
               Find (Position, Code[Index], CipherAl);
               Plain[Index] := RealAl[Position]
            End
    End {Decipher} ;
```

```
Procedure PrintResults (Code, Message: CharLine; Length: Integer);
{This procedure prints the message and the resulting coded text.}
    Var Index: Integer;
    Begin
        Writeln ('When the coded message:');
        For Index := 1 To Length
            Do Write (Code[Index]);
        Writeln;
        Writeln ('is decoded with the above substitutions, the result is:');
        For Index := 1 To Length
            Do Write (Message[Index]);
        Writeln
    End {PrintResults} ;

Procedure ControlProcessing;
{This procedure controls the main steps of data entry and processing.}
    Var RealAlphabet: Alphabet;
        CipherAlphabet: Alphabet;
        Message: CharLine;
        CodedMess: CharLine;
        InputLen: Integer;

    Begin
        EnterAlphabets (RealAlphabet, CipherAlphabet);
        EnterLine (CodedMess, InputLen);
        Decipher (CodedMess, Message, InputLen, RealAlphabet, CipherAlphabet);
        PrintResults (CodedMess, Message, InputLen)
    End {ControlProcessing} ;

Begin {Main}
    Writeln ('Deciphering Program');
    ControlProcessing
End {Main} .
```

This program illustrates several general points. We can declare arrays of characters in the same way that we declare arrays of reals, integers, or Booleans. Then, we can use these arrays to process sequences of characters, by working with our input one character at a time. As we enter our characters, we may need to record the number of characters we have read. Then, in subsequent processing, we can refer to this length.

In working with character data, a space is treated in exactly the same manner as other characters; we cannot ignore spaces. (A space moves the printing element on our keyboard or the cursor at our terminal, so a space makes a difference in what we see.)

This example also shows that in reading from a terminal, we must be careful in processing the end of each line, and we need the *EOLN* function to tell us when we have read the last character on the line. *EOLN* is true when the last character has been read, so no more characters appear on the line. *EOLN* is false if more characters remain. Then, before we wish to enter character data from a new line, we need to use the *Readln* statement to move to the next line.

We now turn to a second problem, which illustrates other ways we can work with sequences of characters.

PROBLEM 12.3B   **Distribution of Letters**

Write a program that reads a line of input, counts the number of times each letter occurs, and displays the final frequency information.

Discussion of Problem 12.3B

In this problem we can read our input line as before. (We will capitalize letters, so no distinction is made between upper- and lowercase.) The new features include counting letters and displaying the information.

In counting letters, we need a count for letter A, a count for letter B, a count for letter C, etc. Thus, we would like variables $Count_A$, $Count_B$, $Count_C$ . . . . This suggests the idea of subscripting we have seen before, but here we want our subscripts to be letters. Thus, in Pascal, we declare

Var Count: Array ['A'..'Z'] of Integer

to record our frequency information.

Once we record this information, we want to print results for each letter which occurred in our line of input. Thus, we want to repeat an activity for the letters 'A', 'B', 'C', . . . , 'Z'. This suggests a For loop where the control variable is a character; that is, we want

For Letter : = 'A' to 'Z'

Each of these capabilities is possible in Pascal, and we have the following outline.

Outline for Problem 12.3B

   I. Enter line of input.
     A. Start with a line length of 0.
     B. Continue reading until we reach the end of line or until we run out of storage space.
       1. Increase the letter count by one.
       2. Read the character.
       3. Capitalize the letter if it was in lowercase.
  II. Count letters. For each character entered:
     A. Determine if the character is a letter.
     B. If so, increase the letter count by 1.
 III. Display the results. Repeat for each letter, 'A', . . . , 'Z'.
     A. Determine if the letter occurred in the line (i.e., if the count > 0).
     B. Print * for each occurrence of the letter.
     C. Print the number of occurrences.

This outline yields the following program.

```
Program LetterDistribution (Input, Output);
{This program reads a line of input, counts the number of times
 each letter appears in the line, and the displays these letter
 frequencies.  No distinction is made between upper case and
 lower case letters.}

Const MaxLen = 80;

Type   CharInput = Array[1..MaxLen] of Char;
       LetterCount = Array['A'..'Z'] of Integer;

Procedure EnterLine (Var Line: CharInput; Var Length: Integer);
{This procedure reads our line of input from the terminal.}

    Procedure CAPITALIZE (Var Ch: Char);
    {This procedure capitalizes lower case letters.}
        Begin
            If (Ch >= 'a') And (Ch <= 'z')
                Then Ch := Chr( Ord(Ch) - Ord('a') + Ord('A') )
        End {Capitalize} ;

    Begin {EnterLine}
        Writeln ('Please enter your input line:');

        Length := 0;
        While (Not Eoln) and (Length < MaxLen)
          Do Begin
            Length := Length + 1;
            Read (Line[Length]);
            Capitalize (Line[Length])
          End;
        If Not Eoln
            Then Writeln ('Your message was to long; ',
                          'message truncated to ', MaxLen:1, ' characters');
        Readln {clear any excess characters from the input line}
    End {EnterLine} ;

Procedure CountLetters (Line: CharInput; Length: Integer;
                        Var Count: LetterCount);

{This procedure counts the frequency of letters in the given line.}
    Var Letter: Char;     {Index variable}
        Index: Integer;   {Index variable for Line}
        Ch: Char;         {Character in the given Line}

    Begin
        {Initially all counts are 0}
        For Letter := 'A' to 'Z'
            Do Count[Letter] := 0;

        {For each letter in line, increment count by 1}
        For Index := 1 To Length
          Do Begin
            Ch := Line[Index];
            If (Ch >= 'A') and (Ch <= 'Z')
                Then Count[Ch] := Count[Ch] + 1
          End;
    End {CountLetters} ;
```

```
Procedure DisplayResults (Count: LetterCount);
{Procedure displays the letter frequencies for the line.}
    Var Letter: Char;
        Index: Integer;  {Control variable to count *'s printed}
    Begin
        Writeln;
        Writeln ('Display of the letter frequencies in the input line.');
        Writeln;

        For Letter := 'A' to 'Z'
          Do Begin
            If (Count[Letter] > 0)
                Then Begin
                    Write (Letter, ' : ');
                    For Index := 1 To Count[Letter]
                        Do Write ('*');
                    Writeln (Count[Letter]:3)
                End
          End
    End {DisplayResults} ;

Procedure ControlPRocessing;
{This procedure controls the main processing steps of data entry,
 analysis, and printing.}
    Var Line: CharInput;
        Count: LetterCount;
        LineLen: Integer;

    Begin
        EnterLine (Line, LineLen);
        CountLetters (Line, LineLen, Count);
        DisplayResults (Count)
    End {ControlProcessing} ;

Begin {Main}
    Writeln ('This program computes the frequency of letters ',
             'in a line of input.');
    ControlProcessing
End {Main} .
```

When this program is run on a sample line of input, we get the following output. The graphic display of frequency information in this output is called a **histogram**.

```
This program computes the frequency of letters in a line of input.
Please enter your input line:
Pascal allows characters both as subscripts and as data.

Display of the letter frequencies in the input line.

A : ********** 10
B : **  2
C : ****  4
```

```
D  :  **    2
E  :  *     1
H  :  **    2
I  :  *     1
L  :  ***    3
N  :  *     1
O  :  **    2
P  :  **    2
R  :  ***    3
S  :  ********    8
T  :  ****     4
U  :  *     1
W  :  *     1
```

As we can see, this program illustrates how we can combine many of the techniques involved in handling characters. We can declare arrays with characters as data or with character subscripts (or both). We can use character variables as control variables in our loops. In addition, to process characters, we can use internal codes to capitalize letters; we can compare characters with each other; we can work with one character at a time; and we can use characters as our subscripts in recording information.

SECTION 12.4   THE CASE STATEMENT

While the previous section illustrates how we may write programs to analyze words of input, another type of application involves the use of character data in making choices. For example, we may have the computer print a list of options, and we may wish the user to enter a letter to choose the option desired. Here, we organize a program on the basis of the various options that the user can select, using a separate procedure to perform each option. The result is called a **menu-driven** program, and we illustrate this approach in the following problem. This problem also illustrates an alternate approach to the *If* statement, which is useful when we need to select from many cases.

PROBLEM 12.4   A Menu-Driven Program

Write a statistics package that will allow us to enter data, modify data, and compute statistics, based on the following menu:

    Statistics Package Menu
        E - Enter Data
        M - Modify Data
        S - Compute Statistics
        Q - Quit
    Enter Option:

After this menu is printed, the user selects the appropriate option by typing the corresponding letter *E*, *M*, *S*, or *Q*, and an appropriate procedure is called.

In determining which choice a user selects, we could use a sequence of nested *If* statements, namely

> If (Option = 'E')
>> Then EnterData
>> Else If (Option = 'M')
>>> Then ModifyData
>>> Else If—

Although this code works, it is hard to read, and it becomes particularly messy if we want to allow both lowercase and uppercase responses.

The following program demonstrates an alternative approach. Note that all procedures involving statistics contain only a stub that identifies the option. Here, the *ProcessMenu* procedure could be used to declare variables needed when we move from one processing step to another.

```
Program Menu (Input, Output);

Procedure PrintMenu;
    Begin
        Writeln ('Statistics Package Menu');
        Writeln ('E - Enter Data');
        Writeln ('M - Modify Data');
        Writeln ('S - Compute Statistics');
        Writeln ('Q - Quit');
    End {PrintMenu} ;

Procedure EnterOption (Var Option: Char);
    Begin
        Write ('Enter Option: ');
        Readln (Option)
    End {EnterOption} ;

Procedure EnterData;
    Begin
        Writeln ('Data entry option');
        Writeln ('    Option not yet available')
    End {Enter Data} ;

Procedure ModifyData;
    Begin
        Writeln ('Data modification option');
        Writeln ('    Option not yet available')
    End {ModifyData} ;

Procedure ComputeStatistics;
    Begin
        Writeln ('Computation of Statistics');
        Writeln ('    Option not yet available')
    End {ComputeStatistics} ;
```

```
Procedure ProcessMenu;
{This procedure handles menu printing and option selection,
 and then calls the appropriate processing procedures.}
    Var Option: Char;
    Begin
        Repeat
            PrintMenu;
            EnterOption (Option);
            Case Option Of
                'E', 'e':  EnterData;
                'M', 'm':  ModifyData;
                'S', 's':  ComputeStatistics;
                'Q', 'q':  ;
                End {Case}
        Until (Option = 'Q') Or (Option = 'q')
    End {ProcessMenu} ;

Begin {Main}
    ProcessMenu
End {Main} .
```

This program prints the desired menu, reads the user's option, and selects the appropriate procedure to do the processing. In this work, the key step is a *Case* statement which has the following syntax:

Case Index *Of*
        Constant(s) : Statement;
        Constant(s) : Statement;
        .
        .
        .
        Constant(s) : Statement;
        End

Here, the *Index* is an integer, Boolean, or character variable or expression. (Reals are not allowed.)

When this statement is executed, the value of the index is evaluated. The machine finds this value on the list below. The machine then performs the statement specified by the constant. In our example, if our *Option* is 'm', the machine finds the value and performs the procedure *ModifyData*.

Within the *Case* statement, each statement may be a simple one such as a *Read, Write,* assignment, or procedure call, or the statement may involve a *Begin-End* block. Further, as we see for cases 'Q' and 'q' in our example, this statement may be empty or null.

Further, the *Case* statement allows us to list as many cases together as we wish, as long as we separate these cases by commas. Thus, we could write a list

        'Q', 'q', 'X', 'x' : —

However, only simple constants are allowed. We cannot use multiple characters such as 'QU' or 'Exit'. Further, our list of choices can involve only constants. Variables are not allowed.

In using *Case* statements, however, we must be careful that the value of our index is included in the list of constants. We may not be able to predict what the computer will do if this constant is not found. For example, if we typed 'B' as our option in this program, the computer might stop executing our program, or it might continue in some way.

On the other hand, some extensions of Pascal allow the inclusion of an *Otherwise* statement, placed before the *End*. When this is allowed, the *Otherwise* statement is executed if the *Index* value is not found. For example, we might write

```
Case Option of
      'E', 'e'    :   EnterData;
      'M', 'm'    :   ModifyData;
      'S', 's'    :   ComputeStatistics;
      'Q', 'q'    :   ;
      Otherwise :   Writeln('Invalid Option')
   End
```

In this case, the computer would print

    Invalid Option

if we entered a choice of 'B'.

As this example shows, the *Case* statement can be very useful whenever our work naturally splits into several cases. Once we identify these cases, the *Case* can help us organize our code accordingly.

This example also shows us a natural way to organize large programs that have many parts. We can divide our large task into small sections with a procedure for each task. Then we can tie the sections together with a general menu in a controlling menu-processing procedure. Further, when we use the technique of stubbing, this organization allows us to write and test a large program in pieces, so we do not have to write all of our code before we start the debugging process.

SECTION 12.5   SUBRANGES

In many of our previous applications, we did not place any restrictions on our data; our numbers could take on any value, and our data could include any characters we could type. However, sometimes we may want to limit ourselves to a specific range of values. For example, in declaring subscripts we specify a range of allowable integers or characters; we do not allow all possible values for our subscripts. Such a limited range of values is called a **subrange.** In this section, we see how we can use these subranges in our programs.

In Pascal, we can define a subrange of values by specifying

Constant .. Constant

in our declarations. For example, we may write

```
Type Capital = 'A'..'Z';        {a subrange of letters}
     NonNegative = 1..MaxInt;   {a subrange of integers}
Var Letter: Capital;
    NaturalNum: NonNegative;
    Little: -10..10;            {values limited to a
                                 subrange of integers}
```

Here, we have defined two new types of data that involve a limited range of values. *Capital* includes only those letters between 'A' and 'Z', while *NonNegative* includes only those integers greater than zero.

These declarations also define three variables whose values are limited to the ranges specified. For example, *Letter* is a variable that can be used to store any character between 'A' and 'Z'; *NaturalNum* can be used to store *NonNegative* numbers; and *Little* can be used to store integers between -10 and 10 (inclusive).

When we declare these new types, we still can use all of the operations available for the nonrestricted data, but we must be sure our final values stored are in the specified range. Thus, we may write

```
Letter := 'Q';
NaturalNum := ABS(-17);
Little := NaturalNum Mod 10;
```

In each case, we are performing operations on some data, and our final results are within the specified subranges for our variables. Thus, we can store the values computed in the given variables.

However, if we try to store values outside the specified range, our program will detect an error, and the computer may stop running our program. For example, suppose we have declared

```
Var A: Array [1..10] of Char;
```

and then we write

```
A[0] := 'Q';
```

From our experience with arrays, we realize that our subscript for *A* is not valid, and we expect the computer to stop with a statement such as

Subscript out of range

A similar result occurs if we try to work with values outside a declared subrange of a variable. For example, with the declarations earlier in this section, we expect the computer to report errors with any of the following:

```
Letter := Succ('Z');
NaturalNum := (15*7) Mod 5;
Little := MaxInt
```

To illustrate how subranges can be used effectively, we consider the following problem.

PROBLEM 12.5   ## Computing a Time Interval

Write a program that reads two times (in hours and minutes), determines which time comes first, and computes the time interval (in hours and minutes) between these two times.

In this problem, base your computations on two times being entered for the same day, with values between 0 hours 0 minutes (midnight, start of day) and 24 hours and 0 minutes (midnight, end of day).

Discussion of Problem 12.5

In this problem, we need to record times in hours and minutes, and we can expect that all hours will be between 0 and 24 and that minutes will be between 0 and 59.

Beyond this form for our data, our problem suggests three basic steps for our solution: recording data, determining which time comes first, and computing a time interval. When we expand these steps into an outline, we get the following.

Outline for Problem 12.5

I. Enter data.
   A. Read first time.
      Check hour is between 0 and 24.
      Check minute is between 0 and 59.
      If hour = 24, check minute = 0.
   B. Read second time.
      Check hour is between 0 and 24.
      Check minute is between 0 and 59.
      If hour = 24, check minute = 0.
II. Determine which time comes first.
   A. If hours are different,
      check which hour comes first.
   B. If hours are the same,
      check which minute comes first.
III. Determine time interval.
   A. If times are the same, time interval is zero.
   B. If times are different, check if minutes of earlier time come before minutes of later time.
      1. If so, compute
         (late hour − early hour)
         and (late minute − early minute)
      2. If not, compute
         (late hour − early hour − 1)
         (late minute − early minute + 60)

Further Discussion of Problem 12.5

In Step I of our outline, we allow the possibility that a user might enter an incorrect time, and we will ask the user to reenter the data in case of an error. However, after this step, all times should be in the range with

$$0 \leq Hour \leq 24 \text{ and } 0 \leq Minute \leq 59.$$

Thus, after data entry, we know we must have a programming error if our times lie outside this range. Therefore, in the following program, we limit our various *Hour* and *Minute* variables to a specific subrange for all work beyond Step I.

```
Program TimeInterval (Input, Output);
{This program reads two times (in hours and minutes),
 determines which time comes first, and computes the interval
 between them.}

Type HourRange = 0..24;
     MinuteRange = 0..59;

Procedure EnterData(Var FirstHr: HourRange; Var FirstMin: MinuteRange;
                Var SecondHr: HourRange; Var SecondMin: MinuteRange);
{This procedure reads two times in hours and minutes, and checks these
times are valid.}

    Procedure ReadTime (Var Hour: HourRange; Var Minute: MinuteRange);
    {This procedure reads a time in hours and minutes, and checks that
    the time is valid.}
       Var HourInput, MinuteInput: Integer;
           LegalTimes: Boolean;

       Begin
           {Read hour and minutes}
           Repeat
               Readln (HourInput, MinuteInput);
               If HourInput = 24
                  Then LegalTimes := (MinuteInput = 0)
                  Else LegalTimes := (HourInput >= 0) And
                          (HourInput < 24) And (MinuteInput >= 0)
                          And (MinuteInput <= 59);
               If Not LegalTimes
                  Then Begin
                       Writeln ('Hour must be between 0 and 24; ',
                                 'Minute must be between 0 and 59');
                       Write ('Please re-enter time: ');
                       End
           Until LegalTimes;

           {Return valid times}
           Hour := HourInput;
           Minute := MinuteInput
       End {ReadTime} ;
```

```
    Begin {EnterData}

        Writeln ('This program reads two times, determines which comes');
        Writeln ('first, and computes the time interval between them.');
        Writeln;
        Write ('Enter hours and minutes of first time: ');
        ReadTime (FirstHr, FirstMin);
        Writeln;
        Write ('Enter hours and minutes of second time: ');
        ReadTime (SecondHr, SecondMin);

    End {EnterData} ;

Function FirstTimeEarlier (FirstHr: HourRange; FirstMin: MinuteRange;
            SecondHr: HourRange; SecondMin: MinuteRange): Boolean;
{This function determines if the first time comes before the second time}
    Begin
        If FirstHr <> SecondHr
            Then FirstTimeEarlier := (FirstHr < SecondHr)
            Else FirstTimeEarlier := (FirstMin < SecondMin)
    End {FirstTimeEarlier} ;

Procedure DetermineInterval (EarlyHr: HourRange; EarlyMin: MinuteRange;
                            LateHr: HourRange; LateMin: MinuteRange);
{This procedure computes and prints the time interval between
 the two times specified}
    Var HourInt: HourRange;
        MinuteInt: MinuteRange;

    Begin
        If LateMin >= EarlyMin
            Then Begin
                HourInt := LateHr - EarlyHr;
                MinuteInt := LateMin - EarlyMin
            End
           Else Begin
                HourInt := LateHr - EarlyHr - 1;
                MinuteInt := LateMin - EarlyMin + 60
            End;
        If (HourInt = 0) And (MinuteInt = 0)
            Then Writeln ('The times specified are the same.')
            Else Writeln ('The time interval between these times is ',
                    HourInt:1, ' hours and ', MinuteInt:1, ' minutes.')
    End {DetermineInterval} ;

Procedure ProcessTimes;
{This procedure guides the solution of the problem}
    Var FirstHr, SecondHr: HourRange;
        FirstMin,SecondMin: MinuteRange;

    Begin
        EnterData (FirstHr, FirstMin, SecondHr, SecondMin);
        If FirstTimeEarlier (FirstHr, FirstMin, SecondHr, SecondMin)
            Then DetermineInterval(FirstHr, FirstMin, SecondHr, SecondMin)
            Else DetermineInterval(SecondHr, SecondMin, FirstHr, FirstMin)
    End {ProcessTimes} ;

Begin {Main}
    ProcessTimes
End {Main} .
```

Two sample runs of this program follow.

First Trial Run

This program reads two times, determines which comes
first, and computes the time interval between them.

Enter hours and minutes of first time: 10 45

Enter hours and minutes of second time: 11 30
The time interval between these times is 0 hours and 45 minutes.

Second Trial Run

This program reads two times, determines which comes
first, and computes the time interval between them.

Enter hours and minutes of first time: 9 75
Hour must be between 0 and 24; Minute must be between 0 and 59
Please re-enter time: 9 10

Enter hours and minutes of second time: 7 00
The time interval between these times is 2 hours and 10 minutes.

As we can see from this example, subranges have several important features.

1. Subranges limit data values to a particular range (e.g., 0..24 or 0..59), and subranges allow the computer to continually monitor that values do not extend beyond the specified limits.
2. When variables have values limited to a subrange, those variables may still be used in computations with other values outside the subrange. For example, while *EarlyMinute* and *LateMinute* are both limited to the range 0 to 59, we still used them with the larger integer 60, in the statement

    LateMinute − EarlyMinute + 60

    Here, only the *Minute* variables are restricted, not the other parts of our expression.
3. Subranges are helpful when we want the computer to halt processing when invalid values are encountered. For example, in Steps II or III, an hour outside the interval 0..24 indicates a bug in the program, and we want the program to stop further processing if such a bug is detected.
4. On the other hand, subranges do not allow us to handle user input errors, as processing may halt if a user enters a value outside a subrange. Thus, for user input, it is better to allow for a wide range of

values and then check for correctness. Once the values are verified as being acceptable, we can perform subsequent processing with values limited to the subrange.

SECTION 12.6	ENUMERATED TYPES

Up to this point, our applications have been selected so we could use rather traditional types of data in our processing. Our data included numbers (real or integers) or Booleans or characters, and our processing involved either these types or subranges of these. However, in some applications we may wish to define a new data type in which we specify exactly which values are possible. Such a data type is called an **enumerated type,** and this section discusses how such types can be defined.

We begin with a problem which may remind us of our letter counting problem in Section 12.3.

PROBLEM 12.6   Write a program that reads a line of input and counts the number of capital letters, small letters, spaces, digits, and punctuation marks.

Discussion of Problem 12.6

In this problem, we need to read our line of input. Then, we need to decide which category each character falls into, and we need to update our category information appropriately.

We begin by defining these categories as a separate data type by declaring

    Type Category = (Capital, Small, Space, Digit, Punc);
    Var Item: Category;

Further, to record our frequency information, we can use these category values as subscripts. Thus, we declare

    Type CounterType = Array [Category] of Integer;
    Var Count: CounterType;

With this setup, we follow the same general approach we used in Section 12.3 to count letter frequencies. Our general plan includes the following outline.

Outline for Problem 12.6

   I. Enter line from terminal.
      A. Read until end of line or until we run out of space.
      B. Record the number of characters read.
   II. Count letters in each category.
      A. Initialize all counts to 0.

B. Repeat for each character in the input line.
    1. Determine which category the character is in.
    2. Increment the count for that category.
III. Display the results for each category.

This outline leads to the following program.

```pascal
Program CountCharactersByCategories (Input, Output);
{This program counts the number of characters in a given line
 of input according to various categories.}

Const MaxLen = 80;

Type CharInput = Array [1..MaxLen] of Char;
     Category = (Capital, Small, Space, Digit, Punc);
     CounterType = Array [Category] of Integer;

Procedure EnterLine (Var Line: CharInput; Var Length: Integer);
{This procedure reads a line of input from the terminal.}

    Begin
        Writeln ('Please enter your line of input:');
        Length := 0;
        While (Not Eoln) And (Length < MaxLen)
          Do Begin
            Length := Length + 1;
            Read (Line[Length])
          End;
        If Not Eoln
            Then Writeln ('Your message was too long; ',
                        'message truncated to ', MaxLen:1, ' characters');
        Readln
    End {EnterLine} ;

Procedure CountCat (Line: CharInput; Length: Integer; Var Count: CounterType);
{This procedures counts the number of letters in each category.}
    Var Item: Category;
        Index: Integer;

    Procedure DetermineCat (Ch: Char; Var Item: Category);
    {This procedure determines which category a given character belongs to}
        Begin
            If (Ch >= 'A') And (Ch <= 'Z')
                Then Item := Capital
            Else If (Ch >= 'a') and (Ch <= 'z')
                Then Item := Small
            Else If (Ch >= '0') and (Ch <= '9')
                Then Item := Digit
            Else If (Ch = ' ')
                Then Item := Space
                Else Item := Punc
        End {DetermineCat} ;
```

```
    Begin {CountCat}
        {Initially, all counts are 0}
        For Item := Capital To Punc
            Do Count[Item] := 0;

        {For each character, find category and update count}
        For Index := 1 To Length
            Do Begin
                DetermineCat(Line[Index], Item);
                Count[Item] := Count[Item] + 1
            End;
    End {CountCat} ;

Procedure DisplayResults (Count: CounterType);
{This procedure displays the frequencies for each category.}
    Var Item: Category;
        Index: Integer;

    Procedure PrintName (Item: Category);
    {This procedure prints the name of the specified category}
        Begin
            Case Item Of
                Capital:  Write ('Captial Letter: ');
                Small  :  Write ('Small Letter  : ');
                Space  :  Write ('Space         : ');
                Digit  :  Write ('Digit         : ');
                Punc   :  Write ('Punctuation   : ');
            End;
        End {PrintName} ;
    Begin
        Writeln;
        Writeln ('Display of the frequencies in the input line by category');
        Writeln;

        For Item := Capital To Punc
            Do Begin
                PrintName(Item);
                For Index := 1 To Count[Item]
                    Do Write ('*');
                Writeln (Count[Item]:3)
            End
    End {DisplayResults} ;

Procedure ControlProcess;
{This procedure controls the major steps of data entry,
 counting of character and printing of results}
    Var Line: CharInput;          {The line of input}
        LineLength: Integer;   {The length of the line of input}
        Count: CounterType;    {The frequency data for each category}

    Begin
        EnterLine (Line, LineLength);
        CountCat (Line, LineLength, Count);
        DisplayResults (Count)
    End {ControlProcess} ;

Begin {Main}
    Writeln ('This program computes the frequency of letters ');
    Writeln ('by category in a given input line.');
    ControlProcess
End {Main} .
```

When this program is run with some test data, we get the following output:

```
This program computes the frequency of letters
by category in a given input line.
Please enter your line of input:
>>>>>This line contains a variety of characters!!! 12345 <<<<<

Display of the frequencies in the input line by category

Captial Letter: *  1
Small Letter  : ***********************************  35
Space         : ********  8
Digit         : *****  5
Punctuation   : *************  13
```

In this program, we have listed (or enumerated) all of the possible categories in our problem, namely *Capital*, *Small*, *Space*, *Digit*, and *Punc*. This program illustrates many features of using these enumerated types.

To begin, we declare our enumerated type, which we called *Category*. In this listing, we indicate what values are allowed; we separate these values by commas; and we put the entire list in parentheses. Some other examples of such declarations are shown below.

Type DayOfWeek = (Sunday, Monday, Tuesday,
                  Wednesday, Thursday, Friday, Saturday);
     SpeechPart = (Noun, Verb, Adjective, Adverb,
                  Conjunction, Preposition, Pronoun, Article);
Var Day: DayOfWeek;
    Word: SpeechPart;
    Month: (January, February, March, April,
                May, June, July, August, September,
                October, November, December);

Once enumerated types are declared, they can be used in many familiar ways. For example, enumerated types can be used in assignment statements, as array subscripts, and for control variables in *For* loops. In addition, they can be compared in Boolean expressions and used as constants in *Case* statements.

Further, the application of enumerated types in *For* loops suggests another aspect of our declarations. When we declare

TypeCategory = (Capital, Small, Space, Digit, Punc)

we are specifying an ordering of these items and an internal coding value. In particular, the computer will consider

Capital as having a code number 0;

Small as having a code number 1;

Space as having a code number 2;

Digit as having a code number 3;

Punc as having a code number 4.

With this ordering, we can establish what happens in a *For* loop. When we write

For Item : = **Capital to Punc**

or

For Item : = **Small to Digit**

Item begins with the first value specified. Then *Item* takes on successive values until the final value is reached. Thus, the first of these examples covers all five values, while the second example continues the loop for *Small, Space,* and *Digit* only.

This coding also allows us to use the functions *Ord, Succ,* and *Pred* (which we discussed in Section 12.2) for characters. In particular, if

Item : = **Space**

then

Ord(Item) is 3;

Succ(Item) is *Digit;*

Pred(Item) is *Small.*

Finally, we note that we are limited in the use of enumerated types in that we cannot read or write these types directly. Thus, when we use enumerated types, we often need to write a procedure that translates from our input data to our special values (Procedure *DetermineCat* in our program). Also, we may need a special output procedure to print the values for these enumerated types. (In this output process, Procedure *PrintName* illustrates a particularly helpful use of the *Case* statement.)

With these comments, our sample program shows us that enumerated types can be quite helpful as we try to solve problems. In our example, we could write our program in the language of our problem, by giving special values for *Capital, Small,* etc. Then, we could record data and establish loops on the basis of these values.

Our program did require procedures to translate from our character input to these special values and from these values to our output. However, in the middle of our processing, our program could follow our solution outline quite naturally.

SECTION 12.7   A SUMMARY OF SIMPLE DATA TYPES

At this point, we have seen all of the simple data types allowed in Pascal, and it is useful to look at these types to see some general patterns. In Pascal, we can organize our simple data types into two main classes: real type and ordinal type.

Real Type

In our work with real numbers, we can perform arithmetic and make comparisons, but we do not think of reals as being isolated entities. For example, there is a vast range of reals between 1.0 and 2.0, and we do not try to work with the real number that comes just after 1.0. With this perspective that reals extend "continuously," we find that we cannot use reals in some contexts.

- We cannot use reals as subscripts, for there are just too many reals in an interval. For example, we would need too much storage for

  Var A: Array [1.0..2.0] of Integer

- Pascal does not allow subranges of reals for a similar reason.
- Functions such as *Pred* and *Succ* do not apply to reals, for we do not know which real exactly precedes or succeeds another.

Ordinal Type

On the other hand, all of the other simple data types do contain distinct, isolated values, and we call these other types **ordinal types.** Included in these are the standard integer, Boolean, and character types we have used in many of our applications. In addition, ordinal type includes enumerated types, where we define our own specific values, and subranges.

With any of these ordinal types, we can consider values in a given interval, and we can ask what precedes or succeeds a given value. This isolated or discrete quality of the data in ordinal types has the following consequences.

- We can define subranges for any ordinal type.
- We can use any ordinal type (including subranges) for array subscripts and for *Case* statements.
- We can use any ordinal type for control variables in *For* loops.
- We can apply *Ord*, *Pred*, and *Succ* functions to any ordinal type. However, in using *Pred* and *Succ*, we must be careful not to go beyond the limits of our type. For example, if

  Category = (Capital, Small, Space, Digit, Punc)

  we cannot try to obtain

  Pred(Capital)

or

Succ(Punc).

This discussion shows that we can view many of our data types as being similar in many ways. Each ordinal type represents a distinct set of values, but we can use these types in many similar ways. On the other hand, real data type is somewhat different from these ordinal types.

SUMMARY

1. This chapter introduces three new data types: **characters, enumerated types,** and **subranges.**
2. With **character data type,** we can read, process, and print individual characters, and several characters can be stored in arrays.
3. With **enumerated types,** we can define new data types containing specific data values. Thus, we are not limited to using only integers, real, Boolean, or character values in processing.
4. When working with integers, Booleans, characters, or enumerated types, we can restrict the range of values being considered to a specific interval or **subrange.**
5. Integers, Booleans, characters, subranges, and enumerated types are all examples of **ordinal data types,** and they share many common features. For example, any ordinal data type can be used as constants in *Case* statements.
6. Ordinal data are stored using an underlying code, and this code allows us to compare data in Boolean expressions and to use any of the ordinal data types for control variables in *For* loops. With this underlying ordering, the functions *Ord, Pred,* and *Succ* can be used in processing any of these ordinal types. (*Chr* is also available for processing characters.)
7. Finally, this ordinal data can be used in a variety of applications, including processing a *Yes* or *No* response, capitalizing letters in a line of input, enciphering and deciphering messages, counting letters or characters in various ways, writing menu-driven programs, and computing time intervals.

EXERCISES

The following four problems all include some aspects of processing a line of input. With some care, the various tasks required can be organized into a few logical procedures that can be reused to solve several problems. Thus, readers are encouraged to spend some time designing procedures that fit together in various ways to meet the requirements of these problems.

Throughout, we will consider a *word* as a sequence of letters without punctuation.

12.1 *Counting Words.* Write a program that reads a line of input and counts the number of words in the line.

12.2 *Capitalizing Words.* Write a program that reads a line of input and then prints the line with the first letter of each word capitalized and subsequent letters in lowercase.

12.3 *Formatting Words.* Write a program that reads a line of input, capitalizes all letters, and prints the words in the line with just one space between words. All punctuation should be·omitted.

12.4 *Average Number of Letters.* Write a program that reads a line of input, determines the number of words and the·number of letters, and prints the average number of letters per word.

12.5 *Caesar Cipher.* Suppose we are given the declarations

```
Const MaxLen = 80;
Type InputLine = Array [1..MaxLen] of Char
```

With these declarations, we will store a line of input as an array of type *InputLine*, and we will record the length of the line.

a. Write a procedure of the form

```
Procedure Shift (Var Line: InputLine; Length: Integer)
```

which replaces each letter in the line by the letter following it in alphabetical order, except that 'A' will replace 'Z'. Thus, the word 'THE' is coded as 'UIF'. Spaces and punctuation are not to be changed.

HINT: Use the *Succ* function.

b. Write a program that reads a line of input and applies *Shift* three times, so that each letter is replaced by the third letter following in the alphabet. Print the resulting coded message.

HISTORICAL NOTE: This code was used effectively by Caesar in the Gallic Wars, and thus this type of enciphering algorithm is called a Caesar Cipher.

KEY TERMS, PHRASES, AND CONCEPTS		ELEMENTS OF PASCAL SYNTAX	
Case Statement	End of Line Processing	*Case*	*Ord*
Character Data	Enumerated Types	*Char*	*Pred*
Type	Histogram	*Chr*	Subranges
Character Codes	Menu-Driven Programs	Enumerated Type	*Succ*
Character	Ordinal Data Types	*EOLN*	
Functions	Subranges		
Comparison of			
Characters			

12.6   *Deciphering a Caesar Cipher.* Write a program that will decipher the messages written using the Caesar Cipher of the previous problem.

12.7   *Enciphering and Deciphering.* In Section 12.3, we used a procedure *Decipher* when we wanted to decode a message using the given real and cipher alphabets. Suppose we use this procedure with the following variable declarations.

```
Var RealAlphabet   : Alphabet;
    CipherAlphabet : Alphabet;
    Message        : CharLine;
    CodedMess      : CharLine;
    NewMess        : CharLine;
    InputLen       : Integer;
```

Then, after entering our message, suppose we have the following procedure calls.

```
Decipher (CodedMess, Message, InputLen, RealAlphabet,
            CipherAlphabet);
Decipher (Message, NewMess, InputLen, CipherAlphabet,
            RealAlphabet);
```

a. How does *NewMess* compare with our original *CodedMess*?

b. Use the answer in Part a. to write a procedure that can help check that the enciphering procedure works correctly.

12.8   *Divisibility by 2 and 3.* Write a program that determines if an integer is divisible by either 2 or 3.

    HINT: If we divide the number by 6, we can identify the following cases.

- If the remainder is 0, then the number is divisible by both 2 and 3.
- If the remainder is 1 or 5, then the number is divisible by neither.
- If the remainder is 2 or 4, then the number is divisible by 2 but not 3.
- If the remainder is 3, then the number is divisible by 3 but not 2.

12.9   *Identifying Months.* Write a program that reads an integer between 1 and 12 and then prints the name of the corresponding month. For example, if the number 5 is typed, the computer should print

    May is the fifth month.

    HINT: Use a *Case* statement.

12.10   *Common Error in Programming-1.* The following procedure for inputing characters contains an error that commonly occurs in using subranges. Find the error.

```
{This procedure assumes the following declarations:

Const MaxText = 80;

Type CharPosition = 1..MaxText;
     TextLine = Array[CharPosition] of Char; }

Procedure EnterText (Var Text: TextLine; Var Length: CharPosition);
{This procedure reads a line of text from a terminal.}
   Begin
       Length := 0;
       While (Not Eoln) and (Length < MaxText)
         Do Begin
            Length := Length + 1;
            Read(Text[Length])
         End;
       If Not Eoln
          Then Writeln ('Message Too Long;  Message Truncated To ',
                   MaxText:1, ' Characters.');
       Readln
   End {EnterText} ;
```

12.11 *Common Error in Programming-2.* A more subtle problem with sub-ranges is illustrated by making the following change in the *Value* function of Section 12.5. The Boolean function *Done* is used in a *While* loop. At first reading, one might think that this Boolean function could be eliminated if we changed the loop to begin

While (Item > Length) Or (Sequence[Item] = '.')
    Do

    .

    .

    .

Find a difficulty with this Boolean expression that motivated us to use the Boolean function *Done*.

CHAPTER 13

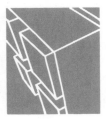

COLLECTIONS

OF OBJECTS:

SETS AND RECORDS

In past chapters, we have worked with individual pieces of data, such as numbers and characters, and we have been able to put these separate pieces together in arrays. This chapter examines the general concept of grouping pieces of data together more fully, and we will suggest an orientation that allows us to think of our data abstractly in terms of the problem we have at hand. We will not want to limit ourselves to thinking about specific values stored in a Pascal program.

In addition, this chapter introduces two specific ways we can work with collections of data. In particular, we consider **sets,** which allow us to store various values as a single entity, and **records,** which allow us to combine various types of data into logical units.

THE CONCEPTS OF GROUPING DATA AND ABSTRACTION

We can think of data on several distinct levels: we can consider each item of data individually; we can group items of data together in various ways; and we can group data items in complex ways, which include operations on data as well as the data themselves.

Up to this point, most of our work has involved the first of these levels, although the second level was introduced somewhat in Chapter 9 when we considered rows in a table as separate entities. In this section, we examine each of these levels more carefully.

Level 1: Individual Data Items

Up to this point, we normally have considered each piece of data individually. We did not need to group our information in any way. This first level is most useful in problems that are simple enough to handle each piece of data separately. For example, in our unit pricing problems in Sections 2.1 and 12.1, we only needed three values (cost per ounce, price in dollars, and weight in ounces), and we could work with each value by itself. We might also choose to focus on individual pieces of information when we are starting to analyze a problem. For example, we might try to find patterns by working with many special cases.

Level 2: Groups of Data

Once we master individual pieces of data, we often want to group the data in various ways. For example, we may form sequences from these pieces. Thus, when data are stored in an array, there is a first item, a second item, and so on.

Alternatively, we may put pieces of information together into groups in which order does not matter. For example, in considering a bridge hand, we care about the cards that we hold, not the order in which they were dealt. We might also want to group various types of information such as numbers and words. For example, an employer may include an employee's name, employee number, address, age, social security number, and telephone number in a single file. This information involves many individual pieces of data, but these pieces are grouped together in the records of the personnel office. At this level, we work with an entire collection of data at once.

In our programming, we have already seen that we can work at this level when we are dealing with arrays. In Chapter 9 we could refer to an entire array as a single entity. (For example, we wrote $A := B$.) Similarly, we could work with entire rows of tables. Later in this chapter, we will see that Pascal allows us to group data in other ways as well.

Level 3: Abstract Data Structures

In more complex problems, we must consider not only the pieces of data that we need to store but also the ways we need to work with that data. For example, if we want to study traffic flow at a traffic light, our individual pieces of data may involve the vehicles turning left or right, the vehicles moving along straight, and the vehicles stopped for a red light. However, beyond these pieces, we also need to consider what happens when another car approaches the light or when a car finishes its turn. In this problem, we want to think in terms of cars entering and leaving the intersection, cars turning, and cars waiting. Our data involve cars, and we can specify various interactions among the cars.

For such complex problems, we need to free ourselves from specific programming details. We will be overwhelmed if we must translate each detail about traffic flow into specifics about numbers or Booleans or characters. Our programs must allow us to work on a more conceptual level.

This is the level of abstract data structures, where we group data items in complex ways and where we specify what operations we wish to perform on these data items. We will see how we can include this level in our Pascal programs in later chapters.

SECTION 13.2   PUTTING PIECES TOGETHER WITH SETS

This section discusses one way that pieces of data can be grouped together, following our second level for working with data. The particular approach uses the concept of a **set,** and we introduce this idea with an example.

PROBLEM 13.2A   Determining Letters and Counting Vowels

Write a program that determines which letters are present in a line that is entered at the keyboard and counts the number of vowels in the line. In this problem, lowercase and uppercase letters should be considered separately.

Discussion of Problem 13.2A

In solving this problem, we can think in terms of three collections of objects: the letters in the alphabet (including both uppercase and lowercase); the letters in the line; and the vowels in the alphabet. Thus, we write our solution in terms of these collections, or **sets.** In our processing, we can describe the first and third of these collections immediately:

The letters of the alphabet include the ranges:
‘a’..‘z’ and ‘A’..‘Z’

The vowels include the specific characters:
‘a’, ‘e’, ‘i’, ‘o’, ‘u’, ‘A’, ‘E’, ‘I’, ‘O’, ‘U’

The second collection depends upon our input. Thus, we will start with this set of letters being **empty,** that is, containing no elements. Then, as we go through our input, we will add the letters.

Also, when we count vowels, we will go through each character in our input. If a character is a vowel, we will increment our vowel count.

This discussion suggests the following outline.

Outline of Problem 13.2A

I. Enter line. (We proceed as in the examples in Sections 12.3 and 12.6.)
II. Process line.

A. Define our collection of letters and vowels.
B. At the start:
    1. We have not found any letters.
    2. Our count of vowels is 0.
C. For each character in the line:
    1. If the character is a vowel, we add 1 to our vowel count.
    2. If the character is a letter, we add it to our collection of letters.
III. Print results.
    A. Print letters in the line. For each lowercase and uppercase letter, if the letter was in our line of input, then we print the letter.
    B. Print the final vowel count.

This outline yields the following program. For clarity in processing, we have used a variable *Ch* for the characters in the line of input. We could use *Line[Index]* in procedure *ProcessLine* instead if we wished.

```
Program DetermineLettersAndCountVowels (Input, Output);
{This program determines what letters appear in a line of input
 and counts the number of vowels in the line.}

Const MaxLen = 80;

Type InputLine = Array [1..MaxLen] of Char;
     CharacterSet = Set Of Char;

Procedure EnterLine (Var Line: InputLine; Var Length: Integer);
{This procedure reads Line from the terminal.}

    Begin
        Writeln ('Please enter your line of input:');
        Length := 0;
        While (Not Eoln) And (Length < MaxLen)
          Do Begin
             Length := Length + 1;
             Read (Line[Length])
          End;
        If Not Eoln
           Then Writeln ('Your message was too long; ',
                         'message truncated to ', MaxLen:1, ' characters');
        Readln
    End {EnterLine} ;

Procedure ProcessLine (Line: InputLine; Length: Integer;
               Var LetterSet: CharacterSet; Var VowelCount: Integer);
{This procedure forms a set of letters and counts the vowels}
    Var Letters: CharacterSet;
        Vowels: CharacterSet;
        Index: Integer;
        Ch: Char;
```

```
Begin
    {Initialize sets and counter}
    Letters := ['a'..'z', 'A'..'Z'];
    Vowels := ['a','e','i','o','u','A','E','I','O','U'];
    LetterSet := [];
    VowelCount := 0;

    {Process each character in line of input}
    For Index := 1 To Length
        Do Begin
            Ch := Line[Index];
            If Ch In Vowels
                Then VowelCount := VowelCount + 1;
            If Ch In Letters
                Then LetterSet := LetterSet + [ Ch ]
        End
    End {ProcessLine} ;

Procedure DisplayResults (LetterSet: CharacterSet; VowelCount: Integer);
{This procedure prints the letters in the input and the count of the vowels}
    Var Ch: Char;
    Begin
        Writeln;
        Writeln ('The following letters were found in the line of input');
        For Ch := 'a' To 'z'
            Do If Ch In LetterSet
                Then Write (Ch:2);
        For Ch := 'A' To 'Z'
            Do If Ch In LetterSet
                Then Write (Ch:2);
        Writeln;
        Writeln;
        Writeln ('There were ',VowelCount:1, ' vowels in the line of input.')
    End {DisplayResults} ;

Procedure ControlProcessing;
{This procedure controls the major steps required to process the line}
    Var Line: InputLine;        {The line of input}
        LineLength: Integer;    {The length of the line of input}
        LetterSet: CharacterSet;{Set of letters from input line}
        VowelCount: Integer;    {Number of vowels in input line}
    Begin
        EnterLine (Line, LineLength);
        ProcessLine (Line, LineLength, LetterSet, VowelCount);
        DisplayResults (LetterSet, VowelCount)
    End {ControlProcessing} ;

Begin {Main}
    Writeln ('This programs processes letters and vowels ',
             'in a given line of input');
    ControlProcessing
End {Main} .
```

When this program is run with some sample data, we get the following output:

```
This programs processes letters and vowels in a given line of input
Please enter your line of input:
This program illustrates some simple ways that sets can help us group data.

The following letters were found in the line of input
 a c d e g h i l m n o p r s t u w y T

There were 21 vowels in the line of input.
```

Sets in Pascal

In the program above, we illustrate several features of sets in Pascal, which allow us to handle groups of data. A **set** is a collection of data items in which duplicate values are not recorded and the order of items is ignored.

We work with groups of data by declaring them as sets. For example, we declare

> Type CharacterSet = Set of Char;
> Var   Letters: CharacterSet;
>   Vowels: CharacterSet;

Alternatively, we could have declared

> Var Letters, Vowels: Set of Char;

These declarations indicate that these variables will be collections or sets of characters. In this problem, all of our collections involved character data. More generally, sets may be constructed from any ordinal type.

Once a variable is declared, we can specify what data we wish to include in a group. Four ways of specifying the data in a group are illustrated in our example.

1. We can specifically list the items in a set. For example,

> Vowels : = ['a', 'e', 'i', 'o', 'u', 'A', 'E', 'I', 'O', 'U']

lists the characters in the set of vowels. Here, each vowel is listed, the characters are separated by commas, and the entire list is placed in brackets [   ].

2. We can specify subranges of elements. For example,

> Letters : = ['a'..'z', 'A'..'Z']

indicates that this set of letters is made up of the two subranges, 'a' to 'z' and 'A' to 'Z'.

3. A special case of this listing of elements is the specification of the **empty set.** For example, the statement

> LetterSet : = [   ]

specifies that the *LetterSet* begins with no elements, just as the statement

> VowelCount : = 0

initializes this integer variable.

4. Once we have initialized a set, we can add elements to it. For example, our program contained the statement

> LetterSet : = LetterSet + [Ch]

Here, we use the " + " sign to add a character *Ch* to our *LetterSet*. Note that the *Ch* is placed in brackets [ ] in this statement. (Later in this section, we will see that " + " can be used more generally.)

While sets do allow us to group data, we note that sets do not keep track of duplicates. Once an element is in a set, the set is not changed if that element is added again. Thus ['a', 'a', 'a'] is the same as ['a']. The multiple copies of 'a' in the first set are ignored.

Next, we note that once a set is created, we can test if a particular element is in that set. For example, we wrote

> **If Ch In Vowels**

to see if the character *Ch* under consideration was a vowel. In general, we may write the Boolean expression

> **Element *In* SetVariable**

to test if the given *Element* is in the set specified by *SetVariable*. This expression is true if the *SetVariable* contains the *Element* and false otherwise.

From our example that analyzes a line of input, we see some ways we can declare sets, group elements together in those sets, and test if particular items are in those collections. Before considering a more extended example, we look at three important operations that we can use to manipulate sets, namely

- union
- intersection
- difference

Unions of Sets

If we have two sets, we can put the elements of these two sets together to form a new set using the **union** or " + " operation. For example, suppose we have

> UpperCase : = ['A'..'Z'];
> LowerCase : = ['a'..'z'];
> Vowels   : = ['a', 'e', 'i', 'o', 'u', 'A', 'E', 'I', 'O', 'U'];

Then, we can put *UpperCase* and *LowerCase* together to get

> Letters : = UpperCase + LowerCase

Here, *Letters* include both capital and small letters, so *Letters* has become ['a'..'z', 'A'..'Z'].

When we put sets together in this way, the union operation discards duplicates; sets only record that an element is present, not the number of times it occurs. In some cases, this means that the union operation does not change what elements we already have. For example, *Vowels* + *Letters* gives us *Letters* again, since all *Vowels* are already included in the *Letters*. Similarly, the union of any set with itself is just the same set.

With this background, we see that our previous statement

LetterSet := LetterSet + [Ch]

is just a special case of this union or " + " operation. Here, we start with the collection *LetterSet*. Then, we make a set out of our character *Ch* by putting *Ch* in brackets. At this point, we have two sets: *LetterSet* and [*Ch*]. Then, we take the union of these two sets, putting their elements together, to get our new *LetterSet*.

Intersection

While the union operation puts elements from two sets together, the **intersection** or "**" operation identifies which elements are in both sets. For example, if we use our earlier declarations, then

Vowels * UpperCase

gives ['A', 'E', 'I', 'O', 'U']. Here, we find elements that are both vowels and capital letters.

As a second example,

UpperCase * LowerCase

is the empty set, [   ]. There are no characters that are both uppercase and lowercase.

Difference

Our third operation, **difference** or " − ", allows us to find all elements in one set that are not in a second. For example,

Vowels − UpperCase

gives ['a', 'e', 'i', 'o', 'u']. Here, we find all vowels that are not capitals; i.e., we obtain the lowercase vowels. On the other hand,

UpperCase − VowelSet

gives a different collection of characters, namely

['B', 'C', 'D', 'F', 'G', 'H', 'J', 'K', 'L', 'M', 'N',
    'P', 'Q', 'R', 'S', 'T', 'V', 'W', 'X', 'Y', 'Z']

Again, set differences may produce the empty set as a result. For example, both

UpperCase − Letters

and

Vowels − Vowels

give the empty set, as every element in the first set is also in the second.

PROBLEM 13.2B

Analyzing Categories of Letters

With the operations we just described, we can consider the following more complex problem involving an analysis of a line of characters.

Scan a line of input to determine

a. the letters (upper- and lowercase) used;
b. the uppercase letters used;
c. the lowercase letters used;
d. the vowels used; and
e. the consonants used.

Discussion of Problem 13.2B

While the statement of our problem involves many categories of letters, our processing need not be complex if we group our letters conveniently.

From Problem 13.2A, we already have seen how to determine which letters are used in a line. Also, we can utilize the following relationships for sets:

Letters := UpperCase + LowerCase
Consonants := Letters − Vowels

Next, we can determine which letters in our line are in each category if we intersect *LetterSet* (letters in our input line) with the appropriate collections of upper- or lowercase letters, vowels, or consonants.

This suggests the following outline.

Outline of Problem 13.2B

  I. Enter line. (We proceed as in the examples in Sections 12.3 and 12.6.)
 II. Determine letters used in line.
    A. At the start:
      1. We have not found any letters.
      2. We have not found any vowels.
    B. For each character in the input line:
      1. If the character is a vowel, then we add it to our list of vowels.
      2. If the character is a letter, then we add it to our collection of letters.
III. Print results. In each case, print a special note if no letters are present in the category.
    A. Print all letters in the line.
    B. Print letters both in line and uppercase.
    C. Print letters both in line and lowercase.

D. Print letters both in line and vowels.

E. Print letters both in line and consonants.

From this outline, we derive the following program.

```
Program GroupingLettersinCategories (Input, Output);
{This program determines what letters from a line of input
 occur in various categories.}

Const MaxLen = 80;

Type InputLine = Array [1..MaxLen] of Char;
     CharacterSet = Set Of Char;

Procedure InitializeSets(Var UpperCase, LowerCase, Vowels,
                           Consonants, Letters: CharacterSet);
{This procedure sets up our sets of upper and lower case letters,
 vowels, consonants, and all letters}
    Begin
        UpperCase := ['A'..'Z'];
        LowerCase := ['a'..'z'];
        Vowels := ['a','e','i','o','u','A','E','I','O','U'];
        Letters := UpperCase + LowerCase;
        Consonants := Letters - Vowels;
    End {InitializeSets} ;

Procedure EnterLine (Var Line: InputLine; Var Length: Integer);
{This procedure reads Line from the terminal.}

    Begin
        Writeln ('Please enter your line:');
        Length := 0;
        While (Not Eoln) And (Length < MaxLen)
          Do Begin
            Length := Length + 1;
            Read (Line[Length])
          End;
        If Not Eoln
          Then Writeln ('Your message was too long; ',
                    'message truncated to ', MaxLen:1, ' characters');
        Readln
    End {EnterLine} ;

Procedure FindLetters (Line: InputLine; Length: Integer;
                    Var LetterSet: CharacterSet; Letters: CharacterSet);
{This procedure forms a set of letters from the input line}
    Var Index: Integer;

    Begin
        {Initialize set}
        LetterSet := [];
```

```
                {Process each character in line}
            For Index := 1 To Length
              Do Begin
                If Line[Index] In Letters
                   Then LetterSet := LetterSet + [ Line[Index] ]
              End
      End {FindLetters};

Procedure DisplayResults (LetterSet, UpperCase, LowerCase, Vowels,
                          Consonants, Letters: CharacterSet);
{This procedure prints the letters in various categories}

    Procedure PrintIntersection (FirstSet, SecondSet: CharacterSet);
    {This procedure prints the letters in the intersection
     of the two given sets}
        Var Ch: Char;
            Intersection: CharacterSet;
        Begin
            Intersection := FirstSet * SecondSet;
            If Intersection = []  {test if intersection is empty}
                Then Writeln ('     No letters found')
                Else Begin
                    For Ch := 'a' To 'z'
                        Do If Ch In Intersection
                            Then Write (Ch:2);
                    For Ch := 'A' To 'Z'
                        Do If Ch In Intersection
                            Then Write (Ch:2);
                    Writeln
                    End;
            Writeln;
        End {PrintIntersection} ;

    Begin {DisplayResults}

        Writeln;
        Writeln ('The following letters were found in the line');
        PrintIntersection (LetterSet, Letters);

        Writeln ('The following capital letters were found');
        PrintIntersection (LetterSet, UpperCase);

        Writeln ('The following lower case letters were found');
        PrintIntersection (LetterSet, LowerCase);

        Writeln ('The following vowels were found');
        PrintIntersection (LetterSet, Vowels);

        Writeln ('The following consonants were found');
        PrintIntersection (LetterSet, Consonants);

    End {DisplayResults} ;

Procedure ControlProcessing;
{This procedure controls the initialization, data entry, analysis, and
printing of the line of input.}
```

```
    Var Line: InputLine;        {The line of input}
        LineLength: Integer;    {The length of the line of input}
        LetterSet: CharacterSet;{Set of letters from line of input}
        UpperCase: CharacterSet;
        LowerCase: CharacterSet;
        Vowels: CharacterSet;
        Consonants: CharacterSet;
        Letters: CharacterSet;
    Begin
        InitializeSets(UpperCase, LowerCase, Vowels, Consonants, Letters);
        EnterLine (Line, LineLength);
        FindLetters (Line, LineLength, LetterSet, Letters);
        DisplayResults (LetterSet, UpperCase, LowerCase,
                        Vowels, Consonants, Letters)
    End {ControlProcessing} ;

Begin {Main}
    Writeln ('This program processes letters and vowels ',
            'in a given line of input.');
    ControlProcessing
End {Main}
```

This program produces the following output:

```
This program processes letters and vowels in a given line of input.
Please enter your line:
pascal's set capabilities allow us to manipulate groups of data easily!!

The following letters were found in the line
 a b c d e f g i l m n o p r s t u w y

The following capital letters were found
    No letters found

The following lower case letters were found
 a b c d e f g i l m n o p r s t u w y

The following vowels were found
 a e i o u

The following consonants were found
 b c d f g l m n p r s t w y
```

This program combines many of the points we have made about sets. We see that we can work conceptually with groups of data by using sets. Once we declare and initialize our sets, then we can manipulate sets in various ways. Finally, we can test if particular elements are in our sets, and we can see if some sets are empty.

SECTION 13.3	PUTTING PIECES TOGETHER WITH RECORDS

In the previous section, we combined various pieces of data of the same type into sets. In this section, we combine different types of data, such as numeric data and alphabetical characters.

We begin with a fairly straightforward problem.

PROBLEM 13.3A	Adjacent Concert Tickets

As part of a job selling tickets for a concert, we must sell pairs of seats. For each ticket, we store

Row: In this hall, rows go between 'A' and 'X'.

Seat Number: Within a row, seats are numbered between 1 and 30.

Cost: Ticket prices are $3.50, $5.00, and $7.35.

When we sell a pair of tickets, we follow these rules:

1. We assign the second seat next to the first. In this pairing, we normally group seats 1 and 2, 3 and 4, and so on, in the same row.
2. We sell the adjacent seat for 70% of the first seat's price.

Write a program that reads the row, seat number, and cost of the first ticket; assigns a seat for the second ticket; and computes the total cost.

Discussion of Problem 13.3A

In this problem, we want to consider *Row*, *Seat*, and *Cost* as part of a single entity called *Ticket*. Then, we want to enter information for the *First* ticket, compute the appropriate information for a *Second* ticket, and print the results.

This suggests the following outline.

Outline for Problem 13.3A

I. Enter data for first ticket.
   A. Row
   B. Seat
   C. Cost
II. Determine second ticket.
   A. Use same row.
   B. Pick the adjacent seat. With the pairing specified, we will add or subtract one from the first seat number, depending on whether the first seat is odd or even.
   C. Cost is 70% of first ticket.
III. Print the data for each ticket.

This outline suggests the following program, in which we first declare a ticket as a separate entity, and then we work with the first and second ticket.

```
Program AssignTicket (Input, Output);
{This program computes the cost and seat number for an adjacent seat}

Type Ticket = Record
          Row: 'A'..'X';
          Seat: 1..36;
          Cost: Real
          End;

Var First, Second: Ticket;

Begin {Main}

    {Enter Data for First Ticket}
    Writeln ('This program determines the Second Ticket of a pair');
    Writeln ('Please enter Row, Seat Number, and Cost of the First Ticket:');
    Readln (First.Row, First.Seat, First.Cost);

    {Determine Second Ticket}
    Second.Row := First.Row;
    If Odd(First.Seat)
        Then Second.Seat := First.Seat + 1
        Else Second.Seat := First.Seat - 1;
    Second.Cost := 0.70 * First.Cost;

    {Print Ticket Assignments}
    Writeln ('          Row    Seat     Cost');
    Writeln (' First Ticket:', First.Row:2, First.Seat:8, First.Cost:9:2);
    Writeln ('Second Ticket:', Second.Row:2, Second.Seat:8, Second.Cost:9:2);
    Writeln;
    Writeln ('The total cost of the tickets is $',
             First.Cost + Second.Cost:1:2, ' .')

End {Main} .
```

Two trial runs of this program are shown below.

First Trial Run

```
This program determines the Second Ticket of a pair
Please enter Row, Seat Number, and Cost of the First Ticket:
C 1 7.35
                Row    Seat     Cost
 First Ticket: C        1       7.35
Second Ticket: C        2       5.14

The total cost of the tickets is $12.49 .
```

Second Trial Run

```
This program determines the Second Ticket of a pair
Please enter Row, Seat Number, and Cost of the First Ticket:
Q 36 5.00
                Row    Seat     Cost
 First Ticket: Q       36       5.00
Second Ticket: Q       35       3.50

The total cost of the tickets is $8.50 .
```

Records in Pascal

The program above illustrates the concept of records in Pascal. A **record** is a collection of several pieces of data, and these pieces may be of different types. Within a record, data are divided into distinct sections, called **fields,** and names are given to each of these fields. When we wish to declare a record, we begin by specifying the word *Record.* Then, we list the various fields that make up the record, and we specify the type of each field. The list of fields concludes with the word *End.* In our example, we declared *Ticket* to be a type with three fields: *Row, Seat,* and *Cost;* and we specified the type of each of these fields. In this case, each field has a separate data type (character, integer, real). In other records, we may wish to have several fields with the same type. We may even want one field to be another record.

Once variables have been defined to be records, we may refer to one of the fields by specifying both the variable and the field, and we use a period to separate the variable identifier from the field. In our example, *First* is a record containing all three fields, and we can specify the seat number for the first ticket by writing

    First.Seat

Here we add the field *Seat* to the variable *First.*

Then, once fields are specified, we can work with the individual fields just as we work with other types of variables. For example,

    First.Row

is a character that enables us to read and write this datum. Similarly, *First.Seat* and *Second.Seat* are integers, so we can apply arithmetic functions, perform arithmetic operations, and assign values to these items.

With this example, we see that once we have defined a record type and declared variables of that type, we can work with each field just as we have previously with other variables.

In solving the following modified problem, we will see that we can work with records as a whole as well as with individual fields.

PROBLEM 13.3B   Modify the previous problem to eliminate the discount for the second ticket. Seat assignment should be done as before.

Outline for Problem 13.3B

In solving this revised problem, we follow the same general outline that we used for the original problem. However, here we place a greater emphasis on the ticket as a whole.

   I. Enter data for first ticket.
      A. Row
      B. Seat
      C. Cost

II. Determine second ticket.

    A. Copy information from first ticket to second ticket.

    B. Modify the seat number.

III. Print the data for each ticket.

    A. Print a heading.

    B. For the first ticket, print row, seat, and cost.

    C. For the second ticket, print row, seat, and cost.

    D. Compute and print the total cost.

Our resulting program is organized into procedures with appropriate parameters.

```
Program AssignTicket {Revised Version} (Input, Output);
{This program computes the cost and seat number for an adjacent seat}

Type Ticket = Record
          Row: 'A'..'X';
          Seat: 1..36;
          Cost: Real
          End;

Procedure DetermineTicket (Var Customer: Ticket);
{Enter Data for First Ticket}
    Begin {DetermineTicket}
        Writeln ('Please enter Row, Seat Number, and Cost ',
              'of the First Ticket:');
        With Customer Do
            Readln (Row, Seat, Cost);
    End {DetermineTicket} ;

Procedure Assign (First: Ticket; Var Second: Ticket);
{Determine seat and compute cost for Second Ticket}
    Begin
        Second := First;
        If Odd(First.Seat)
            Then Second.Seat := First.Seat + 1
            Else Second.Seat := First.Seat - 1;
    End {Assign} ;

Procedure PrintTickets (First, Second: Ticket);
{Print Ticket Assignments}
    Begin
        Writeln ('            Row    Seat    Cost');
        With First
            Do Writeln (' First Ticket:', Row:2, Seat:8, Cost:9:2);
        With Second
            Do Writeln ('Second Ticket:', Row:2, Seat:8, Cost:9:2);
        Writeln;
        Writeln ('The total cost of the tickets is $',
                First.Cost + Second.Cost:1:2, ' .')
    End {PrintTickets} ;
```

```
Procedure ControlProcessing;
{This procedure controls the major steps in assigning tickets.}
    Var First, Second: Ticket;
    Begin
        DetermineTicket(First);
        Assign(First, Second);
        PrintTickets (First, Second)
    End {ControlProcessing} ;

Begin {Main}
    Writeln ('This program determines the Second Ticket of a pair');
    ControlProcessing
End {Main} .
```

This program produces the same output as our previous one, except that the cost of the second ticket is the same as the first.

In this program, we have stressed each ticket as a whole in several ways. First, we have used tickets as parameters in our procedures. We can use both value and reference passage to transmit an entire record between procedures and functions. Next, as we saw with arrays, we can copy all parts of a record from one variable to another. The statement

Second : = First

in procedure *Assign* assigns each field of the record variable *First* to the corresponding field of *Second*.

As a final part of Pascal syntax, when we want to work with various fields of a record, we can use a *With* statement, which specifies the record variable. For example, in procedure *DetermineTicket*, we wrote

With Customer
    Do Readln(Row, Seat, Cost) ;

Here, *Customer* is a ticket record, and we wish to work with each field within that record. More generally, the *With* statement has the form

With RecordVariable
    Do Statement

As before, the *Statement* may be a simple Pascal statement, or it may be a *Begin-End* block. In this statement, we can refer to the fields of our *RecordVariable* directly. We do not need to write out the variable identifier each time. (Thus, we could write *Row* instead of the full name *Customer.Row*.)

In the second program, we see that records allow us to work with collections of data at two different levels. At the first level, we can work with individual pieces of data by specifying both the variable name and the field, as in *Customer.Row*. At the next level, we can consider the entire record as a single entity in parameters and assignments.

In the next chapter, we use both of these levels when we look more carefully at the processing of strings of characters.

SUMMARY

1. In working with problems, we can consider data at any of **three levels,** namely:
   - individual data items;
   - groups of items; and
   - abstract data structures, in which we specify both the type of data and the operations to be performed on the data.
2. In earlier chapters, we considered individual data items as part of the introduction of real, integer, Boolean, and character data, and we grouped data using arrays. The current chapter also introduced two new ways to collect data, sets and records.
3. In Pascal, we can group unordered data of the same type together in **sets.** Sets are unordered collections of data that do not distinguish among duplicate values. In working with sets, we may specify individual elements or ranges of elements that will constitute a set, or we can specify no elements for an **empty set.** Then, once some sets are defined, we can put them together using various operations, including
   - + union
   - * intersection
   - − difference

   Also, we can check if a particular element is *in* a given set.
4. In addition, in Pascal, we can combine various pieces of data together as **fields** within a **record.** Records allow us to work with each piece of data separately. Alternatively, we can consider an entire record as a single entity in assignment statements and in function and procedure parameters.

EXERCISES

13.1 *Letters in a Line of Input.* Write a program that reads a line of input and determines what letters appear in the line. (In this problem, you should not distinguish between upper- and lowercase letters.)

13.2 Write a program that reads a line of input and determines which letters in the line occur both as capital letters and as lowercase letters.

13.3 *Finding Letters.* Write a program that reads a line of input and then determines the first letter of the alphabet that appears in the line. In other words, the program determines if an 'A' occurs in the line; then, if no 'A' occurs, the program searches for a 'B', and so on. (Do not distinguish between upper- and lowercase letters in this problem.)

13.4 *Analysis of Finding Letters.* Analyze the following two algorithms to solve the previous problem.

Algorithm 1:
Read the entire line into an array of characters.
Search the entire line for an 'A'.
If an 'A' is found, stop.
If not, search the entire line for a 'B'.
If a 'B' is found, stop.
If not, search the entire line for a 'C'.
Continue until either a letter is found or until all letters 'A' through 'Z' have been checked.

Algorithm 2:
Read the entire line of line and form a set of characters for these letters.
Check if 'A' is in the set.
If so, stop.
If not, check if 'B' is in the set.
If so, stop.
If not, check if 'C' is in the set.
Continue until either a letter is found or until all letters 'A' through 'Z' have been checked.

In your analysis of these algorithms, assume a full 80 character line of input has been entered. Then count the maximum number of steps that the program might have to make before reaching its conclusion.

In your analysis, count the comparison of one letter with one character of input as one step (Algorithm 1). Also, count each union operation and each test for the inclusion of an element in a set as one step (Algorithm 2).

NOTE: Sets can be implemented very efficiently inside computers, so a union or a test of inclusion can be done very efficiently.

13.5 *Letters in Common.* Write a program that reads two lines of input and determines
• what letters appear in both of these lines;
• what letters appear in the first line, but not in the second; and
• what letters appear in the second line, but not in the first.

(Do not distinguish between upper- and lowercase letters in this exercise.)

13.6

a. Name two syntactical constructions in Pascal where an *End* statement occurs without a *Begin*.
b. Can a *Begin* ever occur without an *End*?

13.7 *Packaging.* In designing a package for a product, a small change in the dimensions of a packing case can make a significant change in the volume of the package. Write a program that reads initial dimensions (width, length, height) of a rectangular box and computes the volume. The program should then ask the user for changes in each dimension and compute the new value. The user should be allowed to continue typing new dimensions until he or she wishes to stop.

NOTES:

1. In this program, try reducing each dimension by 5 or 10% to see the change in volume. (Changes this small may be hard to see in a store.)

2. Try reducing just the depth by a small amount to see the change in volume. (The new box will look the same on the shelf if the front panel is facing the customer.)

3. In this program, store the width, length, height, and volume in a record called *Package*.

13.8 *Nesting* With *Statements—A Caution.* When we put *With* statements together, we must be careful that there is no ambiguity about which fields we mean. Suppose we have the following declarations.

```
Type  Ticket = Record
              Row: Char;
              Seat: 1..36;
              Cost: Real
              End;
           BusinessExpense = Record
              Client: Array [1..30] of Char;
              Transportation: Real;
              Meals: Real;
              Cost: Real
              End;
Var   First, Second: Ticket;
      Evening: BusinessExpense;
```

Find the ambiguities in the following pieces of code:

a. With First
     Do With Second
         Do Begin
            Row := Row;

KEY TERMS, PHRASES, AND CONCEPTS		ELEMENTS OF PASCAL SYNTAX
Levels of Data	Sets	Record ——— End; With ——— Do
Abstraction	Difference	Set Of ———
Individual Items	Elements in Sets	Set Operations
Groups of Data	Empty Set	[ ]
Abstract Data	Intersection	+, −, *
Structures	Union	*In*
Records		
Record Fields		

```
            If Odd(Seat)
                  Then Seat : = Seat + 1
                  Else Seat : = Seat − 1;
            Cost : = Cost
      End
End;
```

b. With Evening
   Do With First
      Do Begin
         Transportation : = 100.00;
         Meals : = 50.00;
         Cost : = Transportation + Meals + Ticket.Cost
      End;

13.9 *Employee Wages.* A program is to compute an employee's wages for a week. In particular, the program reads
- number of hours worked
- hourly rate
- tax withholding rate (entered as a percentage)

Then the program computes
- wages earned
  (The employee earns "time and a half" for any hours over 40 worked during the week.)
- tax withheld
- insurance premium (always $20.00 per week)
- take home pay

   In writing this program, store all employee information in a single employee record. Further, perform the reading, computing, and printing tasks as separate procedures that have the employee record as a parameter.

13.10 *Generating Dates.* We consider a *Date* as the following record:

```
Type Date = Record
               Month: 1..12;
               Day: 1..31;
               Year: 1..2000
               End;
```

Write

```
Procedure NextDate (OldDate: Date; Var NewDate: Date)
```

which takes *OldDate* as one date and computes *NewDate*, which is the following date on a calendar. For example,
- 2/3/1989 follows 2/2/1989
- 3/1/1987 follows 2/28/1987
- 3/1/1988 follows 2/29/1988
- 1/1/1986 follows 12/31/1985

Your procedure should include a check for leap years.

CHAPTER 14

STRINGS

In this chapter, we consider how we might store and process data that involve sequences of characters, such as letters that form words or characters that we type on a line at our terminal. Such sequences are called **character strings,** and we see how we can work with this data. In this work, we will apply many of the ideas introduced in earlier chapters, such as procedures and functions, arrays and records.

COMMON APPROACHES TO STORING STRINGS

A **string** is a sequence of character information. In this section and the next, we see several ways to store strings. In particular, we consider

- Variable-length strings using records
- Fixed-length strings

Variable-Length Strings

In Chapter 12, we used an array to store sequences of characters. In this approach, we first declared a maximum length for our string. For example, in Section 12.3, we allocated space for up to 80 characters of input with the declarations

```
Const MaxLen = 80;
Type  CharLine = Array [1..MaxLen] of Char;
Var    Message: CharLine
```

Then, we declared

```
Var InputLen: Integer;
```

so we could keep track of the actual number of characters that were read. *InputLen* was initialized to 0, and each time we read a character, we increased *InputLen* by 1. We stopped reading either when we reached the end of a line or when we ran out of space in our array.

This program from Section 12.3 demonstrates that in handling strings of characters, we often need two types of information: the characters themselves, stored in an array, and the number of characters actually present.

With the concept of records from the previous chapter, we can combine these pieces into a single unit. For example, we might use the declarations

```
Const MaxLen = 80;
Type String = Record
              Line: Array [1..MaxLen] of Char;
              Length: Integer
              End;
Var Message: String;
```

Here, *Message* involves all of the information we need for our string information.

Message.Line is our array of characters, and

Message.Length gives the number of characters present.

With these declarations, a simple program to read and write a line of input might be as follows.

```
Program ReadAndPrint {Version 1} (Input, Output);
{This program reads and writes a line of input}

Const MaxLen = 80;

Type String = Record
        Data: Array [1..MaxLen] of Char;
        Length: Integer
        End;

Procedure EnterLine (Var Message: String);
{This procedure reads a line of character information from a terminal.}
   Begin
        Writeln ('Please enter your line of input:');
```

```
      With Message
        Do Begin
          Length := 0;
          While (Not Eoln) and (Length < MaxLen)
            Do Begin
              Length := Length + 1;
              Read (Data[Length])
            End ;
        End;
        If Not Eoln
          Then Writeln ('Input is too long; line truncated to ',
                        MaxLen:1, ' characters.');
        Readln
    End {EnterLine} ;

Procedure PrintLine (Message: String);
{This procedure prints a line of character information.}
    Var Index: Integer;
    Begin
        Writeln ('Your input line is shown below:');
        For Index := 1 To Message.Length
            Do Write (Message.Data[Index]);
        Writeln;
    End {PrintLine} ;

Procedure ControlProcessing;
{This procedure controls the reading and printing of character data}
    Var Line: String;
    Begin
        EnterLine (Line);
        PrintLine (Line)
    End {ControlProcessing} ;

Begin {Main}
    Writeln ('This program reads and prints a line of characters');
    ControlProcessing
End {Main} .
```

In subsequent processing, we can work with individual characters and the length of the input, or we can consider this string as a single entity. In this approach to strings, we have counted the exact number of characters in our input, and we have stored that information separately from the characters themselves.

Fixed-Length Strings

In a second common approach to storing strings, we standardize the length of strings. Then, in our processing, we treat all strings as occupying a full array.

In this approach, we must be a bit careful in choosing which extra characters to add, because we do not want to disrupt subsequent processing. Thus, we usually fill up our arrays with a known character that we can take into account in later work. Sometimes, as we will see in Section 14.2, we may use "spaces" for this special purpose. However, more often, we use a character, called a **null,** which is *Chr*(0) in the standard codes. This special character takes up space in arrays, but it is ignored by most terminals. Thus, if we try to "print" this character, our terminal receives the character but does nothing, so our output is not affected by this extra character. (This is different from a space character, which causes the terminal to move its cursor or printing element over one space on the screen or paper.)

In addition, a null has the property that it comes before all other characters. In practice, this means that nulls allow us to alphabetize character strings correctly if we compare strings character by character. In short, a null (or *Chr*(0)) allows us to fill up extra space in arrays without creating special difficulties when we try to print or process character strings.

The following program illustrates this alternative approach to reading and printing strings.

```
Program ReadAndPrint {Version 2, Fixed Length Strings} (Input, Output);
{This program reads and writes a line of input}

Const MaxLen = 80;

Type String = Array [1..MaxLen] of Char;

Procedure EnterLine (Var Message: String);
{This procedure reads a line of character information from a terminal.}
    Var Null: Char;  {The sentinel value, Chr(0), for character strings}
        Length: Integer;
    Begin
        {Initialize Null to the null character, Chr(0)}
        Null := Chr(0);

        {Read input from terminal}
        Writeln ('Please enter a line of input:');
        Length := 0;
        While (Not Eoln) and (Length < MaxLen)
          Do Begin
            Length := Length + 1;
            Read (Message[Length])
          End;
        If Not Eoln
            Then Writeln ('Input is too long; line truncated to ',
                    MaxLen:1, ' characters.');
        Readln;

        {Fill rest of array with Nulls}
        While Length < MaxLen
          Do Begin
            Length := Length + 1;
            Message[Length] := Null
          End
    End {EnterLine} ;
```

```
Procedure PrintLine (Message: String);
{This procedure prints a line of character information.}
    Var Index: Integer;

    Begin
        Writeln ('Your input line is shown below:');
        For Index := 1 To MaxLen
            Do Write (Message[Index]);
        Writeln;
    End {PrintLine} ;

Procedure Control Processing;
{This procedure controls the reading and printing of character data}
    Var Line: String;
    Begin
        EnterLine (Line);
        PrintLine (Line)
    End {Control Processing} ;

Begin {Main}
    Writeln ('This program reads and prints a line of characters');
    Control Processing
End {Main} .
```

In this program, we filled any extra space in the array with nulls after we read the data from the terminal. Once the program has finished the reading process, it processes the entire array. When we run the program, we see the data that we typed, although we may notice a slight delay at the end of the printing of a line while any extra nulls are transmitted to the terminal.

SECTION 14.2   PACKED AND UNPACKED ARRAYS

Each of the approaches to strings in the previous section used arrays to store character information. In this section we look at the way the machine actually allocates this storage, and we identify two distinct forms of array storage.

In Section 9.4, we saw that arrays are stored in a block of main memory, and we can work with a particular piece of data by using a base address and an offset from that base. We also noted that different types of data may require different amounts of storage. For example, we saw that an integer might take 1 unit of storage, whereas a real number might use 2 units. Thus, an array of 100 integers might use 100 units of storage, and 100 reals might use 200 units. (Some technical details of data storage are discussed in Appendix B.)

When we work with Booleans or character data, however, we find that each item may require only a fraction of a unit. For example, depending upon the computer, we may be able to store 16 or 32 Boolean values, or 2 or 4 characters in a unit of storage. Thus, to save space when storing arrays of Boolean or character data, we may want to pack as much information into a unit of storage as we can. This form of storage is called a **packed array.** We give an example to illustrate the difference between a packed array and the **unpacked arrays** we have used up to now.

Example: Suppose we wish to store the phrase *Pascal Programming* in an array, with one character for each array element. Suppose also that our computer is able to store 4 characters of information in each unit of its memory.

In Figure 14–1, we store these characters in an unpacked array, with one character for each unit of memory. Here, our data require 18 units of memory. Also, while each letter is stored in one unit of memory, this memory is only a quarter full. Much of the space in memory is wasted.

Figure 14–2 shows the same phrase in a packed array. Here we fill up each unit of storage with four characters, and we have no wasted space, except at the very end of our storage space. Here, our data require only 5 units of memory, and we have saved 13 units of memory from our previous approach. Thus, we see that packed arrays can save a great deal of space over unpacked arrays.

However, this savings of storage may be offset by increased processing requirements. In particular, since each character in a packed array is embedded in a group, packed arrays may require some special work whenever we want to work with individual characters. In processing, we may

FIGURE 14–1 • **Storage of Pascal Programming in Array [1..18] of Char**

Address	
1	P
2	a
3	s
4	c
5	a
6	l
7	
8	P
9	r
10	o
11	g
12	r
13	a
14	m
15	m
16	i
17	n
18	g

FIGURE 14–2 • **Storage of Pascal Programming in Packed Array [1..18] of Char**

Address				
1	P	a	s	c
2	a	l		P
3	r	o	g	r
4	a	m	m	i
5	n	g		

need to extract the character from the unit of storage before we can proceed.

Packed and Unpacked Arrays in Pascal

Pascal allows us to decide which type of storage we want to use for any particular array. Pascal interprets the declaration

> Var Line: Array [1..Max] of Char

as a specification for an unpacked array. If we add the word *Packed* to our declaration, then Pascal packs our data together. Thus,

> Var Line: Packed Array [1..Max] of Char

compresses our character data into a small space, but possibly increases processing time.

This flexibility of choosing between packed and unpacked arrays in Pascal extends to any type of data, although in practice we rarely specify packed arrays for data other than characters, Booleans, or enumerated types. With each of these types of data, we often can save a considerable amount of space by packing information in our arrays. With other types of data, packed arrays give little, if any, savings.

Beyond this initial declaration of packed and unpacked arrays, a Pascal program does not distinguish between these storage structures, and either form of storage allows us to write statements such as

> Read(Line[7])

> Line[8] := Chr(0)

Our use of array elements in Pascal does not depend on the form of declaration.

Conversion Between Packed and Unpacked Arrays

Sometimes in processing, we want to store data in a packed array most of the time to save space. However, for a brief time during processing, we may need to work with the data in the array a great deal, so we want the data in an unpacked array for efficiency. In this situation, we might move our data from the packed array to an unpacked one first and move the data back later. We can do this with the *Unpack* and *Pack* procedures.

To illustrate the *Unpack* procedure, suppose we have the unpacked array U and the packed array P declared as in Figure 14–3. Then we may move the data from array P to the array U with the *Unpack* procedure. Further, since the array U has more data elements, we need to specify where to place the first elements of the array P. If we want $P[1]$ moved to $U[3]$, $P[2]$ moved to $U[4]$, etc., as shown in the figure, then we write

> **Unpack(P, U, 3)**

More generally, we write

> **Unpack(P, U, S)**

to transfer the data elements in P to U, where the first element in P moves to $U[S]$. Of course, in this case, array U must be able to hold at least as many data elements as array P.

Similarly, we can move data from the unpacked array U to the packed array P, although again, we need to specify where the first element of U will be placed. If we want this first element moved to $P[S]$, then we use the *Pack* procedure with the syntax

> **Pack (U, S, P)**

In contrast to the *Pack* procedure, when we use *Unpack*, the packed array must contain at least as many data elements as the unpacked array.

FIGURE 14–3 • **The Unpack Procedure**

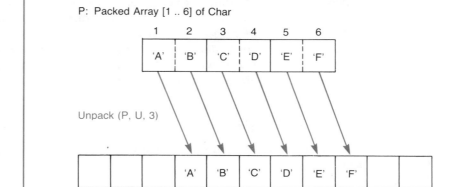

String-Type

In Pascal, packed arrays of characters are considered to be a special type, called **string-type**. With these, we can work with individual characters or with entire arrays as before. However, packed arrays of characters may be used in three additional ways: with literal strings; in Boolean expressions; and in *Write* statements.

Literal Strings. Whenever we place characters in quotes within a program, those characters are considered to be a packed array of characters and are called a **literal string**. Thus, if we declare

        Type String = Packed Array [1..26] of Char;
        Var Alphabet: String;

we may assign

        Alphabet : = 'ABCDEFGHIJKLMNOPQRSTUVWXYZ'

Here, both sides have the same packed array type with the same number of characters, so we may assign the data in one array ('A'..'Z') to the other (Alphabet).

   Similarly, if we declare

        Procedure A(Letters: String)

we could have the call

        A('ABCDEFGHIJKLMNOPQRSTUVWXYZ');

Here, parameter passage by reference is not allowed because the constant array cannot change; however, passage by value is allowed.

   Next, string-type can be used in defining constants, so we could have

        Const Capitals = 'ABCDEFGHIJKLMNOPQRSTUVWXYZ'

Here, the right hand side of our declaration has 26 elements, so *Alphabet* is considered a constant array of 26 elements.

   These capabilities for specifying character strings are particularly useful in setting up entire arrays of characters; we can work with the entire array rather than with individual elements. However, we must be careful that our declared arrays have exactly the same number of characters as the strings we specify. For example, with our previous declaration we could not write

        Alphabet : = 'ABCDE'

for the machine cannot match the 26 elements on the left with the five on the right.

Boolean Expressions. Pascal also allows us to compare two string-type arrays of the same size. For example, given

```
Type String = Packed Array [1..10] of Char;
Var   Line1, Line2: String;
```

we can compare the arrays *Line1* and *Line2*. The expression *Line1* < *Line2* has the usual meaning of alphabetical order. In particular, the computer initially considers the first character of *Line1* and *Line2*. If they are different, then those first characters are compared according to the character codes (e.g., ASCII or EBCDIC). However, if the first characters are the same, the computer looks at the second characters, and the computer continues checking character-by-character until a difference is found or until the entire string is scanned.

Similarly, *Line1* = *Line2* is true if each character in *Line1* matches the corresponding character in *Line2*.

In this comparison of strings, all characters in the string may be checked. Thus, we must be sure that the entire array is being used for our data. For example, if we only read a few characters, we must fill the rest of our array with known values, such as nulls, so we know what the entire array contains. Thus, if we plan to use packed arrays in Boolean expressions, we need to use our fixed-length approach to strings in all our reading and processing.

Writing. Finally, Pascal allows us to use string-type variables in *Write* statements. For example, with our earlier declaration, we could specify

Write (Alphabet)

Here, the entire packed array is printed; we do not have to write each character separately in a loop.

These special capabilities for packed arrays of characters are particularly helpful when we wish to work with character strings, as we see in the following simple problem.

PROBLEM 14.2   Alphabetizing Names

Write a program that reads 10 names and prints out the list in alphabetical order.

Discussion of Problem 14.2

In this problem, we will consider a name as a string (packed array of characters). Then we will use an array of these strings to process the names. Following our work in Section 8.5, we will use a Straight Selection Sort, and we develop the following outline.

Outline of Problem 14.2

  I. Enter names. For each name:
    A. Enter letters.
    B. Fill out name with spaces.
  II. Sort names. (We will use a selection sort for brevity.)
 III. Print sorted names.

Our program, with its sorting algorithm, follows our work in Section 8.5 very closely.

```
Program StraightSelectionSort (Input, Output);
{Program uses a Straight Selection Sort to order names.}
Const Max = 10;      {Number of elements to be sorted}
      MaxName = 20;{Number of characters in a name}
      Spaces = '                    ';

Type String = Packed Array[1..MaxName] Of Char;
     List = Array [1..Max] Of String;

Procedure EnterData (Var Name: List);
{Determine elements to be sorted}
    Var I: Integer;        {Array subscript}
        Length: Integer;      {Number of characters in name}
    Begin
        Writeln ('Enter the names to be sorted');
        For I := 1 To Max
          Do Begin
            {Initialize new name to all spaces}
            Name[I] := Spaces;

            {Read letters for name}
            Length := 0;
            While Not Eoln And (Length < MaxName)
              Do Begin
                Length := Length + 1;
                Read (Name[I] [Length])
              End;
            Readln;  {Go on to next name}

          End
    End {EnterData} ;

Procedure StraightSelectionSort (Var Name: List);
    Var I, J: Integer;       {Array subscripts}
        MaxElt: Integer;   {Subscript of the largest element}
        Temp: String;
    Begin
        For I := Max DownTo 2
          Do Begin
            {Find location of biggest remaining element}
            MaxElt := 1;
            For J := 2 To I
                Do If Name[J] > Name[MaxElt]
                    Then MaxElt := J;

            {Swap}
            Temp := Name[MaxElt];
            Name[MaxElt] := Name[I];
            Name[I] := Temp
          End
    End {StraightSelectionSort} ;
```

```
Procedure PrintData(Data: List);
    Var I: Integer;    {Array subscript}
    Begin
        Writeln;
        Writeln ('The sorted data are shown below:');
        For I := 1 To Max
            Do Writeln (Data[I])
    End {PrintData} ;

Procedure ControlProcessing;
{This procedure controls the reading, sorting, and printing process}
    Var Words: List;
    Begin
        Enterdata (Words);
        StraightSelectionSort (Words);
        PrintData (Words)
    End {ControlProcessig} ;

Begin {Main}
    Writeln ('This program sorts ', Max:1, ' names.');
    ControlProcessing
End {Main} .
```

This program illustrates all of the special capabilities of string-type, and it shows several convenient techniques for working with strings.

We declared *Spaces* as a packed array of 20 spaces. Next, we had to read each name character-by-character. We started by initializing an entire name to *Spaces*. Then, we read each name character-by-character. Thus, after initialization, we read character 1, 2, 3, . . . for *Name[I]*. We followed this by comparing strings just as we compared numbers in Section 8.5. We could compare *Name[J] > Name[MaxElt]* directly to determine alphabetical order; the comparison of individual characters was unnecessary. Finally, we could print the entire name as a whole, using *Writeln(Data[I])*. We did not need to print individual characters in a loop.

With these capabilities, we can consider strings as entire entities in many cases. Initialization, comparison, and writing can all apply to the entire array. We need to consider individual characters only for reading.

SECTION 14.3   COMMON STRING PROCESSING FUNCTIONS OR PROCEDURES

The previous section illustrated how packed arrays allow us to perform some special operations on entire strings of characters. We often use packed arrays to take advantage of these capabilities. However, many applications require further string manipulations. Therefore, in this section, we look at several common functions and procedures that can help us perform more complex operations.

Throughout this section, we will find we need to know the length of

the strings that we are processing, and we will assume the following declarations:

```
Const Max = ——;      {Some positive integer constant}
Type String = Record
              Data: Packed Array [1..Max] of Char;
              Length: Integer
              End;
```

String Concatenation

The first common procedure that we consider involves putting strings together. In this process, called **string concatenation,** we begin with two
strings, S1 and S2, and we want to form a new, longer string NewS, where
the entire S2 string is placed after the S1 string.

In forming NewS, we follow several steps;

1. We copy the characters of S1 to NewS.
2. We compute the length of NewS and the number of letters to be copied
   from S2.
3. We add the characters of S2 to NewS.

Each of these steps is rather straightforward, except that we must be careful
not to exceed the maximum number of characters allowed in the declaration of NewS. Our resulting procedure is as follows.

```
Procedure Concat (S1, S2: String; Var NewS: String);
{This procedure concatenates string S1 with S2 to yield NewS}
    Var Index: Integer;
        NumberFromS2: Integer;      {Number of characters copied from S2}

    Begin
        {Copy S1 to NewS}
        NewS := S1;

        {Compute number of letters to be copied from S2}
        If S1.Length + S2.Length <= Max
            Then Begin
                NumberFromS2 := S2.Length;
                NewS.Length := S1.Length + S2.Length
                End
            Else Begin
                NumberFromS2 := Max - S1.Length;
                Writeln ('Not enough storage space for string concatenation');
                Writeln (S2.Length-NumberFromS2:1, ' characters deleted');
                NewS.Length := Max
                End;

        {Add characters of S2 to NewS}
        For Index := 1 To NumberFromS2
            Do NewS.Data[Index+S1.Length] := S2.Data[Index]
    End {Concat} ;
```

Substring Extraction

The reverse of string concatenation is **substring extraction.** Here, we start with one string, and we extract part of it to form a new string. In general, we can identify three forms that this extraction process can take, and we define three corresponding procedures.

> Procedure Left(Init: String; Number: Integer;
> Var Result: String)

This procedure takes the specified *Number* of characters from the *Left* of the given *Init* string. This part of the *Init* is returned as the *Result*.

> Procedure Right(Init: String; Number: Integer;
> Var Result: String)

This procedure extracts the specified *Number* of characters from the *Right* of the given *Init* string, returning the *Result* string.

> Procedure Middle (Init: String; Start, Number: Integer;
> Var Result: String)

This procedure takes part of the *Middle* of the *Init* string. As with *Left* and *Right*, *Number* specifies how many characters should be taken, and the substring is returned as the *Result*. Here, however, *Start* indicates the position where the substring should start.

To illustrate the use of these functions, suppose our strings have a maximum of 26 characters and suppose

> Alphabet = 'ABCDEFGHIJKLMNOPQRSTUVWXYZ'

is our initial data of length 26. Then,

> Left(Alphabet, 5, Result)

produces a string of length 5 with data 'ABCDE'. Similarly,

> Right(Alphabet 5, Result)

produces a string of length 5 with data 'VWXYZ'. Finally,

> Middle(Alphabet, 10, 5, Result)

produces a string of length 5, starting with the 10th letter of the alphabet. Thus, the data of the *Result* is 'JKLMN'.

To program each of these functions, we copy the appropriate letters from the *Init* string to the *Result* string, and we record the length of *Result*. This process is fairly straightforward, except that we need to be sure that we do not copy data beyond the length of the *Init* string. For example, if *Init* only contained the 10 letters 'ABCDEFGHIJ' as data, then

> Left (Init, 15, Result)

could only copy 10 characters to *Result*, and the length of *Result* would be set to 10.

The following code shows how this checking and copying can be done for the *Middle* procedure.

```
Procedure Middle (Init: String; Start, Number: Integer;
                  Var Result: String);
{Procedure extracts a substring from Init, beginning at the
 given starting position, taking the Number of Characters
 specified, and returning the Result.}
   Var Index: Integer;
   Begin
      If Start + Number > Init.Length + 1
         Then Begin
            Writeln ('Extraction attempted beyond end of string');
            Writeln ('Only ', (Init.Length + 1 - Start):1,
                     ' characters extracted');
            Number := Init.Length + 1 - Start
         End;
      Result.Length := Number;
      For Index := 1 to Number
         Do Result.Data[Index] := Init.Data[Start + Index - 1]
   End {Middle} ;
```

The details of the *Left* and *Right* procedures are left as exercises.

Pattern Matching

The next task that we consider in this section is searching for one string that is contained in another. For example, if

$$Alphabet = \text{'ABCDEFGHIJKLMNOPQRSTUVWXYZ'},$$

then

'ABC' is found in *Alphabet* beginning with the first character of *Alphabet*;

'HIJK' is found in *Alphabet*, beginning with character 8;

'YZ' is found in *Alphabet* beginning with character 25; and

'CBA' is not found in *Alphabet*.

In defining this task more carefully, we often find it convenient to specify this **pattern matching** as

Function Match(SubS, Str: String): Integer

The function *Match* searches for the substring *SubS* in the string *Str*. If the substring is found, *Match* returns the starting position for the match. If the substring is not found, *Match* returns 0. Thus, in our previous matching examples, we have

SubS Data	Str Data	Result Returned
'ABC'	Alphabet	1
'HIJK'	Alphabet	8
'YZ'	Alphabet	25
'CBA'	Alphabet	0

In programming this matching function, we can identify several steps.

I. We begin trying to match the first letter of our substring *SubS* with a letter in the string *Str*.

    A. If the first letter matches, we try subsequent letters.

        1. If all subsequent letters match, we have found our substring. Thus, we record where the match started, and then we stop.

        2. If some subsequent letter does not match, we look back at first letters again.

    B. If the first letter does not match, we try the first letter of the substring against the next letters of our given string.

This general process can continue until we find a match or until we know a match is impossible. A match is impossible if there are not enough letters in our string to match the substring. More precisely, we can stop our search when

$$Position > \text{length of string} - \text{length of substring} + 1.$$

After this position in our string, we do not have enough characters to match our substring.

With this observation about when to stop our search, we are ready to code our procedure.

```
Function Match (SubS, Str: String): Integer;
{This function searches for the Substring SubS in the String Str
 and returns the first position where a match occurs
 or 0 if not match is found.}
    Var Found: Boolean;
        Position: Integer;   {location where match might begin}
        LastPosition: Integer; {last location where match could be}
        Index: Integer;
    Begin
        LastPosition := Str.Length - SubS.Length + 1;
        Found := False;
        Position := 0;
        While (Position < LastPosition) And Not Found
          Do Begin
            Position := Position + 1;
            Index := 1;
            While (Index < SubS.Length) And
                  (SubS.Data[Index] = Str.Data[Position+Index-1])
                Do Index := Index + 1;
          Found := (SubS.Data[Index] = Str.Data[Position+Index-1])
        End;
```

```
    If Found
        Then Match := Position
        Else Match := 0
End {Match} ;
```

As an alternative to this procedure, we may want to require that we begin our search after a given position in the string *Str*. This is left to the reader as an exercise.

Reading Words

The last common task that we consider in this section involves the breaking of a line of input into words. Variations of **reading words** appear in a very large number of applications; we look at one simple version here.

In the typical application, we proceed in several steps. To begin, we read the input character-by-character. Next, we combine characters into units (words), and we continue reading until we detect an end of the input (a sentinel).

Frequently, this work is done with two procedures:

Procedure GetChar(Var Ch: Char);
Procedure GetWord(Var Word: String);

With this structure, the *GetChar* procedure reads successive characters, processes ends of lines, and detects when all of the data have been read. The *GetWord* procedure uses *GetChar* to obtain characters of input and then divides those characters into words. (In this discussion, we will throw away punctuation.) Frequently, this processing also requires a global Boolean variable or function that is shared by *GetChar* and *GetWord* and that is set to true when the end of the data is reached.

More precisely, *GetChar* performs the following.

* returns the next character of input in a line
* returns a "space" at the end of a line (*GetChar* then gets ready for the next line).

Further, if we decide that a blank line will specify the end of our input, then *GetChar* does the following.

1. At the start of each line, *GetChar* sets a shared, global Boolean variable *AllBlanks* to true.
2. During the reading of a line, *GetChar* changes *AllBlanks* to false if a nonblank character is found.
3. At the end of a line, *GetChar* sets a global Boolean variable *InputDone* to true if only blanks have been found on the line. (We assume *InputDone* is initialized to false by the program.)
4. Once *InputDone* is true, *GetChar* performs no more reading, and *GetChar* only returns blanks.

Similarly, we describe the formal specifications for *GetWord*.

1. *GetWord* initializes the length of the word returned to 0.
2. *GetWord* calls *GetChar* successively until either a letter is found or until *InputDone* is true.
3. If a letter is found, that letter is used to begin a word, and the word length is now 1.
4. When the first letter is found, *GetWord* calls *GetChar* successively and adds letters to the word until the maximum word length is found or until a nonletter is encountered.

With these detailed specifications, we are ready to write the code for these two procedures. This code is shown in complete detail as part of the program in Section 14.5.

As with the other string functions, *GetChar* and *GetWord* illustrate many tasks that we may wish to perform with strings. In each case, we identify a task, and we write a procedure or function to perform the details.

As the need arises, other tasks now can be specified in either of two ways. The individual procedures specified in this section can be put together to perform more complex operations. Or, new procedures can be defined similarly to the way we proceeded here.

SECTION 14.4   ALPHABETIZING STRINGS—TWO BETTER WAYS

Up to this point, we have concentrated upon work with individual strings, and we have seen how we can use our earlier sorting algorithms with these strings. Unfortunately, sorting is a very common task in many applications involving strings, and the sorting algorithms we have encountered up to now are very time consuming. Thus, before we are ready to solve many string applications, we need to consider two more efficient sorting algorithms, the *radix sort* and the *merge sort*. Each of these approaches arises from a very different perspective of sorting than we have seen in the past for exchange (or bubble), selection, or insertion sorts.

Radix Sort
We introduce the radix sort with an example:

Suppose we want to put a deck of cards in order. In other words, we want all 2s, then 3s, then 4s, etc. Within this ordering, we want suits ordered 'Clubs', 'Diamonds', 'Hearts', and 'Spades'. Thus, our deck should begin

2C, 2D, 2H, 2S, 3C, 3D, 3H, 3S, 4C, ...

To perform this sorting, we will use several temporary piles for each step. First we go through our cards, putting them into four piles according to their suit. When this process is done, we combine these piles, putting the 'Clubs' pile first, then 'Diamonds', then 'Hearts', and 'Spades'. Next, we go through our cards again, putting them into 13 piles; 2, 3, 4, . . . , 10, J, Q, K, A. When all cards have been put in piles, we again merge them by picking up the 2s, then the 3s, etc. At this point, our deck is ordered.

This approach of moving data into piles and putting the piles back together is called a **radix sort,** and we now apply it to arrays of data. Suppose we are given

Type Word = Packed Array [1..MaxWord] of Char;
    List = Array [1..MaxList] of Word;

In other words, suppose we have a *list* of *words* that we want to alphabetize. The radix sort uses the following algorithm.

Step 1. Place the list of words in piles, according to the last letter of each word, then merge the piles.

Step 2. Place the list of words in piles, according to the next-to-last letter of each word, then merge the piles.

General Step. Continue dividing the list of words into piles by looking at particular letters and merging piles until the first letter has been considered.

We observe that this approach is just the opposite of one that looks at the first letter to get separate piles and then looks at each of these piles individually to consider the second and subsequent letters of each word. This latter approach may seem more familiar but it is harder to use in computers because we cannot put our piles together after each step. The radix sort has the advantage that we can follow the same pattern for each letter of the words, starting from a single pile of data.

When we apply this radix sort to words made up of letters, the possible piles will correspond to the letters 'A' . . . 'Z' and to null. (The null is needed when we run out of letters in a word at the end of our array.) Thus, to sort words, we need 27 piles for our work, and we need to keep track of how many words are in each pile. The result involves a very large amount of memory, but the process can go quite quickly.

Alternatively, we could save memory by going through the words to find all As, then all Bs, and so on for each step. This second approach takes longer, but it requires much less storage.

The following outline shows the radix sort using the 27 piles discussed.

Outline for Radix Sort. Repeat for subsequent letters of a word, from the last to the first.

  I. Initialize all piles to 0.
 II. For each word in the list:
    A. Determine which pile the word belongs to.
      1. The pile depends on the letter of the alphabet.
      2. Nonletters are grouped together in a separate pile.

B. Add word to pile, increasing count for the pile by 1.
III. Merge the piles.

This outline yields the following sorting procedure.

```
Procedure RadixSort (Var Data: List);
{This procedure performs a Radix Sort to order the given Data.}
    Const NumberOfValues = 27;
          MaxList = 10; {Number of words to be sorted}
          MaxWord = 10; {Number of characters in each word}

    Var Pile: Array [1..NumberOfValues] Of List;
        PileCount: Array [1..NumberOfValues] of Integer;
        Letter: Integer;
        ListItem: Integer;
        PileNumber: Integer;

    Procedure InitializePiles;
    {This procedure initializes all pile counts to 0}
        Var Index: Integer;
        Begin
            For Index := 1 To NumberOfValues
                Do PileCount[Index] := 0
        End {InitializePiles} ;

    Procedure DeterminePile (Item: Word; Position: Integer;
                             Var PileNumber: Integer);
    {This procedure determines which pile the word should be placed upon,
     based on the letter position specified}
        Begin
            If (Item[Position] >= 'A') And (Item[Position] <= 'Z')
                Then PileNumber := Ord(Item[Position]) - Ord('A') + 2
                Else PileNumber := 1
        End {DeterminePile} ;

    Procedure Insert (Item: Word; Number: Integer);
    {This procedure inserts the given word on the given pile}
        Var TopOfPile: Integer;
        Begin
            PileCount[Number] := PileCount[Number] + 1;
            TopOfPile := PileCount[Number];
            Pile[Number][TopOfPile] := Item
        End {Insert} ;

    Procedure MergePiles;
    {This procedure puts the various piles back together into one list}
        Var PileNumber: Integer;
            PileItem: Integer;
            ListItem: Integer;
```

```
      Begin
          ListItem := 0;
          For PileNumber := 1 To NumberOfValues
            Do Begin
               For PileItem := 1 To PileCount[PileNumber]
                 Do Begin
                   ListItem := ListItem + 1;
                   Data[ListItem] := Pile[PileNumber][PileItem]
                 End
            End
      End {MergePiles} ;

Begin {RadixSort}
    For Letter := MaxWord DownTo 1
      Do Begin
         InitializePiles;
         For ListItem := 1 To MaxList
           Do Begin
              DeterminePile(Data[ListItem], Letter, PileNumber);
              Insert(Data[ListItem], PileNumber)
           End;
         MergePiles
      End
End {RadixSort} ;
```

After we consider another algorithm, the merge sort, we will analyze the efficiency of the radix sort.

Merge Sort

Our next sorting algorithm is called a **merge sort** because it is based on a simple procedure that combines, or merges, two short lists of ordered data into one large, ordered list. With this procedure, the merge sort divides an initial array into short lists in various ways and a merge procedure then puts the short lists together. At the end, our data are ordered.

To understand this algorithm more clearly, we again consider a deck of cards.

Combining Two Ordered Lists. Suppose we have two piles of cards, and suppose that each pile is ordered. Then we can combine the two piles into one larger, ordered pile as follows: First, we look at the top card in each pile, and select the smaller card to start the new pile. Next, we consider the current top cards in each pile, select the smaller, and add it to the new pile. More generally, as long as cards remain in both piles, we look at the top card from each pile, select the smaller, and add it to the new pile. Finally, after we run out of cards in one pile, we move the cards in the remaining pile to the new pile. This combining or merging operation is very efficient, since we are adding a new card to our new pile at each step.

Combining Lists to Sort Any Data. Once we determine how to combine ordered lists, the merge sort proceeds by dividing a big list of items into very small pieces. Then these items are merged in repeated steps to get bigger pieces until the entire array is sorted. The following uses this approach in our card example. The process is outlined in Figure 14–4.

Step 1. We note that if we divide our deck into piles, where each pile has only one card, then each pile is sorted! Thus, we start with piles of length 1. We merge pile 1 with pile 2, pile 3 with pile 4, and so on. In each case, we get ordered piles, with two cards in each pile.

Step 2. We use the piles from Step 1 and merge pile 1 with pile 2, pile 3 with pile 4, and so on. Here, we get ordered piles, with four cards in each pile.

General Step. Use the piles from the previous step. Merge pile 1 with pile 2, pile 3 with pile 4, and so on. When we are done, our piles have twice as many cards as when we started. Continue this process until all cards are combined into a single pile.

When applying this approach to an array $A_1, \ldots, A_n$ of items, we think of dividing these items up into small pieces. At each step, when we merge the pieces, we store our new piles in a new array. Then, at the end of the step, we copy the new array back into our initial array.

This figure also identifies two details that we must keep track of in

FIGURE 14–4 • **Use of Merge Sort with Array of Eleven Elements**

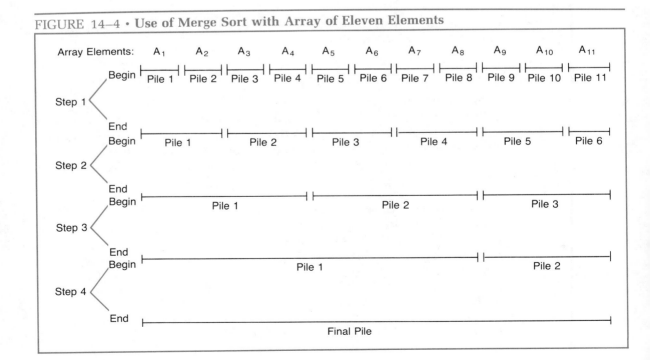

programming. At the end of our array, our piles may not have the full number of items as the rest of the piles; our array may run out of elements. Thus, in merging piles, we must keep track of the end of our array, so we do not try to add items from beyond our data to piles.

At each step, we can perform our merging process if we know where the first pile starts, where the second pile starts, and the size of each pile. From this, we can compute where the first pile ends (one before the start of the second pile) and where the second pile ends (add the size of each pile to the start of the second pile, unless this goes beyond the end of the array).

Outline for Merge Sort.   The following is our formal outline for the merge sort.

I. Repeat for pieces of size 1, 2, 4, 8, 16, . . . , until the size exceeds the number of elements in the array (i.e., until all items are in one pile).
    A. The first pile starts with item 1.
        The second pile starts with item 1 + size.
    B. Repeat until the second pile is empty.
        1. Merge first pile with second pile into new array where starting points of piles are given above.
        2. Update starting points of piles for next iteration.
            a. Next first pile will start at beginning of old second pile + size.
            b. Next second pile will start at beginning of new first pile + size.
    C. Copy new array back to old array.
    D. Double size for next iteration.

This outline suggests the following sorting procedure.

```
Procedure MergeSort (Var Data: List);
{This procedure orders the given data using a Merge Sort.}
    Var Temp: List;
        PieceSize: Integer;
        StartFirst: Integer;
        StartNext: Integer;

    Procedure MergePieces (First, Second, Size: Integer);
    {Procedure merges two parts of an array}

        Var StopFirst, StopNext: Integer;
            NewItem: Integer;
        Begin
            If Second > MaxList + 1
                Then StopFirst := MaxList
                Else StopFirst := Second - 1;
            If Second + Size > MaxList + 1
                Then StopNext := MaxList
                Else StopNext := Second + Size - 1;
```

```
            NewItem := First;
            While (First <= StopFirst)
              And (Second <= StopNext)
                Do Begin
                  If Data[First] <= Data[Second]
                      Then Begin
                          Temp[NewItem] := Data[First];
                          First := First + 1
                          End
                      Else Begin
                          Temp[NewItem] := Data[Second];
                          Second := Second + 1
                          End;
                  NewItem := NewItem + 1;
                End;

            {Finish copying first list}
            While (First <= StopFirst)
              Do Begin
                Temp[NewItem] := Data[First];
                First := First + 1;
                NewItem := NewItem + 1
              End;

            {Finish copying first list}
            While (Second <= StopNext)
              Do Begin
                Temp[NewItem] := Data[Second];
                Second := Second + 1;
                NewItem := NewItem + 1
              End;
        End {MergePieces} ;

Begin {Merge Sort}
    PieceSize := 1;
    Repeat
        StartFirst := 1;
        StartNext := StartFirst + PieceSize;
        Repeat
            MergePieces (StartFirst, StartNext, PieceSize);
            StartFirst := StartNext + PieceSize;
            StartNext := StartFirst + PieceSize;
        Until StartFirst > MaxList;
        Data := Temp;
        PieceSize := PieceSize * 2
    Until (PieceSize >= MaxList)
End {MergeSort} ;
```

Evaluation of Efficiency

In Section 8.5, when we discussed the straight selection sort and the exchange or bubble sort, we also evaluated how much work was required for each algorithm. The actual amount of work depended upon the data that we were sorting, but we were able to estimate the number of times we needed to compare two array elements and the number of times we moved pieces of data. We could perform a similar analysis for the insertion sort of Section 8.7, and we would get the following estimate for arrays of n elements of random data.

Algorithm	Comparisons	Assignments
Straight Selection	$(n^2 - n)/2$	$3n$
Exchange or Bubble	$(n^2 - n)/2$	$n^2 - n$
Insertion	$(n\log_2 n)$	$(n^2 + 7n)/4$

In reviewing each of these numbers, we note that in comparison to n^2, the value n (or $2n$ or $3n$) is quite small when n is large. For example, when $n = 1000$, $n^2 = 1,000,000$ while $4n$ is only 4000. Thus, $4n$ is only 0.4% of n^2. For this reason, we see that the major part of these numbers involve the term n^2, and the total number of operations required is proportional to this term n^2. In this case, we say that these algorithms have **order n^2** or **O(n^2)**. This phrase indicates that the major term in our count of operations is proportional to n^2.

When we evaluate the radix sort and the merge sort, we will find that they are much more efficient.

Efficiency of the Radix Sort.   In the radix sort, we move items to appropriate piles and then we collect piles. This involves the following work.

1. Determine the value of each item to determine the appropriate pile.
2. Move to pile.
3. Move back.

This work requires one comparison (step 1) and two assignments (steps 2 and 3) for each data item. We repeat the process for each character in our array.

Thus, if we have n items and m characters in a name, the work involves:

$(n*1)$ comparisons per pass

$(n*2)$ assignments per pass

and a total of

nm comparisons

$2nm$ assignments

Also, we note that this algorithm requires a great deal of storage. In particular, we need piles for each possible character value we might encounter. (For example, we needed 27 piles in our alphabetizing problem.)

More generally, if d is the number of character values we might encounter, we need extra storage for three types of data:

d lists

n names per list

m characters per name

Thus, we need extra storage for dnm values.

Alternatively, we could go through our list several times, once to find all As, then Bs, etc. This eliminates much extra storage, but then we need many more comparisons because we must go through our data d times rather than just once. Thus, if we save space, the radix sort requires

dnm comparisons

$2nm$ assignments

Since the number of characters is given and the number of characters in a name is constant, the number of operations here is proportional to n. Thus, this is an *order n* or $O(n)$ algorithm.

Efficiency of Merge Sort. In the merge sort, we proceed in several steps, where the size of pieces increases in the progression 1, 2, 4, 8, ... Then, for each step, we move data to a new array, and we have noted that we move data following each comparison. Thus, if our array has n pieces of data, we find we need n comparisons, n moves to new array, and n moves back for each step. Thus, one step requires

n comparisons

$2n$ assignments

To determine the number s of steps needed, we see that the size of our pieces will be

$$1, 2, 4, 8, . . . , 2^s.$$

We continue until all of our data is in one piece. Thus, we need s to satisfy

$$2^s > n$$

or

$$s > \log_2 n.$$

If we round off our logarithm, we have

$$s = \log_2 n + 1.$$

Since each step involves n comparisons and $2n$ assignments, the total work involved is

$n(1 + \log_2 n)$ comparisons

$2n(1 + \log_2 n)$ assignments

Here, for large n, $\log_2 n$ dominates the term 1, so the number of operations is proportional to

$$n\log_2 n$$

Thus, the merge sort has **order n $\log_2$n**.

Comparison of Efficiency.   Our conclusions on the amount of work required for various sorting algorithms are shown in Table 14-1.

The significance of these results is shown in Table 14-2. When we are sorting few pieces of data (n small), almost any sorting algorithm will require little work. However, for large collections of data (n large), order n^2 algorithms take a very long time. In fact, even if we speed up our code by a factor of 2 or 4 or even 10, the time is still prohibitive. Thus, we cannot use a straight selection sort, exchange or bubble sort, or an insertion sort with large data sets. Instead, a radix sort or a merge sort is much more efficient.

Further, Tables 14-1 and 14-2 show that the radix sort is extremely efficient as long as we have adequate storage space. However, we have already noted that storage requirements for the radix sort are often prohibitive. Thus, in practice, we may not have enough space for the radix sort, even though it is efficient.

Finally, the merge sort is a good choice for many sorting needs. This sort does require some additional storage; we need one extra copy of our data during storage. However, Tables 14-1 and 14-2 show that the merge sort offers a substantial time savings over the $O(n^2)$ algorithms we have seen earlier.

TABLE 14-1 · Comparison of Sorting Algorithms

Algorithm	Comparisons	Assignments	Total Operations	Order
Straight Selection	$\dfrac{n^2 - n}{2}$	n	$\dfrac{n^2 + n}{2}$	n^2
Exchange or Bubble	$\dfrac{n^2 - n}{2}$	$n^2 - n$	$\dfrac{3(n^2 - n)}{2}$	n^2
Insertion	$n\log_2 n$	$\dfrac{n^2 + 7n}{4}$	$n\log_2 n + \dfrac{n^2 + 7n}{4}$	n^2
Radix*	dnm or $2nm$	$2nm$	$(d+2)nm$ or $4nm$	n
Merge	$n(1 + \log_2 n)$	$2(1 + \log_2 n)$	$(n+2)(1 + \log_2 n)$	$n\log_2 n$

*Efficiency depends upon storage allocations
n = number of items in array
m = number of characters in word
d = number of distinct letters possible

TABLE 14–2 • Comparison of Number of Operations (and Time) Required* For Various Values of n

n	n^2	$n^2/2$	$n^2/4$	$n^2/10$	$n\log_2 n$
50 (0.01sec.)	2500 (0.25sec.)	1250 (0.13sec.)	625 (0.06sec.)	250 (0.03sec.)	300 (0.03sec.)
100 (0.01sec.)	10000 (1.00sec.)	5000 (0.50sec.)	2500 (0.25sec.)	1000 (0.10sec.)	700 (0.07sec.)
500 (0.05sec.)	250000 (25.00sec.)	125000 (12.50sec.)	62500 (6.25sec.)	25000 (2.50sec.)	4500 (0.45sec.)
1000 (0.10sec.)	1000000 (1.67min.)	500000 (50.00sec.)	250000 (25.00sec.)	100000 (10.00sec.)	10000 (1.00sec.)
1500 (0.15sec.)	2250000 (3.75min.)	1125000 (1.88min.)	562500 (56.25sec.)	225000 (22.50sec.)	16500 (1.65sec.)
2000 (0.20sec.)	4000000 (6.67min.)	2000000 (3.33min.)	1000000 (1.67min.)	400000 (40.00sec.)	22000 (2.20sec.)
4000 (0.40sec.)	16000000 (26.67min.)	8000000 (13.33min.)	4000000 (6.67min.)	1600000 (2.67min.)	48000 (4.80sec.)
8000 (0.80sec.)	64000000 (1.78hr.)	32000000 (53.33min.)	16000000 (26.67min.)	6400000 (10.67min.)	104000 (10.40sec.)
16000 (1.60sec.)	256000000 (7.11hr.)	128000000 (3.56hr.)	64000000 (1.78hr.)	25600000 (42.67min.)	224000 (22.40sec.)
32000 (3.20sec.)	1024000000 (1.19days)	512000000 (14.22hr.)	256000000 (7.11hr.)	102400000 (2.84hr.)	480000 (48.00sec.)
64000 (6.40sec.)	4096000000 (4.74days)	2048000000 (2.37days)	1024000000 (1.19days)	409600000 (11.38hr.)	1024000 (1.71min.)

*Times based upon 10,000 operations performed per second.

SECTION 14.5 EXAMPLE: DIVIDING CHARACTER INPUT INTO WORDS, COUNTING, AND ALPHABETIZING

So far in this chapter, we have seen several ways to store and manipulate strings of characters, and we have seen two new sorting algorithms for ordering data. In this section, we use these various ideas to solve the following problem.

PROBLEM 14.5. Write a program that performs an elementary word analysis. In particular, the program should

- read multiple lines from the terminal until a blank line is entered;
- divide the input into words;
- count the number of times each word appears; and
- print the words and frequencies in two lists (one ordered alphabetically by word and another in decreasing order by frequency).

Discussion of Problem 14.5

We will approach this problem by processing words as they are entered. For each word, we compare it with other words already entered.

Thus, we will store words as packed arrays of fixed length; we will fill any extra space in the array with nulls. We will also need a count of how many times the word has occurred in our input; and we will need to keep track of the number of words we have at any given moment in our list. These comments suggest that our major list of information should have the following declarations.

```
Const WordLength =  30;
      MaxList     = 100;
Type  String      = Packed Array [1..WordLength] of Char;
      WordEntry = Record
                     Word: String;
                     Count: Integer
                  End;
Var   List: Array [1..MaxList] of WordEntry;
      NumberInList: Integer;
```

Here the main list can contain many word entries, where each entry contains a *Word* and a frequency *Count*.

Next, we consider how to structure our processing. As we read each word, we should look to see if it is already on our list of words. If so, we should add to our count. Otherwise, we need to add the word to our list with an initial count of 1.

Once all data has been entered, we need to print it in two ways. Our first listing is to be alphabetical by word. Here, we can use a merge sort, comparing the words on our list. Note, however, that whenever we want to move an item on our list, we must work with the entire record. Our comparisons for ordering will depend only upon the letters of our words, but assignments must include the whole record.

For our second printing, we might wish to print words in decreasing order by frequency. Since we might expect that most words appear relatively few times, we might use a modification of our radix sort for this printing task. In particular, we could search the list to find the largest count for any word. Then, we would go through our list several times.

1st time: print all words with highest count

2nd time: print all words with highest count − 1

3rd time: print all words with highest count − 2

.

.

.

From this discussion, we can develop the following outline, which combines many ideas from this chapter.

Outline for Problem 14.5

  I. Set up to begin.
    A. No characters have been read.
      1. Set *InputDone* to false.
      2. Set *AllBlanks* to true.
    B. No words have been found.
      1. Set *NumberInList* to 0.
  II. Read characters until no more data remains.
    A. Get a *Word*.
    B. If *Word* is not null:
      1. Determine if word is on list.
        a. If so, add to word count.
        b. If not, add word to list.
  III. Print *List* alphabetically by word.
    A. Order *List* using merge sort.
    B. Print *List*, from first word to last.
  IV. Print list in descending order by *count*.
    A. Find highest count.
    B. For Count := Highest Count, . . . , 2, 1
      1. Scan list.
      2. Print words with the given count.

In the following program, we modify several of the procedures in this section to agree with the particular declarations we need for this problem. The ideas behind these procedures follow our earlier discussion.

```
Program WordCount (Input, Output);
{This program reads several lines of input, divides the input into words,
 counts the number of times each word appears, and prints the results}

Const WordLength = 25;
      MaxList = 50;
```

```
Type String = Packed Array [1..WordLength] of Char;

      WordEntry = Record
         Word: String;
         Count: Integer
         End;

      WordList = Array [1..MaxList] Of WordEntry;

Var InputDone: Boolean;      {Shared variables for reading data}
    AllBlanks: Boolean;      {used in GetChar and GetWord Procedures}
    NullWord: String;        {Used as constant string of nulls}

Procedure Initialize(Var NumberInList: Integer);
{This procedure prepares for processing of input}
    Var Index: Integer;
    Begin
        {No characters have been read}
        InputDone := False;
        AllBlanks := True;

        {No words have been found}
        NumberInList := 0;

        {Null word contains only nulls}
        For Index := 1 To WordLength
            Do NullWord[Index] := Chr(0);
    End {Initialize} ;

Procedure GetChar (Var Ch: Char);
{GetChar returns successive characters entered from the keyboard,
 processing ends of lines, and checking when a blank line occurs}
    Begin
      If InputDone
        Then Ch := ' '
      Else If Eoln
            Then {Processing end of line}
              Begin
                If AllBlanks
                   Then Begin {blank line}
                     InputDone := True;
                     Ch := ' '
                     End
                   Else Begin {not blank line}
                     Ch := ' ';
                     Readln;
                     AllBlanks := True
                     End
              End {Processing end of line}
            Else {Processing in middle of line}
              Begin
                 Read (Ch);
                 AllBlanks := AllBlanks And (Ch = ' ')
              End {Processing in middle of line}
    End {GetChar} ;
```

```
Procedure GetWord (Var Word: String);
{GetWord puts characters together to form words}
    Var Ch: Char;
        Length: Integer;

    Function Letter(Ch: Char): Boolean;
    {Function determines if Ch is a letter}
        Begin
            Letter := (Ch In ['a'..'z']) Or (Ch In ['A'..'Z'])
        End {Letter} ;

    Begin {GetWord}
        Length := 0;
        Word := NullWord;

        {Find first letter in input}
        GetChar(Ch);
        While (Not InputDone) And Not Letter(Ch)
            Do GetChar(Ch);

        {Put letters together to get a word}
        If Letter(Ch)
          Then Repeat
              Length := Length + 1;
              Word[Length] := Ch;
              GetChar(Ch)
          Until Not Letter(Ch) Or (Length >= WordLength);
    End {GetWord} ;

Procedure EnterData (Var List: WordList; Var NumberInList: Integer);
{This procedure processes words until no more input data remains}
    Var Item: String;
        Position: Integer;   {Location of Word in List}

    Procedure Find (Item: String; Var List: WordList; Var Position: Integer);
    {This Procedure finds the position of the given item in the List}
        Var Index: Integer;
        Begin
            Index := 1;
            While (Index < NumberInList) And (List[Index].Word <> Item)
                Do Index := Index + 1;
            If List[Index].Word = Item
                Then Position := Index
                Else Position := 0
        End {Find} ;

    Begin {EnterData}
        Writeln ('Please enter your data.');
        Writeln ('Conclude by entering a blank line');

        While Not InputDone
          Do Begin
            GetWord (Item);
            If Item <> NullWord
                Then Begin
                    Find (Item, List, Position);
```

```
                    If  Position > 0
                       Then {Increase count by 1}
                          List[Position].Count := List[Position].Count + 1
                       Else {Add word to list}
                         Begin
                           NumberInList := NumberInList + 1;
                           List[NumberInList].Word := Item;
                           List[NumberInList].Count := 1
                         End;
               End;
      End;
   End {EnterData} ;

Procedure PrintAlphabetically (Var List: WordList; NumberInList: Integer);
{This procedure uses a merge sort to order the list of words, and
 then prints the ordered list}
     Var Index: Integer;

     Procedure MergeSort (Var List: WordList);
     {This procedure orders the given data using a Merge Sort.}
        Var Temp: WordList;
            PieceSize: Integer;
            StartFirst: Integer;
            StartNext: Integer;

        Procedure MergePieces (First, Second, Size: Integer);
        {Procedure merges two parts of an array}
             Var StopFirst, StopNext: Integer;
                 NewItem: Integer;

          Begin
              If Second > NumberInList + 1
                 Then StopFirst := NumberInList
                 Else StopFirst := Second - 1;
              If Second + Size > NumberInList + 1
                 Then StopNext := NumberinList
                 Else StopNext := Second + Size - 1;
              NewItem := First;
              While (First <= StopFirst)
                And (Second <= StopNext)
                   Do Begin
                      If List[First].Word <= List[Second].Word
                         Then Begin
                             Temp[NewItem] := List[First];
                             First := First + 1
                             End
                         Else Begin
                             Temp[NewItem] := List[Second];
                             Second := Second + 1
                             End;
                      NewItem := NewItem + 1;
                   End;

              {Finish copying first list}
              While (First <= StopFirst)
                Do Begin
                   Temp[NewItem] := List[First];
```

```
                        First := First + 1;
                        NewItem := NewItem + 1
                     End;

                {Finish copying first list}
                While (Second <= StopNext)
                   Do Begin
                      Temp[NewItem] := List[Second];
                      Second := Second + 1;
                      NewItem := NewItem + 1
                   End;
            End {MergePieces} ;

        Begin {Merge Sort}
           PieceSize := 1;
           Repeat
              StartFirst := 1;
              StartNext := StartFirst + PieceSize;
              Repeat
                 MergePieces (StartFirst, StartNext, PieceSize);
                 StartFirst := StartNext + PieceSize;
                 StartNext := StartFirst + PieceSize
              Until (StartFirst > NumberInList);
              List := Temp;
              PieceSize := PieceSize * 2
           Until (PieceSize >= NumberInList)
        End {MergeSort} ;

    Procedure Print (Item: String);
    {This procedure prints an item, replacing any nulls by spaces}
        Var Index: Integer;
        Begin
           For Index := 1 To WordLength
              Do If Item[Index] = Chr(0)
                 Then Write(' ')
                 Else Write(Item[Index])
        End {Print} ;

    Begin {PrintAlphabetically}

        MergeSort (List);

        {Print words in order}
        Writeln;
        Writeln ('Printing of words in alphabetical order');
        Writeln;
        Writeln ('Word', 'Count':(WordLength+1));
        Writeln;
        For Index := 1 To NumberInList
           Do Begin
              Print (List[Index].Word);
              Writeln (List[Index].Count:3)
           End
    End {PrintAlphabetically} ;

Procedure PrintByFrequency (Var List: WordList; NumberInList: Integer);
```

```
{This procedure find the highest word count, scans the list for
 each count below this maximum, and prints the words with that count}
    Var Maximum: Integer;
        Count: Integer;
        Index: Integer;
    Begin
        {Find the maximum count}
        Maximum := List[1].Count;
        For Index := 2 to NumberInList
            Do If List[Index].Count > Maximum
                Then Maximum := List[Index].Count;

        {Scan list for count := Maximum, ..., 2, 1}
        Writeln;
        Writeln ('Printing of words in decreasing order by frequency');
        Writeln;
        Writeln ('Count  Word');
        Writeln;
        For Count := Maximum DownTo 1
          Do For Index := 1 To NumberInList
              Do If List[Index].Count = Count
                  Then Writeln (Count:3, '    ', List[Index].Word)
    End {PrintByFrequency} ;

Procedure ControlProcessing;
{This procedure controls the major steps of the word analysis}
    Var List: WordList;
        NumberInList: Integer;
    Begin
        Initialize(NumberInList);
        EnterData(List, NumberInList);
        PrintAlphabetically(List, NumberInList);
        PrintByFrequency(List, NumberInList)
    End {ControlProcessing} ;

Begin {Main}
    Writeln ('This program counts words entered from the terminal.');
    ControlProcessing
End {Main} .
```

A sample run of this program appears below.

```
This program counts words entered from the terminal.
Please enter your data.
Conclude by entering a blank line
the program illustrates
      -- the procedure getchar and the procedure getword
      -- string comparisons and string output
      -- the merge sort and the radix sort
```

```
Printing of words in alphabetical order

Word                    Count

and                     3
comparisons             1
getchar                 1
getword                 1
illustrates             1
merge                   1
output                  1
procedure               2
program                 1
radix                   1
sort                    2
string                  2
the                     5

Printing of words in decreasing order by frequency

Count   Word

  5     the
  3     and
  2     procedure
  2     sort
  2     string
  1     comparisons
  1     getchar
  1     getword
  1     illustrates
  1     merge
  1     output
  1     program
  1     radix
```

From this program, we see how we can combine many of the string processing procedures and functions that we have discussed in this chapter, including processing characters and words with standard procedures; using packed arrays for comparing strings of characters; and sorting with a merge or radix sort for efficiency.

SUMMARY

1. We can store **strings** of characters in several ways. Conceptually, strings may be either variable-length or fixed-length, and the array data can be either packed or unpacked in a machine.
2. **Variable-length strings** are stored in a record, which includes the length of the string as well as an array for the individual characters.

3. **Fixed-length strings** are stored in an array of characters, and **nulls** or spaces are used, if necessary, to fill up the end of the array.
4. In **packed arrays,** data are packed together in main memory as tightly as possible, but processing may require extraction of particular characters.
5. In **unpacked arrays,** one piece of data is stored in an entire unit of main memory. Here, some space may be wasted, but processing is efficient.
6. The *Pack* and *Unpack* procedures allow us to move data easily between packed and unpacked arrays.
7. Pascal defines packed arrays of characters as a **string-type,** and we can perform some special operations with this, including
   - Constant declarations
   - Comparisons in Boolean expressions
   - Use in *Write* Statements
8. Several common string functions or procedures include **concatenation, substring extraction, pattern matching,** and **reading words.**
9. This chapter introduced two new sorting algorithms which are much more efficient than the methods we saw in Chapter 8.
   a. The **radix sort** is a linear or **order n** algorithm, but it requires a great deal of extra storage space.
   b. The **merge sort** has **order n*$\log_2$n** and requires only a modest amount of extra storage.
   c. In contrast, the straight selection, exchange or bubble, and insertion sorts from Chapter 8 were all quadratic, or **order n^2,** algorithms.
10. Our analysis of efficiency showed that for large collections of data (large n), simple improvements in order n^2 algorithms were unlikely to be helpful. Rather, we need different approaches to accomplish our tasks.

EXERCISES

14.1 *Implementing Left and Right.* Implement the *Left* and *Right* procedures discussed in Section 14.3 under substring extraction.
14.2 *Length Function.*
   a. Write

   Function Length (Data: String):Integer

   which returns the length of the variable-length string *Data*.
   b. Write a similar function to find the length of a fixed-length string. Here, assume that nulls are used to fill up the end of a string array.
14.3 *Inserting Commas.* Write a program that reads an integer from a line of input and prints the integer with commas inserted every third

digit from the right. Your program should allow both positive and negative integers up to 60 digits long, and it should not insert a comma before the first digit or just after a " + " or " − " sign.

For example, given the numbers 12345 or − 123456789 or 123456, the program should print 12,345 or − 123,456,789 or 123,456.

14.4   *Pig Latin Translator.* Write a program that will input a word and translate the word into Pig Latin. Recall that to translate a word into Pig Latin, we

1. take the first letter of the word and place it at the end of the word;

2. add the letter *A* at the end of the word.

14.5   *Compare Variable-Length Strings.* Write

Function First(String1, String2: String): Boolean

which returns true if *String1* comes before *String2* in alphabetical order and false otherwise. Here *String1* and *String2* are variable-length strings.

14.6   *InString Function.* Write

Function InString (SubS, Str: String; Start: Integer): Integer

which extends the *Match* function by starting its search in character position *Start*. In other words, *InString* searches for the substring *SubS* within the string *Str*, starting with character position *Start* in *Str*. If the substring is found, *Instring* returns the position of string *Str* where the match begins. Otherwise, *InString* returns 0.

14.7   *Replacing Letters.* Use the functions described in Section 14.3 to scan a line of input and replace all vowels by '*'.

HINT: Define '*' as a variable-length string of length 1. Define similar strings for 'a', 'e', 'i', etc. Then use operations *Match*, *Left*, *Right*, and *Concat.*

14.8   *Replacing Substrings.* Write a program that replaces one substring by another in a line of input. For example, all occurrences of 'any'

KEY TERMS, PHRASES, AND CONCEPTS		ELEMENTS OF PASCAL SYNTAX	
Merge Sort	Reading Words	*Pack*	*Unpack*
Order of an Algorithm	Substring Extraction	String-Type	
Null	String-Type	Comparisons in	
Packed Arrays	Strings	Boolean	
Radix Sort	Fixed Length	Expressions	
String Operations	Literal	Constants	
Concatenation	Variable Length	Use in *Write*	
Pattern Matching	Unpacked Arrays	Statements	

might be replaced by 'some' in the input. The program should ask the user to enter the substrings from the terminal as well as the line of input. (This type of program is very helpful in word processing, as typographical errors can be systematically corrected throughout a manuscript in a single operation.)

14.9   *Name-Address Listing.* Write a program that reads a list of names, addresses, and zip codes and then prints this list in two ways: first ordered by name and then by zip code.

14.10 *Grocery Checkout.* Write a program that simulates part of the grocery checkout process in which product codes are scanned by special sensors. In particular, your program should

- read list of product information, including product name, product code, price;
- order the product data by code;
- ask the user for various product codes;
- use a binary search (Section 8.6) to locate the product; and
- print product name and price.

14.11 *GetToken—An Extended GetWord.* Write

      Procedure GetToken (Var TokenType: Integer;
                        Var Item: String)

which returns the next unit entered from the keyboard. Possible units are

Token Type	Description
1	Punctuation
2	Real Number
3	Integer
4	Word
5	Separator (Tab, Space, Return)

Each time *GetToken* is called, the procedure determines the type of object that appears next on the line. This type is returned as well as a variable-length string, which specifies the object itself. (All separators are translated to a space.)

For example, suppose we enter the line

In this line, we find 16 tokens!

Here, *GetToken* would return the following if it were called 16 times.

Token Type	Length	Item Data
4	2	In
5	1	{space}
4	4	this
5	1	{space}

4	4	line
1	1	,
5	1	{space}
4	2	we
5	1	{space}
4	4	find
5	1	{space}
3	2	16
5	1	{space}
4	6	tokens
1	1	!
5	1	{space for the return}

NOTE: In writing this procedure, you will need a Boolean variable *ReRead* which tells *GetChar* to return the same character it read before. Also, the character read may need to be defined globally.

14.12 *Radix Sort with Cards.* Shuffle a card deck, so the cards are well mixed. Then, follow the steps in the radix sort example of Section 14.4 to order the deck.

14.13 *Merging Two Ordered Piles of Cards.* Divide a card deck randomly into two piles. (The piles need not be of equal length.) Then, follow the description of combining two ordered lists of Section 14.4 to produce one large, ordered pile of cards.

14.14 *Merge Sort With Cards.* Shuffle a card deck, so that the cards are well mixed. Then, follow the steps in the merge sort example of Section 14.4 to order the deck.

14.15 *Alternative Radix Sort.* Write a procedure to perform the alternate radix sort discussed in Section 14.4. Here, the procedure goes through the entire list of data for each character value rather than forming distinct piles. The appropriate outline is shown below.

Outline for Alternative Radix Sort. Repeat for subsequent letters of a word, from the last to the first.
   I. For each possible letter value:
       A. Go through all words on the list.
       B. Add words with the specified letter to a temporary array.
   II. Copy the temporary array back to the original array.

14.16 *Alternative Approach to Problem 14.5.* In dividing character input into words, counting, and alphabetizing, a second approach is to use the insertion procedure of Section 8.7 to keep the words in order as they are entered. Then after each word is identified, we could use a binary search to see where that word should be on the list. If the word appears, we increase the count for the word. If not, we move subsequent words down to make room for this new word. Write a program that uses this alternative approach to solve Problem 14.5.

14.17 *Alphabetizing Numbers.* Write a program that generates the names of the numbers from zero to one hundred and prints them in alphabetical order.

14.18 *Double Words.* One common typographical error is the occurrence of the same word twice in a row. Write a program that reads multiple lines of character input (until a blank line) and determines if any word is repeated twice in a row.

NOTE: Your program should check that the last word on one line is not repeated as the first word on the next line.

14.19 *Counting Words.* Write a program that reads multiple lines of character input (until a blank line), counts the number of words in each sentence, and computes the average number of words per sentence.

a. In the first version of this program, assume a sentence ends whenever one of the marks '.', '!', or '?' appears.

b. Revise your program in part (a). to check that the period is not following a person's initial. (If the period follows a word of length 1 which is capitalized, the program should assume the letter is an initial.)

CHAPTER 15

SIMPLE

FILE

MANIPULATION

All of our programs up to this point have stored their data in the main memory of the CPU. This has the advantage that the computer can process data in main memory more quickly and efficiently than it can if data are stored elsewhere.

On the other hand, storing data in main memory also creates some difficulties. For example, all data must be read into the CPU each time a program is run, and the amount of data is limited by the size of main memory in the CPU. In addition, all data inside the computer itself are destroyed after each program is run, and no data are saved from one run to another.

In this chapter, we see how to overcome some of these disadvantages by studying some basic ways that disk files can be used for long-term, bulk storage, and we apply these files to solve some problems. In these applications, we may give up the efficiency of storing all data in fast memory, but we do overcome the disadvantages mentioned above.

SECTION 15.1   STORING DATA ON A FILE—AN INTRODUCTION

When we analyze the flow of data through our programs up to now, we find that

- we use *Read* or *Readln* to move data from our keyboard or terminal into the program;
- we use *Write* or *Writeln* to move data back out.

This is shown on Figure 15–1.

This flow of data has several implications for our Pascal code. First, we must include *Input* and *Output* in our program header. Then, we use *Read* or *Readln* to enter data and *Write* and *Writeln* to print our data.

For data that involve a disk file rather than the terminal, our picture becomes somewhat more complex, as shown in Figure 15–2. Here we may

- bring data into our program either from a disk file (called "input file" in the figure) or from our terminal (or from both);
- move data out of our program either by putting the data on a disk file (called "output file" in the figure) or by printing at our terminal.

This more complex flow of information requires several additions to our Pascal program. First, we need to specify some file information in our program header, and we need to declare the type of data stored in our files.

Then, when we try to *Read*, we need to specify whether we expect to get data from the terminal or from the input file. When the computer is asked to get data, it must know what source to use. Similarly, when we *Write* results, we must specify where our results are to be sent. The computer must know whether the results should be printed at the terminal or in the output file.

We illustrate how these details are handled in Pascal by considering the following simple problem.

FIGURE 15–1 · **Flow of Data through a Program Using Only a Terminal**

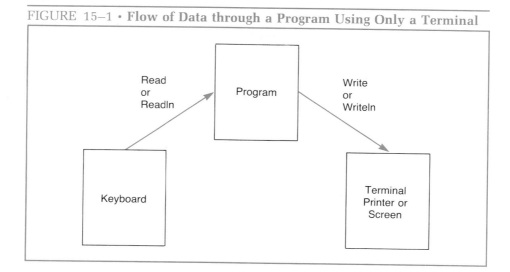

FIGURE 15-2 • **Flow of Data through a Program Using Both Terminal and File**

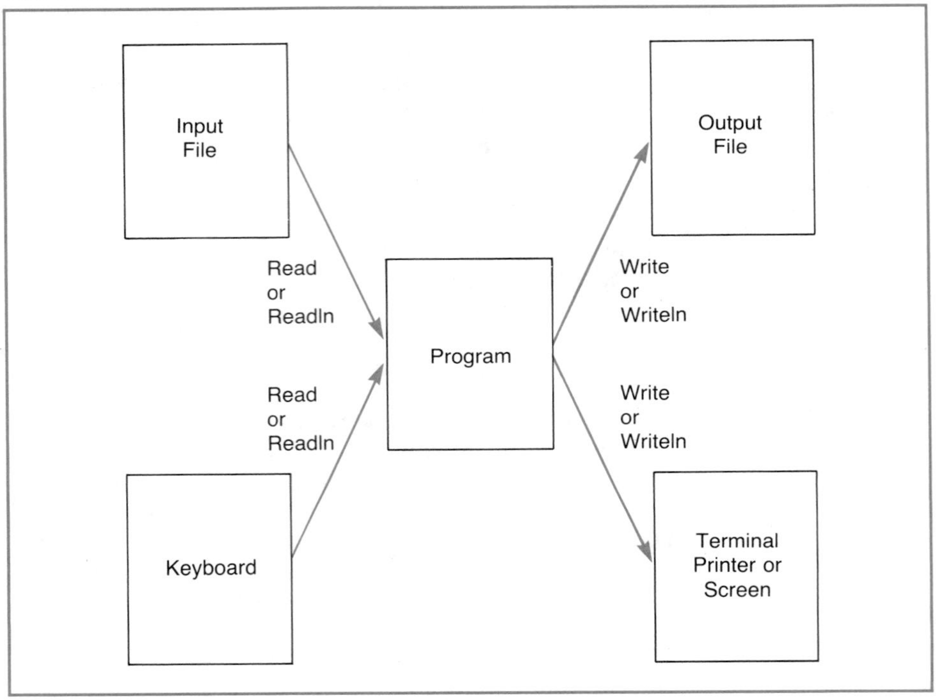

PROBLEM 15.1A — **Creating and Printing Text Files**

A. Write a program that reads some lines of input from a terminal and prints them on a file. Continue reading from the terminal until a blank line is entered.

B. Write a program that reads the lines from a file, copies them to another file, and prints the lines at the terminal.

This flow of data is shown in Figure 15-3.

To solve this problem, we write separate outlines for each part.

Outline for Part A of Problem 15.1A

Common Task: Read a line following the steps used in processing characters in the last chapter.

    A. Read a line.

    B. Record length of line.

    C. Check if line is blank.

  I. Specify file to be used for output.

FIGURE 15–3 · **Flow of Data for Problem 15.1A**

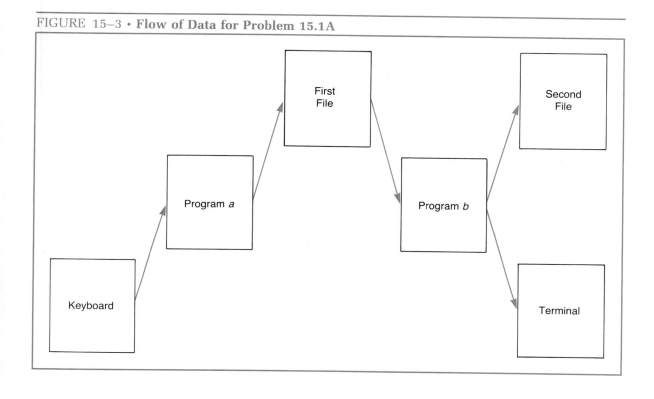

II. Read a line.
III. While input line is not blank:
   A. Print line on output file.
   B. Read a line.

Outline for Part B of Problem 15.1A

I. Specify files for input and for copying.
II. Process successive lines until end of input file is reached. For each line:
   A. Continue processing characters until the end of a line is reached. For each character:
      1. Read a character from input file.
      2. Copy character to new file.
      3. Print character at terminal.
   B. At end of line of input:
      1. Go to new line of input.
      2. Move to new line in output file and at terminal.

These outlines yield the following two programs.

```pascal
Program CreateTextFile (Input, Output, OutFile);
{This program transfers data from the terminal to a file;
 the program continues until a blank line is entered.}

Const MaxLength = 80;        {Length of line typed at terminal}

Type LineType = Array [1..MaxLength] of Char;

Var OutFile: Text;
    Line: LineType;
    Length: Integer;
    Index: Integer;
    BlankLine: Boolean;

Procedure ReadLine(Var Line: LineType; Var Length: Integer;
                   Var BlankLine: Boolean);
{This procedure reads a line of input from the terminal,
 determines its length, and records if the line is blank}
    Const Space = ' ';
    Begin
        Length := 0;
        If Eoln
            Then BlankLine := True
            Else Begin
                Repeat
                    Length := Length + 1;
                    Read (Line[Length]);
                    If Line[Length] <> Space
                        Then BlankLine := False
                Until Eoln Or (Length = MaxLength);
                Readln
                End
    End {ReadLine} ;

Begin {Main}
    {Specify output file}
    Rewrite (OutFile);

    {Read first line of input}
    Writeln ('Enter material to be transferred to a file.');
    Writeln ('Conclude by entering a blank line');
    ReadLine (Line, Length, BlankLine);

    {Transfer lines of data to output file}
    While Not BlankLine
      Do Begin
        {Print line on output file}
        For Index := 1 To Length
          Do Write (OutFile, Line[Index]);
        Writeln (OutFile);

        {Read a new line from the terminal}
        ReadLine  (Line, Length, BlankLine)
      End;

    Writeln ('Data Transferred')
End {Main} .
```

```
Program FileCopyAndPrint (InFile, CopyFile, Output);
{This program reads one file, copies it to another file,
 and writes the file to the terminal}

Var InFile: Text;      {The file which will be read}
    CopyFile: Text;    {The file for the next copy}
    Ch: Char;

Begin {Main}
    {Specify files for input and copying}
    Reset (InFile);
    Rewrite (CopyFile);

    {Process each line of input file until End Of File}
    While Not EOF(InFile)
      Do Begin

        {Process each character until End Of Line}
        While Not Eoln(InFile)
          Do Begin
            Read(InFile, Ch);
            Write(CopyFile, Ch);
            Write(Ch)
          End;

        {Move to new line}
        Readln (InFile);
        Writeln(CopyFile);
        Writeln
      End;

    Writeln ('-----File printed and copied-----')
End {Main} .
```

The following shows a typical run of the first program in which four lines are entered (including the blank line).

```
Enter material to be transferred to a file.
Conclude by entering a blank line
    This material will be transferred from the terminal to a disk file
by the first program run.  This first program continues until a blank line
is encountered.
    The second program then uses the disk file. creating a second file.
and printing out the data.

Data Transferred
```

In this program, we entered our data, but we did not print it out at the terminal. Instead, a new file has been created.

When we run the second program using this new file as input, we get the following.

```
     This material will be transferred from the terminal to a disk file
by the first program run.  This first program continues until a blank line
is encountered.
     The second program then uses the disk file, creating a second file,
and printing out the data.
-----File printed and copied-----
```

In addition, this second program creates a new copy of our original file.

Using Files Like Terminals

The programs listed above illustrate several important points about using files like terminals in Pascal programs.

At the start, when we wish to use file storage in our programs, we declare identifiers to stand for our files. This is done in two steps.

Step 1. We include file identifiers in our program header. In the example, the identifiers *Outfile, InFile,* and *CopyFile* were added. Here, we used *Input* since our program expected us to type some data from the terminal. If we did not need to enter data from the terminal, we could omit *Input* from our header. Similarly, we could omit *Output* if we did not print any data at our terminal.

Step 2. In the main program declarations, we specify the type of file for each identifier. When we use a file like a terminal, for reading and writing lines of data, we are considering our file as a *Text* file. Thus, we declared

Var InFile: Text;

to indicate that the identifier *InFile* would represent a file of *Text*.

Once we have declared our file identifiers, we must tell the machine to prepare to read or write with our file. This is done in one of two ways. We use the *Reset* statement to prepare the file to be read. For example, once we write

Reset (InFile)

we can perform *Read* operations from this file. Alternately, we use the *Rewrite* statement to prepare a new file for writing. For example, when we write

Rewrite (OutFile)

or

Rewrite (CopyFile)

we create a new file to write information out.

After we have declared file variables and prepared files for reading with the *Reset* statement, we can read from files just as we do from the terminal. Thus, we can consider a file as consisting of lines with characters or with numbers, and we can read individual characters or numeric values. Also, we can test for the end of a line and move to a new line in the file. For example,

Read (InFile, Ch)

allows us to get a new character *Ch* of data from a file called *InFile*. Similarly,

EOLN (InFile)

allows us to see if we are at the end of a line in the file. Also,

Readln (InFile)

moves us to a new line in the file. In fact, in reading from the terminal, *Read(Ch)*, *EOLN*, and *Readln* are just abbreviations that we can use in place of *Read(Input, Ch)*, *EOLN(Input)*, and *Readln(Input)*. In using files, we can specify a file identifier or *Input* as the first argument of our *Read*, *EOLN*, or *Readln*. However, if we omit this file identifier, Pascal assumes we are reading from *Input*. Otherwise, these statements work for files in just the same way that they do for the keyboard.

Next, in reading from a file, we can test if we have reached the End Of a *File* using the function *EOF*. The function

EOF (InFile)

is true when we have read the last character in the file *InFile* and false otherwise. Note that in reading our data in Part B of our solution, this function allowed us to determine very easily when we were done. In Part A, we spent much of our code testing for a blank line, but in Part B, we just test the *EOF* function. In fact, this same *EOF* function also can be applied to the keyboard. For example, *EOF* or *EOF (Input)* specifies when we reach the end of our data from the terminal. In typing, we may specify this end in various ways depending upon our terminal. However, once we indicate this end of file, we cannot read any more data from our terminal later in the program.

Similarly, once we declare file variables and prepare for writing with a *Rewrite* statement, we can write to files just as we write to our terminal. As with reading, we can imagine a file as being made up of a sequence of lines, and we can use

Write (OutFile, —)

and

Writeln (OutFile, —)

to print data on these lines in an appropriate format. Further, *Write(Ch)* and *Writeln* are just abbreviations for *Write(Output,Ch)* and *Writeln (Output)* and *Output* is assumed if a file identifier is not specified. In addition, in our printing, we may write numbers, Booleans, and string-type data on files just as we can at terminals.

In working with files, however, Pascal does not allow us to mix reading and writing with the same file. Thus, if we use

Reset (File1)

then we are only allowed to *Read* from this file. If we use

Rewrite (File2)

we can only *Write* to *File2*.

Examples. We illustrate these various capabilities further with two short examples.

A. Set up a text file containing the four lines:

     1A   True
     2B   False
     3C   True
     4D   False

B. Read the letters and numbers from this file, and print the results at the keyboard with the letter followed by the number. (Ignore the 'True' or 'False' at the end of each line for this processing.)

Discussion of Examples. In our processing, we consider two approaches.

Approach 1. We could use four *Writeln* statements to print our file, with one *Writeln* for each line. Then we could read the first two characters of each line, throw away the rest of the line, and then print these characters.

Approach 2. We could print three variables, *Number*, *Ch*, and *TOrF*, on each line. Our program would then have to initialize each of these variables and then recompute them in a loop. Similarly, in a loop, we could read a number and a letter from each line, throw away the rest of the line, and continue until we reach the end of the file.

Each approach to each part of our problem gives rise to a very simple outline, which is left for the reader.

In considering these different solutions, the first approach is quite concise and easy to use in situations where we need to store a very small amount of data in a file. In contrast, this second approach, which uses a loop, can be modified easily to store large amounts of data.

The resulting four programs illustrate many features of using files that we have already seen. First, we list the programs for Example A.

```
Program LoadFile (OutFile);
{This program prints four lines of data on OutFile}
Var OutFile: Text;
Begin
    Rewrite (OutFile);
    Writeln (OutFile, '1A  True');
    Writeln (OutFile, '2B False');
    Writeln (OutFile, '3C  True');
    Writeln (OutFile, '4D False')
End {Main} .
```

```
Program LoadFile {Version 2} (OutFile);
{This program prints four lines of data on OutFile}
Var OutFile: Text;
    Index: Integer;
    Ch: Char;
    TOrF: Boolean;
Begin
    Rewrite (OutFile);

    {Initialize Variables}
    Ch := 'A';
    TOrF := True;

    {Write each line in loop and prepare for next line}
    For Index := 1 To 4
      Do Begin
        Writeln (OutFile, Index:1, Ch, ' ', TOrF:5);
        Ch := Succ(Ch);
        TOrF := Not TOrF
      End
End {Main} .
```

When either of these programs are run, we will not see anything printed at the terminal. Instead, each program places data in a file as specified. The following programs then use this file to solve Example B.

```
Program FileRead (InFile, Output);
{This program reads a digit and a letter from InFile and print
 these values in reverse order.}
Var InFile: Text;
    Ch1, Ch2: Char;
    Index: Integer;
```

```
Begin
    Reset (InFile);

    {Print title}
    Writeln ('This program prints the starting digit and letter ',
         .      'from four lines of a file');
    Writeln ('These characters are:');

    {Read write characters for each line}
    For Index := 1 To 4
      Do Begin
         Readln (InFile, Ch1, Ch2);
         Writeln (Ch2:1, Ch1:2)
         End
End {Main} .
```

```
Program FileRead {Version 2} (InFile, Output);
{This program reads a digit and a letter from InFile and print
 these values in reverse order.}
Var InFile: Text;
    Number: Integer;
    Ch: Char;

Begin
    Reset (InFile);

    {Print title}
    Writeln ('This program prints the starting digit and letter ',
             'from four lines of a file');
    Writeln ('These characters are:');

    {Read write characters for each line until end of file}
    While Not EOF(InFile)
      Do Begin
         Readln (InFile, Number, Ch);
         Writeln (Ch:1, Number:2)
         End
End {Main} .
```

Either program for Example A can be run with either program for Example B. When either program for Example B runs, we get the following output.

```
This program prints the starting digit and letter from four lines of a file
These characters are:
A 1
B 2
C 3
D 4
```

These programs show that we can read and write with files using numbers, characters, and Booleans, just as we have before with the keyboard and terminal, using the *Read, Readln, Write,* and *Writeln* statements. Further, this example illustrates that when we work with files, we may not see any output at our terminal. For example, either program for Example A creates an output file, but we cannot tell this from our terminal. Thus, we often include lines such as

Writeln ('Printing Data On File');

at the beginning of our printing step, and we use

Writeln ('Printing on File Completed');

at the end. Then, we can monitor a program's progress from our terminal, and we know when the task is done. Without these lines, we may wonder if our program is doing anything at all.

SECTION 15.2   MORE GENERAL DATA STORAGE

The previous section illustrated how we can use files just as we do our keyboard or terminal. This is particularly helpful in applications in which we can organize our data into a sequence of lines of input or output. In other applications, this organization of data into lines may be rather awkward, and we may want to organize our files in another way. For example, we may want to store

- the Dow Jones Industrial Average for the past five years;
- words, including letters and length;
- product information for a grocery store, including product name, product code, package size, and retail price.

This section discusses an alternative structure for storing data in files that is more natural in these applications.

Our approach is to define a file for a particular type of data. For example, if we have

```
Const MaxLength = 30;
      SizeLength = 10;
Type  Word = Record
               Letters: Array [1..MaxLength] of Char;
               Length: Integer
               End;
      Item   = Record
               Name:   Array [1..MaxLength] of Char;
               Code:   Integer;
               Size:   Array [1..SizeLength] of Char;
               Price:  Real
               End
```

then we can declare

```
Var DowFile: File of Real;
    WordFile: File of Word;
    ProductFile: File of Item;
```

Here, we declare our files to contain a specified type of data rather than text. To illustrate how such files can be used, we consider the following example.

PROBLEM 15.2 | ## Dow Jones Averages

A. Write a program that reads past Dow Jones Industrial Averages and records these averages on a file. Continue reading data until a negative value is entered. Also, mark the end of the file with a negative value.

B. Write a program that reads the data on file and computes the high, low, and mean of the Dow Averages.

Discussion of Problem 15.2

In Part A, we can continue reading and writing as we did in the last section. However, here our data consist only of real numbers, and these numbers are not naturally organized in lines. Thus, we will not use a text file, but rather a file of reals.

In Part B, we read this file, processing each number as it is read. In our reading, we could read until *EOF*. However, here, for variety, we have used a sentinel, a negative number, to mark the end of our file.

As with the previous problem, we need a separate outline for Part A and for Part B.

Outline for Part A of Problem 15.2

I. Prepare for writing on a file.

II. Continue until a negative number is processed.
    A. Read a value from the keyboard.
    B. Print the value on the file.

Outline for Part B of Problem 15.2

I. Prepare for reading a file.

II. Process first value.
    A. Read value from file.
    B. Record that one value has been read.
    C. This value is both the current minimum and the current maximum.
    D. This value is the current sum of the values read.

III. Prepare for loop to process remaining values.
    A. Read next value from file.

IV. Process remaining values. While value is not negative:
    A. Record that another value has been read.
    B. Check for a new minimum or maximum value.
    C. Add the value to the sum of values read earlier.

        D. Read a new value from file.
     V. Compute mean.
    VI. Print results.

These outlines yield the following programs.

```
Program CreateDowFile (Input, Output, DowFile);
{This program reads Dow Jones Industrial Averages from a terminal
 and prints them on a file.}
Var DowFile: File of Real;
    DowAvg: Real;
Begin
    Writeln ('This program stores Dow Jones Averages for later use');

    Rewrite (DowFile);

    Writeln ('Please enter the averages');
    Writeln ('Conclude by typing a negative value');
    Repeat
        Read (DowAvg);
        Write (DowFile, DowAvg)
    Until (DowAvg < 0.0);

    Writeln;
    Writeln ('Data have been recorded on file.')
End {Main} .
```

```
Program ProcessDow (DowFile, Output);
{This program reads Dow Jones Industrial Averages from a file
 and computes the low, high and mean values.}
Var DowFile: File of Real;
    DowAvg: Real;
    Minimum: Real;
    Maximum: Real;
    NumberAvg: Integer;
    Sum: Real;
    Mean: Real;

Begin
    Writeln ('This program computes low, high, and mean Dow Jones Averages.');

    Reset(DowFile);

    {Process first value}
    Read(DowFile, DowAvg);
    NumberAvg := 1;
    Minimum := DowAvg;
    Maximum := DowAvg;
    Sum := DowAvg;

    {Prepare to process remaining values}
    Read(DowFile, DowAvg);
```

```
{Processing remaining values}
While (DowAvg >= 0.0)
  Do Begin
    NumberAvg := NumberAvg + 1;
    If DowAvg < Minimum
        Then Minimum := DowAvg;
    If DowAvg > Maximum
        Then Maximum := DowAvg;
    Sum := Sum + DowAvg;
    Read(DowFile, DowAvg)
  End;

{Compute Mean}
Mean := Sum / NumberAvg;

{Print Results}
Writeln ('Given the Dow Jones Averages in the file,');
Writeln ('     the minimum was ', Minimum:1:2);
Writeln ('     the maximum was ', Maximum:1:2);
Writeln ('     the mean value was ', Mean:1:2)

End {Main} .
```

When the first of these programs is run with some sample data, we get the following interaction:

```
This program stores Dow Jones Averages for later use
Please enter the averages
Conclude by typing a negative value
1066.0
1067.25
1080.5
1076.25
1093.75
1083.0
1103.5
1111.25
1120.75
1116.5
-3.0

Data have been recorded on file.
```

In this program, note how the addition of the last *Writeln* statement tells the user that the program has completed its work.

With this data, the second program gives the following results:

```
This program computes low, high, and mean Dow Jones Averages.
Given the Dow Jones Averages in the file,
      the minimum was 1066.00
      the maximum was 1120.75
      the mean value was 1091.88
```

These programs illustrate several points about files that are defined for particular types of data. First, we can specify that our files will store character data, numbers, or records by using a declaration:

Var FileName: File of DataType

In this program, we indicated that the *FileName* will contain data of the given *DataType*. As before with text files, the *FileName* is also included in the program header. Next, we use *Reset* or *Rewrite* to prepare a file for reading or writing, respectively.

Once the file is declared and *Reset*, we use the *Read* statement to obtain data from the file. As with text files, our syntax is

Read (FileName, Value1, Value2, . . .)

We add the *FileName* to our *Read* statement to indicate where our data are stored. Here, however, each variable must have the type specified by our file declaration. In the previous problem, we used

Read (DowFile, DowAvg)

where *DowAvg* had type *Real*. We could not read values of other types from the *DowFile*.

Similarly, once we declare and *Rewrite* our file, we can use the *Write* statement to place values on our file. The syntax is

Write (FileName, Value1, Value2, . . .)

and *Value1, Value2, . . .* must have the same type as the *DataType* for the file. Unlike text files, we cannot mix data types on one of these files.

In these files, data are *not* organized into lines. Thus, we cannot use *Readln* or *Writeln* to read or write data with these files. The *Readln* and *Writeln* statements only apply to text files. The following section gives a more extended example using these files.

SECTION 15.3   EXAMPLE: STORAGE OF LARGE DATA SETS

When we want to store large amounts of data on a file, we often find that we want to group pieces of data together in records; to correct or modify our data; and to retrieve particular data items.

These requirements are illustrated in the following problem.

PROBLEM 15.3   Grocery Checkout

At a grocery store cash register, a clerk enters a product code (with a light pen). From this code, the cash register prints the product name, product code, package size, and price.

    Write a program that will retrieve this information from a file given the code number. Also, write programs that allow this information to be stored on a file and modified.

Discussion of Problem 15.3

We consider the pieces of information for a particular product to be part of a single entity. We want to keep product information together in the following record.

```
Const NameLength = 40;
      SizeLength = 10;
Type  Product = Record
              Name: Packed Array [1..NameLength] of Char;
              Code: Integer;
              Size:  Packed Array [1..SizeLength] of Char;
              Price: Real
              End
```

With these declarations, we can use the same type of data entry we have seen before. Because product codes are positive, we will continue processing data until a negative code is entered. Since the outline is similar to what we used for data entry in the previous section, we proceed with the data entry program itself.

```
Program EnterGroceries (Input, Output, ProdFile);
{This program enters grocery information into a file}
Const NameLength = 40;
      SizeLength = 10;

Type Product = Record
         Name: Packed Array [1..NameLength] of Char;
         Code: Integer;
         Size: Packed Array [1..SizeLength] of Char;
         Price: Real
         End;
      GroceryFile = File of Product;

Var ProdFile: GroceryFile;

Procedure Enter (Var Item: Product);
{This procedure reads product name, size and price from the terminal.}
    Const BlankName = '                                        ';
          BlankSize = '          ';

    Var Index: Integer;
```

```pascal
    Begin
        With Item
          Do Begin

              {Read product name}
              Name := BlankName;
              Write ('Product name: ');
              Index := 0;
              While Not Eoln and (Index < NameLength)
                Do Begin
                  Index := Index + 1;
                  Read (Name[Index])
                End;
              Readln;

              {Read size}
              Size := BlankSize;
              Write('Package size: ');
              Index := 0;
              While Not Eoln and (Index < SizeLength)
                Do Begin
                  Index := Index + 1;
                  Read (Size[Index])
                End;
              Readln;

              {Read price}
              Write ('Price: ');
              Readln (Price)
          End
    End {Enter} ;

Procedure LoadFileWithData (Var ProdFile: GroceryFile);
{This procedure controls the reading of grocery data and then
  stores this data on a file}
    Var Item: Product;

    Begin
        Rewrite (ProdFile);

        Writeln ('Please enter product information, ',
                'ending with a negative product code');
        Write('Product code: ');
        Readln (Item.Code);
        While (Item.Code > 0)
          Do Begin
            Enter (Item);
            Write (Prodfile, Item);
            Write('Product code: ');
            Readln (Item.Code)
          End;
    End {LoadFileWithData} ;

Begin {Main}
    Writeln ('This program enters grocery information into a file');
    LoadFileWithData (ProdFile);
    Writeln ('Grocery information stored in file.')
End {Main} .
```

From this program, we see that we can store our product record on a file by declaring

Type GroceryFile = File of Product;
Var ProdFile: GroceryFile

or, more simply

Var ProdFile: File of Product

Then, we can use the *Rewrite* and *Write* statements as we did before. Note, however, that here we must print the data for the entire record at once. We cannot print the fields of the record separately, because the file contains entire records, not just separate pieces of these records.

Discussion of Problem 15.3. (Continued)

Once the product file is created, we can use it to retrieve our product information. Here, for each product code, we start at the beginning of our file and continue reading the product information until we find the code or until we run out of data in the file.

Outline for Returning Data in Problem 15.3

Repeat for each grocery item purchased (e.g., until the next product code is negative).

   I. Prepare to read grocery file from the beginning.
  II. Continue until code found or end of file.
     A. Read data for next product.
 III. Print results.
     A. If code found, print product information.
     B. If code not found, indicate that product information is missing.

This outline yields the following program.

```
Program RetrieveGroceries (Input, Output, ProdFile);
{This program retrieves grocery information from a file}
Const NameLength = 40;
      SizeLength = 10;

Type Product = Record
          Name: Packed Array [1..NameLength] of Char;
          Code: Integer;
          Size: Packed Array [1..SizeLength] of Char;
          Price: Real
          End;

     ProdFileType = File of Product;

Var ProdFile: ProdFileType;
```

```
Procedure Enter (Var DesiredCode: Integer);
{This procedure reads a product code from the terminal}
    Begin
        Write ('Please enter product code ',
               '(enter a negative code to stop):');
        Readln (DesiredCode)
    End {Enter} ;

Procedure Search (Var DataFile: ProdFileType;
                  DesiredCode: Integer; Var Item: Product);
{This procedure searches the DataFile for an Item with the DesiredCode}
    Begin
        {Prepare to read file from the beginning}
        Reset (DataFile);

        {Read file until code found or until end of file is found}
        {Program assumes at least one product item is stored in file}
        Repeat
            Read (DataFile, Item);
        Until EOF(DataFile) Or (Item.Code = DesiredCode)
    End {Search} ;

Procedure Print (Item: Product);
{This procedure prints the product information for the given item}
    Begin
        With Item
          Do Begin
            Writeln('Product Name','Code':36, 'Size':6, 'Price':13);
            Write (Name);
            Write (Code:8);
            Write ('  ', Size);
            Writeln(' $ ', Price:1:2)
          End;
        Writeln
    End {Print} ;

Procedure ControlProcessing (Var ProdFile: ProdFileType);
{This procedure controls the main steps in retrieving grocery data
 from the file}
    Var Item: Product;
        DesiredCode: Integer;

    Begin
        Enter (DesiredCode);
        While (DesiredCode > 0)
          Do Begin
            Search (ProdFile, DesiredCode, Item);
            If Item.Code = DesiredCode
                Then Print (Item)
                Else Writeln ('Product not listed on file');
            Enter (DesiredCode)
          End
    End {ControlProcessing} ;

Begin {Main}
    Writeln ('This program retrieves grocery information from a file');
    ControlProcessing (ProdFile);
End {Main} .
```

A sample interaction with this program appears below.

```
This program retrieves grocery information from a file
Please enter product code (enter a negative code to stop):2020
Product Name                              Code  Size        Price
Soggy Cereal                              2020  Large      $ 1.29

Please enter product code (enter a negative code to stop):1059
Product Name                              Code  Size        Price
Cavities Galore Candy                     1059  8 oz.      $ 1.25

Please enter product code (enter a negative code to stop):1789
Product not listed on file
Please enter product code (enter a negative code to stop):1081
Product Name                              Code  Size        Price
Moo Juice                                 1081  1 Quart    $ 0.98

Please enter product code (enter a negative code to stop):1002
Product Name                              Code  Size        Price
Tantalizing Toasties                      1002  24 oz.     $ 2.53

Please enter product code (enter a negative code to stop):-999
```

This program illustrates several additional features about data files. First, a *Reset* or a *Rewrite* statement prepares a file for reading or writing, respectively, and it places us at the beginning of the file. If we have read part of a file and then want to start over at the beginning of the file, we can use the *Reset* or *Rewrite* again. Each time we use these statements, we move back to the beginning of our file.

We also see that when we want to transfer data in a file from one program to another, the file variables in Pascal must be declared as global variables. Such files are called **external files.** In using these files, we cannot declare them inside a procedure, even if we only work with them in the procedure. All external files must be listed in the program header, so they are global identifiers, and they must be declared in the main program. On the other hand, Pascal does allow us to use file identifiers as reference parameters into procedures. In our example, we passed the parameter filename *ProdFile* into the *Search* procedure. However, Pascal does not permit the identifiers to be passed by value.

Discussion of File Manipulations in Problem 15.3

Finally we look at how we might modify our files in Pascal. First, we observe that files in Standard Pascal are **sequential files.** With Standard Pascal files, we always must start at the beginning of a file and then proceed value-by-value or record-by-record to the end. We cannot back up in our processing, and we cannot skip records. These Pascal limitations mean that we cannot modify a file in one step.

In order to modify a file, we first must find the record where the change is to be made by using *Read* statements. Then, after we determine our revised data, we will need to *Write* the new data on a file. However, since we can use *Read* only with *Reset* and *Write* only with *Rewrite*, we cannot use the *Read* to find our data and then use *Write* on the same file to make the change. Instead, we will copy our file to a second file, making the change when we reach the desired record. After the file is copied to the new file, we can copy the entire file back. Our original file is now modified, and we can follow the same process again if further changes are needed.

Outline for File Modification in Problem 15.3

For each change desired:

I. Determine product code of item to be changed.
II. Copy successive records from the product file to a temporary file until specified product code is found.
III. Enter revised record for the item.
IV. Write the revised product information on the temporary file.
V. Copy the rest of the product file to the temporary file.
VI. Copy the temporary file, with corrections, back to the product file.

In this outline, Steps III through VI only apply if we can find the appropriate record.

In the following program, this outline is implemented as a procedure that we call as needed from our main program. This program uses the same *Enter* procedure that we used in our data entry program earlier in this section. We omit the *Enter* procedure in the following listing.

```
Program ModifyGroceryFile (Input, Output, ProdFile);
{This program allows changed in the grocery information on a file}
Const NameLength = 40;
      SizeLength = 10;

Type Product = Record
        Name: Packed Array [1..NameLength] of Char;
        Code: Integer;
        Size: Packed Array [1..SizeLength] of Char;
        Price: Real
        End;

    ProdFileType = File of Product;

Var ProdFile: ProdFileType;
    TempFile: ProdFileType;
    Answer: Char;

{Procedure Enter (Var Item: Product)
    should be inserted here}
```

```
Procedure Modify;
{This procedure changes a specified item in the file}
    Var Item: Product;
        DesiredCode: Integer;

    Begin
        {Determine product code of item to be changed}
        Write ('Enter code of product to be changed:');
        Readln (DesiredCode);

        {Copy successive records until specified record found}
        Reset (ProdFile);
        Rewrite (TempFile);
        Read (ProdFile, Item);
        While Not EOF(ProdFile) And (Item.Code <> DesiredCode)
           Do Begin
             Write (TempFile, Item);
             Read  (ProdFile, Item)
           End;

        If Item.Code <> DesiredCode
            Then Writeln ('Product not found')
            Else Begin
                {Make change}
                Enter (Item);
                Write (TempFile, Item);

                {Copy rest of file}
                While Not EOF(ProdFile)
                   Do Begin
                     Read  (ProdFile, Item);
                     Write (TempFile, Item)
                   End;

                {Copy back to original file}
                Rewrite (ProdFile);
                Reset   (TempFile);
                While Not EOF(TempFile)
                   Do Begin
                     Read  (TempFile, Item);
                     Write (ProdFile, Item)
                   End

            End
    End {Modify};

Begin {Main}

    Writeln ('This program makes changes in a product file');

    Repeat
        Modify;
        Write ('Do you wish to make another change? ');
        Readln (Answer);
    Until (Answer in ['n', 'N'] );

    Writeln ('Changes completed')
End {Main} .
```

A sample run is shown below:

```
This program makes changes in a product file
Enter code of product to be changed:2020
Product name: Improved Tantalizing Toasties
Package size: 23 oz.
Price: 2.53
Do you wish to make another change? y
Enter code of product to be changed:1059
Product name: More Cavities
Package size: 9 oz.
Price: 1.40
Do you wish to make another change? n
Changes completed
```

This program shows how we can modify and copy files by working from the beginning of a file to the end.

In all our work with files, we first must specify the type of data that we will use, such as text, numbers, characters, or records. Then, we reset or rewrite a file before we use the file and when we want to return to the beginning of the file. Thereafter, we use *Read* or *Write*, specifying our file as we move data between our file and our program.

SECTION 15.4   EXAMPLE: LETTER WRITING

The previous section illustrated one important use of files to store large amounts of data for easy access. A second common computer application involves changing the format of the data in a file. In this section, we outline one such application; we discuss some details for a few simple cases; and we indicate directions for more sophisticated uses. The details for these more complex applications are left as exercises at the end of the chapter.

Form Letters

In one common application, we want to send the same letter to several places, but want each letter personalized. For example, we may want to write to many companies about the possibility of employment, repeating the same basic letter to each firm. However, each letter should be addressed to the appropriate individual at a specific address.

One approach involves three steps.

1. We write our form letter, marking the places where we need to enter our "personalized" information. This form letter is stored in a file.
2. We write a program that copies the form letter many times, asking us for the appropriate special data each time. These completed letters are stored on a new file.
3. We print the completed letters on nice stationery.

To illustrate the general process, we outline one sample form that we might use. In this form, we write a single letter for employment. However, in place of the name, address, and salutation ("Dear . . ."), we include special lines indicating a name or address is needed. Thus, our letter might begin

March 1, 1989

    **Name
    **Address 1
    **Address 2
    **Address 3

    **Salutation
      I am interested in learning about
opportunities for employment in your company.

.

.

.

Here, we have included the appropriate data, and we have written the body of our letter for each company. However, we have also left a line for a person's name, three lines for the person's address, and a line for our salutation.

Outline for Letter Generation Program. As our second step, we write a program that reads our form letter. Whenever the program encounters a line starting with the special code '**', the program asks the user to enter the appropriate special information, and this input is placed in the new file. For all other lines in our form letter, the program simply copies the lines to the new file.

I. Rewrite new file.
II. Repeat for each "personalized" letter desired.
    A. Begin at start of form letter.
        1. Reset form letter file.
        2. Start copy on a new page.
    B. Repeat the following until end of form letter is encountered.
        1. Read line of form letter.
        2. If line begins with '**'
            a. Tell user to supply the desired information.
            b. Read new line from keyboard.
        3. Copy line to new letter.
    C. Ask if user wants to continue.

In the following program, we place the details of reading and writing a line in separate procedures. Then, we use these procedures for reading or writing from files or the terminal through the use of appropriate parameters. Also, note that this program uses a new procedure from the Pascal library called *Pass* that specifies that output should start on a new page.

```
Program LetterGenerator (Input, Output, FormFile, OutFile);
{This program 'personalizes' letters in the FormFile, giving
 completed text in the OutFile}

Var FormFile: Text;
    OutFile: Text;
    Answer: Char;

Procedure CopyLetter;
{This procedure makes one copy of the form letter}

    Const LineLengtn = 75;
        FormFeed = 12;     {This is the ASCII code for a form feed}

    Type LineType = Packed Array [1..LineLengtn] of Char;

    Var Line: LineType;

    Procedure ReadLine (Var Line: LineType; Var InFile: Text);
    {This program reads a line of text from the InFile}
        Var Index: Integer;
        Begin
            {Read line from file}
            Index := 0;
            While Not EOLN(InFile) And (Index < LineLength)
              Do Begin
                Index := Index + 1;
                Read (InFile, Line[Index])
              End;
            Readln (InFile);

            {Add nulls to line if more space remains}
            While (Index < LineLength)
              Do Begin
                Index := Index + 1;
                Line[Index] := Chr(0)
              End
        End {ReadLine};

    Procedure PrintLine (Line: LineType; Var OFile: Text);
    {This procedure prints a line of text on the OFile}
        Var Index: Integer;
        Begin
            Index := 1;
            While (Index <= LineLength)
              Do Begin
                If (Line[Index] = Chr(0))
                    Then Index := LineLength
                    Else Write (OFile, Line[Index]);
                Index := Index + 1
              End;
          Writeln (OFile)
        End {PrintLine} ;

    Procedure AskUser (Var Line: LineType);
    {This procedure asks the user for some 'personalized' data
     and reads this data from the terminal}
        Const Space = ' ';
```

```
        Begin
            Line[1] := Space;
            Line[2] := Space;
            Write ('Enter:');
            PrintLine (Line, Output);
            ReadLine (Line, Input)
        End {AskUser};

    Begin {CopyLetter}
        Reset (FormFile);
        Writeln (OutFile, Chr(FormFeed));
        While Not EOF(FormFile)
            Do Begin
                ReadLine (Line, FormFile);
                If (Line[1] = '*') And (Line[2] = '*')
                    Then AskUser(Line);
                PrintLine (Line, OutFile)
            End
    End {CopyLetter} ;

Begin {Main}
    Rewrite (Outfile);
    Repeat
        CopyLetter;
        Write ('Do you want to make another copy? ');
        Readln (Answer)
    Until (Answer = 'n') Or (Answer = 'N')
End {Main} .
```

A sample run of this program for the form letter described above follows.

```
Enter:  Name
Dr. Mathe Matics
Enter:  Address 1
Department of Quantitative Studies
Enter:  Address 2
The One, Two, Three Company
Enter:  Address 3
Infinity is, Big
Enter:  Salutation
Dear Dr. Matics:
Do you want to make another copy? y
Enter:  Name
Mr. Al Gorithm
Enter:  Address 1
Department of Problem Solving
Enter:  Address 2
Corporation for Pascal Programming (CFPP)
Enter:  Address 3
Good Style,  Counts
Enter:  Salutation
Dear Mr. Gorithm:
Do you want to make another copy? n
```

In addition to applications by individuals, these letter generation programs are used widely by businesses for promoting or selling products. Large numbers of "personalized" letters can be sent easily to a wide audience with very little human effort.

SECTION 15.5	LARGE-SCALE DATA STORAGE

The first part of this chapter has presented some simple ways that data can be stored on a file and then retrieved or modified. Our major techniques involved reading, writing, and copying of files, and our applications involved storing our own data in a convenient way. In these applications, we collected our own data, entered them into our own file, and processed the data for our own personal use. In these cases, the computer serves as a convenient, efficient filing cabinet.

Beyond this ability to store and manipulate data, computers have two capabilities that can allow data files to be used by many people in general applications.

- A single computer can be used by many people at the same time. Thus, computers can provide access to the same data for many users.
- A single computing system can store, retrieve, and process a huge amount of data in a short amount of time.

This section examines some of the consequences that arise when these capabilities are utilized. We will see that some services we may take for granted could not exist without these capabilities. We also see that the storage of data and potential access to many people can have various social implications. By looking at several applications of large scale data storage, we will address these issues.

Applications

We first outline three applications. In each case, computers store the data and also store some relationships among the data. In computer science, this collection of data and relationships is called a **data base.**

TWA Reservation System.[1] In a particularly impressive system, TWA maintains its entire reservation system as a very large data base. With this system, ticket agents around the world are able to accomplish many tasks, including computing fares, making reservations, issuing tickets, and assigning seats.

In this system, current reservation status information is kept on each flight for the next 11 months, and individual ticket information is stored

[1]For more information, see David Gifford and Alfred Spector, "The TWA Reservation System," *Communications of the ACM*, Vol 27, No. 7, July 1984, pp. 650–665.

for each passenger. Thus, ticket agents around the world can receive up-to-the-minute information on what flights are available between any two airports at any time. Also, through a cooperative effort among many airlines, the TWA system can provide information about flights on other airlines as well.

The system provides an excellent illustration in which the capabilities of computers, already mentioned, are needed to provide a service. In this application, reservation information for a flight must be kept in a single place, so two ticket agents at different locations cannot sell the same seat to different travelers. Also, the scope of this operation makes a manual system impractical. In this case, the TWA system includes between 11,000 and 12,000 terminals, and requests for information average 120 messages per second at peak times. The system must maintain records for 1 to 1.5 million passengers at any time, and the total amount of data in storage contains about 2 billion characters. Finally, in making reservations, customers and agents typically want a response very quickly. The TWA system processes 90% of its transactions in under 3 seconds; the average time is 1.5 seconds. With this quantity of data and with this demand for processing, computers are essential to disseminate the information needed by travel agents and to record individual reservations.

National Crime Information Center. The National Crime Information Center (NCIC) is another very large data base. Administered by the FBI, NCIC stores information related to crime, including thousands of active records on

- wanted persons
- wanted vehicles
- license tags
- wanted articles
- guns
- securities
- boats
- criminal histories
- missing persons

Beyond the FBI itself, this system communicates with state and local computers to disseminate information to law enforcement personnel throughout the country. Police officers can use this interconnected system to check for criminal activity or potentially dangerous situations quickly and efficiently. For example, when a police officer stops a car for speeding, the officer can check if the car has been reported stolen. This serves to warn the officer about whether he or she is walking into a potentially dangerous situation before actually approaching the driver of the vehicle.

As with the TWA Reservation System, computers are essential to the NCIC because a large quantity of data must be processed quickly and made available through many terminals.

Internal Company Files. While the previous data files were both very large and accessible by thousands of terminals around the country, more limited files are used by most large companies, governmental agencies, educational institutions, and other organizations. For example,

* companies keep personnel records in files
* educational institutions record registration information and student transcripts
* organizations maintain mailing lists
* hospitals and medical centers store medical records

In each case, information is stored in one or more computers for easy retrieval and processing. Changes can be made in the data easily, and the information can be obtained by the necessary personnel efficiently.

Social Issues

While the establishment of data files is often motivated by the need for efficient storage and retrieval of information, these same qualities raise various social issues. For example, we can ask

Will data be used in the way they were intended?

Will dissemination of data invade an individual's privacy?

How will errors be corrected when they arise?

What happens if the computer goes down?

Each of these questions is the subject for a great deal of discussion and controversy.

Privacy and Security. Whenever several people can retrieve information from a file, the person who entered the data may not be the person who retrieves the data. Thus, we must ask whether information can find its way to people who should not have it. Several examples illustrate some potential problems and solutions. In selling airline tickets, TWA may record an individual's credit card number. Clearly such information should not circulate freely. Thus, TWA's computer system involves various allowed levels of access to data and a system of passwords. In addition, the training of agents includes instruction on what information can be given to whom.

Similarly, license tag information can include name and address data. This can be valuable in locating missing vehicles, but it can also help burglars identify people who have left the state on a trip. (A well packed, out-of-state car is easy to spot, and its owner is likely to be away from home for awhile.) Thus, NCIC must be sure that only authorized law enforcement personnel can obtain license tag information quickly and easily.

In each of these examples, the data stored are very important and useful in the intended application, but there is some potential for data to be misused. More generally, in any large data base, procedures and safeguards are needed to ensure that the data are used responsibly.

In a related area, dissemination of data can also invade an individual's privacy. For example, organizations may sell their membership lists to companies who want to advertise. Thus, by joining one organization, a person may find that his or her address or telephone number has been circulated to various groups. As a consequence, the individual may be bothered by letters or telephone calls.

As another example, in a doctor's office or in a hospital, a patient may volunteer some medical information because it might aid a current diagnosis. That information is given with the understanding that it will be kept confidential. The information simply is not anyone else's business.

In another area, student grades are confidential information. Certainly, a student is free to discuss what he or she received in a course, but the student may choose not to do so. (For example, the student may be embarrassed by doing particularly well or particularly poorly.)

In each of these cases, a person should be able to expect that certain information will not be distributed to other people. However, when that data are stored in a machine that can be accessed by several people, the possibility does exist for that data to be distributed to unauthorized people.

Accuracy and Reliability. When data are stored in a computer, a user normally will expect that the information is complete and correct, and the user may act according to this assumption. For example, if a car is listed as stolen, an officer will assume it has not been recovered. Similarly, if a credit check shows a history of missed payments, a loan officer in a bank may turn down a loan request.

These cases illustrate the importance of maintaining data files in which the data are complete and correct. Thus, whenever large files are being used, procedures are needed to help check data for accuracy, and means are needed to correct errors after they are found.

All of the applications we have discussed assume that a computer system is running smoothly and correctly. However, machinery can fail, so we must consider the possibility that our system may not be working. We need to decide what we will do when the computer goes down. For example, we must ask

Will our entire company operation come to a halt if the system crashes?

What happens if a fire in the computer room destroys the disks attached to our main system?

Can we make contingency plans to do some tasks manually until the system is repaired?

Should we have backup equipment available in case our regular machinery fails?

Once our system is fixed, how can we resume normal operations?

When large quantities of data are essential to a project, such questions cannot be ignored. For example, operations at TWA come to a halt when their computers stop. Thus, they have a considerable amount of backup hardware, and they have well-designed procedures to allow them to switch over to this equipment.

In such large applications, computers allow the storage, processing, and dissemination of data that are needed to do the work required. However, the value of these systems depends upon their working reliably, and the systems must be able to recover if and when they malfunction.

SUMMARY

1. Data can be stored and retrieved from two general types of files.
    a. **Text files** allow the programmer to work with files in the same way that he or she works with a keyboard and terminal. Text files are organized into lines of data.
    b. **Files of data** enable the programmer to organize data in other ways. Such files can contain data of any declared type, including Booleans, characters, numeric data, and records.
2. In using these files, we proceed in several steps.
    a. We include an external file identifier in our program header, and we declare the type of the file. (This is the only instance in Pascal where an identifier must be declared globally. Reference parameters are allowed, but file identifiers may not be declared locally or as value parameters.)
    b. We prepare to work with the file using a *Reset* or *Rewrite* statement.
    c. We work with the file **sequentially;** we start at the beginning of the data in our file, and we work line-by-line or record-by-record to the end using *Read* or *Write* statements.
3. With these simple capabilities, we can store and retrieve data from files, copy data, and modify data.
4. These capabilities also allow us to consider many new applications. For example, we can store data from one program for use later on, we can generate letters, or we can store large amounts of data for use by many people.
5. Some of these applications allow us to solve problems that could not be solved otherwise. However, they also can raise various social issues, including the completeness and correctness of data, privacy, reliability, and the responsible use of data.

EXERCISES

15.1 *Grocery File Updating.*
   a. Write a program that reads a product code from the keyboard and then deletes that product from the grocery file of Section 15.3.
      HINT: Copy the old grocery file to a new one, omitting the specified product. Then copy the new file back.
   b. Write a program that adds new product information to the grocery file of Section 15.3.
      HINT: Copy the old file to a new one. Then copy the information back, adding data entered from the keyboard.
   c. Combine parts (a) and (b) in a program that allows various modifications in a grocery file, including adding new products, modifying data, and deleting products. In this program, the user should be able to continue modifying the information stored until the user asks to quit.

15.2 *Grocery Check Out.*
   a. Modify the grocery program of Section 15.3 so that the computer records all products purchased by customers and then prints a complete listing of items purchased and the total grocery bill for the customers.
   b. Modify part a. so that the product list is printed in order of ascending price.

15.3 *EOLN not defined if EOF True.* The programs in Section 15.1 all assume that a text file ends with a complete line; we assume the file does not end in the middle of a line (before "Return" is encountered). Without this assumption, a programmer encounters the following difficulty.
   • *EOF* always specifies *True* or *False*, depending upon whether the end of a file is reached.

KEY TERMS, PHRASES, AND CONCEPTS		ELEMENTS OF PASCAL SYNTAX	
Data Bases	Large Scale	*EOF*	*Page*
File Initialization	Applications	*File Of*	*Reset*
Reset	Sequential Files	Modified Statements	*Rewrite*
Rewrite	Social Issues	*EOLN*	*Text*
File Manipulation	Completeness	Program Header	
Modifying	Error Correction	*Read*	
Reading	Privacy	*Write*	
Writing	Reliability		
File Type and Declaration	Responsible Use		
File of Data	Text Processing		
Text	Letter Generator		

• *EOLN* is defined only if *EOF* is false.

Thus, at the end of a file, we cannot test *EOLN*.

Write a revised *EndLine* function that will be true at the end of lines and at the end of files and false otherwise. We want to use *EndLine* to test for the end of a line of data anywhere in the program; *EndLine* works even if the file stops in the middle of a line.

15.4 *Storage of Data on a File.* When we perform experiments, it is often helpful to store the data obtained on a file for later processing. Write a program that reads pairs of numbers from a terminal and stores them on a file. Thus, the file will consist of records, when each record contains two values.

15.5 *Least Squares in Stored Data.* Write a program that reads the pairs of numbers

$$(x_1, y_1), (x_2, y_2), \ldots , (x_n, y_n)$$

from the file created in the previous problem and then computes the average x-value and the average y-value for this data, and the standard deviation for the x-values and for the y-values.

[The above two problems were suggested by John Vogel.]

15.6 *Weekly Business Calendar.* Write a program that prints on a file an appointment calendar for a normal business week (Monday to Friday, 8:00 a.m. to 5:00 p.m.). The calendar should have the following form.

```
         Monday      Tuesday    Wednesday    Thursday    Friday
 8:00 +-----------+-----------+-----------+-----------+-----------+
      !           !           !           !           !           !
      !           !           !           !           !           !
      !           !           !           !           !           !
      !           !           !           !           !           !
 9:00 +-----------+-----------+-----------+-----------+-----------+
      !           !           !           !           !           !
      !           !           !           !           !           !
      !           !           !           !           !           !
10:00 +-----------+-----------+-----------+-----------+-----------+
      !           !           !           !           !           !

      .           .           .           .           .           .
      .           .           .           .           .           .
      .           .           .           .           .           .

      !           !           !           !           !           !
 4:00 +-----------+-----------+-----------+-----------+-----------+
      !           !           !           !           !           !
      !           !           !           !           !           !
      !           !           !           !           !           !
 5:00 +-----------+-----------+-----------+-----------+-----------+
```

15.7 *Letter Generator with Embedded Commands.* The Letter Generator of Section 15.4 allowed us to print personalized names and addresses on separate lines, but it did not allow us to include a person's name or a company in the middle of a line. For example, our form letter could not mention a "position as Programmer at The One, Two, Three Company."

Write a new letter generator that permits the user to insert material within a line. The program should scan the form letter for the signal '**', and the program should use the word following '**' as a prompt for the user. For example, given

> . . . ** Position . . .

the computer should print

> Enter Position:

and the user's response should be inserted at this point in the letter.

15.8 *Letter Generator—Automated Salutation.* In the Letter Generator of Section 15.4, we had to enter both a person's name and the salutation. However, we can streamline the process if we make some assumptions about the form of a person's name. For example, suppose we assume that a name will have the form

> Title . . . LastName

such as

> Dr. I. J. Kay

or

> Prof. Henry M. Walker

When names are in this form, we can extract the title and last name information to get a salutation.

> Dear Title LastName:

Modify the program of Section 15.4 so that this salutation is inserted automatically, given the *Name* information.

NOTE: Such programs can produce undesirable results if some names do not follow our assumption. For example, consider the result if we used a name

> Director, Personnel Office

15.9 *Fully Automated Letter Generator.*
  a. Modify the Letter Generator of Section 15.4 to include the modifications discussed in the previous problems. In particular, the program should insert information within lines and determine the salutation automatically.

b. Modify part (a) so that the program reads names and addresses from a file.

c. Modify part (b) so that a person's address may be either 2, 3, or 4 lines long. In this program, assume we end our addresses with a blank line.

NOTE: Programs of this sort are commonly used with mailing lists compiled by publishers and organizations. Businesses may use such lists to send literature or advertising to a wide audience. The resulting mailings may or may not be of interest to those receiving the mail.

Also, due to the automated nature of the process, one often finds some of the assumptions of the generators are not always met. For example, as Chairman of the Department of Mathematics, I once received a special offer for members of the "Mathematics Family." Practically, it usually costs a company more to check for such problems than it does to mail out the letter.

15.10 *Address Book.* A popular application of microcomputers involves the storage of name, address, and telephone information to form an address book. In such an application, a user must be able to
• add entries (including name, address, and telephone number);
• change any part of an entry (which is useful not only when a person moves but also if the user makes a typographical error initially);
• delete entries;
• retrieve an entire entry from a name;
• print the entire name, address, and telephone information in the form of a directory.
Write a program for such an address book.

15.11 *Expanded Address Book.* Modify your program for the previous address book problem so that a single entry can include the first names of each member of a family. Retrieval of information then should be possible using any of these first names with a family's last name.

15.12 *Simple Calendar.* Write a program that prints on a file a calendar for a given month. The program should read the month and year from the keyboard and then print the appropriate calendar on a file.

15.13 *Season's Greetings Card List.* During the December holidays, we may send large numbers of cards to various friends and acquaintances. In this process, records may be kept about where each card is sent and when a card is received.

a. Modify the previous address book program, so that an entry stores information for which cards were sent this year, last year, and the year before, and whether a card was received from an individual for each of these years. The program should allow retrieval of these entries for
• a card sent this year;
• a card sent either of the past two years;

  • a card received this year;
  • a card received either of the past two years;
  • a card sent this year, but one not received;
  • a card received this year, but one not sent.

  b. Write a second program that updates the file after the season is over. In preparation for the next year, records about cards sent or received become a year older, and we can discard the information for two years ago. Also, before the new season begins, no cards have been sent or received for the coming year.

15.14 *Use by Police.* Talk to your local police department about how they use computers in law enforcement. Your questions might include the following:
  • What applications are computerized and why?
  • What data are kept?
  • Who has access to what data?
  • How is individual privacy protected?

15.15 *OCLC and RLN.* Many college and university libraries cooperate in various technical ways through nationwide computerized systems, such as OCLC and the Research Library National (RLN). For example, the computer can eliminate much duplication of work in cataloging books, and large data bases can help locate books for interlibrary loan. Talk to a librarian in your school to see if your school is connected to a computer network. If so, discuss how the computer is used and what benefits are obtained from this application.

15.16 *Social Issues.* Using the resources in your library, investigate further one of the social issues discussed in this chapter, and see how these issues apply in a particular situation.

15.17 *National Data Bank.* In the 1960s, a proposal was made to combine all of the data bases within the Federal Government (excluding some military and IRS data) into a single large data base. Advocates of this system argued that such a system would be much more efficient than spreading the data over the thousands of systems kept by various agencies. Thus, such a system would save considerable sums of money. Opponents cited potential problems involving privacy and responsible use. At the end of the debate, the proposal was defeated. Locate information on both sides of this argument from your library, and write a paper taking a stand on one side of the issue.

CHAPTER 16

THE SOFTWARE
LIFE CYCLE
AND ITS IMPLICATIONS

From the very first section of this book, we have considered computing as part of the overall problem solving process, and our primary motivation for learning various algorithms and programming statements has been to solve problems. In this chapter, we refine and expand our understanding of this process by considering the entire software life cycle. This life cycle begins when we first tackle a problem and extends beyond the writing and testing of programs to include subsequent changes we may wish to make. In this discussion, we find that program modification, done after a program is first written, is an extremely important part of any large software project, and this modification phase has many implications.

SECTION 16.1   SOFTWARE LIFE CYCLE

This section describes the **software life cycle,** which includes the following five phases in the life of a program.

   I. Specifications
  II. Algorithm Design
 III. Coding

IV. Verification and Testing

V. Maintenance

Further, in each of these phases, we need to document our work from two perspectives so that we know what we have done and so that we can tell users how to run our programs effectively. An overview of this software life cycle is shown in Figure 16–1.

Phase I: Specifications

The first phase of the software life cycle is precisely the first step in problem solving; we need to develop a careful **specification** of the problem to be solved. We must describe each type of input (including possible abbreviations and reasonable values), each type of processing request, all required outputs, and any important response times. Often, this work is done largely using terminology familiar to the user or customer, who understands what must be done and how the application can be useful.

Of course, in textbooks, this work is typically written in the form of precise problems, and the student can take this work for granted. However, in real applications, this task can require considerable time and effort in interviewing users, writing proposed plans, and reviewing proposals with customers. On large projects, such writing of specifications may well take up 10% of the entire staff time devoted to the project, and several people may work full-time on this effort for several months (or even years). The resulting written specifications may be several hundred pages long and fill a few notebooks. This first phase of software development is crucial in designing software that meets the users' needs.

Phase II: Design

The **design phase** also parallels the corresponding step in problem solving. Once the specifications tell us what we need to do, we move to the design phase, in which we decide how we will perform these tasks. For example, we may develop algorithms to perform the desired processing, and we may design appropriate ways to store data.

Then, once a general design is completed, we can survey hardware and software packages to see what equipment and software are available. In some cases, we may find that existing packages already will do the work we need, and we may have little additional design or programming work left to do. In other cases, we may find existing hardware and software may do some of the job, but we need to adapt existing packages to meet specific needs. In still other cases, we may find little software available to help us, and we must begin by selecting the computer equipment and programming language(s) to be used.

Next, when existing packages will not do our entire job, we need to concentrate on those parts that remain. Here, we divide the overall project into major pieces, called **modules,** and we describe each in considerable detail, writing pre- and post-assertions and calling formats and developing

FIGURE 16–1 • **Software Life Cycle**

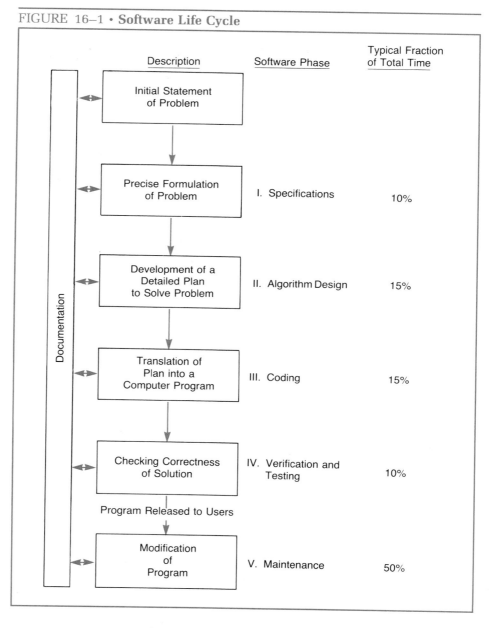

detailed algorithms. This gives us a detailed design for our project, in which the project is divided into pieces using a top-down methodology and in which each piece is described carefully.

Again, in textbooks, much of this work is stated or implied in various problems. For example, one can guess how data will be stored and used for problems in Chapter 8. However, in real applications, this design work can involve great detail, and this work can be the difference between packages that perform poorly and those that work well. For example, in real applications, considerable time can be spent designing the layout of each terminal screen that a user might see. Each character of each screen is analyzed for such things as clarity, ease of use, and uniformity.

On large projects, this design work may consume another 15% of the entire staff time devoted to a project, and the final algorithm designs and module specifications may fill a dozen notebooks and exceed a thousand pages. Detailed design work lies at the heart of the problem solving process, and this phase may involve some of the most difficult work in the entire software life cycle.

Phase III: Coding

Programming or **coding** itself begins only after a complete module is designed. A programmer is given a complete specification of all inputs (including their order and syntax), all outputs (including complete formatting instructions), and all required algorithms. In this context, the programmer's success is measured by the degree to which the module (program, procedure, function) runs efficiently and meets its specifications. In coding, the programmer is expected to follow the detailed design exactly, and the overall system's performance and correctness depend on the interactions of the modules as well as on the efficient functioning of the modules themselves.

In real-world applications, coding takes on a much less significant role than one might expect. For example, in large projects, only 15% of the staff time is spent coding. This involves about the same amount of effort that is directed to the design phase alone, and considerably less time than the total work required prior to coding.

Phase IV: Verification and Testing

In previous chapters, we have observed that we can test our work at many points throughout the development process to identify and correct errors as soon as possible. For example, in Chapter 11, we mentioned walk throughs, design reviews, and module testing. With these techniques, we hope to correct mistakes early, before these pieces are used later on. Each programmer also can use these techniques to test his or her separate modules.

Beyond this testing of individual modules by the programmers themselves, the responsibility for testing entire packages is often assigned to a separate group of people who test all aspects of the overall system to be sure that the final system behaves according to its specifications. This testing group often begins work as soon as specifications are available, and the group spends considerable effort developing test cases, even before any code is finished. Further, this testing group usually works separately from other development groups, and the management of the testing group is often different from the management of the designers and programmers. This allows evaluators to make objective conclusions about any software produced; testers are free from possible repercussions from their boss if they report an error. Thus, in large software development projects, testing is given an important position, separate from the other areas of development.

In testing, considerable time is spent determining how to test, so that each feature of the system will be tested for accuracy and efficiency. Many tests may be run concurrently to determine how various modules interact with each other and how many requests of various types can be run in a specified length of time. Further, special purpose hardware is available to help monitor processing.

This emphasis on testing in large projects may be substantially greater than one sees in a typical programming assignment for a course. In large projects, in which many modules interact and many users may try a wide range of input data, we may find that approximately 10% of the entire staff time is devoted to the testing of an entire system.

Phase V: Maintenance

Following testing, a program is released for general use, and the software enters the final (and, one would hope, long) phase of **maintenance.** This work typically involves two types of activities.

First, some bugs may remain in a program, even after extensive testing. For example:

1. When programs contain many modules, testing may not be able to anticipate all possible execution paths for the modules. An unusual data set may cause modules to be run in a way that was not tested.
2. When programs are used heavily, various parts of a program may be run concurrently by different users with unanticipated results. For example, two parts of a program may update the same file without conflict when only one user runs the program at a time. However, if several users try to update the same file simultaneously, conflicts often arise.
3. Correction of some errors may introduce other problems in other places. Thus, when one bug is corrected, another bug may be created that is not detected in normal testing.

Testing may find many of the more obvious errors, but heavy use frequently uncovers more subtle ones. For large software packages, this process may continue for the entire life of the package.

The second type of maintenance involves the modification of the initial specifications or designs. Such modification may be necessary for several reasons.

1. Users may request new features, once they become familiar with the package.
2. A change in a customer's business or in legal requirements may dictate changes in requirements.
3. New performance demands may force new algorithms to be developed.

In such cases, new specifications must be developed, algorithms modified, new programs or modules written, and the resulting packages tested.

In an academic environment, we tend to minimize this maintenance phase, since we often stress development and our small programs can be changed or rewritten easily. However, maintenance is an extremely significant part of the cost of large software packages, and typically *half (50%) of the staff time devoted to a large project is spent on maintenance.*

Documentation

Another vital area of work that is often ignored or downplayed in an academic environment is **documentation.** With small programs that we are writing and running ourselves, we may not need to write out what we have done in much detail. However, in large projects, documentation is essential for two reasons. First, a user must know how to interact with a program if that program is to be of any value. Complex systems normally have too many options and subtleties for a user to guess how to proceed. Users need to be able to learn how they can use a program efficiently, and they need reference material to refresh their memories after their initial training.

Second, program developers and coders need to know precisely what the software does, how it is organized, and which algorithms are implemented, so that changes can be made during the maintenance phase. In complex software, people cannot remember all of the decisions they made in developing the final product, so reference materials are needed. Further, over the extended period when a package is being used, personnel often change. Thus, the people being asked to modify or correct a program often are not the same people who wrote it. In long-lived systems, personnel may turn over several times before a program is outdated or completely revised. Without adequate documentation, customers cannot use a package, even if the software has all of the required capabilities, and software maintenance people cannot modify the code to meet new demands. A software package's survival depends on good documentation.

SECTION 16.2	MAINTENANCE AND ITS IMPLICATIONS

As we consider the maintenance phase and its implications, we first need to appreciate the size and complexity of many real-world applications, since the scale of a software package has considerable impact upon how the package can be maintained. So far in this text, a typical program might involve a few hundred lines of code organized into relatively few procedures and functions. Few, if any, programs have exceeded 500 lines of code (including comments), and the number of procedures and functions probably does not exceed 5 or 10. For these programs, maintenance is hardly an issue, for we can rewrite an entire program fairly easily.

When we turn to real-world applications, we often find that the simplest problems require coding that runs to several thousand lines, and more sophisticated problems require many times more work. Large software packages with 500,000 lines of code (*excluding* comments) are not uncommon. Such programs are too large and complex for any single individual to understand or modify. The program listing of such a package may take up half a dozen notebooks, and it may require careful indexing to find a particular line of code once one knows what needs to be changed!

With software packages of this magnitude, we cannot leave questions of program modification and correctness to the maintenance phase; rewriting is not the viable option that we have with present exercises. We will need to develop careful strategies if we expect to be able to work with the programs that arise in real applications.

Dependence on Design, Coding, and Documentation

Our first important observation about maintenance is that we must plan for possible changes from the earliest stages of the software life cycle. Thus, designers often try to include flexibility in their work, so that features can be added without affecting existing work. For example, work can be structured so that new modules can be added in the future; and extra (unused) fields may be placed in records and files, so old procedures will not require revision if new information must be stored.

Similarly, coders may use *Case* statements rather than sequences of *If-Then* statements when putting procedures together, so that new procedures can be defined and called easily. In addition, throughout program development, designers and programmers need to write down decisions they have made and the reasons for making them. Then, when changes are needed, the people involved in maintenance can identify which pieces need to be changed and how changes in one piece will affect other pieces.

Without such help, maintenance may be impossible; it may be overwhelming just to determine where to start making a change. Maintenance depends critically on documentation and on the forethought of those involved in development and coding.

Modularity

A second important observation is that changes cannot be made reasonably if one has to scan thousands of lines of code to determine the effects of a particular change. This implies that program structure is not only important in the initial solving of a problem; it is equally important in maintaining the resulting program. The need to maintain programs extends the significance of program structure beyond the initial development phases, and we find that many of the ideas discussed for program development also have important ramifications for maintenance. For example, the concepts of stepwise refinement, module independence, local and global variables and parameters all apply to the maintenance phase as well. In addition, during development we may apply our principles of structure in some special ways to make maintenance easier.

Stepwise Refinement. In problem solving, we divided complex problems into several steps. Then, we tackled each step, refining our analysis and dividing steps into smaller pieces. With this process, we could replace an initially difficult problem by a collection of small, manageable ones. In our design phase, this approach yields an outline with main headings and with various levels of subheadings. In our coding, we maintain this structure with procedures and functions defined at various levels.

When we want to locate errors or make modifications, this structure is precisely what we need to identify the necessary changes. For example, by looking at the main heading in an outline, we can identify which major steps will be affected by a change. Also, within a major heading, we can locate specific places where changes are needed. Thus, our outline allows us to find the particular modules where corrections or changes are needed. Then, since our code follows our outline, we can locate the particular pieces of code that need changing.

Hence, if we have carefully followed the top-down approach of stepwise refinement in our problem solving, we normally find that we do not have to read thousands of lines of code when modifications are required. Rather, we can use the program structure to identify the few short procedures or functions that need attention.

Independence of Modules. Once we have found the procedure or function that we wish to change, we need to know how that module interacts with other modules. We must know how a change in the given procedure or function will affect other parts of our code. We would hope that changes in one place would not affect anything else at all; we want modules to be independent, so maintenance can focus on individual pieces of code rather than on large sections.

Here again, module independence not only aids our development work where such techniques as stubbing and driver programs can help us develop small pieces at a time, but this independence is equally important in maintenance by allowing us to restrict modifications to small sections of code.

Local and Global Variables and Parameters. Even when program structure is planned carefully, module independence can be destroyed with the unnecessary use of global variables and the absence or misuse of parameters. Whenever we use global variables directly, without their declaration as parameters, we are taking two fundamental risks.

1. We are assuming that these variables have been set up in a specific way by earlier modules in the program.
2. When we change global variables, we are assuming that subsequent pieces of code will need these revised values.

In programming one module to perform one task, our use of global variables in that task implies that our assumptions for that piece of code are consistent with other assumptions elsewhere.

When we first develop our modules, this assumption of consistency may even be valid. However, changes in specifications often affect only some modules. Thus, in large programs, these changes may mean that we will want to use global values in new ways in certain places while retaining old meanings elsewhere.

When global values are passed as parameters, we often can control these new interpretations; but when global variables are used indiscriminately, we can no longer retain control. In practice, we find that the misuse of globals (and the corresponding inadequate use of parameters and local variables) is one of the most serious problems that arises in program maintenance. In large programs, the choice among local and global variables and parameters may make the difference between a program that can be modified to meet new or changing needs and a program that must be scrapped and rewritten.

Low-Level Routines.   Another major source of error is the accessing of data from a file or a terminal from many places in a program. When many procedures read and write data, the chances are quite high that an error will arise somewhere, and such an error will have two effects. In the short run, the program will produce incorrect results. Further, since the program error caused incorrect data to be stored on a disk file, future runs of the program will yield incorrect results.

For this reason, large programs often have a few carefully defined and controlled procedures that actually access the data on a file or a terminal. All other modules have to use these low-level, data access routines whenever files are required. These low-level routines can be tested thoroughly so that the chances of systematic errors in file data are minimized.

This use of low-level routines has the additional advantage that changes in the data files themselves can often be made without major code modification. In changing the structure of file data, we may have to change the low-level procedures, but the rest of our program need not even be aware of these changes. (We will see some examples of this in the next two chapters.)

With these low-level routines, other modules not only can be independent of each other, they can be independent of the data files as well.

Fire Walls.   Beyond our striving for top-down design and module independence, we may want to build into our programs specific boundaries that isolate various pieces of code and various data values. Our idea is to contain the damage caused by a bug that happens in one module, so that bug does not destroy the running of the entire program. In large programs, errors almost always arise from time to time, but we can try to limit the consequences to a few procedures or functions. We say that we want to build **fire walls** around parts of our programs, so any errors can be contained in a limited part of a large program.

This containment of errors may take some careful planning, but we often can construct fire walls around our code by consciously keeping major pieces of code completely separate from each other. For example,

- modules may be changed so that they have *no* variables in common;
- modules may access different files.

In these cases, there simply is no possible way that an error in one module will affect another.

Classes of Algorithms

Beyond our planning ahead and our structuring of programs, maintenance has implications for our coding and for our consideration of performance and efficiency. Before discussing this, we need to identify three classes of algorithms.

Sequential Algorithms.   These form the simplest type of algorithm. In these algorithms, we write out all steps of our solution explicitly, and our solution just follows each step. For example, in converting quarts and pints to liters, our solution might be

1. Read value for quarts and pints.
2. Total number of quarts := Quarts + Pints/2.
3. Liters := Total number of quarts/1.056710.
4. Print value of liters.

Here, we can write our steps explicitly, and we have no need for loops.

Iterative or Enumerative Algorithms.   These algorithms involve loops. Each time through a loop, we get closer to our final solution until finally, at the end of the loop, we have our desired result.

Recursive Algorithms.   Recursive algorithms do some processing and then instruct the computer to do the same task on smaller pieces. These pieces are then put back together to produce a solution to our original problem. In Pascal, we program such algorithms by having a procedure call itself at an appropriate time.

Coding

In coding our algorithms, a major objective for maintenance involves clarity, structure, and readability. In maintenance, we need to return to various parts of our code, and we must be able to read and understand what the program is doing before we can make changes.

In earlier chapters, we have discussed the use of comments, descriptive identifiers, and format to simplify debugging and testing. These same issues of style apply equally strongly to maintenance. Further, we make two new points.

Size and Coherence of Modules.   We have said that procedures and functions should be rather short, so we can understand clearly what each piece of code is doing. We also indicated that studies suggest that errors start to arise when modules start to exceed seven or so lines of code. Thus, in writing modules, we will want each piece of code short, clear, and coherent. Each piece of code should have a single, simple theme.

However, in programming individual procedures, we should also take into account the complexity of the algorithms we are coding. For example, sequential algorithms are conceptually quite easy to follow, so we might allow procedures for such algorithms to be somewhat larger than the average. On the other hand, iterative algorithms are more complex, and we might want to break procedures for these iterative algorithms into fairly small pieces.

Programming Shortcuts.   Program readability and maintenance depend not only on various style considerations, but also on the complexity of the underlying program logic. Intricate logic normally produces extremely complex code. Such code often depends heavily upon special details and cases that are present in the original problem being solved. When changes must be made, these details and cases may no longer apply, and the programmer must re-evaluate the entire piece of code. Frequently, logic can be so involved that a programmer will find it much quicker, easier, and more reliable to rewrite a module than to change it.

With these considerations, programmers must avoid the temptation to make shortcuts in their code if those shortcuts make the logic of the code more complex. In many cases, intricate logic may allow a programmer to save a few lines in writing a program originally; however, in the maintenance phase, much extra time is required. Thus, when we consider the effort normally needed in maintenance, we conclude that subtle coding shortcuts are best avoided if these tricks make code harder to understand.

Efficiency Considerations

One common task in the maintenance phase is to improve the speed at which a program performs its task. Often the initial development of a program focuses on obtaining some correct solution to the given problem; efficient results are useless if they are not correct. In addition, in the initial solution of a problem, we may not be sure how long our algorithm is likely to take or just where it can be improved. Once the program is written, we can try to speed it up.

When we try to increase efficiency, we begin by determining how often various tasks are done. For example, an improvement in a line of code will have more of an impact if that line is executed frequently rather than just once. Therefore, we need to identify which statements are done most often. In some situations, computers can monitor how many times each line of code is executed during the running of a program, and they can tell us authoritatively which lines of code are executed most frequently and which are done rarely.

In other cases, we must analyze our code by hand and make an educated guess about where our program is slow. In guessing, a few observations may be helpful.

- Sequential algorithms may take a long time to program, but they execute quickly because each line is done only once.
- Iterative algorithms repeat the same process many times, so each line in an iterative algorithm is done many times.

When loops are nested, the statements in the inside loop are done a very large number of times. For example, if we have

```
For I: = 1 to 50
    Do For J: = 1 to 50
        Do (statement)
```

then the (statement) is done inside both loops and is executed 2500 times. Once these heavily used statements are identified, we can see if some modification of code can reduce the amount of work required.

In many cases, we may find that this streamlining of code reduces runtimes to acceptable levels. However, we have already noted instances where coding probably cannot correct performance problems, and we need to consider more fundamental changes in our algorithms. For example, in Chapter 14, we noted that a bubble sort requires many comparisons, whereas a merge sort requires much less work. In this case, speeding up our coding of a bubble sort by a factor of 3, 5, or 10 probably will not solve any performance problems. Instead, we may need to replace the bubble sort by the vastly more efficient merge sort. In changing these algorithms, we note again that modularity is essential in our coding. If our sorting algorithm is programmed as a separate procedure, then our change only involves this one piece of code. However, if the sorting algorithm is embedded as part of a large procedure, then our change in algorithm might well have broader consequences.

Maintenance Control

With all of these comments about how software can be changed, we also must realize that software developers and maintainers are usually very careful in making modifications to existing packages. If changes are made without careful coordination and testing, different programmers might change various modules in incompatible ways, and users might find these packages producing errors or behaving in new, undocumented, and unpredictable ways.

As a result, most large software packages are never changed without specific authorization. Typically, a project's top management must authorize work on any changes before maintenance can proceed. Then, several changes may be put together in a new version of the software package, sometimes called a **new release** of the software. Before any new release is distributed, the testing group typically gathers the various changes and checks that any enhancements have not altered previously-correct processing. Then the testing group describes all changes in a **release letter** before the release is distributed. Unauthorized changes simply are not tolerated, because reliability is a top priority.

Further, a designated testing group, sometimes called a **change control,** or a **maintenance control group,** is the only group that normally receives direct feedback from customers. Users must channel all requests through change control. Requests are then channeled through management for approval and scheduling. Only after modifications are authorized will a designer or programmer be permitted to work on the change. However, in no instance is a user allowed to interfere with (or even call) a programmer!

Large software projects require a large investment of time and effort, and the maintenance phase of the software life cycle represents a major part of that investment. Thus, we have seen that maintenance activities normally are controlled quite carefully, and many activities in the initial development process try to anticipate possible changes, to increase reliability and to minimize maintenance costs.

SECTION 16.3   DOCUMENTATION

In this section, we look more closely at the needs for documentation both for users of a program and for the maintainers of it. Each of these two groups probably needs different types of documentation, and we must look at how to address these needs. Our conclusions are outlined in Table 16–1.

TABLE 16–1 • Documentation Needs

Audience	Materials	Comments
Users	Tutorial	Introduction to the Package for Beginners
	Reference Manual	Refresher for Experienced Users
Programmers and Maintainers	External Documentation	Specifications, Algorithm Description, Structure
	Internal Documentation	Detailed Comments on Specific Programming Statements

User Manuals and Programmer Information

To begin, users' primary needs involve knowing how to run a program. Thus, documentation for users should include

- a discussion of each possible command;
- a description of each possible input and output; and
- examples of typical sequences of operations, so users know how to put options together.

In presenting this information, user documentation can assume the reader is familiar with the subject matter of the application, since users normally know about their applications and think in the terms of the problem. For example, documentation for an economics program can discuss GNP (gross national product) or marginal revenue freely, as the users of this program will be comfortable with these ideas and terms. On the other hand, users do not want to be sidetracked by computing details. For example, they may need to know that a program updates data in a file, but they do not care that this is done by creating a new file, copying data, and copying it back with the changes. Overall, users want to focus on their applications, and they do not have the time or interest for technical details.

In contrast to these needs of users, program maintenance has a different set of needs that has the opposite orientation. Maintainers need to know the internal algorithms and program structure, so they can make changes when necessary. Maintainers normally do not know a great deal about the particular application, so they may not know terms from the language of the application, and they cannot be expected to be comfortable with the concepts of the application. For example, documentation for maintainers must not assume much background about GNP or marginal revenue.

In addition, maintainers do not want or need to know many details about running the program. They need to be able to check that various options work correctly, but they do not have time for extended examples with combinations of operations.

When we compare the needs of these two groups, we find that in many cases, we cannot use the same documentation for both users and maintainers. For example, if we include enough technical details for program maintainers, then users will have to wade through too much material to allow them to run the programs easily. Similarly, if we use application terminology for the users, we are likely to confuse the maintainers. Of course, if we are working with a rather small software package, user options may be sufficiently simple and algorithm design and program structure may be easy enough to describe so that one manual or report can satisfy both groups. However, once programs become large and complex, the needs of these groups conflict.

In practical terms, then, we must plan to document a software package with two sets of materials: one for users and the other for maintainers.

Reference Manuals and Tutorials

When we focus on the needs of users themselves, we can identify two levels of material that are appropriate. When users begin to use a complex software package, they need detailed, step-by-step instructions, with examples illustrating how various steps go together. On the other hand, more sophisticated users are ready for more of the advanced options that might be available. For most operations, these users just need to refresh their memories about how a particular step is done. They do not want to read extensive examples or detailed instructions; they want a concise summary for fast reference.

As with our distinction between users and maintainers, these two levels of users often require separate pieces of documentation. Materials for beginning users are often called **tutorials;** they tutor the beginners in the use of the system. More advanced users need **reference manuals,** which typically are organized with brief summaries and tables. Occasionally, one document can address both needs, but normally material designed for both is satisfactory for neither.

Internal and External Documentation

Documentation for maintainers can be classified in two forms as well. Throughout the book, we have stressed the use of comments to help us understand what we are doing. Comments allow us to clarify specific pieces of code and to describe the purpose of our procedures and questions. These comments constitute the **internal documentation** for our program.

For small programs, comments also can describe our algorithm and program structure. We can include our algorithm design with our outline at the beginning of our code, so we have all relevant details together. Here, internal documentation may be completely adequate for maintenance.

However, for larger projects, algorithm design and program structure is too extensive to be included in comments. Maintainers still need to have access to this information, but we cannot reasonably include it in part of the program itself. Here, we need a separate document outside our code. Such **external documentation** should contain specifications, design choices together with the reasons for those choices, and the detailed program structure. Programmers still need to comment on specific lines of code, but these details may not be combined with the specifications and design work done earlier in the software life cycle.

The Importance of Documentation

Documentation is often one of the weakest parts of software packages, since many developers and programmers prefer to focus on technical details rather than the presentation of their accomplishments to others. As a result, some truly excellent packages are never used, because users cannot figure out how the software runs. Other fine packages are discarded prematurely, because maintainers cannot figure out how to make even the most modest changes. In either case, the time, effort, and resources that go into a project are wasted, and the software has a short lifetime.

For this reason, developers and programmers must incorporate documentation into their normal work flow. Programmers should write helpful comments as part of their normal coding; they should not be written in later. Designers need to make notes as they develop algorithms and determine structure. Documentation tasks need not be difficult as long as they are done as part of normal work procedures.

SECTION 16.4	USER EXPECTATIONS

Much of our discussion of methodology up to this point has focused on the designers, coders, and maintainers of a software package. With this orientation, we can sometimes forget that the purpose of software is to help solve problems. Thus, throughout our problem solving, we need to consider the needs of users. This section looks at user needs and expectations explicitly in some detail.

Correctness

At the most fundamental level, a user expects that a software package will produce correct results. The user wants to solve a particular problem, and a program is helpful only if it produces useful results.

While this idea of **correctness** may seem obvious, the following examples suggest that some subtleties can arise in this area.

1. In a simulation that uses random numbers to make various choices, our problem may allow a wide variety of "correct" results. Here, the purpose of our program may be to identify the likelihood of various outcomes. For example, in tossing a coin, we may want to know how often two consecutive heads might appear. By the nature of a simulation, we do not expect that our program will produce "exact" results. Rather, we want to obtain a reasonable *estimate* of these correct values.

2. Many applications may depend upon a model of the "real world." That is, we may make some assumptions about our actual application, and then we may investigate how various circumstances affect the application. In studying the stock market, we may assume that stock market prices can be predicted from various economic indicators. Our investigations may suggest some equations for predicting stock prices. In this application, "correct" results depend upon our assumptions; we cannot expect that our software package will predict the future with complete certainty.

3. In an inventory system, we enter new inventory as it arrives, and we subtract inventory levels as items are purchased and shipped. In this system, the inventory in our warehouse is supposed to agree with the levels indicated in our computer files. We expect our program to up-

date levels for specific items correctly as new supplies are added and as other items leave.

These three examples illustrate that "correctness" may have different meanings in different applications. In the first example, we do not expect exact answers; rather, we want good approximations. In the second case, we want our results to be correct, given our assumptions. In the third example, we measure correctness in our system by comparing actual stock levels with the data in our files; we may forget to log items in or out, but our goal is to have complete agreement between our data files and our active inventory.

These distinctions about the meaning of correctness highlight the role of the specifications for a problem. In formulating problem specifications, we must be sure that we address the real needs of the user. We must spend enough time understanding the user's problem, so we can appreciate the various needs of the application. We must be sure that if we write software to meet the specifications then the software will be helpful.

Then, once the problem specifications are written, the correctness of a program is determined by how well the program meets the specifications. In some cases (e.g., the inventory system), we may expect results to be exact, while in other cases (e.g., simulations or modeling), we expect approximate answers.

Predictability

A second important area in the use of a program is **predictability.** In running a software package the user should find that the program proceeds as expected. For example, the running of the program should agree with the user documentation. When the user types a command listed in a manual, the program should respond in the way the manual indicates, and the program should do the task expected. One of the most frustrating experiences for a user occurs when he or she types a command for one operation and the program seems to be doing something else.

In addition, the interface between the program and the user should be carefully designed for ease of use, readability, clarity, and consistency. As a user gains experience with a software package, he or she begins to develop some intuition about how the package will respond. For example, certain commands or options require a particular syntax, and certain reports are generated in a particular format. Once the user becomes comfortable with these commands and reports, the user expects that other options will have a parallel syntax and output format. The user expects that intuition developed for one set of commands will extend to other options as well.

Robustness

In addition to running predictably, a user also expects a program to be **robust.** That is, a program should handle input errors gracefully, without stopping unexpectedly and without destroying data. Also, when typographical errors are made during data entry, the user wants to be able to correct the mistakes easily. Further, if the program detects a problem during processing, the user wants to be able to continue with minimal disruption. All of these issues of robustness imply that the designer must anticipate possible errors and must include procedures to recover from these errors.

Beyond these problems of data entry, we should include tests in our code to find possible bugs, and plan how we will handle such errors in our processing. For example, we may expect that one of three cases will always occur at a certain point, and we may use a *Case* statement to distinguish among the cases. However, before the *Case* statement, we should be sure that a bug in our program has not created another case, and we should decide how to proceed if such a bug is encountered.

In some cases, when errors are encountered, we may want to include code to correct the difficulties and proceed with processing. In other cases, we may want to report the error to the user and then go back to a menu to let the user determine the next step. In still other cases, we may decide that a problem is sufficiently serious that processing should halt and a user should contact an appropriate specialist for help.

Whichever approach is followed for a particular error, our work on software should involve at least three steps.

1. We must make a conscious decision about how the program should respond when a problem is encountered.
2. We must document what response is taken, so the user will know what has happened.
3. We must tell the user how he or she should proceed when an error is reported. The user must know what, if any, data were lost, and what steps should be taken to correct the problem.

In running a program, the user expects a program to handle errors without destroying large amounts of data and without causing a major disruption in processing. Robustness in a program, therefore, depends upon the anticipation of possible errors and the inclusion of procedures to handle such errors when they arise.

Efficiency

Finally, in working with a software package, a user may have some expectations about how long processing should take, and various types of tasks may have different requirements. Some tasks may need to be done very frequently, and answers may be needed while the user waits for a response. Other tasks may need to be done frequently, but the results are not needed immediately. Here, the user expects to enter the appropriate commands or data quickly, but the output is not needed for a while. Finally, some tasks may be done infrequently or the results may not be needed immediately, so the user does not really care how long it takes to enter data or receive results.

These varying needs suggest that specifications should include not only a listing of required tasks but also any relevant demands for **efficiency**. Programs do not have to be written so that every possible output can be obtained quickly. Rather, data can be structured and algorithms chosen so that frequently-executed tasks can be done quickly, while other tasks may take considerable time.

As in our discussion of program correctness, program efficiency must be defined in the context of the problem being solved. Users expect programs to be correct and efficient, but these terms depend upon how the programs are being used. Program specifications need to consider what makes results useful and correct, and specifications need to include any appropriate requirements about how fast the results are needed. With these specifications, our design should ensure that our programs will be predictable and robust in producing the results.

SUMMARY

1. The **software life cycle** includes the following phases:
   * **specifications**
   * **algorithm design**
   * **coding**
   * **verification and testing**
   * **maintenance**
2. The first four of these phases in the development of software agree with the corresponding steps in problem solving. In addition, after a program is developed, software enters a long maintenance phase, in which corrections and modifications are made in programs. This maintenance activity can involve 50% of the entire effort spent on a software package, and thus maintenance has important implications for the earlier phases as well.
3. Many of the considerations we discussed for program development, such as modularity and coding style, also affect maintenance.
4. Throughout this software life cycle, various types of documentation are needed.
   a. **Internal documentation** (comments on details inside our code).
   b. **External documentation** (description of specifications, algorithms and structures, with choices made and reasons for the choices).
   c. **Tutorials** (guides to instruct users how to use the software effectively).
   d. **Reference guides** (materials for experienced users, designed to outline advanced features and to provide quick, summary data).
   Occasionally maintainers and users might find the same documents helpful, but normally these groups have differing needs.
5. While the specific needs of users will depend upon the particular application, we can identify some general user expectations in the areas of correctness, predictability, robustness, and efficiency.

EXERCISES

16.1 *Good and Bad Comments.*

 a. Discuss which of the following comments contribute to the readability of the given program segment.

```
Code Segment A
        Sum := 0;       {Set Sum equal to 0}
        For Index := 1 To 10
                Do Begin {Start of Loop}
                        Read (Value);
                        Sum := Sum + Value
                End;    {End of Loop}
Code Segment B
        {Read 10 Values and Find Their Average}
        Sum := 0;
        For Index := 1 To 10
                Do Begin
                        Read (Value);
                        Sum := Sum + Value
                End;
```

 b. Code Segment A contains more comments and more words of comments than Code Segment B. Can you draw any conclusions from this observation? How does this observation relate to your answer to Part A?

KEY TERMS, PHRASES, AND CONCEPTS

Algorithm Classes	Maintenance
Iterative or Enumerative	Fire Walls
Recursive	Modularity
Sequential	Modules
Change Control or	Release of
Maintenance Control	Software
Documentation	New Release
External	Software Life
Internal	Cycle
Reference Manuals	User Expectations
Tutorials	Correctness
User Documentation	Efficiency
	Predictability
	Robustness

16.2 *Commenting to an Extreme.* The following program illustrates that the quantity of comments is not necessarily related to the quality of internal documentation.

```pascal
Program AverageNumbers (Input, Output);
{This program is called 'AverageNumbers', and the program uses
 both Input and Output}

Var {Var begins the declaraction section of the program AverageNumbers
    {In Pascal, variables must be delcared before they are used in
     a program}

    Value: Real;          {Value is a real number
                           that is used in this program}
    Sum:    Real;         {Sum is another real number
                           that is used in this program}
    Average: Real;        {Average is a third real number
                           that is used in this program}
    Number: Integer;      {Number is an integer variable
                           that is used in this program}

Begin {The Main Program begins at this point}

    Writeln ('This program averages ',       {Writeln is used to print}
            'positive numbers');             {test at the beginning}
                                             {of the program}
    Writeln ('Please enter numbers, ',       {This Writeln is used to}
            'ending with a negative');       {a second line at the}
                                             {beginning of this program}
    Number := 0;                     {The variable Number is set to 0}
    Sum := 0.0;                      {The variable Sum is set to 0.0}
    Read (Value);                    {We Read a Value from the terminal}
    While (Value > 0)                {We will continue the following}
                                     {While Value is greater than 0.0}
      Do Begin                       {Begin the Do part of the 'While' loop}
        Sum := Sum + Value;          {Add Value to Sum to get a new Sum}
        Number := Number + 1;        {Add 1 to Number to get a new Number}
        Read (Value)                 {Read a new Value from the terminal}
      End;                           {This End finishes the earlier Begin}
    Average := Sum / Number;         {Average is given the value of}
                                     {Sum divided by Number}
    Writeln ('Number = ', Number:1); {Write a line with the value of the}
                                     {Variable Number}
    Writeln ('Average = ', Average:1:2) {Use a Writeln statement to write}
                                     {the value of the variable Average}
                                     {on a new line}
End                                  {This is the End of the program}
                                     {called AverageNumbers}
                                     {All Pascal programs must conclude}
                                     {with a period}
```

In this program, each comment restates the meaning of the Pascal statements.

a. Discuss how these comments help or hinder your reading of the program.

b. Revise the comments in this program to improve clarity. In the process, you may want to omit, modify, or add particular comments.

NOTE: While this program may seem extreme, it is typical of many programs that are written by beginners.

MORAL: Comments in every line may not be helpful.

16.3 *User Documentation.* Consider each of the following books.
  • A dictionary
  • This textbook
  • A programming manual for your computer

a. Discuss if each book is primarily in the category of a tutorial or a reference manual. Explain your conclusion.

b. To what extent can each of these books be used for another purpose?

16.4 *Efficiency Techniques—Storage of Intermediate Values.* While it is hardly surprising that it takes less time to do a computation once than it does to do it two or more times, this observation can lead to significant savings in computer time. For example, consider the following code segment.

```
X := A + B / C;
Y := A - B / C;
Z := A * A - 2 * B / C;
```

Here, the quotient *B/C* is computed three separate times. To reduce these computations, we can store this ratio after the first computation and use the result thereafter without repeating the division. The result might be:

```
Ratio := B / C;
X := A + Ratio;
Y := A - Ratio;
Z := A * A - 2 * Ratio;
```

Here we have eliminated two divisions.

Apply this idea of storing intermediate values to improve the efficiency of the following problems.

a. *Quadratic Formula.* Given the equation

$$ax^2 + bx + c = 0$$

compute a solution according to the following quadratic formula:

$$x = \frac{-b \pm \sqrt{b^2 - 4ac}}{2a}$$

This algorithm is programmed with the following procedure.

```
Procedure QuadraticFormula (A, B, C: Real);
{This procedure uses the quadratic forumla to solve the equation
            A*X*X + B*X + C = 0                                    }

Var Root1, Root2: Real;

Begin
    If (B*B-4*A*C < 0)
        Then Writeln ('No Solutions Exist');
    If (B*B-4*A*C = 0)
        Then Begin
            Root1 := -B / (2*A);
            Writeln ('The one solution is ', Root1:1:2)
        End;
    If (B*B-4*A*C < 0)
        Then Begin
            Root1 := (-B + Sqrt(B*B - 4*A*C)) / (2 * A);
            Root2 := (-B - Sqrt(B*B - 4*A*C)) / (2 * A);
            Writeln ('The two solutions are ', Root1:1:2,
                      ' and ', Root2:1:2)
        End
End {Quadratic Formula} ;
```

b. *Computation of the Values X, X^2, . . . , X^{10}.* The following code computes and prints the value of

$$X, X^2, X^3, . . . , X^{10}$$

for a given value of X using a separate function to compute X^n.

```
Procedure DisplayPowers(X: Real);
{This procedure computes and prints powers of X}

    Var N: Integer;

    Function Powers (X: Real; N: Integer): Real;
    {This function computes X to the Nth power}
        Var Index: Integer;
            Prod: Real;
        Begin
            Prod := 1;
            For Index := 1 To N
                Do Prod := Prod * X;
            Powers := Prod
        End {Powers} ;
```

```
Begin {Display Powers}
    Writeln ('Powers of the Number ', X:8:2);
    Writeln ('Exponent    Value');
    For N := 1 To 10
        Do Writeln (N:5, Powers(X, N):13:2)
End {Display Powers} ;
```

In revising each of these procedures to get more efficient code, estimate the amount of work saved by your revision.

16.5 *Efficiency in Loops.* Frequently, we can reduce the amount of work
done by a program by moving part of our code outside of a loop. Use
this idea to improve the efficiency of the following function which
computes

$$3 (1 + 4 + 9 + 16 + \ldots + 100).$$

```
Function ThreeTimesSum: Integer;
{This function computes the value of
    3 ( 1 + 4 + 9 + 16 + ... + 25 )        }

    Var Sum: Integer;
        Index: Integer;
        Factor: Integer;
        Term: Integer;

Begin
    Sum := 0;
    For Index := 1 To 10
      Do Begin
        Factor := 3;
        Term := Sqr(Index);
        Sum := Sum + Factor*Term
      End;
    ThreeTimesSum := Sum
End {ThreeTimesSum} ;
```

CHAPTER 17

STACKS
AND QUEUES:
SOME ADDITIONAL
DATA STRUCTURES

In Chapter 13, we noted that we can work with data on three distinct levels. At the lowest level, we consider individual pieces of data, such as integers, reals, Booleans, or characters. Then, at the next level, we can put some of these pieces together into larger entities using arrays and records. Finally, at a third level, we can think more abstractly of a **data structure,** which involves not only the data themselves but also some operations that we want to perform with the data. At this third level, we want to work with data in a conceptual way in our applications; we do not want to worry about various details of data storage and data operations.

In this chapter, we introduce these general data structures more formally, and we describe two specific examples of these structures, called stacks and queues. In the following two chapters, we continue this study by considering two additional data structures, called linked lists and trees.

SECTION 17.1   DEFINITION OF DATA STRUCTURE

When we want to work with data on a general level, we often need to describe two basic characteristics: the data we will be storing, and the operations we will want to perform on this data. In computer science, these two characteristics combine to give the concept of a **data structure** which allows us to work with data on a conceptual level without worrying about various programming details.

To illustrate this concept of a data structure, we outline two specific examples in this section, called stacks and queues. In this outline, we will consciously omit all details of programming, and we focus on the general data and operations. With these examples, we will be able to give a more careful definition of an abstract data structure. Then, in subsequent sections, we will be able to apply this definition formally.

Stacks

A stack mimics the information that we might keep in a pile on our desk. For example, on our desk, we may keep separate piles for

bills that need paying;

magazines that we plan to read; and

notes we have taken.

These piles have several properties. First, each pile contains the same type of information (e.g., bills, magazines, or notes). In addition, for each pile, we can do several tasks.

1. We can add to the pile by putting information on the top.
2. We can take the top item off of our pile.
3. We can read the item on the top.
4. We can tell if a pile is empty. (There may be nothing at the spot where the pile should be.)

These operations allow us to do all of our normal processing of data at our desk. For example, when we receive bills in the mail, we add them to our pile of bills until payday comes. Then, we take our bills, one at a time, off the top of our pile and pay them until our money runs out.

Queues

A second type of data structure, called a queue, is seen at the checkout counter of a store. Here, a clerk works with one customer at a time, until the customer's bill has been computed and paid. Then the clerk goes on to the next customer. In this situation, while the customer is being served by the clerk, other customers may get into the checkout line to wait for their turn. Normally, customers do not get into line until they have selected all items they wish to buy, and once a customer gets into line, the customer waits until the clerk finishes with those ahead. When we consider this processing at the cash register, we can identify three basic characteristics.

1. Customers wait in a line to be served.
2. People can enter or leave the line as follows:
   a. Customers leave the line at one end, when they have been served by the clerk.
   b. Customers enter the line at the other end.
3. Occasionally, a line may be empty.

These qualities describe the normal flow of customers at the checkout area.

Formal Definition of a Data Structure

In each of these examples, we have stored a particular type of information, and we have organized that data in a particular way. Our discussions have involved the type of data we wish to store and the operations we use to manipulate this information (e.g., entering a queue, removing from a stack). In these discussions, we have not considered how this data might be stored in a computer program.

This description of pieces of information together with the operations required to manipulate the information make up an abstract data structure. A **data structure** consists of two parts: a description of the type of data to be stored, and a description of the operations that can be performed on the data. Later on, whenever we describe a new data structure, we will need to specify both of these parts. In programming terms, we may consider these parts as the declaration of a data type and a complete specification of procedures and functions for the data type. These specifications include pre-assertions, post-assertions, and calling format.

An abstract data structure specifies the data we will store and how we will work with that data on a conceptual level. The structure does not specify how we will perform the details of the operations within our programs.

In our actual programs, we will work with these structures at two levels.

1. We will have to write the code to perform each prescribed operation. Here, we may wish to write some additional procedures to perform the specified operations. Also, we may find we can perform the required work in several ways, so we must pick one particular approach for an actual program.
2. Once the procedures are defined, we can use them on a conceptual level without worrying about the programming details. In fact, we could even change the approach we used to implement the procedures without changing our application code at all.

We illustrate both of these points more fully in the next sections when we consider stacks and queues in more detail. Then, in Chapters 18 and 19, we will introduce two more data structures, called lists and trees.

SECTION 17.2 STACKS

In the previous section, we said that a stack is a structure that mimics a pile of material on our desk. In particular, the stack contains piles of materials, each of which have the same type (e.g., a pile of bills or a pile of magazines). Further, we can use a stack in several ways.

- We can put new items on the top of our stack.
- We can take an item off the top.
- We can read the top item.
- We can determine if our stack is empty.

In working with stacks, the addition of an item to the top of the pile is often called a **Push** operation, and the deletion of an item from the top is called a **Pop** operation. In addition, we may not want to let our pile get too large. In this case, we might specify a maximum size for our stack, and we could ask if our stack was full.

More formally, a **stack** is defined as the structure that has *data* of a specified type, and *operations* described as follows.

1. *Empty*
The *Empty* function returns true or false, depending upon whether the stack contains any items.
2. *Full* {Optional}
The *Full* function returns true or false, depending upon whether the stack contains as much data as it can hold.
3. *Push (Item)*
If the stack is not full, the *Push* procedure adds the specified item to the top of the stack.
If the stack is full, nothing is added, and an error is reported.
4. *Pop (Item)*
If the stack is not empty, the top item on the stack is removed and returned.
If the stack is empty, nothing is returned, and an error is reported.
5. *Top (Item)*
If the stack is not empty, the top item is returned, but the contents of the stack are not changed.
If the stack is empty, nothing is returned, and an error is reported.

This specification says nothing about how we will program the various stack procedures. Rather, this specification tells us about how stacks may be used. We can also infer some limitations on how we can use the data. For example, Stack operations allow us to work with only the top item on the stack. We cannot look at other pieces of data lower in the stack without first using *Pop* operations to clear away items above the desired one.

Secondly, a *Push* operation always puts the new item on top of the stack, and this is the first item returned by a *Pop* operation. Thus, the last piece of data we have added to the stack will be the first item we remove. We say that stacks provide **Last In–First Out** or **LIFO** storage. Similarly, the first item placed on a stack is buried by other items, and we can retrieve this first item only after all other items have been removed. Thus, we can also say that stacks provide **First In–Last Out** or **FILO** storage.

In problem solving, we find that many applications require us to store and retrieve information following a LIFO ordering. The next section illustrates such applications where these stack operations provide just the capabilities needed to solve the specified problems.

SECTION 17.3　EXAMPLES

This section discusses two direct applications of stacks and another application that uses a variation of the concept of stacks. We will see that the LIFO storage of data in stacks allows us to solve our problems fairly easily. Conceptually, stack operations allow us to process data in these applications very simply. To emphasize this point, we omit all programming details from the stack procedures in this section. In the next section, we will see one way such details might be handled.

Our first problem involves checking a line of input.

PROBLEM 17.3　Checking Balanced Parentheses

Write a program that checks whether the parentheses balance in a line of input. More precisely, the program is to process a line of input, and this line may contain three types of parentheses, namely ( ), [ ], and { }. The program is to check that each left parenthesis is closed by the appropriate type of right parenthesis.

For example, parentheses balance correctly in each of the following lines.

{[(abc)]}

a(b((c[d]e)f))

However, each of the following lines is incorrect.

(right parenthesis does not match]

{(right brace is missing)

[[right parentheses in wrong order]}

Discussion of Problem 17.3

One approach to this problem would read the entire line of input, and then move back and forth through the line trying to match up various parentheses. Such a process may seem natural, but it requires the program to scan the input several times, and the details can be a bit tricky.

Instead, we try to solve the problem with a single left-to-right pass through our input line. As we proceed through the line, we keep track of left parentheses. Then, when we encounter a right parenthesis, we see if the right one matches the most recent left one. In this approach, we need to store left parentheses, and we need to retrieve these left parentheses with the last one stored being the first one retrieved. This LIFO storage suggests a stack data structure. With the stack structure, our solution can be stated rather easily.

Outline for Problem 17.3

I. Continue processing successive characters until all characters are processed or until an error is detected. For each character:

    A. Read the character.

    B. Process the character.

        1. If the character is not a parenthesis, ignore it.

        2. If the character is a left parenthesis, then push it on the stack.

        3. If the character is a right parenthesis, then

            a. if the stack is empty, parentheses cannot match and we have an error.

            b. if the stack is not empty,

                i. apply a pop operation to retrieve the most recent remaining left parenthesis.

                ii. compare left and right parentheses to see if they match.

II. After processing has concluded:

    A. Parentheses match if no error has been reported and if stack is empty.

    B. Otherwise, parentheses do not match.

From this outline, we develop the following program, in which we add a procedure *InitializeStack* to set up any necessary details for the stack. As mentioned at the start of this section, the details of the stack operations are omitted.

```
Program BalanceParentheses (Input, Output);
{This program determines whether the parentheses balance in a line of input}

{Declaration of Stack Constants, if any, must be included here}

Type Data = Char;      {Character Data will be stored in a stack}

{Include needed variable declarations for the Stack here}

{Insert the needed stack operations at this point, including
        Procedure InitializeStack;
        Function Empty: Boolean;
        Function Full: Boolean;
        Procedure Push(Item: Data);
        Procedure Pop(Var Item: Data);
        Procedure Top(Var Item: Data);
}
```

```
Function IsLeft(Ch: Data): Boolean;
{Function determines if the given character is a left parenthesis}
     Begin
          IsLeft := Ch In [ '(', '[', '{' ]
     End {IsLeft} ;

Function IsRight(Ch: Data): Boolean;
{Function determines if the given character is a right parenthesis}
     Begin
          IsRight := Ch In [ ')', ']', '}' ]
     End {IsRight} ;

Function ParensMatch (Left, Right: Data): Boolean;
{Function determines if the Left parenthesis matches the given Right one}
     Begin
          ParensMatch := ((Left = '(' ) And (Right = ')' ))
                      Or ((Left = '[' ) And (Right = ']' ))
                      Or ((Left = '{' ) And (Right = '}' ))
     End {ParensMatch} ;

Procedure ProcessRight(Right: Data; Var Error: Boolean);
{This procedure processes a right parenthesis}
     Var Left: Data;
     Begin
          If Empty
             Then Error := True
             Else Begin
                  Pop(Left);
                  Error := Not ParensMatch(Left, Right)
                  End
     End {ProcessRight} ;

Procedure ProcessLine;
{This procedure processes a line of input, checking for balanced parentheses
     Var Ch: Data;              {character read from the terminal}
         Error: Boolean;
     Begin
          {Initialize variables}
          Error := False;
          InitializeStack;

          {Process successive characters}
          Repeat
               Read(Ch);
               If IsLeft(Ch)
                  Then Push(Ch)
                  Else If IsRight(Ch)
                          Then ProcessRight(Ch, Error)
          Until Error Or Eoln;

          {Make conclusion about a match}
          If Empty And Not Error
             Then Writeln ('The parentheses balance')
             Else Writeln ('Parenthesis error')
     End {ProcessLine} ;

Begin {Main}
     Writeln ('Program to check if parentheses balance in a line of input');
     Writeln ('Please enter line');
     ProcessLine
End {Main} .
```

When the stack operations are implemented and included, we can obtain the following sample runs.

```
First Trial Run

Program to check if parentheses balance in a line of input
Please enter line
{[({This [ is ( a ) test ] of } the ) program]}!!!
The parentheses balance


Second Trial Run

Program to check if parentheses balance in a line of input
Please enter line
Here {{{ is another ]]] test
Parenthesis error
```

This example illustrates several important features about the use of stacks in particular and about data structures in general. By choosing an appropriate data structure (a stack), we can often solve problems with efficient, easy-to-read algorithms. We apply appropriate operations to our data, and these operations perform the necessary processing.

In addition, in our solution, we were able to work with our data structures (stacks) at a conceptual level. We did not have to mix the details of the data and its operations with our use of the data.

These comments apply in the same way to the next problem in which we try to evaluate an arithmetic expression. To begin, we consider several alternative ways to write arithmetic expressions, and we note that some of these approaches are actually used in calculators.

Infix, Prefix, and Postfix Notations

Traditionally, when we write arithmetic expressions, we place our operator between the two numbers we want to use. For example, we might write

$$2 + 3, \text{ or}$$
$$30/6.$$

Here, the operator (+ or /) is placed in the middle of our expression. To put these expressions together, we sometimes use parentheses:

$$(2 + 3) * (30/6).$$

Again, * is placed between two values. This traditional form for arithmetic expressions, in which operations are placed in the middle, is called **infix notation.**

Alternatively operations could appear before or after the numbers.

Such approaches give rise to **prefix notation** and **postfix notation,** respectively. For example, in postfix notation, we write

$$2 \ 3 \ + \quad \text{for} \quad 2 + 3$$

and

$$30 \ 6 \ / \quad \text{for} \quad 30/6$$

Further, we can put these expressions together using the same postfix conventions. Thus, we write

$$(2 + 3) * (30/6)$$

as

$$2 \ 3 \ + \ 30 \ 6 \ / \ *$$

Further examples relating expressions in these three notations are shown in Table 17–1.

In practice, we note that some calculators require a user to enter expressions in postfix notation; numbers must be typed first with the operations last. Thus, postfix notation is more than a curious way to write expressions; it is used in real applications.

In addition, we note that prefix and postfix notations allow us to avoid the use of parentheses, while traditional infix notation sometimes requires parentheses. For example, we need parentheses to write

$$(2 + 3) * 4$$

in infix notation. However, the corresponding expressions

$$* \ + \ 2 \ 3 \ 4$$

and

$$2 \ 3 \ + \ 4 \ *$$

in prefix and postfix notations (respectively) do not require parentheses.

Evaluation of Postfix Expressions

When we try to evaluate arithmetic expressions, we find that a particularly simple algorithm is available if our expression is written in postfix notation. In fact, this algorithm motivates the use of postfix notation in some

---

TABLE 17–1 · Corresponding Expressions in Prefix, Infix, and Postfix Notations

Prefix Notation	Infix Notation	Postfix Notation
$- 6 \ 1$	$6 - 1$	$6 \ 1 \ -$
$* \ + \ 4 \ 3 \ 2$	$(4 + 3) * 2$	$4 \ 3 \ + \ 2 \ *$
$/ \ + \ 2 \ 3 \ - \ 9 \ 4$	$(2 + 3) / (9 - 4)$	$2 \ 3 \ + \ 9 \ 4 \ - \ /$

calculators. This algorithm also demonstrates an important application of stacks. Here, a stack is used to store numbers as they are entered. It is also used to store various intermediate values.

Outline for the Evaluation of Postfix Expressions   This algorithm has the following simple outline, which reads our expression from left to right.

  I. Repeat the following for each successive item (operation or number) in the expression.

   A. If the item is a number, push the item onto a stack.

   B. If the item is an operation:

   1. Use a pop operation to get one number (call it a).

   2. Use another pop operation to get a second number (call it b).

   3. Apply the operation to b and a (in that order).

   4. Push the result onto the stack.
  II. When processing stops, the stack will contain exactly one value, and that value will be the desired result.

   Example: To illustrate how this algorithm works, we apply it to the expression

$$5\ 3\ -\ 4\ *$$

that is,

$$(5\ -\ 3)\ *\ 4$$

The various steps in the computation are shown in Table 17–2.

   As in our previous problem about balancing parentheses, stacks allow us to write out a rather straightforward solution to our task of evaluating an expression. The *Push* and *Pop* procedures provide conceptually easy operations that we can apply in solving our problem. We leave the coding of this algorithm as an exercise.

Run-Time Stack

Our final example in this section involves a modification of stacks that is regularly used inside computers to allocate storage when Pascal programs are run. The resulting structure is called a **run-time stack.**

   In Chapter 10, we noted that each time a procedure or function is called, storage must be allocated for various values, such as parameters and local variables. In addition, each time a function or procedure is called, the machine must record where it should return when the new function or procedure is over. Then, when a function or procedure finishes, this space is freed for further use.

   When we consider this allocation and deallocation of space, we observe that procedures and functions finish in the opposite order that they are called. For example, if we call procedure B and then procedure B calls procedure A, we know that A must finish before B does.

TABLE 17–2 · Evaluation of 5 3 — 4 *

Step	Symbol Read	Task Performed	Contents of Stack	Comments
1.	---	---	empty	At the start, the stack is empty.
2.	5	Push(5)	5	
3.	3	Push(3)	3 5	3 is the new top of the stack
4.	—	Pop(a) Pop(b) Compute b — a Push(b — a)	2	a is 3 b is 5 b — a is 2, which is pushed on the stack
5.	4	Push(4)	4 2	4 is the new top of the stack
6.	*	Pop(a) Pop(b) Compute b*a Push(b*a)	8	a is 4 b is 2 b*a is 8, which is pushed on the stack
7.		Processing is complete. The final result 8 appears at the top of the stack.		

With this observation, we see that our allocation and deallocation of space follows the Last In–First Out pattern that we associate with stacks. For this reason, space for procedures and functions in Pascal is allocated in a special area inside the computer, called a run-time stack. A run-time stack stores information for each procedure and function, including

- parameters and local variables; and
- addresses where the function or procedure should return when it is done.

Each time a procedure or function is called, new space is allocated on this stack; each time the procedure or function finishes, that space is deallocated.

For example, consider the program outlined in Figure 17–1. When the program first starts, space for global variables is allocated as shown in Figure 17–2.

After this program executes awhile, procedure B is called. At this point, new space on the run-time stack is allocated for parameters and local variables in B. Further, the computer records where to return in the main program when B finishes. This is shown in Figure 17–3.

FIGURE 17–1 • **Schematic of a Pascal Program**

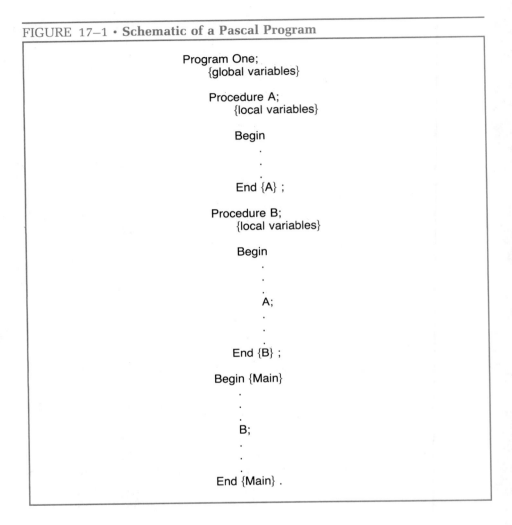

```
Program One;
    {global variables}

Procedure A;
    {local variables}

Begin
    .
    .
    .
End {A} ;

Procedure B;
    {local variables}

Begin
    .
    .
    .
    A;
    .
    .
    .
End {B} ;

Begin {Main}
    .
    .
    .
    B;
    .
    .
    .
End {Main} .
```

FIGURE 17–2 • **Run-Time Stack at Start of Program One**

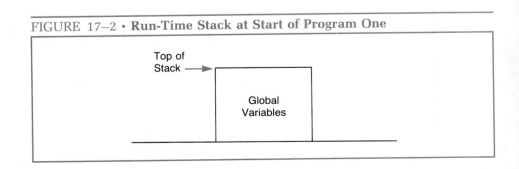

Top of
Stack ⟶

Global
Variables

FIGURE 17–3 • **Run-Time Stack for Program One after Procedure B Is Called**

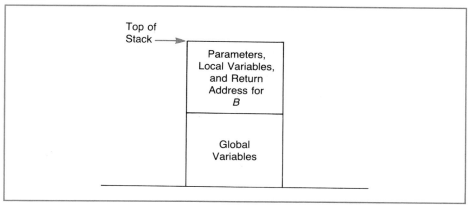

Next, the program continues until procedure A is called. Again, new space is allocated on the run-time stack for parameters, local variables, and a return address for A. This is shown in Figure 17–4.

As processing continues, procedure A will finish, and the space for A can be deallocated. The resulting run-time stack looks as it did before A was called, as in Figure 17–3.

FIGURE 17–4 • **Run-Time Stack for Procedure One after Procedure A Is Called**

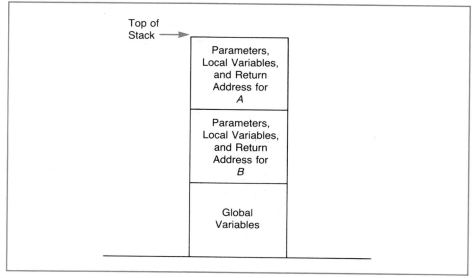

Next, when *B* finishes, more space is deallocated, and Figure 17–2 applies.

This example illustrates how the storage allocation for procedures and functions during program execution follows the LIFO pattern of stacks, and this example suggests why a run-time stack is chosen to allocate this storage.

Beyond this LIFO pattern of storage allocation and deallocation, however, we should note that the space is not necessarily referenced in that way. For example, a procedure may use global variables that are not stored at the top of the stack. Thus, run-time stacks do not follow the strict definition for stack data structures, where only the top item can be accessed at a particular time. Rather, run-time stacks constitute a more sophisticated application of stacks than our previous ones. However, in each case, our motivations for using stacks are the same:

- We need to store and retrieve a certain type of information.
- Our use of data follows a Last In–First Out pattern.
- We can work conceptually with the operations *Empty*, *Full*, *Push*, *Pop*, and *Top*; in our applications, we do not need to focus on the technical details required to implement this data structure.

SECTION 17.4	IMPLEMENTATION OF STACKS BY ARRAYS

Now that we have defined the stack data structure, and we have seen how this structure can be used, we introduce one way that stacks might be implemented based on our picture of a stack as a pile of data (magazines, bills). This pile of data has a form similar to our image of an array as a long sequence of data, and we use arrays to store the piles for our stacks.

More precisely, we store each piece of data as an element of an array. We place the first data item at one end of the array. Then, for a *Push* operation, we add a data item to the next array element. For a *Pop* operation, we return the item at the top of our data, and we record that the top has moved down. This processing requires several parts, including an array (*Stack*) of data to store our data items, a variable (*TopPosition*) to keep track of our top element, and a constant (*MaxStack*) that specifies the total size of our array. This setup fits together as shown in Figure 17–5.

With this figure, we trace what happens in our stack operations. We start with *TopPosition* equal to 0, since we have no data in the array. Then, when we perform a *Push*, we increment *TopPosition* by one, and we store our new item in this new *TopPosition*. Similarly, for a *Pop* operation, we return the item at the *TopPosition*, and we move the *TopPosition* down by one. Finally, for a *Full* or *Empty* function, we can compare the *TopPosition* with *MaxStack* or 0, respectively.

FIGURE 17–5 • An Array Implementation of a Stack

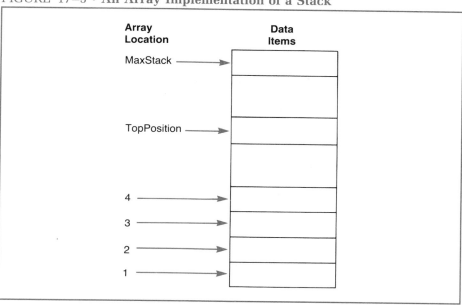

The only additional details arise because we must check if the stack is full or empty before actually performing a *Push* or *Pop* operation, respectively.

The actual code for these operations follows. Here, we declare *Data* as a special type, and our stack handles this special type. In using these stack operations, we need to specify the type of data that we will store. In addition, we think of the *Stack* array and *TopPosition* variables as being shared by the stack procedures and functions, and we declare these as global variables. Finally, these procedures include an initialization procedure, so we can begin with our stack empty (*TopPosition* := 0).

```
{The following procedures implement a stack using an array,
assuming these declarations:

Const MaxStack = 80;      Size of Stack

Type Data = ...           Type of Items Stored on Stack

Var Stack: Array[1..MaxStack] of Data;
    TopPosition: Integer;

}
```

```
Procedure InitializeStack;
{This procedure initializes the stack}
    Begin
        TopPosition := 0
    End {InitializeStack} ;

Function Empty: Boolean;
{This function determines if the stack is empty}
    Begin
        Empty := (TopPosition = 0)
    End {Empty} ;

Function Full: Boolean;
{This function determines if the stack array is full}
    Begin
        Full := (TopPosition = MaxStack)
    End {Full} ;

Procedure Push (Item: Data);
{This procedure pushes the given Item on the Stack}
    Begin
        If Full
            Then Writeln ('Stack Full - Further Data Cannot Be Stored')
            Else Begin
                TopPosition := TopPosition + 1;
                Stack[TopPosition] := Item
                End
    End {Push} ;

Procedure Pop (Var Item: Data);
{This procedure removes the top Item from stack and returns it}
    Begin
        If Empty
            Then Writeln ('Stack Empty - Data Cannot Be Returned')
            Else Begin
                Item := Stack[TopPosition];
                TopPosition := TopPosition - 1
                End
    End {Pop} ;

Procedure Top (Var Item: Data);
{This procedure returns the top Item from the stack;
 the stack remains unchanged}
    Begin
        If Empty
            Then Writeln ('Stack Empty - No Data Returned')
            Else Item := Stack[TopPosition]
    End {Top} ;
```

This code handles all of the details necessary for a stack of the specified type of data. The global variables, *Stack* and *TopPosition*, allow us to apply these functions and procedures easily, and the stack data are shared by other stack operations. Then, once we declare these procedures and functions, we can concentrate on the logical use of our stack operations; we do not need to worry about the details of stacks further in our applications.

QUEUES

We now turn to our second major data structure, queues. In Section 17.1, we introduced a queue to represent a checkout line in a store. Such a line has the following properties.

- Customers enter the line at one end.
- Customers wait in line until being served by a clerk.
- Customers leave the line after being served.
- We can detect if a line is empty.

In addition, if a line becomes too long, customers may decide to purchase their items another time rather than wait in line. In this situation, we might want to specify a maximum size for the queue, and we might want to test if the queue is full.

Unlike stacks where the operational names *Push* and *Pop* are standard, the operations for queues are commonly called by several names. For example, the addition of a customer to a queue may be called an **Enter** or **Insert** operation; the leaving of a customer after being served may be called a **Delete** or **Remove** operation. For parallelism in terminology, we use *Insert* and *Delete* in this textbook.

More formally, a **queue** is defined as the data structure that has *data* of a specified type, and *operations* described as follows.

1. *Empty*
   The *Empty* function returns true or false, depending upon whether the queue contains any items.
2. *Full* {Optional}
   The *Full* function returns true or false, depending upon whether the queue contains as much data as it can hold.
3. *Insert (Item)*
   If the queue is not full, the specified item is placed at one end of the queue.
   If the queue is full, nothing is added, and an error is reported.
4. *Delete (Item)*
   If the queue is not empty, the item at the end opposite where data are added is removed from the queue, and this item is returned.
   If the queue is empty, nothing is returned, and an error is reported.

Normally, queue operations do not allow access to the first or last items on our queue or any items in the middle. Thus, queues have no equivalent to the *Top* operation in stacks.

With these operations, queues provide a rather different pattern of data storage and retrieval than we find with stacks. In particular, once an item is placed on a queue, the item is not retrieved until all items ahead of it have already been removed. Here, the first item placed into a queue is the first one processed, and subsequent items must wait for their turn. We say queues provide **First In–First Out** or **FIFO** storage in contrast to the LIFO storage of stacks.

This FIFO storage and retrieval of information provides the motivation for using queues in problem solving. Queues allow us to simulate various waiting lines, and we can bury the programming details for these lines in our specified functions and procedures.

In the following section, we look at these programming details. Then in Section 17.7, we apply this queue data structure in some typical applications.

<table>
<tr><td>SECTION 17.6</td><td>IMPLEMENTATION OF QUEUES BY ARRAYS</td></tr>
</table>

In this section, we consider how we might implement a queue using arrays. Conceptually, we will find this implementation is reasonably straightforward, but a few details require some care.

Our basic approach is fairly simple. We think of an array as extending to the right indefinitely, and we store our data items in order in this array. We use variables *First* and *Last* to mark where our first element was added and where the last or most recent element was added. Figure 17–6 shows this setup, where we have placed four items on the queue. In the figure, *Item 1* was inserted into the queue, followed by *Items* 2, 3, and 4, in that order. This first item is marked by variable *First* and the final item added is marked by *Last*.

From this figure, we can trace what happens in our insert and delete operations. For the *Insert* operation, we must add 1 to *Last* to mark a new end for the queue, and insert the specified *Item* at this new location. Similarly, to *Delete*, we must return the first *Item* specified, and add 1 to *First* to mark the new head of the queue. With this basic picture, we can tell if a queue is empty by checking if *First* > *Last*. Further, in this figure, the queue has enough space, so it is never full.

In practice, this basic algorithm is complicated by the limitation that

FIGURE 17–6 • **Conceptual Implementation of a Queue**

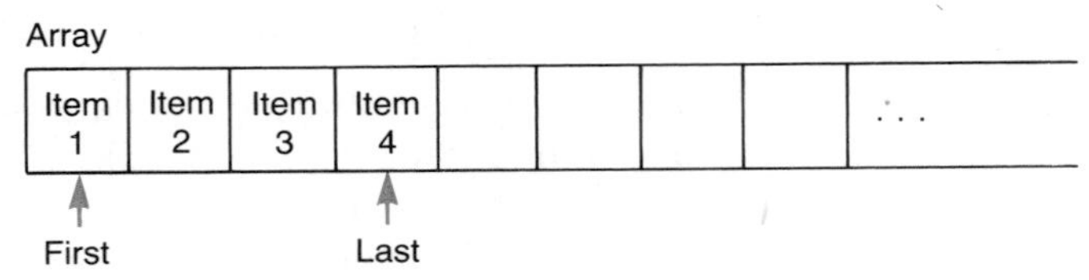

an array has a finite size; the array does not extend indefinitely to the right. With this limitation, we have two choices. As a first choice, when we delete an item from the queue, we could move all of the other items to the left to fill in the extra space. In this way, data in our queue would always start at the left end of our array, and we could keep inserting new items until the array was full. No space would be wasted.

Alternatively, we could think of the first element of the array as following the last element. When *Last* gets to the end of the array, we reuse the space that has been left at the beginning of the array when items have been removed. This approach is shown in Figure 17–7. Here, items 1 through n are waiting in an array, and some room is available at the start of the array. When a new item is added, there is no room at the right end of the array, so we reset *Last* to 1 and add the new item in the vacant space at the start.

Of these two alternatives, the first approach involves much shifting of data and thus is rather inefficient. The second approach allows our code to run much more quickly; however, we do need to be sure that we do not store new items on top of old ones, before the old ones are deleted from the queue. This check can be handled in several ways. One of the easiest is to keep a count of the number of items waiting in the queue. When this number reaches the maximum size of the array, the array is full and further insertions are impossible. This count also allows us to check if the queue is empty.

With these comments, we can write out the code for each of our queue operations. In our code, the queue operations must share data for the Queue array itself, the markers *First* and *Last* (which we call *QFirst* and *QLast*), and the counter for the number of items in the queue (which we call *QCount*). In our program, we write this shared data using global variables.

Also, in this code, we need to be able to increment *QFirst* and *QLast* by 1 easily, with the first element of the array following the last array ele-

FIGURE 17–7 · **Adding an Element to a Queue at the End of the Array**

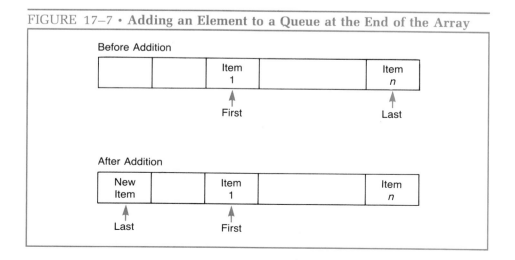

ment. If *MaxQueue* specifies the maximum subscript allowed for the *Queue* array, then this incrementing can be done using modular arithmetic with the statements

QFirst : = (QFirst + 1) Mod (MaxQueue + 1);
QLast : = (QLast + 1) Mod (MaxQueue + 1);

When we start our program, we also need to initialize these variables appropriately, so we include an appropriate *InitiailizeQueue* procedure. The coding of each operation is now rather straightforward.

```
{The following procedures implement a queue using an array,
 assuming these declarations:

Const MaxQueue = 100;          Size of Queue

Type Data = ...                Type of Items Stored on Queue

Var Queue: Array[0..MaxQueue] of Data;
    QFirst, QLast: Integer;    Markers for the Ends of the Queue
    QCount: Integer;           Number of Items on the Queue

}

Procedure InitializeQueue;
{This procedure initializes the Queue}
    Begin
        QCount := 0;
        QFirst := 0;
        QLast := MaxQueue;
    End {InitializeQueue} ;

Function Empty: Boolean;
{This procedure determines if the Queue is empty}
    Begin
        Empty := (QCount = 0)
    End {Empty} ;

Function Full: Boolean;
{This procedure determines if the Queue array is full}
    Begin
        Full := (QCount = (MaxQueue + 1))
    End {Full} ;

Procedure Insert (Item: Data);
{This procedures adds the specified Item to the Queue}
    Begin
        If Full
            Then Writeln ('Queue Full - Further Data Cannot Be Stored')
            Else Begin
                QLast := (QLast + 1) Mod (MaxQueue + 1);
                Queue[QLast] := Item;
                QCount := QCount + 1
                End
    End {Insert} ;
```

```
Procedure Delete (Var Item: Data);
{This procedure deletes the first item from the Queue and returns it}
   Begin
      If Empty
         Then Writeln ('Queue Empty - Data Cannot Be Returned')
         Else Begin
            Item := Queue[QFirst];
            QFirst := (QFirst + 1) Mod (MaxQueue + 1);
            QCount := QCount - 1
            End
   End {Delete} ;
```

This code implements all operations for the queue data structure. These details are conceptually fairly straightforward in using an array to store our queue items; we place the items in order in the array, marking the first and last elements. However, due to the limited amount of storage present in an array, some care is required in doing the actual coding.

Once the specifics are written, we can consider queues more abstractly, storing and retrieving data using specified oprations that result in a FIFO pattern of storage. The applications of queues in the next section suggest how this FIFO storage can be used in practice.

SECTION 17.7   EXAMPLES

Now that we have defined the queue data structure and have seen one way to implement that structure, we consider two typical types of application. The first comes from our original motivation for queues, and we simulate the time spent by customers waiting in a checkout line. The second application involves the scheduling of processing.

PROBLEM 17.7   Checkout Line Waiting Times

Suppose we know the average number of people that buy something at a store, and suppose we know the average time required for a clerk to serve a person at the cash register. Predict how long a customer will spend in line. Also approximate the maximum time a person may have to wait in line. In this problem, assume that only one clerk is available to run the register, so only one checkout line need be considered.

Discussion of Problem 17.7

This problem, and variations of it, involve considerable complexity, and their solutions are quite important for managers, since companies will lose business if customers become discouraged due to long lines. On the other hand, large numbers of clerks can keep waiting times short, but these clerks must be paid. Thus, a balance is needed between customers waiting and the number of clerks hired.

In this problem, we are given an average number of people needing service and an average service time, but we cannot assume that these people enter the line at a uniform rate nor that the service always requires exactly the same amount of time. Thus, while the given averages are easy to compute, they do not tell us directly how long individuals might have to wait.

Our approach to the problem will involve the use of simulation. We use a queue to keep track of individuals as they enter and leave the checkout line, and we record how many customers were served and how long they waited.

More precisely, we divide time into short intervals, and we use the averages given to determine the probability that a person will enter the line during a time interval. We also determine the probability that a person in line will finish at the cash register.

Then, we proceed one time interval at a time. By using a random number generator, we follow people as they enter and leave the queue. We record when they enter. Then, when they finish, we compute how long they waited.

This discussion suggests the following outline.

Outline for Problem 17.7

I. Initialization
   A. Initialize *Queue* and *RandomFunction*.
   B. Set processing totals to 0 for time waited, maximum time waited, and number of people processed.
   C. Determine initial averages.
      1. Average number of people in per hour.
      2. Average time for clerk to serve one customer.
   D. Determine data for one time interval.
      1. Length of interval.
      2. Probability a person will enter line.
      3. Probability a person in line will finish.

II. Repeat for each time interval.
   A. If a person has finished in that interval:
      1. Delete person from queue.
      2. Compute time in queue.
      3. Add time to total.
      4. Check time against maximum waiting time.
      5. Note another person has finished.
   B. If a person enters the queue, record the person's time as a new entry on the queue.
   C. Revise time for start of next interval.

III. Print results.
   A. Print number of people served.
   B. Compute and print the average waiting time.
   C. Print maximum time waited.

While this outline must keep track of several details for our simulation, the main headings and organization are rather clear. Further, the use of a queue allows us to separate the application of queues from the details included in coding queue procedures.

In the following program, we omit the details of both the random number generator (Section 4.4) and the queue procedures. For this program, we simulate the checkout lines for one hour (60 minutes), and we take our time interval as 15 seconds, so there are 4 such intervals each minute.

```
Program WaitInLine (Input, Output);
{This program simulates customers waiting in line
 at a store's check out counter.}

{Constants for the random number generator and the queue
 are given here}

Type Data = Real;          {Real numbers representing starting times
                            are stored in the queue}


{Variables for the random number generator and the queue are declared here}

{Procedures for the random number generator and the queue
 are specified here.  The queue procedures and functions are:
     Function Empty: Boolean;
     Function Full: Boolean;
     Procedure Insert(Item: Data);
     Procedure Delete(Var Item: Data);
}


Procedure Initialize(Var IntTime, TotalTime, MaxWait:Real;
                     Var NumberServed: Integer; IntPerMin: Real;
                     Var Length, EntryProb, ServiceProb: Real);
{This procedure initializes all variables needed for the simulation}
     Var AvgIn: Real;
         AvgLength: Real;
     Begin
         InitializeRandomFunction;
         InitializeQueue;

         {Set totals to 0}
         IntTime := 0.0;
         TotalTime := 0.0;
         MaxWait := 0.0;
         NumberServed := 0;

         {Determine averages}
         Write ('Enter average number of persons served per hour: ');
         Readln (AvgIn);
         Write ('Enter average length at register, in minutes: ');
         Readln (AvgLength);

         {Compute interval data}
         Length := 1.0 / IntPerMin;
         EntryProb := AvgIn / (60.0 * IntPerMin);
         ServiceProb := 1.0 / (AvgLength * IntPerMin)

     End {Initialize} ;
```

```
Procedure CustomerDone(DoneTime: Data; Var TotalTime, MaxWait: Real;
                       Var NumberServed: Integer);
{This procedure updates all totals when a customer finishes}
    Var EntryTime: Data;        {Time person entered line}
        ElapsedTime: Data;      {Total time person in line}
    Begin
        Delete(EntryTime);
        ElapsedTime := DoneTime - EntryTime;
        TotalTime := TotalTime + ElapsedTime;
        If ElapsedTime > MaxWait
            Then MaxWait := ElapsedTime;
        NumberServed := NumberServed + 1
    End {CustomerDone} ;

Procedure PrintResults(EndTime, TotalTime, MaxWait: Real;
                       NumberServed: Integer);
{This procedure summarizes the results of the simulation}
    Var AvgTime: Data;
    Begin
        Writeln;
        Writeln ('During this simulation of ',
                EndTime:1:2, ' hours,');
        Writeln (NumberServed:1, ' people were served,');
        Avgtime := TotalTime / NumberServed;
        Writeln ('these people waited an average of ',
                AvgTime:1:1, ' minutes,');
        Writeln ('and the maximum wait was ',
                MaxWait:1:1, ' minutes.')
    End {PrintResults} ;

Procedure SimulateLines;
{This procedure simulates the lines at a check out counter.}
    Const IntPerMin = 4;       {Specification of number of
                                short time intervals in a minute}
          EndTime = 60.0;      {Length of Simulation in Minutes}

    Var IntTime: Real;         {Starting time of a given interval}
        Length: Real;          {Duration of one time interval, in minutes}
        TotalTime: Real;       {Total amount of time spent waiting
                                by all customers}
        NumberServed: Integer; {Total number of people served}
        MaxWait: Real;         {Maximum time waited by any customer}
        EntryProb: Real;       {Probability that customer enters line in interval
        ServiceProb: Real;     {Probability that customer finishes in interval}
    Begin
        Initialize(IntTime, TotalTime, MaxWait, NumberServed,
                   IntPerMin, Length, EntryProb, ServiceProb);

        {Simulate check-out line for each time interval}
        Repeat
            If (Not Empty) And (Random <= ServiceProb)
                Then CustomerDone(IntTime, TotalTime, MaxWait, NumberServed);
            If (Not Full) And (Random <= EntryProb)
                Then Insert(IntTime);
            IntTime := IntTime + Length
        Until (IntTime > EndTime);

        PrintResults (EndTime, TotalTime, MaxWait, NumberServed)
    End {SimulateLines} ;
```

```
Begin {Main}
    Writeln ('This program simulates customers waiting in a line');
    Writeln ('for service at a check-out counter.');
    SimulateLines
End {Main}
```

Three sample runs of this program follow.

First Trial Run

```
This program simulates customers waiting in a line
for service at a check-out counter.
Enter average number of persons served per hour: 60
Enter average length at register, in minutes: 0.5

During this simulation of 60.00 hours,
52 people were served,
these people waited an average of 0.6 minutes,
and the maximum wait was 1.5 minutes.
```

Second Trial Run

```
This program simulates customers waiting in a line
for service at a check-out counter.
Enter average number of persons served per hour: 30
Enter average length at register, in minutes: 1.5

During this simulation of 60.00 hours,
23 people were served,
these people waited an average of 3.6 minutes,
and the maximum wait was 10.0 minutes.
```

Third Trial Run

```
This program simulates customers waiting in a line
for service at a check-out counter.
Enter average number of persons served per hour: 30
Enter average length at register, in minutes: 0.9

During this simulation of 60.00 hours,
35 people were served,
these people waited an average of 1.0 minutes,
and the maximum wait was 3.5 minutes.
```

In this problem, a queue allowed us to monitor customers by recording the times they entered a line. This structure of a queue, with FIFO storage and retrieval, provided the conceptual framework for our simulation, and we were able to solve our problem without becoming involved in the details required to code a queue.

Job Scheduling

Another type of application of queues is illustrated by the scheduling of jobs within time-sharing computers. In a typical time-sharing computer, many users may request processing at a particular time, and the computer must be set up to divide its time among these requests. This can be done in several ways.

The simplest approach sets up one queue that stores all requests for processing. Whenever a user makes a request, that request is placed on a queue. Then the computer processes the request at the head of the queue. In this simple approach, the computer finishes one request before starting on the next. Such an approach may be used if several people want to obtain output from the same printer. We do not want the output from one user to be interspersed with that from another. Rather, we want one job finished completely before the next starts. A single queue can handle this situation. This approach can effectively handle all requests, and each request will finally be processed. However, this approach does have the disadvantage that short jobs must wait for any long ones that entered the queue first.

A second approach uses a queue together with a time limit. User requests enter the queue as before, and the computer always processes the request at the head of the queue. However, the computer continues processing for only a specified maximum length of time. If the request is satisfied within that time, then the machine goes on to the next request as before. On the other hand, if more processing is still required for that task, any intermediate values are stored and the request is put back on the queue. Processing on that request resumes only after that task makes it way to the head of the queue again. This approach allows short tasks to be done relatively quickly, since long tasks are interrupted after the time limit expires. Particularly long tasks may need to go back through the queue many times before they are finally done.

In a third approach, we refine the idea of a queue with a time limit by adding the idea of a priority. In this approach, a priority for processing is assigned to each request. This priority can be used in several possible ways. For example, the priority level can affect the time limit allocated to a task. High priority jobs may be allowed to run longer at each turn than lower priority ones. Alternatively separate queues may be set up for each priority level. Time limits apply as before, but here the priority of a queue affects which jobs are selected when a time limit expires. When a new task is to be processed, the computer first looks at the top priority queue to see if any tasks are waiting. If so, the task at the head of that queue is selected for processing. If not, the computer looks at the queue with the next highest priority. The computer continues down the priority level of queues until a queue is found with a task waiting. Then the task at the head of that queue is selected.

This third approach allows us to distinguish among various types of requests and gives us considerable flexibility in scheduling jobs. However, if many high priority requests are received, this latter approach may not allow the computer to get to the requests of lower priority.

Other more complex and sophisticated approaches are also possible in which queues, time limits, and priorities are combined in various ways. Within a computer, the approach used depends upon the particular demands anticipated for the system and upon management's perception of the relative priorities for these demands.

Once a particular approach is chosen, the details of that approach are coded and entered into the portion of the computer's main memory that monitors various internal machine functions. Other internal functions include keeping track of the location of files on disks and the communication between the CPU and various terminals. Together these pieces form a computer's **operating system,** which handles many of the detailed internal workings of the computer. We discuss more about operating systems in Chapter 22.

Each of these applications of queues reinforces our motivation for introducing the data structures that we have discussed throughout this chapter. In solving problems, we need to perform certain operations on our data, and we do not want to be distracted by the programming details of these operations. Data structures (e.g., stacks and queues) allow us a convenient way to separate these details from the conceptual view of data with its operations. Thus, data structures allow us to organize and conceptualize our data in the same way that our top-down programming has allowed us to structure our code. In the next two chapters, we continue this abstract approach to data by considering further data structures.

SUMMARY

1. A **data structure** is a way to view data involving two parts: **data** themselves and **operations** on the data.
2. The **stack** data structure mimics a pile of papers on a desk and includes the following operations:

> Function *Empty*: Boolean
> Function *Full*: Boolean   {Optional}
> Procedure *Push* (Item: Data)
> Procedure *Pop* (Var Item: Data)
> Procedure *Top* (Var Item: Data)

3. The **queue** data structure models a line of customers at a checkout counter and includes the following operations:

> Function *Empty*: Boolean
> Function *Full*: Boolean   {Optional}
> Procedure *Insert* (Item: Data)
> Procedure *Delete* (Var Item: Data)

4. In applying these data structures, we focus on the order that data are stored and retrieved. In particular,
   a. Stacks follow a **Last In–First Out (LIFO)** or **First In–Last Out (FILO)** pattern. This approach is useful in balancing parentheses; evaluating expressions in **postfix** notation; and running programs with a **run-time stack.**
   b. Queues follow a **First In–First Out** (FIFO) pattern. This approach is useful in simulating customers in a line and scheduling tasks.

EXERCISES

17.1 *Optional Top Operation.* In some definitions of a stack, the *Top* operation is not included, because it can be written in terms of the *Push* and *Pop* operations.

Write a *Top* procedure that uses only *Push* and *Pop* operations to access the stack.

17.2 *Reversing Input.* Write a program that reads a line of input and prints out the characters in the line in reverse order. In this program, use *Push* operations to store the characters in a stack and return the characters with *Pop* operations.

17.3 *Translating from Prefix Notation.* Translate the following expressions from prefix notation to both infix and postfix notations. Then evaluate each expression.
   a. + * 2 3 4
   b. * + 2 3 4

KEY TERMS, PHRASES, AND CONCEPTS

Data Structures	Queues
Data	Delete or Remove
Operations	Empty
First In–First Out	Full {Optional}
(FIFO)	Insert or Enter
First In–Last Out	Run-Time Stack
(FILO)	Stacks
Last In–First Out	Empty
(LIFO)	Full {Optional}
Notations	Pop
Infix	Push
Postfix	Top
Prefix	
Operating	
Systems	

c. + − 2 3 / 6 3

d. / − 9 3 ∗ 3 2

e. ∗ + 2 3 + ∗ 4 5 6

17.4 *Translating from Infix Notation.* Translate the following expressions from infix notation to both prefix and postfix notations.

a. (2 − 3) + 4

b. 2/3 − 4 ∗ 5

c. (2 + 3) ∗ (4 + 5)

d. (2 + 3 ∗ 4)/(5 − 6)

e. (2 ∗ 3 − 4/5) ∗ (6/7)

17.5 *Translating from Postfix Notations.* Translate the following expressions from postfix notation to both prefix and infix notations. Then evaluate each of these expressions following the algorithm given in Section 17.3.

a. 2 3 ∗ 4 +

b. 2 3 4 + ∗

c. 2 3 4 5 + − ∗

d. 2 3 − 4 5 − 6 ∗ /

e. 2 3 4 − − 80 4 5 ∗ / +

17.6 *Evaluating Postfix Expressions.* Write a program that reads an arithmetic expression written in postfix notation and evaluates it. In your program, you will need to read the expression as a line of input. Then you will have to identify successive operations and numbers in the input line. In this scanning of input, you will need to write a procedure that reads a number as a sequence of characters and then computes the value of that number.

NOTE: For simplicity, you may assume all numbers read in this problem are positive integers.

17.7 *Translation from Infix to Postfix Notation.* In converting from infix to postfix notation, we observe that all numbers remain in the same order. The only work is to move operations from between numbers to an appropriate point after them. This conversion is done by the following algorithm[1] in which we read the infix expression from left to right, and we assume that we type the symbol '$' as a sentinel at the end of this expression. We also use the symbol '$' to mark the bottom of a stack. The algorithm then proceeds according to a system of priorities given to symbols located in the input and on the stack. This system is shown in Table 17–3.

I. Push ('$'). (This initializes the stack.)

II. Read successive items of input.

A. If the item is a number, move the number to the output.

---

[1]Algorithm taken from Robert J. Baron and Linda G. Shapiro, *Data Structures and Their Implementation*, Van Nostrand Reinhold Company (New York, 1980), pages 58–60.

TABLE 17–3 · Priorities for Symbols in Infix-Postfix Conversion

Operator	Input Priority	Output Priority
*	2	2
/	2	2
+	1	1
−	1	1
(	3	0
)	0	—
$	0	0

B. If the item is a right parenthesis, ')'
    1. Continue until top of stack is '('
        a. Pop stack to get operator.
        b. Move operator to output.
    2. Discard (pop) the '(' from the stack.
C. If the item is an operator or a '('
    1. As long as the input priority of this item is smaller than the stack priority of the operators at the top of the stack
        a. pop stack to get operator
        b. move operator to output
    2. Push input item onto stack.

    a. Apply this algorithm (on paper) to the expressions in Exercise 17.4.
    b. Write a program that reads an expression in infix notation and then applies this algorithm to convert it to postfix notation.

17.8 *Declarations for Stacks or Queues.* In an application of stacks (or queues), we used the stack by specifying simply *Empty, Push (Item),* etc. We preferred not to use other parameters for *Stack* and *Top-Position.* Instead, we thought of *Stack* and *TopPosition* as shared variables.
    a. Why does this preference require that all stack declarations must be global?
    b. Use our conclusions about program correctness and maintenance to discuss the dangers of declaring these stack variables as global.
    c. How could we redesign the stack procedures and functions so that global variables are not needed?

17.9 *Revision of Single Line Checkout.* Modify the simulation program of lines in a store from Section 17.7 to include the following.
    a. Record the time in line for each customer. Then print a histogram displaying these times at the end of the program.

b. At the end of the simulation, some customers may be left in line. Use queue operations to determine the number of such customers, and include this result in your output.

NOTE: In part (b), you may *not* access *QFirst* and *QLast* directly to make your computation.

17.10 *Palindromes.* A palindrome is a sequence of characters that reads the same from either end, such as *abcdedcba*, *otto*, or *madam*. Write a program that reads a line of input and determines if the line is a palindrome. In your program, use a queue to store the characters in the line in the order they were read and use a stack to store the characters in the reverse order. Then use the queue *Delete* operation and the stack *Pop* operation to obtain characters from each end of the line, and compare successive characters.

17.11 *Scheduling Computer Jobs.* Section 17.7 presents three ways that tasks in a computer can be scheduled. In evaluating these different approaches, it is useful to determine the minimum, mean, and maximum times required for differing jobs to be completed. Write a program that simulates each of these algorithms and computes these processing times. In this simulation, generate jobs whose processing requirements vary randomly between 0.1 second and 5.0 seconds.

17.12 *Traffic at a Stop Light–1.* Traffic flow can be simulated by making various assumptions. One of the simplest situations involves the intersection of two roads, where one lane goes each direction. At the intersection, we assume the following.
   • A car may encounter either a red or a green light. (For simplicity, we omit the possibility of an amber light.)
   • If a car encounters a red light, it stops for the light.
   • If several cars have stopped for the red light, they wait in a queue.
   • When a light changes to green, cars waiting in a queue may continue. (We might assume they leave the queue at a specified rate, such as 1 car leaving every 10 seconds.)
   • If a car encounters a green light, there are two possibilities.
      a. If there are cars ahead that are still in a queue from a previous red light, then the car stops in the queue.
      b. If there are no cars ahead, the approaching car proceeds through the intersection.
   • In all cases, cars proceed straight ahead. (We do not complicate the situation by allowing turns.)
   Write a program that simulates this situation. The program should request
   • the average number of cars coming in each direction, and
   • the length of the red and green lights.
Then, the program should record and print the average waiting times for the cars going in each direction.

NOTE: The following two problems require several queues, which we may implement as an array of queues. With these queues, a new operation is needed to identify which queue is the shortest. (If queues are each the same length, this new operation may identify any of the queues.)

17.13 *Traffic at a Stop Light–2.* Extend the previous stop light problem, so that two lanes of traffic go in each direction. You may assume that when a car encounters a red light, it will always enter the queue in the lane with the smallest number of cars.

17.14 *Multiple Checkout Lines.* Write a program to simulate waiting times in a store that has several cashiers and checkout lines. In this simulation, you may assume each cashier is equally efficient, so the average time a cashier takes with a customer is the same for all lines. Also, you may assume a customer coming to the checkout area always enters the shortest line.

17.15 *Several Clerks—One Queue.* In some situations (e.g., at some banks and airports), several clerks are available to serve customers, but customers all wait in a single queue. When a customer wants service, the customer enters the queue. Then, when the customer gets to the head of the queue, the customer is served by the first available clerk. (If a customer arrives when no one is waiting in line and when a clerk is free, then the customer can go immediately to the clerk for service.)

a. Write a program to simulate waiting times in this situation.

b. Compare the times for this allocation of clerks with the waiting times for the multiple queue approach of the previous exercise. Is one of these strategies for employing several clerks better than the other? Justify your answer.

CHAPTER 18

LINKED LIST
DATA STRUCTURES:
AN INTRODUCTION
TO POINTERS

T he previous chapter introduced the definition of a data structure, and we saw two examples of these structures, stacks and queues. In this chapter, we consider another such data structure, called a **linked list.** As in previous discussions, our work will include both a description of lists on a conceptual level and a consideration of how these structures can be implemented in Pascal. As part of this implementation of linked lists, we will need to introduce a new type of data called **pointers.**

LINKED LISTS AND THE CONCEPT OF POINTERS

To motivate what we mean by a linked list structure, we begin with an illustration involving lists that we might maintain for work we need to do. In preparing these lists, we initially might write down the tasks that we must do as we think of them. Then, we might number these tasks in the order in which we plan to do them. As we think of additional work to do, we would write down each new task (perhaps at the bottom of our paper)

557

FIGURE 18–1 • **List of Tasks Written on Paper**

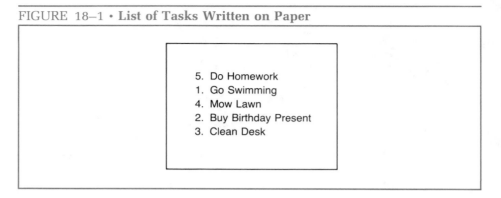

5. Do Homework
1. Go Swimming
4. Mow Lawn
2. Buy Birthday Present
3. Clean Desk

and then revise our numbering, which indicates our order for doing the work. Such a list is shown in Figure 18–1.

When we analyze the list in Figure 18–1, we can identify several important characteristics.

- One task, *Go swimming*, is designated as the first item.
- Another item, *Do homework*, will be done last.
- If we follow our numbering, each entry in our list (except the last) has exactly one item following it.
- In using this list, we do not attach any special significance to the order in which we wrote the tasks. For example, we thought of our homework first, and *Do Homework* appears as the first line of our figure. However, that task will be done last in our work schedule. On the other hand, *Go swimming* appears on the second line of our list, but that task is done first.

With these observations, we may write our list in a different form to better reflect what we have identified as being important. Such a representation of our list is shown in Figure 18–2.

FIGURE 18–2 • **List of Tasks Using Pointers**

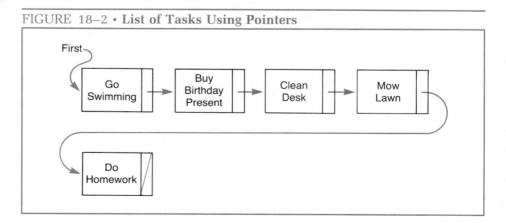

In this figure, we have not tried to write separate tasks on different lines on paper. Rather, we represent each item on our list as a box that has two parts:

- the name of the task for our list entry, and
- a place to indicate which box is next. (In our diagrams, we indicate this next box with an arrow.)

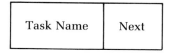

In this representation, the *Task Name* includes alphabetic characters which we have worked with before. However, the arrows for the *Next* part of the box are something new, called **pointers.** Pointers represent a new data type and indicate where other pieces of information are located. In our figure, a box contains both a task name and an arrow or pointer which points to another box. Arrows do not contain our task names; rather arrows point to boxes, and the boxes contain the task names.

In using pointers to put our boxes of data together, Figure 18–2 also illustrates two other features that we must include in this representation of lists. First, we use a special pointer to specify the location of the initial item on our list. In addition, we need a special symbol to indicate the last element on our list, since the last box does not have an arrow pointing onward. In our diagram, we drew a diagonal line through the *Next* part of our box for the last item, *Do Homework.*

More generally, a **linked list** contains list items, which are made up of data (such as a task name) and a pointer to the next item. This list also contains a special pointer to indicate the first item on the list. With this structure, each item on the list can be reached starting with the first item and following the pointers from one item to the next. Here, we emphasize that the physical location of each item is unimportant; rather, we stress the linking of one item to the next by pointers. We illustrate this general form in Figure 18–3.

Operations on Linked Lists

When we use linked lists to store our data, we often perform one of four types of operations on the list: finding and perhaps changing a data item, printing data, deleting an item, or inserting a new item. Conceptually, each of these operations is quite simple, but some details for item deletion and insertion require a bit of care. We now look closely at the specifics of these operations. In each case, we begin with the simple linked list shown in Figure 18–4, where our data consists of the numbers 2, 4, 6, and 8.

FIGURE 18–3 • **A General Linked List**

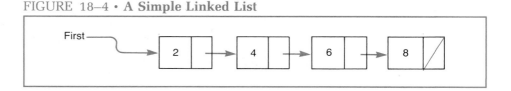

Finding a Data Item

Outline for Finding a Data Item. In locating a particular data item in a linked list, we start with the first item on our list and then proceed from one item to the next until we find our desired piece of data or until we reach the end of the list.

 I. Prepare to examine first item.
 II. Continue until data found or no more items remain.
   A. Compare the data desired with the data stored in this item.
     1. If the data match, note data found.
     2. If the data do not match, prepare to examine the next item.

As an example, we try to find the number 6 on the list of Figure 18–4. We proceed in several steps. (See Figure 18–5.)

   Step 1. We prepare to examine the first item.
   Step 2. The 2 of the first item does not match the 6 we want, so we move to the next item on the list.
   Step 3. The 4 of this item does not match the 6 we want, so we again move to the next item on the list.

FIGURE 18–4 • **A Simple Linked List**

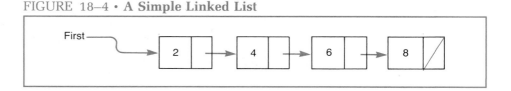

FIGURE 18–5 · Locating a Data Item on a List
Locating "6" on the List of Figure 18–4

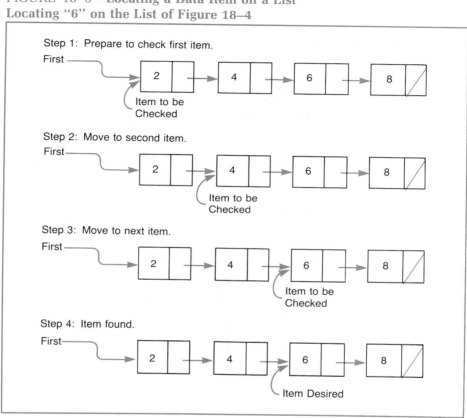

Step 4. The 6 of this item does match our desired number, and we are done.

This process illustrates the distinction between list items and pointers. Throughout our work, we first use a pointer to identify the item that we want to check. Then, we consider the data within that item. Further, in this process, we maintain a pointer that tells us what item we wish to examine next. That pointer begins at the first item. Then we move that pointer along from item to item as we check data in subsequent items.

Printing the Data on a List

We can print the data on a list following much the same process as for finding a particular item, except that we keep printing successive items until no more items are present. We do not stop partway through.

Outline for Printing List Data. The following outline for printing follows the same general form as our previous outline.

I. Prepare to print data in first item.
II. Continue until no more items remain.
    A. Print the data at the current item.
    B. Prepare to examine the next item.

Deleting a Data Item

The deletion of an item from a list is illustrated in Figure 18–6, where we delete the third item. In the new list, the "4" box no longer specifies that the "6" box comes next. Rather, the pointer for the "4" box indicates that the "8" box comes next. Thus, within a linked list structure, we can delete an item by changing pointers; the "6" box is no longer on our list, because we cannot reach that box by starting at the beginning of our list and moving from one item to the next. Even if the box is physically present somewhere, it is lost for all future work, since we cannot find this box by searching, starting from the beginning of the list. Beyond this changing of pointers, we also may decide to throw away the old item that we deleted, so we can use that space again.

This example illustrates the main steps involved in deleting an item from a linked list.

Step 1. Find the item to be deleted.
Step 2. Change the pointer of the previous item to specify the next item. (This deletes the item from the list itself.)
Step 3. Free the space occupied by the deleted item, if desired.

These steps are shown more carefully in Figure 18–7.

As the figure shows, the ideas behind this deletion are fairly simple. However, in actually writing an outline to perform this task, we find two complications. First, the deletion of the first item in a list requires a special case. Specifically, we must now designate a new "first" item. Secondly, when we find the item we wish to delete, we still must keep track of the previous item. For example, in Figure 18–7, when we locate the "6" box, we must also be able to locate the "4" box.

FIGURE 18–6 • **List Deletion**

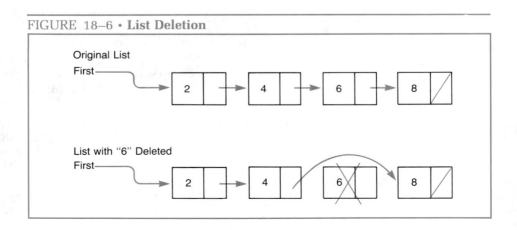

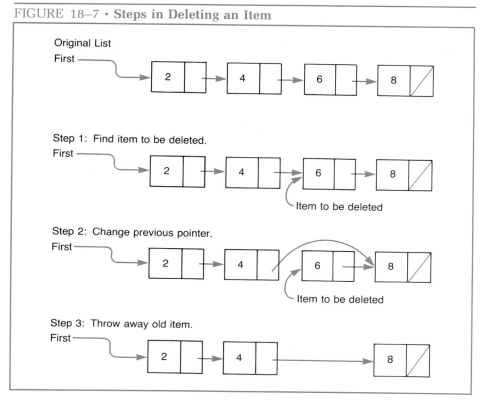

FIGURE 18–7 · **Steps in Deleting an Item**

This second point illustrates an important characteristic of linked lists that requires explicit mention. When we consider a particular item on a list, it is easy to find items that come later in the list; we can just follow the arrows. However, a linked list does not allow us to back up toward the front. At each list item, we have information about the next item, but we do not have information about previous ones, so we cannot follow our arrows backward. Thus, when we delete an item from a list, we must explicitly keep track of previous items as we perform our search. More specifically, when we write a search procedure, we might return a pointer to the previous item on the list. From this previous item, we can move ahead easily to the item we will actually delete.

With this observation, we now outline the operation to delete an item from a list.

Outline for Deleting an Item.   Determine if the item to be deleted appears first on the list.

I. If so:
   A. Move the first pointer to the new "first" item on the list.
   B. Throw away the old item.

II. If not:
  A. Find the item to be deleted on the list, keeping track of the previous item as the search continues.
  B. Change the pointer of the previous item to specify the next item.
  C. Throw away the old item.

Inserting a Data Item

The insertion of an item into a list is illustrated in Figure 18–8, where we insert a "5" into a new third box in our list. In the new list, we have created a new box, placed the "5" as the data for this box, made the pointer of the "5" box indicate that the "6" box comes next, and changed the pointer of the "4" box to this new list item. In this insertion process, we can build our "5" box at any convenient place; then we can add this box to our list by changing pointers appropriately.

This example illustrates the main steps involved in inserting an item into a linked list.

  Step 1. Determine where item will be inserted.
  Step 2. Create a new box.
  Step 3. Place data in the new box.
  Step 4. Make pointer of new box specify the appropriate next element.
  Step 5. Update the pointer in the previous box to specify the newly created box.

As with list deletion, the details of list insertion include two complications. If we wish to insert an item at the beginning of a list, then we must update the "first" pointer rather than the pointer in the previous list item. Secondly, when we are finding the place to insert the new item, we must be able to identify the item that will precede our new item. In our example,

---

FIGURE 18–8 • **List Insertion**

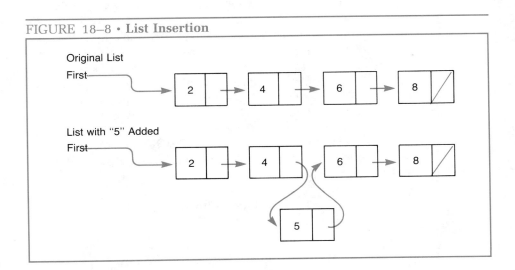

we must know that the "4" box will precede the "5" box. When we keep these details in mind, we can expand the above steps for list insertion into a complete outline.

IMPLEMENTATION OF LINKED LISTS WITH POINTERS

In the previous section, we saw how to represent linked lists in picture form, where arrows or pointers allowed us to move from one list item to the next. In this section, we translate this representation of lists into Pascal code. In this translation, we will meet a new Pascal data type called **pointers.** Then, with these Pascal pointers, we will find that the pictures of our list operations carry over in a rather straightforward way into corresponding procedures.

As with our conceptualization of pointers and lists in the previous sections, we must be careful in programming to distinguish between the pointers themselves and the item which the pointers specify. In Pascal, the upward arrow ↑ is used in conjunction with pointers, and this symbol helps us make this distinction. On some terminals, the upward arrow is printed as a caret ˆ. Alternatively the "at sign", @, may be used instead of the upward arrow or caret. In using pointers and this upward arrow or caret in programming, we must consider several important topics:

- pointer type and type declarations;
- variable declaration and initialization;
- manipulation of pointers and items; and
- storage of list items.

To illustrate our discussion, we consider the following problem.

Write a program that will maintain a list of tasks. In particular, the program should allow us to

- insert a new task after a specified task;
- delete a task; and
- print the list of tasks.

To solve this problem, we need to address each programming topic mentioned above.

Declarations

In our declarations, we must specify two types of objects: list items and pointers to list items. Following our discussion of list items in the first section, the list items themselves will contain two parts, data and a pointer to another item.

The following declarations define these objects.

```
Const Max = 20;
Type  ListData = Packed Array [1..Max] of Char;
      ListPointer = ^Item;
      Item = Record
            Data: ListData;
            Next: ListPointer
            End;
```

In this declaration,

```
^Item
```

designates a pointer to an *Item*. In declarations, we use the ^ to declare a new **pointer data type,** which is a pointer or arrow to a specified type of item.

This declaration specifies our list items as having two parts by defining an *Item* to be a record. Here, the *Data* field is a packed array of characters holding our task names, and the *Next* field points to another *Item*. Thus, this declaration exactly parallels our concept of a list item as a box with two parts.

After we declare these new types that involve pointers, we also need to declare a variable that will indicate the first item on our list. Thus, we write

```
Var First: ListPointer;
```

Alternatively, we could write

```
Var First: ^Item;
```

In either case, our variable declaration specifies a new variable that we will be able to use to find the beginning of our list.

Initialization

In the previous section, we noted that in reading through a list, we need to know when we come to the end of our list. We must know when an arrow does not point to a new box, and we notated this end by placing a line through the *Next* part of a box.

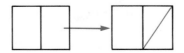

In Pascal, the value **Nil** is used to indicate that a pointer does not specify a new item.

Using this value, we normally initialize our first pointer to *nil*

First := Nil;

at the beginning of our program, since we start our program with no items on our list. Then as we add items to our list, *First* is updated to point to these new items. Also, we can use this *nil* value to check when we reach the end of our list. When a *Next* field is *nil*, we know we have found the last list item.

Manipulation of Pointers and Items

Suppose we have built a list of tasks, such as that shown in Figure 18–2. We now consider how to manipulate pointers and items to print our list.

From our discussion of printing in the previous section, we need to declare another variable that we can move along our list as we print. Thus, we begin

Var ListElt: ListPointer;

Then, our processing starts by examining the first element on our list. At first, *ListElt* points to the same item as the *First* pointer, and we use the assignment

ListElt := First;

The assignment statement makes the two pointers indicate the same item. At this point, *First* and *ListElt* are arrows that point to our first list item. (See Figure 18–9.)

Next, we want to work with the box at the end of our arrow. In Pascal, this is the second use of the upward arrow or caret ˆ. When we want the information that an arrow points to, we follow our pointer with the ˆ. Here,

- *ListElt* is the arrow, and
- *ListElt*ˆ is the item specified by the arrow.

(See Figure 18–9.) Thus, by using the upward arrow, we can distinguish between a pointer and an item itself.

Once we have our item *ListElt*ˆ, we work with it just as with any of the variables we have encountered before. In this case, *ListElt*ˆ specifies an item which is a record. In printing, we want to write the data in the record. As in the past, we precede a field by a period, so

.Data

specifies the task name within our box. Putting this field together with the box specification, we find

ListEltˆ.Data

allows us to work with the data field inside the box pointed to by the

FIGURE 18–9 • **Distinguishing Pointers and Items**

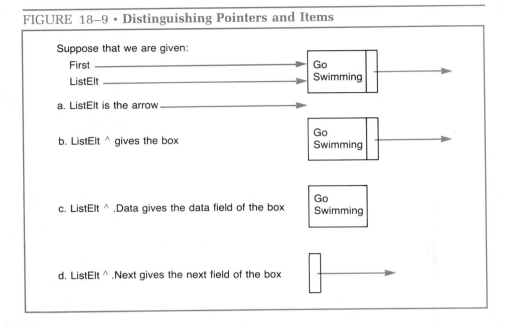

pointer *ListElt*. Then, to print out this field in our program, we state

Writeln(ListElt^.Data);

When we want to move from one box to the next, a similar sequence allows us to update our *ListElt*. In particular,

- ListElt   points to the box in the list we are currently considering;
- ListElt^   is the current box itself; and
- ListElt^.Next is the next pointer in the current box.

Then, in moving from one list item to the next, we need to update *ListElt* to the next pointer, *ListElt^.Next*. Again, this involves the assignment:

ListElt := ListElt^.Next

With this discussion, we now can write out the entire code for printing our list.

```
Procedure Print (First: ListPointer);
     Var   ListElt: ListPointer;
     Begin
          ListElt := First;
          While  (ListElt <> Nil)
             Do Begin
                Writeln(ListElt^.Data);
                ListElt := ListElt^.Next
             End
     End {Print} ;
```

This procedure illustrates several important features about using pointers in Pascal. We can use assignment statements to change what a pointer is pointing to. In addition, a *nil* value allows us to determine when we come to the end of a list. Finally, we can move from a pointer to the item pointed to by adding an upward arrow or caret ˆ to our variable. Here, we say we are **dereferencing** the pointer. The pointer itself gives a reference to an item. Adding the arrow or caret ˆ gives us the item itself.

Storage Allocation

Now that we have seen how to move from one list item to another when we print our list data, we turn to the creation and elimination of list items. Here, we find that list items are stored differently than other information. Up to now, storage for variables was created each time functions and procedures were called, and this space was freed when the functions and procedures finished. Such storage represents **static storage allocation;** within a function or procedure, this storage does not change.

In contrast, items that are specified by pointers can be created and destroyed within a function or procedure. Such storage is called **dynamic storage allocation.** For example, when we want to add an item to a list, we will need to explicitly create some space for the new data; when we want to delete an item, we will explicitly dispose of the old item.

This dynamic creation and deallocation of storage space are performed with two new procedures, *New* and *Dispose*. To see how these procedures work, suppose we have the declaration:

Var Elt:ˆ Item

Then

New(Elt)   allocates a new box for an item, and the variable *Elt* points to that new space.

Dispose(Elt) deallocates the box pointed to by the variable *Elt*.

Special Cases for Insertion and Deletion

To illustrate how these procedures are used, we consider two special cases that occur in our task problem.

Case 1: Insertion of New Task at Start of List.   To add an item to the start of our list, we declare a pointer variable.

Var NewItem: ListPointer;

After this declaration, we start our insertion by allocating the space for *NewItem* with the statement

New(NewItem); {Create Box for NewItem}

Next, we read the name of the task as data for the item. If we do this reading in a procedure *ReadData,* we might write

ReadData (NewItemˆ.Data)

Then, we need to change arrows, so that *NewItem* appears at the start of our list. In particular, the previous head of the list should come after *NewItem*:

NewItem^.Next : = **First**

Then, the *NewItem* should be put first:

First : = **NewItem**

These steps are shown in Figure 18–10.

FIGURE 18–10 • **Insertion of New Task at Start of List**

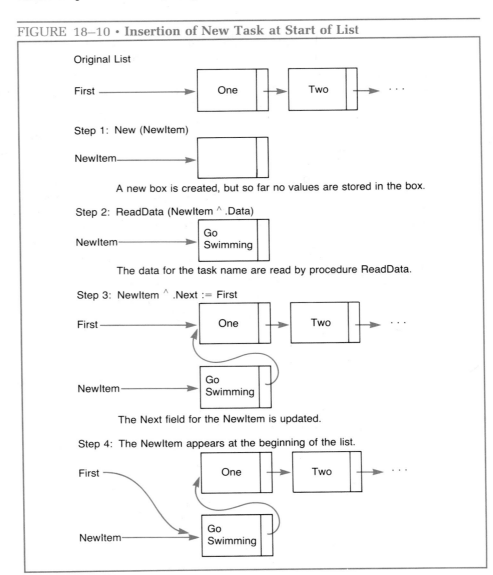

Case 2: Deletion of an Item from Middle of List.   To delete an item from a list, we follow our steps from Figure 18–7 (Section 18.1) carefully. Recall that in this process we need to keep track of the item to be deleted and the previous item on the list. Thus, our declarations include

Var PrevElt, ListElt: ListPointer;

Then, we search our list to find the item that we wish to delete. Such a search may be performed by a procedure call

FindPrevious (Name, PrevElt, First)

which locates *PrevElt,* the item that precedes the *Name* on the list given by the *First* pointer. Then

ListElt : = PrevElt^.Next

gives the item actually deleted. Next, we remove our element from the list by changing the previous list item. Again, following Step 2 of Figure 18–7, we write

PrevElt^.Next : = List Elt^.Next

Finally, we can throw away the old item with

Dispose (ListElt)

With these cases, we see that our insertion and deletion steps follow our discussions and figures from the previous section. We just translate the pictures into Pascal. We also have to be careful about those possibilities where our list does not contain any elements or when we need to work with the first item on our list.

The final program to perform these operations for Problem 18.2 is given below. Here, we will define two separate procedures, *ReadData* and *FindPrevious,* to read names from the terminal and to find names on our list. We will also write the program as a series of procedures which are driven by a single menu.

```
Program TaskList (Input, Output);
{This program maintains a list of tasks}

Const Max = 20;      {Length of task names}

Type ListData = Packed Array [1..Max] of Char;
     ListPointer = ^Item;
     Item = Record
          Data: ListData;
          Next: ListPointer
          End;
Var NullChar: Char;           {the null character, Chr(0)}
```

```
Procedure Initialization(Var First: ListPointer);
{This procedure initializes all appropriate variables}
    Begin
        First := Nil;
        NullChar := Chr(0)
    End {Initialization} ;

Procedure ReadData (Var Name: ListData);
{This procedure reads a name from the terminal}
    Var Index: Integer;
    Begin
        Index := 1;
        While (Index <= Max) and Not Eoln
          Do Begin
            Read (Name[Index]);
            Index := Index + 1
          End;
        Readln;
        While (Index <= Max)
          Do Begin
            Name[Index] := NullChar;
            Index := Index + 1
          End
    End {ReadData} ;

Procedure FindPrevious (Name: ListData; Var PrevElt: ListPointer;
                        First: ListPointer);
{This procedure locates the task that comes before given name on the list.
 If the name is not found, PrevElt^.Next will be Nil.
 The procedure assumes the Name is not the first list element.}

    Var ListElt: ListPointer;   {This pointer gives the list item
                                 where the Name is checked}

    Function Done: Boolean;
    {This function determines if more items must be searched on the list}
        Begin
            If ListElt = Nil
                Then Done := True
                Else Done := (Name = ListElt^.Data)
        End {Done} ;

    Begin {FindPrevious}
        PrevElt := First;
        ListElt := PrevElt^.Next;
        While Not Done
          Do Begin
            PrevElt := ListElt;
            ListElt := PrevElt^.Next
          End
    End {FindPrevious} ;

Procedure AddName( Var First: ListPointer);
{This procedure reads a task name and inserts it into the list}

    Var NewItem: ListPointer;
        OldName: ListData;
```

```
      Procedure InsertFirst (NewItem: ListPointer; Var First: ListPointer);
      {This procedure inserts the new item at the beginning of the list}
          Begin
              NewItem^.Next := First;
              First := NewItem
          End;

      Procedure InsertAfterFirst (NewItem, First: ListPointer);
      {The procedure inserts the new item after the start of the list}
          Var PrevElt: ListPointer;

          Begin
              FindPrevious (OldName, PrevElt, First);
              NewItem^.Next := PrevElt^.Next;
              PrevElt^.Next := NewItem
          End {InsertAfterFirst} ;

  Begin {AddName}
      New(NewItem);
      Write ('Enter new task: ');
      ReadData (NewItem^.Data);
      If First = Nil
          Then InsertFirst (NewItem, First)
          Else Begin
              Writeln ('Enter old task which new task should preceed, ');
              Write ('or enter a blank if new task should be ',
                      'placed "last": ');
              ReadData(OldName);
              If OldName = First^.Data
                  Then InsertFirst (NewItem, First)
                  Else InsertAfterFirst(NewItem, First)
          End
  End {AddName} ;

Procedure DeletionName(Var First: ListPointer);
{This procedure reads a task name and deletes the name from the list}
    Var Name: ListData;

    Procedure DeleteName (Name: ListData; Var First: ListPointer);
    {This procedure deletes the name from the specified list}
        Var PrevElt, ListElt: ListPointer;

        Begin
            If First^.Data = Name
                Then Begin {delete first element on list}
                    ListElt := First;
                    First := ListElt^.Next;
                    Dispose(ListElt)
                    End
                Else Begin
                    FindPrevious (Name, PrevElt, First);
                    ListElt := PrevElt^.Next;
                    If ListElt = Nil
                        Then Writeln ('Task not found on list')
                        Else Begin
                            PrevElt^.Next := ListElt^.Next;
                            Dispose(ListElt)
                            End
                    End
        End {DeleteName} ;
```

```
      Begin
          If First = Nil
              Then Writeln ('List is empty - no deletions are possible')
              Else Begin
                  Write ('Enter task name to be deleted: ');
                  ReadData(Name);
                  DeleteName (Name, First)
                  End
      End {DeletionStep} ;

Procedure Print(First: ListPointer);
{This procedure prints the current data items on the list}
    Var ListElt: ListPointer;
    Begin
        Writeln ('The list of tasks are:');
        Writeln;
        ListElt := First;
        While (ListElt <> Nil)
          Do Begin
            Writeln (ListElt^.Data);
            ListElt := ListElt^.Next
          End;
        Writeln;
        Writeln ('End of List');
        Writeln
    End {Print} ;

Procedure ProcessFromMenu;
{This procedure presents the menu options and calls the requested task}
    Var First: ListPointer;     {pointer to the first list item}
        Option: Char;           {user response to menu selection}
    Begin
        Initialization(First);
        Repeat
            Writeln ('Options available');
            Writeln ('I - Insert a task into the list');
            Writeln ('D - Delete a task from the list');
            Writeln ('P - Print the tasks on the list');
            Writeln ('Q - Quit');
            Write   ('Enter desired option: ');
            Readln (Option);
            If Option in ['i','I','d','D','p','P','q','Q']
                Then Case Option of
                    'I', 'i': AddName(First);
                    'D', 'd': DeletionName(First);
                    'P', 'p': Print(First);
                    'Q', 'q':
                    End
                Else Writeln ('Invalid Option - Try Again!')
        Until (Option = 'Q') Or (Option = 'q')
    End {ProcessFromMenu} ;

Begin {Main}
    Writeln ('Program to Maintain a List of Tasks');
    ProcessFromMenu
End {Main} .
```

A sample run of this program follows.

```
Program to Maintain a List of Tasks
Options available
I - Insert a task into the list
D - Delete a task from the list
P - Print the tasks on the list
Q - Quit
Enter desired option: I
Enter new task: do homework
Options available
I - Insert a task into the list
D - Delete a task from the list
P - Print the tasks on the list
Q - Quit
Enter desired option: i
Enter new task: go swimming
Enter old task which new task should preceed,
or enter a blank if new task should be "last": do homework
Options available
I - Insert a task into the list
D - Delete a task from the list
P - Print the tasks on the list
Q - Quit
Enter desired option: p
The list of tasks are:

go swimming
do homework

End of List

Options available
I - Insert a task into the list
D - Delete a task from the list
P - Print the tasks on the list
Q - Quit
Enter desired option: i
Enter new task: mow lawn
Enter old task which new task should preceed,
or enter a blank if new task should be "last": do homework
Options available
I - Insert a task into the list
D - Delete a task from the list
P - Print the tasks on the list
Q - Quit
Enter desired option: p
The list of tasks are:

go swimming
mow lawn
do homework

End of List
```

```
Options available
I - Insert a task into the list
D - Delete a task from the list
P - Print the tasks on the list
Q - Quit
Enter desired option: d
Enter task name to be deleted: do homework
Options available
I - Insert a task into the list
D - Delete a task from the list
P - Print the tasks on the list
Q - Quit
Enter desired option: p
The list of tasks are:

go swimming
mow lawn

End of List

Options available
I - Insert a task into the list
D - Delete a task from the list
P - Print the tasks on the list
Q - Quit
Enter desired option: q
```

SECTION 18.3   MAINTAINING ORDERED DATA

One particularly important application of linked lists involves the maintaining of data items in an alphabetical or numerical order. For example, consider the following problem.

Problem 18.3   Alphabetical List of Names

Write a program that maintains a list of names in alphabetical order. In particular, the program should allow

- names to be inserted in alphabetical order on the list;
- names to be deleted from the list; and
- all names on the list to be printed.

For simplicity, assume the names are entered with the last name first.

Discussion of Problem 18.3

In this problem, we are performing the same basic operations as in our list of tasks problem (Problem 18.2) in the previous section. However, here we keep all of our data items in alphabetical order. With this ordering of data, we no longer have to ask the user to specify where the new item should be inserted into the list. Thus, data entry by the user is simpler than in Problem 18.2.

In addition, in searching for an item in our list of tasks, we had to continue going through our list until either we found the desired item, or we reached the end of the list. We had to check all items on our list before we could conclude that a given name was not present. On the other hand, once a list is alphabetized and we want to insert a new item, we do not have to go through the entire list. Instead, we can stop checking items on the list when we reach an item coming after the desired one in alphabetical order. Once we reach a name that comes later in alphabetical order, the ordering implies that all subsequent names will also come later. Thus, we can stop searching before reaching the end of the list.

Each of these observations affects our code for finding, inserting, and deleting items, and we need to modify

- Procedure FindPrevious
- Procedure AddName
- Procedure DeleteName

in program *TaskList* from the previous section.

The simplest change can be seen in the *FindPrevious* procedure. Here, we need to change the condition in our loop invariant that is specified in the function *Done*. In the revised function, we need to check for alphabetical order as well as for equality, and the revised function reads

```
Function Done: Boolean;
    Begin
        If ListElt = Nil
            Then Done : = True
            Else Done : = (Name < = ListElt^.Data)
    End;
```

In the insertion procedure, we must consider alphabetical order to find the appropriate location for a new item. As with our previous insertion procedure, we also need to write special cases for when the list is empty or when the new item goes first on the list. This suggests the following outline for insertion into an ordered list.

I. Check if list is empty.
    A. If so, new item becomes first item in list.
    B. If not, check if new item comes first in list.
        1. If so, place new item first.
        2. If not,
            a. search list, finding where item goes and keeping track of previous item on list;
            b. insert new item at designated location by adjusting pointers.

The code that results from this outline is quite similar to procedure *AddName* that we wrote in Section 18.2. As before, we check our special cases first. Then, if these cases do not apply, we use the *FindPrevious* procedure to locate the appropriate spot for the new item on the ordered list.

Turning to the deletion procedure, the revised search conditions change our conclusions about when an element is found. In the previous section, we searched until we found the appropriate item for deletion or until we reached the end of the list. Thus, after searching, procedure *DeleteName* could check if the specified item was found by testing if we had reached the end of the list (i.e., *ListElt = Nil*). In this revised program for ordered lists, we must be more careful in determining if our element is present. The desired item will not be on the list if we reach the end of the list or if we find a name coming after the desired item in alphabetical order. In both our outline for deletion and in our *DeleteName* procedure, we must check for each of these cases before we can conclude the item specified is present on the list. We leave the details of the outline and coding as exercises.

FIGURE 18–11 • 'a', 'b', 'c', 'd', 'e' Stored as a List with Pointers

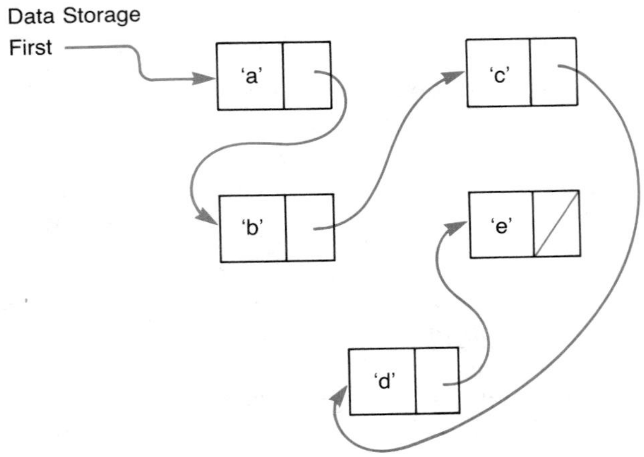

```
Declarations
              Const MaxLen = 20;

              Type ListData = Packed Array [1 .. MaxLen] of Char;
                   ListPointer = ^ Item;
                   Item = Record
                          Data: ListData;
                          Next: ListPointer
                          End;

              Var First: ListPointer;
```

Comparison with Array Storage

Now that we have seen how to maintain data items in alphabetical order using lists and pointers, it is useful to compare this list structure with the arrays that we used in discussing strings in Chapter 14. To facilitate our discussion, we consider the five data items 'a', 'b', 'c', 'd', 'e' stored in order using both pointers and arrays.

In the list/pointer structure, each data item is stored as part of a box, where one box points to the next. We also specify the start of the list. The appropriate declarations and structures are shown in Figure 18–11.

In the array structure, we form a large array, where each entry in the array is an element of data, and we keep track of the number of elements in our list. Figure 18–12 shows the appropriate declarations and structure. (This structure is analogous to our list of words from Section 14.5.)

FIGURE 18–12 • 'a', 'b', 'c', 'd', 'e' Stored in an Array

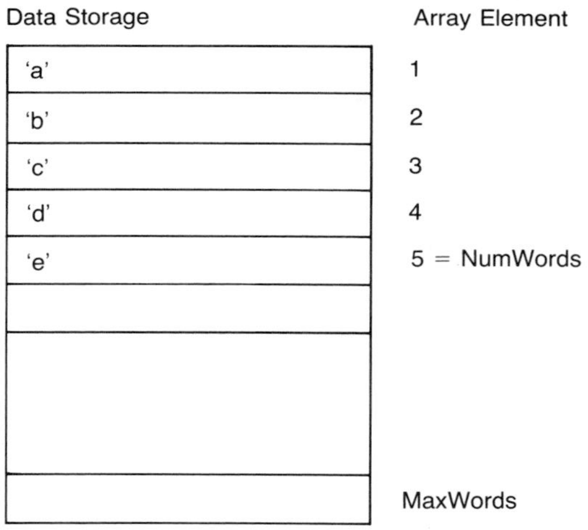

Data Storage | Array Element

'a' — 1
'b' — 2
'c' — 3
'd' — 4
'e' — 5 = NumWords

MaxWords

Declarations

```
Const MaxLen = 20;
      MaxWords = 40;

Type ListData = Packed Array [1 .. MaxLen] of Char;
     WordTable = Array [1 .. MaxWords] of ListData;

Var List: WordTable;
    NumWords: 0 .. MaxWords;
```

In comparing the effectiveness of these structures, we need to consider the topics of data insertion and deletion, searching, and maximum capacities. We will see that lists with pointers offer several advantages, while arrays also have one definite advantage.

Data Insertion and Deletion.   In data insertion in ordered arrays, we have noted (Sections 8.7 and 14.5) that we may have to move large amounts of data to make room for a new item. For example, in Figure 18–12, we would have to move 'c', 'd', and 'e' down if we wanted to add 'ba' to our list. A similar movement of data may be needed in deletion (e.g., 'c', 'd', 'e' must be moved up if we delete 'b'). In contrast, in lists with pointers, we only need to change a few pointers to perform our insertion or deletion.

Searching.   When we want to locate an item on our ordered lists, the linear search applies to both arrays and lists with pointers. In this searching algorithm, we start with the first element of data and proceed item by item through the data. While this method works, we have noted in Chapter 8 that the linear search takes some time.

We also noted in Section 8.6 that when we use ordered arrays, the binary search allows us to divide our data in half with each step, so the search can proceed very quickly. The binary search looks at the item in the middle of the array and then makes conclusions about where to search next. However, when we use lists with pointers, the binary search cannot be used since we have no way of knowing where the "middle" item is. For example, Figure 18–11 shows that the various boxes containing data can be spread around, and we cannot guess where any particular item might be located.

Thus, while the relatively slow linear search applies to either type of ordered data, the fast binary search can be applied only to arrays.

Storage Capacity.   In the previous section, we noted that storage is allocated differently for lists with pointers than for arrays. Array storage is allocated when a procedure is called, and the size of the array is determined by constants in the program. With this static storage allocation, the size of an array is determined by the programmer when the code is written, and this size cannot be changed when the program is run. Thus, with array storage, the programmer must guess at the number of items that will be needed in the array, and this guess cannot be exceeded.

In contrast, in lists with pointers, storage is allocated as it is needed while the program is running; the programmer does not have to guess at the size of storage necessary for the problem. Further, storage can be used for one list and then freed to be used in another list. Thus, with pointers, new items can be added as long as space remains in the CPU's main memory, and space can be reused. The number of items does not depend on a specification made before the program started. This suggests that the dynamic storage allocation of lists with pointers allows substantially more flexibility than the static allocation of arrays.

Putting these parts together, we find that lists with pointers allow easy insertion and deletion of data and dynamic storage. Thus, such linked lists are particularly useful in problems where list items will be changing frequently. However, array storage of ordered data does permit the very efficient binary search. Thus, if we expect to do many searches through our data, array storage can be particularly effective.

In the next section, we see how we can retain the flexibility of linked lists for insertions, deletions, and storage allocation while minimizing the time required for linear searches.

SECTION 18.4   HASH-CODED STORAGE AND SEARCHING

In the last section, we saw that linked lists can provide a very flexible and effective structure for inserting and deleting items, but the searching of linked lists can be time consuming. In this section, we discuss a general technique that can reduce the search time considerably.

Analysis of Search Time

We begin by noting that searching a linked list always starts with a first element and then proceeds from one item to the next. This approach has two limitations.

1. If the list is unordered, we must check all elements on the list to conclude a given item is not present.
2. If the list is ordered, we cannot jump to the middle or the end of the list to speed our processing.

In each of these cases, the amount of search time depends upon the length of the list in question.

More precisely, suppose our list contains n items of data. In Chapter 8, we noted that if we perform a linear search, we can expect to find a given item about half way through the list, requiring us to check about $n/2$ elements. Thus, for either ordered or unordered lists, we will need about $n/2$ checks to find an element if it is there.

We see that the time required for searching a linked list is proportional to the length of the list. If the list is short, little search time is required. However, as lists become longer, so will our average search time. For example, if the number of data items on our list doubles, we can expect the average search time to double as well.

Strategy for Reducing Search Time

After analyzing these search times, it is clear that search times will be rather short if we can keep our lists rather short. When we have a large number of items, this observation suggests that we divide these items into several relatively short lists.

In practice, the division of a large list into pieces requires two basic steps for the operations of searching, insertion, and deletion. First, for a particular item, we must determine which short list to consider. Then, after choosing the short list, we perform the desired searching, insertion, or deletion operations. The following example shows one way that we can accomplish this division into smaller lists. We look at a more general approach later in the section.

PROBLEM 18.4   Rewrite the ordered list program of the previous section so that the list of names is divided into several smaller lists. In particular, maintain a separate list for names starting with each letter of the alphabet. Thus, names

FIGURE 18–13 • **Storage of Names**

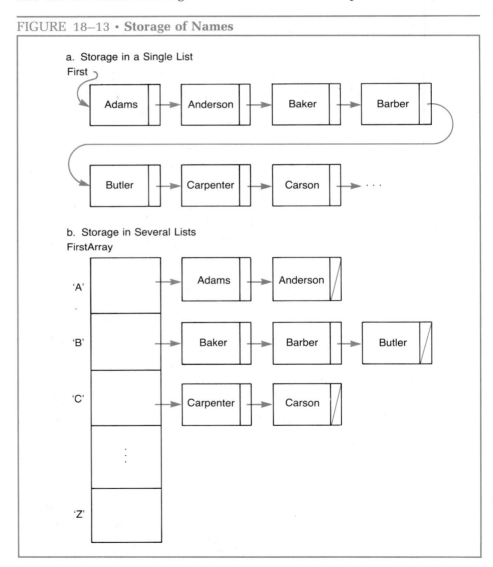

beginning with 'A' form one short list; those beginning with 'B' form a second; and so on.

Discussion of Problem 18.4

In this problem, we are replacing one long list by 26 lists, one for each letter of the alphabet. In coding these lists, we no longer have a simple pointer for the start of our names. Rather, we will use an array of pointers, as shown in Figure 18–13. Thus, our first pointers have the declaration

Var First: Array ['A'..'Z'] of ListPointer;

Here *First*['A'] will point to the 'A' list, *First*['B'] will point to the 'B' list, and so on.

Outline for Printing. With this revised data structure, our printing step might have the following major outline.

I. Repeat for Letter := 'A', 'B', 'C', . . . , 'Z'.
  A. Print the list starting with the given letter.
    1. Prepare to print the first item on the list.
    2. Continue until reaching the end of the list.
      a. Print the given item.
      b. Prepare to print the next item.

This outline yields the following structured code.

```
{The following code assumes these declarations:

Const Max = 20;

Type ListData = Packed Array [1..Max] of Char;
     ListPointer = ^Item
     Item = Reecord
          Data: ListData;
          Next: ListPointer
          End;
     PointerArray = Array ['A'..'Z'] of ListPointer;

}

Procedure Print (First: PointerArray);
{This procedure prints the current data items on the list}
     Var Index: 'A'..'Z';
         ListElt: ListPointer;
```

```
Begin
    Writeln ('The list of tasks is');
    Writeln;
    For Index := 'A' To 'Z'
      Do Begin
        ListElt := First[Index];
        While (ListElt <> Nil)
          Do Begin
            Writeln (ListElt^.Data);
            ListElt := ListElt^.Next
          End
      End;
    Writeln;
    Writeln ('End of List'):
    Writeln
End {Print} ;
```

In the middle of this code, we follow the same process we used in previous sections to print the list specified by *First[Index]*. Our major change in coding involves the repetition of this code for Index := 'A', 'B', etc.

Similarly, we can use the same basic structure of our searching, insertion, deletion, and printing procedures as long as the appropriate first pointer is passed as a parameter to the various list procedures.

Outline for Insertion Step. The major outline for the insertion process might be revised as follows.

   I. Read name to be inserted.
   II. Use first letter of name to determine list for insertion.
  III. Insert name on given list.

With this outline, our program follows much the same structure that we used in Section 18.2. Only a few lines in the main body of procedure *AddName* need to be modified. The main points of the revised code for insertion follow.

```
Program TaskList (Input, Output);

Const Max = 20;      {Length of task names}

Type ListData = Packed Array [1..Max] of Char;
     ListPointer = ^Item;
     Item = Record
           Data: ListData;
           Next: ListPointer
           End;

     Pointer Array = Array ['A'..'Z'] of ListPointer;
```

```
Procedure Initialization(Var First: PointerArray);
{This procedure initializes appropriate variables}
    Var Index: 'A'..'Z';

    Begin
        For Index := 'A' To 'Z'
            Do First[Index] := Nil
    End {Initialization} ;

Procedure ReadData (Var Name: ListData);
{This procedure reads a name from the terminal}

Procedure FindPrevious (Name: ListData; Var PrevElt: ListPointer;
                        First: PointerArray);
{This procedure locates the task that comes before given name on the list.
 If the name is not found, PrevElt^.Next will be Nil.
 The procedure assumes the Name is not the first list element.}

Procedure AddName(Var First: PointerArray)
{This procedure reads a task name and inserts it into the list}

    Var Let1: Char;
        NewItem: ListPointer;
        OldName: ListData;

    Procedure InsertFirst (NewItem: ListPointer; Var First: ListPointer);
    {This procedure inserts the new item at the beginning of the list}

    Procedure InsertAfterFirst (NewItem, First: ListPointer);
    {The procedure inserts the new item after the start of the list}

    Begin {AddName}
        New(NewItem);
        Write ('Enter new task: ');
        ReadData (NewItem^.Data);
        Let1 := NewItem^.Data[1];
        If First[Let1] = Nil
            Then InsertFirst (NewItem, First[Let1])
            Else Begin
                Writeln ('Enter old task which new task should preceed, ');
                Write ('or enter a blank if new task should be placed "last": ');
                ReadData(OldName);
                If OldName = First[Let1]^.Data
                    Then InsertFirst (NewItem, First[Let1])
                    Else InsertAfterFirst(NewItem, First[Let1])
                End
    End {AddName} ;
```

In this code, we have expanded our *Initialization* procedure so that all list pointers are initially set to *nil*.

Then, in the *AddName* procedure, we added a variable *Let1* for the first letter of the new name. Then *First[Let1]* points to the appropriate list for our new list item, and we use *First[Let1]* as our actual parameter in place of the pointer *First* in our earlier versions of this program.

We leave further details of this operation, as well as all details of deletion, as exercises.

Throughout this work, our basic outlines for using a list remain the same. We always start at the beginning of a list and move from one item to the next. The additional steps involve locating the start of the appropriate list.

Hashing

In Problem 18.4, we divided our long list into pieces by using the first letter of the name. This division into pieces is easy to do, but it does have the disadvantage that our various lists may not all be short. For example, the 'S' list might contain many names while the 'Q' list might be short. Here, names beginning with 'S' might require a rather long search, while names starting with 'Q' may be processed very quickly.

More generally, we may decide to break up long lists into short ones in a variety of ways. For example, we might consider the first two letters of a name, or we might put several letters of the alphabet together on one list. Our only requirement is that given a name, we must be able to determine which short list to consider.

In computer science, this general technique of dividing a long list into small pieces is called **hashing,** and a **hashing algorithm** or a **hashing function** describes the way that we determine which list to use in processing, given a specific name.

SECTION 18.5   DOUBLY LINKED LISTS

Up to this point, our lists have been structured so we can start at the front and move efficiently item by item to the end. However, in many applications, we need more flexibility than this. For example, consider the following:

PROBLEM 18.5   Recording and Retrieving Golf Scores

In recording scores for a golf tournament, we enter the name and score of the player as the player finishes. This information is to be retrieved in each of the following ways.

- Scores and names can be printed in order by ascending or by descending scores.
- Given the name of a player, other players with the same score can be printed.

Discussion of Problem 18.5.

This problem requires the frequent updating of names and scores and the ordering of the information. Such requirements naturally suggest a linked list structure. However, here a simple linked list is difficult to use efficiently because all of the pointers move in one logical direction from the start to the end. This structure makes it hard to print the list in reverse order or to move backward from a given name.

To resolve these difficulties we consider a new type of structure, called a **doubly linked list,** where each item contains a pointer to the previous item as well as to the next one. A doubly linked list for this problem is shown in Figure 18–14.

This figure illustrates several important features of a doubly linked list. Each item on the list contains two pointers as well as some data. Thus, this doubly linked list might use either of the following declarations.

```
Const Length = 30;
Type  ListPtr = ^Item;
      Name = Packed Array [1..Length] of Char;
      Item =   Record
                 Score: Integer;
                 Player: Name;
                 Previous: ListPtr;
                 Next: ListPtr
                 End;
Var   First:  ListPtr;
      Last:   ListPtr;
```

In this declaration, we list *Score* and *Name* as two separate data fields. In the next declaration, these fields are combined as parts of a single data field.

```
Const Length = 30;
Type  ListPtr = ^Item;
      Name = Packed Array [1..Length] of Char;
      Item = Record
                   Data = Record
                       Score: Integer;
                       Player: Name
                       End;
                   Previous: ListPtr;
                   Next: ListPtr
                   End;
Var   First:  ListPtr;
      Last:   ListPtr;
```

FIGURE 18–14 • **A Doubly Linked List with Golf Data**

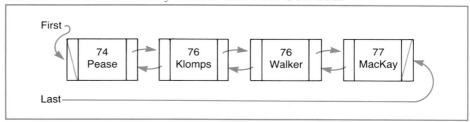

With these declarations, the data fields store appropriate scores and names, the *Previous* field points to the previous item on the list, and the *Next* field specifies the next item on the list. The *First* and *Last* pointers give the ends of the list, and we use nil to specify an end of our list.

With this structure, we can perform the same general operations we discussed for simple lists, namely

- printing the data on the list;
- inserting or deleting an item; and
- finding and perhaps modifying an item.

However, here the pointers going backward as well as forward simplify some of these operations and expand our capabilities.

Printing.   We now can print the list in reverse order just as easily as in the normal order. To print from the first to last item, we start with the item specified by the *First* pointer, and we then proceed item by item using the *Next* field of each item. To print in reverse order, we start with the item specified by the *Last* pointer. Then we proceed item by item using the *Previous* fields of each item.

Insertion and Deletion.   In these operations, we can follow the same general steps that we discussed for simple lists in Section 18.1. However, now we must take care of backward pointers as well as forward ones. This suggests the following main steps for insertion into a doubly linked list.

FIGURE 18–15 • **Insertion into a Doubly Linked List**

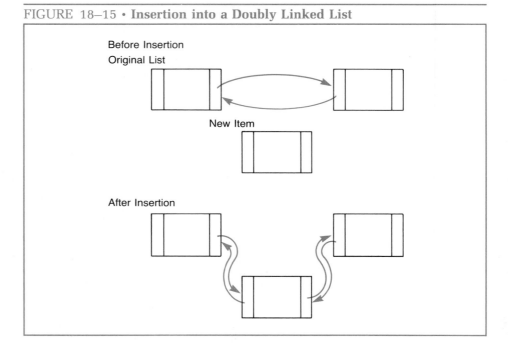

Step 1. Determine where item will be inserted.

Step 2. Create a new box or record.

Step 3. Place data in new record.

Step 4. Make *Previous* and *Next* pointers of new record specify the appropriate list elements.

Step 5. Update the *Next* pointer in the previous record to specify the newly created record.

Step 6. Update the *Previous* pointer in the next record to specify the newly created record.

The final pointers are shown in Figure 18–15.

With this outline, the programming details for doubly linked lists now proceed in much the same way as singly linked lists. However, in this process, we must remember to modify the *Previous* pointers as well as the *Next* ones. The necessary details are seen in the following revised *Find* and *Insert* procedures for doubly linked lists.

```
Procedure Insert (Var First, Last: ListPtr);
{This procedure inserts a new element into an ordered, doubly linked list}
   Var Element: ListPtr;

   Procedure Enter (Var Element: ListPtr);
   {This procedure reads a name and score from the terminal
    and creates a new record for this data}
      Var Index: Integer;
      Begin
          New (Element);
          With Element^
            Do Begin
              Write ('Enter player''s name: ');
              {Read Name From Terminal}
              Index := 0;
              While (Index < Length) And Not Eoln
                Do Begin
                  Index := Index + 1;
                  Read (Player[Index])
                End;
              Readln;

              {Fill rest of string with nulls}
              While (Index < Length)
                Do Begin
                  Index := Index + 1;
                  Player[Index] := Chr(0)
                End;

              Write ('Enter player''s score: ');
              Readln (Score);

              Previous := Nil;
              Next := Nil
            End;
      End {Determine} ;
```

```
Procedure InsertInOrder (Element: ListPtr; Var First, Last: ListPtr);
{This procedure inserts the given Element on the List}

    Var PrevElt: ListPtr;

    Procedure Find (Var PrevElt: ListPtr; Element, First: ListPtr);
    {This procedure returns the record on the list that preceeds the
     specified element}

        Function MoveNeeded: Boolean;
        {This function determines if the specified element must be
         inserted further in the list}
            Begin
                If PrevElt^.Next = Nil
                    Then MoveNeeded := False
                    Else MoveNeeded :=
                              (PrevElt^.Next^.Score <= Element^.Score)
            End {MoveNeeded} ;

        Begin {Find}
            PrevElt := First;
            While MoveNeeded
                Do PrevElt := PrevElt^.Next
        End {Find} ;

    Procedure InsertAfter (PrevElt, Element: ListPtr; Var Last: ListPtr);
    {This procedure inserts the Element after the PrevElt on the list}
        Begin
            Element^.Next := PrevElt^.Next;
            Element^.Previous := PrevElt;
            If (PrevElt^.Next = Nil)
                Then Last := Element
                Else PrevElt^.Next^.Previous := Element;
            PrevElt^.Next := Element
        End {InsertAfter} ;

Begin {InsertInOrder}

    If First = Nil
        Then Begin {List is empty}
            Element^.Next := First;
            First := Element;
            Last := Element
            End
        Else If (Element^.Score < First^.Score)
            Then Begin {Insert before head of list}
                Element^.Next := First;
                First^.Previous := Element;
                First := Element
                End
            Else Begin {Insert after head}
                Find (PrevElt, Element, First);
                InsertAfter (PrevElt, Element, Last)
                End;

End {InsertInOrder} ;
```

```
Begin {Insert}
    Enter (Element);
    InsertInOrder (Element, First, Last)

End {Insert} ;
```

These procedures are quite similar to the corresponding ones for singly linked lists; the major changes involve the updating of *Previous* pointers as well as *Next* ones and some modification of our search operation. The deletion operation for doubly linked lists requires similar modifications; we leave the details as an exercise.

Discussion of Problem 18.5 (continued)

Now that we have introduced this doubly linked structure, we return to Problem 18.5. In storing scores and names, we will maintain a doubly linked list, ordered by name. With our comments on printing, we can print our data in ascending and descending order quite easily. Our remaining task involves printing the names of all people who shot the same score as a given person. This task illustrates further the considerable flexibility that we can obtain by adding the *Previous* pointers to our list elements.

One natural way to print these names involves the following general steps.

    I. Determine name
   II. Find name on list.
      If name not found, stop.
  III. Look up score for given name.
  IV. Move backward along list to find first item with the given score.
      A. If a previous field is *nil,* we have the first entry.
      B. If previous field not *nil,* look at previous record.
          1. If previous record's score is same, move to previous item and repeat this step.
          2. If previous record's score is different, stop.
   V. Move forward along list. Continue until end of list or until score changes.
      A. Print name and score.
      B. Move to next item.

This outline gives rise to the following procedure.

```
Procedure PrintSameScore (First: ListPtr);
{This procedure prints the names of those players that scored the same
 as a given player.}

    Var Element: ListPtr;
        Person: Name;
```

```
Procedure Determine (Var Person: Name);
{This procedure reads a name from the terminal}
    Var Index: Integer;
    Begin
        Write ('Enter Player''s Name: ');
        {Read Name From Terminal}
        Index := 0;
        While (Index < Length) And Not Eoln
          Do Begin
            Index := Index + 1;
            Read (Person[Index])
          End;
        Readln;

        {Fill rest of string with nulls}
        While (Index < Length)
          Do Begin
            Index := Index + 1;
            Person[Index] := Chr(0)
          End;
    End {Determine} ;

Procedure Find (Person: Name; Var Element: ListPtr; First: ListPtr);
{This procedure finds the Element on the List where the
 player's name is the given Person}

    Function Done: Boolean;
    {This Function determines when the search of the list is done}
        Begin
            If Element = Nil
                Then Done := True
                Else Done := (Person = Element^.Player)
        End {Done} ;

    Begin {Find}
        Element := First;
        While Not Done
          Do Element := Element^.Next
    End {Find} ;

Procedure FindFirstScore (Var Element: ListPtr);
{This procedure moves backward along the list to find the first
 element with the given score}

    Function BackUp: Boolean;
    {This function determines if we should move to the previous
      element in the list}
        Begin
            If (Element^.Previous = Nil)
                Then BackUp := False
                Else BackUp :=
                        (Element^.Score = Element^.Previous^.Score)
        End {BackUp} ;

Begin {FindFirstScore}
    While Backup
        Do Element := Element^.Previous
End {FindFirstScore} ;
```

```
Procedure PrintPlayers (Element: ListPtr);
{This procedure prints the names of the players with the same score as
 found in the given element}

    Function Continue: Boolean;
    {This Function determines if printing should continue
     with the next element}
        Begin
            If Element^.Next = Nil
                Then Continue := False
                Else Continue :=
                        Element^.Score = Element^.Next^.Score
        End {Continue} ;

    Begin {PrintPlayers}
        Writeln ('The following players shot a score of ',
                Element^.Score:1);
        Writeln (Element^.Player);
        While Continue
          Do Begin
            Element := Element^.Next;
            Writeln (Element^.Player)
            End
    End {PrintPlayers} ;


Begin {PrintSameScore}
    Determine (Person);
    Find (Person, Element, First);
    If (Element = Nil)
        Then Writeln ('Player not found on list')
        Else Begin
            FindFirstScore (Element);
            PrintPlayers (Element)
            End;
End {PrintSameScore} ;
```

With this procedure, we see that doubly linked lists allow us to move both backward and forward along our lists very easily. The backward pointers have added considerable flexibility to our capabilities for processing.

In the next section, we see how the addition of other pointers can increase this flexibility and capacity even further.

SECTION 18.6   MORE GENERAL LINKED STRUCTURES

In the previous section, we used pointers to previous list items as well as pointers to later ones to permit more flexibility in our retrieval of data. In this section, we further expand our retrieval capabilities by adding more pointers to form more general structures.

First, we consider a problem where we need to maintain our data records in several lists. Here, we will need to store several different types of information, and pointers will be needed to organize records of different types. Further, we will find that some records will need several pointers, with one set of pointers for one type of data and a second set of pointers for another type of data.

PROBLEM 18.6

A Very Simple Date Book

A date book contains information on special events, scheduled meetings, and important commitments for various days throughout the year. For this date book, we need the following capabilities:

> adding appointments for any specified day;
>
> printing appointments for a given day; and
>
> printing all appointments.

Develop a data structure for this date book.

Discussion of Problem 18.6

In this problem, we must deal with two types of information:

1. dates (month, day, year)
2. appointments for a given date

In considering this data and the requirements we have for processing, we can make several observations and conclusions. First, we can expect many additions to our list as our schedule fills up. Thus, we will want the flexibility of a linked structure to store our data. Second, there will be some days on which no appointments are scheduled, while other days are heavily scheduled. Overall, we must be prepared to handle a large number of commitments, which may not be evenly distributed through the year. Finally, once we have scheduled many appointments, we do not want to take the time to search through all of them when we add new ones or print our schedule for a given day. A list of all our appointments is likely to be too long for a linear search to be adequate.

With these observations, we conclude that a simple linear list of appointments is unlikely to meet our processing demands. However, we do need the flexibility that a list structure gives us. To meet these needs, we use a structure that separates the dates and the appointments for the day. In particular, we form one linked list for the dates that have appointments. Then, for each date, we have a list of appointments for that day. Such a structure is shown in Figure 18–16.

Such a structure requires two separate types of records. Dates must include month, day, and year information, a pointer to the first appointment on that date, and a pointer to the next date. Appointments must contain character data and a pointer to the next appointment. The appropriate declarations follow.

FIGURE 18–16 · A Data Structure for a Simple Date Book

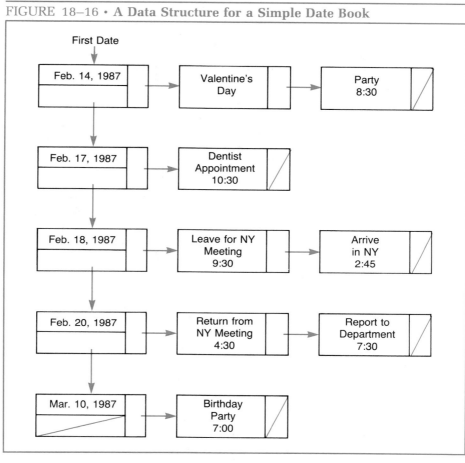

```
Const Length = 60;
Type  DatePtr = ^Date;
      ApptPtr = ^Appointment;
      Date = Record
              Month: 1..12;
              Day: 1..31;
              Year: Integer;
              FirstAppt: ApptPtr;
              NextDate: DatePtr
              End;
      Appointment = Record
              Data: Packed Array [1..Length] of Char;
              Next: ApptPtr
              End;
Var   FirstDate: DatePtr;
```

With these declarations, we consider the dates as a simple linked list, with *FirstDate* specifying the initial item on our list and the *NextDate* field indicating how to proceed from one date to the next.

Then, for a given date, we have another simple list. Here the *FirstAppt* field for our date specifies the initial item on our list and the *Next* field for each appointment indicates how we can proceed from one appointment to the next.

Outline for Insertion of A New Appointment.   Next, we consider the operations we will need to solve our problem. In outlining the insertion operations we find we need to proceed in two steps (plus data entry), following the organization of our data.

I. Enter date and appointment information.
II. Starting with date specified by *FirstDate*, search the date list for the specified date.
  A. If the date is found, work with the existing date record.
  B. If the date is not found:
    1. Create a new record for this date.
    2. Store day, month, year data in the record.
    3. Set *FirstAppt* field to *nil*.
    4. Insert new date record into date list.
    5. Work with this new date record.
III. With the given date record, insert appointment.
  A. Create new appointment record.
  B. Store new appointment data.
  C. Insert new appointment into appointment list for the given date.

In this work, both Steps II and III follow the same procedures that we used before in singly linked lists. The new feature here is the combining of these lists as part of a more complex structure.

Outline for Printing Appointments for a Given Date.   Similarly, our printing requires two steps (beyond data entry).

I. Enter date.
II. Search list of dates to find the one specified.
  A. Start with date specified by first date.
  B. Use *NextDate* field to find successive dates.
III. When date record is found, print list for that date.
  A. Start with appointment specified by the date's *FirstAppt* field.
  B. Continue while appointment pointer is not *nil*.
    1. Print appointment information.
    2. Use next field to find next appointment.

The printing of all appointments combines Steps II and III in a loop.

In analyzing this structure, we can identify several important features. By using list structures, we maintain the flexibility that we need for easy insertion and deletion of items. In addition, by separating dates from appointments, we can reduce our search time considerably, since we only have to search one record for each date. We may have several appointments on certain dates, but our data structure does not require us to look at all of these appointments as we go from one date to another. Thus, we are able to ignore many appointments that occur on dates that do not interest us in a particular processing request. Finally, if we want to reduce searching time further, we could break down this data into more pieces. For example, we could consider

months,

days within a month, and

appointments for a given day.

Here, we could search a month list until we found the correct month, then we could search a day list for that month to find the correct date. Finally, the day record would specify our desired list of appointments.

More generally, the list structures in this example illustrate that pointers allow us to organize our data in many ways that allow easy storage and retrieval. We can order the same data records in several ways by using distinct pointers for separate lists. We also can separate our data into different types of records and then use distinct lists to tie these pieces together. In these data structures, the details of data organization may vary from one application to another. However, the basic ideas behind the list operations for insertion, deletion, and searching all depend on the simple cases for singly and doubly linked lists that we saw in the previous sections.

SECTION 18.7   POINTER IMPLEMENTATIONS OF STACKS AND QUEUES

To conclude this chapter, we consider two more examples of lists and pointers. In particular, in Chapter 17, we saw how we could implement stacks and queues using arrays. In this Section, we implement the same operations using lists and pointers.

Implementation of Stacks

In Chapter 17, we considered the following stack operations:

```
Function Empty: Boolean;
Procedure Push (Item: Data);
Procedure Pop (Var Item: Data);
Procedure Top (Var Item: Data);
```

In this structure, we specify the top of our stack, and we work with the stack by adding and deleting items from it.

FIGURE 18–17 • A List/Pointer Implementation of a Stack

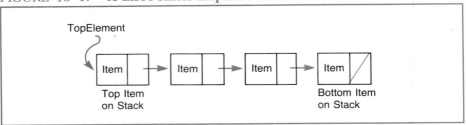

With these ideas in mind, we can work with a stack if we can keep track of its top and if we can locate subsequent items in the stack after we perform a *Pop* operation. Figure 18–17 shows how such a structure could be organized.

In this picture, we store a stack item in a record with a pointer to the next lower item on the stack. Also, we use a pointer variable that specifies the top record. The appropriate declarations for a stack with data are

```
Type Ptr = ^Stack;
      Stack = Record
            Info: Data;
            Next: Ptr
            End;
   Var   TopElement: Ptr;
```

With these declarations, we initialize *TopElement* to *nil* at the beginning of our program, and the Boolean expression

```
TopElement = Nil
```

allows us to test for an empty stack. Then the *Push, Pop,* and *Top* operations involve inserting, deleting, and reading items at the top of this list structure, respectively. The outlines of these operations are quite similar to our work in Chapter 17. However, we do not have to declare a list size initially, and we do not need the *Full* function we used before. Also, in the *Pop* operation, we *Dispose* of the list item once we have returned the appropriate information. The coding details for these operations are now shown below.

```
{Operations implementing a stack using lists and pointers.}

{Required Declarations
Type Data = ...            Type of Items Stored on Stack
     Ptr = ^Stack;
     Stack = Record
             Info: Data;
             Next: Ptr
             End;
Var TopElement: Ptr;
}
```

```
Procedure InitializeStack;
{This procedure initializes the stack}
    Begin
        TopElement := Nil
    End {InitializeStack} ;

Function Empty: Boolean;
{This function determines if the stack is empty}
    Begin
        Empty := (TopElement = Nil)
    End;

Procedure Push (Item: Data);
{This procedure pushes the given Item on the Stack}
    Var NewElement: Ptr;
    Begin
        New (NewElement);
        NewElement^.Info := Item;
        NewElement^.Next := TopElement;
        TopElement := NewElement
    End {Push} ;

Procedure Pop (Var Item: Data);
{This procedure removes the top Item from the Stack and returns it}
    Var Element: Ptr;
    Begin
        If Empty
            Then Writeln ('Stack Empty - Data Cannot Be Returned')
            Else Begin
                Element := TopElement;
                Item := Element^.Info;
                TopElement := TopElement^.Next;
                Dispose (Element)
                End
    End {Pop} ;

Procedure Top (Var Item: Data);
{This procedure returns the top Item from the Stack;
 the stack remains unchanged}
    Begin
        If Empty
            Then Writeln ('Stack Empty - No Data Returned')
            Else Item := TopElement^.Info
    End {Top} ;
```

Once these functions and procedures are defined, we can use them just as we did before. In a program, we must include the appropriate stack declaration (shown earlier in this section). We must write out these procedures, and we must call our *Initialization* procedure. However, once these details are completed, we can use *Empty*, *Push*, *Pop*, and *Top* without change. These revised procedures and functions perform exactly the same tasks as our earlier ones that used arrays, and the calling formats for these operations are the same. For example, when we fill in the details of these declarations and operations, our Parentheses Balancing program of Section 17.3 can be run without change. Thus, while our implementation of stacks has changed dramatically, our use of stacks in applications is identical.

Implementation of Queues

As our final example in this chapter, we consider a list/pointer implementation of queues. As with our discussion of stacks, we want to retain the same operations and calling formats that we defined in Chapter 17. Only the implementation details will change.

Chapter 17 defined the following queue operations:

> Function Empty: Boolean;
> Procedure Insert (Item: Data);
> Procedure Delete (Var Item: Data);

In this structure, we must work with both ends of the queue, inserting items at the bottom and deleting them from the head. (See Figure 18–18.) Here, we can view the queue as ordering items from the head to the bottom; the head is the first item we will remove, and the bottom is our last item.

In this picture, our queue consists of a list of records, where each record contains an item of data and points to the record that comes after it. The appropriate declarations are

> Type Ptr = ^Queue;
>   Queue = Record
>   Info: Data;
>   Next: Ptr
>   End;
>   Var Head, Bottom: Ptr;

With these declarations, we initialize *Head* and *Bottom* to *nil* at the start of our program, and the Boolean expression

> Head = Nil

allows us to test if the queue is empty. Then, the *Insert* operation proceeds by adding an element at the bottom end of the list. Also, the *Delete* operation proceeds by returning the data at the head of the list, moving the *Head* pointer to the next element, and disposing of the old record. In each of these operations, we also must be careful to account for the special cases where the queue is empty and where it contains only one item. We leave

---

FIGURE 18–18 • A List Implementation of a Queue

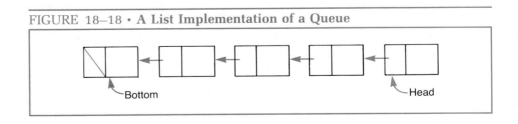

FIGURE 18–19 • An Alternate List Implementation of a Queue

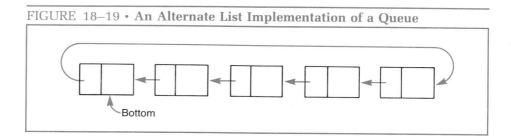

Bottom

the complete outline and coding of this implementation as an exercise.

An alternate approach to this implementation is possible if we modify the list structure so that the head of the list follows the bottom element, as shown in Figure 18–19. This structure is an example of another list structure, called a **circular list.** In such a list, each item points to the next, and this chain of pointers eventually forms a loop back to the first one. Here, we need only one pointer to the bottom of the queue. From this bottom element, we can follow the *Next* field to obtain the head. Again, we need special cases for queues with no elements or with just one element.

Conclusions

These new implementations of stacks and queues demonstrate several important points. First, lists and pointers can be useful in a variety of ways when we need to keep data in an ordered form. Lists allow particularly easy insertion and deletion of data, thus providing considerable flexibility in organizing data.

Second, in some cases, we may be able to choose among several different ways to store data. For example, here lists provided a reasonable alternative to arrays for implementing stacks and queues.

Finally, in defining data structures, we need to distinguish between the operations that we want to perform and the implementation of those operations. For example, in defining stacks and queues, we describe such operations as *Empty, Push, Pop, Top, Insert,* and *Delete,* and we write applications completely in terms of these operations. Then, when we implement these operations we can proceed in several ways. We can choose between writing the details with arrays or with lists, and our coding for these operations may change significantly from one implementation to another. However, these details do not affect our application code at all; our use of data structure operations does not depend upon these underlying details.

SUMMARY

1. **Linked list data structures** allow us to store individual data elements, and these list elements are interconnected by **pointers.**
2. In a **singly linked list,** we declare a **pointer** variable that specifies the

location of the first element on the list. Then, each subsequent list element includes a pointer to the next element until a *Nil* pointer marks the end of the list. With this structure, we include the operations *insert, delete, search,* and *print.*

3. These lists also motivate a discussion of storage allocation in computers.

   a. ***Static storage*** depends upon declarations in a Pascal program. This space is allocated when a function or procedure is called. In this allocation, all space requirements depend upon the variables declared, and the amount of this space does not change during procedure execution.

   b. With ***dynamic storage,*** a program can allocate and deallocate space as the program is running. The total amount of space used is not fixed by the variable declarations.

4. Beyond the singly linked structure, we find several variations of list structures.

   a. We can divide long lists into short pieces using a ***hashing algorithm.*** Then to find an item of data, we could search an appropriate short list rather than proceeding linearly through all the data.

   b. We can add pointers to previous data elements as well as to the next ones, and we can specify last items on lists as well as first ones. These additions introduce ***doubly linked lists.***

   c. We can organize our data into several types of records, using pointers to move from one type of record to another. These ***general linked structures*** allow us great flexibility in organizing our information.

5. We use lists and pointers to solve a variety of problems where we need to insert and delete data easily. These applications include alternate implementations for the stack and queue structures discussed in the previous chapter. In these new stack and queue applications, we retain the same operations and calling formats defined earlier, so our applications using these operations do not depend on the implementation details. Only the internal coding of these functions and procedures change with new implementations.

EXERCISES

18.1 *Outline for List Insertion.* Section 18.1 gives the basic steps required to insert a new piece of data into a list. The section also notes some complications that arise when insertion is actually attempted. Write an outline for list insertion that takes these complications into account.

18.2 *Changing List Items.* Section 18.2 includes a program that inserts, deletes, and prints items on a list. Modify this program so that a user can change a task. In particular, write

Procedure ChangeListItem (Var First: ListPointer);

where ChangeListItem
* reads the name of a current task;
* finds the task on the list;
* asks for a revised task name; and
* changes the task name on the list.

18.3   Write a complete outline for the solution of the problem in Section 18.2.

18.4   *Steps in Searching Lists.* Determine the number of checks that are required to conclude that a given item is not on a linked list.
  a. Assume the list is ordered.
  b. Assume the list is unordered.

18.5   *Deletion of Duplicates.* Write a procedure that deletes duplicate records from a list.
  a. Assume the list is ordered.
  b. Assume the list is unordered.
  After writing your procedures for parts (a) and (b), compare the number of steps required for each case.

18.6   *Insertion and Deletion for Ordered Lists.* Section 18.3 contains a detailed outline for the insertion of a new item into an ordered list.
  a. Write the Pascal procedure that follows this outline.
  b. Write a corresponding outline and procedure for deleting an item from an ordered list.

18.7   *Using a Hashing Algorithm.* Section 18.4 includes a problem where a single alphabetical list is to be divided into 26 shorter lists, according to the first letter of each word. The section also discusses some of the steps involved in inserting and deleting elements from this revised list structure.
  a. Write detailed outlines for these insertion and deletion operations.

KEY TERMS, PHRASES, AND CONCEPTS		ELEMENTS OF PASCAL SYNTAX	
Circular Lists	Pointers	*Dispose*	*New*
Doubly Linked Lists	Dereferencing	Pointer, ↑ , ˆ, or @	*Nil*
General Linked	Singly Linked Lists		
Structures	Storage Allocation		
Hashing	Dynamic		
List Data Structure	Allocation		
Operations	New		
Delete	Dispose		
Find	Static Allocation		
Insert			
Print			
Nil Pointers			

    b. Use these outlines to write a program to solve the problem in Section 18.4.

18.8 *Deletion and Modification of Doubly Linked Lists.* Section 18.5 introduces the concept of doubly linked lists and also presents the details required to insert new elements into such lists.

    a. Write similar detailed outlines and procedures for deleting and for modifying elements in doubly linked lists.

    b. Put these procedures together in a program that expands the golf scoring problem from Section 18.5.

18.9 *Two-Round Golf Tournament.* A local golf tournament consists of two rounds of golf, played on different days. On the first day, names and scores in the first round are entered into the computer as the players finish their rounds. On the second day, the second round scores will be added. This information is to be retrieved in each of the following ways.

- Scores and names can be printed in ascending order of scores for either round.
- Total scores, with names, can be printed in either ascending or descending order of scores.
- Given the name of a player, other players with the same total score can be printed.

    a. Write a detailed outline to solve this two-round golf tournament scoring.

    b. Write a program for this problem based on your outline.

18.10 *Player Withdrawing from a Tournament.* Expand the program for the Two-Round Golf Tournament to allow a person to withdraw from the tournament. This operation will require a procedure that deletes the person's name from the first round list and sometimes from the second round list and total list.

18.11 *Queue Implementation by Pointers.*

    a. Write a detailed outline for the pointer implementation of the queue that uses both *Head* and *Bottom* pointers. Your outline should include the details for

- Procedure InitializeQueue;
- Function Empty: Boolean;
- Procedure Insert(Item: Data);
- Procedure Delete (Var Item: Data);

    b. Implement these procedures following your outline.

18.12 *Parentheses Balancing Revisited.* Revise the Balance Parentheses program of Section 17.3, so that the required stack is implemented by a linked list structure.

18.13 *Improving Average Search Time.* One way to improve the average time required for the linear search of a list is to group the frequently accessed items near the head of the list. A practical way to approximate this grouping involves the modification of the list after every search. In particular, whenever an item is found on the list, that item is moved to the front of the list. (Thus, if an item is found often, that item will stay close to the start. If an item is not used often, that item will gradually move back.) Write a search procedure that implements this list modification as a side effect.

18.14 *Telephone Directory.* This problem applies the search improvement of the previous problem to the storage and retrieval of records for a telephone answering service that keeps track of commonly used names and telephone numbers. In particular, a program for a telephone answering service must perform the following tasks.

I. The user specifies a name, which is searched in an abbreviated telephone directory.

II. If the name is found:
   A. The person's name and telephone number are printed.
   B. The entry printed for that person is moved to the beginning of the list of names and numbers.

III. If the person is not found:
   A. The user is asked to verify that the name was typed correctly. (If the name was incorrect, the processing goes back to Step I.)
   B. The user is asked to look up the person's telephone number in a more complete directory (or call directory assistance, etc.) and enter the number from the terminal.
   C. A new entry, with the new name and telephone number, is added to the beginning of the list.

Write a program to perform these tasks.

18.15 *Expanded Directory.* Modify the program in the previous exercise so that retrieval by individual names uses this efficient list organization but also so that an alphabetical listing of names, with telephone numbers, is possible.

18.16 *Dentist's Office Waiting Room.* In a dentist's office, patients enter and immediately notify a receptionist that they have arrived for their appointments. The dentist then sees patients in the order that they arrive. (The first patient to arrive is the first patient to see the dentist.)

   a. Design a data structure to keep track of who is waiting for the dentist and whom the dentist will see next. (You may assume that patients never leave the waiting room before seeing the dentist.) In your design, you should describe
      1. the format in which data will be stored (e.g., include fields for all records); and
      2. how data will be stored and retrieved.
   b. Write a program that implements your design.

18.17 *Dentist Office with Technician.* Modify your work in the previous problem so that the office employs several dental hygienists, where each has a separate list of appointments. Thus, for a given hygienist, the first patient to arrive is the first patient to see the hygienist. However, the patients for one hygienist do not have to wait for patients of other hygienists.

18.18 *Recording Prescriptions.* A doctor keeps records on all her patients, including their names and all medicines prescribed.

   a. Design a data structure to store each patient's name and all medicines prescribed for each patient. The structure must allow the doctor to obtain a complete list of her patients' names and a complete list of medicines for any specific patient. Your design should describe

      1. the format in which data will be stored (e.g., include fields for all records); and
      2. how data can be added, modified, and searched.

   b. Write a program to implement your design.

      CAUTION: In this problem, it should not be necessary to scan the entire data structure to obtain the desired results.

18.19 Modify your work in the previous problem so that the doctor will also be able to obtain a list of all patients who have used a specified medicine.

CHAPTER 19

TREE

DATA STRUCTURES

AND RECURSION

This chapter discusses **trees,** which constitute the fourth and final formal data structure considered in this book. As with previous data structures, we consider trees both on a conceptual level and on the detailed level of programming trees in Pascal using records and pointers. In this discussion, we will find that many of our needed operations are best performed by procedures and functions that call themselves, and this introduces the subject of **recursion,** where tasks call themselves. Finally, these subjects of trees and recursion will provide us with powerful tools to solve a wide variety of problems.

SECTION 19.1   INTRODUCTION TO TREES

To introduce the concept of tree data structures, we first consider an organizational chart for a company. (See Figure 19–1.) This chart organizes personnel in a hierarchical structure and has the following characteristics.

1. Exactly one person, the president, appears at the top of the structure.
2. Under the president, several people, called vice presidents, are in positions that report directly to the president.

FIGURE 19–1 • **A Simple Hierarchical Structure Illustrating the Organization of a Corporation**

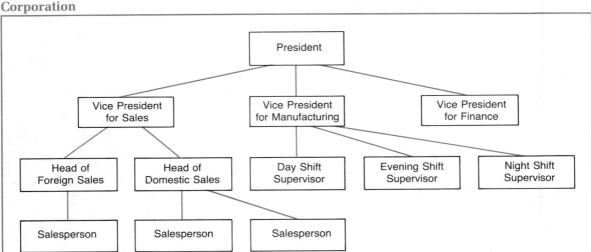

3. Moving down the structure, each person reports directly to exactly one person, and each person may supervise zero, one, or more others.

In the tree data structure, we generalize these characteristics. (See Figure 19–2.) In this structure, we store data in positions called **nodes.** In Figure 19–2, these nodes are shown as circles, and we have stored the letters 'a' through 'o' as our data. In Figure 19–1, the nodes contained the positions in the company as data. Further, these nodes are organized in a hierarchy. We now look at these nodes in more detail.

First, we introduce some terminology. Throughout this terminology, we might think of the structure as a family tree starting with one ancestor as the "root." The single node containing 'a' at the top of the tree structure is called the **root** of the tree. Further, each node, except the root, has exactly one other node above it. For example, the node containing 'e' has the 'b' node above it. In this situation, we say that the 'e' node has the 'b' node as its **parent,** and the 'e' node is the **child** of the 'b' node. We note that several nodes may have the same parent and one node may have several children. For example, the nodes containing 'g', 'h', and 'i' all have the 'c' node as parent. Further, it is not necessary for two nodes to have the same number of children. For example, the 'c' node and the 'l' nodes have three children each, but the 'b' and 'h' nodes have only two children. We say that two nodes with the same parent are **siblings.** Also, some nodes may not have any children. In a mixing of metaphors, such nodes are called **leaves.** In our example, the nodes containing 'j', 'f', 'g', 'k', 'm', 'n', 'o', 'i', and 'd' are leaves.

FIGURE 19–2 • A Typical Tree Structure

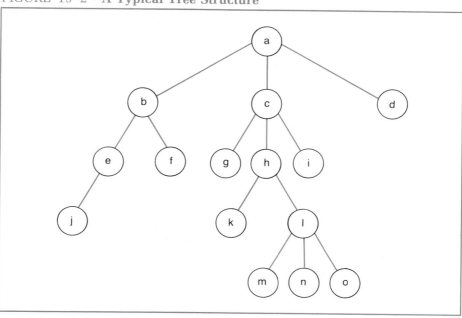

For any node, we may proceed upward from parent to parent. This line upward gives us the **ancestors** of the given node. For example, the ancestors of the 'k' node are the nodes containing 'h', 'c' and 'a'. As a special case, the root is an ancestor of every node in the tree (except itself). Similarly, starting at any node, we may move away from the root by selecting one child at each subsequent node until we reach a leaf. For example, starting with the 'c' node, we may pick the nodes containing 'h', 'l', and 'm'. Such a collection of nodes is called a **branch** of the tree, and the branch has the same general structure as a linked list. For any branch, there is a first element. Each element (except the final leaf) has a single successor.

This last observation that a branch of a tree forms a linked list also suggests another observation. We can view any singly linked list as a tree if we consider the first element of the list as the root and if we think of each successive item in the list as a child of the previous item. In this special tree, all list items or tree nodes lie on a single branch that starts with the root.

Finally, in any tree, we may get another tree by starting at any node and including all its descendants. For example, starting with the 'b' node, we include the nodes containing 'e', 'f' and 'j'. This small collection of nodes fit together in a hierarchical structure called a **subtree** of the original tree.

Tree Operations

Now that we have identified the basic structure of a tree, we need to consider which operations we might want to apply to trees. As in our work with lists, the most common tree operations include

- finding and perhaps modifying a piece of data in a tree;
- printing the data in a tree;
- inserting a piece of data; and
- deleting data.

For insertion, we might place data in the middle of trees and at the end of trees to form new leaves. In this text, we will consider insertion of new data items only in the form of new leaves. Insertion within a tree can be more complex and is best left to more advanced texts.

Next, in considering the deletion operation, we can delete individual nodes and entire subtrees. In practice, deleting individual nodes can be more complex than deleting an entire subtree. This is because the children of a deleted node must be attached to a new parent node, for instance, the parent of the deleted node. Such an operation may require considerable care so that no nodes are lost by mistake.

Binary Trees

Finally, within this general discussion of trees, we identify one special type of tree structure that arises frequently in applications. In this type of tree, each node may have only zero, one, or two children, as illustrated in Figure 19–3. Here, below each node, we think of children on the left and the right sides of the parent. In this situation, we also can add operations *Left* and *Right*, which move us from one node to the appropriate child of that node.

FIGURE 19–3 • **A Typical Binary Tree**

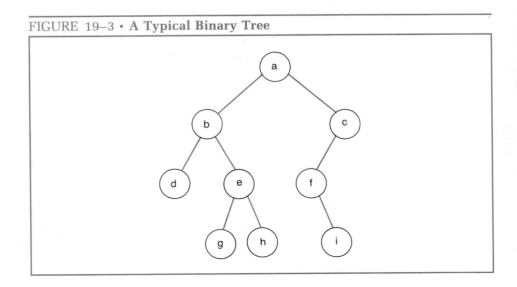

Trees with this special structure are called **binary trees,** and we will see several applications of them in the next section.

EXAMPLES

The last section considered the general structure of a tree, and it described some typical operations that we might want to perform on such a structure. In this section, we consider three applications that illustrate many of the common uses for these tree structures. In particular, we discuss

- tree representations of arithmetic structures;
- game trees; and
- ordering data in trees for efficient searching.

In each case, we will be able to utilize the hierarchical structure of trees to organize data efficiently.

Tree Representations of Arithmetic Expressions

In our first example, we use trees to clarify the structure of arithmetic expressions. Specifically, we store both arithmetic operations ($+$, $-$, $*$, $/$) and numbers as the data in our nodes, and we use the connections between nodes to specify which operations are applied to which numbers and expressions. Several typical representations are illustrated in Figure 19–4.

The tree representation of the number 2 (Figure 19–4a) contains only one piece of data, and the tree contains only one node.

In the expression $2*3$, the operation $*$ is applied to the numbers 2 and 3. In this situation, we place $*$ in the root node, and this node contains two children containing the numbers 2 and 3. (See Figure 19–4b.) As our expressions become more complex, these individual pieces are linked in the tree. For example, when we represent $2*3 + 4$, we first need to apply the $*$ operation to the numbers 2 and 3. Then, we apply the $+$ operation to the 4 and the result of the $*$ operation. This process of evaluation is seen in the tree of Figure 19–4c, where the $+$ has children ($*$ and 4) and where the $*$ in turn is applied to its children (2 and 3).

When we evaluate the operations in a different order, the corresponding changes are seen in the tree structure. For example, if we perform the addition before multiplication by adding parentheses in the expression $2 * (3 + 4)$, the root of the tree changes as do various relationships. (See Figure 19–4d.)

These examples illustrate several important properties of tree representation of arithmetic expressions.

1. The structure of a tree provides us with an unambiguous way of determining which operations should be applied to which objects.
2. In structuring the tree, we do not have to store parentheses; the tree structure defines the appropriate relationships without parentheses.

FIGURE 19–4 • **Tree Representations of Arithmetic Expressions**

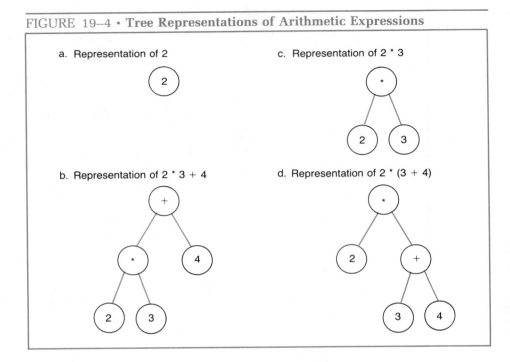

a. Representation of 2

c. Representation of 2 * 3

b. Representation of 2 * 3 + 4

d. Representation of 2 * (3 + 4)

3. In this application, the leaf nodes always contain numbers as data, and the nonleaves always contain operations.

Game Trees

A second major application of trees involves the recording and analyzing of various possible moves in games. In this application, each node contains data for a particular situation that can arise in a game, and a connection from one node to its child represents a move in the game. This structure is seen more clearly if we look at two examples from Tic-Tac-Toe.

Example 1: In playing Tic-Tac-Toe, we can consider the current board position as the root of a tree, as shown in Figure 19–5. Then, from this root, we can consider all possible moves starting with a given board position, assuming X is to move next. Thus, in Figure 19–5, four squares are filled, and X could be placed on any of the remaining five squares. Then for each move by X, O could move into any of the remaining squares.

This game tree also illustrates one way that these structures are used in programming games in computers and in analyzing different potential moves. In particular, if X first moves into the lower right square, then any move for O can be followed by a win for X. Thus, from this position, our analysis of the tree shows that by a proper selection of moves, X can be assured of a win.

FIGURE 19–5 • A Complete Game Tree for a Specified Position

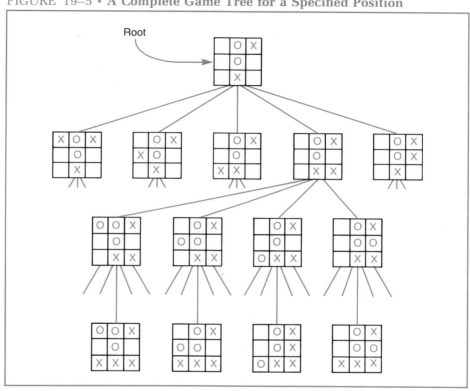

This observation is the basis for many of the game-playing programs now in existence. For a given position, a computer can build a game tree to determine what might happen after every possible move it could make. Then, by analyzing these possible consequences, the computer can select a move which is best.

Example 2: The previous example also shows one potential difficulty with the use of game trees in analyzing possible moves. In particular, starting with all possible first moves, the full game tree for Tic-Tac-Toe contains something like 900,000 nodes. Thus, even for a simple game, complete game trees can become very large, and the creation and analysis of such trees can take an unacceptably long length of time. For this reason, game trees that are used in game programs are abbreviated, or "pruned," in a variety of ways.

One way this may be done is to consider only a certain number of moves in the future in the tree. In this situation, we call the move by each player a "ply", and we may record only a specific number of "plies." A two-ply tree is shown in Figure 19–6. Such limited trees do not allow us

FIGURE 19–6 • A Two-Ply Tree for a Specific Tic-Tac-Toe Position

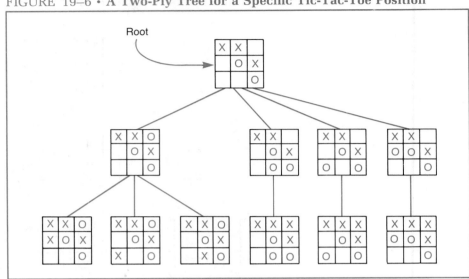

to see all possible consequences of our moves, so in some cases we may not be able to be sure which of several moves is best. On the other hand, Figure 19–6 shows that even a two-ply tree can be enough in some cases. In that figure, all but one move for O results in an immediate win for X. Thus, the only hope O has is to move into the upper right box.

A second method tries to eliminate some branches by clever analysis. Once one branch can be identified to include a sure loss or a sure win, then no further analysis along that branch is needed.

In practice, sophisticated game programs use a variety of methods to prune trees in careful ways.

Ordering Data in Trees for Efficient Searching

As our final application of this section, we consider an important way that data can be arranged in a tree so that searching can be done very efficiently.

A basic approach to arranging data is shown in Figure 19–7. In the figure, we start with a binary tree, with names entered as the data in each node. Then these nodes are arranged in a special way so that for any node the descendants along the left branch precede their ancestor in alphabetical order, and all descendants along a right branch follow their ancestor.

For example, in the figure if we start with the root, we obtain the name *MacKay*, and we find that the descendants along the left branch (*Bliven, Colpitts*, and *Klomps*) all come before *MacKay* in alphabetical order. Similarly, if we look at the *Colpitts* node, we find that *Bliven* appears along the

FIGURE 19–7 • **A Binary Tree with Data Arranged for Efficient Searching**

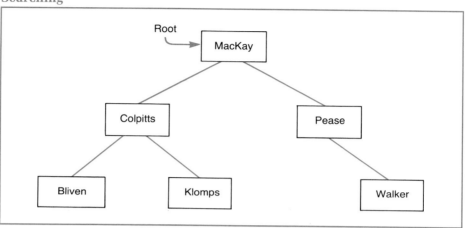

left branch and *Klomps* along the right branch. With this placement of the *Klomps* node, we note that *Klomps* comes after *Colpitts* but before *MacKay* in alphabetical order.

Once we have ordered data in this way, we can search a binary tree very quickly. In particular, we start at the root of the tree, and if this is our desired item, we stop. Otherwise, we check if our desired name comes before the name at this node. If the desired name comes before, we move to the child on the left and repeat the process. If the desired name comes after, we move to the child on the right and repeat this step.

This search strategy is very efficient, just as was the binary search from Section 8.6, because after working with one node we can rule out half of the remaining nodes. For example, if our desired name comes after *MacKay*, then we know all nodes along the left branch from *MacKay* can be ignored in our search.

Of course, such a search strategy requires that the names are split up evenly, so the number of nodes to the left is about the same as the number to the right. However, if a tree is arranged properly, it can be a particularly effective way to store and retrieve data. Thus, this structuring of data is seen in a great number of applications, where quick retrieval of data is needed.

More generally, the examples in this section have illustrated several important ways that trees can be of considerable value in applications. In each case, we stored relevant data in the nodes of a tree, and we used the tree structure to organize this data in a conceptually clear and effective way. In the next section, we see how to translate this conceptual structure into Pascal code.

IMPLEMENTATION OF BINARY TREES WITH POINTERS

Now that we have seen several applications that use trees, we turn to various techniques for implementing these trees. In this section, we look at the special case of binary trees, and we see how such trees could be built. Then in Section 19.5, we look at ways to implement more general trees.

In considering a binary tree, a typical node must contain the three pieces of information:

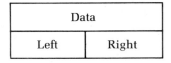

First, the node must contain the appropriate data, such as arithmetic operations or numbers, game board positions, or names. Next, the node must contain information about the child on the left (if any) and about the child on the right (if any). We might also want to record information about the parent of the node, but in practice we often can omit this information. This description of a node suggests the following declaration.

```
Type Data  =  . . .    ;
     Ptr   =  ^Node;
     Node  =  Record
                Info: Data;
                Left: Ptr;
                Right: Ptr
              End;
Var Root: Ptr;
```

This node information is analogous to our list item declaration. In each case, we store our appropriate information in a cell. Then we use pointer fields (*Next* for lists, *Left* and *Right* for binary trees) to specify the next objects in the list or tree.

To see how these declarations can be used to form a tree, we consider the following problem.

PROBLEM 19.3 ## Building an Ordered Binary Tree

We wish to build an ordered tree of names, such as shown in Figure 19–7, so that we can locate specific names efficiently as discussed earlier. To this end, we include the following declarations:

```
Const Max = 20;
Type  Data = Packed Array [1..Max] of Char
```

Write a procedure that adds a name, in an appropriate node, to an ordered binary tree. More precisely, write

Procedure Insert (Name: Data; Var Root: Ptr);

which places the given *Name* into a new node and then inserts that node into the ordered tree with the given *Root*.

Discussion of Problem 19.3

Procedure *Insert* must perform two operations: create an appropriate new node; and insert the new node into the tree. The creation process is similar to our creation of new list items. The insertion process is a bit more complex. In particular, we must start at the root of the tree, and we must see if the new name comes before the name stored in the root. If so, we move left; otherwise, we move right.

This process continues from node to node as we work down the tree. Finally, when the appropriate left or right pointer is *nil*, we insert the new node as a new leaf of the tree.

This suggests the following outline which also includes the special case where the tree is *nil*.

Outline for Problem 19.3

I. Create a new node.
  A. Allocate space for the node.
  B. Place the name in the data field.
  C. Initialize left and right pointers to *nil*.
II. Insert new node.
  A. If root is *nil*, insert new node as root and stop.
  B. If root is not *nil*, then start with root node.
  C. With the given tree node
    1. If new name comes before name in the tree node, then move left.
      a. If left pointer is *nil*, insert new node and stop.
      b. If left pointer is not *nil*, move on to the left tree node and repeat step C.
    2. If new names come after name in the tree node, then move right.
      a. If the right pointer is *nil*, insert new node and stop.
      b. If the right pointer is not *nil*, move on to the right tree node and repeat step C.

Throughout Step II, we move steadily down the tree from the root, going left or right as needed to maintain our ordering. Then, when we finally reach the bottom of the tree, we insert our new node. This outline gives rise to the following code.

```
Procedure Insert (Name: Data; Var Root: Ptr);
{This procedure creates a new node for the name and inserts the
new node in the tree with the specified root.}

    Var NewNode: Ptr;

    Procedure InsertNode (NewNode: Ptr; Var Root: Ptr);
    {This procedure inserts the new node on the tree with a simple loop.}
        Var Done: Boolean;
            TreeNode: Ptr;

        Begin
            If  Root = Nil
                Then Root := NewNode
                Else Begin
                    Done := False;
                    TreeNode := Root;
                    While Not Done
                        Do Begin {Move down tree}
                            If  NewNode^.Info < TreeNode^.Info
                                Then Begin {Move Left}
                                    If TreeNode^.Left = Nil
                                        Then Begin
                                            TreeNode^.Left := NewNode;
                                            Done := True
                                            End
                                        Else TreeNode := TreeNode^.Left
                                    End {Move Left}
                                Else Begin {Move Right}
                                    If TreeNode^.Right = Nil
                                        Then Begin
                                            TreeNode^.Right := NewNode;
                                            Done := True
                                            End
                                        Else TreeNode := TreeNode^.Right
                                    End {Move Right}
                            End {Move down tree}
                    End
        End {InsertNode};

    Begin {Insert}
        {Create and initialize new node}
        New (NewNode);
        NewNode^.Info := Name;
        NewNode^.Left := Nil;
        NewNode^.Right := Nil;

        {Insert new node into tree}
        InsertNode (NewNode, Root)
    End {Insert} ;
```

This processing with Pascal pointers follows many of the same ideas that we saw in writing our procedures for lists. If we were to follow this procedure when it is called six times for the names *MacKay, Pease, Col-*

pitts, Bliven, Walker, and *Klomps*, we should find that the resulting tree agrees with the structure shown in Figure 19–7. From this code, we see that much of our work with pointers for lists carries over to our manipulation of binary trees. Our initial declaration of a node is new, but the techniques of pointers for building trees are similar.

In the next section, however, we encounter a new type of algorithm that prints a listing of data stored in a tree.

SECTION 19.4   PRINTING DATA (TREE TRANSVERSALS)

In much of our work with data up to now, we have started at one end of our data and moved to the other end. When we try to print out all of the data stored in a binary tree, however, we cannot proceed linearly from one end to another. Rather, from any particular node, we may have to move left for some data and then right for more data. Thus, if we use our previous printing techniques, we may become overwhelmed with the complexity of our task. We must keep track of what we have printed at a node and on its left and right, and our code can become quite messy.

Instead of trying to keep track of all details of printing, we consider an alternate approach that turns out to be extremely powerful. We begin by focusing on a typical node in an ordered tree. If we want to print names in alphabetical order, we identify three steps.

1. Print names (if any) on the left of the node.
2. Print the name at the given node.
3. Print names (if any) on the right of the node.

Further, we observe that we want to repeat this process at each node.

In implementing this simple outline, we write procedure *Print* so that it will process a single node. Then, as part of our work, we have *Print* call itself to process its left and right children. After we look at this code itself, we analyze in some detail why the procedure works.

```
Procedure Print (Base: Ptr);
{This procedure prints all node on the tree with the given base,
 focusing on the printing for the given node}

    Begin
        If Base <> Nil
        Then Begin
            Print (Base^.Left);
            Writeln (Base^.Info);
            Print (Base^.Right)
            End;
    End {Print} ;
```

Details of Processing with a Recursive Print Procedure

To understand why procedure *Print* works, we follow the execution of statements for the data in Figure 19–8. In this analysis, we need to refer to each arrow from parent to child and to consider *nil* pointers at the leaf nodes. Thus, for reference, we have numbered all of the pointers in Figure 19–8. We now follow the steps involved when procedure *Print* is called. These steps are shown pictorially in Figure 19–9.

To begin, procedure *Print* is called with *Root* (or pointer(1)) as the actual parameter, and formal parameter *Base* becomes pointer(1).

The first part of *Print* involves a test. Here pointer(1) is not *nil*, so we continue with the *Then* clause of the procedure. Within this *Then* clause, *Print* is called again, with *Base^.Left* (or pointer(2)) as actual parameter. Here, when *Print* is called, we know a new storage location is created for the new parameter *Base*, and we know pointer(2) is used for this new *Base* parameter.

Again, *Base* (now pointer(2)) is not *nil*, so *Print* is called another time, with *Base^.Left* (or pointer(4)) as actual parameter. At this point, *Print* has been called three times, each with a different value parameter for *Base*. These three calls are shown as nested boxes in Figure 19–9. Once again, the new *Base* (pointer(4)) is not *nil*, and *Print* is called with actual parameter *Base^.Left* (or pointer(8)). This gives the first inside box in our figure. Finally, pointer(8) is *nil*, so this last procedure call can finish.

We return to the next box, where *Base* is pointer(4). Now

Print (Base^.Left)

FIGURE 19–8 • **An Ordered Binary Tree with All Pointers Numbered**

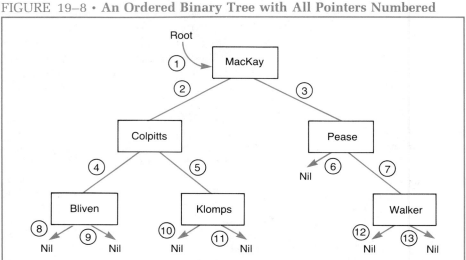

FIGURE 19–9 • **Steps Involved when Procedure Print Acts on the Tree of Figure 19–8**

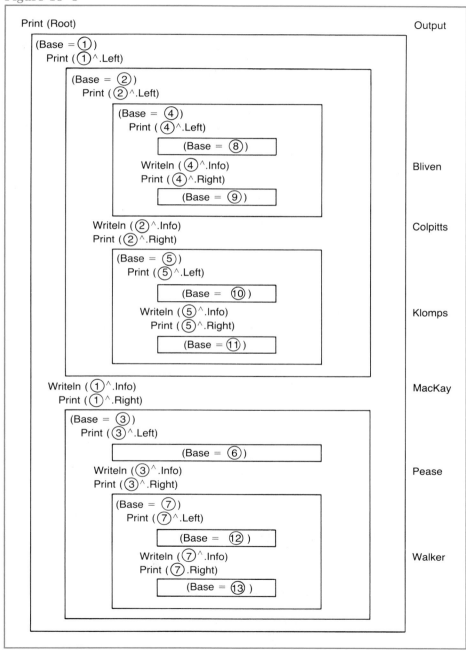

with *Base* = (4) is complete, so we continue with

> **Writeln (Baseˆ.Info)**

This prints our first name, *Bliven*. Next, the procedure states

> **Print (Baseˆ.Right)**

with *Base* = (4) so we call *Print* again, this time with actual parameter pointer (9).

This new *Base* (pointer (9)) is *nil*, so *Print* returns, and *Base* = (4) as before. However, now we have completed all steps for this *Print* procedure as well; our processing with *Base* = (4) is done, and we return to our previous work. In the figure, we have left the box where *Base* = (4), and we continue in the box where *Base* = (2).

The next step with *Base* = (2) involves

> **Writeln (Baseˆ.Info)**

and the name *Colpitts* is printed.

Moving along, *Print* is again called with *Baseˆ.Right* (pointer (5)) as actual parameter. This procedure call allows the program to process the *Klomps* node in much the same way we have already seen for the *Bliven* node. When the *Klomps* node is done, the machine returns to the *Colpitts* node where *Base* is pointer (2). This completes the processing of this node, and the machine returns to the first call of *Print* where *Base* = (1).

Next, *MacKay* is printed, and the machine calls *Print* with actual parameter pointer (3). This leads to the printing of the right hand part of the tree.

Overview of Processing with the Print Procedure

Now that we have followed the details of what happens when we call procedure *Print*, we need to organize these details on a more conceptual level, and we focus on the work required at each node.

1. We process the left child node.
2. We print the name at the node itself.
3. We process the child node on the right.

When we repeat these steps at one node, the first step processes the left child which in turn handles all nodes on the left. The computer repeats these steps at each node in turn by a sequence of procedure calls, and the entire data eventually are printed. In this example, we have reduced the details of all nodes to the specific steps for a single node by having the procedure *Print* call itself.

Recursive Programming

This example illustrates a more general technique that is very useful in programming. In a more general setting, we may proceed in two steps. In the first step, we identify a small part of the task or some simple cases that are easy to handle. In our problem, we focused on the work required at a node. Then, in the second step, we reduce more complex situations to these easier ones. In our example, we instructed the computer to repeat the same process for each child.

In applying this approach to solving problems, we often want a procedure or function to call itself. In such cases, we write out the details for one situation and have the computer repeat these steps by having the function or procedure refer to itself.

For example, in printing the data in a tree, we identified what we needed to do at a particular node. Then we reduced our general printing task to a single node problem by telling the computer to repeat this process with both the left and the right children.

In general, **recursion** is a technique in which a function or procedure calls itself, and a **recursive algorithm** is one in which a process refers to itself. Such algorithms often can yield very clean solutions to problems that otherwise could be quite complex. Our example of printing data in a tree structure is a good illustration of this technique, and we will find that many other tasks involving trees also can be solved rather simply by recursive algorithms. Later in this chapter, we will see other examples where recursion is useful when no trees are being considered.

Before turning to a second example using trees, we need to make two practical points about recursion in our programming. To start a recursive algorithm, we need a procedure call outside of our recursive procedure. For example, in our printing procedure, we assume that the printing process begins with a procedure call:

Print (Root)

In addition, in a recursive algorithm, we expect procedure calls to move us from one case to another. However, if this process is to stop eventually, we must include some condition in our code so that further procedures are not called. For example, in our printing procedure, we started with a test to see if a pointer was *nil*, and work on a node continued only if a non-*nil* was encountered. With this condition, we could be sure our printing would stop eventually whenever we reached the leaves of our tree.

Insertion by Recursion

With these comments about recursion, we now turn to a second example, and we reconsider the insertion of a new node into an ordered binary tree from Section 19.3.

In reviewing the insertion process, we can identify one particularly simple case: when we reach a *nil* pointer, we know we need to insert our new node. Further, we can work our way down the tree with the simple observation: if our new name comes before the name at a tree node, then we should move left. Otherwise, we should move right.

Outline for Tree Insertion.   Putting these ideas together, we obtain the following outline.

I. Start at root of tree.
II. General step.
  A. If we are at the end of the tree (i.e. if our pointer is *nil*), then insert the new node.
  B. If we are not at the end, then compare the new name to the name in the tree node.
    1. If the new name comes first, repeat this Step II, moving left.
    2. If the new name comes later, repeat this Step II, moving right.

In this outline, the details in Step IIB tell us to repeat the entire Step II with a new node. This suggests that our procedure for node insertion should call itself with a new, revised parameter for the repetition step. Thus, this outline suggests the following recursive procedure for insertion.

```
Procedure Insert (Name: Data; Var Root: Ptr);
{This procedure creates a new node for the name and inserts the
new node in the tree with the specified root.}
{The insertion process itself is done recursively}

    Var NewNode: Ptr;

    Procedure InsertNode (NewNode: Ptr; Var Base: Ptr);
    {This procedure inserts the new node on the tree recursively.}
        Begin
            If Base = Nil
                Then Base := NewNode
                Else Begin
                    If NewNode^.Info < Base^.Info
                        Then InsertNode (NewNode, Base^.Left)
                        Else InsertNode (NewNode, Base^.Right)
                End
        End {InsertNode};

Begin {Insert}
    {Create and initialize new node}
    New (NewNode);
    NewNode^.Info := Name;
    NewNode^.Left := Nil;
    NewNode^.Right := Nil;

    {Insert new node into tree}
    InsertNode (NewNode, Root)
End {Insert} ;
```

In this code, the recursive *InsertNode* procedure is much simpler than the nonrecursive version in the previous section. Here, we have been able to focus on a single node where the work is quite easy, and we can move from one node to another by appropriate procedure calls. In tracing through this code, we can see how recursion has allowed us to handle each node simply and to move easily from node to node down the tree. In the next section, we describe another application of recursion: solving a puzzle.

SECTION 19.5   APPLICATIONS OF RECURSION TO SIMPLE PUZZLES

In the previous section, we were able to insert nodes into ordered trees and to print all nodes in a tree by focusing on a single node and then telling the computer to repeat this work at the children of a node. In this section, we see an example of recursion that arises in a rather different context. As in the previous section, our approach will be to solve a simple case and then to have the computer repeat this case as often as necessary.

First, we state a problem that is the basis for several commercially available puzzles.

PROBLEM 19.5   The Towers of Hanoi

One classic puzzle is often called "The Towers of Hanoi." It contains three rods and several rings of different sizes that can fit over the rods.

At the start, the rings are placed over one rod, so that each ring rests on the next larger one. This initial configuration is shown in Figure 19–10, where all rings are positioned around Rod 1.

With this starting point, the goal of the puzzle is to move all rings from Rod 1 to Rod 2 so that at the end the rings again are in order.

FIGURE 19–10 · **Initial Position for the Towers of Hanoi**

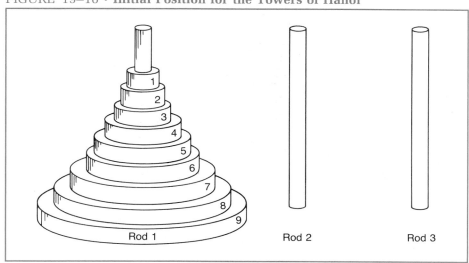

The challenge of the puzzle arises from the following rules for moving these rings.

1. Only one ring may be moved at a time.
2. Only a ring on the top of a rod may be moved to the top position on another rod.
3. A ring may never be placed on top of a smaller ring.

For example, looking at Figure 19–10, initially we may move the smallest ring (ring 1) to either Rod 2 or Rod 3. So suppose we move Ring 1 to Rod 2. Then, on our next turn, we may move Ring 2 to Rod 3, but we may not move Ring 2 to Rod 2, because the smaller Ring 1 is already there.

Discussion of Problem 19.5

In attacking this puzzle, our first approach might be to describe the motion of each ring in detail, establishing a pattern for each move. However, if the number of rings is large, this level of detail can become quite complex and hard to program. Instead, we take a broader view of the problem. We begin our analysis by identifying the three rods as follows.

Original Rod: Where all rings start (e.g., Rod 1)

Final Rod: Where all rings are to end (e.g., Rod 2)

Spare Rod: Neither the starting nor ending Rod—the rod we can use for intermediate steps (e.g., Rod 3)

Further, if we have N rings that we want to move, we can imagine performing our task by

Procedure Move (Original, Final, Spare: Rod; Number: Ring);

With this procedure, we solve our puzzle with the initial procedure call

Move (1, 2, 3, N)

This moves N rings from Rod 1 to Rod 2, using Rod 3 as a spare.

Now that we have set up this general framework, we consider the work we need for the moving of Ring N. In our analysis, our major breakthrough is to identify the following general steps:

1. Move the top $N-1$ rings from the original rod to the spare rod.
2. Move the Nth rod from the original rod to the final rod.
3. Move the $N-1$ rings from the spare rod to the final rod.

With these steps, we can perform Step 2 as one move of a single ring from one rod to another. Thus, this step can be done directly. Further, Steps 1 and 3 can be done with the same *Move* procedure, applied to a pile of one fewer rings.

This discussion suggests the following program which depends upon recursion to repeat Steps 1 and 3.

```
Program TowersOfHanoi (Output);
{This program prints solution of the Towers Of Hanoi problem.}
   Const Total = 4;   {Number of rings given in the problem}

   Type Rod = Integer;
        Ring = Integer;

Procedure Move (Original, Final, Spare: Rod; Number: Ring);
{This procedure moves the ring with the given Number from the original
 rod to the Final rod, using the Spare rod as necessary}
   Begin
       If Number > 1
           Then Move (Original, Spare, Final, Number-1);

       {Move ring with given Number}
       Writeln (Number:8, Original:11 ,Final:9);

       If Number > 1
           Then Move (Spare, Final, Original, Number-1)
   End {Move} ;

Begin {Main}
    Writeln ('This program prints a solution ',
             'to the Towers of Hanoi puzzle,');
    Writeln ('where ', Total:1, ' rings are move from Rod 1 to Rod 2.');
    Writeln;
    Writeln ('List of turns');
    Writeln ('Move Ring:  from Rod:  To Rod:');
    Move (1, 2, 3, Total)
End {Main} .
```

When this program is run for 4 rings, we get the following output:

```
This program prints a solution to the Towers of Hanoi puzzle,
where 4 rings are move from Rod 1 to Rod 2.

List of turns
Move Ring:  from Rod:  To Rod:
       1          1        3
       2          1        2
       1          3        2
       3          1        3
       1          2        1
       2          2        3
       1          1        3
       4          1        2
       1          3        2
       2          3        1
       1          2        1
       3          3        2
       1          1        3
       2          1        2
       1          3        2
```

As with our recursive tree procedures, this program illustrates several major features of recursion. First, we concentrate on a simple part of the puzzle that we want to solve, and we reduce the general problem to this simple case. Then, we solve the simple case (Step 2 in our current solution). Next, if our problem is more complex, we apply the same process to the rest of the problem after solving the simple case. Finally, our procedure involves a Boolean condition, and the procedure is called again only in some cases. When we put the various cases together, we must be sure that our work will stop eventually.

SECTION 19.6   IMPLEMENTATION OF GENERAL TREES

Whereas in the past sections we implemented binary trees, in this section we return to our study of other types of tree structures. In fact, we find three alternative approaches for defining various types of trees.

To illustrate the various ways we might implement more general trees, consider the following problem.

PROBLEM 19.6   Department Store Organizational Chart

Write the appropriate Pascal declarations necessary for creating the tree of Figure 19–11, which shows a simple organizational chart for a small department store.

FIGURE 19–11 • **Personnel Organization in a Small Department Store**

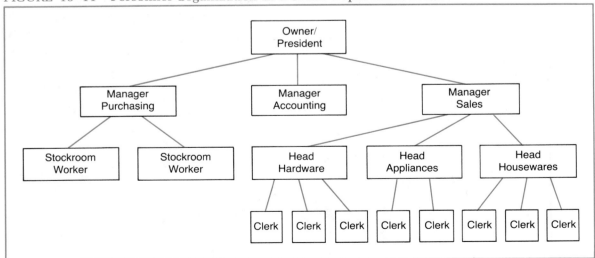

Discussion of Problem 19.6

While the tree of Figure 19–11 is not a binary tree, we can observe that no node has more than three children. Thus, this tree is a special structure called a **ternary tree.** In developing the declarations for this tree, we will find some approaches that make use of this ternary tree structure, and we will find another approach that will work more generally.

Approach 1. Since Figure 19–11 pictures a ternary tree, our first approach might involve modifying our binary tree declarations to include three possible children at each node. In particular, each node might have

1. a child node on the left
2. a child node underneath (in the middle)
3. a child node on the right

With this structure we use the following declarations:

```
Const Max = 20;
Type  Data = Packed Array [1..Max] of Char;
      Ptr = ^Node;
      Node = Record
              Name : Data;
              Left : Ptr;
              Middle : Ptr;
              Right : Ptr
              End;
Var   Root : Ptr;
```

With these declarations, the root variable can specify the root node of the tree. Then, at each node, we have pointers available to specify the left, middle and right children.

More generally, if we knew that each node in our tree would contain no more than N children, we could declare:

```
Const Max = 20;
Type  Data = Packed Array [1..Max] of Char;
      Ptr = ^Node;
      Node = Record
              Name : Data;
              Child1 : Ptr:
              Child2 : Ptr;

                   .
                   .
                   .

              ChildN : Ptr
              End;
Var   Root : Ptr;
```

In this first approach, we simply write out a pointer field for each possible child of a node. Then, in processing, we explicitly refer to the appropriate child whenever necessary. In practice, we have already seen that this approach can work very well for binary trees, when a node has no more than two children. Similarly, this approach can work well for ternary trees, where we need only three pointer fields for the three possible children of a node.

However, this approach is cumbersome if each node can have many children. With even four or five possible children, we need four or five pointer fields, and working with these different specific fields requires writing special code for each field. Thus, in more general trees, we may want another, less cumbersome approach.

Approach 2. Our second approach for declaring nodes in trees uses arrays for pointers. In particular, we use the following declarations, where we store our pointers to descendants in an array *Child*.

```
Const Max = 20;
      MaxChildren = 3;
Type  Data = Packed Array [1..Max] of Char;
      Ptr = ^Node;
      Node = Record
               Name : Data;
               Child : Array [1..MaxChildren] of Ptr;
               End;
Var   Root : Ptr;
```

In this structure, our node pointers have the form

```
Child[Index]
```

Thus, if we want to create and initialize a node using a specific name for data, we might write the following code:

```
Procedure Create (Item : Data; Var NewNode : Ptr);
      Var   Index : Integer;
      Begin
            New (NewNode);
            NewNode^.Name := Item;
            For Index := 1 to MaxChildren
                Do NewNode^.Child[Index] := Nil
End;
```

Here, we create the node, insert the appropriate name in this node, and set all pointers in the node to *nil*.

This approach has two advantages over the previous approach. First, we can refer to each child easily, using the child field and a subscript. Secondly, this form works well whenever we know the limit on the number of children that a node might have; we just need to choose the constant *MaxChildren* to reflect this limit.

Thus, this approach allows us to work with general trees whenever we know a reasonable limit for the number of children at each node. However, this approach is still inadequate if we cannot anticipate this limit. Hence, in working with general trees, we must consider one more approach as well.

Approach 3. Another alternative is suggested by Figure 19–12, which shows the same personnel structure for the small department store from Figure 19–11, but the lines connecting the positions are drawn differently. For example, in this revised figure, the purchasing manager, the accountant, and the sales manager are all shown as being under the owner/president, but we have arranged these three positions in a row. Similarly, the clerks are shown in a row under their department head.

This organization of children in a row suggests the third implementation of trees, and this implementation places no restrictions on the number of children a node may have. Rather, in our declarations, we consider all children of a node as forming a linked list of children; and we use the parent node to specify the head of this list of children.

This discussion suggests the following declarations:

```
Const Max = 20;
Type  Data = Packed Array [1..Max] of Char;
      Ptr = ^Node;
      Node = Record
            Name : Data;
            NextSibling : Ptr;
            FirstChild : Ptr
            End
```

FIGURE 19–12 • **Alternate Description of Personnel Organization in a Small Department Store**

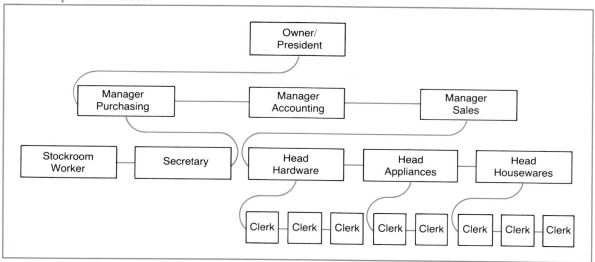

FIGURE 19–13 • **Children of a Parent Node**

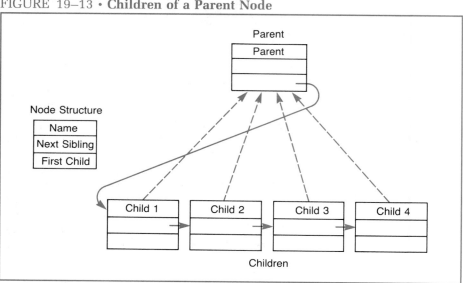

With these declarations, we use the *NextSibling* field to form a linked list of children of a given node, and the *FirstChild* pointer of the parent specifies the first of these siblings. Such a structure is shown in Figure 19–13.

This approach to trees has the disadvantage that we must use lists to record our tree information, and we may have to perform a linear search if we want to find a particular child. On the other hand, this approach has the advantage that all children are handled by the same list structure. We do not have to distinguish here between left and right children or among *Child*[1], *Child*[2], etc.

As a final note, with the linked structure, we sometimes find it appropriate to record explicitly the parent of each node. In this case, we may add a parent field to our declarations of a node. With this field added, we include the dotted lines of Figure 19–13 as well.

SECTION 19.7   SORTING WITH TREES OR RECURSION

Earlier in this chapter, we applied trees and recursion to solving puzzles. In this section, we use these same ideas in developing two excellent sorting algorithms.

Correspondence Between Binary Trees and Arrays

To begin, we need to impose a binary tree structure on an array. In order to see how this can be done, we look at a full binary tree in Figure 19–14. In this figure, we have created nodes for ten pieces of data. To condense

FIGURE 19–14 • A Binary Tree with Nodes Numbered Top to Bottom, Left to Right

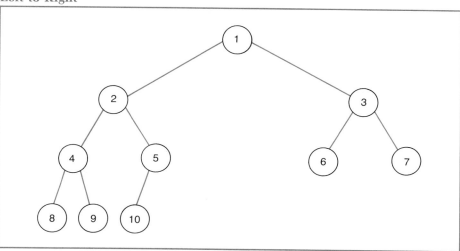

this tree as much as possible, we started at the root. Then, we worked down the tree, one row at a time; within a row, we worked left to right. At each stage, we established two children for each node until we had created all ten desired nodes.

In Figure 19–14, we also have numbered all ten nodes, again starting from the root and then moving downward row by row. As before, within a row, we have numbered the nodes from left to right. With this numbering of nodes, we can establish a natural correspondence between binary trees and elements in arrays. In particular, in the tree, we see that for any node I, its left child, if any, is numbered $2*I$; and its right child, if any, is numbered $2*I + 1$. This pattern suggests that whenever we have an array $A[1]$, . . . , $A[N]$, we can think of the array elements as being in a tree if we consider

$A[2*I]$ as the left child of $A[I]$

$A[2*I + 1]$ as the right child of $A[I]$

$A[I \; Div \; 2]$ as the parent of $A[I]$

In this way, we can work with an array as if its elements were arranged in a tree.

Heap Sort

Our first new sorting algorithm, called a **heap sort,**[1] illustrates a use of trees that does not involve recursion. With this connection between binary trees and arrays, we can describe the heap sort. To begin, we suppose the binary

---

[1]The Heap Sort was devised by J. W. J. Williams. For more details, see *Communication of the Association for Computing Machinery*, Vol. 7 (1964), pages 347–348.

tree is partially ordered, so each parent is greater than or equal to each of its children. (See Figure 19–15a).

Once our tree is partially ordered, the elements can be completely ordered fairly easily as follows.

Step 1A. (See Figure 19–15b.) The first (and largest) element on the

---

FIGURE 19–15 • **Ordering Data Given a Partially Ordered Array**

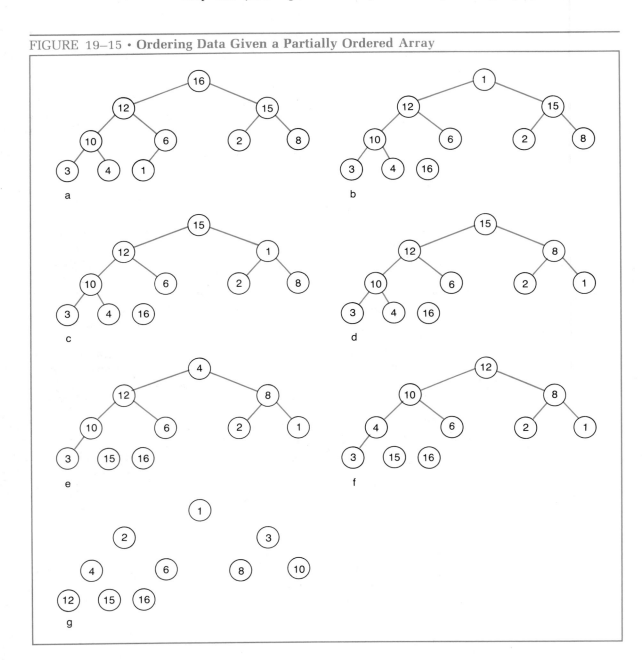

tree is interchanged with the last element, and the last element is then ignored.

Step 1B. (See Figures 19–15c and d.) We now put the resulting tree back into a partially ordered state. Since only the (1) node has been moved in the present tree, that is the only node that we must work with. When we compare (1) with its two children, we observe that if the (15) and (1) are swapped, the left half of the tree will be partially ordered (as 15 > 12 and 15 > 1).

After this swap is made (Figure 19–15c), we again look at the (1) node and its offspring. By interchanging the (1) and (8), the tree again becomes partially ordered (Figure 19–15d).

Step 2. We repeat this process again. We interchange the first and last elements in the tree and the last element is ignored (Figure 19–15e). We move the (4) node down the resulting tree to obtain another partially ordered tree. In particular, we compare the (4) node with each of its offspring and swap the (4) with the larger of its two children as necessary. In this case, the (4) node moves along the leftmost edge of the tree until it reaches the present (10) node. The result is shown in Figure 19–15f.

General Step. We continue the above process. We interchange the root with the last element in the tree, and we ignore the last element. We move the new root down the tree as necessary to obtain a new, partially ordered tree. This process continues until there are no more elements remaining on the tree. (See Figure 19–15g.) The ordered elements can now be read off, one row at a time, from top to bottom. In other words, our initial array is now ordered.

To complete our description of the heap sort, we must consider how we might obtain our first partially ordered array. For example, we must determine how we can transform Figure 19–16a into Figure 19–15a.

For this work, we proceed from the bottom of the tree toward the root.

Step 1. We consider the last node that has an offspring (Figure 19–16b). This small subtree is already partially ordered, so we do nothing.

Step 2. We consider the next small subtree at the end of the big tree (Figure 19–16c). Here, we can interchange nodes (4) and (12) to obtain a partial ordering.

Step 3. We consider the next small subtree (Figure 19–16d). Here the (2) and (15) nodes must be swapped.

Step 4. Again, moving up from the bottom of the tree, we consider the next subtree (Figure 19–16e). As before, in this structure only the root is out of order, and we can move the root into place by interchanging the (6) and (16) nodes.

Step 5. We now can consider the entire tree (Figure 19–16f). As in the previous step, only the root remains out of order in this tree, and we can move it down into an appropriate place as we have several times earlier in our discussion. In particular, we interchange nodes (10) and (16) to obtain the partially ordered tree with which we began this discussion.

FIGURE 19–16 • **Moving Data to Obtain a Partially Ordered Array**

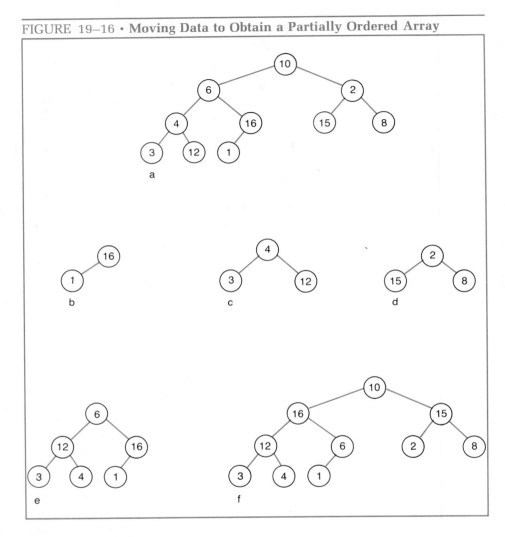

Programming the Heap Sort

When we try to program the heap sort, we first observe that the major step involves the consideration of a part of a tree, where the root of the tree may be out of order but where the rest of the tree is partially ordered. Thus, the key step in programming is to develop Procedure *SearchDown*, which moves the root data down to the appropriate place in the tree.

Further, in specifying this procedure, we need to indicate what part of the tree we wish to consider at a particular step. Since the tree in a heap sort is represented by an array, this specification corresponds to indicating which part of an array is to be used in this *SearchDown* procedure. Hence, in declaring the *SearchDown* procedure, we include two parameters, *First* and *Last*, which give the appropriate bounds on the array elements. Next, once *SearchDown* is defined, we need to use it in two ways.

1. To set up the partially ordered array at the beginning, we need a sequence of calls:

> For Index : = (ArraySize Div 2) DownTo 1
> Do SearchDown (Index, ArraySize)

2. Then, once the initial tree is partially ordered, we need to finish the ordering by another sequence of procedure calls:

> For Index : = ArraySize DownTo 3
> Do Begin
> Swap (Data[Index], Data [1]);
> SearchDown (1, Index − 1)
> End
> Swap (Data[1], Data[2])

In this code, the *Swap* procedure just interchanges the two data elements specified in the array.

With these notes, we leave the remaining programming details as an exercise, and we turn to our final sorting algorithm.

Quicksort[2]

Quicksort is a recursive approach to sorting, and we begin by outlining the principal recursive step. In this step, we make a guess at the value that should end up in the middle of the array. In particular, given the array

$$A[1], \ldots, A[N]$$

of data, arranged at random, then we might guess that the first data item $A[1]$ often should end up in about the middle of the array when the array is finally ordered. ($A[1]$ is easy to locate, and it is as good a guess at the median value as another.) This suggests the following steps.

I. Rearrange the data in the A array, so that $A[1]$ is moved to its proper position. In other words, move $A[1]$ to $A[Mid]$ and rearrange the other elements so that

$$A[1], A[2], \ldots, A[Mid − 1] < A[Mid]$$

and

$$A[Mid] < A[Mid + 1], \ldots, A[N].$$

II. Repeat this process on the smaller lists

$$A[1], \ldots, A[Mid − 1]$$

and

$$A[Mid + 1], \ldots, A[N].$$

A specific example is shown in Figure 19–17.

---

[2]The Quicksort was originally devised by C. A. R. Hoare. For more details, see the *Computing Journal*, Volume 5 (1962), pages 10–15.

FIGURE 19–17 · **Main Steps in a Sample Quicksort**

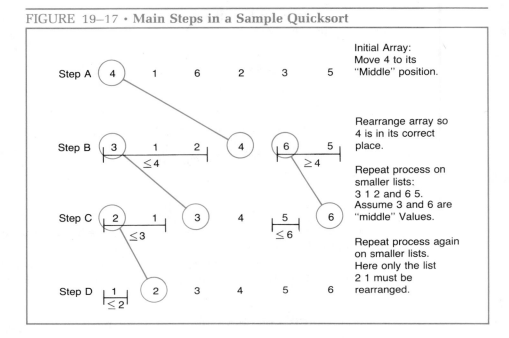

Step A ⓸ 1 6 2 3 5   Initial Array:
Move 4 to its
"Middle" position.

Step B ⓷ 1 2 ⓸ ⓺ 5   Rearrange array so
4 is in its correct
≤4 ≥4   place.

Repeat process on
smaller lists:
3 1 2 and 6 5.

Step C ⓶ 1 ⓷ 4 5 ⓺   Assume 3 and 6 are
"middle" Values.
≤3 ≤6

Repeat process again
on smaller lists.
Here only the list
2 1 must be

Step D 1 ⓶ 3 4 5 6   rearranged.
≤2

Outline to Move the First Array Element to the Appropriate Middle.
With this outline, we now need to consider how we might move the first
element to its appropriate location in the array. Here the basic approach is
to work from the ends of the array toward the middle, comparing data elements to the first element and rearranging the array as necessary. The outline details are given below.

I. Compare $A[First]$ to $A[Last]$, $A[Last - 1]$, etc. until an element $A[U]$ is
found where $A[U] < A[First]$. Then $A[U]$ and $A[First]$ are swapped. At
this point:
 A. the first element has moved to $A[U]$
 B. $A[U] < A[U + 1], \ldots, A[Last]$
 C. $A[First] < A[U]$.
II. Compare $A[U]$ with $A[First + 1]$, $A[First + 2]$, etc. to find an element
$A[L]$ where $A[L] > A[U]$. Then $A[L]$ and $A[U]$ are swapped. At this
point:
 A. the original first element has moved to $A[L]$
 B. $A[L] < A[U], A[U + 1], \ldots, A[Last]$
 C. $A[First], \ldots, A[L - 1] < A[L]$.
III. We continue Steps II and III, comparing the original first element
against the ends of the array until the "first" element is placed into
$A[Mid]$ where
 A. $A[Mid] < A[Mid + 1], \ldots, A[Last]$
 B. $A[First], \ldots, A[Mid - 1] < A[Mid]$.

This process is illustrated in Figure 19–18, where $A[1]$ is put in its appropriate place. The circled numbers in the figure follow the movement of this element. The elements in color show which parts of the array have already been checked.

Programming the Search Up and Down Steps

In programming this process, it is convenient to use several variables to record what we have done at each point.

We use *First* and *Last* to indicate that we want to work with the list

$$A[First], \ldots , A[Last].$$

We use *Mid* to indicate where our "first" element is located on its way to the middle. (Initially, $Mid = First$. Then Mid changes as this element is moved.)

Finally, we use *LowerCheck* and *UpperCheck* to note how far we have checked the list. The use of these variables is illustrated in Figure 19–19, which follows the work in Figure 19–18.

With these comments, we now can write the code for a quicksort. In this code, the parameter *Data* is an array to be sorted. In addition, we assume we have declared *Bigger* as a Boolean function that indicates if the

---

FIGURE 19–18 • **Putting the First Array Element in Its Place**

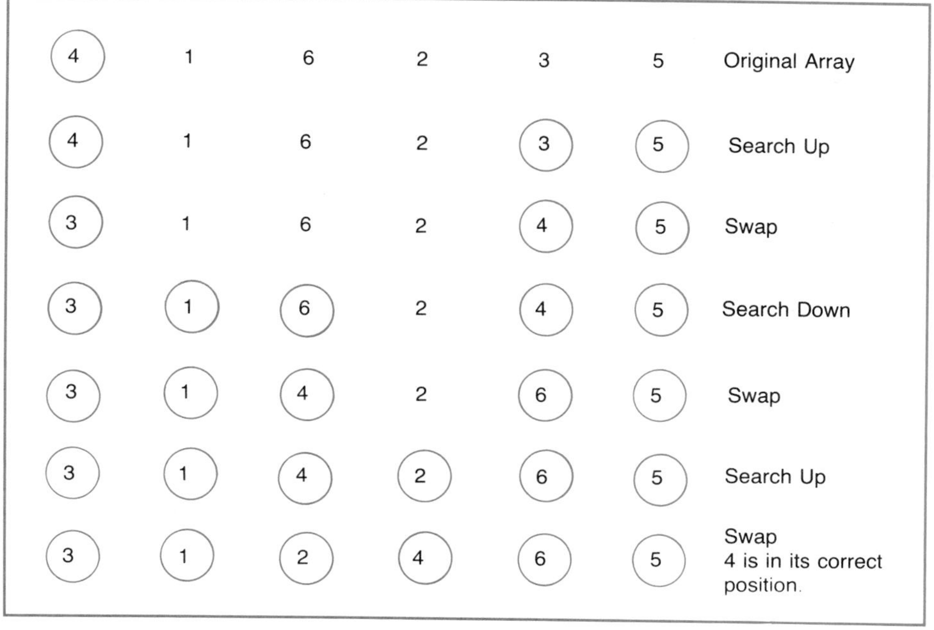

FIGURE 19–19 • **Use of Variables in the Quicksort Searching Process**

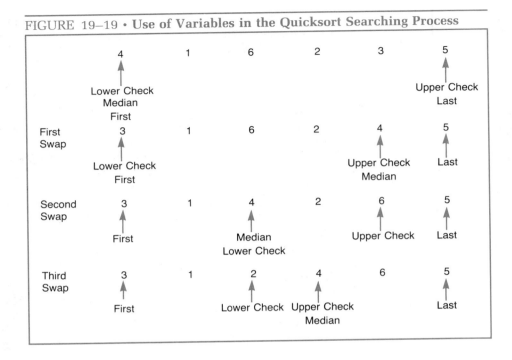

first data element is bigger than the second. Also, we assume *Swap* is a procedure that interchanges the elements specified. Finally, to start this quicksort procedure, we use the call

Quicksort (Data, 1, **N**)

which indicates that we are to sort elements 1 through N of the *Data* array.

```
{This procedure assumes the following declarations}

Const ArraySize = ... ;   {Number of items to be sorted}


Type  ArrayData = Array [1..ArraySize] of Integer;

Procedure QuickSort (Var Data: ArrayData;
                  LowerArrayBound, UpperArrayBound: Integer);
   {Procedure performs a QuickSort on the array Data}
   Var
      Median, LowerCheck, UpperCheck: Integer;
      ExitLoop, Quit: Boolean;
```

```
Procedure CheckUp;
    Begin
        Quit := False;
        While (Median < UpperCheck) And Not Quit
            Do Begin
                If Bigger(Data[Median], Data[UpperCheck])
                    Then Begin {Swap Variables}
                        Swap(Data[Median], Data[UpperCheck]);
                        LowerCheck := Median + 1;
                        Median := UpperCheck;
                        Quit := True
                        End;
                UpperCheck := UpperCheck - 1;
                End;
    End {CheckUp};

Procedure CheckDown;
    Begin
        Quit := False;
        While (LowerCheck < Median) And Not Quit
            Do Begin
                If Bigger(Data[LowerCheck], Data[Median])
                    Then Begin {Swap Variables}
                        Swap(Data[Median], Data[LowerCheck]);
                        UpperCheck := Median - 1;
                        Median := LowerCheck;
                        Quit := True
                        End;
            LowerCheck := LowerCheck + 1;
            End
    End {CheckDown};

Begin {Main Part of QuickSort}

    {Set Up Procedure Variables}
    LowerCheck := LowerArrayBound;
    UpperCheck := UpperArrayBound;
    Median := LowerArrayBound;

    {Put "Median" value in its proper place}
    ExitLoop := False;
    Repeat
        CheckUp;
        If (LowerCheck < Median)
            Then CheckDown
            Else ExitLoop := True
    Until (Median >= UpperCheck) or ExitLoop ;

    {Repeat Process on Smaller Lists}
    If LowerArrayBound < Median - 1
        Then QuickSort (Data, LowerArrayBound, Median - 1);
    If Median + 1 < UpperArrayBound
        Then QuickSort (Data, Median + 1, UpperArrayBound)
End {QuickSort} ;
```

Evaluation of Efficiency

With these descriptions of the heap sort and the quicksort, we now need to consider how efficient each of these algorithms is. In previous chapters, we have seen a wide variety of other sorting algorithms, and it is interesting to see how these new ones compare to the others.

One approach to evaluating efficiency involves the same general process we have followed in evaluating other sorting algorithms in previous chapters. This analysis always involves two basic parts:

1. Determine how many basic steps are needed to perform the algorithm.
2. Determine the number of comparisons and interchanges required within each step.

When we apply this approach to either of the new algorithms in this chapter, we find that the number of comparisons and interchanges is proportional to $nlog_2n$. Thus, both of these algorithms have *order* $(nlog_2n)$.

A second method for evaluating the efficiency of these algorithms is to run each algorithm on some data and count the number of comparisons and interchanges required. Here, rather than perform the sophisticated mathematical analysis required for each algorithm, we can use simulation techniques to see how the algorithms compare with different types of data. Then, we can compare our results. For example, Table 19–1 shows what happens when most of the sorting algorithms mentioned in this text are applied to three data sets containing 100 elements. In particular, we consider the work done when the data are already ordered in ascending or descending order and when the data are quite random. The results illustrate several points.

1. The work required for n^2 algorithms, such as the bubble sort and the straight selection sort, is always very high.
2. The work required for $nlog_2n$ algorithms, such as the merge and heap sorts, is much less.

TABLE 19–1 · This Table Compares Sorting Routines by Running Various Algorithms on Data Sets of 100 Elements.

Sorting Algorithm	Ascending Data		Descending Data		Random Data	
	Compare	Assign	Compare	Assign	Compare	Assign
Bubble	4950	0	4950	14850	4950	8298
Improved Bubble	99	0	4950	14850	4848	8298
Straight Selection	4950	297	4950	297	4950	297
Insertion	99	198	4950	5148	2860	2964
Merge	372	1400	316	1400	550	1400
Quicksort	4950	0	4950	150	712	657
Heap Sort	1081	1920	944	1548	1026	1740

3. Some algorithms can be very efficient at processing some types of data but very poor on other data sets. For example, the improved bubble sort is outstanding if the data are already in ascending order, but it is very poor otherwise. In contrast, the quicksort, which we developed for random data, is outstanding for that random data, but it degenerates to a bubble or straight selection sort on data that are already ordered.

4. Some algorithms are very stable for all types of data. For example, the heap sort is rarely the most efficient algorithm for any one type of data, but its performance is always quite good. The heap sort always can be counted on to work fairly well, even though other algorithms may work better in certain cases.

These observations demonstrate that in solving a problem our choice of algorithm often must take into account the type of data we expect to encounter. Some algorithms may work particularly well in certain cases, but quite badly in other circumstances. Other algorithms may be quite consistent in their performance under many circumstances.

These heap sort and quicksort algorithms also demonstrate that the concepts of trees and recursion can be applied effectively in many different situations. Initially, we considered trees as a data structure that helped us organize data in a certain way, and we introduced recursion as a useful technique in working with these trees. These new sorting techniques show that both subjects can be useful in other contexts as well.

SUMMARY

1. The **tree data structure** allows us to organize data in a hierarchical structure, and this structure is helpful in many applications such as
   a. Representing arithmetic expressions graphically.
   b. Illustrating the moves that can be made in a given situation in a game, and allowing us to analyze various possible moves in a game.
   c. Organizing data for fast retrieval.
2. Conceptually, we can consider three basic types of trees.
   a. In **binary trees,** each node has at most two children, a right child and a left child.
   b. In **ternary trees,** each node has at most three children.
   c. In **general trees,** nodes can have arbitrarily large numbers of children.
3. Beyond the conceptual structure of trees, we can implement trees:
   a. by explicitly declaring a pointer field for each possible child. (For example, binary tree nodes might have left and right pointer fields.)
   b. by declaring an array of pointers to specify the children of each node.
   c. by organizing the children of each node into a linked list.
   d. by placing the elements of a binary tree into an array structure.

4. **Recursion** is a technique in which a function or procedure may call itself. In developing recursive algorithms, we typically
   a. identify and solve simple cases;
   b. reduce harder cases to these simple ones by appropriate function or procedure calls.
5. Recursive algorithms are particularly helpful in working with trees, where we can focus our attention on individual nodes and then ask the computer to repeat the processing for all descendant nodes. Recursion also is useful in solving some puzzles such as the Towers of Hanoi.
6. Both trees and recursion are helpful in developing some new, efficient sorting algorithms.

EXERCISES

19.1 a. In the Tree Insertion procedure of Section 19.4, suppose procedure *Insert* is called with the tree shown in Figure 19–7 and with the name Ellen. Describe the sequence of events that results, including all procedure calls and the results of these calls.
      b. In the same Tree Insertion procedure, why is the parameter *Base* passed by reference and not by value?
19.2 *Ordered Binary Tree.* Write a program that performs each of the following tasks.
      1. Names can be entered from the keyboard and stored in an ordered binary tree.
      2. A specific name, entered by the user, can be searched for on the tree.
      3. Names can be printed in alphabetical order.
      Include each of these tasks as part of a main menu that drives your program.

```
+-------------------------------------------------+
|     KEY TERMS, PHRASES, AND CONCEPTS            |
+-------------------------------------------------+
|                                                 |
|     Ancestor       Sorting Algorithms           |
|     Branch            Heap Sort                  |
|     Child             Quicksort                  |
|     Leaf           Subtree                       |
|     Node           Trees                         |
|     Parent            Binary                     |
|     Recursion         General                    |
|     Root              Ternary                    |
|     Sibling                                      |
|                                                 |
+-------------------------------------------------+
```

19.3 *Binary Tree Search Analysis.* Suppose data are stored in an ordered binary tree as discussed in Section 19.2. Estimate the average number of comparisons needed to find a given item.

a. Assume the tree is as balanced as possible so that all branches are about the same length.

b. Assume the tree is as unbalanced as possible.

What other structure does part (b) remind you of?

19.4 Consider the following:

```
Program One (Input, Output);
Const Length = 10;

Type NodePtr = ^Node;
     Node = Record
            Text: Packed Array[1..Length] of Char;
            Size: Integer;
            Left, Right: NodePtr
            End;

Var Root: NodePtr;

Procedure Enter;
    Var NewNode: NodePtr;
        Entry: Integer;

    Procedure ReadText (Var Ptr: NodePtr);
        Var Index: Integer;
        Begin
            New(Ptr);
            Index := 0;
            While (Index < Length) and (Not EOLN)
              Do Begin
                Index := Index + 1;
                Read(Ptr^.Text[Index])
              End;
            Readln;
            Ptr^.Size := Index;
            While (Index < Length)
              Do Begin
                Index := Index + 1;
                Ptr^.Text[Index] := Chr(0)
              End;
            Ptr^.Left := Nil;
            Ptr^.Right := Nil
        End {ReadText} ;

    Function First(Node1, Node2: NodePtr): Boolean;
        Begin
            If Node1^.Size <> Node2^.Size
                Then First := (Node1^.Size < Node2^.Size)
                Else First := (Node1^.Text < Node2^.Text)
        End {First} ;
```

```
   Procedure EnterNode(Var Base: NodePtr);
      Begin
         If Base = Nil
            Then Base := NewNode
            Else If First (NewNode, Base)
                     Then EnterNode (Base^.Right)
                     Else EnterNode (Base^.Left)
         End {EnterNode} ;

   Begin {Enter}
      Root := Nil;
      Writeln ('Enter Data');
      For Entry := 1 To 10
         Do Begin
            ReadText(NewNode);
            EnterNode(Root)
         End
   End {Enter} ;

Procedure Print (Base: NodePtr);
   Begin
      If Base^.Left = Nil
         Then Writeln (Base^.Text)
         Else Print (Base^.Left);
      If Base^.Right <> Nil
         Then Print (Base^.Right)
   End {Print} ;

Begin {Main}
   Enter;
   Print (Root)
End {Main} .
```

Suppose this program is run with the following data: ONE, TWO, THREE, FOUR, FIVE, SIX, SEVEN, EIGHT, NINE, and TEN.

a. After the entire procedure is completed, describe the data structure pointed to by the variable *Root*. (For instance, draw a picture of the appropriate nodes created with their data, left pointers, and right pointers.)

b. What is printed by this program?

19.5 *Tree Searching.* A tree is defined with the following declarations:

```
Const Length = 3;
Type String = Packed Array [1..Length] of Char;
     NodePtr = ^Node;
     Node = Record
              ChData: String;
              Number: Integer;
              Left: NodePtr;
              Right: NodePtr
            End;
Var Root: NodePtr;
```

Here, *Root* specifies the root node of the tree, and the *Left* and *Right* fields specify the children of each node. (A pointer of *Nil* specifies no offspring.) Write

Function Value (Item: String; Base: NodePtr): Integer;

which considers a tree, starting at the node specified by *Base*. The function searches this tree for a node where *ChData* matches the given *Item*. When a match is found, the function returns the *Number* at the node. If no match is found, then 0 is returned. For example, consider the tree

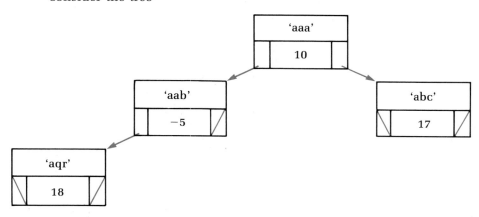

Here, Value ('abc', Root) returns 17, while Value ('cba', Root) returns 0.

HINT: Use recursion.

19.6   *Printing Leaves.* Using the tree declaration of the previous problem, write

Procedure PrintLeaf (Base: NodePtr)

which prints out all data at all leaves of the tree with the given *Base*.

19.7   *Erase a Tree.* Using the declarations for Exercise 19.5, write

Procedure Erase (Base: NodePtr)

which erases (disposes of) all nodes in the tree with the given *Base*.

HINT: For any node, erase all descendants and then erase the node itself.

19.8   A list is defined with the following declarations

```
Const Length = 3;
Type  String = Packed Array [1..Length] of Char;
      Ptr = ^Item;
      Item = Record
               Data: String;
               Next: Ptr
             End;
Var FirstItem: Ptr;
```

Write

Procedure PrintReverse (First: Ptr)

which prints out the data in the list of items, from the last item in the list to the *First*.

HINT: Use recursion.

19.9 *Heap Sort Procedure.* Write a procedure which sorts an array using the heap sort algorithm.

19.10 *Heap Sort Analysis.* Analyze the heap sort algorithm to determine its efficiency. In particular,

a. Estimate the number of comparisons and interchanges needed for the basic step that moves the root of a tree into its appropriate position. (Here, you should assume that the rest of the tree is ordered.)

b. Determine the number of times the basic step of part (a) must be executed.

c. From part (a) and part (b), estimate the overall efficiency of the heap sort algorithm.

19.11 *Quicksort Analysis.* Follow the analysis outline of the previous exercise to estimate the work required for the quicksort algorithm, assuming the data begins in random order.

19.12 a. *Quicksort Degeneration.* Write out in detail the steps that the quicksort follows when sorting the array: 1 2 3 4 5.

b. Discuss why the quicksort requires as much work as the bubble sort on ordered data, as illustrated in Table 19–1 of Section 19.7.

19.13 *Computing Powers.* In computing x^n, where x is any real number and n is a non-negative integer, we can proceed by noting

$x^0 = 1,$
$x^1 = x,$ and
$x^n = x(x^{n-1})$, for $n > 1.$

a. Use this observation to write

Function Power (x: Real; n: Integer): Real;

which computes x^n using recursion.

b. What happens in your function if N is negative? How might you correct this problem for negative values of N?

19.14 *The Fibonacci Sequence.* In the thirteenth century, Leonardo of Pisa, nicknamed Fibonacci, used a simple model to study the breeding of rabbits. In this model, the number of rabbits in one generation is thought to be equal to the number of rabbits in the previous two generations combined. Thus, if *Fib* (n) is the number of rabbits in the nth generation, then Fibonacci's model says that

$$Fib(n) = Fib(n-1) + Fib(n-2).$$

In practice, this same formula turns out to apply in many other situations as well.

Today, we usually start with

$$Fib(1) = Fib(2) = 1,$$

(although we might argue that only 1 rabbit in an entire generation would be unlikely to produce offspring). With this start, the first few generations are

1, 1, 2, 3, 5, 8, 13, . . .

a. Write

Function Fib(N: Integer): Integer

which uses the formula (recursively) to compute the Nth number in the Fibonacci sequence.

b. Use your function in part (a) to compute and print all terms of the Fibonacci sequence that do not exceed 1000.

c. Let R be the ratio of successive terms in the series, so

$$R = Fib(N)/Fib(N - 1).$$

Modify part (b) so that the ratio R and the expression $(2R - 1)^2$ are also printed for each term.

NOTE: It can be shown that R approaches

$$1 + \sqrt{5}/2.$$

Thus $(2R - 1)^2$ should approach 5.

19.15 *Combinations.* In dealing cards, we may ask how many different possible hands we could get. In poker, this is a question of how many ways we can get 5 cards from a 52 card deck. More generally, we can ask how many ways we can select m things from a collection of n objects. In mathematics, this is called the number of combinations of n things, taken m at a time, and we sometimes say "n choose m," and write

$$\binom{n}{m}.$$

One can show that

$$\binom{n}{m} = \frac{n!}{m! \, (n - m)!}$$

where n! (or n factorial) is the product

$$n*(n - 1)*(n - 2)* . . . *3* \, 2*1$$

In practice, n! can be very large, and this number may be larger than a computer can store. Thus, the computation of these computations is often done following the formulas

$$\binom{n}{0} = \binom{n}{n} = 1$$

$$\binom{n}{m} = \frac{n}{m}\binom{n-1}{m-1} \qquad \text{for } n > 1, n > m > 1$$

Write

Function Comb (M, N: Integer): Integer

that uses these formulas (with recursion) to compute

$$\binom{n}{m}$$

Apply your function to compute the number of possible poker hands and the number of possible bridge hands.

19.16 One can show that the number of combinations (mentioned in the previous problem) also satisfies the formulas

$$\binom{n}{0} = \binom{n}{n} = 1$$

$$\binom{n}{m} = \binom{n-1}{m} + \binom{n-1}{m-1} \qquad \text{for } n > 1, n > m > 1$$

Revise your function in part (a) to reflect these new formulas.

19.17 *Tic-Tac-Toe Playing Program.* (A particularly challenging exercise.) Write a program that plays Tic-Tac-Toe. In your program, you may decide to look ahead only a prescribed number of moves in determining the "best" next move.

CHAPTER 20

BUFFERS

AND

FILES

In Chapter 15, we learned some ways to store information on a disk. We saw how to open a file for input or for output, and we saw how to enter and print lines or sequences of records with only minor modifications in our *Read* and *Write* statements. Throughout this processing we started at the beginning of a file and then proceeded line by line or record by record to the end.

In this chapter, we extend this discussion of files by studying some of the details that underlie the actual use of files. We also consider a basic extension of files that moves beyond Standard Pascal syntax so that we are not limited to the sequential access of data in files from Chapter 15. Each of these extensions will allow us to develop efficient solutions to a wide range of problems. This discussion also leads us to a study of how files are normally structured and cataloged on a disk itself.

SECTION 20.1   BUFFERS—AN OVERVIEW

To use files effectively for storing and retrieving data, we first need to have some understanding of how this data transfer takes place. As we will see, there are differences between how data are accessed within main memory and how data are accessed from a disk file. These differences affect not only how our data are stored but also how we organize and process our data.

To appreciate the difference, we first consider data in main memory. Here, technical details of circuitry may vary from one machine to another, but in any machine all storage and retrieval is performed electronically, not mechanically. All parts of main memory are linked by some type of electrical path, and data can be moved using this circuitry alone. Here, the key point is that all processing can be done quite quickly. The computer never needs to wait for a mechanical operation to occur.

In contrast, disk storage does involve some mechanical processes. To begin, a simple disk looks like a flat, round platter, much like a phonograph record without grooves. This platter is coated with a magnetic substance, and data are stored on the platter by placing appropriate magnetic charges at various locations on the disk.

Next, the computer accesses this information in much the same way that we might play a phonograph record. The disk turns at a high rate of speed, and a read/write head (like a tone arm) moves back and forth to the appropriate spot on the disk. Thus, to obtain one piece of information from a disk, the computer must do three things:

1. move the read/write head to the appropriate position;
2. rotate the disk to the correct location;
3. read or write the desired data at the correction location.

See Figure 20–1.

This process clearly requires considerable mechanical activity, and mechanical work is much slower than electrical work. Thus, the disk access of a particular piece of data is much slower than the access of similar data stored in main memory.

FIGURE 20–1 · Organization of a Disk

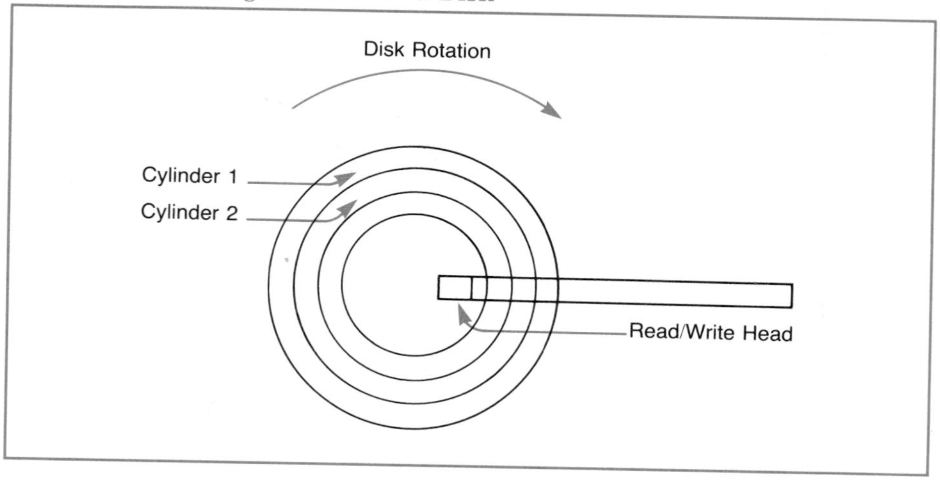

With this inherent delay in working with data on disk, computers are designed to incorporate several features to speed up data transmission. The initial accessing of data never can be done quickly, but with care, subsequent data can be obtained somewhat more efficiently in several ways. First, instead of scattering individual pieces of data around the disk, some pieces are put close together. Then, once we move the read/write head to a particular location, we can let the disk continue to rotate, processing data as they go by. Thus, data on disks are organized onto **tracks** or **cylinders** just as phonograph records contain bands for separate pieces. With this structure, we still must move the read/write head, and we must wait for the disk to turn to the start of a track before we can begin processing data. However, once we start, we can process a whole track of data relatively quickly.

We can also increase efficiency by working with several items on a disk file at about the same time. For example, we may want to read or write several characters of text, or we may want to work with a whole record of data. Combining this observation with our previous point, we find that processing disk data is often most effective if we can read or write several pieces of data at a time. We may not need all pieces of data in a record immediately, but we can save time if we read an entire record at once. Similarly, we may want to accumulate all fields of a record before transmitting it to disk.

Buffers for Disk Files

With these considerations, we find that working with disk files involves several steps. First, the computer allocates some space, called a **buffer,** in main memory, so we can read or write several pieces of data at a time. In fact, a separate buffer is set up for each file that we use in a program. Then, transmission of data *into* a program proceeds in two steps.

1. Several pieces of data are moved from the disk to the appropriate input buffer.
2. Data are moved, as requested, from the buffer to the program itself.

Similarly, transmission of data *from* a program to disk involves two steps.

3. Data are moved piece by piece from the program to an output buffer.
4. The data are moved from the output buffer to the appropriate disk file.

This division of reading and writing into steps is shown in Figure 20–2, where Steps 1 and 2 are followed for reading data and where Steps 3 and 4 are used in writing.

Buffers for Transmission to a Terminal

In practice, we also find that buffers are used with terminals and printers for much the same reason. In particular, typing at a terminal or printing on a printer is a slow, mechanical process. For example, while a printer is typing out data, the computer's CPU is fast enough to be doing other work.

FIGURE 20–2 • Transmission of Data

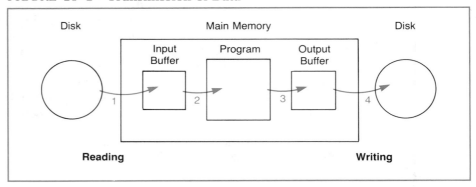

Thus, a buffer is reserved in main memory for a user's output, so the CPU does not have to wait for mechanical processes to be completed.

Similarly, when a buffer is used for input, a user can anticipate the data that will be needed next by a program, and this data can be entered ahead of time. The data are simply saved in an input buffer until the program actually needs them. Alternatively, if data are not already typed by a user, then the CPU may work on other jobs until the data for a particular job are entered.

Buffers and Read or Write Statements

With this discussion of buffers, we need to make two final comments before we see how these buffers can be used effectively in our code.

While we have not explicitly used buffers in our coding up to this point, we should understand that these buffers have been present behind the scenes. Our input and output have always involved special buffer areas inside main memory. Similarly, our *Reset* or *Rewrite* statements of Chapter 15 cause the computer to allocate buffer space. The *Read* and *Write* statements offer a convenient way to do both steps of input and output. For example, the *Read* first moves data to a buffer and then into the program. With these *Read* or *Write* statements, we have not had to worry about the details of buffers, but internally, the computer still performed both steps.

SECTION 20.2   STANDARD FUNCTIONS

Now that the concept of a buffer and its role in transmitting data have been introduced, we consider how we can control this transmission of data within a Pascal program.

As we saw in Chapter 15, we can use an identifier to refer to a specific file, and we declare this identifier in two steps.

1. We placed the identifier in parentheses, after the word *Program* in our program header.
2. We declared the identifier as a variable of the appropriate file type.

We then refer to our file by using the identifier. For example, we write

Reset(Infile)

when we want to prepare to read a file designated by the *Infile* variable. Then, we can read from this file using

Read(Infile, . . .)

and we can determine when we reach the end of the file by using the Boolean function

EOF(Infile)

Now that we have expanded our understanding of file processing to include buffers, we find we must distinguish between two types of references: the reference to the file and its buffer, and the contents of the buffer. In Pascal, we will continue to use an identifier (e.g., *Infile*) to refer to the file and its associated buffer. Then, we add an up-arrow ↑ or caret ˆ (e.g., *Infile*ˆ) to refer to the contents of the buffer.

With these general conventions, we now outline the appropriate steps for using a file. Our work involves two new procedures: *Get* for moving data from the file to the buffer and *Put* for moving data back.

Input from a File

I. Prepare to use the file. (These steps are accomplished by *Reset (Infile)*, which is the same statement we used in Chapter 15.)
   A. Set up buffer.
   B. Move first record from file to buffer.
II. Use the data within the buffer. (By adding the up-arrow or caret to the buffer/file identifier, we can refer to a buffer record the same way we refer to any record.)
III. Use a *Get* statement to move the next record in the file to the buffer. Thus, *Get (Infile)* updates the data in the buffer so that it refers to the next record on the file. (Note that a *Get* statement throws away any previous data in our buffer, although any data in our file is still present.)

Output to a File

I. Prepare to use the file. (As in Chapter 15, these steps are accomplished by *Rewrite (Outfile)*.)
   A. Throw out any data that had been in the file, so the file starts fresh.
   B. Set up buffer.
II. Move data from the program to the buffer. (Again we refer to the con-

tents of the output buffer by adding an up-arrow or caret to the buffer/file variable.)

III. Use a *Put* statement to add the contents in the buffer to the output file. Thus, *Put (Outfile)* causes the data in the buffer to be appended to any previous output.

To illustrate how these various steps are implemented in a Pascal program, we write the code for the following simple task.

PROBLEM 20.2A | **Sequential Access, Reading and Writing Files**

A file is to be created with the two records shown in Figure 20–3. Then, this file is to be read, and the data displayed at the terminal.

To solve this problem, we need two programs, one to create the initial file and the second to read it. In each program below, we demonstrate various ways to perform this work, following our outlines for input and output.

First, we write an appropriate output program.

```
Program FileWrite (Outfile, Output);
{This program writes two records to a file.}

{Specify File Characteristics}
Type
     FileItem = Record
          Number: Integer;
          Letter: Char
          End;
Var
     Item: FileItem;
     Outfile: File of FileItem;

Begin {Main}

     Writeln ('Starting to create file');

     {Open File}
          Rewrite (Outfile);

     {Write First Record}
     {Move Data to Output File Buffer}
          Outfile^.Number := 1;
          Outfile^.Letter := 'A';

     {Move Data from Buffer to Disk File}
          Put(Outfile);

     {Write Second Record}
     {Move Data to Output File Buffer}
          Item.Number := 2;
          Item.Letter := 'B';
          Outfile^ := Item;
```

```
{Move Data from Buffer to Disk File}
      Put(Outfile);

  Writeln ('File Created')

End {Main} .
```

In this program, we declare *Outfile* as our file identifier, and we begin by resetting this file. At this point, we have a buffer available for data, but we still need to place data into that buffer.

In this example, the buffer is a record containing both a number and a letter, and our program illustrates two ways to place data into this buffer. In the first approach, we move data into the buffer one field at a time, using the following syntax.

Outfile   is the buffer/file variable

Outfile^   refers to the buffer record, containing a number and letter

Outfile^.Number   refers to the number field within the buffer record

Thus,

Outfile^.Number := 1

places the integer 1 into the *Number* field within the buffer. Similarly,

Outfile^.Letter := 'A'

places a character in the buffer's *Letter* field. With these two statements, we now have placed data in each field of the buffer.

Our second method involves placing data in a record within our program, and then moving an entire record of data into the buffer at once. In our program, we first placed the number 2 and the letter 'B' into a record called *Item* with the statements

Item.Number := 2;
Item.Letter := 'B';

FIGURE 20–3 • **A Very Simple File**

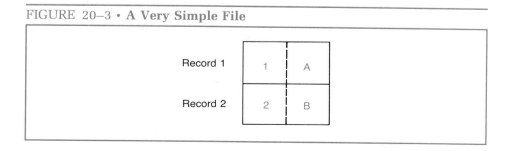

Then we copied this entire record into the buffer with the statement

Outfile^ : = Item;

Here, *Outfile^* refers to the contents of the buffer, and we want to copy all data in the *Item* record into the buffer.

In either case, the program has placed appropriate data in the output buffer. Then, we write

Put (Outfile)

to move the data from the buffer to the file. If we omitted the first *Put* statement, then the data '1', 'A' would never get to the file. Instead that data would be lost, when the buffer data was superceded by '2', 'B'.

With this explanation of a file creation program, we now write a program to read this newly created file, following our outline for output.

```
Program FileRead (Output, Infile);
{This program reads two records from a file and prints them
 at the terminal.}

{Specify File Characteristics}
Type
     FileItem = Record
           Number: Integer;
           Letter: Char
           End;
Var
     Item: FileItem;
     Infile: File of FileItem;

Begin
     {Open File and Move First Record from Disk File to Buffer}
          Reset (Infile);

     {Move Data from Buffer}
          Item := Infile^;

     {Write Out Record}
          Writeln (Item.Number, Item.Letter);

     {Process Second Record}
     {Move Data From Disk File to Buffer}
          Get(Infile);

     {Move Data From Buffer to Terminal}
          Write(Infile^.Number);
          Writeln(Infile^.Letter)

End {Main} .
```

In tracing this program, we see that it involves the following elements.

1. The *Reset* statement sets up the buffer and then moves the first record of data (i.e., '1', 'A') into the buffer.
2. The entire contents of the buffer are moved to a record variable with a simple assignment *Item := Infile^*. Again, we use the up-arrow or caret to specify the contents of the buffer.
3. The next record in the file is read using *Get(Infile)*, which moves the next record of data into the buffer.
4. Individual fields within the buffer can be referenced separately instead of treating the buffer as a whole. For example, in our write statements, *Infile^.Number* refers to the *Number* field of the buffer record; while *Infile^.Letter* refers to the corresponding letter field.

These programs illustrate the mechanics of using buffers for input and output. The next example shows how to use buffers to streamline file processing tasks.

PROBLEM 20.2B	Copying Text Files

Write a program to copy text files. (Recall that in Chapter 15 text files include character data organized into lines.)

Discussion of Problem 20.2B

Following our work in Chapter 15, one approach to solving this problem would be to read the first file, character by character, until we reach the end of the file. In this process, we would write each character on the new file as soon as it was read. However, while this code is easy to write, the actual work would involve four steps.

1. Move character from initial file to input buffer.
2. Move character from input buffer to program.
3. Move character from program to output buffer.
4. Move character from output buffer to new file.

This flow of data was shown earlier, in Figure 20–2.

To make this code more efficient, we combine Steps 2 and 3 into a single step, which moves each character from the input buffer to the output buffer. Here, we do not bring the data into the program at all, since we never want to examine the data; we only want to copy it, as we see in the following program.

```
Program Copy (Output, Infile, Outfile);
{This program copies a file of text to another file.}

Var
     Infile, Outfile: Text;
```

```
Begin {Main}

    Writeln ('Starting to Copy File');

    {Open Files}
        Reset (Infile);
        Rewrite(Outfile);

    {Copy Files}

        While Not EOF(InFile)
          Do Begin

              {Transfer Data From Input Buffer to Output Buffer}
                  Outfile^ := Infile^;

              {Move Data From Output Buffer to Disk File}
                  Put(Outfile);

              {Move Data From Disk File to Input Buffer}
                  Get(Infile)

          End;

        {Transfer last character}
            Outfile^ := Infile^;
            Put(Outfile);

    Writeln ('File Copied')

End {Main} .
```

Here, the main loop has been streamlined to save the step we discussed. The loop simply

1. moves a character into the input buffer: *Get (Infile)*
2. copies the character to the output buffer: *Outfile^ := Infile^*
3. moves the character to the new file: *Put (Outfile)*

Thus, by using buffers, this program is more efficient than it would be using only *Read* and *Write* statements.

Finally, to explain the order of statements in our loop, we emphasize that the *Reset* statement already brings the first piece of data into the input buffer. Thus, at the start, we already have data that need processing, so we transfer data from input to output first in our loop. If we performed the *Get* operation at the start of the loop, this first data item would be thrown away before it was copied, and our new file would have lost some data.

This example shows that careful control of data in buffers can help us write code that uses files quite efficiently. This ability for handling file data is particularly important in some more complex applications.

SECTION 20.3 · FILE MANAGEMENT

In the last section, we saw how we might be able to use buffers effectively when processing data in individual files. In this section, we use some of the data structures we learned in previous chapters to help us manage multiple files.

File Directories

Before we can use information stored on a disk, the computer must be able to locate that information. One way such data could be found would be to have the computer search through the entire disk. However, with the amount of information that might be present, such an approach is clearly impractical and inefficient.

Instead, the computer normally maintains some type of index, called a **directory,** which contains information about each disk file. For example, a simple directory containing four files is shown in Table 20–1. In this directory, we find the text of a memo, and we find several parts of an inventory system: the Pascal program, the compiled program or object code, and the file of data. In more sophisticated systems, a directory might also contain such information as

- date and time file was first created;
- date and time file was last used; and
- information about who can use the file.

With such a table, the computer can always find an appropriate piece of data in a file by looking up a file name to see where the file is physically located. The actual process of looking it up, however, may vary considerably from one machine to another, and therefore, directories may be structured in several ways. For example, directories may be set up as arrays of records, where each record contains information for one file. Here, file look-up may involve a linear search if the file names are unordered or a binary search if the file entries are ordered. Alternatively, directories may be structured as linked lists, where each entry contains the data for one file. Here, a linear search must be used to look up the entry in a table. In

TABLE 20–1 · A Very Simple Disk Directory

File Name	Starting Point of File	Length of File
Memo.Text	Track 2	2 Tracks
Inventory.Pascal	Track 5	4 Tracks
Inventory.Object	Track 11	9 Tracks
Inventory.Data	Track 20	308 Tracks

fact, any structure may be used to maintain this file information, as long as the information about each file can be found and updated efficiently. Also, we note that the actual location information (e.g., track number) may be considered a type of pointer; the starting track number for a file directs the computer to a file just as a Pascal pointer can direct the computer to a record in main memory.

Directory Tree Structures

In small computer systems, each disk may contain a single directory for its files, and searching the entire directory is quite manageable. However, on larger systems that serve many users and contain large numbers of files, this single directory is not very efficient. Searching a single large directory for a file can involve considerable time, particularly if a linear search is used.

Therefore, on large computer systems and on many smaller ones as well, several directories are organized into a tree. (Such an organization is shown in Figure 20–4.) With tree structures, each node can specify a few files and a few further directories. Then, by moving through this structure, we can find the location of each desired file without forcing the computer to handle large lists of files all at once. This separation of file information into distinct pieces also allows different users to use the same file names for their various tasks. For example, the entry under *Memo* in the *H.Walker* directory can be different from the entry with the name in the *N.Levy* directory.

To carry this one step further, a computer system also may allow us to

FIGURE 20–4 · **Simple Tree Directory Structure**

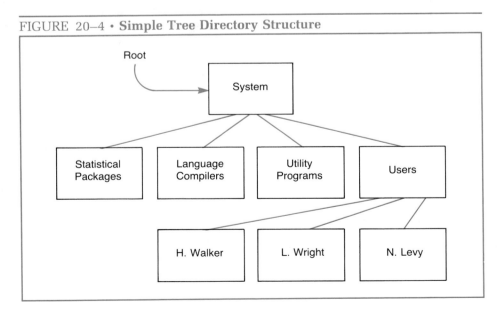

organize our own work into pieces. For example, under our root or base directory, we may be able to define smaller directories for

- separate courses, so each course has its own directory;
- different types of work, where papers are listed in one directory, Pascal programs in another, etc.;
- work from different years or semesters, so our first semester freshmen work is separated from our work as juniors.

With this structure, directories not only allow the machine to find the files, directories also can help us manage several distinct projects by allowing us to organize each task into small, manageable pieces.

File Management Routines

With this discussion of complex tree structures for file information, we now identify some of the common tasks that are needed to work with this file structure. In actual computer systems, each of these file management tasks is performed by a few simple, carefully designed routines that allow for the strict control of data access while allowing for a wide variety of general file management capabilities.

In considering the work we might need to perform in managing files, some tasks are quickly identifiable, such as

- creating new directories,
- adding, deleting, or updating directory entries for a particular file,
- listing the entries of a node in the directory tree structure,
- moving a file entry from one directory node to another, and
- copying a file, so a new copy appears as a second file with an entry in an appropriate directory.

However, some additional tasks arise from security or control issues. For example, access to programs or data collected by one person may need to be restricted, so other users cannot read, use, or modify this work. In addition, certain users may be authorized to delete or modify system packages, such as statistical programs or language compilers. However, not everyone can be given this authority.

As another example, in deleting a file, we certainly need to remove the appropriate entry from a file directory. However, that file of information may still be physically present on a disk. Thus, we may need to consider if that data should be rewritten with blanks or other characters, so others cannot stumble upon that data later on.

In still another area, we may want to allow users to send messages to each other. Such mail systems can allow users scattered around the campus (or even around the world) to communicate easily and quickly. However, when such mail systems exist, we must be sure that correct messages are sent to the appropriate person. In these cases, a file might be set up under each person's main directory to receive mail, and the computer's mail program must be sure that messages are placed in this special file as they are received.

With any of these applications, the file structure can be very helpful in organizing files so users can work with them easily and quickly. However, in managing this tree structure, the programs or routines that perform file management also have to include capabilities to restrict access in various ways so that one user cannot always work with data collected by another.

SECTION 20.4   RANDOM FILE ACCESS

Throughout most of this book, we have stressed concepts that generally apply in computing, and we have focused on Standard Pascal syntax, so our programs will run on most systems.

In this section, we look at general concepts for modifying files that are commonly found in many data processing applications but that are beyond Standard Pascal syntax. Thus, while the concepts we discussed are quite general, there is not a Standard Pascal syntax for performing these tasks.[1] Users may have to inquire about their individual computer systems to see if and how these concepts can be implemented on their machines.

To begin, we consider a file as a long sequence of records stored on a disk. For example, each record might contain the name of a city. Then, if we want to print a list of cities, we could start at the beginning of our file, and we could read successive names, printing them as we get to them. With this **sequential access,** the files contain many records, but we only process them one at a time from first to last. In particular, we use *Reset* or *Rewrite* to move us to the first record. Then, *Get* or *Put* moves from one file record to the next. No procedures are available to skip ahead or to back up in our processing. We have already seen that such files can be useful in many applications, and we have written several programs that utilize these sequential files.

However, they also have limitations; we cannot obtain any record unless we start at the beginning of the file and read successive records until we reach the desired one. Further, in Chapter 15, we noted that this limitation restricts our ability to update a particular record, because a whole file must be copied, making the one desired change, when we want to revise one entry. Therefore, instead of the sequential processing of files, we need random access to the data in files.

Random access allows us to skip around in a file and alternately to read and modify a particular entry in the file. This requires us to proceed in several steps. In our first step, we need to index the records in our file

---

[1]The syntax followed in this section conforms to a proposed extension of Pascal that may be included in a revised Pascal Standard in the future. For more information, see "Pascal: Foreword to the Candidate Extension Library" in *SIGPLAN Notices*, Vol. 19, No. 7, July 1984, pp. 28–44.

in some way, so we can refer to them. For example, we may number the records from 0 to 99999 as shown in Figure 20–5.

Then, when we want to change a specific record, we must

1. determine which record we need to modify (e.g., change record number 31415);
2. move to that record in the file;
3. load the buffer with the desired revised data; and
4. use the *Put* procedure to move the new information from the buffer to the appropriate record.

Similarly, when we want to read a specific record, we must

1. determine which record we need to find;
2. move to that record on the file; and
3. use the *Get* procedure to move the desired information from this record to the buffer for processing.

With this sketch of what we might like to do, we consider the following problem.

PROBLEM 20.4	**A Zip Code Directory**

Write a simple zip code directory, which will enable us to print out the city that corresponds to a given zip code. Such à directory project involves several distinct operations:

I. Directory maintenance.
   A. Enter names initially.
   B. Correct spelling of names.
   C. Add new names. (After we type in some names, we may want to rest before entering the next batch.)
II. Directory look-up.
   A. Given a specific zip code, find the corresponding city name.

Discussion of Problem 20.4

One natural way to store this zip code/city information is to write the city names in a long array of names, where

City[0] is the name of the city with zip code 00000;

City[1] is the name of the city with zip code 00001; and so on.

However, such an array of 100,000 names is often too big to store in main memory, so an array cannot be used. Also, storage of all names in main memory would require us to retype the data every time we run the program, and such effort seems excessive.

Instead, we store our sequence of names in a file of records, and we index these records by zip codes (i.e., by integers between 0 and 99999). Again, our picture in Figure 20–5 is appropriate.

FIGURE 20–5 · Diagram of a File as a Sequence of Records
For Illustration, Records Are Numbered 0..99999

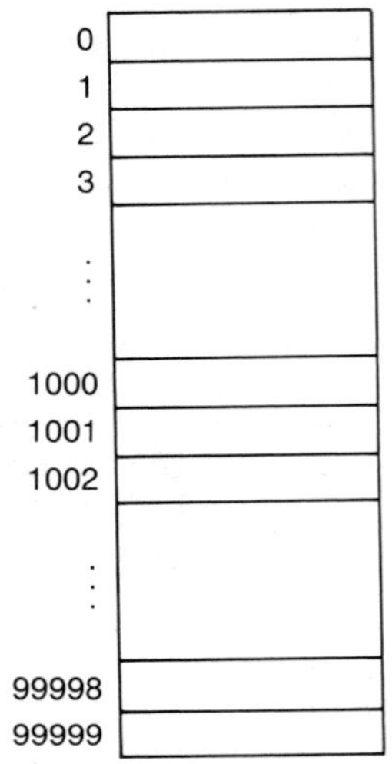

To work with this file, we will need to specify particular zip codes and then work with the appropriate name records. In this work, two new procedures and three new functions have been proposed by the American National Standard Pascal Committee.[2] In defining these items, *f* specifies the file variable and *n* indicates the index of the record under consideration.

> *Procedure SeekRead (f,n)*: prepares the computer to read record *n* on the file *f*. Thus, after *SeekRead (f,n)*, we may call *Get(f)* to move the data in the desired record to our buffer.
> NOTE: If *SeekRead* attempts to position the machine beyond the end of the file, then the computer just moves to the end of the file.
>
> *Procedure SeekWrite (f,n)*: prepares the computer to write record *n* on the file *f*. Thus, after *SeekWrite (f,n)*, we must load our output buffer and then apply *Put(f)* to update the appropriate record.
> NOTE: While *SeekWrite* may move to any record in the file, including the end of the file, it is an error to try to write beyond the end of file.
>
> *Function Position (f)* returns the index of the current record under consideration.
>
> *Function EndPosition (f)* returns the index of the last record in the file.
>
> *Function Empty (f) Boolean*: returns true if there are no records currently in the file.

---

[2]From the "Foreword to the Candidate Extension Library," Ibid, pp. 39–40.

To see how some of these new pieces can be put together, we consider a program that will print the city name corresponding to a given zip code. The outline for the program follows.

Outline for Problem 20.4 (Part 2)
I. Declare file to have records for zip codes 0..99999.
II. Open zip code directory file.
III. Read zip code.
IV. Obtain appropriate city name.
  A. If zip code exceeds the highest code in the directory, report an error and stop.
  B. Prepare computer to read zip code record from file.
  C. Use *Get* to move city name to buffer.
  D. Print name.

This outline yields the following non–Standard Pascal program.

```
Program GetCity (Infile, Input, Output);
{This program obtains an appropriate city name from a directory,
 given the zip-code.}

Const Max = 25;

Type City = Packed Array [1..Max] of Char;
     IndexType = 0..99999;
     FileType = File [IndexType] of City;

Var ZipFile: FileType;
    ZipCode: Integer;

Begin {Main}
    Writeln ('This program prints a city name with a specified zip code.');

    {Open zip code directory file}
    Reset (ZipFile);

    {Read Zip Code}
    Write ('Enter a zip code:');
    Readln (ZipCode);

    {Obtain appropriate city information}
    If (ZipCode < 0) Or (ZipCode > EndPosition(ZipFile))
        Then Writeln ('Zip Code is not in the directory')
        Else Begin
            SeekRead(ZipFile, ZipCode);
            Get (ZipFile);
            Writeln ('The city''s name is ', ZipFile^ )
        End

End {Main} .
```

This program uses several of the new functions and procedures mentioned in our outline. This program also has a different form of file declaration, since we need to specify that our records will have indices in the subrange 0..99999. In our program, we declared

Var ZipFile: File [0..99999] of City;

More generally, we could insert any ordinal type into the square brackets to indicate an appropriate range of indices for file records.

As a second example, we consider a procedure that allows us to update or revise a particular file entry in our zip code file. Here, we combine our reading and writing capabilities in the same modification procedure. The following code assumes the same global declarations as the previous example.

```
Procedure Update (Var ZipFile: FileType; ZipCode: IndexType);
{This procedure revises the city name in the ZipFile with the given ZipCode}
    Var Index: Integer;      {Used for entering the new name}

   Begin
       If (ZipCode < 0) Or (ZipCode > EndPosition(ZipFile))
           Then Writeln ('Invalid Zip Code - File Not Updated')
           Else Begin
               {Obtain the old name with the given zip code}
                 SeekRead (ZipFile, ZipCode);
                 Get (ZipFile);
                 Writeln ('The current city name is:  ', ZipFile^ );

               {Update the city name}
                 SeekWrite (ZipFile, ZipCode);
                 Writeln ('Please enter the revised name: ');
               {Read name character by character into file buffer}
                 Index := 0;
                 While (Index < Max) And Not Eoln
                   Do Begin
                     Index := Index + 1;
                     Read (Zipfile^[Index])
                   End;
                 Readln;
               {Fill rest of buffer with nulls}
                 While (Index < Max)
                   Do Begin
                     Index := Index + 1;
                     ZipFile^[Index] := Chr(0)
                   End;
               {Move revised name to file}
                 Put (Zipfile)

           End

   End {Update} ;
```

Finally, we note that this random access capability also allows us to organize file records as linked lists, so we can store many of our previous data structures on disk as well as in main memory.

More precisely, the purpose of pointers in Pascal has been to specify a particular record of information. The record index can perform the same task in files. Thus, we can implement linked lists in file records if we replace pointer fields by record index fields. Such a parallel structure is shown in Figure 20–6.

In this figure, variable *First* shows where the first record is located; in the file, we find the first element on our list is located at record 3. Then, each element on the list specifies where the next element is found. For example, the *A* record on the file specifies that record 1 comes next. Then *B* is followed by record 2, and *C* by record 4. Finally, we have a special code to indicate the end of each list. In the figure, we used -1 for this code; in other applications, another code might be more appropriate.

Then, with this structure, we can read through an entire list with code, such as the following:

```
Item : = First;
While(Item > = 0)
    Do Begin
        SeekRead(f,Item);
        Get(f);
        Writeln(f^.Data);
        Item : = f^.Next
    End
```

FIGURE 20–6 • **Lists with Pointers and with File Indexing**

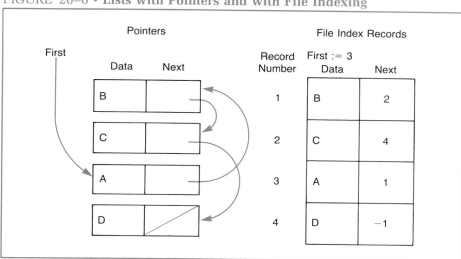

As before, the *Next* field allows us to move from one record to the next. However, in this example, we no longer use pointers to specify next elements. Rather, we use a record index, and then we use *SeekRead* (or *SeekWrite*) and *Get* (or *Put*) to move along our list. To summarize, we find that random access files allow us several capabilities for enhancing our processing.

1. We can index all data records so we can refer to each file record separately.
2. Using these indices, we can move to specific data records to read, write, or modify data.
3. We can include these file indices in the file records themselves, so that one record can point to the next.
4. When records point to one another, we are able to implement all of our list and tree structures on disk files as well as in main memory. When using disks, we just replace pointer fields by the corresponding record indices. Then we can move from record to record in files using *SeekRead*, *SeekWrite*, *Get*, and *Put* just as we did with records in main memory that used pointers.

In the next section, we outline how this expanded access of data in files is used in practical ways in large programs called Data Base Management Systems.

SECTION 20.5   APPLICATION: DATA BASE MANAGEMENT SYSTEMS

In the past sections, we have seen how to work efficiently with individual files using random access for storage and retrieval and using record indexing to move from one record to another. In this section, we apply these ideas to more general applications that include data in several files.

In particular, we consider applications that may involve a vast amount of data and that require processing in a wide variety of ways. For example, a college or university registrar's office must maintain records on such things as

> students: including name, address on and off campus, telephone on and off campus, class standing, and grade point average;

> courses: including course name, instructor, time of meeting, room, students enrolled, and final grades of students;

> instructors: including name, department, and home and office data.

With such applications, we may organize our data into several files, and we need to specify various relationships among the data in these files. When these files and relationships are set up, we typically need to update data, inserting new data, deleting old data, and modifying current data. In addition, we need to be able to interrogate our stored data, scanning the data files to answer various questions.

For example, in our registrar application, we might specify the following.

Add *Henry Walker* to the list of instructors (insertion of new data).

List all students in Henry Walker's Introductory Computer Science course (data interrogation).

In such situations, where data are organized into several pieces with relationships among these pieces, we say the data are placed in a **data base.** In practice, many software packages have been designed to perform many of the normal tasks required to update and interrogate these data bases, and such packages are called **Data Base Management Systems (DBMSs).**

The details of such systems involve considerable complexity and study, and we cannot develop these details in any great depth here. Rather, data bases are the subject of advanced courses by themselves. However, we can apply some of the structures we have developed to introduce how such data base systems might be organized.

Division of Data into Pieces

First, we observe that if we wish to maintain a large amount of data efficiently, we must organize it so we can work with various pieces separately. For example, in our registrar's example, we might separate the overall data into three pieces:

- a student file,
- a course file, and
- an instructor file.

With this division, we can include student names, addresses, and telephone numbers in a single student file. Then, in the course file, we can include just a name for each student; we can get address information from the student file.

This division into pieces does introduce some duplication of effort (e.g., student names are entered in both the student file and the course file). However, with some care, this division into pieces also can make each piece reasonably manageable. Any DBMS must allow individual entries in each file to be added, deleted, and modified easily.

Indices or Directories for a File

In many cases, this division of data into files still results in each file being quite large. (For example, the list of students enrolled may include thousands of names.) With such large files, we can always find any particular item by a linear search, but we also know from Section 8.3 that such searches are very inefficient. Thus, as an adjunct to our large files, a DBMS also may introduce various hashing algorithms or indices for speeding up a search. For example, the DBMS may contain a directory based on the first three letters of a last name. Then, when a student name must be found in the file, the directory indicates where names starting with the appropriate three letters can be found. In large systems, the details of such directories or hashing algorithms may be complicated, but the concept depends on the ideas we discussed for linked lists in Chapter 18. Alternatively, a directory may be based on the ordered tree structure we discussed in Section 19.2.

Relationships Among Files

Beyond the data located in each file, a data base also must include various relationships among files. For example, in our registrar application, we may ask for the name and address of each student who has a given instructor. Here, the course file is needed to find the names of the students. Then, a program can put these names together with the addresses in the student file.

As with our discussion of searching, one way this work might be done involves the linear searching of files to find each needed address. However, often more efficient methods are needed to make this work more feasible. For example, when searching in one file, we could make a separate list of items that we need (e.g., we could make a list of students in a class). Then, we could use this list to search in another file. As a second improvement, we could include pointers from one file to another in various records. For example, in a course record, we could include an index to the student record containing the student name. Then when we find a student's name in a class, we would also know where the address information is located in the student file.

Combining Relationships

Next, we can consider more complicated questions that require several intermediate steps. For example, we might ask for all students from Iowa who are enrolled in a given class. Here, we might proceed in three steps.

1. Make a list of all students in the class.
2. Make a list of students from Iowa.
3. Find names common to both lists.

In such situations, a DBMS must be able to construct lists of items satisfying certain conditions, and then the DBMS must be able to compare multiple lists efficiently.

In working with large sets of data, DBMSs must involve extremely efficient, sophisticated algorithms for extracting and combining data from various files. However, even with the complexity involved, it is also encouraging to note that much of the work for these algorithms depends on just the ideas we have already seen. In particular, we find considerable use of trees and lists to organize data records, to specify relationships between records, and to improve searching efficiency. Further, we find the records in each file are indexed in an appropriate way, so direct access is available to each record as part of a random access file.

SUMMARY

1. Disk files require a mechanical process to store and retrieve data.
2. In this process, the most time is spent in obtaining the first piece of data in a file. Thereafter, subsequent data in a file can be transmitted relatively quickly. Thus, in practice, the computer reads or writes several pieces of data at a time to increase efficiency.
3. In the transmission process, a **buffer** is used to store these pieces of data.
   a. In reading, an entire record of data is read into a buffer. Then various fields of the record can be read into the program as needed.
   b. In writing, various fields of a record are gathered in a buffer before being sent to the file on a single operation.
4. Within a Pascal program, buffers are created by a *Reset* or *Rewrite* statement. Thereafter, we can move data from disk to buffer or back using the special procedures *Get* and *Put*, respectively. Then, adding an up-arrow or caret to a file/buffer variable allows us to access the contents of the buffer itself.
5. Beyond this simple **sequential access** to files, this chapter also introduced **random access files.** In a random access file, each record on the file is indexed. Then, using this index, the computer is able to move from one record to another to read and write using several new procedures and functions.
6. This indexing of records within a file also allows us to specify individual records. In particular, this enables one record to indicate another one that might come next. Thus, record indexing also allows files to be organized into lists and trees.
7. We can organize several different files using **file directories,** which organize files into a tree structure. This allows each directory to be manageable in size. Also, individual users may specify their own private files.
8. With these directories, we use **file management routines** to create, delete, and modify directories and files. However, these routines also must control access to various files. The routines need to prevent some users from reading, using, or modifying the work of others.
9. **Data bases** allow us to store large amounts of data in several files, and these data are tied together with relationships among the various records. Then, large software packages, called **Data Base Management Systems (DBMSs),** process this data, allowing general file updating and allowing data to be combined and extracted in many ways. For efficiency, the DBMSs often make use of lists, trees, and other structures.

EXERCISES

20.1 *Input and Output Buffers.* When we type at many terminals, material goes directly from the terminal to an input buffer. Then, for most processing, the CPU copies this information to an output buffer where it is transmitted back to the terminal to be displayed on a screen or printed. Use this flow of data to explain the following phenomena that are observed on many computing systems.

    a. There may be a time delay between when a user types at the keyboard and when the data appears on the screen.

    b. In entering a password, nothing appears on the screen at all. (Thus, people looking over one's shoulder during log-on cannot see one's password.)

    c. When an instructor types on one keyboard, the same information can be displayed on many different terminals, even when others are logged on to other terminals.

20.2 In the file copying program of Section 20.2, we observed that the transfer of data

    Outfileˆ : = Infileˆ

had to come first in the loop so that we did not lose the first piece of data. Is it also necessary that

    Put(Outfile)

comes before

    Get(Infile)

Explain your conclusion, and write a Pascal program to check your answer.

20.3 *Print End of File.* Write a program that prints out the last record in a file.

    HINT: For efficiency, there is no reason to move most of the records into main memory beyond the buffer.

KEY TERMS, PHRASES, AND CONCEPTS		ELEMENTS OF PASCAL SYNTAX	
Buffers	Directory Tree	**Standard**	**Non–Standard**
Data Base Management	Structure	*Get*	*Empty*
System (DBMS)	File Directory	*Put*	*EndPosition*
Disk Cylinder	Random Access		*File [. . .] of*
Disk Track	Sequential Access		*Position*
			SeekRead
			SeekWrite

20.4 a. Write a program that reads a list of grocery items, including product codes, names, and costs from the terminal and stores them on a disk file.

b. Write a second program that copies this disk record of codes, names, and costs to another file, decreasing all costs by 35%. (Such a program might be used to price all items during a store-wide sale.)

20.5 *Lists Stored on File.* Write a program that will store a list of names on a file as a linked list, using record indices to point from one record to the next. Your program should include procedures to insert new items and to print all list items.

20.6 *Location of Disk Directories.* Microcomputer diskettes can be changed easily, and files can be read from diskettes as soon as they are purchased. How do you think the computer can find the directory for each new disk?

20.7 *Random Access in Standard Pascal.* While random access procedures are not built into Standard Pascal, these tasks can still be performed if one is willing to sacrifice some efficiency and if one is willing to add some global variables.

For example, we could specify *Position* as a global variable, and we could use this variable to keep track of how many records we have read or written. Thus, we might initialize *Position* to 0. Then, we might revise the *Get* or *Put* operations to obtain revised procedures *GetR* and *PutR*, which not only transfer data between disk and buffer but also update the file *Position*. Similarly, *SeekRead* could perform an appropriate number of *Get* procedures to move to the desired record from the present one. (If the desired record is after the current record, then we perform the correct number of *Gets*. Otherwise we start from the beginning.)

The *SeekWrite* procedure is harder, because we may have to copy earlier parts of a file to get to the desired new record. (After a *Put* and before a new *SeekRead* or *SeekWrite*, we may also have to finish copying a file before we can start from the beginning again.)

a. Use these examples to outline how the new procedures *Seek-Write*, *SeekRead*, *Position*, *EndPosition*, and *Empty* might be implemented using Standard Pascal functions. Also, outline new *GetR* and *PutR* procedures that include any needed revisions in *Get* and *Put*.

b. Write Standard Pascal procedures and functions to implement the outlines of part (a).

NOTE: The next two exercises require random access files. If such files are not available on a particular system, then either these exercises should be skipped or the extra work from the previous exercise will be necessary. If random access files are available, then the reader should use the capabilities of the local system to implement the five new procedures listed in Exercise 20.7a.

20.8 *Zip Code Directory*—1. The zip code directory of Problem 20.4 is to be expanded to allow a listing of records ordered by city name, and to allow searching for a zip code by city. To do this, we first add a *Next* field to each file entry, where this field will give the entry number of the next city in alphabetical order. Thus, file records will have the form

```
Const Max = 25;
Type Entry = Record
     City: Packed Array [1..Max] of Char;
     Next: −1..99999
     End;
```

Also, in the file, we will use a record −1 and we will use its *Next* field to give the name of the first city in alphabetical order, and we use the code −1 in a *Next* field to show that the city comes at the end of the alphabetical listing. Write a program that
- reads cities and zip codes;
- prints a list of cities and zip codes in alphabetical order;
- given a name, searches the city list linearly to find the appropriate zip code; and
- inserts cities into the appropriate record, based on zip code, and maintains the records in alphabetical order as a linked list using the *Next* fields.

20.9 *Zip Code Directory*—2.
   a. Write a program that expands the one in Exercise 20.8 to maintain a brief index to city names, based on the first two letters of the name. (See Section 18.4 or Section 19.2 for ideas of how an index or directory might be organized for fast retrieval.) In each case, the brief directory would specify where in the zip code directory we should begin a linear search. Thus, instead of searching an entire file for a name, the directory allows us to start at a place in the file close to the desired name.
   b. Discuss how such a directory might be stored on a separate file for permanent reference.

20.10 *Design of a Spelling Checker.* Suppose you were asked to write a spelling checker program. Your program should read words from a file of text, look them up in a dictionary stored on another file or files, and print out an alphabetical listing of misspelled words.

   Design the data structure(s) used by this program. In particular,
   1. specify how you would organize the words in the dictionary for efficient look-up;
   2. specify how you would organize your listing of misspelled words for printing.

   For efficiency, you might organize your program so that each word is looked up only once. (There is no reason to look up the word "the" each time it appears in the text.) How could you organize your work to avoid repeated dictionary references for the same word?

20.11 *Data Structure Design for Course Scheduling.* A program is to be written that will keep track of the course schedule used at pre-registration. The program reads the following course information for each course: department, course number and section, course title, instructor(s), room(s), and time period(s).

NOTE: Multiple rooms and times are possible, as some lectures have separate laboratories or discussion sections, and some classes meet four times a week.

With this data, the program provides the following output.

- Course information, sorted by department, course number, and section
- Course listing by room, ordered by time period
- Schedule conflicts for a given time and room
- Schedule conflicts for a given instructor

NOTE: Labs might overlap several time periods.

Design the data structure(s) for this information.

1. Outline how this information will be structured. (You may want to draw a picture of a typical structure.)
2. Specify the declarations needed for these structures.
3. Outline how the data will be retrieved at the end to produce the desired lists.

20.12 *Storing Prescription Data.* A druggist must keep a record of all prescriptions that she has filled. In particular, she must keep track of

- drug prescribed,
- patient's name, and
- date prescription filled.

For various reasons, the druggist must be able to retrieve this information by any of the following:

- patient's name (for refill information);
- patient's family name (for tax purposes);
- date (for doctor's inquiries);
- month (for billing purposes).

Design a data structure that could be used to store and retrieve this information. Your structure should be practical, because the druggist fills many prescriptions each day and new customers arrive in town frequently. Also, your design should assume that there is too much information to rely solely upon storage in main memory. Thus, disk storage is needed.

In discussing your data structure, specify the declarations that you would use for these structures. Also, describe the techniques you would use to store and retrieve the data. For example, you should identify which search or sorting algorithms you would use, and you should describe how new records would be added.

20.13 *Indexing.* A program is to be written which will produce an index for a manuscript. The program will read a list of key words or phrases from one file, and this list will specify the entries to be used in the index. Then, the program will read the formatted manuscript.

Each word or phrase in the manuscript will be checked against the list of key words or phrases, and the page number will be recorded whenever a word or phrase matches. When the entire manuscript has been read, the program will print the index, with entries in alphabetical order.

Design the data structure(s) for storing the data (key words or phrases, corresponding page numbers) needed in this program. In particular, you should
1. specify the declarations needed for these structures
2. outline how the list of keywords or phrases will be organized and searched
   (a) assuming the list of keywords and phrases is stored in the file in alphabetical order
   (b) assuming the list of keywords and phrases is *not* stored in the file in alphabetical order
3. outline how page numbers will be recorded
4. outline how the data will be retrieved at the end to produce the printed index.

CAUTION: If this program is to perform well, we must be able to search for key words and phrases very efficiently. Thus, long linear searches are not appropriate in this program.

CHAPTER 21

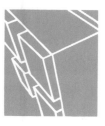

UNCONDITIONAL
BRANCHING

T hroughout this text, we have stressed a top-down approach to problem solving and a corresponding structure in our programs. This orientation prompted our discussion of procedures and functions and motivated our consideration of how to control the execution of programs. For example, the *While, Repeat,* and *For* control structures for loops and the *If* and *Case* conditional statements all evolved from a structured analysis of a problem. In this chapter, we consider one more control structure, called unconditional branching, which can be of considerable help in structuring certain types of solutions. Unconditional branching also provides a way for us to implement more general control structures in Pascal.

SECTION 21.1   ELEMENTS OF UNCONDITIONAL BRANCHING

In most problem solving, we organize a program in one of several ways, depending on what we wish to do. For example, we may want to perform a sequence of steps, proceeding one step at a time (sequential execution). Alternatively, we may want to repeat certain steps several times (repetitive execution), or we may want to execute some steps only under certain circumstances (conditional execution). For each choice, we use a different structure to organize our program. We organize sequential execution into blocks using procedures and functions; we use *For, Repeat,* or *While* loops for repetition; and we use *If* or *Case* statements for conditional execution.

Occasionally, however, our work requires an additional capability. For example, we may need to jump out of the middle of a loop, or we may want to leave the middle of a procedure. Here, we do not intend to return to our current processing at a later time; instead, we want to move directly to a new section of code. Thus, this jump is not the same as a normal procedure or function call where we perform a task and return. Rather, this **unconditional branch** moves us out of our current code, and we will not return later. Unconditional branching breaks the normal flow of program execution.

To make this concept more concrete, we first introduce some Pascal syntax in a simple program. Then we look further at applications of this capability and some natural constraints on its use.

Syntax

When we need to make a jump within our program, we logically must specify where the machine should jump and when the jump should occur. In Pascal, the first of these parts is addressed by labeling a particular statement. Then, we perform the second part with a *GoTo* statement. These points are illustrated in the following program.

```
Program GotoExample (Output);
{This syntactically correct program demonstrates the use
 of the Goto statement}

Label 1;      {"1" will be the label of a statement}

Procedure P;
{We will use a Goto statement to jump out of the middle of this procedure}
    Begin
        Writeln ('Start of Procedure P');

        { . . . First part of procedure P }

        Goto 1;  {Jump directly from here back to the main program}

        { . . . Second part of procedure P}

        Writeln ('Normal end of Procedure P');
    End {P} ;

Begin {Main}
    Writeln ('Start of Program');
    P;
    Writeln ('Line after call to P');
    1: Writeln ('Main Continues');
    Writeln ('End of Program')
End {Main} .
```

When this program is run, we get

```
Start of Program
Start of Procedure P
Main Continues
End of Program
```

This program illustrates the syntax for unconditional branches, which consists of three elements: a label declaration, a label within a statement, and a *GoTo* statement. A statement in a Pascal program can be labeled following two steps.

1. We use a *Label* statement in our declarations to indicate that a particular integer will be used as a label. For example,

    ```
    Label 1;
    ```

    indicates that we will use "1" to label a statement within our main program.

    More generally, we can declare any integer in the range 0 . . 9999 as a label in the program. Note that the *Label* statement, if present, is always the first declaration, coming before any constants, types, etc.

2. We label a specific statement by placing the declared number before the statement, followed by a colon. For example, we labeled a *Write* statement by specifying

    ```
    1: Writeln ('Main Continues');
    ```

When a statement is labeled, we can instruct the computer to jump directly from one point in our program to another by writing *GoTo* and the appropriate label. For example, in our sample program,

```
GoTo 1;
```

told the computer to jump out of procedure *P*, back to the designated point in the main program. When a *GoTo* is executed, the machine skips any intervening statements in our code. In our example, the last *Write* statement in procedure *P* was skipped. Similarly, the *Write* statement

```
Writeln ('Line after call to P');
```

was not executed. Rather, the machine returned directly from the procedure to the spot designated by the *GoTo* statement.

With this example, we see that the *GoTo* causes the computer to interrupt its normal flow of execution. Such a jump allows us to skip steps in our program, and occasionally this is very helpful. However, such jumps also can introduce difficulties if the *GoTo* is not carefully controlled.

Constraints on GoTo Statements

Some of the possible abuses of the *GoTo* are reduced in Pascal by specific restrictions imposed by the Pascal language itself. To illustrate these limitations, we consider several cases where the *GoTo* could yield ambiguous code. We then state the rules in Pascal that address the problem.

The first case where code becomes ambiguous involves variables within loops, since jumping into a loop can cause variables to be undefined. For example, consider the following:

```
Label 2;
        .
        .
        .
Sum : = 0.0;
GoTo 2;
For Index : = 1 to Max
     Do Begin
          2: Sum : = Sum + A[Index]
          End;
```

In this code, the statement

```
For Index : = 1 to Max
```

gives *Index* a specific initial value. However, a jump into the middle of such a loop would skip this initialization, so *Index* would not be defined correctly. Thus, our first rule in Pascal becomes:

Branches into loops (or into any block) are prohibited.

Pascal allows us to jump out of loops prematurely, but it does not allow us to jump into a loop or a *Begin-End* block.

Another problem occurs when we jump into a procedure or function without allowing the computer to allocate needed space on the run-time stack. In addition, needed return addresses cannot be stored. Thus, the second rule in Pascal is:

Branches into a procedure or function are prohibited.

Pascal does allow jumps out of procedures, and in such cases, the computer must deallocate space on the run-time stack. For example, in our program *GoTo*, space for procedure *P* is popped from the run-time stack when the machine jumps from the middle of *P* back to the main program. However, jumps into a procedure or function are not allowed. (This prohibition also resolves initialization difficulties that might arise if we jumped into a procedure without specifying needed parameters.)

Finally, in coding, we want to avoid "global labels" wherever possible, just as we want to avoid global variables. Instead, labels should be used to designate a point in a particular task; they should not be embedded in the details of the task. Thus, the third rule in Pascal is:

Labels must be declared at the same level that they are used.

For example, labels cannot be declared globally and then used to designate a statement in a procedure.

This is the same restriction that we have already discussed in Section 5.4 for control variables. We can declare and use labels or loop control variables within procedures and functions, but our top-down methodology prevents us from declaring them at one level and then using them to specify statements or index loops at a lower level.

With this general discussion of the syntax and constraints for branches, we now turn to two specific examples that illustrate how this new idea of unconditional branching can be used effectively in our programs.

| SECTION 21.2 | THE LOOP/EXIT CONCEPT |

An important characteristic of all Pascal loop control structures is that the condition for terminating the loop always appears once, at the beginning or at the end of the loop. For example, when we write

```
While ---
    Do ---
```

the computer checks our condition at the very beginning of our loop, before any other work is done. In contrast, the statement

```
Repeat
    .
    .
    .
Until ---
```

checks at the end of our loop.

This checking at the start or end of loops has never seriously impaired our problem solving and programming, but occasionally it has required us to add a few lines of code. At times this code also has destroyed some parallelism between cases. For example, when we wish to read values and compute their sum until we reach a sentinel value, we write

```
Sum := 0.0;
Read (Value);
While (Value <> Last)
    Do Begin
        Sum := Sum + Value;
        Read (Value)
    End;
```

Here, we need an initial *Read* statement to check if our first value is the sentinel value.

Similarly, in our quicksort algorithm from Section 19.7, we needed to work alternately with the top and bottom parts of an array. Here, our main loop was

```
Repeat
     Checkup;
     Done = (LowerCheck > = Median)
     If Not  Done
        Then Begin
             Checkdown;
             Done : = (Median > = Uppercheck)
             End
Until Done;
```

Our code must treat the *CheckUp* and the *CheckDown* procedures in different ways, because once we start the loop we cannot stop in the middle. Rather, we need to place *Checkdown* in the middle of an *If* statement, and the parallelism between the two cases is lost.

In each of these cases, more natural code results if we can leave a loop in the middle as well as at the beginning and the end.

LOOP and EXIT Statements in Ada[1]

To illustrate how we can apply this concept of checking loop conditions in the middle, we first see how we might incorporate this concept into our thinking about program code. Unfortunately, the Pascal language itself does not have a simple statement for checking loop conditions. Thus, to make this concept concrete, we borrow our syntax from a more recent language, Ada, which has evolved from Pascal and other structured languages. Similar statements may be found in some other relatively new, higher level languages.

In Ada, the body of loops is placed between the statements

```
Loop
End Loop;
```

Further, Ada allows us to use *For* and *While* statements in conjunction with loops. For example, our code to sum values could be translated into Ada as follows:

```
Sum : = 0.0;
Read (Value);
While (Value < > Last)
     Loop
          Sum : = Sum + Value;
          Read (Value);
     End Loop;
```

Thus, Ada permits much of the same coding that we have done in Pascal with very little change.

---

[1] Ada is a registered trademark of the U.S. Government, Ada Joint Program Office.

However, Ada also contains an *Exit* statement that allows us to test a condition in the middle of a loop. With this new statement, we can rewrite our summing code without the initial *Read*, and the result is a bit more natural, as shown below.

```
Sum := 0.0;
Loop
      Read (Value);
      Exit When (Value = Last);
      Sum := Sum + Value;
End Loop;
```

In this code, our loop contains three steps.

1. We read a new value.
2. We leave the loop when we reach the sentinel.
3. We add the new value to the previous sum.

This code also has the important characteristic that once we test our *Exit* condition, we can assume the result of the test in the rest of the loop. In our example, the third step can assume that the value is not the sentinel.

The importance of this last characteristic is illustrated when we rewrite our main loop in the quicksort using these *Exit* statements.

```
Loop
      CheckUp;
      Exit When (LowerCheck >= Median);
      CheckDown;
      Exit When (Median >= UpperCheck);
End Loop;
```

This code restores the parallelism between the two parts of our algorithm. Here, we alternate working with each end of our array until we reach the middle, and we exit the loop whenever the middle is found. This code also eliminates the Boolean variable *Done*, which we needed in the Pascal version of this code.

With these examples, we see that in some circumstances code can be streamlined and clarified if we can leave loops in the middle as well as at the start or end.

LOOP and EXIT in Pascal

Returning to our programming in Pascal, we find that this *Loop/Exit* concept can be implemented if we are willing to use the *GoTo* statement. In particular, we can program the loop concept using the Pascal *While* structure:

```
While True
      Do Begin
      End;
```

Similarly, we can code the exit concept in Pascal using an *If* statement with a *GoTo:*

```
If ---
    Then GoTo ---
```

The resulting code has the logical structure that we want for a *Loop/Exit,* and we use the *GoTo* for our *Exit* statement. For example, our code to sum values might be written as follows:

```
Label 3;
    .
    .
    .
Sum : = 0.0;
While True
    Do Begin {Loop}
        Read(Value);
        If Value = Last
            Then GoTo 3;
        Sum : = Sum + Value
    End {Loop}
    3:    ;
```

Here, we label the statement that immediately follows the *While* loop. Then, the *Exit* is equivalent to an unconditional branch from the middle of the loop to that label.

A similar use of *GoTo* allows us to write clean Pascal code for the main quicksort loop.

```
Label 17;
    .
    .
    .
While True
    Do Begin {Loop}
        CheckUp;
        If (LowerCheck > = UpperCheck)
            Then GoTo 17;
        CheckDown;
        If (Median > = UpperCheck)
            Then GoTo 17
    End {Loop};
    17:    ;
```

Again, this testing and loop exit allows us to maintain the parallelism between the two parts of our algorithm.

In each of these cases, we first wrote our loop in a structured form, and we identified natural places in the loop where we needed to exit. Once these exit points were identified, we then could use the Pascal *GoTo* statement to implement this *Loop/Exit* in our code.

SECTION 21.3	**EXAMPLE: EXCEPTION HANDLING AND ERROR RECOVERY**

A second important use of the *GoTo* statement arises in complex programs when we must handle unusual situations in our code. To begin, we look at three cases where this might occur. In our first case, we might be writing a compiler, where we want to read a correct program and translate it into machine language. However, we must allow for the possibility that the program being read is not syntactically correct. A second, more general case occurs in reading commands or data, where our program must process correctly formatted commands in the appropriate way. However, the program also must behave predictably when errors in the input are found. Our third case deals with processing data in a tree where we often move from node to node recursively. However, if we detect an error in our tree data, then we may need to change our approach to processing.

In each of these cases, we need to take special action when an unusual situation occurs. Here, we may divide our possible responses into one of two categories: we may be able to correct a difficulty immediately and then continue normal processing, or we may need to abandon normal processing completely.

Already in this text, we have seen several examples that fall into the first category. For example, our discussion of data entry errors in Section 11.6 showed how we sometimes can check input as it is entered. Then, if the data seem incorrect, we can ask the user to re-enter the data immediately. Here, all checking can be confined to a data entry procedure, and the rest of the program can assume that all data are correct. In such situations, we can identify an error easily and correct it before continuing.

However, in the more complex examples mentioned at the beginning of this section, such immediate correction may not be possible. For example, a compiler often uses several procedures that call each other recursively. Each procedure processes part of a Pascal statement, and the recursive calls put these parts together. When an error occurs, this entire process must be modified. In particular,

1. the error must be identified and reported to the user;
2. much processing up to that point must be discarded; and
3. the compiler must then try to resume processing, so it can identify any further errors. For example, the compiler may scan for the next semicolon and then continue processing from that point.

In general, this activity of discarding previous processing and then trying to resume is very complex and difficult. To illustrate this, we consider the following example, which demonstrates how programs can respond to errors identified in processing.

Example: A binary tree is constructed to store real numbers in nodes using the following declarations:

```
Type Ptr = ^Node;
        Node = Record
                    Value : Real;
                    Left   : Ptr;
                    Right : Ptr
                    End;
Var   Root : Ptr;
```

Write a procedure that determines the sum of the square roots of these numbers.

Solution: Part 1. A natural solution to this problem uses recursion in much the same way that our tree printing procedures did in Chapter 19. The appropriate outline is as follcws:

I. If a node is empty, return a value of 0.
II. If a node is not empty:
    A. Compute the sum of the nodes on the left.
    B. Compute the sum of the nodes on the right.
    C. Compute the square root of the value at the given node.
    D. Add the results of A, B, and C and return this sum.

This outline suggests the following procedure.

```
{Procedure Compute assumes the following declarations:}

Type Ptr = ^Node;
     Node = Record
            Value: Real;
            Left: Ptr;
            Right: Ptr;
            End;

Var Root: Ptr;

Procedure Compute (Root: Ptr);
{This procedure computes the sum of the square roots of the data in a tree}
{Version 1}
    Var Sum: Real;

    Function FindSum (Base: Ptr): Real;
    {This function finds the sum for the tree with the given base as root}
        Begin
            If (Base = Nil)
                Then FindSum := 0
                Else FindSum := FindSum(Base^.Left) + Sqrt(Base^.Value)
                                    + FindSum(Base^.Right)
        End {FindSum} ;
```

```
Begin {Compute}
    Sum := FindSum (Root);
    Writeln ('The Sum of the square roots of the tree data is ', Sum:1:2)
End {Compute} ;
```

This procedure works well for any trees as long as we can compute the needed square roots. However, this procedure fails if we allow the possibility that our data may contain negative values. Thus, for a more complete solution, we must decide how to respond if we encounter a negative value.

Solution: Part 2. First, we note that once we find a negative value, we cannot proceed with our computation. Instead, we should report that an error has occurred, and we should stop further processing.

However, halting further processing in this context can be rather awkward, since we will find this negative value only after some amount of work within the tree. We cannot just stop work in the *FindSum* function and then return, because this function may have been called recursively. Rather, after reporting the error, we need to go back to procedure *Compute* itself.

One way to handle this problem is to check *FindSum* each time it is used to see if an error has been found. (*FirstSum* might return −1 if an error has been identified.) However, such checking greatly complicates our code.

A more common approach involves the definition of a separate error procedure that reports the appropriate error and then returns directly to procedure *Compute*. In general programs, we may even pass an error code to the error procedure, so an appropriate error message can be printed. With this approach, we have the following expanded outline.

Error Procedure

I. Report appropriate error message.
II. Jump back to original compute procedure, skipping any intermediate evaluation that might have occurred.

Normal processing

  I. If the node is empty, return a value of 0.
 II. If the node value is negative, then report an error.
III. If the node value is non-negative:
    A. Compute the sum of the nodes on the left.
    B. Compute the sum of the nodes on the right.
    C. Compute the square root of the value at this given node.
    D. Add the results of A, B, and C and return this sum.

This outline yields the following procedure, which shows the general structure that is commonly used to handle such unusual situations. Note that a *GoTo* is used in the *Error* procedure to jump back to procedure *Compute*.

```
{Procedure Compute assumes the following declarations:}

Type Ptr = ^Node;
     Node = Record
            Value: Real;
            Left: Ptr;
            Right: Ptr;
            End;

Var Root: Ptr;

Procedure Compute (Root: Ptr);
{This procedure computes the sum of the square roots of the data in a tree}
{Version 2}
     Label 1;
     Var Sum: Real;

     Procedure Error (ErrorCode: Integer);
     {This procedure handles any errors that are found in the summing
      computation}
     {This procedure is structured so it may be expanded to handle
      additional errors as they are identified}
          Begin
               Writeln ('* * * * Processing Error * * * * *');
               Write ('Error Number ', ErrorCode:1, ':  ');
               Case ErrorCode Of
                    1: Writeln ('Tree data include negative value - ',
                                'square roots not defined');
                    End {Case} ;
               Writeln ('Computation terminated');
               Goto 1
          End {Error} ;

     Function FindSum (Base: Ptr): Real;
     {This function finds the sum for the tree with the given base as root}
          Begin
               If (Base = Nil)
                    Then FindSum := 0
                    Else If Base^.Value < 0.0
                         Then Error(1)
                         Else FindSum := FindSum(Base^.Left) + Sqrt(Base^.Value)
                                       + FindSum(Base^.Right)
          End {FindSum} ;

     Begin {Compute}
          Sum := FindSum (Root);
          Writeln ('The Sum of the square roots of the tree data is ', Sum:1:2);
     1: End {Compute} ;
```

When this procedure is called with non-negative data at all nodes, then this procedure produces the same results as before. However, when some data value is negative, the following message is produced.

```
* * * * * Processing Error * * * * *
Error Number 1:   Tree data include negative value - square roots not defined
Computation terminated
```

A similar approach may be used in writing compilers, where Pascal programs are being scanned and then translated into machine language. In particular, an error procedure may be developed to

1. print an appropriate message (the *Case* statement of the example is simply expanded to include more messages);
2. scan input to find a good place to resume (e.g., read until finding a semi-colon); and
3. jump back to the initial scanning process, throwing away the parts of the incorrect statement already processed.

Beyond this error procedure, processing can proceed normally. Procedures can call each other as necessary, processing input piece by piece as appropriate. However, when an error is detected, execution shifts to the *Error* procedure, which handles all of the needed details of error handling. Thus, the rest of the program can remain free of these possible error conditions.

In reviewing this handling of unusual conditions, we find that we have applied the general top-down structure that we have used consistently in the past. We define a common task, procedure *Error*, to handle processing details for these unusual situations. Procedure *Error* prints appropriate messages and takes appropriate corrective action, if necessary. When procedure *Error* finishes, it uses a single *GoTo* statement to return control to an appropriate point for resuming processing. Awkward intermediate steps can then be skipped. As in the previous section, this example illustrates ways that the *GoTo* can be used effectively within a program to clarify code and enhance structure.

In the next section, however, we also note ways that the *GoTo* can destroy structure.

SECTION 21.4   STYLE, DESIGN, AND TESTING: SOME WARNINGS

In both Sections 21.2 and 21.3, we approached a particular problem in a structured, methodical way, and we concluded with a useful application of the *GoTo* statement. In Section 21.2, we saw a need to leave a loop in the middle using the *Loop/Exit* concept. In Section 21.3, we isolated error handling in a special procedure, which needed to return control to a fresh starting point. In each case, we first developed a well-structured algorithm to solve a particular problem, and then we found we needed the *GoTo* statement to implement this algorithm.

Unfortunately, the *GoTo* statement also can be used in many other circumstances that may destroy the advantages of structured programming emphasized throughout this text. Thus, before we leave our consideration of the *GoTo*, we identify some possible abuses of this statement so we will be able to avoid them.

Perhaps the most common difficulty with the *GoTo* is that it allows us to link parts of a program that should be independent. As a simple example, consider the following code fragment:

```
1: {Task A}
   Begin
           .
           .
           .
       If ---
           Then GoTo 2;
           .
           .
           .
   End {A} ;
2: {Task B}
   Begin
           .
           .
           .
       If ---
           Then GoTo 1;
           .
           .
           .
   End {B} ;
```

Here, the *GoTo* allows the computer to jump freely between the two tasks A and B. Thus, these pieces of code have become interdependent, and we cannot test one without the other. Hence, instead of working with two small, manageable pieces, we now have to contend with a larger piece of code that may be more complex and thus more error-prone.

In a related matter, *GoTos* may confuse the logic of a program, for there may be many paths that lead to the same piece of code. For example, consider the following code fragment:

```
Begin
    If A > B Then GoTo 1;
        .
        .
        .
2:
        .
        .
        .
    If A < B Then GoTo 1;
    If A > D Then GoTo 2;
1:  If C > B Then GoTo 2;
```

With such code, we may have a very difficult time knowing what we can assume at a particular point. For example, at the statement labeled 2, we might be

going through the code the first time with A <= B;

returning from the A > D test; or

executing statement 2 the first time, having jumped from the first test (A > B) to statement label 1 and then up.

From these examples, we see that program logic can become quite complex if various conditions can lead to the same place in our code, and the *GoTo* can compound this problem.

Both of these difficulties are found in many programs written by inexperienced programmers and by people who have not had to read, test, correct, or maintain large programs. Before using *GoTos*, we should review the following principles, which have evolved from much practical experience in solving problems and programming.

Principle 1: The use of a *GoTo* often indicates that we have not analyzed a problem carefully. Code containing a *GoTo* often can be replaced by cleaner, more concise code if more time is spent in algorithm design.

Principle 2: When we use a *GoTo*, we should always start with a top-down analysis of our problem. We should not consider using the *GoTo* at an early stage of our analysis.

Principle 3: *GoTos* are not necessary to solve a wide range of problems, and before using a *GoTo* we should check if another construction might be more appropriate. Without the *GoTo* statement, Pascal still contains a rich repertoire of control statements and conditional statements, including

```
For --- Do ---
Repeat --- Until
While --- Do ---
If --- Then ---
If --- Then --- Else ---
Case
```

With all of these statements available, we have not had to use *GoTos* for solving any problems prior to this chapter.

Principle 4: When we need to use the *GoTo* statement with a label, we should limit its use to a very few points in our code. Further, when a procedure or function contains two separate pieces of code, we should never use *GoTos* to move from the middle of each piece to the other. In our examples in Sections 21.2 and 21.3, each program fragment contained just a single label and only one or two *GoTos*. In a loop, we used the label and *GoTo* simply to leave the loop. In error handling, we used a single *GoTo* to skip intermediate steps before resuming processing.

To summarize, we find that the *GoTo* can be a useful statement when we need to jump out of the normal flow of processing. Such situations may arise from an organized, top-down analysis of a problem, and in such situations, the *GoTo* can clarify and simplify our code. However, the *GoTo* also can have the opposite effect of blurring the structure of our work and increasing the complexity of the code. Thus, in writing programs, we always should consider the effect of the *GoTo*, and we should use this statement only in special circumstances.

SUMMARY

1. An **unconditional branch** instructs the computer to jump from one point in a program to another. In Pascal, this branching involves: the declaration of a specific *Label*, specifying a statement in the program; and the use of a *GoTo* to cause the computer to jump to the specified statement during processing.
2. In this branching, Pascal permits us to jump out of loops, procedures or functions, but we are not allowed to jump into any of these.
3. Unconditional branching can be useful in certain, controlled applications.
   a. *GoTos* allow us to **Exit** from a loop at any designated point, following a concept from Ada.
   b. *GoTos* allow us to apply special processing to unusual or exceptional cases without significantly disturbing the normal processing.
4. The *GoTo* statement may be abused. It can destroy program structure and can make program logic extremely complex. Thus, while unconditional branching can be used effectively within a structured program, we must be careful not to abuse this capability.

EXERCISES

21.1 *Repeat–Until as a Special Case of Loop Exit.* The *Loop/Exit* concept is a general looping control structure that can replace many more limited looping structures.
   a. Explain how the *Repeat–Until* of Pascal could be implemented using *Loop* and *Exit* statements.
   b. Give an example to illustrate your answer to part a.

KEY TERMS, PHRASES, AND CONCEPTS		ELEMENTS OF PASCAL SYNTAX
Exception Handling and Error Recovery Loop/Exit	Unconditional Branching Potential Hazards Uses	*GoTo* *Label*

21.2 *Loops in Early Languages.* One of the reasons for the popularity of Pascal is its inclusion of a wide variety of control structures, including *For, While,* and *Repeat* loops and *If–Then, If–Then–Else,* and *Case* statements. Many earlier languages did not have all of these features, and structured code was not emphasized. For example, both BASIC and standard FORTRAN contain only *For* and *If–Then* statements.

With these limitations, structure is still possible if we use the *GoTo* statement with *If–Then* statements to expand the types of loops possible, just as we used the *GoTo* in Pascal in Section 21.2 to implement the *Loop/Exit* construction.

a. Use *GoTo* statements, with any necessary labels, to implement a *While* loop.

b. Use *GoTo* statements, with any necessary labels, to implement a *Repeat–Until* loop.

These problems suggest general ways that Pascal loops might be handled in BASIC or FORTRAN.

21.3 *Nested Loops and Exit Statements.* The *Loop/Exit* concept can be extended to include nested loops. In Ada this is done by placing an identifier at the end of each loop to label the loop and by specifying the appropriate identifier in the *Exit* statement. For example, the summation loop of Section 21.2 could be rewritten

```
Loop
          Read(Value);
          Exit Loop1 When (Value = Last);
          Sum := Sum + Value;
     End Loop Loop1;
```

Here, the loop is identified as *Loop1,* and the *Exit* statement refers to this loop.

a. Rewrite the main loop of the quicksort in Section 21.2, labeling this loop *Main.*

b. Expand the summation problem of Section 21.2 so that several data sets are read. In this case,
   1. compute and print the sum of each set separately;
   2. compute the total sum of the data sets; and
   3. end each data set with a negative number as sentinel, except that the final data set will use the sentinel 0.

In each of these parts, write the program using *Loop/Exit* statements and label each loop.

21.4 *Nested Loops and Exit Statements in Pascal.* Translate the Ada-like code of the previous problem into strict Pascal, using the *GoTo* to implement an *Exit* statement.

21.5 *Translation of Loop/Exit Statements to Pascal.* With the labeling of loops mentioned in Exercise 21.3, it is possible to translate *Loop–Exit* statements into Standard Pascal mechanically, as follows.

1. We can maintain a table that associates a number with each label identifier.

Then, we read the program.

2. When new identifiers are declared, a new number can be entered into the table.

3. When *Exit* statements are encountered, we can insert a *GoTo* with the appropriate number from the table.

4. When *End Loop* statements are encountered, we can add the appropriate label number to the next statement after the loop.

With this outline of major tasks, write a program that will read as input a Pascal program containing *Label* identifiers, and *Loop* and *Exit* statements. Your program should then produce a revised program, written in Standard Pascal, which translates the *Loop/Exit* statements to appropriate *GoTos* with labels.

21.6 *Avoiding GoTos.* An important classical result of theoretical computer science states that *GoTo* statements can be eliminated from any program, as long as the language contains certain loops (*Whiles*) and conditional expressions (*Ifs*) and as long as additional variables can be added.[2] However, although this result guarantees that *GoTos* are not strictly necessary, it does not directly address the issue of program structure or clarity. To illustrate this, rewrite procedure *Compute* (Version 2) from Section 21.3, eliminating the *GoTo* statement.

HINT: In this revision, you will need to test for errors every time function *FindSum* is used.

---

[2] This result was first proved in Corrado Bohm and Guiseppe Jacopini, "Flow-diagrams, Turing machines, and languages with only two formation rules," *Communications of the ACM,* Vol. 9, No. 5, May, 1966, pp. 366–371. This result is expanded in H. D. Mills, "Mathematical foundations for structured programming," Report FSC 72–6012, IBM Federal Systems Division, Gaithersburg, MD, February, 1972.

CHAPTER 22

HARDWARE AND

OPERATING

SYSTEMS

We began this text by describing the problem solving process and by giving a brief overview of the pieces of hardware involved in a computer. We described the main pieces of this environment that we encounter when we write Pascal programs. Since the first chapter, we have gained considerably more expertise in solving problems, and we have studied many aspects of programming and data structures while trying to solve problems.

In this final chapter, we return to the machine environment for a closer look at the hardware and operating systems that we have come to take for granted. In this discussion, we will be able to apply many of the principles that we have developed for problem solving and software design. For example, the machine environment, like well structured programs, is divided into several distinct pieces. Further, with the interplay of software with the machine environment, we find that in some cases, a machine may be built to take advantage of well organized code. Thus, well structured programs not only may be easy to read, correct, and modify; they also may run very efficiently.

SECTION 22.1   OPERATION SYSTEM FUNCTIONS

Throughout our work with computers, we have taken for granted many features of the computing environment. For example, we have certain expectations in the following situations.

1. When we ask for a program or a data file that is stored within the machine, we expect the machine to locate the appropriate information.
2. If several people are using terminals connected to the same CPU, we expect not only that the machine will keep track of which user is doing what operations but also that the computer will schedule its time fairly among the various users.
3. If several tasks require the same equipment, we expect the computer to allocate that equipment in a reasonable way. For example, if several files are to be printed, we expect the machine to print one file at a time, while it keeps track of pending print requests.
4. When we type at a terminal, we expect the terminal and CPU to communicate correctly. Further, if we change terminals, we expect the CPU to accommodate the new equipment.

These examples illustrate the wide variety of tasks that must be performed within a computer. In practice, some such tasks may be done by the electrical circuitry (or hardware) itself, and other tasks may be done by programs that other people have written and that are stored within the machine for our use. As we move from one machine to another, we may find that a particular task is performed by hardware in one case but by software in the other. However, in each machine, we can expect that many such tasks are performed by some combination of hardware and software.

In computer systems, many of these programs are grouped in a single conceptual entity, called an **operating system.** In this section, we discuss some of the primary tasks that are performed by operating systems. If we think of the activity within a computer as being analogous to the flow of traffic in a city, then the operating system behaves as the "traffic cops" of the city, regulating the flow so that everyone gets to his or her destination.

Storage and Retrieval

In Section 20.3, we noted that a computer normally stores file information in a directory. One function of the operating system is to maintain file directories and to perform the detailed tasks of locating the needed data and transferring that data between disk and main memory. For example, when processing involves the use of a file, the computer uses the directory to find the file on the disk. In addition, the CPU must tell a disk drive to move its read/write head to an appropriate track and then move the needed data between the disk and a buffer.

Section 20.3 also noted that in many machines, file directories might be organized into a tree structure, where different nodes might correspond to different types of data or different users.

Further, with this structure, we noted that the computer has routines to update file directories, insert new files, delete or erase old files, move files from one place to another, and check if a file may be accessed by a specified user.

These tasks all represent one important aspect of an operating system, which includes the general storage and retrieval of information within the computer. In this text, we have limited our discussion of such work to file storage on disks. The operating system must perform similar work when storage involves other devices as well, such as tapes and drums.

Scheduling

Virtually all large computers and many small ones have the capability of allowing several processing tasks to occur in parallel. For example, a microcomputer might allow a user to print one file on a printer while the user goes on to another job. A minicomputer or a larger machine may allow several users to work at terminals at the same time. This scheduling of processing is another major task performed by the operating system.

In such situations, a single CPU must handle several separate tasks; the computer must split its time among various requests. Typically, this division of work is done by setting an interim time limit for each processing request and by maintaining a queue of requests. With such a time limit, the CPU works on one job until the time limit expires or until the job is done. If the job finishes early, the CPU goes on to the next request. However, if the time limit expires before the job is done, then the work is interrupted and the task is put back on the queue so that processing can resume later.

Resource Allocation

Beyond issues of scheduling, processing several tasks in parallel also requires the computer to allocate various machine resources among these tasks. As with storage, retrieval, and scheduling, this **resource allocation** is included in the work of operating systems.

For example, when several users are working at different terminals, the computer must keep track of the data and instructions that are needed by each user. The work on one user's job must not be confused with the work for another. Again, the operating system is responsible for keeping processing requests separate. At the very least, such bookkeeping involves the division of main memory into various pieces, so that each user will have some room for his or her data. The operating system then must keep track of which data belong to which user.

More generally, this allocation of resources among tasks may extend well beyond the simple division of main memory to the allocation of other devices as well. We can look at three examples to demonstrate that this can become quite complex.

As our first example, suppose that two users want to print files at the same time on the same printer. The operating system can start one job printing, but the other file must wait. (We would not want various lines of the files interleaved.)

As a more subtle example, suppose two people share the same checking account and suppose each person wants to withdraw $50. The typical code might follow this outline:

I. Read old balance from file.
II. Deduct $50 from balance.
III. Write revised balance to file.

This outline works fine unless the two people go to different automatic teller machines and request the transaction at the same time. The difficulty of concurrent processing is shown for a balance of $200 in Figure 22–1. Here, the machine could read the same $200 balance for both Mary and Fred. Then, each person would receive $50 and this amount would be deducted from the $200. The new balance of $150 would then be written back to the file twice.

The difficulty here is that both transactions start with the original $200, since that was the original balance and since Step I. for both Mary and Fred occurred simultaneously before either transaction finished. To resolve this situation, an operating system must require one task to finish before the other starts. (First one job can use the file, then the other.)

As a third example, while an operating system can allocate resources to tasks, this allocation is complicated when two tasks request the same resources. In such situations, it is possible for each task to be waiting for the other. This is illustrated in the following example, where both Mary and Fred want to transfer money from a savings to a checking account. The previous example shows that the operating system must allow only one user to have access to the account file at a time. This could result in the following sequence.

Mary

• Gain access to savings
• Gain access to checking

FIGURE 22–1 • **Concurrent Deduction of $50 from a Checking Account**

	Mary's Processing		Fred's Processing
Step I.	$200	Read Old Balance from File	$200
Step II.	$150	Deduct $50	$150
Step III.	$150	Write Revised Balance	$150

- Transfer money
- Relinquish access to checking
- Relinquish access to savings.

Here, Mary's job specifies that she be given access to each file. Once this access is achieved, money is transferred, and the access rights are relinquished. The idea here is that Mary's request for access of a file prevents others from using that file until she is done.

This approach is fine, again, as long as Fred and Mary process their requests separately. However, consider this request.

Fred

- Gain access to checking
- Gain access to savings
- Transfer money
- Relinquish access to savings
- Relinquish access to checking

With this code, it is possible for Mary to gain access to savings while Fred gains access to checking. Then, each person would have to wait to gain access to the other account before transferring money. However, since each account is now tied up, further access is impossible. Such a situation is called **deadlock,** and this problem can complicate considerably the issues of resource allocation and scheduling.

Terminal Handling

Still another task that is often performed by the operating system involves the transmission of data between the CPU or main memory and a terminal. Here, transmission difficulties can arise because different terminals have distinct characteristics. For example, different terminals may expect data to be transmitted at different speeds; the format of data may vary; the capabilities of terminals may vary; and terminals may interpret characters differently.

With all of these variations among terminals, the operating system often maintains a table for each terminal containing various details of data transmission. Then, before the operating system actually sends data to a terminal, the operating system may look up details of transmission in the table, so the appropriate data will be sent and received correctly.

In all of these areas—storage and retrieval, scheduling, resource allocation, and terminal handling—the operating system keeps track of various technical details that are needed for processing users' requests. In each case, these details may include considerable subtlety and complexity, and individual users normally do not want to worry about these low-level tasks. Thus, they are grouped in an operating system, which frees users for other work.

SECTION 22.2   A TYPICAL MACHINE ENVIRONMENT

We can think of the operating system of a computer as running behind the scenes of our Pascal programs. At a still more hidden level, we can consider the physical hardware that follows our instructions. This level of the computer involves the actual circuitry and mechanical devices that fit together to form the computer. These physical objects comprise the **hardware** of a computer. (See Figure 22–2.) In Chapter 1, we reviewed hardware at a general level; in this section, we consider machine organization in more detail.

A typical organization of machinery in a computer is shown in Figure 22–3. In general, this equipment can be organized into the following categories:

- Central Processing Units
    Instruction decoder
    Arithmetic and logic unit
    Registers
- Memory
    Cache memory
    Main memory
    Secondary storage devices
- Other peripherals
    Terminals
    Printers
    Graphics equipment

In the rest of this section, we look at each of these categories more carefully.

FIGURE 22–2 • **Levels of Activity within a Computer**

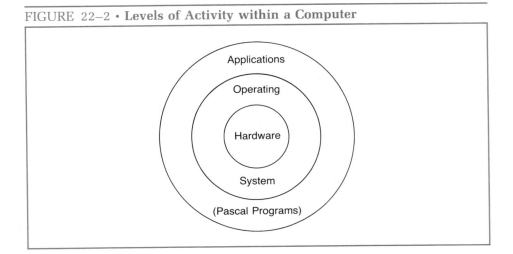

FIGURE 22–3 · **A Typical Machine Environment**

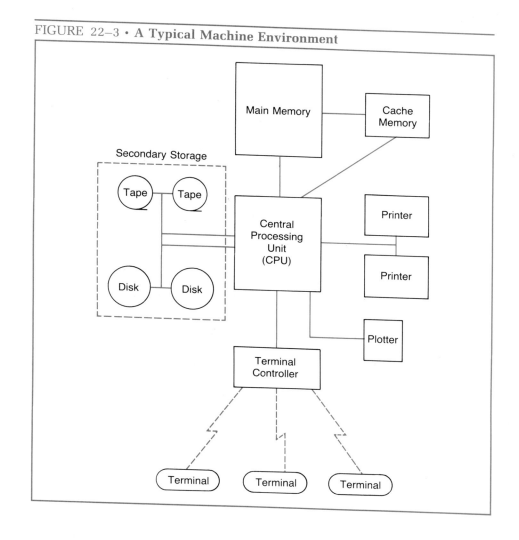

Central Processing Unit (CPU)

We have noted that the CPU is the piece of equipment that controls all activity within a computer. Within the CPU itself, this control responsibility may be broken down further into several tasks, including

decoding software intructions;

following arithmetic and logic instructions; and

storing intermediate values.

Some of these tasks may be obvious; others are more subtle. Figure 22–4 shows a more detailed view of a typical CPU.

FIGURE 22–4 • **Central Processing Unit (CPU)**

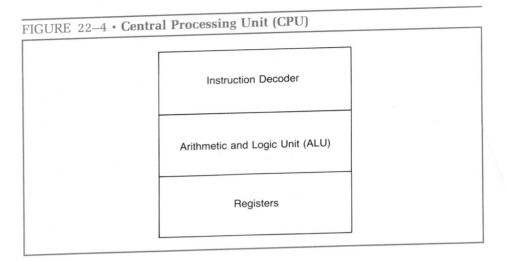

Instruction Decoder

Arithmetic and Logic Unit (ALU)

Registers

Decoding. Clearly, a computer must be built to follow instructions that it is given. Thus, it must contain circuitry that can recognize each machine language instruction. The CPU must be able to decide what each instruction means before processing can proceed. Thus, each computer contains some circuitry that acts as an **instruction decoder.**

In practice, such decoding may involve several steps, and the decoder may take advantage of several shortcuts to speed up the process. For example, structured code proceeds linearly through a program much of the time. The machine does not need to jump from one point in the program to another. Thus, an instruction decoder may try to overlap some of its interpreting of various instructions. For example, consider a simple piece of machine code to perform the Pascal statement

    A := B + C

In machine language, this may take the form of three instructions.

    Find the value of B.

    Add the value of C.

    Store the result in storage location A.

Some overlapping of this processing is shown in Figure 22–5. At Time 1, the computer starts decoding the *Find* instruction. At Time 2, the computer continues decoding *Find* and begins decoding *Add*. At Time 3, the computer executes the *Find* instruction, continues decoding *Add*, and begins decoding *Store*. With such overlapping, different circuits in the CPU can be working at the same time, and processing can be speeded up substantially.

FIGURE 22–5 • **Decoding and Executing A := B + C**

Time			
1	Begin decoding *Find.*		
2	Begin decoding *Add.*	Finish decoding *Find.*	
3	Begin decoding *Store.*	Finish decoding *Add.*	Execute *Find.*
4		Finish decoding *Store.*	Execute *Add.*
5			Execute *Store.*

Of course, with this overlapping, the machine must make allowances in case the instruction being executed involves a jump (e.g., a *GoTo* or a procedure call). In this case, any partial decoding must be thrown away, and the machine must locate, decode, and execute the appropriate new instructions.

Overlapping of processing strongly supports arguments that *GoTo* statements should be minimized, for they interrupt the efficient overlapping of instruction decoding and execution. Thus, *GoTos* not only make programs harder to read; they may also make programs run more slowly.

Other parts of a CPU.   Beyond the instruction decoder in a CPU, two specialized pieces of circuitry also may be identified.

The **Arithmetic and Logic Unit (ALU)** executes instructions once they are decoded. This normally involves two basic tasks.

1. Arithmetic, such as addition, subtraction, multiplication, and division, may be required for the instruction.
2. Values may need to be compared and the machine may need to act on the basis of that comparison. (For example, the execution of an *If* statement depends upon comparisons in a Boolean expression.)

When the ALU operates, it typically uses some particularly fast storage locations, called **registers,** for some of its work. For example, when we suggested a translation of *A := B + C* into machine language, we wrote

Find the value for *B.*

Add the value of *C.*

Store the result in the location *A.*

In each case, the work involved uses one of these registers. Thus, the value for *B* is stored in one register; the value for the sum is stored in a second register; and this final value is copied from the second register to location *A.*

Similarly, when we use arrays in our work, base addresses and offsets are often stored in registers for fast, efficient reference.

Memory and Storage

So far in this text, we have identified two basic areas for data storage, **main memory** and **disk storage.** After we look at main memory more carefully, we will also identify two additional storage areas.

Main memory.   This is a rather fast storage area, relying exclusively upon electrical circuitry. We can identify several parts of main memory that have specific functions. (See Figure 22–6.)

In many machines, some instructions are permanently stored within main memory; the instructions are coded in the circuitry itself. This type of memory is called **Read Only Memory** or **ROM.** For example, parts of an operating system may be stored in ROM, so the machine will know what to do when it is turned on.

As a second example, some programming packages, such as language compilers for microcomputers, may be packaged so that they are physically plugged in to the memory of the machine. Here, instructions are placed in ROM for permanent reference.

These examples illustrate the primary features of ROM: information in ROM is stored permanently and cannot be erased or modified. This infor-

FIGURE 22–6 • **Main Memory-Single User**

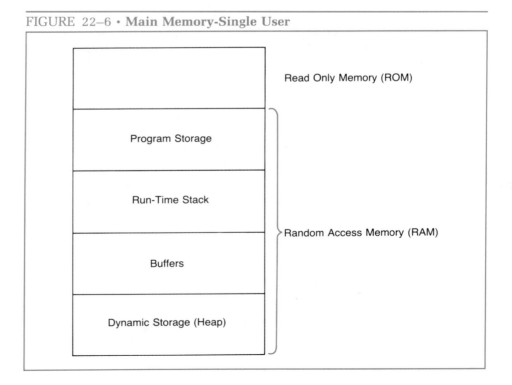

mation remains when electric power is turned off, and ROM instructions therefore can be used for permanent storage.

In contrast to ROM, users' programs and most other data involved in the processing of a task is stored in **Random Access Memory** or **RAM.** Data in RAM may be accessed quickly, changed as needed, and retrieved in any order. Thus, RAM is particularly useful in storing programs and data while processing is under way.

However, such storage normally is erased when a computer is turned off, so RAM is not helpful for long-term storage.

Within RAM several distinct areas are often allocated when a program is compiled. In particular, room is reserved for the instructions of the program; the run-time stack; buffers; and dynamic storage allocation.

When a machine is used for a single application, the overall allocation of main memory is as shown in Figure 22–6. When several tasks are scheduled concurrently, the large RAM is divided into pieces for each user. Then for each user, RAM may be subdivided as shown in Figure 22–7. Here, multiple users may share instructions in ROM, since no user data can be stored in these locations. Only RAM needs to be divided into pieces when multiple tasks are processed.

FIGURE 22–7 • **Main Memory-Multiple Users**

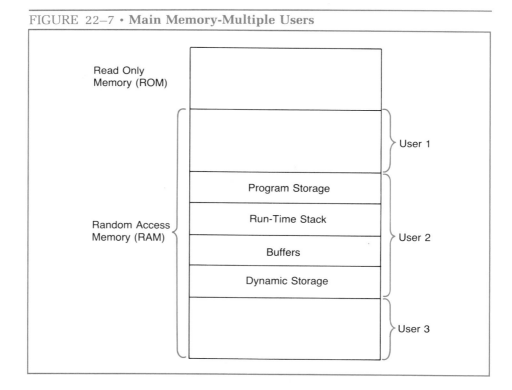

Beyond main memory and disk storage, we also mention a couple of additional types.

Tape Storage.   This has many of the same characteristics as disk storage; the major difference is that data are stored on tape (much like audio tape) instead of on disk.

- Tape storage involves mechanical activity as well as electrical activity. Tape must be moved from one reel to another before appropriate data can be found.
- Buffers are normally used to help increase tape efficiency because blocks of data can then be transferred between main memory and tape.
- Tape storage must be done sequentially, from start to finish, just as Pascal disk files. We cannot jump to a middle point in a tape without first reading all data starting at the beginning of the tape. Unlike Pascal disk files, however, there is no convenient way to bypass this sequential nature of tape files, and random access to tape is not possible.

Cache Memory.   Finally, some machines include yet another type of memory, called **cache memory,** which duplicates some information in main memory to improve performance.

We have already noted that program execution often proceeds linearly through code, and we have seen that instruction decoding may take advantage of this observation. When we expand this idea to include loops, we find that most work is localized in small pieces of code. (This is called the **Principle of Locality.**) We may loop through one section of code many times, but that section is not likely to contain large numbers of instructions. For this reason, some computers use a very fast main memory to store small sections of instructions or data. Each time the CPU finds some information in main memory, that information is also placed in the cache. Then if the same information (instructions or data) is needed again soon, the CPU can go to the higher speed cache memory so that processing can proceed more quickly than if only main memory is used.

The details of cache memory, like the details of instruction decoding, may be quite complex and may vary greatly from one machine to another. (Some machines may not use a cache at all; others may use it extensively.) However, even without these details, we still can conclude that processing is likely to go more quickly if we organize our code into small pieces, so our various program pieces will fit well into any cache memory that might be available. Since this orientation toward organization again follows from our structured programming principles, we see that cache memory provides yet another argument in favor of our top-down methodology.

Other Peripheral Devices

We have already identified disk drives and tape units as devices that are physically distinct from the CPU and main memory. In addition to the peripherals, such as terminals, we are already familiar with, we note one further type of device that is commonly used in many computers, called the **controller.**

We have noted that data from terminals or to printers must be interpreted by the operating system, so that this data will be formatted correctly and interpreted properly. When computers need to communicate with several devices, the communication details can require a significant amount of processing, and the CPU may spend much of its time on these matters. Thus, in many computers, a large portion of these details may be split off onto a separate device, called a controller, which handles communication processing. For example, a terminal controller might monitor several terminals waiting for a user to enter data. Then, when the data are received, the controller may place them in a buffer and tell the CPU that information is now ready for processing. Such work by a controller can free up the CPU considerably, and the overall computer then may be able to process large tasks relatively quickly.

SECTION 22.3   EXAMPLE: TRACING THE EXECUTION OF A SIMPLE PROGRAM

Now that we have taken a closer look at the various functions of operating systems and the various hardware components of a computer, it is instructive to trace the execution of a simple program through this array of individual pieces to see how they work together. To begin, we assume the following simple Pascal program has been compiled and stored in a disk file.

```
Program Convert (Input, Output);
{This program converts quarts to liters}
Var Quarts, Liters: Real;

Begin
    Write ('Enter value of quarts: ');
    Readln (Quarts);
    Liters := Quarts / 1.056710;
    Writeln (Quarts:1:1, ' quarts = ', Liters:1:2, ' liters.')
End {Main} .
```

Throughout the processing of this program, the CPU controls all operations within the computer, so we must understand that the CPU must constantly direct the various pieces of hardware and execute instructions from the operating system. Beyond this activity of the CPU, we consider work involving the

terminal,

terminal controller,

terminal input and output buffers in main memory,

program storage area in main memory,

run-time stack area in main memory,

disk, and

CPU registers.

and we follow the necessary instructions from the operating system. The overall flow of activities is outlined in Figure 22–8.

FIGURE 22–8 • **Running a Simple Program**

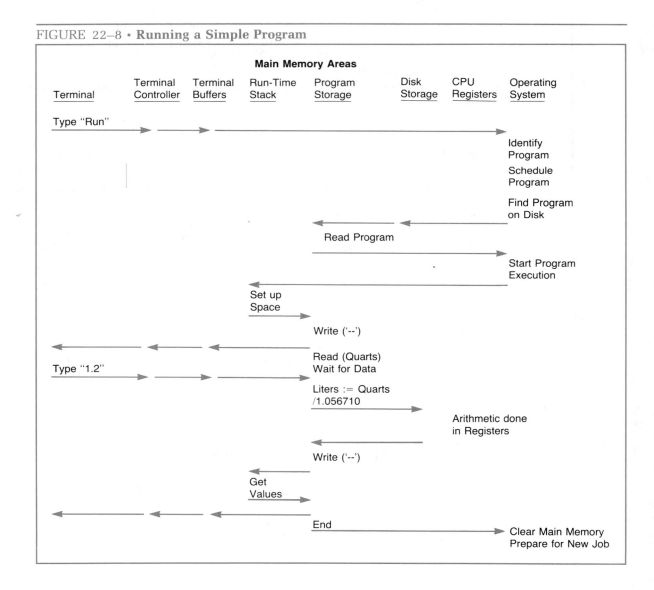

To begin running our program, we type an appropriate command at our terminal, such as

Run Convert

As we type these characters, our terminal transmits them to a terminal controller, and the data are placed in an input buffer within main memory to await processing.

When we hit the return key, the operating system takes over, by following several steps.

1. The operating system interprets the word *Run* to mean that we want to execute a specific program.
2. The operating system identifies the desired program *Convert* and places it on a queue of tasks awaiting processing.
3. When the time comes for *Convert* to be run, the operating system looks up *Convert* in a disk directory to identify where this program is stored.
4. The operating system issues a command to the disk drive unit to read the program information from the appropriate location on disk and place it in the program storage area of main memory. (This reading of data from disk may first transfer data to a disk buffer and then to the program storage area of main memory, or the data transfer may proceed in one step.)
5. The operating system initializes the run-time stack for the program. (At this point, the size of the stack is initialized to 0.)
6. The operating system starts the program. As the program proceeds, the operating system may monitor that work is progressing correctly.

When the program itself begins, again the computer proceeds in several steps.

Step 1: Space for global variables is allocated on the run-time stack. Buffer space for input and output is also created.

Step 2: The computer begins executing the instructions for the program.

Step 3: The first statement executed is a *Write* statement, and this requires several activities:

a. The character string to be printed is placed in the output buffer.
b. The terminal controller is notified to transmit these characters to the terminal. (This may be done directly, or our program may call the operating system which in turn signals the controller.)
c. The terminal controller sends the data in the appropriate format to the terminal, where our message is printed.

Step 4: The next statement involves a *Readln*. Here, the CPU must wait for data to be typed. While the CPU waits,

a. We type our data (e.g. "1.2") at the terminal.
b. These data are transmitted to the terminal controller, which places the data in a terminal input buffer.

c. When we hit the return key, the controller (or the operating system that monitors this reading) identifies that the needed data are now present.

The program instructions now move this data from the buffer to the appropriate storage location on the run-time stack. (This movement of data may actually require two steps, first going from the buffer to a CPU register and then from the register to the stack.)

Step 5: The third Pascal statement involves a computation of liters. Here, the value for *Quarts* and the conversion factor 1.056710 are moved to CPU registers so the actual arithmetic can be performed. The result is then stored back on the run-time stack.

Step 6: The last Pascal statement involves another *Writeln*. As in Step 3, this requires data transfer to buffers for transmission to the terminal. Here, however, some preliminary steps are needed.

a. Values for *Quarts* and *Liters* must be retrieved from the run-time stack.
b. These values must be formatted correctly following the specification in the program.
c. The formatted data must be transformed to character data, so it can be transmitted.
d. Other characters in the *Writeln* statement message string must be added.
e. The complete, formatted character string must then be moved to the terminal output buffer.

At this point, printing can proceed as in Step 3.

Step 7: When we reach the end of the Pascal program, control must be returned to the operating system. At this point, the operating system

a. clears main memory,
b. removes our task from the queue of tasks awaiting processing, and
c. prepares for a new processing task.

Beyond this outline, we may make a few general observations. First of all, whenever we type data into the computer, either the operating system or some other module must interpret what we type. For example, when we type a value for *Quarts* (e.g., "1.2"), this data must be transformed from a sequence of characters to a number. Such work may be embedded within the Pascal *Read* procedure, or it may be part of a standard operating system task. In any case, such processing is always part of any reading operation.

Throughout program execution, the operating system normally monitors activities in several ways. For example, if the program has run for a long time, the operating system may interrupt processing so that other tasks can proceed as well. Then, when these other tasks have had their turn, our program may be allowed to continue. Similarly, if our program encounters various difficulties, the operating system may intervene. For example, our program may be halted if we try to divide by 0; or our program may be stopped if the operating system cannot find a file that we try to *Reset*. In each case, the operating system may detect that an error has occurred, and it may step in to prevent further processing.

In many of the tasks described, various procedures (e.g., Pascal *Read* and *Write* procedures or operating system functions) often use the CPU registers for holding intermediate values. Thus, while our discussion only referred explicitly to the CPU registers at a few places, these registers are normally used during most other steps as well.

Tracing this program illustrates how various components of a computer can work together effectively in executing a program. This example also shows that whole computing systems follow the same structured principles that we have stressed throughout this text. In particular, in running an entire program, the computer must perform a great many tasks, and these tasks are divided into many smaller units, spread over pieces of hardware and software. Each individual piece plays a specific role, and these pieces are structured within a computing system so they can work together to perform our entire task.

SECTION 22.4	SYSTEM CONFIGURATIONS

Now that we have identified various parts within a computer system, we need to look at larger systems, where several computing units may be placed together to form a single entity.

Chips

To begin, we consider the individual pieces of hardware in which much electrical circuitry is found. Circuitry for computers typically is integrated into complex pieces, called **chips,** and each chip contains a logical piece of the computer. For example, the CPU may be composed of a single chip in a microcomputer. Other chips may comprise main memory.[1]

In recent years, this integration of circuitry has involved placing more and more capacity on a single chip. Thus, with **Very Large Scale Integration (VLSI),** we find single chips that have very great storage capacity and computing power.

For a given computational or storage capacity, the cost of individual chips generally is decreasing. This trend implies that more chips can be put together within a system to provide more power with no increase in cost compared to previous years. With a decrease in costs of chips, more computing power is now placed in terminals, disk devices, controllers, etc.

---

[1]Normally, memory is specified in terms of the number of words or bytes that it contains. Traditionally in science, size is measured in thousands (kilo-) or millions (mega-). In computer science, however, the binary system has dominated terminology. Thus, 1 kilobyte is $1024 = 2^{10}$ bytes and 1 megabyte is $1,048,576 = 2^{20}$ bytes.

Thus, more work is now done outside the main CPU than has been possible in the past.

Greater storage capacity on chips has allowed the size of main memory in computers to increase dramatically. In the past, main memory often was rather small, since such memory was quite expensive. Memory sizes are now much larger without being prohibitively expensive. The recent developments allowing the manufacture of powerful, inexpensive chips have dramatically affected the ways that pieces are now commonly put together.

Master–Slave Configurations

In large centralized systems, we typically find that one CPU may control the overall flow of processing, but several other CPUs may work following the commands they are given. Here, the main CPU acts as a **master,** performing the critical functions and making the major decisions. If this CPU is particularly powerful, it may also do major processing tasks. In this context, other CPUs function as **slaves,** following the commands of the master and performing tasks that free the master to do other work. For example, upon instructions from the master, a slave CPU may process all input from a terminal, removing any characters deleted by the user and placing a corrected message in a buffer in main memory. The slave then may tell the master CPU that the input is available, so the master can proceed with processing.

Networks

In contrast, with the availability of small microcomputers, systems may be built in which each CPU functions relatively independently. In this context, computers may be linked together to form a **network.** In a network, individual computers may work separately on some types of processing. Then, as the need arises, one machine may send another machine a message requesting information. Once a request is made, processing for the job on the first machine may be suspended until an appropriate message is received from the other machine. In such networks, each computer largely works by itself, processing its own work and responding to questions from other machines. Here, no one computer controls the activities of the others; rather, machines work in parallel, and we say that processing is distributed over several machines. Between these two extremes of master/slave configurations and **distributed processing** networks, we find many intermediate configurations, where a central computer controls certain functions for the overall system but where local, distributed machines also have some independent control for other tasks.

With this configuration, it is interesting to note that the general trend of recent years has been from the large, centralized systems to the networks of computers. Much of this trend has been made possible by the decreasing cost of chips and the advent of powerful, relatively inexpensive microcomputers. Developments with the transmission of messages and the linking procedures for computers have also aided this process.

SECTION 22.5   SYSTEM RELIABILITY

Now that we have reviewed the hardware involved in computers, we need to ask how reliable that hardware might be. In using computers, we need to know how much we can rely upon the results that we might obtain.

In Chapter 11 and in Section 16.4, we have considered part of this question in relation to software and data entry. Now we need to consider the reliability of hardware in performing the operations it is instructed to follow.

Hardware Errors

Generally, we find that current hardware circuitry is extremely reliable, and any hardware errors that do occur normally are detected automatically. This level of accuracy arises for several reasons. First, hardware circuitry often contains extra bits of data and extra electrical circuits to constantly monitor the validity of data that it stores. For example, in Section 11.6, we saw that we could add check digits to numbers so machines could catch various data entry errors. This same approach is commonly used within circuitry so that hardware can determine if data within a chip is miscopied from one address to another. When errors are detected, hardware may contain circuitry to repeat an instruction so that a correct result may be obtained on a second try.

Similarly, in transmitting data from one machine to another, various formal rules, or **communication protocols,** are followed to verify that data are sent and received correctly. It is quite possible that electrical static, or "noise," is present on transmission lines, and extra bits of data may be received during data transmission. However, with various protocols involving check bits, such transmission errors are routinely detected, and retransmission can be attempted automatically.

Many machines contain specific programs or circuitry that allows hardware components to be tested explicitly. For example, main memory may be tested by storing known data in each storage location and then checking that the actual data returned from main memory agree with the data sent to memory.

With such checking built into hardware circuitry, few undetected errors are likely to arise from circuitry or data transmission. We normally can be quite confident that any unknown errors we encounter are not due to circuitry itself; such errors usually are detected as they occur. However, storage of data on disks or tapes does involve somewhat greater risks of error because these storage devices require both electrical and mechanical activities. In practice, many electrical checks may be used for disks and tapes just as checks may be used for testing main memory storage or data transmission. Thus, when using disk or tape storage, electrical errors usually are not a primary problem. Rather, we need to focus more on physical difficulties with a disk, tape, or read/write mechanisms.

For example, an individual disk or tape stores data in patterns of magnetic charges. Thus, if we bring a disk or tape near a magnetic field, we may change the data stored. In this context, we need to be aware that data storage actually involves very low magnetic levels, and the static electricity in our fingers may be enough to modify data. Hence, we must be particularly careful in handling tapes or disks so that we do not touch an area where data are stored.

As a second example, a disk read/write head must move to a specified location before reading or writing data can occur. Such work requires the careful alignment of the read/write head so that data will be placed at an appropriate place. Unfortunately, if this alignment is altered, an entire disk may become unreadable.

As a final example, disks must turn for appropriate data to be found, and read/write heads must be located close to the disks so that magnetic charges can be detected. This mechanical activity must be done within small, precise tolerances for data storage and transmission to occur. Unfortunately, such tolerances create a potential for errors to arise in several ways.

"Hard" disks rotate constantly at high rates of speed. In such a situation, vibration or a misaligned disk head may cause the head to touch the disk itself. Such a head touch on a fast moving disk may cause the entire disk to disintegrate, ruining the whole disk and the disk drive itself. Such problems arise only rarely; however, hard disks can store large amounts of data, so much can be lost.

Soft or "floppy" disks rotate at lower speeds and often remain stationary until specific data are needed. On the other hand, floppy disks are more fragile than hard disks and are often handled more frequently. Thus, there is a reasonable likelihood that physical damage may occur.

In both of these cases, electrical circuitry in a computer may be able to detect that data read from a disk have been corrupted, and a user may be able to tell that a problem has been detected. Unfortunately, tapes and disks often contain large amounts of data, so correcting this problem may be very difficult and time consuming.

Recovery

Now that we have identified the possible sources of hardware problems, we need to consider how we might respond to such trouble. Obviously, the first part of our corrective work must be to fix the hardware; we might replace a chip or a circuit board or install a new disk drive. However, this repair resolves only part of our problem. We also need to recover the data we might have lost due to the error.

Here, we can identify two types of recovery: restoration of information in the CPU or main memory, and restoration of secondary memory, such as disks or tapes.

Restoration of Programs/Main Memory. The most common way to recover programs that have been running is to start them over again. This approach is particularly useful when programs are short. We just repeat our previous work, duplicating what happened when the computer detected an error.

With larger programs involving considerable data or processing, we may need to be somewhat more careful, however. We may want to record our data on a disk during processing, and we may want our program to record what it has done on a file as well. Then, if the program is interrupted, we can go to the disk file to determine what work had been done. With this information, we may be able to resume processing close to where the machine stopped.

Restoration of Disks or Tapes. The problem of recovery is more severe, however, if a disk or tape becomes unreadable, because these storage devices hold large amounts of data that may be difficult to duplicate. Thus, for disk or tape files, we may need to take some special actions to guard against possible disk problems. Here, we mention three of the common preventive measures that may be taken.

1. On a regular basis, we may copy our data from one disk or tape to another. This copying gives us a **backup** disk or tape. Then, if a problem arises with one disk or tape, we will have another copy that we can use.
2. As information comes into the CPU or as files are updated, we may log all incoming messages or file changes on a separate disk or tape. With this **audit trail,** we have a permanent record of all activity involved with processing, so we can reconstruct any processing that has occurred since our last disk or tape backup.
3. We may record all data in parallel on different disks, so that we have at least two duplicate copies of all data at any moment. Then, if one disk becomes unusable, the **duplicate copy** may be used. With this approach, we must be careful that the two drives really work independently, so that one failure does not destroy both copies.

With any of these techniques, we must allocate some extra time, effort, or resources to record or duplicate data, so these techniques are not without some cost. However, this cost is offset by reducing the potential risk of loss that could occur if all data were lost.

In business, it is not unknown for a company to go bankrupt because it lost all of its records when a disk drive damaged a disk. In such cases, the company could no longer function because it no longer knew the status of any of its accounts. Similar problems may arise if inventory is stored exclusively on a disk. In such circumstances, special care must be taken so that data can be reconstructed if machinery malfunctions. Thus, backup disks, extensive audit trails, and duplicate copies are often used for sensitive company data. In some cases, such measures may even extend to storing copies in several locations to guard against possible damage from fire, water, lightning, etc.

Distributed Processing

Each of the above issues of reliability involve the recovery of data on a single computer, and in practice such issues are fairly well understood. These topics have been studied extensively, and common procedures have been developed to safeguard single computer systems. However, when several machines are linked together in a network, recovery problems may be somewhat more complex.

Certainly, when one computer in a network becomes disabled, we can use the ideas we have already encountered to restore its data fairly well. However, in a network, we may find that other computers may have sent requests to the disabled machine, and these computers may be awaiting a reply. In such cases, our recovery of the one machine must involve a response to pending questions so that processing elsewhere can continue. However, in this recovery, we do not want to answer requests a second time if answers have already been sent. Such practical problems can be quite hard to resolve.

Similarly, before one computer goes down, it may have sent requests for information out along a network. Thus, when we repair a computer and try to recover our data, we need to know how to respond to these replies from the network.

Theoretically, this detail of recovery may seem reasonably straightforward; in practice, this recovery of a distributed system is not as clearly understood as simple system recovery, and hard details still remain.

Social Ramifications

So far in this section, we have focused primarily on some technical aspects of computer failure, and we have considered some technical approaches to system recovery. Before leaving the subject, however, we also need to realize that computer failure has social implications as well. Below we suggest just three of the many areas where computer failure can have a major impact.

We have mentioned some implications of computer failure in business. As companies store more and more of their data on disks and tapes, they rely upon the computers more and more to be able to function. Any disruption of normal computer operations may have a considerable impact on the running of the business. For example, in Section 15.5, we noted that a single processor handles the entire TWA reservation system. In such situations, loss of a disk could be devastating unless the data stored there could be recovered, so the company must utilize many of the techniques mentioned earlier to protect itself.

In banking, account processing is sometimes distributed among several branches or regional centers. In such instances, risk of a single failure may be somewhat decreased, as each machine holds information on only a part of the bank's overall accounts. However, here, much attention also must be paid to keeping machines synchronized, so credits to one account in one branch are balanced by withdrawals from another account, perhaps in another branch. When one machine goes down and then recovers, we must be sure that no credits or withdrawals are made twice.

In the military, large numbers of computers may be tied together to monitor and track the movement of a wide variety of aircraft and ships. In such work, vast amounts of data are collected and tabulated, so that current locations of various craft can be monitored regularly. Further, these data must be sufficiently accurate and reliable, so that hostile attacks can be detected quickly and so that appropriate responses can be started. Here, computer failure must be anticipated so that an electrical or mechanical malfunction will not trigger an inappropriate or premature response. In particular, the possibility of nuclear warfare has such devastating consequences that computer reliability is an extremely vital concern in this aspect of military computing.

These three examples suggest that computer reliability, failure, and recovery are crucial issues in many computer systems, particularly those involving large or sensitive data sets. Thus, whenever such systems are being designed and built, error detection and system recovery must be considered as important parts of the overall computing environment.

We have identified some ways that we might use to help protect systems from catastrophic failure. For more information on computer reliability, particularly in the area of military systems, the interested reader might consult the *Bibliography on Reliability* compiled and published by the Computer Professionals for Social Responsibility (CPSR), P. O. Box 717, Palo Alto, CA 94301.

SECTION 22.6	CONCLUSION

With the descriptions of operating systems and hardware in this chapter, we have completed our introduction to computer science, and we have a foundation for moving on to a more concentrated study of specific topics within computer science. As we conclude, we need to observe that while this discussion of operating systems and hardware has focused on different topics in computing than our earlier topics of problem solving, algorithm design and analysis, programming, and data structures, we still have encountered many of the same common themes from this earlier work. For example, operating systems and hardware are structured in the same top-down, modular way that we used in designing our own programs. Overall, an operating system or a piece of hardware may perform several tasks, but these tasks may be divided logically into relatively small, independent modules.

This modularization within operating systems or hardware can help us isolate errors or bugs when they occur. For example, in working with files, we can determine if our troubles occur on only one disk drive. If so, we may be able to identify a mechanical problem with that drive. Also, we may find that our troubles occur only with files specified within one file directory. Such trouble may signify an operating system problem with directories. In interacting with a computer, we may encounter difficulties with a specific terminal or group of terminals. Such problems suggest hardware problems with a terminal or a controller. While working with a printer, we may find that the paper regularly advances too far for a new page or that unusual characters are printed at the start of each file. Such problems suggest an error in the device table within the operating system.

In each case, we may run tests to identify errors as being of a particular type. Then, we can trace the errors to a small module within the operating system or to a small hardware component. As with our discussion of structured programming, this modularization can help us correct hardware or operating systems as well.

In many cases, hardware may be built to take advantage of linear or structured code; instruction decoding and cache memory both help improve efficiency if our code does not jump around too much. In this way, structured code not only allows us to write, correct, and maintain programs easily; such code also may run more efficiently than nonstructured code.

Hardware and operating systems face the same issues of reliability and error handling that we addressed earlier for our programming. We did encounter some new techniques in this chapter, such as backups, audit trails, and duplication of data. However, we also saw that some of our earlier techniques, such as check digits, can be used as well.

All of these observations suggest that while each area of computer science has specialized algorithms and techniques, several areas also may depend upon some common principles. In moving beyond this introduction to computer science and studying more advanced topics, it is important to maintain this general perspective, so ideas in one field can suggest approaches or ideas in another.

SUMMARY

1. **Operating systems** perform many of the common tasks required for the smooth running of a computer, including storage and retrieval, scheduling, resource allocation, and terminal handling.
2. We can divide the functions of some hardware components into smaller pieces. Pieces of hardware might fit together in various system configurations.
3. Many of the same issues of reliability and correctness apply to hardware and operating systems as they do for general applications programming.
4. Some familiar themes carried over from our previous work in problem

solving, programming, and data structures to these new areas of operating systems and hardware. For example, we found that modularization was an important element in these newer topics just as in our previous subjects of study. Further, we found that in some ways, a well structured program not only may be easier to read, correct, and maintain than poorly structured code; the well structured program also may run more efficiently.

EXERCISES

22.1 *The Delete Key on a Terminal.* When we are typing at a terminal, each character normally is transmitted to the terminal controller as we type. However, we know we can type the delete key to discard a previous character, and our program normally is not even aware that the discarded character was once present. Use the description of operating systems and hardware in Sections 22.1 and 22.2 to show how this discarding process might take place.

22.2 *Tracing Activities Within a Computer—1.* Section 22.3 outlines the steps in the running of a simple, compiled program. Expand this outline to include the steps in compiling the program. Your outline

---

KEY TERMS, PHRASES, AND CONCEPTS

Central Processing Unit
  (CPU)
    Arithmetic and Logic
      Unit (ALU)
    Instruction Decoder
    Registers
Chips
Controllers
Communication Protocols
Deadlock
Distributed Processing
Hardware
Master-Slave Configuration
Memory
  Cache
  Main
    Random Access
      (RAM)
    Read Only (ROM)
  Secondary (disk, tape,
    etc.)

Network
Operating System
Principle of
  Locality
Resource
  Allocation
Scheduling
Storage and
  Retrieval
Terminal
  Handling
System Recovery
  Audit Trail
  Backup
  Duplicate
    Copies
Very Large Scale
  Integration
  (VLSI)

should begin as the program is first being entered into the computer, and your outline should finish when the compiled program is stored on disk, ready for running.

22.3 *Tracing Activities Within a Computer—2.* Consider the functions involved in a normal Pascal program, in an operating system, and in hardware. Then describe what tasks are required for each of the following and determine which modules (program, operating system, hardware) are involved in performing each of these tasks.

a. A program is halted when a user types "Control C" or *Reset* at the terminal.

b. A program is halted when a subscript goes out of range.

c. An error message

   Division By Zero

   is printed at the terminal, and the program continues. (On some systems, the program would be halted by this error.)

d. A program opens a file with a *Reset* statement.

e. A program rewrites a file that already existed.

f. A program halts with the error message

   Disk Read Failed on Drive A:

g. A program halts with the error message

   Invalid Memory Address

22.4 *Addresses of RAM and ROM.* When new main memory is being added to a computer, appropriate boards containing chips are normally plugged into outlets that have been installed in anticipation of such expansion. In many cases, we may add RAM at various places, so that the new memory may have any of several addresses. However, ROM must always be added at a designated location. Further, RAM boards often can be interchanged without affecting the operation of the machine, while ROM boards normally cannot be shifted around.

On the basis of the information stored in ROM and RAM and the general description of these types of memory, explain why we can be flexible in adding a RAM, while we are constrained in adding ROM.

22.5 *System Configurations—Business.*

a. Visit a local business that uses computers, such as a bank, to determine which hardware components and configuration are used.

b. Are several processors connected by a network, are machines in a master-slave hierarchy, or is some other organization used?

c. What procedures are followed to aid in the recovery of essential data? For example, are disk backups, audit trails, or data duplication techniques used?

22.6 *System Configuration—Schools, Colleges, or Universities.* Answer the questions from the previous problem for an application from your school. For example, you might talk with an administrator, a librarian, or the Registrar to see what computer applications are being used.

APPENDIX A: PASCAL LANGUAGE SUMMARY

This Appendix concisely outlines significant elements of Pascal syntax in pictorial form. The interpretation of this form follows a few simple rules.

For each syntax element, we start at the top left of a picture and follow the arrows. Then, when arrows divide, we may follow any of the possible paths. For example, Section 2.2 stated that an identifier is any sequence of letters and digits starting with a letter. On page A3, the corresponding pictorial specification begins with a <u>LETTER</u>. Then, we can follow the arrows to the end or in a loop for additional <u>DIGIT</u>s or <u>LETTER</u>s.

Next, definitions of one syntax element may include references to other elements. For example, on page A2, a <u>PROGRAM</u> starts with the reserved word **program,** followed by the <u>IDENTIFIER</u> just discussed, and possibly a list in parentheses (for Input and Output). Various declarations may follow in a specified order. In this work, each of these separate <u>PART</u>s are defined as separate syntax elements elsewhere in the Appendix. The <u>PROGRAM</u> concludes with some <u>ACTION</u> elements enclosed within the keywords **begin** and **end**.

Throughout, reserved words are printed in boldface, pre-defined identifiers are in regular lowercase letters without underlining, and syntactical elements are in capital letters and underlined.

Finally, note that this Appendix does not include a few relatively minor Standard Pascal elements, such as the *GoTo* statement of Chapter 21 and *Variant Records* of Appendix B.

SECTION A.1   SYNTAX DIAGRAMS FOR REFERENCE

PROGRAM

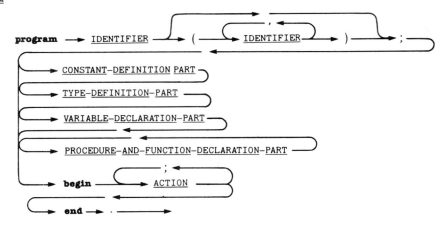

CONSTANT-DEFINITION-PART

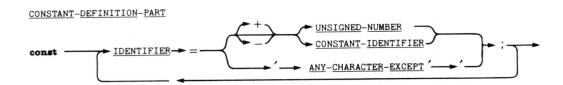

TYPE-DEFINITION-PART

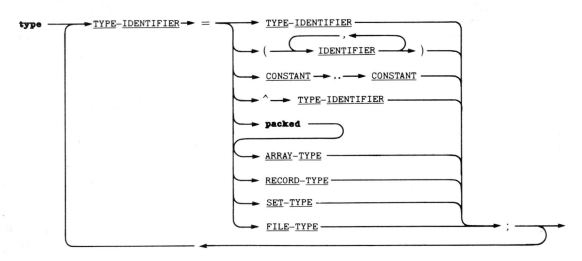

VARIABLE-DECLARATION-PART

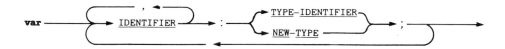

IDENTIFIER

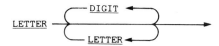

ARRAY-TYPE

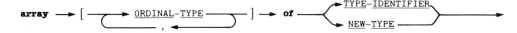

RECORD-TYPE

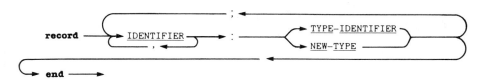

SET-TYPE

set ──▶ of ──┬─ ORDINAL-TYPE-IDENTIFIER ─┬──────▶
             └─ NEW-ORDINAL-TYPE ─────────┘

NEW-ORDINAL-TYPE

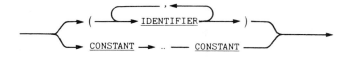

FILE-TYPE

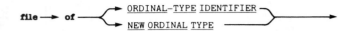

ACTION

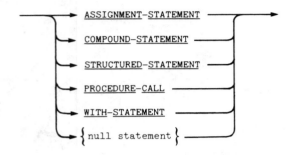

STRUCTURED-STATEMENT

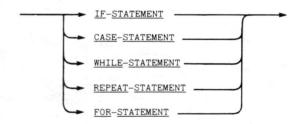

ASSIGNMENT-STATEMENT

IDENTIFIER ⟶ : = ⟶ EXPRESSION ⟶

EXPRESSION

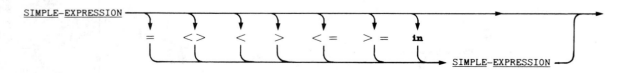

SIMPLE-EXPRESSION

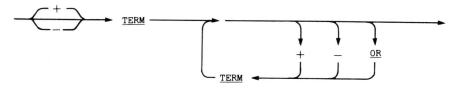

TERM

FACTOR

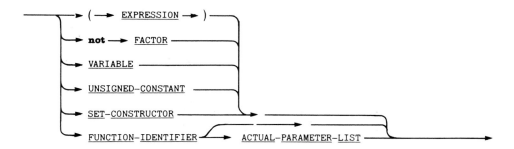

COMPOUND STATEMENT

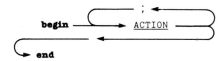

IF STATEMENT

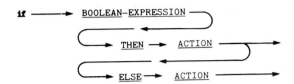

CASE STATEMENT

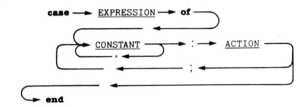

WHILE STATEMENT

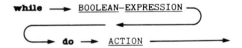

REPEAT STATEMENT

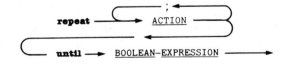

WITH STATEMENT

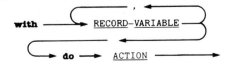

FOR STATEMENT

PROCEDURE-CALL

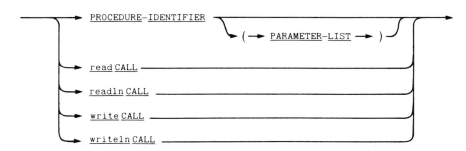

read CALL

readln CALL

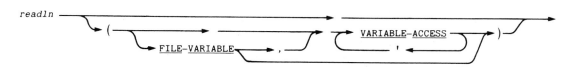

write-CALL

writeln <u>CALL</u>

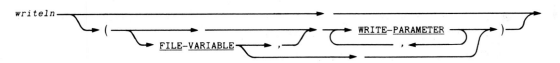

<u>WRITE-PARAMETER</u>

APPENDIX B: MACHINE REPRESENTATION OF DATA

This Appendix discusses the machine representation of data at two levels, first giving an overview of machine storage and then looking at that storage in more detail.

SECTION B.1 ## STORAGE OF REALS AND INTEGERS: AN INTRODUCTION

Chapter 2 observes that Pascal distinguishes between real numbers and integers. For example, real numbers must be written with decimal points and with at least one digit on each side of this decimal point. On the other hand, integer data contain no decimal points at all. In addition, we find that some operations, such as addition, subtraction, and multiplication, can be used for both real numbers and integers, while other operations, such as division, depend upon the type of data that we have. The properties of real numbers and integers depend upon the way each of these data types are stored.

Storage of Real Numbers

Real numbers are stored using "scientific notation," with an "exponent" and a "mantissa." The actual storage involves binary numbers (base 2), and we discuss the details of this storage in Section B.2. For now, we can think of real numbers in a decimal form (base 10). For such numbers, it turns out to be most efficient for computers to shift a decimal point, so the decimal point occurs after the first digit. Then the amount of the shift is recorded as a power of 10. (See Figure B–1.) The number with the shifted decimal point is called the **mantissa** and the power of 10 is called the **exponent**.

FIGURE B–1 · **Examples of Scientific Notation (Base 10)**

Number	Written as	Mantissa	Exponent
500.0	5.000×10^3	5.000	3
.035	3.5×10^{-2}	3.5	-2
3.1416	3.1416×10^0	3.1416	0

In computers, real numbers are stored in two parts:

mantissa	exponent

and both are considered part of the number. Further, a machine allocates the same number of digits to each mantissa. This number of digits may vary from one machine to another, but within any particular machine, all real numbers have the same number of significant digits. Figure B–2 shows the storage of numbers for a machine that allocates eight digits to each mantissa.

In this storage, some real numbers cannot be stored exactly. For example, in base 10, the number ⅓ has the decimal form 0.3333. . . . The threes go forever. If only eight digits are available, ⅓ will be stored 3.3333333×10^{-1}, and we will be off in the ninth decimal place. Further, if we multiply this value by 3, we get 9.9999999×10^{-1}, which is *not* the number 1. Therefore, while real numbers can be stored to several digits of accuracy, arithmetic need not be exact. Our example shows that

$$(1.0/3.0) * 3.0 = 0.99999999.$$

On the other hand, we can store a wide range of exponents, so real numbers may lie in quite a large range. Again, each machine has its own limits for exponents. For many machines, the (decimal) range from -38 to 38 is allowed for an exponent, so 3.257×10^{23} is an acceptable real number as is 1.583×10^{-32}. Real numbers may not be exact, but they can be used for very large and very small numbers.

Storage of Integers

In contrast, integers are stored directly, without conversion to scientific notation. This storage is exact, and all arithmetic is done exactly. Since integers do not contain decimal points, we never have to worry about how many significant digits are present.

On the other hand, each computer must allocate space for integers, just as space is needed for the mantissa and exponents of real numbers. In most

FIGURE B–2 • **Examples of Base 10 Machine Storage of Real Numbers (Here 8 digits are allocated to a mantissa)**

Number	Scientific Notation	Machine Storage Mantissa	Exponent
3.1415926535	$3.1415926535 \times 10^{1}$	3.1415927	0
500.0	5.000×10^{2}	5.0000000	2
.000003789	3.789×10^{-6}	3.7890000	-6

cases, this space constraint limits the range of integers considerably. For example, on many minicomputers and microcomputers, integers must be between -32768 and 32767 (inclusive). Thus, while integers are stored exactly and integer arithmetic does not introduce any errors, integers are restricted to a relatively narrow range of values.

SECTION B.2	BITS, BYTES, AND WORDS

On a hardware level, all work within a computer is done with electrical circuitry, and all data must be stored in a form that can be detected by that circuitry. In some early computers, data was encoded by various voltage levels. For example, zero voltage might represent a "0," a little voltage a "1," and so on, until full voltage might be a "9." However, with this encoding, circuitry had to be relatively complex so it could distinguish various voltage levels. In contrast, in all modern computers, data are stored with a simpler encoding that is based on circuits either being on or off (current flowing or not, an electrical charge being present or not). With this encoding of data, we may represent a single piece of data by

0   no current or voltage or charge

1   some current or voltage or charge

Such a single piece of data is called a **bit,** and we find that all information in a computer ultimately is translated into one or more bits.

Beyond this simplest unit of data, we often want to group bits together so that we can consider larger pieces. This is normally done in two ways: bytes and words.

A **byte** of data is composed of 8 bits. For example, the following represent one byte of information:

01001101,

11111111,

00000000,

10101010.

In practice, we find that 8 bits provide enough possible combinations so that we can encode character data easily into a byte. Such encoding is discussed in Chapter 12, and there we find that several standard codings are in common use. For example, in the ASCII Code, we may encode:

A as 01000001
[as 01011011

Here, each character is given a specific 8-bit code, and each character takes up precisely one byte of storage.

A **word** of data is composed of several bytes, although the size of a word may vary from one machine to another. A word is often the amount of data that a computer will work with at once, and the size of a word dictates the size of numbers and programs.

- If a word consists of 2 bytes (16 bits), then there is enough room in a word to encode 65536 pieces of information. Thus, in 16-bit machines, integers may be restricted to the 65536 numbers in the range

$$-32768 \ldots 32767.$$

- If a word consists of 4 bytes (32 bits) then there is enough room in a word to encode about 5×10^9 numbers. Thus, in 4-byte machines, main memory may include up to about 5×10^9 addresses. (Here each address corresponds to a different pattern of 0s and 1s within a word.)

Representation of Booleans and Characters

Within a computer, a single Boolean value of true or false can be encoded in a single bit of storage, with 1 for *true* and 0 for *false*. Then, when we have arrays of Boolean values, we can put these bits of storage together. Following the discussion in Section 14.2, this can be done using either packed or unpacked arrays. With the current discussion of bits, bytes, and words, we now can look at the details of these types of arrays more carefully.

In packed arrays, these bits are put together in a single word. For example, if a word contains 2 bytes, we can store an array of 16 Boolean values in a single word of storage, as shown in Figure B–3a. Here, each bit of a word is utilized to store data, and there is no wasted space.

In contrast, in unpacked arrays, only one bit is used within each word, so an array of 16 Boolean values extends over 16 words. (See Figure B–3b.) Here, if a word consists of 2 bytes, 15 bits of each word are not utilized for storage. More generally, the amount of unused space will depend upon the word size of a particular machine.

Similarly, we may place one or more characters in a word of storage. In a packed array, several characters may be placed together in a word, while in unpacked arrays only one character is placed in each word. We have already noted that one character takes up one byte of space. Thus, if a word takes up 4 bytes, we may store 4 characters in a word in a packed array, while we waste 3 bytes of storage for each word of an unpacked array.

These examples illustrate three points.

1. Booleans may be translated naturally into single bits of data, with *True* being 1 and *False* being 0.
2. Characters need to be encoded into bit patterns, and we may use a variety of such encodings. Some common encodings exist, but these

FIGURE B–3 · **Storage of Boolean Values in Packed and Unpacked Arrays**

A. Var T: Packed Array [1 . . 16] of Boolean

Word₁

T[1] T[2]   T[16]

B. Var T: Array [1 . . 16] of Boolean

Word₁ ←T[1]
Word₂ ←T[2]

Word₁₆ ←T[16]

encodings are somewhat arbitrary, and they may vary from one machine to another. However, in each case, one character normally fills one byte of storage.

3. Data may be packed together into words, or each datum may be placed in a separate word.

Representation of Numbers
When we turn to the storage of numbers, we find that the encoding of positive integers depends on a notation called the **binary system.**

Positive Numbers—Binary Notation
To see how a sequence of 0s and 1s can represent a positive integer, we first consider an example. Suppose we have the sequence

01101011,

which is a 2-byte (8-bit) number. With such a sequence, we proceed in two steps.

Step 1: Label each digit by successive powers of two, from right to left

$$
\begin{array}{cccccccc}
0 & 1 & 1 & 0 & 1 & 0 & 1 & 1, \\
2^7 & 2^6 & 2^5 & 2^4 & 2^3 & 2^2 & 2^1 & 2^0, \\
\text{or } 128 & 64 & 32 & 16 & 8 & 4 & 2 & 1.
\end{array}
$$

Step 2: Add the powers of two where a 1 appears

$$
\begin{array}{cccccccc}
0 & 1 & 1 & 0 & 1 & 0 & 1 & 1 \\
 & 64 + & 32 & & + 8 & & + 2 & + 1 = 107.
\end{array}
$$

Thus, our number 01101011 represents the decimal number 107.

This same process may be applied to any sequence, as shown in Table B–1. Here, we see all numbers expressed as 8-bit (2-byte) positive integers, and from the last line of the table, we see that the largest 8-bit positive number represents the decimal number 255.

Addition of Positive Integers. Now that we can represent positive numbers, we need to consider how to add such numbers. Here, the basic ideas are similar to decimal addition as long as we notate our answers in binary when we finish. In particular

$$
\begin{aligned}
0 + 0 &= 0 \\
1 + 0 &= 1 \\
0 + 1 &= 1
\end{aligned}
$$

Further, we want to write $1 + 1 = 2$. However, the number 2 in binary is written 10. So,

$$
\begin{array}{r}
1 \\
+1 \\
\hline
10
\end{array}
$$

where we write down the 0 and carry the 1.

TABLE B–1 · Representation of Positive Integers as Binary Numbers

Label of Bits

2^7 (128)	2^6 (64)	2^5 (32)	2^4 (16)	2^3 (8)	2^2 (4)	2^1 (2)	2^0 (1)	Decimal Number
Binary Number								
0	0	0	1	1	1	0	0	$= 16 + 8 + 4 = 28$
0	0	0	0	0	0	0	0	$= 0$
1	0	0	0	1	0	0	0	$= 128 + 8 = 136$
0	1	0	1	0	1	0	1	$= 64 + 16 + 4 + 1 = 85$
1	1	1	1	1	1	1	1	$= 128 + 64 + 32 + 16 + 8 + 4 + 2 + 1 = 255$

We illustrate these rules of addition in Figure B–4. In that figure, we see that we may add digit by digit, right to left, as we do with decimal numbers. For each digit, we add the numbers, and we keep track of any carries that extend from one digit to the next. The process is quite similar to addition of decimals, except that we only have 0 and 1 to work with.

Negative Numbers

For much processing, negative numbers must be represented as well as positive ones. We identify three reasonable notations:

sign and magnitude,

one's complement,

two's complement.

In each of these approaches, we will find it convenient to agree on the number of bits that we will write down for each integer. For example, we may agree to use 8 bits as shown in Table B–1.

Sign and Magnitude Notation.   With this specification of a number of bits, perhaps the most common approach is to use the first bit to record if the number is positive or negative and subsequent bits to store the number itself. Here, we will use the convention 0 represents " + " and 1 represents " − " With this convention, we use the first bit as a plus or a minus sign, and the rest of the bits are interpreted as before. Such an approach is illustrated in the examples of Table B–2. Here, we see that the size of our number is given as 7 bits and the sign requires one extra bit so we have a total of 8 bits for an integer.

Conceptually, this storage of integers is quite similar to our writing of decimal numbers; we are accustomed to writing numbers with an initial plus or minus sign, and this binary notation is familiar. However, in computers, this approach has several difficulties that may complicate electrical circuitry or programming significantly.

1. In adding two numbers, we first must look at their signs to see how to proceed. In fact, circuitry must check at least three cases:
   • both are positive,
   • one is positive and the other is negative, and
   • both are negative.

FIGURE B–4 • **Sample Additions of (Positive) Binary Numbers**

(Carry)	1 1	111	
First Number	100101	1001	10101
Second Number	110101	1111	01010
Total	1011010	11000	11111

TABLE B–2 · Representation of Integers in Signs and Magnitude Notations

Label of Bits

Sign ('+'=0) ('−'=1)	2^6 (64))	2^5 (32)	2^4 (16)	2^3 (8)	2^2 (4)	2^1 (2)	2^0 (1)	
Binary Number								**Decimal Number**
0	0	0	1	1	1	0	0	= "+" 16 + 8 + 4 = +28
0	0	0	0	0	0	0	0	= "+" 0 = 0
1	0	0	0	1	0	0	0	= "−" 8 = −8
0	1	0	1	0	1	0	1	= "+" 64 + 16 + 4 + 1 = +85
1	1	1	1	1	1	1	1	= "−" 64 + 32 + 16 + 8 + 4 + 2 + 1 = −127

2. Subtraction involves cases similar to addition.
3. Although the numbers +0 and −0 both represent zero, they are notated differently.

In addition or subtraction, sign bits must be analyzed before operations can be performed. In comparing a value against zero, the computer must compare the value against two forms: +0 and −0. In each case, the use of a sign bit complicates the circuitry or programming needed to perform the operations desired.

One's Complement Notation. A second way that negative numbers can be stored follows a different approach. Again, we proceed in two steps.
Step 1: Ignore the negative sign and write the remaining number in a binary form, being sure to use an initial 0 as a plus sign.
Step 2: For each digit in the number, change 1s to 0s and 0s to 1s.
For example, using an 8-bit integers as before, we may write

$$28 \text{ as } 00011100.$$

Then,

$$-28 \text{ is } 11100011.$$

This last form is called the **one's complement notation** for negative numbers.

This allows many calculations to proceed without making special cases for positive and negative numbers. For example,

$$\begin{array}{r} 28 = 00011100 \\ +35 = 00100011 \\ \hline 63 = 00111111 \end{array}$$

$$28 \ = \ 00011100$$
$$\underline{+(-35) \ = \ 11011100}$$
$$-7 \ = \ 11111000$$

However, in some cases, this arithmetic produces a carry that would normally require an additional bit of storage. In such situations, this carry must be added to the right digit of the sum. For example,

$$(-28) \ = \ 11100011$$
$$\underline{+ \quad 35 \ = \ 00100011}$$
$$100000110$$

↑ extra carry

$$00000110 \qquad \text{8 bits}$$
$$\underline{+ \qquad 1} \qquad \text{carry}$$
$$\text{result } 7 \ = \ 00000111$$

$$(-28) \ = \ 11100011$$
$$\underline{+(-35) \ = \ 11011100}$$
$$110111111$$

↑ extra carry

$$10111111 \qquad \text{8 bits}$$
$$\underline{+ \qquad 1} \qquad \text{carry}$$
$$\text{result } -63 \ = \ 11000000$$

In general, this one's complement notation has two features. First, addition can be performed following the same algorithm for any combination of positive and negative numbers. To complete this addition algorithm, two additions are needed.

1. The numbers are added.
2. An extra carry, if present, must be added as an extra 1 to the sum.

Second, one's complement notation still gives two forms for zero,

$$00000000 \ = \ 0, \text{ and}$$
$$11111111 \ = \ -0$$

For many purposes, this one's complement notation is much simpler than the sign and magnitude notation, since we do not need to make special cases for adding various combinations of positive and negative numbers. However, a third notation is still better in many situations.

Two's Complement Notation.   To write a negative number in two's complement notation, we follow these steps.

Step 1: Write the number in one's complement notation.
Step 2: Add 1.
As an example, we write -28 in this notation. We have seen that -28 is written 11100011 in one's complement form. Thus in two's complement form, we have

$$
\begin{array}{r}
11100011 \\
+ \quad\quad\quad 1 \\
\hline
-28 = \quad 11100100
\end{array}
$$

Similarly

$$-35 = 11011100 + 1 = 11011101$$

With this notation, we can perform our additions without making special cases for positives and negatives, and we can ignore any carry into an extra digit, as shown in the following examples.

$$
\begin{array}{rl}
28 & = 00011100 \\
+(-35) & = 11011101 \\
\hline
-7 & = 11111001
\end{array}
\qquad
\begin{array}{rl}
(-28) = & 11100100 \\
+ \quad 35 = & 00100011 \\
\hline
7 = & 100000111
\end{array}
$$

                 ⌐ignore
                 extra
                 carry

$$
\begin{array}{rl}
(-28) = & 11100100 \\
+(-35) = & 11011101 \\
\hline
-63 = & 111000001
\end{array}
$$

             ⌐ignore
             extra
             carry

In each case, addition can follow normal rules for binary numbers, and we do not need special conditions for negatives. Further, additions can be done in one operation with this notation, in contrast to the two addition operations sometimes needed with one's complement notation. For these reasons, we find that negative numbers are represented in two's complement notation in many computers. This notation allows addition circuitry to be relatively simple. Further, we find that this notation specifies zero in only one form, namely

$$00000000$$

Thus, checking numbers for zero is also simplified when this notation is used.

Variant Records

To conclude this discussion of machine storage of data, we now consider how to write a program to display data storage in binary.

  The major step involves an extension of records, where we include a

Case statement in our record declaration. Such records are called by various names, including **variant records, record variants,** and **records with variants.** The required form of declaration is illustrated below.

```
Const WLen = 16;
Type  Word = Record
            Case Flag: Integer of
                1:(Int : Integer);
                2: (BArray: Packed Array [1..WLen] of Boolean)
            End;
         Var Item: Word;
```

In this declaration, the word *Item* may hold different types of data depending upon the value of a *Flag* field. This field is called a **Tag Field** for the variant record. For example, if *Item.Flag* = 1, then the word *Record* has an integer field called *Int,* and we can refer to *Item.Int.* In contrast, if *Item.Flag* = 2, then the *Int* field is not defined, and we use the *BArray* field instead. With such variant records, we can use the same variable in different contexts to store different types of data, and we can shift from one type of data to another if we are careful.

In the following program, we take advantage of the shifting to analyze the form of data stored inside a word of memory. In particular, we expect the *Int* field and the *BArray* will be allocated the same storage space within the computer's memory. (Here, we pick *Wlen* to be the number of bits per word for our machine.)

If *Flag* = 1, then this word of storage will be considered an integer. If *Flag* = 2, this same storage will be considered a (packed) array of Boolean. In our program, we consider *True* to be represented as "1," False to be represented as "0."

Thus, to print out a word of memory, we write

```
For Index : = WLen Downto 1
    Do Begin
        If Item.BArray[Index]
            Then Write ('1')
            Else Write ('0')
        End;
    Writeln;
```

With this in mind, our approach for analyzing the form of integers follows this outline.

  I. Set *Flag* to 1 for integer data.
 II. Read integer.
III. Reset *Flag* to 2 for Boolean data.
IV. Write word of memory from Boolean array.

In writing a program from this outline, we note that Standard Pascal does not allow us to change the flag of a variant record and then write data without first reinitializing the new data type. However, if these shifts, reads, and writes are in separate procedures, few compilers will be able to check that the shift has occurred without reinitialization, and our outline will work.

This outline suggests the following non-Standard Pascal program, which shows some uses of variant records.

```
Program Coding (Input, Output);
{This program reads integers and displays the binary
 notation used by the machine to store those numbers}

Const WLen = 16;  {The number of bits per word in a machine}
      Sentinel = -10;

Type Word = Record
        Case Flag: Integer of
            1: (Int: Integer);
            2: (BArray: Packed Array [1..WLen] of Boolean)
        End;

Var Item: Word;
    Number: Integer;

Procedure ReadNum (Var Number: Integer);
{This procedure reads a value from the terminal}
    Begin
        Write (' Enter an integer value ',
            '(Conclude by typing ', Sentinel:1, ' ): ');
        Readln (Number)
    End {ReadNum} ;

Procedure ShiftInt (Var Item: Word);
{This procedure shifts the Word Flag to 1 for integer data}
    Begin
        Item.Flag := 1
    End {ShiftInt} ;

Procedure AssignInt (Number: Integer; Var Item: Word);
{This procedure reads an integer from the terminal}
    Begin
        Item.Int := Number
    End {ReadInt} ;

Procedure ShiftBool (Var Item: Word);
{This procedure shifts the Word Flag to 2 for Boolean data}
    Begin
        Item.Flag := 2
    End {ShiftInt} ;

Procedure PrintBits (Var Item: Word);
{This procedure prints the bit pattern in the specified word}
    Var Index: Integer;
```

```
    Begin
        Write ('The bit pattern for this word of data is: ');
        For Index := WLen DownTo 1
          Do Begin
            If Item.BArray[Index]
                Then Write ('1')
                Else Write ('0')
          End;
        Writeln;
        Writeln
    End {PrintBits} ;

Begin {Main}
    Writeln ('This program prints the bit pattern for integer storage');

    ReadNum (Number);
    While (Number <> Sentinel)
      Do Begin
        ShiftInt (Item);
        AssignInt (Number, Item);
        ShiftBool (Item);
        PrintBits(Item);
        ReadNum (Number)
      End

End {Main} .
```

When this program was run on one specific 16-bit computer, the following output was printed.

```
This program prints the bit pattern for integer storage
 Enter an integer value (Conclude by typing -10 ): 1
The bit pattern for this word of data is: 0000000000000001

 Enter an integer value (Conclude by typing -10 ): 2
The bit pattern for this word of data is: 0000000000000010

 Enter an integer value (Conclude by typing -10 ): 3
The bit pattern for this word of data is: 0000000000000011

 Enter an integer value (Conclude by typing -10 ): 4
The bit pattern for this word of data is: 0000000000000100

 Enter an integer value (Conclude by typing -10 ): 8
The bit pattern for this word of data is: 0000000000001000

 Enter an integer value (Conclude by typing -10 ): 28
The bit pattern for this word of data is: 0000000000011100

 Enter an integer value (Conclude by typing -10 ): 35
The bit pattern for this word of data is: 0000000000100011
```

```
Enter an integer value (Conclude by typing -10 ): -1
The bit pattern for this word of data is: 1111111111111111

Enter an integer value (Conclude by typing -10 ): -2
The bit pattern for this word of data is: 1111111111111110

Enter an integer value (Conclude by typing -10 ): -8
The bit pattern for this word of data is: 1111111111111000

Enter an integer value (Conclude by typing -10 ): -28
The bit pattern for this word of data is: 1111111111100100

Enter an integer value (Conclude by typing -10 ): -35
The bit pattern for this word of data is: 1111111111011101

Enter an integer value (Conclude by typing -10 ): -10
```

From our discussion earlier, this output shows that the specific computer used to run this program uses two's complement notation for negative numbers.

EXERCISES

B.1 *Storage of Character Data.* Figure B–3 illustrates the difference between packed and unpacked arrays of Boolean values. Draw a similar illustration for character data, assuming each character requires one byte of storage space.

B.2 *Largest Integers.*
  a. What is the largest 16-bit integer? (Assume here that only positive integers are to be encoded in binary.)
  b. Suppose a machine uses a 16-bit word size, and suppose that each memory address is stored in one word. (These assumptions hold in many of today's microcomputers.) With these limitations, how large a main memory can the CPU utilize? Explain your answer.

B.3 Translate the following positive integers from binary to decimal notation.
  a. 01101110
  b. 00011011
  c. 01101101
  d. 00011111
  e. 00011100

B.4 Translate the following positive integers from decimal to binary notation.
  a. 18
  b. 43
  c. 64
  d. 79
  e. 100

B.5 Consider the following negative decimal integers: -18, -43, -64, -79, and -100.
  a. Translate these to binary, using sign and magnitude notation.
  b. Translate these to binary, using one's complement notation.
  c. Translate these to binary, using two's complement notation.

B.6 Consider the following negative binary integers
  - 10101010,
  - 11001110,
  - 10000111,
  - 10010100, and
  - 11100001.
  a. Translate each of these into decimal form, assuming these binary numbers are written in sign and magnitude notation.
  b. Repeat part a, assuming one's complement notation.
  c. Repeat part a, assuming two's complement notation.

B.7 *One's Complement Notation Revisited.* Suppose that a word contains n bits, and suppose we want to store integers in one word. Then, we think of the first bit as being related to the sign of the number, while the remaining $(n - 1)$ bits can store a positive integer.
  a. Show that the largest positive number that can be stored with $n - 1$ bits is $2^{(n - 1)} - 1$.
  b. Show that the bit pattern for corresponding to n ones is $2^n - 1$.
  c. If we represent a positive number x in binary, show that $2^n - 1 - x$ is the binary number that can be obtained from x by changing all 0s to 1s and all 1s to 0s. (That is, the one's complement notation of the negative number $-x$ is given by $2^n - 1 - x$.
  d. (Optional) Use this notation, with $2^n - 1 - x$ representing $-x$, to explain the addition examples in Section B.2, where we used one's complement notation.
    NOTE: In n bits, the number after $2^n - 1$ looks like 0, as 2^n must be represented by a 1 in the $(n + 1)$ bit.

B.8 *Two's Complement Notation Revisited.* Let x be a positive integer, and assume the results of the previous problem.
  a. Show that the two's complement notation for $-x$ is given by $2^n - x$.
  b. Use this notation to explain the addition examples in Section B.2 where we used two's complement notation.

B.9 *Representation of Large Numbers.*
  a. Assuming a word size of 8 bits, write out the value for *MaxInt* in sign and magnitude notation. (The first bit will be 0.)
  b. Use binary arithmetic to compute *MaxInt* + 1.
  c. Interpret the bit string obtained in part b. using each of the three binary notations for integers.

B.10 *Machine Representation of Data—I.*
  a. Determine the word size of a computer that you can use. Then modify the binary integer program of Section B.2 to print the binary representation of integers on your local machine.

b. From your work in part a, determine which notation is used to store negative integers in your machine.

B.11 *Machine Representation of Data—II.* Expand your program from the previous problem so that it will print the binary representation of

a. characters

b. real numbers

within your machine.

NOTE: In many machines, real numbers may require two or more words of storage, and your program will have to take these storage requirements into account.

APPENDIX C: MATHEMATICAL DETAILS

Computer science applies various topics from mathematics in important ways, and an understanding of these topics is essential for many applications. For example, the analysis of many algorithms requires an understanding of logarithms, and the simulation of many activities requires some background with random number generators. This Appendix introduces the necessary material for this work.

SECTION C.1   INTRODUCTION TO LOGARITHMS

Logarithms are functions that allow us to work with exponents effectively. For this reason, much as we might wish otherwise, logarithms arise naturally in several contexts. However, most of these uses in computer science require only a very elementary knowledge of logarithms, and we focus on this minimal necessary background in this section. We do *not* cover many of the interesting properties of logarithms that are not used regularly in computer science or in applications.

For quick reference, the major conclusions of this Appendix are shown in Table C–1.

Definition of $\log_b a$

We begin by raising various positive numbers to various powers. (See Table C–2.) We construct this table as follows. We start with a number (e.g., 2) and we raise it to a power (e.g., 3) to get a result: $2^3 = 8$. If we wish, we could extend the table in many ways. For example, since we know

$$b^{-n} = 1/b^n$$

TABLE C–1 • **Basic Properties of Logarithms**

Property 1:	$\log_b b^a = a$
Property 2:	$b^{\log_b c} = c$
Property 3:	$\log_b c^n = n \log_b c$
Property 4:	$\log_b s / \log_b c = \log_c s$
Application 1:	a^r may be translated to exp $(r*\ln(a))$ in Pascal
Application 2:	(The Definition of Logarithms)
	$\log_b c = a$ answers the question:
	"b to what power is the number c?"
Application 3:	$\log_2 c$ may be computed by $\ln(c)/\ln(2)$ in Pascal

---

TABLE C–2 · Various Positive Numbers Raised to Various Integral Powers

$2^0 = 1$	$3^0 = 1$	$10^0 = 1$
$2^1 = 2$	$3^1 = 3$	$10^1 = 10$
$2^2 = 4$	$3^2 = 9$	$10^2 = 100$
$2^3 = 8$	$3^3 = 27$	$10^3 = 1000$
$2^4 = 16$	$3^4 = 81$	$10^4 = 10000$

we could consider $2^{-3} = 1/2^3 = 1/8$ and $3^{-2} = 1/9$. Also, we could add fractional powers to our table. For example, since $\sqrt{b}$ corresponds to $b^{1/2}$, we could write $2^{1/2} = \sqrt{2} = 1.414$. Thus, with appropriate additions, we could have a very extensive table of powers.

From such a table, we can imagine trying to work backward from our final number to the exponent. For example, we can ask: 3 to what power is 81? From our table, we discover $3^4 = 81$. Thus, the answer to our question is 4. We may even imagine this process as sort of a children's game.

I am thinking of a number n where $2^n = 8$.

What is my number?

From our table, we see $n = 3$. Of course, in some cases, the answer may not be so easy to find. For example, if we said

I am thinking of a number s where $2^s = 1.414$.

What is my number?

we might have trouble. (The careful reader will realize that we have already noted that $2^{1/2} = 1.414$, so here $s = 1/2$ will work. Without that note, however, we might not be able to find the answer without great effort!)

In general, our question has the following form.

Suppose b and c are positive real numbers.

What is the number a so that $b^a = c$?

If we have an extensive table such as Table C–1, we may be able to answer such questions easily. Otherwise, we may find that the answers are hard to determine. However, in either case, we can still *ask* the question. It turns out that this question arises fairly frequently in many contexts. For example, this question is the key to understanding the work involved in storing and retrieving data in various ways. Therefore, we find that we need to be able to get a, given b and c. This gives rise to the following definition.

Definition: Given positive numbers b and c, we say $a = \log_b c$ or a is the

logarithm base *b* of *c*, if $b^a = c$. Thus, from our earlier example, we have

$$4 = \log_3 81 \quad \text{since } 3^4 = 81$$
$$3 = \log_2 8 \quad \text{since } 2^3 = 8$$
$$0.5 = \log_2 1.414 \quad \text{since } 2^{1/2} = 1.414$$

Similarly from Table 4–3, we can determine many other logarithms.

$$\text{Log}_{10} 10000 = 4 \text{ since } 10^4 = 10000.$$

Other log values derived from Table C–2 are shown in Table C–3.

Similarly, since $b^0 = 1$ for any positive number b, we know that $0 = \log_b 1$. (0 answers the question "*b* to what power is 1?")

Basic Properties of Logarithms

With this definition of logarithms, several properties follow quickly.
Property 1:

$$\log_b b^a = a$$

Discussion: While the left side of this equation may look formidable, the meaning of the terms makes this computation trivial. Remember that $\log_b c$ is asking the question "*b* to what power gives the number *c*?" Thus, $\log_b b^a$ asks the question

"*b* to what power gives the number b^a?"

The answer is a, since b to the ath power gives the number b^a. Thus, $\log_2 2^3 = 3$ and $\log_3 3^4 = 4$. (You can also check these computations by looking at Tables C–2 and C–3 since $\log_2 2^3 = \log_2 8 = 3$, and $\log_3 3^4 = \log_3 81 = 4$.)
Property 2:

$$b^{\log_b c} = c$$

Discussion: As in the previous discussion, this property follows from our definitions once we understand what all the symbols mean:

$$\log_b c \text{ is the number } a \text{ where } b^a = c.$$

Using a for $\log_b c$, we get

$$b^{\log_b c} = b^a = c.$$

TABLE C–3 · Logarithms for the Powers in Table 4–3

$0 = \log_2 1$	$0 = \log_3 1$	$0 = \log_{10} 1$
$1 = \log_2 2$	$1 = \log_3 3$	$1 = \log_{10} 10$
$2 = \log_2 4$	$2 = \log_3 9$	$2 = \log_{10} 100$
$3 = \log_2 8$	$3 = \log_3 27$	$3 = \log_{10} 1000$
$4 = \log_2 16$	$4 = \log_3 81$	$4 = \log_{10} 10000$

For example, from Tables C–2 and C–3,

$$\log_2 8 = 3 \text{ so } 2^{\log_2 8} = 2^3 = 8$$

and

$$\log_3 81 = 4 \text{ so } 3^{\log_3 81} = 3^4 = 81.$$

Property 3:

$$\log_b c^n = n\log_b c$$

Discussion: As in our earlier discussions, suppose

$$b^a = c \text{ or } \log_b c = a.$$

Now let us consider what the left side of the above equation means. $\log_b c^n$ asks the question "b to what power gives c^n?" In trying to answer this question, we look at our starting point $b^a = c$. When we raise both sides to the nth power, we get

$$c^n = (b^a)^n = b^{na}.$$

Thus, we see that b to the na power gives c^n. We conclude that $\log_b c^n = na$. But we said that $a = \log_b c$. Thus,

$$\log_b c^n = na = n\log_b c.$$

When we look at our tables, we see this relationship in several places. For example

$$\log_{10} 10 = 1.$$

Thus, by Property 3,

$$\log_{10} 1000 = \log_{10} 10^3 = 3\log_{10} 10 = 3 \times 1 = 3,$$

and the value agrees with our table.

Property 4:

$$\log_b s / \log_b c = \log_c s$$

Discussion: In understanding the formula, we first look at the left side, and then we think about what the right side means.

Suppose t and a are two numbers where

$$b^t = s \text{ and } b^a = c,$$

so

$$\log_b s / \log_b c = t/a.$$

With this information, we try to compute the right side of the equation. $\log_c s$ asks the question "c to what power gives s?" From what we have above,

$$b^a = c.$$

Taking the ath root of each side, we get

$$b = c^{1/a}.$$

Taking both sides to the t power, we have

$$s = b^t = (c^{1/a})^t = c^{t/a}.$$

Thus, we see that $c^{t/a} = s$ or

$$t/a = \log_c s.$$

Above, we found

$$t/a = \log_b s / \log_b c,$$

so we conclude

$$\log_b s / \log_b c = \log_c s.$$

Applications of Logarithms

Throughout the text, we find that these properties of logarithms are needed in three types of applications.

Application 1: Compute a^r, given a and r.

Many times our problems will require us to compute a positive number a to some power r. For example, we may need to compute

$$4^3 \text{ or } 4^{13} \text{ or } 4^{15}.$$

However, Pascal does not have an arithmetic operator for powers. Thus, while we can compute 4*3 easily, we cannot compute 4^3 directly.

Sometimes, these computations can be performed by replacing the power with other operations that we do have. For example, we can rewrite 4^3 as 4*4*4, and $4^{1/2}$ as *sqrt*(4). This approach also works for big powers such as 4^{15}, but this approach is awkward. For example, we could write

$$4^{15} = 4*4*4*4*4*4*4*4*4*4*4*4*4*4*4,$$

or

$$4^{15} = sqr(sqr(sqr(sqr(4))))/4.$$

These expressions allow us to perform the desired computations, but they are difficult to use and are error-prone. In other cases, such as $4^{1/3}$, this approach breaks down completely.

An alternative approach uses logarithms and the functions available in Pascal. First, we write e for the number 2.718281828459. . . . Then we note that

$$\begin{aligned} a^r &= e^{\log_e a^r} &\text{(Property 2)} \\ &= e^{r\log_e a} &\text{(Property 3)} \end{aligned}$$

When we look at this last form, we see that Pascal does allow us to do all operations required. In particular,

$\log_e a$ translates to the Pascal function $Ln(a)$, and

e^s translates to the Pascal function $Exp(s)$.

Thus, we can translate a^r to Pascal notation by

$$a^r = e^{r\log_e a}$$
$$= Exp(r*Ln(a)).$$

For example,

$$4^{1/3} = \exp(1.0/3.0*\ln(4.0)).$$

Application 2: Find a so that $b^a = c$.

When we analyze the work required to perform certain algorithms, we find we often are faced with the above problem. To be more specific, we may want to know how many steps are needed to find a particular item in a list of items. When we use the binary search of Section 8.6, we find

a = number of steps
b = 2
c = number of data items

and $2^a \geq c$.

Thus if we start with c items of data, we will need at most $\log_2 c$ steps to find a particular item. A similar analysis is required when we consider sorting our data, that is, putting our data in order. (For example, see Sections 14.4 and 19.7.)

Application 3: Compute $\log_2 c$.

In Application 2, we saw that we will need to compute $\log_2 c$ to determine the number of steps required for an algorithm to produce a desired result. However, when we look at the functions available in Pascal, we see that the $\log_2$ function is not available; only $\log_e$ or Ln is readily computed. This is when we use Property 4, since we have

$$\log_2 c = \log_e c/\log_e 2 = Ln(c)/Ln(2).$$

Thus, in Pascal, whenever we need to compute $\log_2 c$, we can write

$$Ln(c)/Ln(2)$$

using the Pascal function available to us.

Final Notes on Logarithms

In practice, only three bases commonly arise for logarithms: $\log_{10}$, $\log_2$, and $\log_e$.

We have already noted that $\log_2$ is used to analyze various algorithms. We see much of this analysis in several chapters.

Historically, $\log_{10}$ or **common logarithms** were used widely for various types of computations, and slide rules were based on principles of common logarithms. Further, common logarithms formed the basis for certain measurements. (The pH scale to measure acidity is based on common logarithms.) Now, with the widespread use of calculators, the computational features of common logarithms are rarely used, and common logarithms are limited to relatively few applications.

Finally, $\log_e$, ln or **natural logarithms,** are used extensively in mathematical, scientific, and engineering applications. The motivation for $\log_e$ comes from calculus and is well beyond the scope of this book. Some applications of probability and statistics also involve the number e.

SECTION C.2	RANDOM NUMBER GENERATORS

Section 4.4 describes a special type of function, called a *random number generator,* which is of considerable use to us in many applications. However, while the concept of the random number generator described in that section is correct, the code given does involve one possible technical difficulty. In particular, in that section, we use integers A, C, M, and *Seed,* and we say

set M = MaxInt + 1

compute (A*Seed + C) Mod M

In each case, we compute values larger than the maximum allowed in Pascal. On some machines, such computations will still be run correctly; on other machines, our program will not compile or run as desired.

When such programs will not run on the computer available, we still can use the same approach for computing random numbers. However, the details are more complex. We proceed by working with only part of each number at a time. To use a decimal analogy, suppose we want to work with a large number, such as 314159. If we are limited to only three or four digits in our computations, we might break this large number into pieces, such as 314 and 159. In this process, we must be careful to use the pieces correctly so that we can produce the desired results.

For our random number generator, we use A and C as before. As M is too large an integer, we instead keep track of the number of binary digits we may use for integers. (This is called the length of a word in the computer, and we discuss this more in Appendix B.2.) Then, we divide our numbers into pieces, which we will need as global variables.

A is divided into *HighA* and *LowA;*

C is divided into *HighC* and *LowC;*

Seed is divided into *HighSeed* and *LowSeed;* and

M is split several ways, giving rise to *HighSize, LowSize, HighFactor,* and *LowFactor.*

With these comments, we revise the random number generator from Section 4.4. This revision clearly is more cumbersome but it does conform to Standard Pascal. Thus, the revision can be run on any computer, when we make appropriate choices for *WordLength* (i.e., M), A, and C.

```
{The following constants are needed for the Random Number Function}
    Wordlength = 16;    {In this machine, 1 word = 16 bits}
    A = 3373;           {A should satisfy four conditions:
                            Sqrt(MaxInt) < A < MaxInt-Sqrt(MaxInt)
                            MaxInt/100 < A < MaxInt/2
                            A mod 8 = 5
                            Binary digits not in a simple, regular pattern}
    C = 6925;           {Set C odd with C approximately
                            (MaxInt+1.0)*.2113248654}

{The following variables are needed for the Random Number Function}
HighSize, LowSize, HighA, LowA, HighC, LowC: Integer;
HighSeed, LowSeed: Integer;
HighFactor, LowFactor: Real;

Procedure InitializeRandomFunction;
    {Procedure initializes variables for the Random Number Function}
    Var Seed, Index: Integer;
    Begin
        LowSize := 2;
        For Index := 3 to (WordLength Div 2)
            Do LowSize := LowSize * 2;
        HighSize := LowSize * 2;
        HighA := A Div LowSize;
        LowA := A Mod LowSize;
        HighC := C Div LowSize;
        LowC := C Mod LowSize;
        Seed := trunc(time * 500.0);
        HighSeed := Seed Div LowSize;
        LowSeed := Seed Mod LowSize;
        HighFactor := 1.0 / HighSize;
        LowFactor := HighFactor / LowSize
    End {InitializeRandomFunction};

Function Random: Real;
    {Function returns a random number between 0 and 1}
    Begin
        HighSeed := (HighSeed Mod 2) * (HighA Mod 2) +
                    ((HighSeed * LowA) Mod HighSize) +
                    ((LowSeed * HighA) Mod HighSize);
        LowSeed := LowSeed * LowA + LowC;
        HighSeed := HighSeed + (LowSeed Div LowSize) + HighC;
        HighSeed := HighSeed Mod HighSize;
        LowSeed := LowSeed Mod LowSize;
        Random := HighSeed * HighFactor + LowSeed * LowFactor
    End {Random};
```

APPENDIX D: STYLE SUMMARY AND CHECKLIST

PROGRAM FORMAT, STYLE, AND READABILITY

Never 1	Sometimes 2	Almost Always 3	Always 4	
				Structure
—	—	—	—	Program divided into appropriate functions and procedures.
—	—	—	—	Procedures and functions of appropriate length and complexity.
				Comments
—	—	—	—	Program and each function and procedure begin with appropriate comments describing purpose.
—	—	—	—	Other comments added as needed to interpret program.
—	—	—	—	Comments aid program readability.
				Variables and Parameters
—	—	—	—	Descriptive identifiers used.
—	—	—	—	Variables initialized.
—	—	—	—	Use of global variables minimized.
—	—	—	—	Parameters used effectively to control passage of data in and out of procedures and functions.
				Format and Statement Use
—	—	—	—	Program easy to read and understand.
—	—	—	—	Indenting helps clarify program logic and readability.
—	—	—	—	Appropriate selection of repetitive statements (For, Repeat, While).
—	—	—	—	Appropriate use of conditionals (If, Case, Boolean expressions).

Never	Sometimes	Almost Always	Always	
1	2	3	4	**Input and Output Format**
—	—	—	—	User reminded what input is required.
—	—	—	—	Output labeled clearly.
—	—	—	—	Output put in columns when appropriate.
—	—	—	—	Input and output neat; not cluttered.
				Testing
—	—	—	—	Test cases appropriate to the problem.
—	—	—	—	A sufficient number of test cases considered.
—	—	—	—	Hand calculations provided when appropriate.
				Algorithm Design and Correctness
—	—	—	—	Program meets specifications of problem.
—	—	—	—	Algorithms used correctly solve problem.
—	—	—	—	Algorithms used are sufficiently efficient.

SECTION D.2   OVERALL STYLE AND FORMAT

Bad				Good	
1	2	3	4	5	
—	—	—	—	—	Program
—	—	—	—	—	Input and Output
—	—	—	—	—	Testing
—	—	—	—	—	Algorithms

INDEX

OPERATIONS AND PRECEDENCE RULES

Operations are arranged in groups according to precedence. Within each group, operations have the same precedence, and evaluation proceeds from left to right.

Operation	Type of Arguments	Type of Result	Description
Highest Precedence			
Not	Boolean	Boolean	Logical Negation
Second Highest Precedence			
*	Integer or real	(1)	Multiplication
*	Set (2)	Set	Intersection
/	Integer or real	Real	Real division
Div	Integer	Integer	Integer quotient
Mod	Integer	Integer	Integer remainder
And	Boolean	Boolean	Logical "and"

Notes:
1. Result is integer if both arguments are integer; Result is Real otherwise.
2. Arguments are sets of the same type; Result also has the same set type.